WOMEN  L

Adventures, Advice and Experience

Acknowledgements:

This book would not have been possible without the sustained encouragement, help and patience of our contributors, whom, as far as possible, we have tried to acknowledge within the relevant chapters. But there were many other people who helped in ways less easy to classify, spreading word about the project, passing on information and lending their judgement to the problems of selecting and editing pieces.

We take this chance to thank: Daphne Toupouzis, Christine Georgeff, Ilse Zambonini, Harriet Gaze, Peggy Gregory, Cath Forrest, Pilar Vazquez, Dörte Haarhaus, Marilyn Hayward, Amanda Sebestyen, Beverley Milton-Edwards, Kate Sebag, Deborah Birkett, Alison Woodhead, Ann Light, Jessica Jenkins, Clare Bayley, Carey Denton, Elaine Wilson, Sara Hovington, Marifran Carlson, Anita Peltonen, Jo Siedlecka, Jackum Brown, Marta Rodriguez, Edie Jarolim, Dana Denniston, Salli Ramsden, Valerie Unsworth, Myra Shackley, Sheena Phillips, Mark Thompson, Amy Erickson, Sabrina Rees, Peggy Jansz and Clifford Jansz.

Also, thanks to all those connected with the *Rough Guide* office who shared their knowledge and enthusiasm for many of the destinations covered and guided us through the practicalities of putting this book together, especially Richard Trillo, who helped shape the Africa chapters, Susanne Hillen, Greg Ward, Dan Richardson, Karen O'Brien, Shirley Eber, Jules Brown, Mark Salter, Jack Holland, Martin Dunford, Kate Berens, Kate Chambers, Andy Hilliard, Melissa Kim and Andrew Neather.

We acknowledge a special debt to Bridget Davies, Michael Reed and Litza Jansz for encouragement and practical help at times of crisis . . .

. . . and Mark Ellingham who, by a combination of unfailing support, editorial prowess and insistence that the project could work, helped bring this idea to fruition.

Published by Harrap Columbus, Chelsea House, 26 Market Square, Bromley, Kent BR1 1NA.
Typesetting by Greg Ward and Mark Ellingham.
Design by Andrew Oliver.
Typeset in Linotron Univers and Century Old Style.
Printed by Cox & Wyman, Reading, Berks.

560p.

British Library Cataloguing in Publication Data
Women Travel; Adventures, Advice and Experience. (The Rough Guides).
  1. Travel by women, history.
  I. Jansz, Natania II. Davies, Miranda III Series
910.82

ISBN 0-7471-0213-9

WOMEN TRAVEL

Adventures, Advice and Experience

Edited by

MIRANDA DAVIES and **NATANIA JANSZ**

with

Alisa Joyce (USA) and Jane Parkin (New Zealand)

Consultant editors
Laura Longrigg and Lucinda Montefiore

HARRAP COLUMBUS ■ LONDON

Contents

CONTENTS

CONTENTS

Introduction

When Baedeker launched the first modern guidebooks in the 1830s it was clear whom he was addressing: gentlemen travelling alone or acting as the guardians, protectors and second-hand guides to the less able travellers accompanying them, namely the "ladies of the party". The fact that many women were making the grand tour of European sites on their own – and often seizing the chance to act as companions and chaperones – could not have escaped his notice. It just wasn't the concern of a travel writer to recognise or encourage this particular phenomenon.

Things are very different now. No one doubts that with the explosion of mass tourism, women, just as much as men, are taking up opportunities to set off abroad. More importantly, no one doubts that we have as much right as men to do so. Yet how many of our super-abundant travel books, guides, brochures, magazines, articles, films and journals really prepare us for the experiences we might have; describe how we are likely to be perceived and treated; deal with the concerns we share about sexism and harassment, or even consider these issues when recommending options for getting around, sleeping and socialising? More radically still, how many break with the Baedeker tradition altogether and talk first and foremost to the woman who is planning the journey?

The problem is not simply that the books and articles are written by men – many are not. But, in following the conventions of "objective" and "authoritative" journalism – where any information of specific relevance to women is considered of marginal interest – women can all too easily write themselves out of the picture.

Consequently, most would-be travellers try to get in touch with other women who have recently returned from a country in order to gain the necessary advice and reassurance. *Women Travel* is an attempt to provide some sort of alternative. The book concentrates on personal accounts, describing the problems and pleasures of travelling in countries as different as Iceland and India. To give some context to the travels, we have added country-by-country introductions, and, as practical pointers, each section ends with contacts for women's organisations and resources, and suggestions for further reading. We don't intend the book to replace regular guidebooks, but instead to fill in some of the gaps, and to give first-hand experience that, hopefully, will both prepare and inspire travels.

Setting off

In our selection of accounts we have concentrated on women travelling alone, with other women or with children. This was not the result of any hardline rejection of travelling with men but a recognition that such experiences tend to be one step removed and therefore less useful to those who want to set out alone. As Margaret Hubbard, travelling in Morocco, put it:

> I used to feel cheated that I was no longer at the forefront and that any contact would
> be made through (the man) . . . I was prepared to go on alone, however uncomforta-
> ble it might become, so long as I was treated as a person in my own right.

Except in cases where there's no choice, as in Albania or Vietnam, we kept the focus on independent travel. Many women, especially those travelling with children, choose package trips as the cheapest, most convenient and "safest" option for setting off alone. But these are, by definition, insulated experiences; encounters with local people, where they occur at all, tend to be brief, impersonal and dominated by the business of buying and services. Some notion of ordinary, everyday human contact seemed essential if we were to provide material of any use. For this reason a large space is given to women who have lived or worked in a country for a while.

Attitudes towards travel were an equally important consideration. Travel, we are told, broadens the mind, but it can also reinforce prejudices. Visiting or working in a country previously colonised by a Western power, there is a pressure to re-enact the old colonial relationships – to treat the problems or pitfalls you come up against as confirmation that we in the West know better. This was graphically illustrated by the experience of Adrienne Su, an American of Chinese descent visiting China for the first time:

> (The privileges accorded tourists) feel more like the privation of the human rights of the Chinese than the extension of hospitality to their visitors . . . When I came across other Westerners on the road their attitude towards me was high-flown and condescending until I spoke English. It wasn't entirely their fault, they had been deluded by the environment into seeing the Chinese as less than people.

We wanted to hear from women who questioned the values they brought to bear in judging societies very different to their own, who were sensitive about their status as affluent Westerners, and who had a genuine interest in crossing cultural divides.

Last, but not least, we wanted to get across the excitement of travel. Not just the adventurous spirit but the fact that for so many women the act of setting off alone, adapting to a new way of life, and coping with the logistics of getting around, amounts to a personal test of ability and independence. As Ann Stirk wrote, having given up twenty years of factory work and cashed in all her savings to ride a motorbike across America:

> I learned my strengths and my weaknesses. I experienced the exhilaration of the ups and the despairs of the lows and most of the feelings in between . . . I learned courage and I learned it myself.

Writing home

Having already been through the process of advertising and sifting accounts for our previous travellers' anthology, *Half the Earth*, we should not perhaps have been surprised by the response we received for *Women Travel*. We were. In addition to the thousand-odd accounts submitted for publication, many other women wrote to share information that they thought might be of help – books to read, contact addresses, women-only resources, gay listings, notes on campaigns of interest to women. And much the same response was arriving in regular packages from our editors in the USA and New Zealand.

In the accounts themselves, it was the depth and the range of experiences that surprised and gratified us the most. If proof was needed of women's ability to embrace new cultures, let go of the comforts and conveniences of a familiar and privileged lifestyle, contend with new customs, and battle with the elements – surely this was it. Some of the travels were astonishingly intrepid: Terri Donovan's epic bike ride across the sands of the Nubian desert; Alison Gostling's illegal hitch across the China/Tibet border; Wendy Dison's lone trip across Iran;

Lesley Reader's account of trekking across the Himalayan mountains of Bhutan; Helen Scadding's motorbike journeys across Ghana. And there were many more.

But demonstrating that women can and do plunge themselves into potentially difficult or dangerous situations did not seem enough in itself. A feature of almost all of the "adventurous" journeys in this book is the extraordinary opportunities they provided for contact and a new depth of understanding between people of entirely separate cultures. The arduous task of hauling a bike over sand dunes was, for Terri Donovan, eclipsed by the unobtrusive warmth and kindness she met from the workers manning the remote transNubian railway maintenance stations. Lesley Reader stayed on for two years with the villagers of Buli, in Bhutan, primarily because these were the people whose friendships she most valued:

> My friends here in Buli are women of all ages. Just as I am a woman alone, the major-ity of them are either widows, women with husbands absent in the army, or single women. They arrived in my house the evening after I reached Buli bearing many bottles of local brew and we all got drunk. We have been together ever since. They teach me to plant, harvest and thresh rice and cook me dinner of rice and chillis when they see that I'm struggling . . . I take their photographs, cook them egg and chips, help out with the cash and tell them about my life and country.

And there were many other, equally inspiring, accounts of finding a new place amongst new people. Naomi Roberts lived for a year and a half in a Ghanaian compound; Rosie Ayliffe (one of many English language teachers) spent a year living in one of the shack dwellings of Istanbul; Valerie Mason-John, a black woman from London, set out to support the Aboriginal cause in Australia; Jan Wright settled with her family in a remote peasant village in the Portuguese Alentejo; Susanna Rance struggled to adapt to the harshness of life in the Bolivian Andes.

Choosing destinations

All in all, a large proportion of the accounts that we chose cover travel to so-called Third World countries. This was not deliberate, but contributors generally felt that they had less to say of relevance or use to women about places closer to home. For every piece we received on Greece, for example, there were perhaps ten or twelve each on India or Morocco. The only country that we actively excluded was South Africa, although we were well aware that many other coun-tries pose a similar moral dilemma for travellers – where your presence and foreign cash might be seen as lending credibility and support to a corrupt or authoritarian regime. As one writer put it, "the nastiest regimes often have the nicest hotels". It is an issue that Jane Schwartz contends with in her account of travelling around Turkey.

As editors, we felt in no position to pronounce judgement on one regime's fail-ings versus another's. We have, however, tried to present a political context in the country introductions and to give precedence to accounts that seem to consider the needs and concerns of the host population; Israel/Palestine is absent because we failed to find sufficient articles which did this.

If we had been able to choose our moment for bringing out a book that covered contemporary experiences worldwide, we probably wouldn't have chosen this one. The world has changed in extraordinary ways since we started work on the project. Pieces on East Germany, Czechoslovakia, Romania and much on the Soviet Union had to be dropped, relegated in the space of a few months to salutory reminders of the old totalitarian days.

It is not that life in these places has altered unrecognisably – social problems and, particularly, attitudes towards women take time to shift – but the premise of travel is different. As borders have opened, so too have the opportunities for contact, and recent cold-war scenarios of reticent conversations and surveillance by the secret police seem strangely out of place. We hope that in those accounts included of places in transition – Christina Gajda's on the dilemmas of being a guest in Poland, for example, or Lynne Attwood's description of the contrasting pressures on women in the different Soviet Republics – the focus on dealings with ordinary people has produced something of enduring relevance.

Harassment and safety

Most women recognise that, much more than bad roads, visa restrictions or poor hotels, it is the fear of sexual attack that most limits the scope of their travels. Yet the issue is still glossed over by the majority of travel accounts. We asked contributors to broach the subject of safety head on, to provide information on the assumptions that were made about them as unattached foreigners, whether harassment was a problem, how they were defined and limited by customs and laws concerning women's roles.

Harassment and safety, of course, are not just an issue for women setting off abroad. It seems easy to forget the limitations we routinely face at home; to forget how habitual it is for us to avoid wandering alone in certain parts of our cities by day and almost everywhere by night; to brace ourselves for comments and jeers if we happen to pass crowds of men; to be far more cautious than men about accepting help from strangers or hitching alone. Belinda Rhodes found Norwegian women "incredulous when they come to Britain and get whistled at by builders", while Susan Bassnett discovered that for Colombians the violence of their own country pales into insignificance against the dangers of New York, "where doors were fitted out with more padlocks than a Colombian would ever dream of and where you cannot be assured safe delivery from a mugger if you simply hand over two dollars or an old watch".

Statistically, we may well be less safe at home. The problem with travel is that we can no longer rely on an instinctive knowledge of what might be considered dangerous, provocative or offensive. In general terms women share an unease about situations where they might feel isolated and exposed. An obvious example is in fundamentalist Muslim cultures where the absence of women on the streets (either actual or because they are hidden behind robes and veils) can in itself be unnerving. Yet sticking to the beaten track is by no means always the safest or easiest option. It is in areas most frequented by tourists, where an easy-going holiday culture has been grafted onto a traditional way of life, that the most damaging stereotypes of Western women have developed – as free-spending, immodest and more available for sex.

Pat Chell, in her piece on Morocco, gives some insights into the sort of attitudes travellers might encounter:

> As for tourists how do Moroccans see them? If a woman is alone or only with women, what kind of woman can she be? No father would put his daughter at risk by letting her travel unless she was already "worthless". Her nearest equivalent in Moroccan society is the prostitute. She sits in cafés, drinks alcohol, smokes cigarettes or hashish and will even comb her hair in public. She often dresses "indecently" – not even a prostitute would do this. She will also be prepared to have sex if you can charm her into it.

And much the same point was made by Sarah Wetherall in Pakistan;

> The combination of sexually liberated women in the bygone age of the hippy trail, pictures of Sam Fox and widely circulated Western pornography make up a formidable myth of the Western woman as a whore. A myth that cannot easily be dispelled by a single woman traveller wearing a *dupati* (headscarf) for protection.

Attitudes as extreme as this are by no means limited to the Muslim world. Helen Lee in her account of living in Sicily described the commonplace experience of being hemmed in by groups of men "leering and touching". And, as Valerie Mason-John pointed out, a black woman traveller in Europe and Australia is burdened by men's fantasies of her as a more exotic and desirable sex object.

Most women are all too familiar with these forms of sexism. However, in travelling, this picture becomes complicated by the fact that you are also a symbol of the affluent West. You have money, status and can perhaps provide access to a more privileged lifestyle – and you may be resented or desired accordingly. In many Third World tourist resorts (notoriously in Jamaica, Kenya, The Gambia and, according to Jane Schwartz, parts of Eastern Turkey) a gigolo culture has emerged where the exchange of sex and male companionship for money is explicitly made. Travelling in these areas, it may well be assumed that you're looking for a "holiday boyfriend" – someone who you might feel genuinely attracted to and wish to share your holiday funds with, but will nonetheless "dump" when you go back home.

The ambivalence men feel about this reversal of sexual exploitation (and the wider inequalities between North and South that make it possible) can find its expression in propositions and harassment. As Valerie Walkerdine comments:

> The attitudes of Mexican men towards *gringas* are about the hate and envy of an exploited people. White women, especially with fair hair, are about the most hated, envied and desired of all. Any glance at the television screen makes it immediately obvious that white skin equals wealth and class in the Mexican popular imagination. Hence many Mexican men's desire to "have" a white woman is matched by their secret (or sometimes not so secret) contempt.

It is also important to note that local reactions are bound up with differing cultural attitudes towards sex. A woman traveller condemned for being "loose" and "immoral" in Asia or the Middle East might be viewed as "uptight" and "aloof" in Jamaica, Brazil and many parts of Africa, where sex is less ridden by taboo. It can be hard to get used to the idea that sex might be offered in a casual way on the understanding that you have the option of saying no.

Strategies

It's impossible to completely avoid harassment – and a list of do's and don'ts strikes us as colluding with the idea that women create the problem. However, as many women point out, to close yourself off entirely would be to miss a great deal. Once you get accepted as part of a community, once you make friends and learn the language, these problems noticeably fade.

Prior experience of dealing with street hassle certainly helps. Lindsey Hilsum, who had travelled to Kenya after a long stay in Latin America, was amazed by the contrast between her first experiences and those of a woman friend arriving fresh from Norway:

As I showed her around Nairobi that afternoon, men shouted and stared at her. Talking to other women later, I understood the problem. Because I had already learned to walk with confidence and aggression, no one perceived that I was vulnerable. But my friend gave off an aura of uncertainty – she was obviously a newcomer, a tourist, and, as such, fair game.

We found the same observations being made about first-timers in New York.

There were many strategies that women used to try and merge in more easily. Following the lead of more Westernised women in the country (adopting their more conservative style of dress and behaviour) was an obvious one. We point out in each chapter the prevailing attitudes, customs or even laws about clothes. For instance, shorts are illegal in Malawi, and any clothes that indicate (let alone accentuate) the figure or that leave hair, arms and legs uncovered are illegal in Saudi Arabia and Iran. In the Pacific Islands, thighs and ankles are far more taboo than breasts and should be covered. Trousers get a mixed reception in most parts of Africa. The variations are endless.

It should be mentioned, too, that the tendency to dress down, reject ostentatious fashion, or make a personal statement by wearing old or ethnic clothes is very poorly understood outside of the affluent West. People don't flaunt poverty and in many countries bright, colourful, or brand new clothes are a symbolic escape from it. Cleanliness and neatness are similarly valued – it helps to be aware of such factors and to follow suit.

Pregnant women and women with children tend be treated as a category apart and accorded far more respect. As Jo Crowson observed, in her account of setting out as a single parent around Morocco, "having a child labels you as another man's possession". Not only did she suffer less harassment but she found that people welcomed her three-year-old daughter with an openness unthinkable in Britain. She was particularly moved by the hospitality and companionship offered her by Moroccan women. In fact the only undermining encounters she had were with other (male) travellers who took it upon themselves to criticise her for "exposing her child to danger". Despite the dire warnings both mother and daughter had a great time.

Contact with women

In many parts of the world, you're unlikely to have much contact with women. This is not only because men have more interest in making, and following up, the first approaches. But the fact that you are free of family or domestic responsibilities, with time to while away in cafés and bars, places you much more in the male sphere of life; women generally have less opportunities to meet, or leisure to entertain, passing strangers.

In the more developed Western societies this is less of a problem, as there are the possibilities of seeking out women with common interests or politics and tapping into established networks of women-only resources, or lesbian bars and nightclubs. We've either given direct listings or have pointed out ways of getting up-to-date information in the "Travel Notes" section of each country's chapter. Jane Basden in her piece on Germany describes some of the problems and pleasures of linking up with women there.

Elsewhere, divisions are more clearly drawn between the woman traveller as "honorary man" and the women of the country concerned. Many of the travellers who wrote to us expressed an uneasy guilt about identifying more closely with men, whose greater access to education and contact with the outside world provided a more immediate common ground. Language can be more of a barrier with women – who are more often limited to the local dialect – and without the shorthand of shared experience it can be hard to find ways to overcome it.

But beyond this it is the relentless nature of "women's work", and the sheer physical demands of stretching scarce resources to meet the needs of a family (and also any guests that are brought home), that creates obstacles to contact. As Kate Kellaway comments, in her acount of living in a Zimbabwean township, "I wasn't so much lazy as frightened by the routine of housework that shaped the women's day". Her experience, like that of many contributors who lived as guests in village compounds, was that her interest and company were appreciated but her attempts to help were treated as little more than a joke – fortunately one that both sides were able to share.

In such societies, the fact of being childless or husbandless, with no apparent family to protect you, marks you out as an object of pity and concern in many women's eyes – as, too, will ignorance of local custom and lack of any knowledge of importance to women. But it's only on rare occasions that you are blamed for your "unnaturalness". Most of the contributors, such as Naomi Roberts in Ghana, found that concern went hand in hand with a spontaneous urge to offer comfort and help.

In the same way, many women travelling in segregated cultures had positive experiences of being drawn into and protected within the women's community. In Egypt Kate Baillie found:

> There is a communion between women who share and work in and outside the home, in ways that our Western conception of sisterhood could never emulate. In Cairo I experienced this almost instinctive kind of care and protectiveness. On several occasions women who were strangers to me, and who spoke no English, rescued me from situations in which I was unwittingly at risk.

And her sentiment is one that was echoed in most of the accounts of Third World travel.

A final, sensitive issue touched upon by many contributors was the clash between Western feminist values and the very different priorities and concerns of the women they met. It is all too easy for a traveller, disturbed by overt forms of sexism and apparently restrictive customs and laws, to condemn a culture out of hand and view the women who have to contend with it as victims, ignorant of their own oppression. It's a perspective that is rarely well received. As Lindsey Hilsum wrote from Nairobi:

> A Western feminist is often resented. There is good reason for this – many Western women simply do not know about the issues which affect Kenyan women, but nonetheless push their own priorities. On the other hand, the widespread denunciation of feminism (which finds its most outrageous expression in the letters pages of newspapers) is a way of keeping women down, by telling them that any change is "unAfrican" . . . issues such as male violence and access to healthcare and contraception are as important in Kenya as in any Western country, although the starting point for pushing to achieve these things is different.

In Eastern Europe travellers found that feminism got a similarly guarded reaction, but as part of an old and discredited Party ideology. Feminism imposed from above has had little impact on sexual relations and the division of domestic labour. "Maintaining a rightful place in the workforce", often in low-pay, low-status jobs, has become an untenable burden to many women faced with the logistics of queueing and searching for scarce foodstuffs. Emma Roper-Evans pointed out in her account of life in Hungary:

> The Communist Party has for years issued great tracts on equality and heroised certain women who took part in the struggle for communism between the wars, but nothing was done and nobody believed it was anything but a propaganda ploy. Feminism tends to be viewed as something that the West can afford to dabble in but which has no place in Hungary.

Obviously you can't and don't suspend your political beliefs and critical abilities as soon as you set off abroad – it's just that private battles and denunciations are unlikely to be viewed as expressions of solidarity. Some of the contributors, notably Jane Schwartz in Turkey and Jackie Mutter in the Philippines, used the opportunity of travel to make contact with women's groups, and present an inspiring picture of the different paths women take towards emancipation. As far as possible we've also tried to point out, in the introductions to each country, the issues and campaigns that women are organising around, and, in our listings, to provide contact addresses of local groups who might welcome international support.

Privileges

Our purpose in putting together this book was to bring women's experiences to the fore – to highlight the invisible travellers who are pounding the beaten track or finding new paths away from it. Inevitably, this is something of a select group. Travel is a privilege (a fact reflected in the preponderance of white, middle-class experiences in this book) and, beyond the Western routes it's a privilege we seldom share with the people of the countries we visit. In setting out, our hopes are high that we will be well received, greeted with hospitality and friendship and accommodated as uninvited guests. But what welcome do we offer in return? Deborah Rutter ends her account of living in Nepal with a question. We would like to do the same:

> It is strange now to remember with what trust they took me into their kitchens to feed me. They would wave aside any thanks and say, "If we came as strangers to your country, you would feed us, wouldn't you?"

Natania Jansz and Miranda Davies, London, 1990.

WOMEN TRAVEL : THE NEXT EDITION

We plan to produce a new edition of WOMEN TRAVEL in a couple of years' time, and would welcome any information of use in keeping the chapters as up-to-date as possible – as well as new, personal accounts of travel (including to those countries we have not been able to cover this time around). Should you wish to contribute or have information on contact listings, books or travel notes that you feel should be included please write to:

Natania Jansz and Miranda Davies
Women Travel, Rough Guides, 149 Kennington Lane, London SE11 4EZ.

Albania

. . . .

At the time of writing Albania stands alone – the last closed and determinedly obscure nation in Europe, Stalinist in politics and closely guarded against the prying eyes of independent visitors and journalists. Rumours of revolutionary activity are rife but hard to substantiate in such an inaccessible country. Since the death of Enver Hoxha, president since independence was gained in 1945, small but grudging concessions have been made towards opening up and for the last few years visitors have been allowed in on carefully organised and restricted tours. Visiting is a bit like going into a time warp, so tightly insulated is Albania from the outside world. Private cars are banned, people work the fields with their hands and there is virtually no sign of modern prosperity.

As a foreigner, you will be constantly stared at and women venturing out alone may experience a degree of verbal harassment, though you are unlikely to feel in any physical danger. While all images of Albanian women remain strictly within the framework of mother, worker and soldier, any visitor inevitably tends to be seen to represent the decadence of the capitalist world.

Despite the government's dismantling of any religious buildings, including mosques, Albania's people remain faithful to Muslim traditions, inherited from early centuries of Turkish domination. Women wear trousers under skirts or dresses and usually cover their heads. Except out in the fields, where women do a major share of the work, men are far more visible, monopolising the streets, bars and cafés after dusk.

Officially, there is equality between the sexes: state childcare is freely available and **women** and men receive equal pay for equal work. But old-fashioned attitudes die hard, especially in such a closed society, and women no doubt have their grievances, not least the double burden of paid work and heavy domestic responsibilities. However, there is no recognised forum for dissent and, if Albania's dubious human rights record is anything to go by, any signs of organised protest would soon be quashed.

The Noise of People Walking

. . . .

Jane McCarten went to Albania out of pure curiosity, having gazed at it from the nearby tourist haven of Corfu.

Albania has at least one thing going for it. Or so I thought as I crossed the border from Yugoslavia. The tight security, searches of cases and bags and stern border guards had led to the confiscation of *Penthouse*. Albanian customs are famed for their ferocity, but this was a decision I would have welcomed at home.

It was to be an enlightening few days. When I returned to customs on my way out of the country, I was not surprised to see a soldier poring over that same magazine. Some things are the same the world over.

I'd decided to go to Albania several years before when I was in Corfu. Wouldn't it be great to have Greece without the tourists? This was my bright idea as I looked across the four miles of deceptively calm water which separates Corfu from the Albanian coast. After the death of Enver Hoxha, president since Albania gained independence just after World War II, I had heard that the country was gradually opening up and thought I'd go there before it changed.

It's not possible to travel on your own, and you are always supervised by tourist guides, but at least you can get a taste of the country. A number of companies offer trips ranging from long weekends to a full two week tour. I went for a long weekend. This is probably about right to get the flavour.

So what is it really like? The nearest I can get to describing the experience is that it's like time travel. Albania is a small country, about the size of Wales, extremely mountainous and with one main metalled road running from north to south. Before I went, I read *High Albania,* an account of travelling in the country in the early years of this century. The author, Edith Durham, found the people warlike and tribal, describing how one night seventeen were shot dead in an argument over which star was the biggest in the sky!

Maybe the book is not so outdated. Enver Hoxha is reputed to have shot one of his cabinet ministers dead in a fit of pique. The men I encountered also seemed to have inherited this tradition of aggression.

"I quickly learned the Albanian for 'whore'. Several men called something out to me and it didn't take long to dawn on me what it was."

Within minutes of arriving at Shkodër, our first stop, we had encountered the Albanian stare. We – two journalists, a lecturer and myself – went for a walk in the main square of the town. Wherever we went, people, mainly men, stopped dead in the street and simply stared at us. It was hard to fathom the expressions on their faces. It could have been curiosity or hostility, or any number of other emotions. Whatever, it was extremely unnerving.

The reaction was less ambivalent when I ventured out alone the next morning. I quickly learned the Albanian for 'whore'. Several men called something out to me and it didn't take long to dawn on me what it was! After that, I always went out with a male companion. It is definitely not a country for the faint-hearted.

On the other hand, a young girl we met picked a huge bunch of red flowers for me and thrust them into my hands before retreating to a safe distance.

Albania is a very odd mixture of cultural references. It proclaims itself to be a socialist state, and has been helped at various times by both China and the USSR before breaking off relations with each in turn. It has spent most of its history under the domination of one European country after another – from Italy to Turkey.

What has emerged is a country with an overlay that any traveller in Eastern bloc countries would recognise: prefabricated modern buildings, state rejection of religion, pride in factories and progress, and an obsession with facts and figures, especially those relating to production and output.

But under the surface, what you find is quite different. Despite the painted slogans on the walls, the churches turned into cinemas and the legislated equal rights, people adhere to Muslim traditions brought centuries ago by the Turks. Women sweeping the streets wear crimplene or nylon dresses and, under them, trousers. They cover their heads with scarves.

Rules of dress for visitors follow the same pattern. Despite being told that there are no restrictions, there quite obviously are. My companion brought a whole factory to a halt as he jogged past in shorts, and the men in our party were asked not to show their shoulders in the hotel. You should certainly try to dress unobtrusively if you want to feel at ease.

During our visit we spent a night at the seaside, at Durrës, and there were seemingly fewer restrictions on the beaches. Women and men mixed together, the women wearing bikinis. But when we went to a bar at the end of the pier we found that it was almost exclusively male. The women appeared at the end of the evening to meet their men and go home with them.

Alcohol seems to be accepted, and even quite cheap. Visitors' food is of the minute steak and chips variety and varies from edible to appalling. But this is to judge harshly a country where the standard of living is low and where meat is a luxury. Rejecting food or complaining about it makes life unbearable for your waiters and may subject you to a lecture from your guide, so it's better just to eat. I took snacks with me for variety.

Evening entertainment for visitors was the same as in most Eastern bloc countries – small bands miming to Western records. You can guarantee a rendering of Stevie Wonder songs in any tourist bar from Tirana to the wastes of Siberia, which is a great pity because of the mutual misunderstanding it represents. We would far rather know how they live, and they are only trying to please us by showing us that they understand our culture.

Glimpses of Albanian leisure were a lot more tantalising. One evening we wandered from our hotel and, attracted by the sound of music, crossed the square to a restaurant with a crowd around the door. Inside a wedding feast was in full swing, with two large families and friends drinking, dancing and singing to an accordion accompaniment. The bride and groom sat rather stiffly between their respective parents, he a lot older than her and rather uncomfortable in a suit.

"Sightseeing is a bit surreal in Albania"

Two tourists who had arrived earlier had been invited in and were enthusiastically dancing and drinking. The rest of us stood outside with the local children, craning our necks to see in through the windows. Now and again members of the wedding party waved their glasses at us in an altogether friendly though not very sober way. It looked like a lot of fun.

Another evening we arrived in a hill town to find the municipal brass band playing to a large crowd. We watched them and the crowd watched them and us in equal measure, impassive as usual. When the band stopped, we climbed self-consciously into our coach and drew out. I waved at the old woman who had been standing stony-faced next to me. She grinned broadly. So sometimes the barriers do come down.

Sightseeing is a bit surreal in Albania. In the 1960s the churches and religious buildings were destroyed, so there is very little in the way of monuments to see. The tourist board is now aware of this and is trying to repair what is left of the traditional architecture. The usual trips to museums and workplaces are arranged, but they are very loath to take visitors to farms and rural areas where they perceive themselves to be backward.

One of the most extraordinary things about Albania is the lack of cars. There are buses and ox-carts, as well as ancient Chinese and Russian farm equipment and trucks packed with people, but few cars. When you open the window of your hotel, there is an amazing noise of people walking.

And life for Albanians? It is obviously hard. Women do much physical labour, from hard work in the fields to washing clothes in the river; and there is a government-sponsored population drive to provide much needed labour. On the other hand, the climate is Mediterranean and living conditions have improved out of recognition since the 1940s.

It's easy to deride this small, fiercely nationalistic and independent country which has been the butt of so many jokes for so long. I'd advise going to see and try to understand and enjoy the process as I did. Looking across the water from Corfu, I dreamed of a land which combined the best of the Greek way of life, without the trappings of commercialism and cheap tourism. Looking back across the water towards Corfu, I reflected that reality can indeed sometimes be stranger than dreams.

TRAVEL NOTES

Languages Albanian.

Transport Your movements as a tourist are largely restricted to official buses.

Accommodation Again, there is no choice since all arrangements are made through the state tourist agency, *Albturist*. Hotels are simple and clean.

Tour operators *Voyages Jules Verne*, 21 Dorset Square, London NW1 6QJ, ☎071-730 9841; *Regent Holidays*, 13 Small St., Bristol BS1 1DE, ☎0272-211711.

Special Problems It is best to dress modestly, avoiding bare shoulders or shorts away from beach areas. Journalists, and citizens of America, Israel, the USSR and South Africa are banned from entry.

Guides Philip Ward, *Albania – A Travel Guide* (The Oleander Press, 1983) is knowledgeable, if slavishly official, full of historical as well as practical information. *Albania, A Guide and Illustrated Journal* (Bradt Publications, 1989) is a bit quirky but up-to-date.

Contacts

There are no women's organisations in Albania. **The Albanian Society**, 26 Cambridge Road, Ilford, Essex 193 8LU, is a useful general contact in Britain.

Books

Edith Durham, *High Albania* (Virago, 1985). Account, first published in 1909, of a Victorian traveller's intrepid journeys in the region.

Thanks to Joy Chomley for additional background information.

Algeria

$\cdot$ $\cdot$ $\cdot$ $\cdot$ $\cdot$ $\cdot$ $\cdot$ $\cdot$ $\cdot$ $\cdot$ $\cdot$ $\cdot$ $\cdot$ $\cdot$ $\cdot$ $\cdot$ $\cdot$ $\cdot$ $\cdot$ $\cdot$ $\cdot$ $\cdot$ $\cdot$ $\cdot$

Algeria has a reputation as one of the most adventurous parts of North Africa to travel. Having featured for years as the starting point for overland journeys to Mali and the West African routes, the country is now developing its own small tourist industry, centred around the spectacular desert landscapes and ancient sights (such as the Tassilli Plateau rock paintings) within its southernmost borders. As yet, there are few facilities for travellers and getting around requires a great deal of patience and stamina. However, the low-key approach

to tourism has its advantages. Coming from Morocco you will be immediately struck by the relative absence of hustlers and guides; although harassment does occur, it's nowhere like as persistent and oppressive as in, say, Tangiers. Travelling alone you are bound to attract attention (in the more traditional southern areas women have a low profile in public) but the curiosity people may feel about you is often tempered by a traditional and very generous hospitality to strangers. Travelling with a man makes things easier, although you can feel hidden and removed from ordinary contact; as in any Islamic society respect is shown by addressing the man first and foremost.

For many years a combination of Socialist welfare provisions and Islamic charity provided a buffer from the worst effects of poverty but as the oil recession has taken hold this safety net has worn thin. Many Algerians are now struggling to maintain a subsistence living in the face of increased austerity measures and unemployment. The non-aligned socialist government which has been in power throughout the country's 26 years of independence is currently facing an unprecedented wave of protest and dissent, which surfaced in the food riots of October 1988.

There's a noticeable lack of adverts, pornography and Western films in Algeria, in line with the government's rejection of Western cultural influences (though *Dallas*, with its extended family, was shown and proved popular). As yet, this hasn't coincided with any overt antagonism towards Westerners themselves; any resentment you experience is likely to be a legacy of the French colonial war. It took fourteen years up until 1962 for the French to cede independence.

During that struggle, women fought conspicuously and bravely at the fore-front of the resistance movement – and **women's liberation** was a central nationalist issue. Post-Independence betrayal of revolutionary promises has been a key theme, keenly felt, for Algerian feminists. They have had to fight for all advances, and to retain the most circumscribed freedoms. In the 1960s huge numbers of women mobilised against dowry payments, polygamy and disparities in wages, and for better birth control and divorce laws. Twenty years on women organised again, in opposition to a proposed family code, derived from conservative interpretations of Islamic law and directly at odds with the Independence constitution. The proposal was withdrawn after demonstrations led by women veterans of the Revolution, but was passed in secret only three years later. Opposition continues with annual demonstrations on International Women's Day.

With the exception of occasional reunions of veteran revolutionaries, women are unable to hold public meetings or actively engage others in campaigns. Meetings are sabotaged and members physically threatened by Muslim fundamentalists. Algerian women are looking to the international Muslim women's community to co-ordinate legal actions against governments who pass unconstitutional legislation and also to a wide range of international groups to help secure the release of women political prisoners.

Overland with Children

. . . .

Jan Wright travelled through the Sahara by Landrover with her husband and three small sons, aged one, two and four.

It was with relief that I crossed into Algeria from Morocco. I was fed up with being hassled and so hoped that Algeria would be different. It was, and as we steadily made our way along the northern coastal strip our mood lightened and we relaxed.

We had come to see the desert, but before we could do that we had to spend several days in Algiers – fighting our way through traffic jams and looking for goods that weren't in the shops. We were soon feeling frustrated again. Even camping was a problem. There was no campsite and we had great difficulty finding a private spot along the coastal strip, partly because of the heavy military presence and partly because of the spread of the population and cultivation. The seaside resorts offered little consolation. Whilst obviously splendid in French colonial times, they are now decaying and depressed, with rubbish piled high in the streets. Eager to get away from the industrialised and "civilised" north, we drove south.

> *"To eat breakfast watching the sunrise, to write by moonlight, and to roll down sand dunes ... are things I will not easily forget. To the boys it was one big beach"*

We were heading down the trans-Saharan highway, which is extremely broken-up tarmac, to Tamanrasset, the centre of the desert. This once sleepy desert oasis is now a tourist centre with visitors being flown in on package tours to luxury hotels. By the time we arrived I was in love with the desert. The freedom and solitude of that great expanse was something I had never before experienced. To eat breakfast watching the sunrise, to write by moonlight, and to roll down sand dunes perhaps previously untrodden are things I will not easily forget. To the boys it was one big beach.

Tamanrasset is also accessible by bus (once or twice weekly from Ghardaia – gateway of the Sahara) and from the town there are organised tours into the desert by Toyota land-cruiser. In many ways to travel with your own vehicle is to do it the hard way. It's tough driving over long distances, but the obvious advantage is the freedom to explore, and we decided to do just that. We drove through the Hoggar mountains and then up north, stopping at the Touareg village of Ideles.

There we were then invited into a *zeriba* – a grass house – by a young Touareg girl to drink tea with her family. The Touareg children were crying with hunger and were given sand to eat to put something in their bellies. Our hostess could speak French and asked us for eye ointment to cure blindness. We learnt later that blindness is very common and could be prevented by the use of antibiotics. Peripatetic teachers reach many of the

desert villages but not healthcare. We gave what we could, and left feeling a mixture of anger and sadness for their situation.

Three hundred and fifty kilometres south of Tamanrasset, near the border with Niger, is Gara Ecker, a weird landscape of wind-eroded sandstone rocks. We spent two whole days without seeing another person. It was magic. From here many tourists continue south into Niger. Instead, turning northwards, we set off to recross the Sahara, travelling the lesser used eastern route via Djanet and In Amenas.

This route is much more spectacular than the highway, but it is also much more difficult to drive and there is little traffic. Certain parts have to be driven in convoy for safety. In the hot summer months it can be weeks between one vehicle and the next and a breakdown could mean disaster. We spent the next two weeks in the eastern part of the desert and I enjoyed every minute of it – far more so in fact than the southbound Saharan journey. I think that was partly because I was so much more relaxed with myself and the people, but also because we were so far off the beaten track and there was an unspoilt air about things.

At Fort Gardel, which is 560km north-east of Tamanrasset, we spent several days living in a *zeriba* whilst our excellent Touareg guide showed us famous rock engravings in the Tassilli mountains. He also drove us right out into the desert to where his brother was camping with the camels. Whilst a Touareg boy caught camels for us to ride, we sat in the sand and ate delicious dried meat, which had been wrapped in dung and buried in the sand.

Our guide had two wives, and twelve children – all from his first wife. The wives lived in separate *zeribas* and shared their husband. To marry a second wife is a sign of wealth and status and I believe our guide was the only man of his village to do so. We felt very sad when the first wife asked my husband if, in his eyes, the second wife was pretty.

"Driving into Djanet, you are struck by the absence of women on the streets. The men do all the shopping, socialising and business while the women stay at home"

My memories of the drive between Fort Gardel and Djanet are of baking delicious desert bread in the sand under the embers of a fire, of a hummingbird singing on top of our tent at sunrise, and of a sandstorm which kept us huddled in our tent for twenty-four hours. Temperatures dropped to freezing as the fog of sand completely blocked out the sun.

Driving into Djanet, you are struck by the absence of women on the streets. The men do all the shopping, socialising and business while the women stay at home. Throughout Algeria there are government-run food shops, called national galleries, in an attempt to standardise food prices and it was in one such shop in Djanet that I found myself the only woman amongst a crowd of men pushing and shoving for cheese and eggs after a new consignment had been delivered. These were luxury items.

Further north we visited a really isolated oasis village at the bottom of a canyon. The village chief came out to meet us, or rather my husband Chris, as he totally ignored me. Chris was directed to the chief's house, while I was taken to the women's compound, where numerous women and children were congregated, feeding and washing babies and small children.

I was requested to sit in the centre and breastfeed my youngest son, which I did, much to the delight and amusement of the women. They also insisted on taking off Ed's nappy to discover his sex. Needless to say I was complimented for having three sons and no daughters.

We continued to drive north, over tortuous black rock strewn with corrugations that shook the vehicle nearly to pieces, and past the wrecks of others that had failed to make it. Then, passing Illizi, we picked up a newly scraped gravel road that felt like a motorway in comparison, and a day later we were on tarmac again, and almost out of "our" desert. The last thousand kilometres to the coast were "civilised" as a result of the oil industry, and for us the magic of the desert was already a memory.

Whilst we as a family were not hassled at all in Algeria, we did meet five Dutch girls at Tamanrasset who, travelling together in a van, had been followed into the desert by some Algerian border guards and pestered for sex. It might be worth pointing out that they were dressed in shorts which is usually seen as an invitation in Islamic countries. They did manage to retain control over the situation and nothing dire happened. On the other hand, two French girls we spoke to had hitched across the Saharan highway with truck drivers and had no problems whatsoever. I feel pretty sure that had the Dutch girls been travelling the eastern route they would not have encountered the same problem. One is less likely to be hassled the further one is from the main tourist route. By the same token, however, one can also expect to be treated as invisible the further one gets from the beaten track.

Camel Trek to Tassilli

. . . .

Janey Hagger first went to Algeria to visit her sister, who was working in the north. Looking for a small, remote yet accessible spot they flew to Djanet, an oasis town close to the Libyan border. She has returned there many times on her own, once for a three week camel trek into the desert.

It was early morning when I set out from Djanet with Abdou, my guide and friend, Lakdar, a Tuareg friend and Laura, an Italian woman whom I had met by chance on the day of arrival, for a long trek up to the Tassilli plateau.

We had three camels loaded with supplies consisting of, among other things, four jerry cans of water and a few dozen eggs strapped precariously on the top of the bedding. Throughout our journey we would be alternating between riding and leading the camels on foot, although Abdou and Lakdar would rarely allow themselves a ride.

The first night was spent at the foot of the plateau in a dry *wadi*, where I lay contemplating the great bulk of the cliffs that loomed out of the darkness, against a sky pierced by tiny stars.

My eyes opened as the sun began to rise; it was cold, but the colours gave a hint of what was to come. The fire was already crackling and coffee, bread and jam were produced. There is a Tuareg tradition that says, when travelling in the desert the men do all the work and the women nothing. Cooking being one of my pet hates this suited me fine, although I became an honorary male when it came to learning about camel handling. This latter bit of sexual role reversal was the dubious domain of the Western woman.

The climb began in the pleasant warmth of the early sun when the rocks and boulders were infused with a warm, pink glow. We continued up and up the almost sheer cliff face along a carefully meandering path. The camels seemed hesitant and disgruntled at this; with wide feet designed for the softly moving sand they do not welcome steep, rocky climbs.

As the heat became oppressive, I shed some clothes and brought out my *shesh*, a long piece of muslin traditionally used as a headdress by the men and an all purpose sun and wind screen by me. While on their own business the Tuareg move at a near run, but we took a more modest pace, stopping to revive ourselves every so often with mint tea and plenty of sugar. The tea acted as a natural amphetamine helping us to buzz up the slopes.

We reached the top on the second day and rewarded ourselves with a longer than normal midday rest before setting off again across the flat volcanic stone. We paced out the miles on foot, talking to the camels, lizard watching and spotting serpent trails that zigzagged across the ground beneath our feet.

Donkeys are excellent at raising the alarm if there is a snake on or near the route, their noses being so close to the ground they can pick up the scent of a fatal reptile, stop dead in their tracks and refuse to go further until the danger has passed. They are also brave rock climbers, leaping across sizeable gaps with grim determination. Camels, with their aristocratic noses in the air, have neither of these advantages but are unsurpassed on the vast tracts of desert dunes.

The rocks began to change formation, some mushrooming out of the earth like small sculptured atomic clouds, others seemed almost fluid, like great waves of rock. We came across fossilised sea-shells, ostrich eggs, arrowheads and the pure white skeletons of camels. Soon the horizon that had seemed like a limitless dome closed in and pillars of rock rose above our heads.

We searched for the most comfortable place to stop for the night. Sometimes we had to make do with a sheltering rock, at other times there would be a small paradise with sand, shade, water and wood offering a respite from the winds. At certain months of the year the winds can blow hot, like air from a hair dryer, for days at a time, but in January we managed to escape the worst of this.

After finding a place we would unload the camels, hobble them and set them free to find their own food. Sometimes the "boss" camel was tethered to prevent him leading the others astray. We collected dead wood, gingerly picking out the thorny branches of acacia trees. The continual need for timber is causing an ecological crisis in the desert, those who live there having to make lengthy excursions from their settlements to find the fuel necessary for survival. A few tourist agencies leave a supply of gas at the more popular places to be used by their tour groups.

Dinner, also made by Abdou, usually consisted of *cous-cous*, a few vegetables and *galet*(bread), baked in the hot embers beneath the fire. During the early part of the journey there was mutton and we also carried some rice and pasta.

As night settled over the desert the silence would be broken by the occasional screech of a jackal searching for breakfast or a mate. We would wait for the fire to burn down, passing round more tea and playing music (the jerry cans doubling up as drums) or telling stories. I would wrack my brains in order to offer a little of my history but the long forgotten art of story-telling can be hard to resurrect.

Sometimes a figure would appear from behind a rock, share tea and pass the time of day with us or rest in silence beside the fire and then rise and disappear in the direction from which he had come. After wrapping up the supplies to protect them from the sand-coloured rodents and sharp-eyed crows, who loved to polish off a bag of sugar, we would bed down for the night. I wore more clothes in bed than at any other time. The nights on the plateau were bitingly cold with frosts that could crack stone. Volcanic rock, however, is tougher than the weather.

"After the fifth day our water supply was getting uncomfortably low. While I had already learnt to bathe in a cupful of water, now even this was forbidden"

After the fifth day our water supply was getting uncomfortably low. While I had already learnt to bathe in a cupful of water, now even this was forbidden. We went to a well-known watering hole and found it dry. A day of hard walking in shadeless countryside stretched out ahead of us. The mountainous rocks had disappeared leaving a plain of black, cracked earth, hard on the feet. Singing kept our spirits up and by early evening we descended into a small valley to find a stairway of three *geltas* (water holes) nestling in its slopes.

The lowest pool was shielded by rocks to offer a perfectly private bathing space. Although we were in the middle of the Sahara, this place, being one of the few water supplies between Djanet and Libya, had become a veritable Piccadilly Circus. Many Malians, fleeing the hardships of the Sahel to find work in Libya, gathered here. We exchanged greetings and gave away some food as is customary for those with the more plentiful supply and being the group closest to its destination. I bathed with the aid of a jerry can and bowl – it is certainly not etiquette to leap bodily into the precious water supply armed with a bar of soap, although, sadly, this is not unknown among tourists.

That evening had a very special quality to it. Having washed the dust temporarily out of my system, cleaned my hair, put on clean clothes and pencilled kohl around my eyes I felt enveloped in a pocket of luxury.

The next stage of the journey was once again among cliffs but this time in the form of alleyways and labyrinths that robbed you of any sense of direction. It is here that some of the oldest rock paintings in the world can be found, providing a clear illustration of a Sahara of water, boats and cattle, a fertile ground where people danced, hunted, fought and made love. Because of these paintings the area is becoming more and more popular with travellers. Our arrival is beginning to threaten the balance of life in the region, although now that border controls and modern transport have almost wiped out the caravan trade routes, the Tuaregs are welcoming the chance of extra work as guides. As yet they are a proudly independent people and hopefully they will be allowed to remain so.

"Everyone, even the Algerian military, has to rely on guides – not least to find the hidden sources of water"

Looking out at the vast horizon, through the large gaps in the rocks, the desert stretched on to Libya in the east and to the edge of the plateau, below which lay Djanet in the west. This, like the land we had just crossed, appeared so different when you turned to look back, that I would have had no chance of finding my way alone. Everyone, even the Algerian military, has to rely on guides – not least to find the hidden sources of water.

The final week of our journey was spent travelling among the main tourist sites. The desert is easily big enough to accommodate all its visitors although a litter problem is gradually developing due to the amount of tinned food consumed by the parties.

In travelling, our hours were set by the sun. We would rise in the pink light of dawn and rest at midday when everything seemed locked in a sizzling heat. My favourite times were the evenings when a golden light saturated the dunes and it would be cool enough to clamber up their slopes and descend in soft, easy cushions of sand.

Eventually we came back down the plateau to re-enter leafy Djanet. The descent the camels disliked even more than the vertical climb. They were tired and hungry. The gravel-like slopes sent us all slipping and sliding, thankfully not all the way to the bottom (not unknown). Once we hit the lower ground, where the air was much warmer, the camels suddenly picked up speed. They were heading for home; I no longer had to guide them towards the easiest path between the boulders as they already had the soft, familiar home ground beneath their feet. It was as much as I could do to keep them in line with the rest of the party.

Soon the palms of Djanet were visible. It seemed like a metropolis after the wide desert landscapes. I dismounted to walk the final mile, turning back as the sun sank low to gaze at the last outcrops of rock.

TRAVEL NOTES

Languages Arabic and (in the south) Berber dialects. French is very widely spoken.

Transport Plenty of buses on main routes, including the Algiers–Ghardaia–Tamanrasset run. Hitching is possible with trucks and other tourist vehicles. Camel treks can be organised through agencies in the south.

Accommodation Most hotels are expensive. Cheaper categories tend to be incredibly basic, like the *zeriba*, a compound of grass huts, which might have a café and camping space for overlanders.

Special problems Sexual harassment – particularly if you're on your own. It helps to dress modestly in long loose-fitting clothes. Coping with a feeling of threat can be difficult. People generally respond intuitively to foreigners and a constantly wary and suspicious approach will lose you many potential friends and guardians. All travellers have to deal with stringent currency exchange regulations, occasional food shortages and a dearth of commodities. You should take any sanitary protection, contraceptives or medicines out with you.

Guides *Morocco, Algeria and Tunisia: A Travel Survival Kit* (Lonely Planet, 1989) is good for general practicalities. *Sahara Handbook* (Roger Lascelles, 1985) is useful for overlanding through the desert.

Contacts

Union Nationale des Femmes Algeriennes (National Union of Algerian Women), 22 Avenue Franklin Roosevelt, Algiers, Algeria. Produces a journal **El Djazairia**.

Books

Fadhma Amrouche, *My Life Story: The Autobiography of a Berber Woman* (The Women's Press, 1988). Born at the end of the last century, Fadhma Amrouche tells of her life in a Berber village, her travels to Paris and eventual acclaim as a singer of the wild and plaintive *Kabylia* songs. Her style of writing draws on the same folk tradition.

"Bound and Gagged by the Family Code" in **Miranda Davies, ed., *Third World – Second Sex*** (Zed Books, 1987). An interview with an Algerian feminist, Marie-Aimée Hélie-Lucas, that details the restrictions imposed on women by an increasingly fundamentalist culture.

Isabelle Eberhardt, *The Passionate Nomad* (Virago, 1987). The recently translated diaries of one of the nineteenth century's most astonishing adventurers. Dressed as a man she mixed freely with the nomadic tribes of the Sahara, even gaining admission to its fiercely protected Muslim Brotherhoods.

Touatti Fettouma, *Desperate Springs: Lives of Algerian Women* (The Women's Press, 1987). Follows the life of one girl growing up in a traditional Berber family.

Ali Ghalem, *A Wife for my Son* (Zed Books, 1985). The painful yet determined struggle of a woman becoming conscious of her own strengths and possibilities.

Juliette Minces, *The House of Disobedience* (Al Saqi, 1984). Introduction to the legal status of women in the Arab world and everyday forms of oppression. Case studies on Algeria and Egypt.

Bouthaina Shaaban, *Both Right and Left Handed* (The Women's Press, 1988). A series of interviews with women from Algeria, Syria, Lebanon and Palestine, highlighting the rapidly changing world that challenges Arab women today.

Pontecorvo, *The Battle of Algiers* (a film – 1965). A classic, clear and powerful on women's involvement in the resistance.

Anguilla

nguilla is a small, serene island at the top of the Lesser Antilles Leeward Islands chain. With a population of roughly 7000, it is dwarfed both in size and in number of tourist trappings by its nearest neighbour, St Martin. Anguilla did not even get electricity until 1977 and the casinos, high-rise hotels and European opulence which are the lifeblood of so many Caribbean islands are thankfully absent.

Anyone planning to visit Anguilla should probably do so in the next ten years. Life is changing so quickly that many of the islanders are reeling from recent events and from developments in the name of progress. The young have become especially disillusioned, and their difficulties in coping with these changes have been exacerbated by the introduction of cable television. These overseas programmes, most of them from America, expose Anguillans to the corruptions of the West: violence, racism, sexism and rampant materialism. Tourism is expanding rapidly as more people discover Anguilla's beauty, the sheer loveliness of mile after endless mile of isolated, quiet beaches, and the kindness of the Anguillan people.

As a lone female tourist you may cause a few raised eyebrows but, provided you respect local custom, people will generally treat you as a welcome curiosity. However, the unsolved murder of two American women on Anguilla in 1988 is a shocking reminder that, even on a remote and seemingly tranquil island, there's no guarantee that you're totally safe.

A dry climate and poor soil long ago forced people to turn to the sea for a living and, at least until tourism catches up, fishing remains the island's prime source of income. People also survive through farming. On top of working on the land and tending the animals, **women** no doubt carry most of the burden of domestic responsibilities. But the extended family is very strong and, despite the escalating number of teenage pregnancies, there are no signs as yet of organised female discontent.

An Island in Transition

. . . .

A black American, Viki Radden had long wanted to visit the Caribbean, intrigued and inspired by tales of her people's history. When the opportunity finally came, she chose Anguilla for its tranquillity and comparative lack of tourist exploitation.

It has been four months since I heard about the brutal murder of two American women on a deserted Anguillan beach. After having spent some time on this tranquil, idyllic island, I still find the news of these women's deaths shocking and incomprehensible.

As a black American woman, I have had an interest in the West Indies since I was a young girl, when my mother told me that there were black people, descendants of slaves, living throughout the Caribbean. Later I discovered reggae music; the day I first heard Bob Marley, my life was changed forever.

When I was finally able to go to the West Indies, I read extensively so that I could find out just which islands I wanted to visit most. I was looking for an undeveloped island, somewhere without gambling or huge international airports and the maddening sight of black people having no choice but to work in bars, casinos and hotels, helping to keep alive and thriving the very industry which debilitates them and irreversibly alters their way of life. From what I read, Anguilla sounded like the place for me.

I sailed to Anguilla from St Martin on the midnight boat, under a giant full moon. I was escorted there by the island's chief of police, with whom I had shared the flight from Miami. When the boat docked at Blowing Point, the police chief led me through customs and helped me find an inexpensive guesthouse.

When I awoke the next morning I went out on the balcony and saw what was, for me, an especially beautiful sight: black people, some of them as dark as their African ancestors, working, walking barefoot in the summer sun, balancing baskets on their graceful heads. There were goats and chickens everywhere.

"The people are so intact, so sure of their dignity, that there is little evidence of a slave mentality"

Anguillans are unique in the African diaspora in that they, unlike most other blacks brought to the Americas during the slave trade, were never actually enslaved. The British reached the shores of Anguilla with a boatload of West African slaves, but when they saw the flat, arid land, so unsuited to the growing of sugar cane, they packed up and sailed away, leaving behind the Africans, who continued to live according to their tradition as farmers, fishers, and keepers of goats and fowls.

On Anguilla the people are so intact, so sure of their dignity, that there is little evidence of a slave mentality. Anguillans are proud and hardworking, and incredibly friendly. There is also a strong sense of family, not only in individual nuclear or extended families, but in the island as a whole. With such a small population, it is not surprising that almost everyone knows nearly everyone else, and visitors, who can't help standing out, will be regarded with friendly interest.

I am black, but I stood out as well. My light-brown skin seemed absolutely pale compared to the darker-skinned Anguillans. Not only that, but most Anguillans I met told me they had never met a black American woman (or man), but that they were anxious to talk to me and to find out what it was like to live in America, a place towards which they naturally have ambivalent feelings.

The Anguillans I met, young and old, were a little surprised by my travelling alone. Some of the women seemed not to understand my reasons for doing so, and some men immediately assumed that I was looking for a man. But they were more surprised that I was thirty and single and didn't have any children. This is nearly unheard of in Anguilla. Marriage is not seen as necessary, or even particularly desirable, but having children is something Anguillan women are expected to do. A friend I met there told me that when young girls get pregnant, there is a lot of community pressure on them not to have an abortion, but to have the baby and let the extended family help with the childrearing.

I met some wonderful people in Anguilla, although there was an initial language barrier until I became used to hearing Anguillan English. One young woman, a 23-year-old mother of two, worked at one of the larger, upscale hotels. She was grateful for her job and didn't seem to worry too much about the influx of tourists and facilities to accommodate them. She lived with her mother and father in a three-bedroomed house on the north end of the island.

But the most meaningful connection I made was with a twenty-year-old rasta-man who was the manager of a vegetarian restaurant. One night we hired a rental van and cruised endless back roads that led to once-deserted beaches now filled with skeletons of hotels, houses and restaurants under construction. He told me how Anguillans, mostly the elderly who don't know the long-range ramifications, are selling off their land at an alarming rate. Rich Americans and Europeans, who have no respect for Anguilla and its culture, are buying property, purchasing entire beachfronts and restricting the property from trespassers. These elite newcomers have no interest in maintaining the traditions of Anguillan life,

quite the contrary. It is in their best interests to bring even more tourists and to build more hotels, all of which are priced beyond the reach of most Anguillans.

The rastaman and I drove to the newly-built house of American movie star Chuck Norris, the he-man who is known for fending off attacks from pesky communist invaders with his endless array of big guns. As we sat and looked at his sprawling house, complete with private beach and huge swimming pool, we were silent. My imagination wandered back to a time not so long ago when Anguilla was virtually unheard of, when no one but Anguillans lived there; I began to see the devastation that comes with each passing day.

I must say that I felt completely at ease as a woman travelling alone. During my stay the worst crime that took place was the theft of various potted plants and flowers from porches of the locals' homes. Tourists to Anguilla can expect to be treated with hospitality, particularly if they respect the customs of the island. For example, Anguillans are modest and frown on nude swimming and sunbathing. I had a wonderful time there, exploring the many beaches, the ruins of the island's original inhabitants, the Arawak Indians, and talking with Anguillans, all of whom seemed to have quite a story to tell.

My most moving experience was spending an afternoon with the children of Island Harbour Primary School. The children lit up the minute they saw me, and whisked me off to a stunning white sandy beach lined with coconut palms. We played in the warm aqua-coloured sea, sat in boats that lined the shore, and took each other's pictures. I saw all of the children home that afternoon, and I am pleased to still be in regular contact with a beautiful little girl I met that day.

TRAVEL NOTES

Languages English, though it may take a while to get used to the island dialect.

Transport Car rental costs about $25 per day, but Anguilla's size – not much more than sixteen miles long by four miles wide – means that it's possible to explore a fair part of the island on foot. Bicycles and mopeds are also available.

Accommodation During the off-season (May–November) prices are about half the amount you'd pay during the rest of the year. The island has a surprising number of guesthouses, starting at roughly $15 per night. There are no established campsites and camping wild is not worth the risk.

Guides *Insight Guides, Caribbean, The Lesser Antilles* (APA Publications/Harrap) is a bit glossy but contains good detailed information. The section in *Caribbean Islands Handbook* (Trade and Travel Publications) is excellent on practicalities.

Contacts

We haven't traced any specific women's contacts on the island. However, it is worth writing for information to the **Caribbean Association for Feminist Research and Action**, PO Box 442, Tuniapuna PO, Tuniapuna, Trinidad and Tobago. Founded in 1985, CAFRA aims to develop and co-ordinate the feminist movement throughout the Caribbean.

Books

Pat Ellis, ed., *Women of the Caribbean* (Zed Books, 1987). Gives a good general introduction to the history and lives of Caribbean women.

Jamaica Kincaid, *A Small Place* (Virago, 1988). Although the author grew up in Antigua, this often lyrical essay against colonialism and the modern ravages of tourism could apply equally to the changes taking place in Anguilla.

Thanks to Viki Radden for her contribution to the introduction and Travel Notes.

Australia

Australia is a vast country, almost the size of North America, yet with 16 million people, concentrated largely on the southern and eastern coasts, it has the same population as Holland. This enormous scale and emptiness make it in some ways a difficult place to explore. Temporary jobs, however, well paid by British standards, are relatively easy to find and travellers often gain most from working their way around.

Long distances and the high cost of living mean that public transport is expensive; the cheapest way to travel is to team up with a group and share a vehicle. Women do hitch, but there are obvious dangers, especially in remote areas and along the Queensland coast. It is certainly not advisable alone. Australian men have been slow to accept the notion of women's rights and the bigotry prevalent in country towns may sometimes make you feel uncomfortable. In general though, people are easygoing and friendly and offer a warm welcome to strangers.

Australia's population is very mixed. It was not, as popular belief would have it, "discovered" by Captain Cook in the eighteenth century. Aboriginal people had lived there for some 40,000 years when white colonisers arrived to disrupt and destroy their harmony with the land. Thousands were wiped out, either brutally murdered or killed off by imported diseases. Their descendants now form a tiny minority – roughly 1.5 percent of the total population – increasingly prepared to fight for self-determination. The rest of the population are first, second and third generation Australians originating mainly from Europe and, most recently, the subcontinent of Asia.

Aboriginal women hold "Women's Business" involving women only, but their main concerns focus on their people's rights rather than the specific rights of women. Current issues at stake include the high imprisonment rate of their men, Aboriginal and Islander deaths in custody, high infant mortality and a life expectancy rate which is some twenty years lower than that of whites. Aboriginal women also played an active part in protest demonstrations surrounding Australia's 1988 Bicentenary. For years a blank on the political agenda, issues of Aboriginal rights were highlighted during the Bicentennial celebrations which, by their very nature, excluded Aboriginal claims.

Australia has a strong **women's movement**, active on government, local and community levels. The Hawke government has a women's advisory committee and even conservative Queensland has a female senator. Equal opportunity and anti-discrimination laws introduced by the 1970s Labour government have laid the foundations for an impressive network of women's refuges, rape crisis centres and health centres throughout the country. However, recent changes in state and federal governments have meant that women have had to fight hard to maintain these services. Recently feminism has also been very much linked to the environmental and anti-nuclear movements and to issues of racial equality and racism.

Working from Coast to Coast

. . . .

Jennifer Moore runs her own solicitor's practice in Glasgow. Before taking on this commitment she spent a year travelling and working her way around Australia. Her jobs included a gruelling month's fruit-picking and a spell as crew member on a yacht.

Driving through Sydney suburbia from Kingsford-Smith airport, my first impression was one of American-ness: long straight highways, lush green lawns, low, neat, red-roofed bungalows, drive-in movies and McDonalds. Later I was to discover how Australians dislike comparisons with either the US or Britain and that they are very conscious and proud of their national identity. Rightly so, for this huge empty continent is like no other.

Although I enjoyed the bustle and nightlife of the large cities of Sydney and Melbourne, I was drawn by the beautiful rain forests and islands of Queensland and the arid red and ochre plains and escarpments of the outback.

"I found the only real way to meet Australians was to work among them"

Travelling first from Sydney west to Adelaide, then north to Alice Springs, you realise that the "red centre" really is red. Ayers Rock, though crawling with tourists, is well worth a climb despite the commemorative plaques at the bottom to those who have died in the attempt. I did not need to find work until I reached North Queensland. Although it is easy to meet lots of fellow travellers in hostels I found the only real way to meet Australians was to work among them.

Travellers seem to congregate in Cairns, where the emphasis is on partying. Due to the crowds of mainly penniless young people, competition for work is fierce. I moved south to Townsville where I spotted a notice on the hostel board for "female crew on a yacht sailing to Brisbane". Though a bit suspicious of the emphasis on female, I went to the yacht club to meet the skipper and was relieved to find another girl from the hostel. Our tasks were to be cooking, cleaning and generally helping with the sailing. The skipper, who lived aboard his forty-foot yacht, could sail alone, but preferred having company to share the load. We both signed on.

Our journey took us through the Whitsunday islands, calling alternately at deserted bays and resorts. The whole experience was tremendous: warm azure seas, dark leafy mounds of islands, clear skies, the rush of water and roar of wind in the sails. Each day we trawled for fish, catching mackerel and tuna, occasionally supplemented with oysters chipped from the rocks with a chisel. Cooking facilities were cramped, but I soon became adept at

improvising with yet another mackerel and at sieving cockroach maggots from the flour. Our dinghy doubled as a washing machine; when half filled with sea water and washing-up liquid the clothes were sloshed about by the waves.

We often sailed along with other boats and visited them in the evenings to swap stories and have dinner, staying in radio contact during the day. Talking to other female crew members, it seems that on the whole women encountered few problems. Nevertheless I did hear of two or three girls being harassed once out at sea, and in a couple of cases it actually seemed to be expected that they would sleep with the skipper. It is probably better to go aboard with another girl, at least to start with.

I arrived back in Sydney at Christmas to visit friends. It was 25°C, but we had turkey and Christmas pudding and artificial snow on the tree. Having spent all my money in the city I again had to find work. Everyone seemed to be converging on Sydney for the holidays, so once more competition was fierce. I decided to head for the country and, through the Fruit Growers' Association, found a job picking pears in north Victoria.

"By 11am the heat was oppressive and the flies appalling, crawling into your eyes, ears and even mouth as you tried to take a drink from a water bottle"

The main town in the area was Shepparton, Sheppo to its friends. I was stationed six miles away, in the midst of vast orchards at Ardmona. The "barracks" were basic – concrete blocks in a dusty yard, with mattresses on wooden benches and water piped from the irrigation channel. Still, there was all the good money to be earned that I'd heard so much about. My illusions were soon dispelled. It was piecework that was on offer at around $14.50

per large bin, each of which took two or more hours to fill. Expert pickers who follow the seasonal crops each year could fill ten bins a day, but a beginner would be lucky to fill four. My average was three.

We would start in the cold dew-damp early light, but by 11 am the heat was oppressive and the flies appalling, crawling into your eyes, ears and even mouth as you tried to take a drink from a water bottle. Our legs were badly scratched and torn by twigs and my skin came up in a rash from the chemicals in the trees. I stuck it out for four weeks and made about $500.

Despite the hardships, they were some of my happiest days. The warmth and friendship among those staying in the barracks made up for the miseries of the day. We were a mixed bunch: other travellers, whole families with children aged between six and sixteen, all working, lone wolves and students. We were organised into gangs and allotted different areas of the vast orchards.

I shared a trailer, on which were loaded two bins, with my room-mate, an Irish girl. Buried in the branches, we used to sing to keep our spirits up and play guessing games. The voices of fellow pickers would join in from inside the leaves of other trees. We all became quite obsessive and in the evenings could sit for hours discussing pears: how well the trees had been pruned, whether the stalks snapped easily, how best to position your ladder. It was everyone's dream to be moved into the sorting shed and put on wages.

After four weeks, twelve of us hitch-hiked to the New South Wales coast where we spent a fortnight camping on the beach, fishing, swimming, eating round the camp fire and generally recovering. It was wonderful to feel clean again.

After visiting friends in Melbourne, my next stop was Perth. I treated myself to a train journey on the Indian Pacific Railway across the Nullabor Plain. It was a three-day journey and cost $300 for a sleeper and all meals. I think this was when the sheer vastness of Australia finally hit me. Looking out of the window the first morning I could see only a flat, red plain with dull silvery green scrub stretching to the curve of the horizon. The next morning it was exactly the same!

Perth is a very attractive, clean city like a large small town. Work was again quite scarce, but I was lucky enough to find a job waitressing in an Italian restaurant in Northbridge, the arty quarter and rather tame red light district. My employers spoke mostly Italian; the kitchen hands spoke Cantonese and with my own Scottish accent we were often reduced to shouting at each other in an effort to communicate. I rented a room in a flat nearby for eight weeks. Though it was probably quite a bad area, I never felt threatened even when walking home from work late at night.

"Sharing a car is the cheapest way to go and probably the most fun"

My next plan was to travel up the 400km of the west coast to Darwin. Sharing a car is the cheapest way to go and probably the most fun. All the hostel noticeboards have offers and requests for lifts. My notice was only up for a day before I had three offers. I shared a beaten-up Falcon station wagon with one other English girl and two men. We camped most of the time and did our own cooking, stocking up in Perth before we left. The main highway north only has room for two cars, the tarmac simply falling away into gravel and scrub at the sides. You can often drive for half an hour or more without having to turn the steering wheel, the road narrowing to a point at the skyline.

One of my most memorable experiences was at Monkey Mia, a beach on

Shark Bay which wild dolphins have been visiting for over twenty years. They are not fed, but just come to meet the human visitors. The campsite at the beach has resident rangers to protect the dolphins and provide information. We got up to watch the sunrise and the sight of those swooping curved backs cruising in the cold, red stillness was pure magic. Stand knee deep in the sea and the dolphins will approach and eye you up. They will offer strands of seaweed which it is rude not to accept. It was moving to feel that we were perhaps communicating with these gentle intelligent animals.

"The whole town goes to watch the sunset, then wanders round the stalls filling up on Asian food and fruit shakes"

After Monkey Mia, we stopped at a campsite at Carnarvon, a rough little coastal town, where we were woken in the night by wet canvas flapping in our faces. It was Cyclone Herbie. All the campers spent the night in the toilet block, sitting on the edge of urinals, brewing tea. Although it seemed an adventure, the uncertainty of how bad the "blow" would be was frightening. In the end the damage was minor.

Further up the coast, we turned inland to the Pilbara region. Here the only settlements are mining company towns. The area is red and dry, but has some beautiful escarpment and gorge systems around Wittenoom. This was once a thriving town of several thousand people, all servicing the asbestos

mine; now it has a population of 26.

Although sad and deserted, it's one of the friendliest places I visited. We were taken walking in the gorges and were roped into the local darts and badminton matches. Life centred around the pub. Heavy rains caused the creeks to flood the roads and we were trapped there for a week. Once on our way again, we were forced by floods to camp on the road, waiting for the water to go down. The four of us felt very small around our fire, pressed by the dark of the desert night.

Our journey continued north through the pearling port of Broome and the largely unexplored Kimberley region, to arrive in Darwin four weeks later.

I spent two months in Darwin doing casual work: cleaning a youth hostel and tourist buses. The city has a tremendous atmosphere: cosmopolitan, lazy, hot and welcoming. It is closer to Bali than Sydney, has temperatures of 32°C every day and a beautiful sunset in the evening, though in the wet season storms and humidity can be trying. My favourite night was a Thursday, when a market is held at Mindil Beach. The whole town goes to watch the sunset, then wanders round the stalls filling up on Asian food and fruit shakes. If you get there early you can find a place for your table and chairs on the grass under the palm trees. It's a great meeting place; I met many travellers who had come to Darwin for a few days and slowed down to the tropical pace so much that they stayed for months.

A Black Woman's Perspective

· · · · · · · · · · · · · ·

Valerie Mason-John is an investigative journalist and researcher based in London. She travelled to Australia in support of Aboriginal protest against the Bicentenary and to research a book on the Aboriginal struggle.

Seven years old, female and black, sitting in a classroom listening to my teacher tell the class about the world and its colourful people: "Africans and Aborigines are the evolutionary link between man and monkey; they swing from trees and are cannibals", she said. The only difference was that Aborigines were a dying race, almost extinct.

"Miss, what does evolutionary, extinct and cannibals mean?" Each word was explained with vivid images.

Ten years old, female and black, sitting in a classroom listening to my teacher tell the whole class about the world and its discoverers. Columbus and Cook were the heroes, two people we should be very proud of and grateful for. "When Captain Cook discovered Australia it was a vast, empty land with only a few savages who were nomadic", she said.

"Miss, what does savage and nomadic mean?" Both words were explained in vivid detail. I believed my teacher. After all, it was she who awarded the gold stars.

Twenty-five years old, female and black, sitting in the outback, living a traditional life among the Yolngu of Arnhemland in the Northern Territories, I pondered on the facts that I had been brainwashed with eighteen years before. I was visiting Australia, home of the oldest civilisation in the world, and this time my teachers were the indigenous people of that country. I lived on missions, reserves, in urban areas and in the outback. My teachers shared their culture with me, which comes from the Dreamtime when the spirits roamed the universe and created the oceans, rivers, plains, valleys, sun, moon and all living creatures.

During the Dreamtime, these ancestral spirits gave the law to the Aboriginal people. This law is told and retold in *corroborees*, when the people dance and sing their own rituals and ceremonies. Proof of these ancestral spirits lies in the landscape which continues to determine the seasons and cycle of life. Spirits dwell in the caves, mountains, places where the sea thunders against rocks, a pool, a tree or perhaps a spring. These places are the sacred sites today.

"I could hear them asking me: 'Why go to Australia, Valerie? It's so racist out there'"

Historical facts which I had stored for years became historical lies. I soon learned that when Captain Cook first hoisted his flag in 1770 there were over 500 tribal boundaries, clans, languages and dreamings, each clan with its own culture, myths, structures, systems and laws that came from the Dreamtime. Within the first forty years of white settlement, rape, disease, genocide and the partition of land had shattered the fabric of Aboriginal society.

While travelling around Australia, the effects of colonisation became obvious. On the surface Australia appeared so white, only because many of the indigenous population were still tucked away on old government missions and reserves. In Tasmania, Victoria and New South Wales the majority of Aborigines are fair-skinned – those who refused assimilation were wiped out.

Being coastal, these areas were easier for the white man to colonise. Further north, in the Kimberleys, Western Australia and the Northern Territories, the land was rugged and inhospitable for the nineteenth-century settler; and so missionaries were sent in to round up the Aborigines and settle them on reserves. These are the areas where many of the full-blooded Aborigines and traditional elders live today.

"We don't have a colour bar here, we have a dirt bar. The Abos are dirty and drunks; they litter our streets with their filth," I heard the owner of a camel ranch in Central Australia tell a group of tourists. Attitudes like this, typical of many of the pastoralists living in red-neck country, reminded me of my friends back home. I could hear them asking me: "Why go to Australia, Valerie? It's so racist out there."

I was in Australia to support the Aboriginal struggle against the Bicentenary in 1988 – white Australia's celebration of a nation, her two hundredth birthday party. The indigenous people had nothing to celebrate. Inviting them to the party was like asking the Jews to celebrate the Holocaust. The Bicentenary marked 200 years of mourning and colonisation for the Aboriginal people, who continue to struggle for a national form of land rights, self-determination, equal status in society and basic human rights.

Visiting Australia was no easy task. Black women who travel round the globe must be prepared for stress caused by combined racism and sexism. Anyone who says only blond hair, blue eyes and fair skin are a hazard for women travellers is a comedian. Black women travelling in Western attire in Islamic and black countries are considered bizarre, while in Western countries we're regarded as a novelty or exotic.

We black women inevitably encounter different experiences from white women who travel. It is rare to see a black woman travelling on her own. In fact it is only those of us from the African diaspora, Asia and the subcontinent, living in the US and Britain, who have easy access to travel.

Seven years ago I travelled for nine months with another black woman through Palestine and Greece, and then hitched back from Turkey to England. We were picked up so many times because people found it a rare sight to see what they thought were two black men hitching. When they realised we were women, backpacking, most drivers were beside themselves. As black women, we were offered thousands of shekels by Palestinian men to sleep with them, kidnapped by a black cult in Domona, Israel, offered work as prostitutes everywhere we visited in Europe . . . But we survived.

"Because I was a foreign black woman, I was perceived as exotic, beautiful and a whore"

It irks me when I read or hear that Arab or Turkish men are the worst. As far as I'm concerned, men all over the world can be as bad as each other. They just have different ways of harassing you, different chat-up lines and charm. After travelling for thirteen months in Australia I could quite easily complain that white Australian men are the worst. Cars would follow me, beep me, wait for me, the drivers seriously expecting me to hop in beside them. Because I was a foreign black woman, I was perceived as exotic, beautiful and a whore.

In Australia every black looks alike. I was always somebody else, not me. "You're the girl who presents on ABC television, Tricia Goddard," I would be told while out shopping. In most states I was stopped and asked for my autograph, only to be abused because people wouldn't believe that I wasn't Whoopi Goldberg. In Sydney I was often mistaken for Sandra, the black American friend I was staying with.

It can be difficult for black women who travel since there are often no other black women from their part of the world to identify with, or offload on to. And in countries like Australia, with a black indigenous population, foreign blacks can be treated with suspicion because the system uses them to oppress the indigenous blacks. The first black woman to present on ABC, national television, was British. Aboriginal people found this a big insult and felt that in 1988 ABC could at least have found an Aboriginal person to do the job.

"I had to acknowledge that as a foreign black woman I had certain privileges and access, being considered better than an Aboriginal"

I noticed how my status went up while living in Australia. I was no longer at the bottom of the pile. I had to acknowledge that as a foreign black woman I had certain privileges and access, being considered better than an Aboriginal. There were occasions when nightclubs allowed me entry but not my Aboriginal friends. Once I opened my mouth everything was OK. However, I was forced to travel by air because coach stops in Australia refused to serve me. Ten hours to go without

refreshments is a long time, and a severe price to pay for the colour of your skin.

The sunshine, the stunning landscape, the ocean and the life of a lotus-eater somehow made life a lot easier to cope with. My skin sparkled, my hair glowed like red embers and I realised that I was not meant to live in a cold climate. Like any other place, Australia is what you make of it, a country where you can choose what you want to see and ignore what you want to miss. Despite the beauty and the fact that it is one of the wealthiest countries in the world, I could not ignore that some of the indigenous population are living in Third World conditions, suffering from Third World diseases; and although they make up 1.4 percent of the population, Aborigines are the most institutionalised race in the world.

Yet with all their hardship I found the communities I visited in Queensland, Tasmania and the Northern Territories immediately friendly and warm – and, living traditionally among the Yolngu of Arhemland, I came across the most gentle men I have ever met.

Six Months in the Outback

· · · · · · · · · · · · · ·

Nerys Lloyd-Pierce is a freelance journalist, originally from North Wales. After some time in Asia she travelled widely around Australia, starting with six months working on a remote cattle station in the west of the country.

Having spent four months travelling around Asia, a trip to Australia seemed

a logical progression. My reasons for visiting that country were ambiguous. On a mercenary note, I knew I would be flat broke by then and had a good chance of earning money. The prospect of warm, sunny weather was also appealing after a succession of chilly English winters.

I arrived with the usual preconceptions about heat, flies and Bondi beach, but was soon to learn that Australia had considerably more to offer. My first preconception was shattered as I flew into Perth. It was green! Greener in fact than the subdued winter face of the England I had left behind.

On the flight from Bangkok I had my first encounter with Australian hospitality. The young guy I started chatting to on the plane was shocked when I remarked that I had nowhere to stay, no connections and very little money, and offered me an indefinite place on his sitting-room floor. This gave me an invaluable base from which to look for the work I now desperately needed.

Finding casual work in Australia shouldn't be a problem and the pay is good. It helps, however, to have a working holiday visa as the government is trying to clamp down on people working illegally. Those I met working without a permit hadn't had any problems, but the penalty if you are caught is instant deportation. Having enough money to tide you over does ease the pressure; I arrived at my first job with only thirty cents left in my purse.

"I saw a newspaper advertisement for a stock camp cook on a remote cattle station . . . Only later did I learn that the job had been advertised for three months and I was the only applicant"

Despite dire financial straits I really didn't want to do a mundane job like waitressing or working behind a bar. Having travelled halfway across the world I wanted to do something which was as much an experience as a job. The chance came when I saw a newspaper advertisement for a stock camp cook on a remote cattle station. I was accepted for the job with an alacrity which surprised me. Only later did I learn that the job had been advertised for three months and I was the only applicant!

To the horror of my Perth friends – urban Australians rarely seem to venture into the bush – I set off, leaving them convinced that I would loathe every minute.

The bus journey from Perth to the cattle station brought home to me the vastness of Australia: close on 2000km of open space and travel for hours without seeing a solitary sign of human habitation. The station itself was situated 260km from any town with over 60km to the nearest neighbour.

The homestead formed a small cluster of houses in a vast bowl skirted by rugged magenta hills. A deep slow-moving river curled in crescent shape around these homes, creating an effective natural fire break. Families had their own houses while the unmarried stockmen lived in bedsits. I was lucky enough to have a house to myself, which gave me both space and privacy, essential elements in what could very easily become a claustrophobic environment.

Everyone used to meet up for coffee and a chat at morning "smoko" when I, being the "cookie", had to produce vast quantities of cake or biscuit. Food was of great importance to people leading such active outdoor lives. There was no television and evening entertainment revolved around barbecues, fishing, playing cards and scrabble. I was always amazed how the same group of people managed to laugh and joke together in spite of seeing each other every day. On the other hand, living in such close proximity you can't afford to fall out with anyone as there's no way you could manage to avoid them.

Coming from a tiny country like England, the isolation of the outback is hard to imagine. The four-hour drive between station and town naturally made conventional shopping quite impractical; fresh produce was flown in on the mail plane every fortnight. If you ran out of anything in the meantime, too bad.

Every four months a road train brought in supplies of non-perishable goods, absolutely essential in the wet season when it was often impossible for the mail plane to land. During this period the dirt road connecting properties with the outside world would become altogether impassable, sometimes for weeks at a time.

Communications were made by means of a two-way radio with a shrill continuous call sign to clear the airwaves in the event of an emergency. In such a case the flying doctor plane would land on the nearest airstrip, but the patient still had to be transported from the scene of the accident to the waiting plane. Radio also plays an important role in children's education. The school of the air is part of their daily routine, the teacher no more than a disembodied voice. To qualify for a government governess a community must have seven or more children of school age.

"We worked on the basis of three weeks mustering cattle in the bush, when we slept on 'swags' (bedrolls) under the stars, and a week at the homestead"

The cattle station covered one-and-a-half million acres, a distance that I found hard to assimilate. Stand on a high point and literally all that the eye can see is one property. On arrival I naively commented that fifty horses seemed a lot in one paddock, only to be told that the paddock stretched over 12,000 acres.

My job out in the bush was to cook meals for fifteen stockmen, or ringers as they're known, on an open fire. We worked on the basis of three weeks mustering cattle in the bush, when we slept on "swags" (bedrolls) under the stars, and a week at the homestead. Every day we loaded up the gear on to the creaking chuck wagon and moved to a new camp, each of which had a name: Corner Billabong, Eel Creek, Old Man Lagoon.

This itinerant lifestyle led me to discover the hidden corners of a region that might simply appear barren and hostile to the casual observer: an arid outcrop of rocks hiding a tumbling waterfall, a pool framed by the luxuriant growth of pandanus palms, the sudden blooming of hibiscus on a dry plain or the strangely contorted branches of a boab tree clawing the sky.

At first I was afraid of getting hopelessly lost between camps – after all there was no one I could stop to ask for directions – until Phil, the manager, put my mind at rest with the wry observation, "No worries, if you've got the tucker they'll always come and look for you."

Despite the obvious novelty of being in a new place and seeing a different way of life, being a stock camp cook was far from easy. At times I felt very isolated from anything familiar and comforting. Physically the job was often hard work and the hours were long as the cook is always the first up and last to finish. On occasions, struggling to lift billies of boiling water from the fire, sweat dripping down my face and clothes smeared in grime, I wondered why the hell I was doing it.

It's not easy to conquer the vagaries of cooking on an open fire. In order to bake a cake or loaf of bread I had to build up the fire, only to wait for it to die down to a heap of glowing coals. The temperature of these coals was all important; too hot and the cake would burn, too cool and it would simply never cook. I can't remember how many times I found myself frantically piling on more coals in an effort to cook a loaf, while the middle remained stubbornly soggy.

"To his amazement I socked him across the back with an axe handle. Cooks are notoriously bad-tempered and I can see why"

Having put so much effort into cooking you become strangely possessive about the results! On one such occasion I had been labouring over melting moments (biscuits which literally melt in the mouth), a task I wished I had never started, when John, the youngest of the ringers, strolled up remarking, "These look good, cookie" and grabbed a handful. Seeing him munching so indifferently after my labours was too much and to his amazement I socked him across the back with an axe handle. Cooks are notoriously bad-tempered and I can see why.

Eight of the fifteen stockmen were Aboriginals. Relationships between the two communities on the station were amicable but distant. I found the Aboriginal men good humoured, easy-going company. The oldest among them couldn't have been more than fifty, though the deeply etched lines on his face suggested a much older person. He would tell me stories of how he first came into contact with white Australians – how, at the age of fifteen when he saw his first car, he got on his horse and chased it off his land. Despite their superficial friendship, a certain segregation clearly existed between the two communities. The Aboriginals always built a separate campfire in the evenings. This was done by tacit agreement and both groups seemed to accept the arrangement. During the twelve months I lived there I never met a white Australian who mixed socially with an Aboriginal and was shocked to find racial intolerance common, even among the educated elite.

"Male attitudes perhaps resemble those in Britain twenty or thirty years ago"

Generally speaking women in the bush tend to adopt the conventional female roles, and male attitudes perhaps resemble those in Britain twenty or thirty years ago. It is considered unladylike for a woman to swear and, by the same token, it really isn't on to swear in front of a "lady". On one occasion at camp I burnt my foot quite badly on the hot coals; all alone, angry and frustrated, I let loose the tirade of swearing I had so carefully been suppressing!

The three women on the station stayed at the homestead while the men and I went out into the bush. I was worried this might create friction, or that they might simply resent me for being an outsider intruding on their close-knit community, but nothing could have been further from the truth. I was welcomed and accepted from the beginning.

The women's role was different, though no less important than that of the men. They were responsible for the smooth running of the station during the men's absence; they organised the vegetable garden and the orchard and kept chickens. They also provided a balance in a male-dominated environment. The station manager's wife was a nursing sister and fortunate enough to be able to pursue her career as organiser of community health in outlying areas. She told me that without the job she could easily have found the lack of intellectual stimulation hard to handle.

Even though I was alone in the bush with fifteen men, I never at any point encountered sexual harassment. Both women and men went out of their way to make sure I settled in and felt happy and at home. Working on the station was an incredible experience, probably the last vestige of frontier spirit left in Australia. Several things will remain imprinted on my mind forever: the cloud of dust on the horizon heralding the return of stockmen and cattle; riding all day across that immense parched land; the sheer delight of coming across a cool shady water hole.

It was not without regret that I decided after six months that the time was right to move on. I wanted to see more of Australia and now had the finances to do so. As a leaving present the Aboriginal men gave me three boab nuts, carved with the traditional pictures of emu, goanna and kangaroo.

Returning to the city was like emerging into another world, only this time it was urban life that felt alien.

Alternative Living

. . . .

Philippa Back was 21 years old and recovering from the break-up of a five-year relationship when she set off for Australia. She eventually found her peace in Nimbin, a haven of alternative culture.

I started saving with my mind set on India, since I had no reason to stay in London. I ended up going to Australia not by choice but because of the salesmanship of the local travel agent who convinced me it was better value for money and a country where I could work to cover my costs.

Looking back, I would barely have survived Bombay airport. What I needed was confidence boosting and inner strength. I travelled to feel like myself again.

"I was aware that my English accent provided an unjust passport to acceptability"

Now, I really appreciate the advantages of, superficially at least, knowing the language and culture of a country: being able to find out where it is safe to hitch and where to avoid (like Queensland), getting money transferred easily and finding out all those essential travel tips almost straight away. In comparison with my other trips, Australia felt easy. "No worries, mate", as they say.

Arriving in Sydney, however, was a complete letdown: it looked so much like London. Why had I spent three days in an aeroplane travelling to the other side of the world to experience mildly less culture shock than I'd feel landing in Scotland? Three months later I was extending my visa and in love with this continent of astounding variety and quite unimaginable space.

I worked for two-and-a-half months in Sydney, as a waitress, packing boxes

and video cassettes, selling soft toys and signing on. (I had a work permit.) Aussie officialdom, like the post, has a rough and ready flavour and tourists are given a welcome blind eye, despite mounting paranoia about the immigrant invasion of the so-called lucky country. At the same time I was aware that my English accent provided an unjust passport to acceptability. Aussies seem predominantly racist and arrogant when it comes to sharing their wealth, and though white Europeans get a good deal, it is not the same for Asian people or for Islanders from the Pacific.

I still had my ticket for India, but through a fateful meeting with an astrologer who showed me the *Nimbin News* I never used it. In good alternative style she convinced me that I needed to visit Nimbin – Aboriginal Sacred Territory, subtropical rainforest and so-called hippy centre of Australia. I arrived two days later and had one of my most memorable experiences ever. Sitting on the bus as we rolled in through the hills, tears poured down my cheeks on first seeing those magnificent Nimbin rocks and I immediately knew that this was where I wanted to be.

Walking into Nimbin I had the remarkable fortune to find a place to rent in the hills almost straight away. I stayed for ten months, working six days a week on the *Nimbin News*, the community newspaper and ecology campaign.

Nimbin is located in northern New South Wales, near Byron Bay, a haven of utopian ideals in a basically conservative land. It is a noble experiment of over thirty communes scattered across acres of hills, jungle, waterfalls and green valleys. Paradise, Bohdi Farm, Dharmananda, Crystal Kookaburra and Heaven are the names of these hamlets of hand-built houses where people grow herbs, keep goats, bake bread and bathe outside; where water wheels in streams provide electricity for televisions and videos; where staircases are built from tree trunks that look like tree trunks; where children go to "free" schools and babies are born at home. Nimbin has community shops, a newspaper, a circus, rebirthing and alternative technology.

"Nimbin is a haven for middle-class drop-outs, for junkies, homeless people, Aborigines, for mystics, astrologers, health freaks and Buddhists"

The community was set up to preserve the rainforest, which it did successfully over years of sit-ins and demonstrations. Living there means spiders and snakes and lots and lots of leeches, and being cut off for two weeks up the mountain in the wet season. My home was on the top of a hill, an hour's walk from the track and a half-hour hitch from the village. I shared it with wallabies, kookaburras, parrots and possums on my doorstep, and sometimes on the kitchen table.

Nimbin is a haven for middle-class drop-outs, for junkies, homeless people, Aborigines, for mystics, astrologers, health freaks and Buddhists. Home too for German and English migrants and the many who fit into no such stereotype, but like myself warmed to the carefree moonlit nights of guitars and festivity, of craft markets, down-to-earth living and wild country. I'll never forget walking into the *Rainbow Café* on the high street, seconds from the cupboard-size police station, to find drugs and carrot cake and an ambiance of gentle rebellion.

Nimbin is laid back yet active. Yet I read more newspapers than ever before. I wrote to more politicians and campaigned more actively for the rights of people in South America, Papua New Guinea and South Africa than during my "right on" days in London. I wrote about incest and women's experiences of violence in the home. I spent five days walking through the bush and waterfalls with a woman friend and her two-year-old child, without seeing a soul, nor fearing if we did. I met women who peed on the beach like men, and for all my feminist training I found myself to be far more romantic, idealistic and naive about men than these Aussie women who, despite driving trucks and working on prawn trawlers, still had a hard time being seen as anything more than a "Sheila". Their lack of willingness to compromise taught me a lot.

Nimbin is an island in Australia, a space that probably only exists because the country is so large, and those who hate its every association live a long way up north. However, survival is not that easy, as people campaign again and again for their community to be recognised by the government so as to ensure its protection. I recommend anyone to visit, for the magnificent countryside if nothing else. Stay a little longer at the Youth Hostel and in the café, and you'll find warm and friendly people and get a chance to visit the communities up in the surrounding hills. It took me a long time to recognise the subtle differences between here and Australia, but they grew on me. I finally left knowing that my experience had changed my life.

TRAVEL NOTES

Languages English is the official language, but you'll also find Italian, Greek, Serbo-Croat, Turkish, Arabic, Chinese and numerous Aboriginal languages.

Transport A good system of trains, buses and planes connects major cities. Public transport is expensive, but prices are competitive and it's a good idea to look around. Petrol is cheap by British standards so it's worth buying your own vehicle if you have the time and money. Hitching alone is not advisable.

Accommodation Suburban motels tend to be much cheaper than those in central locations. Sydney, especially, has lots of hostels geared up to travellers. Australians are very hospitable so don't be afraid to use any contacts you may have. University noticeboards can also be good sources (and for lifts too).

Special Problems Working visas are becoming increasingly hard to get, especially for visitors older than 26. Applications should be made well before you leave home and you will need evidence of sufficient funds to cover your trip.

Guides *Australia: A Travel Survival Kit* (Lonely Planet) is thorough, though written from an Australian perspective and sometimes assuming a bit too much knowledge. *A Traveller's Survival Kit to Australia and New Zealand* (Vacation Work) is the latest in this new series, worth checking out.

Contacts

It would be impossible to include here all Australian **feminist groups**. The following list focuses on some of the major cities – for more details take it from there.

ADELAIDE: **Women's Liberation House**, 1st Floor, 234A Rundle St., Adelaide 5000 ☎223-180.

BRISBANE: **Women's House**, 30 Victoria St., West End 4101 ☎44-4008. For women's radio in the city tune into Megahers on 102FM (5pm Tuesdays).

CANBERRA: **Women's Centre**, 3 Lobelia St., O'Connor 2601 ☎47-8070; **Women's Shopfront Information Service**, Ground Floor, CML Building, Darwin Place, Canberra 2600 ☎46-7266.

DARWIN: **Women's Information Service**, PO Box 2043, Darwin 5794 ☎81-2668.

MELBOURNE: **Women's Centre**, 259 Victoria St., West Melbourne 3000 ☎329-8515. Groups at this address include Women Against Rape, Lesbian Line, Women's Radio Collective and Women's Liberation Newsletter.

PERTH: **Women's Information and Resource Centre**, 103 Fitzgerald Rd., North Perth 6006 ☎328-5717.

SOUTH HOBART: **Women's Information Service**, 4 Milles St., South Hobart 7000 ☎23-6547.

SYDNEY: **Women's Liberation House**, 62 Regent St., Chippendale 2008 ☎699-5281.

Selected women's bookshops

ADELAIDE: **Murphy Sisters Bookshop**, 240 The Parade, Noward 5067 ☎332-7508.

BRISBANE: **Women's Book, Gift and Music Centre**, Cnr Gladstone Rd. and Dorchester St., Highgate Hill 4101 ☎332-7508.

SYDNEY: **The Feminist Bookshop**, 315 Balmain Rd, Lilyfield 2040 ☎810-2666.

VICTORIA: **Shrew**, 37 Gertrude St., Fitzroy 3065 ☎419-5595.

Books

Robyn Davidson, *Tracks* (Paladin Books, 1982). Compelling, very personal story of how the author learned to train wild camels and eventually sets off with four of them and a dog to explore the Australian desert.

Helen Garner, *Postcards from Surfers* (Bloomsbury, 1989). Recommended short stories by one of Australia's finest women writers. **Dorothy Hewett, *Bobbin Up*** (Virago, 1985). Entertaining portrait of working-class life in Australia in the 1950s and only novel by one of the country's leading women playwrights, first published in 1959. Also look out for her forthcoming autobiography, ***Wild Card*** (Virago, 1990).

Pearlie McNeill, *One of the Family* (The Women's Press, 1989). Vivid account of her often unhappy life growing up in Sydney during the 1940s and 1950s.

Glenyse Ward, *Wandering Girl* (Virago, 1988). The author, an Aboriginal from Western Australia, tells her own story of growing up in a white world.

John Pilger, *Secret Country* (Jonathan Cape, 1989). This investigation into Australia's hidden history by one of the country's leading journalists incorporates a strong indictment against the persistent maltreatment of Aboriginal people.

Robert Hughes, *The Fatal Shore* (Pan, 1988). Riveting account of Australian settlement.

Jill Julius Mathews, *Good and Mad Women* (Allen and Unwin, 1984). Traces a history of Australian traditions behind the national ideal of the "good woman".

Susan Mitchell, *Tall Poppies* (Penguin, 1983). These profiles of ten successful Australian women make an inspiring and well-balanced read (the women come from all backgrounds and nationalities). The book has been a phenomenal best seller in Australia.

Sally Morgan, *My Place* (Virago, 1988). A powerful and widely acclaimed account of a young Aboriginal woman's search for her racial identity.

Bruce Pascoe et al., eds., *The Babe is Wise* (Virago, 1988). Excellent collection of contemporary short stories by Australian women writers.

Isobel White et al., eds., *Fighters and Singers: The Lives of Some Australian Women* (Allen and Unwin, 1984). Collection of stories focusing on the lives and strong characters of a number of Aboriginal women.

David Adams, ed., *The Letters of Rachel Henning* (Penguin, 1985). Written between 1853 and 1882, the letters give a vivid account of life in colonial Australia as seen through the eyes of a previously sheltered young Englishwoman.

Also novels by **Miles Franklin, Henry Handel Richardson and Christina Stead** – classics by and about women.

Other publications

Keith D. Suter and Kaye Stearman, *Aboriginal Australians* (Minority Rights Group, Report No. 35, 1977). This excellent report, revised and updated in 1988, includes useful addresses and a select bibliography.

There are many feminist magazines in Australia, among them *Girl's Own, Hecate, Womanspeak, Scarlet Woman* and *Liberation*.

Thanks to Christine Bond, Karen Hooper, Tessa Matykiewicz and Jenny Moore for their individual contributions to these Travel Notes.

Bangladesh

In the minds of most Westerners, Bangladesh remains synonymous with the worst ravages of war, famine and disaster. Whilst a superficial "stability" has been reached under President Ershard, who gained control of the military junta in 1982, the country continues in a state of devastating economic crisis made worse by the ever more frequent out-of-season floods.

In recent years very tentative attempts have been made to entice travellers from the usual subcontinent routes – "Come to Bangladesh before the tourists get here", being the main airline slogan. However this is not a country to visit casually. The degree of poverty experienced in the villages (where most of the country's 100 million people still live) can come as a shock even if you've travelled extensively around

India. Also as a predominantly Muslim country, although not formally an Islamic state, women are expected to conform to Islamic codes of dress and behaviour, a pressure which increases as the fundamentalist movement gains political ground. In the main towns, women are rarely seen in public and those who are, will usually be covered by a *burqua* (a form of veiling).

A number of Western women work in Bangladesh with the development agencies and relief organisations, and reports are that it is easier to travel alone here than in Pakistan. As a stranger (particularly if you are white) you are bound to attract attention – people may be intensely curious about you and astonished by your freedom to travel independently but this is usually expressed in a welcoming, friendly way, often showing great concern for your safety.

Aid and development agencies within the country are increasingly recognising that the long-term survival of impoverished rural communities will depend on how much **women** can be supported in their role as care-givers and providers. Operating at a very local level – and within the confines of Muslim custom – projects have been set up to educate women in healthcare, nutrition and literacy.

Working in Development

· · · · · · · · · · · · ·

Christina Morton went to Bangladesh as a volunteer with a development project. She spent three-and-a-half months there, living mainly with Bengali families in Dacca and the surrounding villages.

During my stay in Bangladesh I experienced complete and profound culture shock – I doubt even now I can write objectively about what it's like to visit the country. I did not go as a tourist – few people do. My purpose was to observe, and as far as possible to participate in, some of the innumerable development projects which have sprung up since the war of independence with Pakistan.

In Bangladesh poverty permeates every facet of human existence, and emotional, cultural, social and political interactions are all to some extent determined by this. I would not, though, discourage anyone from visiting the country provided they were really prepared to open their eyes, their ears, their hearts and their minds to the society around them. This of course takes time and commitment, and it's debatable whether a very short stay would afford great insights.

I was lucky in that for most of the time I wasn't forced to stay in hotels but was able to live with Bangladeshi families, urban and rural, poor and not so poor. Also, though my status of

single woman closed a few doors (inevitably of mosques and shrines), it brought me the huge advantage of contact with Bangladeshi women. Having been given initial introductions – most often, from men – I was allowed behind the veil of purdah to see the harshness of women's lives and feel their warmth, their gentleness and generosity.

This process was never easy and I would be emotionally exhausted at the end of a day. Bangladeshi women lack any comprehension of Westerners wanting privacy, and in addition I sometimes felt that I was not appearing as a person with depth, humanity and personality but as a symbol of promiscuity perhaps, of beauty – they have a high regard for white skin – but above all of affluence. Yet it was an unfailingly rewarding process to strip away layers of cultural differentiation, to build a bridge across the gulf that separated us in terms of economic circumstance, and to achieve, on occasion, that truly human contact which is the reward of all travellers.

"One of the names that was called after me was the Bengali word for eunuch"

Language was sometimes a problem. I never picked up as much Bengali as I could have wished, but there are sometimes better ways of communicating – signs, touch, laughter. Indeed there were times when I was positively glad to be unable to understand Bengali. Bangladesh is an Islamic country (not, like Pakistan, an Islamic State but under the influence of aid-giving Middle Eastern countries such as Saudi Arabia it becomes more dogmatically religious every day) and women are simply not seen in public places without the veil, or at least a male escort. Women who do venture out, women who like me walk about alone in the streets, are considered whores and are called after as such.

Sometimes my short hair and my unconventional clothing (I usually wore for modesty's sake – and I would advise any women to do the same – a long-sleeved hip-length shirt over trousers or a longish skirt) invited men to speculate about my sex and one of the names which was called after me was the Bengali word for eunuch. This did not really upset me, because on the whole I had anticipated far worse sexual harassment than I ever actually experienced, and indeed I often felt safer travelling alone in Bangladesh than I do crossing my home town in England.

My hosts, my fellow travellers and the friends I made were often beside themselves with anxiety on my behalf. "Where are your brothers?", they would ask, "Don't you need your father to protect you?", "Don't you miss your mother?" An independent and self-sufficient woman is indeed an enigma to them.

People are what a visit to Bangladesh is all about. There is little point in going if you are more interested in monuments (there are none) or a fun time (forget it). The only places that could be described as being of "tourist interest" are Sundarbans in the south (last remnants of genuine jungle, where people motorlaunch into the forest waterways in search of wildlife) and the 70-mile beach at Cox's Bazaar. But even if the will is there, the near total dearth of tourist facilities makes the usual indulgent "holiday resort" lifestyle impossible.

People, however, are everywhere, over a hundred million of them squashed into a country which is no bigger than England and Wales together. The vast majority live in the villages but even the ten million or so who form the urban population are sufficient to throng the streets and cram the public transport system to bursting. Every bus and railway carriage has almost as many bodies hanging from the outside as are squashed into the interior.

"I would be surrounded by crowds, sometimes scornful, suspicious or even hostile, sometimes merely curious, but mostly, or so it seemed to me, gentle and welcoming"

On a few occasions I visited villages where a white face had never been seen and where England (*Bilat*) was the stuff of legends and faded memories. In any such place I would be surrounded by crowds, sometimes scornful, suspicious or even hostile, sometimes merely curious, but mostly, or so it seemed to me, gentle and welcoming and always ready with hospitality – water, rice, the juice of the date palm, precious eggs.

Women in Bangladesh carry simultaneously the burdens imposed by economic exploitation, from both national and international sources, and a society which in both its religious and secular aspects is stubbornly patriarchal. Uncharacteristically, however, the government has legislated for a quota of ten to fifteen percent of women in employment in all areas of administration and industry, and several of the leading figures in the opposition political parties are women.

Far more significant, I felt, was the relative effectiveness of development schemes which have grasped that the recovery and advancement of the entire country would stand or fall on the improvement of the position of women – their health, their education, their nutrition and their participation in the political and economic organisation of their society.

Bangladesh is, in the villages at least, and particularly where endemic landlessness has rotted the social fabric from within, an embryonic gathering together of the fragments of a ravaged social structure into what is as yet the flimsiest of edifices, so fragile in the face of the odds stacked against it that you tremble for it.

What hope have 100 million souls, half of which hover at or below the poverty line, chronically malnourished, in the face of increasing landlessness among the peasants, a rocketing population (which is predicted to reach 150 million by the end of the century), an escalating national debt, a dearth of commodity resources and a heritage of feudalism and imperialism? All the problems which we now so glibly label "Third World" are concentrated in Bangladesh to a degree which will inevitably shock.

But projects such as *Gonoshastraya Kendra* (the People's Health Centre) just north of the capital, Dacca, and those working under the auspices of the Bangladesh Rural Advancement Committee (both entirely indigenous organisations, incidentally) have recognised the enormous potential for radical change and development which lies in the hands of women.

Women who are healthy, properly fed, basically literate and skilled, who have, in other words, access to the opportunities available in their society now and the chance to create further opportunities for the future – in their hands lies not merely *a* hope, but *the* hope of Bangladesh's future generations. I could not avoid reflecting that this is a concept of social development with which the most advanced Western nations have in large measure yet to grapple.

Learning Village Life

. . . .

Katy Gardner, a British research student in anthropology, spent a year-and-a-half living in a village in the north of Bangladesh.

As the plane began its slow descent, a flat expanse of endless paddy fields and long winding rivers spread out beneath us. Closer down, scattered village compounds came into view: men driving bulls through mud, fishing nets spread across waterways, people working in their yards. At last we had arrived in Bangladesh.

It was the beginning for me of a sixteen-month stay. As a student of

anthropology my task was relatively simple – to find myself a village and live in it, as much a part of the community as possible, to let the village people teach me about their lives. I had travelled fairly widely in India and Pakistan before, as well as in other parts of the Muslim world, and had always felt strongly drawn to the Indian subcontinent. I had also always found the role of a tourist, unable to speak the local languages, inherently frustrating. This time would be different. I would learn Bengali and actually get close to people where previously I had felt apart.

I made my base in Dacca, a sprawling and chaotic city which by any standards is hard to love, and tried to connect to its modern streets and shopping arcades, its pristine parliament building and ghetto of luxury mansions owned largely by aid donors, to what I felt must surely be the "real" Bangladesh – a country which is mainly rural, with a depressingly large percentage of its population below the poverty line.

Like many of the foreigners I stayed in the district of Gulshan with a friend in a huge house owned by an American donor agency. There was a 24-hour guard service, a full staff, and more rooms than could ever be used. Dacca, like most South Asian cities, is a place of contrasts. Close to this area, although well hidden from sight, were the horrific *bustees* of Dacca – vast areas of huddled huts made from polythene sheeting and jute matting, and down the road, the smog and crowds of the central city.

I was to visit Dacca many times in the months to come, taking breaks from my periods in the village, and although I enjoyed those spells of getting away from it all, I found it disturbingly easy to lead a life there quite separate from Bangladeshi people. Sadly, many of the expatriates have little to do with Bangladeshis socially, and rarely leave Dacca. Perhaps because of this lack of contact, and because the middle classes usually speak good English, many never get round to learning Bengali properly. I was shocked, but perhaps not really surprised by how quickly and easily some of the Westerners took to the master-servant relationships they were involved in. In some ways the Raj, albeit in the form of international aid, still continues.

But although foreigners driving smart jeeps around the city are a common sight, once outside the relative peace of the middle-class suburbs, they attract the usual crowds and stares common in the rest of Bangladesh, especially in the warren-like alleys and roads of the old city.

Foreign women are even more of an oddity; the streets of Dacca are crammed with people, but they are almost exclusively men. In the old city women, if seen at all, are hurrying past, wrapped up in their *burquas*, with faces averted. This does not mean that the atmosphere is hostile to foreign women, but women wandering about alone are conspicuous, an easy target, and I always took the warnings not to walk alone around the city at night seriously.

"A middle-class Bangladeshi said I would never survive the rigours of life without electricity, or eating rice with my hands"

So, after about a month of leading a lifestyle far more luxurious than I had at home, a development worker whom I had met on a trip up north to Sylhet introduced me to a family in his wife's village, and we decided that I should move in. Back in Dacca, a middle-class Bangladeshi said that I would never survive the rigours of life without electricity, or eating rice with my hands. White expatriates talked in terms of rabies injections and medicines, and I bought myself a mosquito net and a hurricane lamp.

I eventually moved into my new home one night in September, travelling by boat from the nearest road with a small group of villagers returning home from a trip to Sylhet. From June to October much of the country is under water, and even under normal, non-flooded conditions (the recent floods which have been so disastrous are not part of this seasonal pattern), many places can only be reached by the painted wooden boats of the villages. In November, the clouds and heat clear, and with the cooler, dry weather, fields and paths miraculously appear from a morass of mud. When the rains start in the spring these are inundated, and the landscape becomes watery once more.

"Although I never enjoyed it, I gradually became used to the excitement my appearance inevitably generated"

That evening we passed straggling villages, waterlogged fields, and groups of children on the paths calling out "Inreji! Inreji!" (English) when they saw me. Very few white people venture outside the urban areas and those that do are always assumed to be English. They are viewed with a mixture of amazement and extreme curiosity.

At the politest end of the continuum this leads to the eternal question: "What is your country?", at the other end huge crowds gather to gape and comment on your every move ("What is she doing? . . . Look, she's alone . . . She doesn't speak our language, she's white . . . Look, she's opening her bag . . . " etc, etc). Although I never enjoyed it, I gradually became used to the excitement my appearance inevitably generated.

Six hours later, and about five miles from the potholed road (the boat being not exactly speedy), long after the sun had set and the Bangladeshi sky turned violet, I arrived. Immediately I was surrounded by clusters of children and the many faces of my new adoptive family. I had of course already met them a month earlier, but I still had no idea who was who, especially as many of the children and younger women had felt unable to come out in front of me and the distantly-related town man who had been my escort.

Now, everyone was present: Amma, my new mother, who took my hand and pronounced immediately that I should be just like a daughter to her; Abba, my dad, who shuffled in to receive my Salaam and then with a chuckle went back to his hookah; and numerous young women – my sisters who were to become my closest friends. I understood hardly anything that was being said to me but it didn't really matter. In

a process which was to be repeated many, many times in the following weeks by every family in the village, I was inspected and commented upon. "Look, she's so tall," they said, "Look, she doesn't wear a sari . . . Why don't you wear oil in your hair? . . . Yallah, she's not a proper Londoni, she isn't fat enough . . . Look at her great earrings . . . " and so on.

I didn't really mind these appraisals, since they were a quick way of striking up friendships and of proving that I was no threat and quite prepared to make a fool of myself. More or less everything I did caused outbursts of laughter (whether I'd intended it to or not) and nothing more so than my pathetic attempts to speak the Sylheti dialect. Not surprisingly nobody understood why I should possibly want to live with them and learn. "How can you learn here?", they asked, "Where are your schoolbooks?"

Eventually most people accepted that for some extraordinary reason, I spent hours writing and asking exceedingly stupid questions and wanted to live in their village. "But why come here?", I was often asked, "Your country is a land of peace and richness. Why are you here when we all want to be there?"

Everyone agreed that I had to start at the basics if I wanted to live as they did. "Katy," one of my sisters, Khaola, announced as she eyed me making a mess with my supper of rice that first week, "you're just like a baby, but don't worry, after a year with us we'll make you into a proper Bengali." She was right, I had a long way to go.

Everything I did at first was watched, criticised, laughed at, and corrected. I had to learn how to tie a sari, bathe in the family pond, how to wash out my clothes properly on the stone steps, how to eat my rice, spit, use water in the latrine and much, much more. Compared with the other women, I was a complete oaf and indeed, hardly female. I was clumsy at cutting bamboo or vegetables on the great blades the women squat over, unable to light the fire, and hopelessly inelegant in a sari, which kept riding over my heels. Worse than that, I kept forgetting to cover my head.

As I let the village people mould me, however, I began to learn much about the essence of being a Muslim woman in rural Bangladesh. To be approved of, you must be as feminine and submissive as possible. You must dress in a certain way; your hair must be tied back and smoothed with oil, otherwise you will be seen as "mad" and manly; your sari must be tied properly and your blouse fit in the correct way. There are certain bits of you which must never be shown, especially your legs and ideally your head should always be covered. You must talk quietly, not call out or run; you must be shameful and obedient to your menfolk. An old adage, which village women often quote, is that: "A woman's heaven is at her husband's feet".

"When strange men came into the family compound, I jumped up with the other women and ran inside, feeling genuinely ashamed"

I certainly failed on most counts of modesty, especially as I never succeeded in changing into a new sari after bathing without revealing myself, or in keeping it continually over my head. But slowly, as I stayed longer in the village, I noticed that a transformation had happened in my values as well as my appearance. Not only had I begun to sit, dress and talk like the village women, but to my amazement I began to express the same sorts of ideas. "It is the will of Allah", I heard myself telling people, and when strange men came into the family compound, like the other women I too jumped up and ran inside, feeling genuinely ashamed. If I went out without an umbrella to keep my face hidden, I felt naked.

It was alarming, to say the least. If fourteen months can have effects like that on such a product of Western feminism as I had considered myself to be, what would happen after two years or more? And what did it imply about the security of my beliefs if they could be so easily moulded by a new environment?

Of course this doesn't happen to all Western women who visit Bangladesh. My need to be open to the culture and customs of my hosts left me peculiarly vulnerable. Bangladesh is a very difficult country to get to the heart of, and many visitors leave feeling unsympathetic towards it. This is perhaps because although extremely friendly, Bangladeshis tend to be on their guard with foreigners. The country has had a short, violent and politically unstable history, and foreigners, who originally came to Bengal to rule, now usually come as dispensers of aid or advice. "What project do you work for?", is almost as ubiquitous a question as "What is your country?", and many foreigners inadvertently end up as the patron of a Bangladeshi. I was continually asked for money by people in the village. Poor women would come into my room and ask for saris or *taka* – they felt that since I was rich, which I must have been since I was white, it was my duty to give. I nearly always refused, knowing that I could not manage the stream of requests and people's expectations of me had I taken those initial steps. However frequent this became I never managed to get accustomed to the requests and demands made of me, or my hollow excuses that I wasn't *really* rich. When I left, I gave away all my clothing, bedding, etc and even my bras, which various women had been eyeing all year. One of the last things which one old destitute woman said to me was: "Now you have your own poor, we are your responsibility now."

Just as relationships with foreigners can be coveted, leading as they might to patronage and help, they can also be regarded with horror, due to our dirty ways, loose women and alcohol consumption. This ambivalence is especially strong towards young white Western women. We are respected because we are probably involved in aid, and certainly rich, yet viewed with unease because of our independence. One of the most common reactions I had when meeting people from outside the village was a horrified: "But are you alone? Aren't you married?" So that after sixteen months I too began to see myself as some kind of freak.

Although people may be surprised, even affronted, to see a woman alone, I always felt that Bangladesh was a relatively safe place to travel in. Wherever I went, people were anxious to help me (whether I needed it or not) and get talking. I travelled by trains, local buses, planes and ferries, and always ended these journeys with new friends. Speaking the language helps of course, as does dressing appropriately – I always wore *shalwar kameez* (baggy trousers and long tops), and an *orna* (scarf worn over the chest), or in the village, a sari.

"'Why should we be afraid of you, sister?' I was told so many times, 'Aren't we all women?'"

My sex was far more of a blessing than a curse, which I have sometimes felt it to be in other countries. Whilst most rural women would never talk to foreign men, wherever I went I was welcomed into women's quarters. Our Western inhibitions do not exist in these places and friendship is easily and unquestionably offered. "Why should we be afraid of you, sister?"

I was told so many times, "Aren't we all women?"

Sixteen months after landing in Dacca, I began to prepare for leaving the village. Many of the villagers asked me to stay, "You can become a Muslim, we'll arrange a husband for you." I wasn't so sure about the conversion or the husband, but leaving was certainly extremely difficult.

The day I went, many people came to our homestead. A tinsel garland was put around my head, and Amma fed me the special sweetmeats she had made. A crowd of people then led me down to the river where a boat was waiting to take me back to the road across the flooded fields, this time for good. As was expected of us, we all cried. The boat punted me away while I looked back at the figures, dwindling against the green fields behind. I knew that my return to Britain would not mean that I would stop being their daughter and that we would write regularly. Now, after a few months in London I am already planning my return.

Bangladesh is a powerful and very beautiful place, with golden winters, lush greenness and kingfishers darting over great rivers of water lilies. My image of the country had been largely of a poverty stricken land, precariously surviving an endless cycle of famine, and bloody coups – swollen-bellied children with begging bowls staring out at me from the TV news or Sunday supplements. That poverty and suffering are very real, yet throughout my time in Bangladesh I was constantly reminded that the ways in which it is portrayed by the Western media conceal in a cloak of sensationalism that the majority of Bangladeshis are extraordinarily resilient. They do as they have always done – they carry on.

TRAVEL NOTES

Languages Bengali. English is widely spoken.

Transport Flights between towns are incredibly cheap. There's a limited rail network and a few buses but these tend to be old, decrepit and massively overcrowded. Boats, paddle launches and steamers are the usual forms of transport in the south. Bangladeshi women tend not to travel without a male escort and can easily be overprotective towards a lone woman. It's often possible to arrange lifts with foreign workers, many of whom have jeeps.

Accommodation Outside Dacca there are very few hotels (or any sort of tourist facilities). You may find rooms in guesthouses but there's nothing like the range in India or Pakistan. Bangladeshis can be very hospitable – the responsibility is yours to pay for as much as you can. As a guest you should always offer some sort of gift.

Special Problems As in any Muslim country, you should dress extremely modestly with loose clothes covering arms and legs. (Non-Muslims are not allowed into mosques or shrines.) Only a few hotels in Dacca sell alcohol and it would certainly be frowned upon for a woman to drink alone.

Guides *Bangladesh – A Travel Survival Kit* (Lonely Planet) is the best-known but can be inaccurate in places. *Bangladesh – a Traveller's Guide* (Roger Lascelles) gives a useful overview.

Contacts

Bangladesh Rural Advancement Committee (BRAC), 66, Mohakhali Commercial Area, Dacca 12. A private, non-profit making organisation of Bangladeshis engaged in development work. BRAC initiated the Jamalpur Women's Programme in 1976, which focuses on skills training, health education and literacy. It has also set up many women's work co-operatives and produces a regular mimeographed newsletter.

National Women's Federation, Rumy-Villa, 88 Santinagar, Dacca. Organises income-generating and health education projects.

Bangladesh Mohila Samity, 104-a New Bailey Road, Dacca. A new group geared towards campaigning for equal status and providing educational and employment opportunities, especially for rural women. It has branches all over the country and runs two educational institutions and a number of cottage industries.

Books

Betsy Hartmann and James Boyce, *A Quiet Violence – View from a Bangladeshi village* (Zed Books, 1983). An account of the role of women in a rural society.

Katy Gardner has written a book of her experiences in a Bangladeshi village, to be published by Virago, 1991.

Bhutan

. . . .

After centuries of almost complete isolation from Western influences, the Himalayan kingdom of Bhutan has recently and very guardedly begun to admit Western visitors. It's a privilege, however, well beyond the means of most ordinary travellers. Whilst willing to make some concessions in the interests of foreign exchange, the government of King Jigme Singye Wangchuck is determined to avoid the cultural havoc wreaked by open tourism in nearby Nepal.

His solution has been to limit the number of tourist visas to approximately two thousand a year, and restrict them to visitors arriving on accredited (and incredibly expensive) "luxury tours".

Even after gaining access to the country there are only a few permitted areas of travel. The terrain is difficult and, in order to get away from the capital and into the villages, where the majority of people live, your only option is to trek. There are companies that organise such expeditions but, again, with a hefty charge levied for each day spent in the country. The only way round this is if you arrive on invitation from someone working in the country – foreign workers are allowed a quota of two visitors a year.

Due to its strategic importance, as a borderland between northeast India and Tibetan China, Bhutan was one of the first British protectorates to be established in the Indian subcontinent and English continues to be taught in the state schools. It's a predominantly Buddhist country (with a large Hindu minority in the south) and although formally governed by a constitutional monarchy, the Buddhist clergy still wield considerable power at a local as well as national level. Away from a few urban centres, life continues more or less unchanged from the centuries-old traditions of Himalayan subsistence farming. Communication by roads, wireless, radio and newspaper is still in its early stages and although attempts are being made to introduce formal education to the villages (as part of a general modernisation programme) many still rely on monastic teaching.

Lacking a developed professional class of its own, Bhutan has had to import foreign advisers and teachers, mainly from India and Nepal, although recently work visas have been given to Western volunteers. There are a few women working in the country on two- or three-year contracts. From our correspondence with Lesley Reader (see below) it would seem that Westerners are becoming more familiar in the fairly affluent valley of the capital, Thimpu, but in the more remote Himalayan villages are an incredibly rare sight and a source of both fascination and fear. The conventions and popular beliefs that shape village life vary greatly from area to area. Whilst men on the whole occupy positions of status in the community, **women** are valued as the mainstay of the extended family and in many areas property is inherited through the female line. Attitudes regarding divorce, adultery, illegitimacy, or education for girls can differ even between villages only a day's walk apart.

From Sunderland to Ura

. . . .

Lesley Reader came to Bhutan, from England, in 1986 on a three-year voluntary contract. As part of a project that aimed to improve the quality of state primary schooling she took up a post first in Ura, a small village in the centre of the country, and then in Buli, lower, warmer and more remote. She was the first Westerner to make her home in these villages.

"Well, there are jobs in Zimbabwe, Nepal, Kenya or Bhutan. What do you think?" The voice on the telephone paused. I looked out of the window on to the depressed and depressing Sunderland landscape and tried hard to conjure up the distant and exotic worlds itemised by the woman from the London Headquarters of Voluntary Service Overseas (VSO). It was impossible.

"I'd like to go to Bhutan," I said.

"What do you know about it? Where is it?" she asked. Not unreasonable questions in view of its size, inaccessibility to most people and absence from the world media.

"It's to the right of Nepal and I know enough," I claimed boldly.

I had applied to VSO in a state of boredom with my job, disillusionment with house owning, disgust at the rat race and horror of the increasing materialism of life in England. It seemed to me that I could run away from it all or I could stay and try to improve matters by involving myself in politics at some level. I decided to run.

Four months after the phone call I was actually among the mountains of Bhutan. And two-and-a-half years later, as I write, I am still here. I realise now that I didn't know enough when I arrived, don't know enough now and, indeed, even if I stayed forever, would never know enough about this foreign land and its people where I feel so much at home.

It seems that there are two distinct Bhutans for me. One is the remote Himalayan Kingdom, last remaining Shangri-la, mystical, almost magical place described in guidebooks and glossy travelogues, with scenery beyond words, peace beyond imagining and people of such friendliness, generosity of spirit and contentment that they are special indeed. Remarkable as it seems, this is a true picture.

But it exists alongside the other Bhutan. The Bhutan of sheer slog and drudgery for its people, where ill health, illiteracy, ignorance, and a terrifyingly low life expectancy prevail; where people lead short lives made painful, both physically and emotionally, by hardship. I sat in my friend's house in the village the other evening and her mother looked at me carefully, and said "we go to the fields every day and we become old women very quickly. You teach in school all day and you will become old very slowly". She is right. Yet slowly things are changing.

"I met a group of women on the path a few days ago. They closed their eyes at the sight of me, covered their ears and shook with fear at my approach"

Increased contact with other nations, both by foreigners being allowed into the country and with Bhutanese people being sent abroad to study, has increased the awareness of the potential for improving the situation. But this is only among some. Much of the country is isolated and unvisited either by tourists or aid workers. I met a group of women on the path a few days ago. They closed their eyes at the sight of me, covered their ears with their hands and shook with fear at my approach. They had never seen a Westerner before and thought I was a white ghost. It will be a long time before any of the advantages of development touch their

lives. But it will also be a long time before they have to cope with its disadvantages.

In the more urban centres crime has increased, consumerism raised its ugly head and dissatisfaction at the disparity between rich and poor affected the normal equilibrium of the Buddhist temperament. The balancing act being attempted by the royal government between improving the lives of the people while avoiding the worst pitfalls of "civilisation" makes a tightrope walk across Niagara Falls look like a gentle stroll in the park.

The majority of the Bhutanese are subsistence farmers. In harsh terms that means if you don't farm well you don't fill your stomach. It means working sixteen-hour days of hard physical toil when the work has to be done: dragging yourself weary from your bed well before dawn to get to the fields so as to make use of every second of daylight. The people of Buli did this for more than three weeks at a stretch during rice planting. In my enthusiam to take an equal part I managed a day- and-a-half with them one weekend and lurched back to the classroom on Monday morning, certain I would never walk upright again. For me it was a new experience, for them the stakes are higher.

In addition to the inexorable demands of the land they must expend considerable ingenuity to find a source of cash as money has become increasingly necessary, perhaps to take a relative to hospital. Sometimes the family or a neighbour helps out, sometimes they can sell butter, cheese or eggs. It isn't easy. They must live with the knowledge that they, their crops and their livestock are at the mercy of unseasonal weather, wild animals or disease. Most cannot read or write although the majority now send at least some children to school in the hope that they will eventually get a job away from the land and so have a steady income. One son, or maybe more if the family is large and the lands sufficient to support them, may be sent to a monastery to become a monk.

"Into this land I arrived from my comfortable terraced house in Newcastle-upon-Tyne"

The main source of information is oral; the weekly government newspaper is incomprehensible to many villagers and any printed matter must be taken to a sympathetic teacher or Lama for understanding. There may or may not be someone in the village with a radio (and the necessary batteries) to listen to the daily broadcasts of news, information or music from the capital which is often many days' journey away. People do not travel much; there is no reason and it is expensive and time consuming.

Knowledge of the outside world is limited, very often, to a few visits to the local "town" and administrative head-quarters. In many ways people have little control over their lives, they either have to work to grow food or starve. Fortunately very few Bhutanese go hungry; there is adequate land for a small number of people. But as the government realises, the population is growing and improved farming methods are going to be needed for the picture to remain so rosy.

Into this land I arrived from my comfortable terraced house in Newcastle-upon-Tyne; central heating, automatic washing machine, freezer, a garden that was a wilderness as I knew nothing about growing anything, a car and deep feelings of wanting something different. As I passed my first few days in late winter at over ten and a half thousand feet in Ura, the tiny village in the Himalayas that was to be my home for the next two years, it dawned on me that I had certainly found it.

I was alone and relished what lay ahead, whatever that may turn out to be. I decided to learn the language, find out what life in this beautiful but harsh environment was about and participate in as much as I could. Of course, in some matters there was no choice: I had to adopt local ways; my water was in the stream with everyone else's, I had a pile of wood and an earthen cooking stove to get my food cooked and my pit latrine was out the back. The wind scythed through the myriad tiny cracks in the house walls as it funnelled up the valley every afternoon and the closest electricity was a long way over the horizon. For many weeks I considered it quite a feat just to feed myself, wash my clothes and keep warm. It was to be a long time before I even bothered about washing myself!

In other respects I did have a choice. I could have just spoken English and restricted my social contacts to the staff at school and the few other people in the valley who would understand me. I need not have adopted the national costume. I could have declined to drink the local distillation. I could have stayed in my school quarters and not moved out to live in the temple. I could have refused blessings from the local Lamas. I could have stayed home and not sallied forth with the archery team for a weekend in a neighbouring valley. I could have, but I didn't. And the fact that I had the pleasure of so many remarkable experiences was due to my Bhutanese neighbours.

I was the first Westerner to live in Ura. As such I was the subject of considerable curiosity. For my first two weeks there were twenty faces peering in at my windows each morning watching me eat breakfast. Their disappointment was palpable as they realised I opened my mouth, put food in, chewed and swallowed just like they did. The favourite occupation of some of the smaller children was to stand next to my washing line and watch my multi-coloured knickers, bra, jeans and other exotic clothes flap in the wind.

My entertainment value was considerable and every activity was scrutinised. As their confidence grew I was questioned as to why I took all my clothes off to wash, why I used paper after I'd been to the toilet, why I walked up the mountain at the weekend when I had no work to do there. And to their, and my, delight, after much struggle they could do this in their own language.

> *"'I know who you are,' he said, 'you're the Ura teacher, I'd heard tell there was a teacher there who could speak our language.'"*

At first no one understood why I wanted to learn, then they despaired of me ever managing it, then every person I encountered took it upon themselves to teach me until I thought my brain would explode. Finally after two years they would proudly inform any visitor to the valley, "You know our foreign teacher? She speaks our language."

Once, when visiting a school a day's walk to the north of the village I met an old man walking towards me down the mountain path. We began the usual greetings. He stopped after a short while, "I know who you are," he said, "you're the Ura teacher, I'd heard tell there was a teacher there who could speak our language," he nodded, "it's true, you can." With encouragement like this it was hardly surprising I succeeded. It is the greatest achievement of my life.

In all their curiosity and interest there seemed to be no malice; they enquired, noted the differences and let me carry on, however bizarre they obviously found me. One question that came up again and again related to my family. As an only child (that was considered peculiar and sad enough in itself), they wanted to know how I could leave my elderly parents to travel for so many days across the sea to live amongst strangers. I tried, oh I tried, to convey curiosity, the reality of city life, itchy feet, philanthropy and whatever else my confused motives contained.

But I know that although they might be able to imagine themselves, if they tried very hard, in some of the strange situations I described; living with electricity, driving a car, buying everything from a shop, having a tap in the house, they could never imagine journeying so far from one's family and staying away for so long out of choice. Such a thing was strange indeed.

In Bhutan, the family are your mainstay in times of crisis; they and neighbours will rally round if food runs out, if someone falls sick, if someone dies or if more help is needed in the fields. They are the buffer in misfortune, easing your burdens physically and psychologically. In my case contact with my family was limited to letters. In Buli the postman came every ten days or so, he can rarely have had anyone waiting with such anticipation for him to amble along the path.

The other means by which people achieve control over their fate lies in religion. In the northern part of Bhutan this is Tibetan Buddhism. Seeing its influence on the everyday lives of people, I sought to find out more about this gentle religion. Unfortunately I wasn't fluent enough to grasp the deeper philosophy but I began to attend ceremonies, leave offerings, receive blessings, and later I was given a Bhutanese name. I don't know what much of it means but I do know that it is about living in the present, and that's fine by me.

And where do women fit into all of this? Well, it depends. In the south of the country the majority of the population orginate from Nepal and have retained their language, culture and Hindu religion. Of this I know nothing. My life is among the Buddhists in the north. I have been told on many occasions by people far better travelled than I, that compared to the rest of Asia "it's not too bad".

I am not knowledgeable enough to argue. But to my mind there are considerable inequalities. In the village where

I live some work is divided between the sexes; both men and women work in the fields, tend the cows and fetch firewood. Some work seems to be the province of one or the other; men usually do the ploughing, women plant the paddy, women care for the children and do the housework. It isn't rigid and if circumstances dictate then the completion of the work is more important than who does it. However, within the community, the majority of those with status are men; Lamas, village headmen, elected representatives are all men, most teachers and the vast majority of headteachers are men; most health workers, animal husbandry workers and agricultural extension workers are men.

At school the drop-out rate among girls is far higher than for boys. At the local school in Class X, the equivalent to "O" level year, there is one girl and 59 boys. Double standards prevail about sexuality; boys are allowed and indeed expected to be promiscuous, girls are expected to be faithful to one partner. Yet the society is tolerant, the extended family absorbs illegitimate children and the victims of broken marriages just as it absorbs widows and orphans. Many marriages end in divorce, usually when a man tires of his wife and finds a new one. Not many women initiate divorce although there is no legal or social prohibition against them doing so.

My own perceptions have been that more women than men are victims in unsatisfactory relationships, they remain tied to husbands who beat them, are unfaithful to them and generally treat them shabbily. But I admit to a biased view. It needs to be stated that the expectations from marriage are very different from those in the West. In Bhutan it is the cement to bind the social fabric, it brings an additional worker into a household, and through children forms an insurance for old age. Emotional support from a spouse may be an added bonus but in general is found elsewhere.

The women I met were strong, vibrant, outspoken, bawdy and the mainstay of the community. On marriage a man moves to his wife's house and becomes part of her family.

> **"Coming back late from my friend's house I am warned only about ghosts and bears. I have never met either"**

Consequently the birth of a daughter is greatly celebrated as she will later bring much needed manpower to the house. In their everyday lives the women are not constrained as long as the work is attended to. They travel if they need to, they decide on their own work and they drink alcohol if they wish. It's the same for me; I am free to travel where and when I wish. Bhutanese custom dictates that one must offer all possible hospitality to visitors and travellers, and arriving anywhere at any time of the day or night one is immediately looked after. Any man approaching me to ask who I am and where I am going merely wishes to know who I am and where I am going. Coming back late from my friend's house I am warned only about ghosts and bears. I have never met either.

Women speak out at village meetings and, on social occasions, more than hold their own in the verbal sparring that inevitably takes place between the sexes. Yet in their everyday life it would be impossible to have a simple friendship with a member of the opposite sex. These expectations applied to me also; my friends in the village were all women. If any man were seen walking or talking with me it would be instantly assumed we were having an affair. And if he was married the wrath of his wife would traditionally descend upon me, as the "other woman", rather than upon the errant husband.

My friends here in Buli are women of all ages. Just as I am a woman alone, the majority of them are either widows, women with husbands absent in the army or single women. They arrived in my house the evening after I reached Buli bearing many bottles of local booze and we all got drunk. We have been together ever since. They bring me rice, vegetables, local alcohol, they teach me to plant, harvest and thresh rice, and cook me dinners of rice and chillies when they see that I'm struggling.

They try to understand why I don't want a husband and children, they worry about the fact that I will have no one to carry me to my cremation when I die and they answer my innumerable questions about their life, Universe and everything. I take their photographs, cook them egg and chips, read and write letters, cut their hair, help them out with cash and tell them about my life and country.

"As far as people here are concerned, to be on one's own is to be lonely and true friends make sure that I am never in that unfortunate state"

In their attempts to try and understand more about this strange, but entertaining phenomenon in their midst they ply me with questions; why the double-decker buses in the picture of London had no driver on top, where were our rice fields, where did we keep our yaks, how did we cook and keep our saucepans clean? They wanted to know about my parents' house and were astonished to see a picture of a block of flats. They sat mesmerised as I explained how my parents use a lift to get to the thirteenth floor and couldn't understand why I didn't know every single person in my village (London). I fear they have ended up with strange ideas of England. In some ways it doesn't matter, and in other ways it does.

I am rarely completely alone. As far as people here are concerned, to be on one's own is to be lonely and true friends make sure that I am never in that unfortunate state. Sometimes this can feel a burden. I once became sick. As is my habit I took to my bed to sleep. Every five minutes somebody arrived to wake me up and talk to me, they came in relays of two or three for three days. I was demented, I craved sleep, healing sleep. If I had possessed enough strength, the expression "bugger off and leave me alone" might have been verbalised. As it was I lay and suffered.

Inevitably I recovered and questioned my tormentors, although obviously torment was the last thing on their minds. They had come to protect me from the spirits. For spirits are particularly aware of vulnerable souls: those of the sick and anyone who sleeps during the day. They had come to look after me and I in turn have gone to visit sick people for this reason.

So I live all day in a crowd, I live with the constant knowledge that something strange and unexpected may be about to happen; my friends arrive to take me to a wedding, to the temple to get a blessing from an important Lama or from some sticks that have come by magical means from Tibet. I'm aware, however, that I can still only appreciate from the outside what it means to have been born here, to grow up and to expect to die in this tiny valley. To say there is never a dull moment is absolutely true. No it certainly isn't Shangri-la. It's better.

Walking with Margaret

· · · · · · · · · · · · ·

Before setting off on a three-day trek from Ura to her new post in Buli, Lesley Reader met Margaret, an English science teacher who had been working in Bhutan for two years. They completed the trek together.

The first hiccup came when I left the monks. Or maybe they lost me, or avoided me, or ran away. I wanted to walk from Ura, ten-and-a-half thousand feet up in the mountains, my home for two years, to Buli, lower, warmer, three-and-a-half days' walk away. The monks were heading in that general direction, perhaps to meet their Lama, escape from work, or do whatever the large numbers of monks who seem forever to be roaming the Bhutanese countryside do. They had been asked by the headmaster to take me along; then they had vanished. Perhaps they had heard about my unique walking style.

At that point Margaret came to my rescue. A teacher in the far west of Bhutan, her trekking exploits have entered local mythology. "Ah, the tall foreign woman, no friend", villagers in remote corners of the country reminisce about the solitary visit, her fearlessness, her remarkably fast walking and her consumption of the local booze. Fortuitously she arrived as my plans disintegrated and took me in hand. We'd go to Buli together; I was daunted.

She seemed so much better equipped than I was for striding the hills. Uphill my lungs go on strike, downhill my knees creak and along the flat I look at the scenery and trip over my own feet. Added to this I get vertigo when more than ten inches off the ground, so all in all, wandering about in the middle of the highest mountains on earth I was hardly in my element. Margaret took seven-eighths of the

baggage, leaving me the feeble rest. She said it would even out our walking speeds. It didn't, but she complained not a syllable, looked not a dagger and more importantly, refused to leave me in the wilderness.

We left Ura in the freezing cold with snow swirling in flurries around us. The first day-and-a-half took us 800 feet to bananas in the forest and leeches (indescribably yucky) in the shoes. The path winds down, down and yet more down from blue pines at the top to tropical ferns and lushness at the bottom. It follows a river gorge as the raging, white water plummets down on its southwards journey to India; the roar of its passage a constant counterpoint to my gasping for breath and frequent comments, "Oh, shit" as I slithered once again on my, fortunately well-padded, backside.

> *"I concentrated on putting one foot successfully in front of the other when all I really wanted to do was sit down and cry"*

The scenery is truly remarkable. On either side of the river massive forested hills rise up thousands of feet, enormous spurs of the hillside encroach into the main gorge for as far as the eye can see until they vanish into the mists of the horizon. Perched way up, on what passes as flat land in these parts are small villages; each house surrounded by steeply terraced fields. Pitifully small pools of cultivation are carved painfully out of the oceans of jungle waiting just metres away to take over again.

"We'll sleep the first night in a cave," said Margaret, who'd done this sort of thing before. Her concept of "cave" however was a little different to mine. I couldn't tell you the exact critical point at which a rock turns into a snug, secure and inviting dwelling, but it seemed to me that lying along the bottom of the cliff face with just enough overhang to stop the rain drenching us, we were not even close to it.

I slept the sleep of the dead tired, putting aside all thoughts of bears, snakes, wild pigs and other beasties and woke the next morning with aches I could never have imagined. Every moving part hurt. Stunned by pain (mine) and beauty (Bhutan's), the day passed in a blur as I concentrated on putting one foot successfully in front of the other when all I really wanted to do was sit down and cry.

As pitch darkness surrounded us (why is there never a moon when you want one?) we arrived at the first house we had seen since leaving Ura. The people, obviously poor, and totally bemused at finding two foreign women wandering around in the night, took us in. They gave us floor space to sleep on and the use of their fire to cook our supper. Gradually they became less shy and as I could understand some of their dialect, we began to converse. Suddenly they asked, "In your village, foreigner's village, we have heard you have machines to do your housework." I nodded. "Tell us," they demanded.

It would take these people at least two days' hard walk, up the 8000 feet we had already come, to reach a road. They would then need to journey further to find anything even resembling a town. I didn't know if they had ever encountered electricity. How on earth had they heard about machines? My language was simply not good enough to find out. I searched my mind and, hands providing action where words failed, told them about washing machines. I had never seen people stunned into silence before.

When I finished my monologue they looked at each other, shook their heads in amazement and carried on eating as though I had never spoken. Who knows what thoughts of wonder, disbelief and perhaps irritation at the, no doubt, fantasising foreigners were going through their minds.

The next morning we left late. My aches and pains were settling down. Instead of every single part of my body hurting I now had distinct spots of

agony; about two thousand of them. Coming over the crest of a hill we saw a beautiful white *chorten*. They dot the Bhutanese countryside containing relics, prayers and sacred objects representing the Buddhist universe.

"Waiting for us and us alone, was a Lama, the Lama from the village near Ura – my Lama who had given me my Bhutanese name"

Sitting resting at the base, as though waiting for us and us alone, was a Lama, the Lama from the village near Ura – my Lama, who had given me my Bhutanese name. Not old, not young, pious, bawdy, serious and startlingly funny, without a word of English, he had the most amazing desire and ability to understand and communicate.

I knew him well and he'd met Margaret the previous winter. He sat and watched us approach as though it was a prearranged appointment. Maybe it was. For him. We chatted, gossiped, exchanged gifts and drank far too much alcohol. He set up a makeshift altar and began his prayers, stopping after a while to pick up a metal statue that had obviously been broken and repaired. Carefully he explained to us that when the statue had been damaged it had been heard to scream. Sittting in the middle of the most dramatic scenery I had ever encountered, beside the Lama, with my brain whirling from the amount I had had to drink, it all seemed perfectly possible. And strangely enough it still does.

Blessings accomplished, regretful farewells completed and promises to meet again sworn, we set off on our separate ways; the Lama back up to Ura, Margaret and I in search of Buli, which I was beginning to imagine was transporting itself by some magical means further and further away from me. By this time it was ridiculously late. Time keeping was not helped when we decided to wash off the worst of the grime and inebriation in a freezing cold stream.

We didn't manage to reach a village that night and slept in a hut on stilts in a rice field. The inadequacies of the roof only became apparent in the middle of the night when the rain began; merely another discomfort to add to the multitude. I was beginning to get the hang of living in agony. I had reached a stage of acceptance of my fate, which seemed to be to slog for the rest of my days up interminable slopes only to slip and slide right down the other side.

As I contemplated the path ahead it seemed to ascend straight up a terrifying looking mountain. Surely my eyes were deceiving me? They weren't. Up we went, then up a bit more, then a bit more, and then further still, round, down a touch, round, down and then steep, steep down some more. Finally, unbelievably, we reached Buli.

In pitch darkness, still no moon, and pouring rain (this was supposed to be the dry season for goodness sake), I staggered to the first house. "I'm the new teacher," I gasped. Traditional hospitality took over. We were fed, watered (with something much stronger and more invigorating than water) and bedded down. The following morning I started school and Margaret left to stroll over some impassable looking mountains and create more amazement wherever she trod.

TRAVEL NOTES

Languages There's a great deal of regional variation in languages and dialects – all of which are hard to pick up. Dzongkha, the national language, is taught in schools but spoken only in the west of Bhutan. English remains the language of instruction, but with formal education being so limited very few people outside of the towns will speak it.

Transport is extremely rudimentary. There are no airports; entry to the country is by bus from Darjeeling in India to the capital, Thimphu. Tour groups usually have coaches laid on but though there are local buses, many villages are a long trek from the roads. Travelling and trekking is sturdy work but helped by the open-handed generosity of the Bhutanese people. From June to September (monsoon season) travel is likely to be severely disrupted.

Accommodation Besides the air conditioned hotel in Phuntsoling built for the luxury tours and a scattering of government rest houses, there are a few spartan hostels for local people.

Special Problems The biggest. is gaining entry. Visas are by direct application only to the Director of Tourism, Thimphu, three months in advance; tours available through *Bhutan Travel.* Transit permits can be gained from the Indian High Commission but travelling through can be very expensive ($150 a day at present). Most large overseas voluntary agencies – VSO, VSA (New Zealand), WUSC (Canada), UNV, FAO, WHO, other branches of the UN and Helvitas (Switzerland) – supply workers to Bhutan. Once there, the obvious problems are language, altitude, and the many and various physical demands of rural subsistence in the Himalayas. Take everything you need by way of contraception, sanitary protection and medicine with you.

Guides *The Insight Guide to Asia* (Harrap Columbus) has a small section on Bhutan, with good pictures.

Contacts

As far as we know, no autonomous women's groups have been established.

Books

Katie Hickman, *Dreams of the Peaceful Dragon: Journey into Bhutan* (Coronet, 1989) and **Tom Owen Edmunds, *Bhutan, Land of the Thunder Dragon*** (Elm Tree, 1988). Katie Hickman and Tom Owen Edmunds travelled together through Bhutan. Her version of their epic Himalayan journey is complemented by his book of photos.

Francoise Pommaret-Imaeda and Yoshiro Imaeda, *Bhutan. A Kingdom of the Eastern Himalayas* (Serindia Publications, 1984). A superbly illustrated, informative book by two eminent Tibetologists who have been living in Bhutan for many years.

Thanks to Lesley Reader for help with Travel Notes and introduction.

Bolivia

I n Bolivia things are seldom straightforward. Schedules can be disrupted by anything from floods through strikes and road blocks to plain bureaucracy – all hazards you have to take philosophically. The country itself, though, is one of the most exciting for travellers in South America. The scenery, ranging from a height of zero to 16,000 feet, is often spectacularly beautiful and the people (two-thirds Indian) are still steeped in tradition.

From the point of view of sexual harassment, the overwhelming presence of indigenous people make this a relatively peaceful country to travel around. Probably the biggest threat is from black-market moneychangers who see a woman as an easy target to short-change. In this case, ignore the sweet talk, be firm and make absolutely sure you check your money. With an inflation rate not far off 450 percent, poverty is rife, even by Latin American standards, so it's hardly surprising if tourists are seen as a tempting source of income.

The **women's movement** in Bolivia continues to develop as more and more women demonstrate for economic and political change. They were a key factor in the defeat of the Banzer dictatorship in 1978 when women from the mines staged a hunger strike in the capital, La Paz, in demand for an amnesty for political exiles. They have also won themselves a strong platform in the COB (Bolivian Workers Federation), where women delegates have long insisted on the need for more representation on its committees and participation in general.

There are women's groups and organisations of all types, from conservative upper-middle-class associations through all shades of the political spectrum to the far left. Two of the most notable are the widespread Women's Peasant Federation and the Amas de Casa de la Ciudad, a group of poor women who run a health clinic and various education programmes in the slums of La Paz. Both are remarkable in being grass-roots women's organisations who believe in the value of excluding men from specific discussions and decisions in order for women to gain the confidence to stand up for their rights.

An Inside View

. . . .

Susanna Rance has been living and working in Bolivia since 1980. Former editor of the bi-monthly news analysis *Bolivia Bulletin*, her special interest is in grass-roots and development journalism, especially relating to popular women's organisations.

When I first arrived in Bolivia nine years ago, I came with the idea of settling here permanently. Not just because La Paz was my husband's birthplace: on previous travels through Mexico and Central America en route for Venezuela, where I lived for two years, I had already got the "bug". I had fallen in love with Latin American culture, music, language, politics, a certain flavour of life which I found – and still find – warming and exhilarating.

On returning to London from Venezuela in 1977, I joined the Latin American Women's Group and became involved in discussion and solidarity work with women from a variety of backgrounds and countries. That experience confirmed my desire to live permanently in South America, and at the same time to change the course of my work, then teaching English as a foreign language, to something linked with the international struggle for social change.

I flew into La Paz airport, reeling from the 13,000ft altitude, in May 1980. Winter, the cold dry season, was beginning, but La Paz was spectacular with its crystal clear air, blue skies and bright Andean sun. The beauty of the descent from the high plateau into the basin of the city has never lost its impact for me. The narrow back road winds down steep hillsides covered with a pastel-coloured hotchpotch of improvised dwellings, a sharp contrast to the avenues and high-rise buildings of the city centre.

"As a gringa, I expected to feel out of place, even rejected. None of my fears were confirmed"

As a *gringa*, arriving in the midst of a fairly traditional Aymara household, I expected to feel out of place, even rejected. None of my fears were confirmed. My husband's extended family welcomed me warmly and did all they could to make me feel at home.

Each of the small rooms around the cobbled courtyard housed several people, yet there were always invitations for us to visit, sit and share a meal or borrow what we needed. Twenty of us used one cold tap in the yard, the only source of water, which frequently dried up. Washing and cooking, both done squatting at ground level, were social activities, a time for the women of the household to chat, complain and catch up on family news. My husband was thought odd for joining in with these tasks, and our attempts to involve our nephews in household chores were firmly rejected.

Although our lifestyle was clearly different from that of the rest of the family, I found an atmosphere of tolerance, generated largely by my mother-in-law, a generous and open woman who was always loving and supportive to me, up until her recent death. "La Mama" was the hub of the household, a true matriarch.

Only three of her nine children had survived. In my terms, the others died of poverty; in hers, from a variety of supernatural causes: the evil eye, a sudden shock which sends the soul fleeing from the body, a strange illness called *larphata* which has all the symptoms of malnutrition.

My parents-in-law lived for most of the year in the subtropical Yungas valley, growing coffee, citrus fruits, bananas and coca on land which they had cleared from virgin forest. Our honeymoon was a month spent with them up in the woods, harvesting coffee, talking in the evenings by candlelight, preparing lunch at dawn on a wood fire before we set off to work.

La Mama worked energetically on the land, dressed in trousers and boots, wielding a machete. On her weekly trips to the nearest town, she would run the two-hour stretch down rocky paths, stopping at intervals to take off one of her work garments and replace it with a petticoat, a long vest, a layered skirt, Cinderella-style shoes and finally her bowler hat.

Despite the family's usual openness towards me, there was one period when I felt isolated. In our second year my husband, a folk musician, went abroad for months on tour. I was "sent to Coventry" by his younger brother's family for carrying on my life as usual, going out at night and staying over with friends: unseemly behaviour for a woman, which I could only get away with in their eyes if my husband was around to give his permission.

Nevertheless, I know that even now a lot of allowances are made for me because I am a *gringa*. One of my sisters-in-law, a Quechua from rural Potosi, often feels as much at sea as I do in the midst of Aymara customs and rituals. Yet as a Bolivian, she is expected to merge totally with the dictates of local and family tradition. Only I, as a foreigner, receive praise for any efforts to integrate, and understanding when I opt out!

"After the coup, I felt panicked, ignorant, impotent to do anything about the repression we witnessed daily"

Two months after I arrived in La Paz there was a military coup. I still knew very little about the country, and it wasn't until some time later that I realised this wasn't just another of the frequent changes of government for which Bolivia is notorious.

Being stopped in the street by military patrols after curfew, hearing sinister shots late into the night, seeing tanks blocking the university gates and the media censored – these were just symptoms of the more hidden violence imposed by the cocaine generals. Their two-year rule, ended by the virtual collapse of the Armed Forces, left a trail of exile, massacre and corruption, which remains a brutal reminder of the fragility of the Bolivian democratic system.

After the coup I felt panicked, ignorant, impotent to do anything about the repression we witnessed daily. I looked for ways of finding out more about what was going on. A couple of months later, I was offered the chance to join a small group of people in the clandestine task of collecting and processing information about the abuses committed under the military regime, to send to solidarity and human rights organisations abroad.

Through this work, I started to learn not just about the current situation but also about Bolivia's history and culture. Gradually the information project began to take up most of my time and I was able to leave my English teaching job and change my line of work, just as I had wanted to do before leaving England.

Meanwhile, I had also become politically involved, in the Women's Front of a party active in the resistance to the dictatorship. Our group, made up mainly of middle-class professionals, represented the first attempt to bring women's issues into the forefront of Bolivian left-wing party politics.

We fought against being relegated to tea-making and sticking up posters while the men met to make the "serious" decisions. We were criticised for doing popular education with women's groups in the shanty towns, instead of pushing the party line and rallying female masses to the demos. We were accused of dividing the struggle at a time when the urgency of the situation required unquestioning discipline. Eventually, the Women's Front was dissolved, but a women's education and information centre grew out of that first initiative.

My first three years in Bolivia were a time of almost total immersion in the life, culture and work around me. Most of my friends and workmates were Bolivian and I had little time to miss my own country or people. Then two things happened to change my experience of Bolivia: I got hepatitis and lost a pregnancy; and we moved out of the family house to have our first child.

It wasn't until I was pregnant that I realised I was malnourished. Although my weight had fallen to a little over six stone, I had never given a thought to my diet. When the doctor asked me exactly what I ate each day, I said it was the same as the rest of the family, but I had to admit it wasn't very nutritious: dry bread and herb tea for breakfast, rice or noodle soup with potatoes or boiled bananas for lunch and the same again for tea and supper. No milk, butter or jam. Very little meat, cheese or eggs.

Cooking together at home, we all ate from the same pot, just adding a cup of water to the soup if there was a visitor. The main difference between me and the rest of the family was that they were used to eating large quantities of carbohydrates to compensate for the lack of protein. Often, rice, potatoes and bananas would make up most of the meal, with a tiny sliver of meat and some spicy chilli sauce to give it all flavour. I couldn't take that much bulk, so I just ate less and lost weight.

"I suddenly realised that I couldn't go on subjecting myself to that diet, to that poverty. For the first time since arriving in Bolivia I felt horribly foreign and apart"

Soon after this discovery I got hepatitis and had a miscarriage as a result. The next time a plate of watery rice soup was put in front of me I burst into tears, and I've never been able to eat it since. I suddenly realised that I couldn't go on subjecting myself to that diet, to that poverty. For the first time since arriving in Bolivia I felt horribly foreign and apart. I started to sort out what things I could and couldn't accept in the way of life around me. Some months later, when I had recovered and was pregnant again, we moved out into our own house, on a market street not far down the road.

The birth of my daughter was a wonderful experience. Apart from the joys of motherhood, encountered for the first time at 31, I discovered firsthand how children are welcomed and loved in Bolivian society, how they are accepted as part of everyday life, not segregated into a subculture of mums and toddlers as in my own country. Relatives and neighbours would ask for a turn with the baby. Market sellers would hold out their arms to give her a cuddle. As a mother, I had a new-found bond with the women around me, even if they shrieked with horror to see Nina being carried down the street in a baby sling, unswaddled and hatless.

I went back to my job a couple of months after Nina was born, working partly from home and sitting breast-feeding her in office meetings with the full support of my colleagues. However, I found it impossible to continue my political activity. Carrying my daughter on long, bumpy bus rides to smoky meetings, coming out late and waiting for transport in the cold, arriving home exhausted, with a broken night ahead of me – it was too much. Aside from the incomprehension of the male party militants, the women my age had all started their families ten years before me and weren't into babies any more.

Another isolation point. My life became a shuttle between home and work, and I started to miss the company of other foreign women who were late-starting mothers like myself, or could understand what I was going through. When I did start to find such allies, I was faced with a hard fact of having chosen to live so far from my own culture: the departure of a succession of friends who left Bolivia when their period of work or study ended.

One year, I withdrew and refused to make new contacts, knowing they would just leave again. But gradually I came to terms with the fact that despite the yearly exodus, these friends greatly enrich my life while they are here. Contact with many of them has continued and some, smitten with the Bolivia bug, return periodically to visit.

When Nina was two-and-a-half, our son Amaru was born. I carried on working full-time, thanks to the support of helpers, friends and neighbours. My husband took on the main parenting role during the months he was in La Paz, but continued to tour with his group for several months each year. Like working mothers everywhere, I felt the inevitable strain of combining parenting with a demanding job, and there was little time for relaxation or social activities.

Meanwhile, the work of our small team had grown and developed into a documentation and information centre.

With the demise of the military regime and the return to democracy in 1982, we were able to open an office, print and mail our news bulletins in Spanish and English and offer our services to students, researchers and journalists in Bolivia and abroad.

My own work was taking a clearer line as I alternated writing and editing on general topics with following up my specific interest: popular women's organisations. I started writing for publications in Bolivia and abroad on grass-roots organisations grouping women from the countryside, factories, mines and shanty towns, writing about their experiences and activities on the basis of direct testimonies.

"A stay of several months in England had convinced me that, despite some nostalgia, I far preferred living in Bolivia"

The end of my eighth year in Bolivia marked a watershed in my personal and professional life. A stay of several months in England had convinced me that, despite some nostalgia, I far preferred living in Bolivia, which offered me many more opportunities to develop as a person, worker and mother than Thatcher's Britain. I returned feeling confident in this choice, ready to start a new phase in my life. It was this new confidence which enabled me to make some unsettling changes: I left my job of eight years and my marriage, also of eight years, in the space of three months.

Belonging to the information centre had been a kind of umbilical cord for me almost since my arrival in Bolivia. It was there that I had become accepted as part of a team, made friends, learned about Bolivia and developed a new career. Finally, I was ready to branch out on my own.

As well as writing articles on development issues, I began to research a report for the National Population Council on the hot debate around (voluntary) family planning versus (imposed) birth control. This work has opened up new channels: the opportunity for training in population and development planning and the prospect of running a programme on legislation and women's rights.

Soon after I changed jobs, my husband and I reached the point of recognising that our lives had become distanced and we had come to relate more as "co-parents" than as a couple. I started to experience the problems of being a single woman in Bolivian society, where stable couples are the accepted norm and *machismo* sets out the rules for most relationships.

But through it all, after nine years in Bolivia, I've finally found my own identity here as a *gringa*, person, mother and worker. I now have close Bolivian women friends with ideas and experiences in common. And I know that this is where I want to stay, where I want my children to grow up, the country I want to keep enjoying, discovering and writing about.

TRAVEL NOTES

Languages Spanish, Quechua, Aymara and other minor Indian languages.

Transport *Flotas*, or long-distance buses, run from the main bus terminal in La Paz to most other towns in the country. Trains are slow, but the journeys often picturesque. Air travel is very cheap.

Accommodation Although prices are rising fast, there are still plenty of cheap, basic hotels by European standards. Only La Paz tends to get booked up, so try to arrive early in the day.

Special Problems Avoid going to a doctor, dentist, clinic or hospital unless absolutely necessary. The Bolivian medical profession has an unhealthy reliance on the prescription of (unnecessary) drugs. Take with you all the sanitary protection you will need as tampons are incredibly expensive. Most varieties of contraceptive pills can be bought at chemists.

Don't bring British currency to Bolivia. If you manage to change sterling it will be at a very low rate. Everything revolves around the dollar.

Guides The excellent *South American Handbook* (Trade and Travel Publications) includes roughly 60 pages on Bolivia.

South America on a Shoestring (Lonely Planet), aimed more at the budget traveller and a lot cheaper to buy, is especially strong on maps and trails.

Contacts

Ms. Guided Tours, 16B Vicars Terrace, Leeds LS8 5AP, UK, organise women-only tours to Bolivia and Peru. Their aim is to combine adventurous travel with introducing and informing Western women about women's lives in the so-called Third World.

Centro de Promoción de la Mujer Gregoria Apaza, Edificio Muritto, 3rd Floor Office no. 2, Calle Murillo, La Paz, ☎327932. Postal address: Casilla 21170, La Paz, Bolivia. Women's centre carrying out research and popular education sessions with poor urban women.

Centro de Información y Desarrollo de la Mujer (CIDEM), Avenida Villazon 1950, Of. 3A. 3rd floor (opposite University). Postal address: Casilla 3961, La Paz, Bolivia. Women's Information and Development Centre – activities include the provision of health and legal advice, participatory research and the build-up of an audiovisual archive on the lives of Bolivian women.

Centro de Estudios y Trabajo de La Mujer (CETM), Calle España 624, Cochabamba, Bolivia. Information and research centre, again concerned with working with women's organisations in poor urban areas. Publishes a weekly bulletin, *Nosotras*.

Books

Domitila Barrios de Chungara, *Let Me Speak* (Stage 1, 1978). First-hand account of the life of one of the founder members of the Housewives Committees of Siglo XX, one of Bolivia's largest mining complexes. A more recent pamphlet by Domitila is included in **Miranda Davies, ed., *Third World – Second Sex*** (Zed Books, 1983). See General Bibliography.

Audrey Bronstein, ed., *The Triple Struggle: Latin American Peasant Women* (War on Want Campaigns, 1982). Includes interviews with Bolivian women.

Alicia Partnoy, ed., *You Can't Drown the Fire: Latin American Women Writing in Exile* (Virago, 1989). Moving anthology bringing together essays, stories, poetry, letters and song by women in exile.

James Dunkerley, *Bolivia: Coup d'Etat* (Latin America Bureau, 1980); and ***Rebellion in the Veins: Political Struggle in Bolivia, 1952–82*** (Verso, 1984). Excellent, well-informed studies of Bolivia's recent political history.

Susan George, *A Fate Worse than Debt* (Penguin, 1987). Provides a clear account of Latin America's biggest collective problem, debt, including some information on Bolivia.

Thanks to Ruth Ingram of **Ms. Guided Tours** for background information.

Botswana

B otswana is relatively affluent by African standards, and it can be an expensive place for independent travellers. The government has a policy of trying to promote luxury tours and squeeze out the ordinary backpackers, and has recently introduced a daily levy for visitors, payable in the game parks and the magical wildlife reserve of Okavango. In these areas there is also little option but to stay in the upmarket accommodation provided. However, if you do manage to escape official tours – possible if you're determined – travel can still be affordable and very rewarding. What's more it is one of the easier African countries for women travelling alone. Harassment, whether on racial or sexual grounds, is uncommon.

Botswana's economic mainstays are diamonds and beef. The country's predominant tribal group, the cattle-herding Batswanas, have benefited considerably from the export of beef to the EC. Few, however, grow rich from the nation's hefty mineral deposits, which are primarily exploited by South African companies or siphoned off by smugglers. Even before independence from the British in 1966, Botswana's leaders stood firmly against apartheid, but the economy remains heavily dependent on its imperialist neighbour. However, changing expectations in Botswana – largely a nation of young people – combined with upheavals in South Africa, may herald a dramatic shift in relations, as well as other changes in what remains one of the few multi-party democracies in the continent.

Nearly half of all households in Botswana are headed by women, due to male migration to urban centres and to South Africa. The majority work on the land. Though

more are beginning to occupy ministerial and embassy positions, women in towns, hampered by lack of education, are mainly employed in the service industries as cooks, cleaners, hotel workers, etc. Widows and single mothers often supplement their incomes by brewing beer.

Botswana has a growing **women's movement** in the sense that, as the backbone of the country's economy, more and more women are demanding respect and recognition for what they do. Women's agricultural co-operatives are on the increase and, largely through the government's Department of Women's Affairs, many are calling for information about their legal rights.

A Personal Safari

· · · · · · · · · · · ·

Adinah Thomas is a writer and dramatist based in London. She went to Botswana at the invitation of two friends, but spent most of her two-month stay exploring alone.

During my visit, I went off alone into the hinterland using a variety of forms of transport. There is basically only one tarmac road in Botswana, running from Gaborone, the capital in the south, to Kasane in the north. Apart from a few good side-shoots, most roads are little more than dirt tracks, some quite reasonable but most impassable in anything other than a four-wheel drive vehicle. A single railway runs from Gaborone to Bulawayo in Zimbabwe. I never travelled by train, but the service is said to be reliable provided you can find someone to explain the timetable.

Despite primitive road conditions, I found travelling through the endless variations of desert fairly easy. I began by catching a bus from Francistown to Nata, a village on the edge of the Makgadigkaki Pans. The bus went on to Kasane where I waited for three

hours with six white people and about thirty Batswana, all wanting to go on across the desert to Maun. Eventually I camped in a field belonging to the Sua Pans Lodge, a clean and friendly establishment owned by possibly the most supportive man in Africa, and his efficient wife. That night I had a minor hassle with an extremely drunk and callow youth who wanted to share my tent. I was rescued by "Mr Supportive", who got rid of him with a mixture of firmness and tact. "What sort of opinion do you want this lady to take back to her country about our people?" The youth vanished.

That was the one and only hassle I had while travelling well over a thousand miles alone. The local men were polite, helpful, sometimes amused, sometimes a little reserved and always delighted by my pathetic attempts to string together my few words of Setswana.

I eventually got a lift to Maun with two South African farmers in a massive lorry that averaged 20km per hour. They were kind enough, but every time the engine boiled over, which was often, and we sat in the middle of nowhere, waiting for it to cool down, they would moan about how dreadful it was, not being allowed to shoot everything in sight any more.

The Nata–Maun road is renowned for its bad surface: 300km through desert that varies from scrubby savannah to the vast and lifeless saline pans, empty of water in November, to the palm tree belt, then sandy wastes followed by more scrub and trees, and more sand. It is not soft golden sand like you find in the Sahara, but a much grittier substance, tufted with dry grasses and thorn bushes and the ever-present acacias. When it rains, parts of the road get washed away. I was lucky and actually made the trip four times without either drowning or dying of heat.

In Maun I borrowed floor space from Barbara, an Australian teaching at the secondary school. Maun itself is set on thick, pale sand, with a shopping mall, Riley's Hotel, and a collection of rather upmarket Safari centres. I walked out of town several times, partly to explore and partly to find a swimming pool. On most occasions I got lifts at least part of the way, though I did once walk eighteen kilometres in blazing sun, with a towel draped around my head.

"Travelling on the back of a truck, ostrich-spotting, sharing canned drinks at every bottle store ... is an exhilarating way of getting about"

Local buses exist, but they are on the erratic side and tend to break down; either all the tyres blow, or the springs give way under the weight of what seems like hundreds of Batswana and their bundles. I frequently found myself with a lapful of parcels, a sleeping baby in one arm and my own luggage in the other. Very local public transport, connecting small villages, can comprise anything from converted lorries to open trucks, and vary accordingly in discomfort. But travelling on the back of a truck, ostrich-spotting, sharing canned drinks at every bottle store on the way and trying to understand what the hell people are talking about is an exhilarating way of getting about..

The Batswana usually charge hitchhikers. The most I ever paid was ten pula from Nata to Maun, and I paid far less for shorter and less bumpy rides. Sometimes I paid nothing at all. Whites don't normally charge, but do get uptight about their insurance policies and tend to make you promise not to sue them if they accidentally almost kill you. Lorry drivers, doing the north–south run will sometimes pick up passengers, but many are forbidden to do so by their contracts. Wherever you are, though, you will eventually get a lift, even if you have to wait a day or two in the more remote areas. Some people will ask for beer (drinking is pretty heavy in Botswana) or food, or even money – if you are white it is assumed you are rich, and by most Botswana standards you are – but it's unlikely that you will ever feel threatened in any way.

Tourism in Botswana concentrates on safaris, aimed pretty exclusively at the very wealthy. It is possible, I was told, to be set down by chartered plane in the middle of the Kalahari amid carpeted tents, with a chance to drink French champagne between taking the occasional blast at leopard from the back of a Landrover. I preferred to spend three unimaginably wonderful days being poled through the watery mazes of the Okavango Delta by a quietly polite and generous-hearted Bushman whose name I never did learn how to pronounce.

It is not only foolish but positively dangerous to roam the ever-changing Delta without the help of an expert, and Kubu Camp, who more or less organised my guide, mentor and transport, came up with a marvel. I was collected from the school gates in a battered jeep, and driven through the bush for three-and-a-half hours to the pick-up point where the *mokoro*, a dug-out canoe, was waiting. My tent, tins of food, lotions, potions and water bottle were carefully loaded and I was arranged equally carefully in the prow, so that I wouldn't upset the balance.

We pushed off into the whispering silence and beauty of the Delta. The poler knew exactly where he was going. Punting soundlessly though great beds of pink, white and lilac water lilies, swishing through reeds and rushes, nosing through rhododendrons, we paused only to gaze at the brilliant birds glittering about their business. At one point, I swam in warm water soft as silk, watching dark red weeds wrap themselves round my legs and getting tangled in lily roots. It was a new, clean, pristine world with its own laws and legends. The Bushman poler knew these laws. Alone, I would have been lost within minutes in those winding secret channels.

I was punted to a small island where I found I was to share a campsite with three Dutch tourists. There was just time to brew a cup of tea and set up my tent before setting off across the bay for a game walk, until the sun did its vanishing act for the day. The Bushman moved softly, perfectly at ease; he belonged to the Delta, his knowledge was awesome and profound. We tracked – he tracked – a herd of buffalo, massive yet gentle until they saw us and vanished. We saw reedbuck, warthogs, assorted boks and beasts, and more species of bird than I could count. We met two giraffe, who loped off with easy elegance, and saw ostrich racing furiously through the grass. There was nothing but the wind, the tart, warm smell of animals and grasses, the clacking of palm leaves, the silky swish of water. The world suddenly made sense.

The next day we set off in the *mokoro* again to do a bit of hippo-spotting. We were lucky to come across a family of hippos, hugely enjoying a late splash, their vast jaws agape, almost grinning at us as they heaved and floundered, snickering to each

other. On land, like elephants, they move almost soundlessly. It seems incredible that all these prehistoric creatures have such grace and gentleness. They won't attack unless they feel threatened, although probably any one of these massive beasts could kill a man. They prefer to back off, to merge into the background, or in the case of hippos, submerge, only their bright eyes alert and visible above the water. A couple of birds dive-bombed the mother hippo, who snapped at one amiably, knowing she would never catch it, and the cabaret continued until slow, warm rain sent the animals underwater and me back to the camp.

"The poler stopped about halfway . . . and led me cautiously through tall grass to stare at what I thought was a tree until it moved forward"

The final day meant another game walk, just after dawn. That night, I heard a lion roaring in the distance, and the poler found its spoor. We tracked it for a while, then lost it in churned-up mud. The poler, while knowing everything, kept his respect and excitement for the wildlife intact. We went back to the beasts and the boks, endlessly graceful, their huge eyes dark and inscrutable.

I left with great reluctance in the *mokoro*. The poler stopped about halfway along the journey, and led me cautiously through tall grass to stare at what I thought was a tree until it moved forward and I found myself so close to a giraffe that I could see its eyelashes. We stared at each other, the Bushman grinning from ear to ear with pride and love and satisfaction before the giraffe became a tree again. We continued pushing through the lilies, pausing to swim and fill our water bottles from the clear river or simply to stop and watch the birds.

There was no sign of the jeep when we arrived at the pick-up point, so the poler and I sat in companionable silence, smoking, dozing, dreaming, until dusk. Out of nowhere a tall, thin man appeared, driving a safari truck with all the trimmings, and offered us a lift. We had gone about 2km when we met our jeep pulling three new *mokoros*. We swapped vehicles and drove at

breakneck speed, first to the poler's hut then back to Maun, bouncing over potholes, grinding to a halt in sandpits, narrowly avoiding being pounded to death by startled kudu, and driving into one of the most magnificent electric storms I have ever seen.

TRAVEL NOTES

Languages English and Setswana.

Transport Hitching is widely accepted, as there are few buses away from the main roads, but you're expected to pay. Entering the country from Zimbabwe, it's best to take the train.

Accommodation Hotels are few and expensive, catering to luxury tour groups. There are hostels, mostly run by the different voluntary services, but most places have somewhere you can camp, though clearly at your own risk.

Guide *The Rough Guide: Zimbabwe and Botswana* (Harrap Columbus) has a hundred or so pages on Botswana and is very much geared to independent travel.

Contacts

Women's Affairs Unit, Ministry of Home Affairs, Private Bag 002, Gaborone. Run almost single-handedly by Joyce Anderson, the Department is largely concerned with supporting women's agricultural co-operatives. It also produces publications and helps organise workshops to spread information on women's legal rights.

Books

Bessie Head lived in Botswana as an exile from South Africa until her death in 1988. Of her novels, the best is **A Question of Power** (Heinemann Educational, 1974). Set in the village in Botswana where she lived, this is a beautifully written exploration of a woman's sanity. Heinemann have also published three other of her novels/short story collections: **Maru** (1972), **The Collector of Treasures** (1977) and **Jerowe, Village of the Rain Wind.**

Brazil

. . . .

Arriving in Brazil from any neighbouring country, let alone from the States or Europe, can be something of a culture shock. Besides the shift from Spanish to Portuguese, the sudden vast distances and extraordinary blend of people and landscapes, the country holds some of the worst pockets of urban poverty in the world. Personal safety has to be taken seriously, as robbery, notably on deserted beaches, in Rio de Janeiro, and in the larger towns of the poverty-stricken northeast, is a very real threat.

Women travellers are also likely to suffer a fair amount of sexual harassment. In general, Brazilians are open, easygoing people with a very relaxed attitude to sex, encapsulated in the often outrageous eroticism of Carnival. At the same time, this is a strongly *machista* society; whether it feels threatening clearly depends on the situation, but a woman alone, especially a foreigner, will inevitably attract a lot of physical attention from men. Hitching is definitely out and it is inadvisable to walk in any city streets on your own at night.

Brazil's diverse landscape, ranging from the threatened tropical rainforest of the Amazon Basin, to partially arid Highlands, down to the heavily industrialised coastal strip, is matched by its population. After the centuries of decimation which began with colonisation, only a fraction of Brazil's indigenous Indian population remains. The rest of the population is mainly descended from the Portuguese colonists, the African slaves they brought with them, and the millions of European families who more recently flocked to the country for work. Today whites or near-whites hold most of the nation's wealth, while black and mixed-race people constitute the bulk of the population pouring into the cities in search of work. Along with high inflation, the problem of internal migration is one of the key symptoms of Brazil's ongoing economic crisis.

Despite periods of economic growth and social reform enjoyed earlier this century, Brazilian politics have a tendency to degenerate into turmoil. Instability and corruption finally led, in 1964, to twenty years of military rule, from which the country has only comparatively recently emerged. During the army's most repressive period in the Sixties, hundreds of students, trade unionists and other political activists went into exile. Among them were feminists who later returned with ideas from Europe and the United States. They are just one of the influences behind Brazil's growing **women's movement**. Today groups range from autonomous feminist organisations campaigning on issues such as reproductive health, sexist education, racism, male violence and women's legal rights, to more hierarchical organisations directly linked to political parties. Brazil has a national feminist paper, *Mulherio,* and groups dedicated to working with low-income women, such as the Carlos Chagas Foundation in São Paulo, produce excellent cartoon pamphlets to get their messages across.

A Different Rhythm

. . . .

Rebecca Cripps visited Brazil on the last stage of a year-long trip to South America. She spent much of the time in São Paulo, teaching, writing and helping out at a centre for single-parent families. She works as a freelance writer in London.

I took the 24-hour "death train" out of Santa Cruz, Bolivia, and arrived in Brazil bone-rattled and worn out. While having my passport stamped at the train station in the border town of Corumbá, sweating in the stifling midday heat, I asked the policeman in the office where I could go for an immediate and everlasting swim. "At my house," he replied, looking at his watch, and he locked up the office for his lunchbreak.

The woman I was with at the time and I refused to go at first; in the previous few months of travelling through South America, we had both already risked our lives more than once, in the cause of spontaneity and the desire to trust. But the man expressed such an earnest wish to have a chance to speak with foreigners – "sin compromiso, you are my guests" – besides which the idea of a cool swim seemed so miraculous, that we finally agreed. Having begged us to stay on, two days later Miguel held a party in our honour and invited forty other federal policemen and their wives for a celebratory barbecue. We became firm friends and two months later he came to stay with me in São Paulo, where I was teaching English.

Such is the generous spirit of hospitality in Brazil that I was constantly invited to stay with people, some of whom I had barely met, and probably I need never have paid for a hotel room. However, I quite often chose to rent somewhere, as basic accommodation is cheap and plentiful throughout the country.

After experiencing Peru and Bolivia, to cross into Brazil involves a certain amount of culture shock. Immediately the atmosphere seems greatly relaxed (police presence is minimal in comparison) and attitudes more liberal, and the Brazilian people move to a different rhythm altogether. They have a languid, graceful motion and a lazy, vibrating way of speaking Portuguese, so unlike the pure clipped tones of *castellano*.

"I was many times touched and stroked against my will by men, and was always unnerved by the strange intimacy inflicted upon me"

Brazilians give the impression of being extremely laid-back – as well as displaying an intense passion for living – while at the same time they are incredibly friendly and open-minded. After the mistrust and hostility I had experienced so often before, particularly in Peru, in Brazil it crossed my mind at first that people were either behaving with extreme cynicism or were overwhelmingly naive. I was wrong on both counts: Brazilians are just unbelievably open.

The whole country seems to breathe in time to some original, sensual drumbeat; sex is everywhere – youth, fire and rhythm. Teenagers make love as soon as their bodies are able and sex is universally proclaimed as the greatest possible pleasure. However, men assume a "liberal" attitude which is often offensively infringing. In São Paulo, where I lived for three months, I was many times touched and stroked

unwillingly by men, and always unnerved by the strange intimacy inflicted upon me in often very public places.

I spent a year in South America, my last five months being in Brazil, and by the end of it all I was sick and wary of macho men and their continual harassment. I found it hard not to become cynical, and even harder sometimes not to just give up and go along with it, to save energy. A very few men I met had managed to break away from *machista*, but for most the indoctrination starts too young and is too deeply ingrained.

Once, on a beach, I was offered money for sex by an eleven-year-old boy, whose persistence and expectations of success appalled me. Miguel, the policeman, warned me on my first day in Brazil: "Don't smile at men or they will think you want to go to bed with them", and his assumption proved to be frustratingly correct. He bemoaned to me the virtual impossibility of building a non-sexual relationship with a Brazilian woman and claimed that he was required to "perform" on a first date or risk being considered freakish, and questioned as to his "problem", so expected is the macho way. Although in Brazil there is more acceptance of homosexuality than in other countries on the continent, homophobia is widespread, and the behaviour of men and women is controlled by an uncompromising heterodoxy. If you break the rules you may get into trouble, and if you are rescued it will probably be, ironically, by chivalry.

São Paulo, the skyscraping business and finance centre of Brazil, does not attract many tourists, and most sightseeing visitors are warned off by descriptions of its vast and sprawling ugliness and dirt. There is certainly not much to see there in terms of beauty or history or ancient culture, and it is a city motivated by a work ethic which supersedes the traditional siesta-happy image of sleepy Latin America and lazy hammock lie-ins. What makes it such a vibrant, vital place is the inhabitants: over fourteen million people from an astonishingly diverse mix of racial origins and cultural backgrounds.

If you haven't got long in Brazil, a visit to São Paulo will probably not seem worth the trouble of working out its inordinately complex system of buses (it takes about two months!). However, as a place to live in, it has many advantages over other Brazilian cities, the greatest being availability of work. Also, in terms of street crime and violence, it is reputedly much less dangerous than Rio de Janeiro – I certainly found the atmosphere generally much more relaxed.

In certain areas of Rio at night, the tension can reach quite unbearable levels. Romantic as it looks from the lofty peak of Sugarloaf Mountain in the softness of evening, this is a city in decline, and the effects of economic collapse and crippling inflation are apparent everywhere on street level and reflected in its mood of suppressed violence and instability. São Paulo, in contrast, is a place of industrial and economic growth, where opportunities for financial success are there for the grasping. It is one of the few places in Brazil where you can make your fortune, or at least earn enough in order to eat. (To breathe, however, is a different matter – pollution is dense.)

At the same time, against this optimistic background of financial and industrial success, São Paulo has a population of slum-dwellers almost as large as that of Rio. Many are transplanted villagers, attracted from the interior and impoverished northeast by the potent appeal of employment and a vision of existence higher than that of mere survival; many cannot subsist anywhere else. *Favelas*, or slums, which have become a dominant feature in Rio's cityscape – almost a tourist attraction – have sprung up all over São Paulo.

"Children younger than ten have been busted for selling cocaine, often to support their own habit"

There are more than half-a-million homeless children in the city, living on the streets of the *favela* districts in whose dirt and squalor they lack access to even the most basic amenities. Many have been abandoned by their parents, who are simply unable to provide for them, and often at a very early age children are forced on to the streets to live as best they can with no permanent shelter, nor food nor clothes. In order to eat, many have to steal, and the downtown streets of the financial centre of São Bentão and Se are crowded with child pickpockets who are often organised into gangs.

Exposed to the starkness of slum life and surrounded by examples of corruption and crime, children are armed as soon as they can walk and take drugs as soon as they can sell them. Children younger than ten have been busted for selling cocaine, often to support their own habit, but as one policeman sighed to me: "They have to escape like their parents, and I can't blame them. They wake up under no roof, to nothing."

In order to try to curb the increasingly alarming situation and provide at least some support for *favela* children, several schemes have been set up in the city over the past couple of decades, to varying degrees of success. In São Paulo I stayed with an American nurse who works as a volunteer at the Sabia centre, a virtually self-sufficient community of single-parent (mother) families situated about an hour away from the city centre in an area of debilitating poverty. It is run in close association with the Hospital of São Paulo which buses volunteer nurses and helpers to the centre each day, but it remains solely reliant on private investment and donations and has no state funding. Between teaching and writing, I occasionally joined the group to help out.

Sabia was built about fifteen years ago on a site donated by a philanthropic landowner, and constructed out of the rubble and waste found abandoned on the land at the time. The founders were single women with children – from its original four families there are now over forty – and the centre remains as a shelter for mainly women and children, with about four men living and working there at the moment. Apart from the family shacks, Sabia is comprised of a set of common buildings, the most important of which are the creche and the daycare centre. There is also a sewing room, a carpentry workshop and a kitchen and garden, which provide all the children and volunteers with two meals a day. A school has been set up with morning and afternoon sessions, plus provision for learning practical skills during any free periods.

"The Brazilian knack of living with a focus on the present . . . helps put off till tomorrow what could happen today"

There was a wonderful atmosphere at Sabia, a feeling of unity and strength in the face of what seem insurmountable obstacles. But the centre is by no means secure. It could not survive without its private funding, and in a country of such economic and social instability as Brazil its stream of donations could dry up at any moment with a lot of work going to waste. Sometimes it

seems as though the whole country could go down too when inflation rises by thirty percent in one day. But the Brazilian knack of living with a focus on the present, an attitude so often mistakenly identified as hedonistic but simply rising from a necessary short-sightedness, helps put off till tomorrow what could happen today.

After three months in São Paulo, I spent my last four weeks in Brazil on my back on the beaches of the Bahia, eating watermelon. I decided that if I were to choose to live anywhere in South America, it would be in this state, which seems to harbour the essence of Brazil. The people here have an endemic closeness to nature and a habitual knowledge of tides, moon cycles, star formations, trees, plants and animals. They celebrate the full moon without any kind of hippy pretension and constantly express their wonder at the natural beauty of their country.

Poverty here is a way of life and of a different make-up than the consumer-deprivation visible elsewhere; as such it seems far less oppressive than in the cities, where living poor is a struggle with many complications. In the Bahia, which has a mainly black population, life is more immediate. It is yearly attracting more and more visitors seeking palm trees and a good time, and of all the places I have been there is nowhere better for kicking off your shoes, dancing all night and flopping into your hammock without a thought of what is life. Only living.

TRAVEL NOTES

Language Portuguese. Don't assume everyone speaks Spanish. It won't be appreciated.

Transport Cheap, fast and comfortable buses criss-cross the country almost any time of day or night. Hitching is difficult and potentially dangerous. Internal air travel is highly developed.

Accommodation There are plenty of cheap hotels throughout Brazil.

Special problems Avoid going alone to isolated beaches or walking around alone at night in any city. Robberies and assaults on residents and travellers alike are becoming increasingly frequent.

Guide *The Rough Guide: Brazil* (Harrap Columbus) is a new addition to the series – up to date and comprehensive.

Contacts

There are far too many women's organisations to list here; also, groups are forever moving and changing. Probably the best central organisation to contact is **Centro Informação Mulher** (*CIM*). Rua Leoncio Gurgel, 11-Luz 01103, São Paulo/SP, ☎229 4818, or Postal 11.399, 05499 São Paulo/SP, Brazil. *CIM* publishes regular lists of different women's organisations throughout the country.

Books

Elizabeth Jelin, ed., *Citizenship and Identity: Women and Social Change in Latin America* (Zed Books, 1990). Edited by an Argentinian sociologist, this book examines women's increasing involvement in grass-roots social change, from the *favelas* of São Paulo to the Bolivian Highlands.

June Hahner, *Women in Latin American History – Their Lives and Views* (UCLA Latin America Center Publications, Los Angeles, 1976). Includes Brazil.

John Hemming, *Amazon Frontier: The Defeat of the Brazilian Indians* (Macmillan, 1986) and ***Red Gold*** (Macmillan, 1987). Excellent detailed histories tracing the plight of Brazilian Indians from the early days of colonisation.

Jorge Amado, *Dona Flor and Her Two Husbands* (Serpent's Tail, 1986). Exhilarating story set in Bahia by one of the country's leading novelists.

Britain

For many travellers, Britain begins (and quite possibly ends) with London. The capital, with its individuality, cultural mix and entertainment, largely lives up to its myths and reputation. At the same time, along with much of southern England, it can often seem unwelcoming – and for visitors it is outrageously expensive. Without friends to stay with, the cost of accommodation can be crippling, whilst the city's transport charges are the highest in Europe.

Expense, in fact, is a problem throughout Britain and if your funds are limited, you may have to be prepared to rely on youth hostels (or else camp in all weathers), spend a lot of time hitching and cook for yourself. However, there is plenty of scope for walking and cycling holidays, and there are parts of the north of England, and certainly Scotland and Wales, where you can wander for miles without seeing a soul.

Politically, Britain is at a low ebb, after more than a decade of Conservative Party rule under the increasingly autocratic Margaret Thatcher. Her government has overseen a dramatic widening of the gap between rich and poor, mirrored by the marked differences in prosperity between north and south and the growing number of homeless people and beggars at the heart of commercial London – a shock for many who have not visited for a while. Parts of Wales, Scotland and the north of England have been especially hard hit by government spending cuts, and the poverty and unemployment in cities like Glasgow, Liverpool, Bradford and Newcastle are the worst Britain has seen since the war. But don't be put off exploring these parts of the country. Northerners tend to be more open and friendly, with less of the traditional English reserve; accommodation is cheaper; and much of the countryside is spectacular and wild.

Sexual harassment varies little between England, Wales and Scotland. Apart from the odd wolf-whistle, you're unlikely to be bothered by men in rural areas, except in pubs. Big cities, however, pose a definite problem at night when you're likely to feel uneasy wandering around alone. Racism is an additional problem, rooted in Britain's history as a leading imperialist power. You're undoubtedly more prone to abuse if you're black, but even white Australians report patronising, colonial attitudes, especially at work.

The double issue of racism and sexism has become a strong focus of the **women's movement** in England, which has many more Asian and Afro-Caribbean communities than neighbouring Wales or Scotland; to understand this commitment you need only turn to Britain's long-standing national feminist magazine, *Spare Rib*. The movement as a whole, as in the US and most of Europe, has greatly diversified since its inception in the early 1970s. As well as racism, questions of equal opportunity, reproductive rights, education and violence have been joined by a growing commitment to environmental issues. There is also mounting concern about poverty and homelessness, of which some of the worst sufferers are single mothers. British feminism may have lost its unity as a national movement but all in all, in spite of economic recession and a Prime Minister devoted to traditional Conservative values, its spirit and aims remain very much alive.

"I am not a Tourist; I live here"

. . . .

A German national, Ilse Zambonini lives and works in north London. She has seen many sides of the city over the past twelve years.

The first time I came to Britain, I was eighteen and on my own; I travelled widely, through England, Scotland and Wales, by coach, train and hitchhiking. Protected as much as anything by my naivete, nothing nasty happened to me and I retained a nagging love for this country. In 1976, I decided to return to London for a while, and I have lived here ever since.

I did not know anyone in London, but I had an idea of what kind of people I wanted to meet and where to look for them. I also managed to find a teaching job through the Central Bureau for Educational Visits and Exchanges. Luck – but also my determination to find a way of staying here. Many people who have moved to London from abroad have told me how difficult it is to meet "English people"; they end up in ghettoes of immigrants, give up and go home. I did not find this a problem; it helps if there is a context of shared interest, for instance feminism, politics, education . . . perhaps being a parent.

Within a year, I had moved into a communal house full of English and

Scots. At first I couldn't understand a word the Scots were saying: I thought they were speaking a foreign language. Now, like everyone else in Britain, I can place people by their accents – and people can place me, too.

I have never lost my German accent – it just won't shape into clipped English noises – which puts me outside the class structure. I could be anybody and I enjoy that. The only time I get a little short-tempered is when someone talks to me as if I were a tourist, very slowly and just a little patronisingly. How many English people speak German, let alone accent-free?

However, I never experienced any hostility directed at my being German, except for one English lady in the Portobello Road who called me a "stupid German cow" because I was in the way of her smart car – and she would have found something else to blame me for if I hadn't had a foreign accent. No one has ever complained about my taking jobs away from the British. They are too busy blaming black people for it. And Nazi films on television, where English actors speak with terrible German accents, have thankfully gone out of fashion.

"This was the first time I had come into contact with people who were culturally different from myself and my friends in age, race and class background"

In 1977 I joined a band and found myself in the middle of the Rock Against Racism movement. I was living on Social Security, and upon my return from a tour abroad with the band, I discovered that I had been turned out of the country. I was only admitted back on the condition that I would never again be a burden to the British tax payer. Under the Treaty of Rome, EC nationals are entitled to work and live in any member country. They are entitled to unemployment benefit once they have worked for a certain number of months or years, but not to Social Security benefits. So, I became a resident working alien!

My life changed. I started out as a youth worker and began to get to know intimately the young unemployed of Islington and Hackney: whites, blacks, Cypriots, Asians. This was the first time I had come into contact with people who were culturally different from myself and my friends in age, race and class background. I felt that I was beginning to understand more about London. I had to think about poverty, racism, about being white and working with young black people, and about being a childless woman and working with young single mothers.

When I moved to London, I had been warned about the dangers from muggers, burglars, murderers, rapists, all waiting there for me. At first, I walked about warily. One evening, on my way home, a group of young men walked up to me. "Here it comes, my first encounter with male violence," I thought. They stopped, looked at me, and one of them said: "You look like a hippie." I giggled all the way home.

How exciting, how amusing everything was then: having a key to a boyfriend's flat in Hackney; cycling from Holloway to Mare Street and finding shortcuts through parks; living in a decrepit squat that had open fires in every room but no electricity; having breakfast in my own garden; going on women's day marches dressed in purples, pinks and high lace-up boots, carrying the small children of women friends ... even the weather was glorious.

Nowadays, I am aware that violent attacks happen all the time, in London as everywhere else. But I move around as though I had a right to, day or night. The area I live in, Archway, in the north of the city, is on the way to "gentrification", though being burgled remains a day-to-day possibility. Sometimes I resent living as if in a fortress, with locks on the windows, locks on every door; lock up after you've let the cat out and unlock when she comes back in (and don't forget to lock up again!). But in a country where the divide between rich and poor is becoming as extreme as in the so-called Third World, this is the price I pay for not being at the bottom of the pile.

In Munich, there are people I know who leave their doors unlocked during the day, some even at night. In London, crime is all around you, and it is just another thing to live with. The dirt, the feeling of neglect, the ugliness of some parts of London, where you find yourself either in a shantytown or in a post-modern theme park, can be extremely depressing. Most of the housing estates are disgusting – full of dogs and dogshit, with dangerous lifts, broken windows and no lighting. But then I go to Hampstead and daydream about living in one of those mansions on the hill, where you breathe London's cleanest air.

"There is a Third World feel to many parts of London"

There is a Third World feel to many parts of London: people queueing outside post offices and benefit offices; beggars; plastic bags full of rubbish everywhere; tatty goods in the shops. In a city with tens of thousands of homeless people, and as many brand new cars, the contrast between private wealth and public poverty has become almost intolerable over the last ten years, and now healthcare is set to go the same way. During the last two elections, I swore to myself that if Thatcher was elected again I'd go back home to Mother, where everything is nice, clean and egalitarian, and ecologically sound. But I never did.

There have also been changes for the better. When I first moved here London was a culinary desert with no decent cup of coffee to be found. The word "café" was synonymous, not with coffee and cake but with greasy food, and wine with overpriced sugarwater.

During my first few years all visitors from Germany had to bring enormous food parcels full of real bread, real coffee, real chocolate, etc. Maybe I felt insecure. Now every supermarket sells ground coffee, and I can buy *Lebkuchen* from my local garage. Everybody knows what *tagliatelle* are (also no one knows how to pronounce them), and cafés with shining espresso machines can be found in Stroud Green Road, Clapham and even Dalston. Thanks to those deplorable yuppies, off-licences now have affordable as well as drinkable wines, and I can swill champagne in wine bars instead of going to a pub – the only British institution I have never learned to love.

London is, of course, different from other big cities in Britain. No other city is so much like a whole country in itself, a whole continent; it is hard to think of leaving, once established. Life in London is anonymous, certainly, and many people are isolated. But isn't this also why they came to live here? If you want to know all your neighbours and all the gossip, you live in the villages. London is a city of privacy, but a place where you can also say hello to the greengrocer or the garage cashier. It is exciting, full of things no one needs, full of useless discoveries, cinemas you will never go to, bands you will never hear, restaurants you might one day go to. The one really negative factor is provided by its size – visiting a friend in another part of town can be a day trip.

I also enjoy the feeling of living in a city I still don't quite know. After twelve years here I still discover new walks by the river or along the canals, parks I have never walked in, or some old bridge or railway station. There are dozens of galleries and museums which I still haven't seen, and I can shop at any time of day or night. In Munich, I hated the deadness that descends on the city at the weekend. Life there stops by noon on Saturday, and if you don't do your shopping by then, you eat out or not at all. No sweat in London.

When I feel like going out to see live music, there is always some band over from Africa, the Caribbean, or some brilliant local musicians no one in Germany will ever hear. There are clubs and events where forty-year-olds can go and dance. There are hundreds of record shops, and dozens of radio stations. In London I'll never run out of music. And the cultural and style climate here is almost anarchic – people wear practically anything. You really appreciate this coming from dull and decent Munich, or from Rome, where you feel like a freak unless you wear something brand new or at least crisply ironed.

What if I get a bit exhausted by all the excitement in London? I have discovered ways of getting out of it. Papers like *Dalton's Weekly* and the Sunday papers advertise cottages all over the country, often incredibly cheap. You don't need to own a second home to have weekends away. I now have two places, one in Cornwall and one in Shropshire, where I go regularly, and I love reading about all the other ones I could go to. The weather, of course, is hardly Mediterranean, but then, if it were, the country would be full of tourists. As one of our cottage landladies said: "We have good weather at the most inconvenient times".

Under the Eyes of the Home Office:

. . . .

Luisa Handem first visited Britain at the age of seventeen from Portugal, where her family had settled after leaving their native Guinea Bissau. She has since made her home in England despite a long history of struggling with the country's forbidding immigration laws.

In Portugal, as a teenager of African descent, I was never quite aware of the fact that, although we all live on one planet, freedom of movement between countries is strictly regulated. Upon my arrival at Gatwick Airport I was kept waiting much longer than everyone else before finally being granted a six-month visitor's visa – and I had only intended staying a couple of months.

"My experience as an au pair was horrendous"

That first hurdle overcome, I went back home to resume my studies, full of wonderful memories of the United Kingdom and its people, and resolved to return the following year to work as an au pair. This time I satisfied all requirements (a letter from my host family inviting me to stay as an au pair for an unspecified period), but the immigration officer decided that only a seven-month visa was appropriate, even though the accepted timespan for an au pair is one year. On being asked what I was coming to do in England, I replied "I intend studying to improve my English." The answer I got was that my English sounded quite good enough and that au pair girls weren't expected to attain a high level of fluency.

My experience as an au pair was horrendous. To begin with the family whose address I had given to the immigration officer had decided not to wait any longer and had taken on another girl. After spending the night at an au pair agency I was allocated a family with one child. A brief interview ensued during which I stated my desire to have some afternoons off to attend a language school. Several weeks later I realised that the agreed two afternoons off a week (plus all of Sunday) were simply not enough.

Unable to negotiate any more free time, I found another family. But my problems weren't over. Not happy with my success in finding an alternative household, the woman I was working for first threatened to have the Home Office deport me and then phoned my next family and told them that I was no good and that I had stolen some envelopes and a half-full can of hairspray (which I had picked out of the rubbish bin in the bathroom). As a result, by the time I moved in they were already looking for a substitute, and, given my bad references, only agreed to keep me for a couple of weeks. The nature and long hours of work aside, I found au pairing a depressing and insulting experience, but it was the only way I could legally stay and work in the UK.

Later on, giving up on the work, I stayed at an all girls Catholic hostel, from where I could at least attend daily classes in English. However, restrictions on closing time (10.30pm weekdays and 11pm on weekends) interfered with my happy discovery of London nightlife and I eventually moved to the newly built YWCA, which doubled as a hotel and youth hostel. From there I attended a full-time "A" level course in order to be able to apply for a university place, applied to a charitable organisation for a grant and worked for up to thirty-five hours a week at a local cinema.

At the age of nineteen I still didn't know enough about immigration laws and the consequences of failing to strictly comply with them. Despite having "employment prohibited" stamped on my passport, I had heard from several people that I could work part-time as long as I was a student receiving more than fifteen hours of tuition a week. Confident of my status, I went on a two-week holiday to visit my parents in Lisbon. Upon my return, I was again faced with a menacing immigration officer and was this time kept waiting for hours while my luggage was taken away and searched in detail. My address book and any letters or notes in my handbag were photocopied and kept for further investigation. One of the letters contained the offer of another cinema job, revealing my intention to work in this country – a point which immigration officers can legitimately use to refuse leave to enter the United Kingdom.

"I was kept for 72 hours in a detention centre at Heathrow, sharing a small cell with three women from Latin America"

I was kept for 72 hours in a detention centre at Heathrow, sharing a small cell with three women from Latin America. When the decision was finally taken to deport me, I was transferred by helicopter to Gatwick Airport where a flight had been booked for my return to Portugal.

All along I was treated as an arrested criminal. One day, while being driven back and forth for questioning, I tried to be human and make a joke about the bitter winter and heavy snow to the woman police officer at the wheel. I was soon shut up by her retort: "If it was so much warmer in Portugal why didn't you stay there?" The only kind words I ever received from officialdom during my detention came from another policewoman. "Why on earth do they keep detaining and sending back polite, decent girls like yourself when we need to be concentrating on dealing with drug traffic?" she said, angrily. I shall always be thankful for those words, which proved to me that not all British people were xenophobic and racist.

After spending nearly a year in Portugal, where post-colonial turmoil was still very much the order of the day, with a huge shortage in housing, work and university places, I was forced once again to contemplate returning to Britain. Despite everything, I stood a better chance of resuming my education. This time I entered successfully as a visitor and, after seeking advice from many friends, decided to apply once again to stay for a year as an au pair.

Months of awaiting a reply from the Home Office followed, during which time I had enrolled at a polytechnic and found myself a family. I finally got in touch to enquire about the fate of my passport. To my astonishment what followed was a visit by an immigration policeman who, using threats and remarks about the poverty of Portugal, wasted no time in suggesting that I was hiding in the country. By the time my hostess's allegiances had switched in favour of the policeman, I was nearing a complete nervous breakdown.

In the end I survived without being deported. My polytechnic supplied good references to back up my assurance that I was only in Britain to pursue my education and I was lucky enough to find a fun-loving Anglo-American family who took such a liking to me that they put in a new application for the extension of my leave to remain in the country. While my case was being considered I managed to secure a university place with a full grant for three years. This in turn helped my case and I was finally granted a visa for the duration of my studies.

Before completing my degree I married a foreign student and, soon after graduating, moved to Sweden where I stayed for two years. I couldn't stand the snow, the country or my marriage, and, refusing to succumb to destiny, I decided one day to return with my young son to Britain. I took the ferry over to Harwich, and as the boat sailed into the port, found myself reassuringly greeted with kindness by strangers.

However, I had come back to join the ranks of single parents struggling in a society which far from meets their needs. I was shocked to find that in London – I still knew nothing of the country outside and the capital was my natural choice – my child was an obstacle. Now that I could neither be sheltered in a hostel, nor housed by a rich family as an au pair, accommodation was very hard to find. Having previously lived in wealthy areas like Hampstead, I now joined the long queues of homeless people waiting to be rehoused.

"I had come back to join the ranks of single parents struggling in a society which far from meets their needs"

Mine was not one of the worst cases; I was kept waiting only six months between bed and breakfast accommodation and incredibly poor temporary housing.

Having grown used to the advanced Swedish welfare state, I was depressed to discover the difficulties of travelling with a child on public transport – something which policy-makers don't seem to take into consideration. This, coupled with the lack of facilities for babies in shops and restaurants, makes it very hard to get around. There are also far too few nurseries to meet the demands of working mothers. My child was on a waiting list for two years.

Despite these setbacks I stayed on. I had been uprooted from my home country as a child and somehow still associated Britain with a sense of liberalism and freedom. Although I'm not so sure about the freedom anymore, to me this is one of the best countries for cultural interchange. I feel I am in the centre of the world. I love the art galleries, the television, the markets; I have been to the Cotswolds, Derbyshire and other parts of northern England and I loved these places too. To deal with British people is not always easy, though. The lack of openness, the silence of the London underground, all contribute to a grim picture of the capital itself. And anyone having to face the bottom line here would certainly not view this as a country of hope.

My child is growing up now, with mixed ideas about his identity. I have noticed improvements in race relations over the years but any mention of African origins still triggers racist senti

ments. I have recently noticed that, even in schools, children seem to be confused about the meaning of being African. On being asked by a seven-year-old where I came from, the laughter that followed my reply only served to remind me of my own childhood in what was then Portuguese Guinea, where my dark mother was often an embarrassment in social places and the cause of much humiliation.

A Scottish Journey

· · · · · · · · · · · · ·

Cathy Roberts works for an independent research service in London. Fuelled by childhood lullabies and enthusiastic reports from women friends, she explored Scotland for the first time in autumn with a friend.

I had wanted to see Scotland since the days when my mother would sing me "The Skye Boat Song" as a lullaby, and had a very clear vision of the country – peopled by strong women in shawls and long skirts, either striding across the heather or weaving famous tweeds. The chance to test the reality came when my best friend returned from abroad and we wanted space and time together. What better than the Western Isles, we thought, and set off to gather information from the Scottish Tourist Board. We didn't want to rough it, feeling we were past the backpacking days (always more fun if the sun shone), and coupled with the fact that my friend was pregnant, we decided to find out about train timetables and the availability of guesthouses and small hotels.

Once we had worked out a route on the Scottish mainland which did not

entail a sequence of five-hour stop-overs in Inverness we set off. It was the last week in September. We had wanted to travel from London by sleeper train, then by ferry to Lewis, but the tourist season really ends in mid-September, after which timetables shrink dramatically. In the end we flew to Glasgow, then travelled by train and ferry to Skye.

The train journey, from Glasgow to Mallaig, up the western coast, was superb. There must be something in the atmosphere of the highlands which calms nerves normally shredded by late trains and bad time-keeping. Our train was delayed because it had waited for a steam train to get through on a single track line, making us late for the ferry to Skye, but that was okay, because the ferry waited for us. That first day, the sky was blue, the sun shining and the air cold. We were settling into a marathon talk and boarded the ferry thinking, "Isn't Skye going to be beautiful . . ."

By the time we crossed the narrow stretch of sea and landed at Armadale on Skye, it was raining. It was also the start of a night and a day of upset and anger, as we had been badly misled by the manager of the hotel we were booked into. "Get the bus from the ferry", he had said; we arrived on Skye on the one ferry a bus does not meet, with no transport to travel the 25 miles to our hotel. "I can't help and, no, I can't hold dinner for you if you're going to be late," were the reassuring words of the manager. A fully booked town of Armadale meant we had to get a taxi – an expense we could have done without. Mind you, at least it led us to meet Mrs Morrison, owner of one of the isle's few taxis and lover of Hebridean folk songs and culture. We cheered up a little as she drove us along the night-time roads, explaining the nuances of the songs of the women weavers on the Isle of Harris.

"We felt decidedly isolated and vulnerable, stuck on a cold, wet island, in an ugly hotel"

It was Mrs Morrison we turned to the next day, to take us away from the hotel, which, with its tall tales of original character and sympathetic adaptations of William IV fisherfolks' cottages, had originally attracted us. The reality was 1950s institutional decor. We felt decidedly isolated and vulnerable, stuck on a cold, wet island, in an ugly hotel, with a manager who appeared to have lied about everything when we had phoned from England. I was nervous, and more than a little angry. There was no hire car ("yes, of course, no problem, but you'll find the bus service good"), no buses, no food and certainly no hint of regret. The uncomfortable, noisy rooms were too much for sensitive souls like us, as was the cost of this blot on the harbour.

We called Mrs Morrison, who understood perfectly – in fact, I would swear she was waiting for us to call – and took us to a Victorian hunting lodge in the middle of nowhere, where all the guests but us spent all day standing thigh deep in water, fishing. Here we were handed over to a good old-fashioned house-keeper, began to feel like houseguests and really began to relax.

We did get a car, and discovered how useless they are for sightseeing when there is fog outside and the windows steam up. But it did at least get us around an island where buses are few and far between, leaving little alternative apart from walking. We spent happy hours in and around our wondrous hotel, by Loch Snizort, curled up in comfy old armchairs before a log fire, walking around the loch between rainstorms and seeing the river grow from a pleasant flow to a raging torrent in 24 hours. I phoned my mother, who said, "Well, they do call Skye the 'misty isle'", and giggled. I'm glad I inherited her sense of humour.

We visited Dunvegan Castle to get out of one rainstorm and called in at a few of the many craft workshops during more drizzle. Strange shapes looming in the sky were identified as mountains when the clouds lifted slightly, and we sat coughing in a smoke-filled old "black house", a rebuilt crofter's house made of mud and turf, with a peat fire burning in the middle of the one windowless room. The newer, squat, whitewashed houses dotted over the hills and moors, though bleak, looked beautiful in comparison.

The appalling weather eventually drove us to escape to the mainland. Mrs Morrison, playing us the women weavers' songs as we drove, waved us off at Kyleakin and the sun shone brightly over Skye as we watched the shore recede. We saw more of the isle from the mainland than we did while we were there.

Once on the mainland, we were back on the train. After a few days' pottering on the west coast, we were lucky to stumble upon the tiny seaside village of Plockton, which, together with some of the surrounding hills, is owned by the National Trust for Scotland. And so it should be. There were palm trees and pampas grass in the bay, and pleasant little Bed and Breakfasts where we really did have good value for little money. Our main evening entertainment was to eat out, as pubs and bars didn't hold much attraction. By day, the scenery was all we had hoped for. We spent a wonderful afternoon walking in the new forest nursery owned by the National Trust at Balmacara. We were escorted by a sturdy grey cat who seemed determined to ensure we found the right paths. She stayed with us, fussing and rolling against us, only cross when we stopped too long to enjoy the views. It was beautiful – and dry.

Back on the trains for the journey east and south, we really appreciated rail travel in bad weather. Where the landscape is the main attraction, the problem has to be what to do when the weather stops all but the most intrepid (or waterproof) traveller from getting out into it. The train provided a journey through the mountains, moorlands and lochs, and no steamed-up windows (as long as the carriage was a little draughty!). We felt it was a safe and relaxing way for women to travel together, certainly less stressful than a car. We also appreciated the loos!

We finished up in Edinburgh, in fine weather, and started walking around the city. We didn't appreciate the military presence in the Castle, but we did like the views of the city. I wish we had had the chance to check out some of the women's places in the city, which has quite a flourishing network of groups. I find it hard to make contact in strange places, but I think I would try if I went back. It would help give a female imprint to Scotland as a whole, for I think it sad that a country which has produced some strong women in its history – we were there for the 400th anniversary of the death of Mary Queen of Scots – denies its female past.

Scottish history, like that of most countries, seemed to be all wars and male heroics. We were put off by the blood and guts histories of the castles and museums. The thing that really upset me in Dunvegan Castle, in Skye, was not the sight of the hole in the

ground through which prisoners were dropped and left to die, but the hole in the kitchen wall next to it, which had been cut through into the dungeon so that the starving people could smell the food. That's really warped.

"Public transport systems are really important to women ... and Scotland let us down."

Looking back now, there are general pictures I have, other than rain and puddles. If you are interested in alcohol, then the whisky distilleries can provide a fascinating hour or two in the dry, trying the different types. If you don't like drinking, then the heavy emphasis on pubs, beer and whisky can be off-putting – it certainly doesn't challenge the stereotype of the heavy drinker, usually male, for which Scotland is renowned.

There is some attempt to develop Scottish cuisine, and that is brave in a country famous only for rolled oats and salmon. It is often expensive to eat out, though, and the standard is patchy to say the least. Long will we remember, as food never to be eaten again, "Plaice with Bananas" and weird desserts like strawberry mousse with oats.

Public transport systems are really important to women, whether visitors or residents, and Scotland let us down. Not being able to walk five miles from a station to a hotel, or twenty miles to a ferry, we found ourselves stuck time and time again. Hotels didn't necessarily have transport arrangements either, though the good ones were willing to help out when needed. Perhaps most people take their own cars, which is a shame. The railways have a good network of lines but, out of high season at least, run a slow and infrequent service, much of it stopping in Inverness.

I must admit, I came back wondering a little what my women friends had seen in Scotland. Though I look back fondly now, I'm still left with a very masculine image of drinking, of wars and clans. Then I hear the female voices singing as they stamped the tweed, picture the women cutting peat and living out their lives within its smoke, and think of Mrs Morrison running her taxis and her B & B. I also remember the prevailing sense of space, even in towns, and realise how comfortable we two felt travelling around.

TRAVEL NOTES

Languages English and Welsh; plus many dialects and languages spoken by different ethnic groups.

Transport An efficient, if costly, network of buses and trains connects all main centres, coaches being cheapest for long distance travel. Services in remote areas, especially parts of Scotland and Wales, are often slow and irregular. Hitching alone carries the usual risks, although it's fairly easy to get a ride.

Depending on the exact area, big cities can be unsafe at night; if you're going to be out late it's wise to work out in advance how you'll get home. Public transport tends to shut down around midnight and taxis can be extortionate. London at least has a special minicab service, *Ladycabs*, run by women for women, though it doesn't operate around the clock. The service is based at 150 Green Lanes, N16 (☎01-254 3501/3314).

Accommodation In general expensive, especially in London which is renowned for having some of the most highly priced hotels in the world. Rooms advertised as Bed and Breakfast can be reasonable and very comfortable, but fill up quickly in the summer, as do youth hostels. Most tourist information offices carry a list of rooms available in the area. If you don't mind the regulations, youth hostels are widespread and some of the cheapest places to stay. Camping is safer than in many countries and often feasible outside of organised sites.

Special Problems Getting into Britain can be a harrowing experience, especially if you're arriving from a Third World country. Admission is at the discretion of the immigration officer and even marriage to a British citizen won't guarantee you secure entry. Make sure you have all the relevant documents, including entry clearance from the British Embassy in your home country where applicable, and proof of sufficient funds to cover your stay. Black women have been particularly discriminated against by the UK Nationality Act. If in trouble, contact the *United Kingdom Immigrant Advisory Service* (☎01-240 5176), which has offices at Heathrow and Gatwick airports; and/or the *Women's Immigration and Nationality Group*, c/o 115 Old Street, London EC1V 9JR (☎01-251 8706).

Guides *Let's Go Britain and Ireland* (St Martins Press, US) is good on practicalities, if sometimes a little crass. *Hitchhiker's Manual: Britain* (Vacwork, Oxford) has invaluable route information. *Summer Jobs in Britain* (Vacation Work) is a fairly comprehensive, annual work directory.

Contacts

We only have space for a small selection of **women's organisations** here, but the **Spare Rib Diary** contains a fairly comprehensive list that includes women's centres and local groups, holiday places, bookshops and publications. The diary is obtainable from feminist and radical bookshops (see below) or by writing to *Spare Rib*, 27 Clerkenwell Close, London EC1 0AT.

London (highly selective)

Kings Cross Women's Centre, 71 Tonbridge St., WC1 (☎01-837 7509). Multiracial women's drop-in, resource, advice and information centre.

Women's International Resource Centre, 173 Archway Road, London N6 5BL (☎01-341 4403). Mainly geared to linking up and giving solidarity to Third World women.

Lesbian Archive and Information Centre, BM Box 7005, London WC1N 3XX.

Women's Health and Reproductive Rights Information Centre, 52/4 Featherstone Street, London EC1Y 8RT (☎01-251 6332). National information and resource centre.

Feminist Library, 5 Westminster Bridge Road, London SE1 (☎01-928 7789).

London has two feminist **bookshops**: **Silver Moon**, 68 Charing Cross Road, WC2 (☎01-836 7906; and **Sisterwrite**, 190 Upper Street, N1 (☎01-226 9782, closed Monday). There are also a number of radical bookshops, among them **Compendium**, **Housman's** and the **Africa Book Centre**, with extensive women's sections.

England outside London

The following are a few **feminist/radical bookshops outside London**. All of these should be able to provide you with some information on women's activities in the area.

BIRMINGHAM: **Key Books**, 136 Digbeth, Birmingham B5 6DR (☎021-643 8081).

BRISTOL: **Greenleaf Bookshop Co-operative**, 82 Colston Street, Bristol 1 (☎0207-211369). Also a wholefood café.

CAMBRIDGE: **Grapevine**, Unit 6 Dale's Brewery, Gwydir Street, Cambridge (☎0223-61808).

LEEDS: **Corner Bookshop**, 162 Woodhouse Lane (opposite university), Leeds 2 (☎0532-454125).

LIVERPOOL: **Progressive Books**, 12 Berry Street, Liverpool L1 4JF (☎051-709 1905).

MANCHESTER: **Grassroots**, 1 Newton Street, Manchester M1 1HW (☎061-236 3112).

NEWCASTLE: **The Bookhouse**, 13 Ridley Place, Newcastle-upon-Tyne NE1 8JQ (☎ 091-261 6128).

SHEFFIELD: **Independent Bookshop**, 69 Surrey Street, Sheffield S1 2LH (☎0742-737 722).

YORK: **York Community Books**, 73 Walmgate, York (☎0904-37355).

Scotland

EDINBURGH: **West and Wilde Bookshop**, 25A Dundas St., Edinburgh EH3 6QQ (☎031-556 0079).

GLASGOW: **Changes Bookshop**, 340 West Princes St., Glasgow G4 9HF.

Wales

CARDIFF: **108 Bookshop**, 108 Salisbury Road. You should also make contact with the **Women's Centre**, 2 Coburn Street (☎0222-383024), for information about women-only/lesbian bars and discos.

Women-only hostels/holiday centres

Again, only a selection:

England

Shiplate Farm, Shiplate Road, Avon BS24 ONY (☎0934-14787). Bed and Breakfast in a converted eighteenth-century farmhouse.

The Only Alternative Left, 39 St Aubyns, Hove, Sussex, BN3 2TH (☎0273-24739). Feminist-run Bed and Breakfast, also used for small residential conferences.

The Hen House, Hawerby Hall, Thoresby (☎0472-840278). A large Georgian mansion converted into a women's holiday centre. Slightly more expensive and luxurious than usual.

Women-Only Guest House, 19 Crossroads, Haworth, West Yorkshire, BD22 9BG (☎0535-45711; eves and weekends). Women-run Bed and Breakfast in the heart of Bronte country.

Scotland

Belrose Guest House, 53 Gilmore Place, Edinburgh EH3 9NT (☎229-6219). Women-owned and operated Bed and Breakfast.

Wales

Oaklands Women's Holiday Centre, Glastonbury-on-Wye, nr Hereford, Powys (☎04974-275). Tends to be booked up in advance by groups and can be chaotic and not always very friendly, but worth trying out.

Lan Farm, Graigwen, Pontypridd, Mid Glamorgan, CF37 3NN (☎0443-403606). Traditional Welsh farmhouse run as a hostel by two gay women.

Books

The 1980s saw a rapid development of feminist presses and feminist writing in Britain. Below are just a few personal favourites

Non-fiction

Beatrix Campbell, *Wigan Pier Revisited, Poverty and Politics in the 1980s* (Virago, 1984). A devastating record of the extent of poverty and unemployment in the north of England, and a passionate plea for a feminist socialism that responds to real needs. Also by the same author, ***The Iron Ladies: Why Women Vote Tory*** (Virago, 1987) provides some astute insights into the Margaret Thatcher phenomenon.

Angela Carter, *Nothing Sacred* (Virago, 1982). Collection of essays and writings, many of them autobiographical, by one of Britain's leading contemporary writers.

Jennifer Clarke, *In Our Grandmothers' Footsteps. A Virago Guide to London* (Virago, 1984). The author plus photographer Joanna Parkin have unearthed the memorials to 271 women – famous, infamous and unknown.

Anna Coote and Beatrix Campbell, *Sweet Freedom – The Struggle for Women's Liberation* (Picador, 1982). Two long-term active feminists chronicle the progress of the movement since the late 1960s when it began.

Hannah Kantner, Sarah Lefnu, Shaila Shah and Carole Spedding, eds, *Sweeping Statements: Writings from the Women's Liberation Movement 1981-3* (Women's Press, 1984). Collection of articles and conference papers, demonstrating the range of feminist involvement, analysis and action during this period.

Barbara Rogers, *52%: Getting Women's Power into Politics* (Women's Press, 1983). Compelling argument for the urgent need for more women's involvement in British politics.

Beverley Bryan, Stella Dadzie and Suzanne Scafe, *Heart of the Race* (Virago, 1985). Insights into what it's like growing up as a black woman in Britain.

Sharan-Jeet Shan, *In My Own Name* (The Women's Press, 1985). Autobiographical story of an Indian woman, born in the Punjab and forced into an arranged marriage which brought her to England, where she finally refuses to renounce her right to live her own life. Simply written and very moving.

Amrit Wilson, *Finding A Voice* (Virago, 1978). Experiences of Asian women in Britain recorded in their own words.

Rosalind K. Marshall, *Virgins and Viragos – a History of Women in Scotland from 1080-1980* (Collins, 1983). Over-academic but interesting in its exploration of little known ground.

Fiction

Zoe Fairbairns, *Benefits* (Virago, 1979). Feminist science-fiction set in a not too distant London future where men try to control women's reproduction and the "victims" fight back.

Pat Barker, *Union Street* (Virago, 1982). About the lives and struggles of seven working-class women and their men in the north of England during the 1973 miners' strike. Also recommended is ***The Man who Wasn't There*** (Virago, 1988). An optimistic novel about the bridging of age and class barriers.

Maggie Gee, *Grace* (Heinemann, 1988). Based on the events surrounding the extremely suspicious death of Hilda Murrell, an anti-nuclear campaigner, this novel deals with the threats inherent in British life.

Sara Maitland, *Telling Tales* (Journeyman Press, 1983). Collection of short stories, some set in the present, others featuring women from ancient and biblical history. Very readable. Her latest book, **Three Times Table** (Chatto, 1989), interweaves the lives of three women, combining fantasy with everyday observations.

Jeanette Winterson, *Oranges are not the Only Fruit* (Pandora Press, 1985). A quirky, funny and original book based on the author's own experiences of growing up in a pentecostal community in Lancashire. Barred from expressing her lesbian sexuality she breaks away, establishing her independence via university. Her later novels, ***The Passion*** (Penguin, 1988) and ***Sexing the Cherry*** (Bloomsbury, 1989) are both highly acclaimed works of history, fantasy and magic, inventive if not quite so much fun.

Buchi Emecheta, *Adah's Story* (Allison & Busby, 1983). Having left Nigeria to join her violent husband, Adah finds herself living alone in London with five children to look after. An account of an indomitable woman who fights against the odds to realise her ambition to be a writer. Look out also for Emecheta's other novels and children's books.

Canada

· · · · · · · · · · · · · · · · · · · ·

Compared with the US, Canada is a country of less outrageous extremes, more famous for its great outdoors than the hype and excitement of city life. There are far fewer people and, for many, mountains, forests, rivers and vast empty plains really are the principal attraction. You should have little trouble travelling alone or with another woman although, as in the States, most cities have areas it is best to avoid. Getting around to the main centres is straightforward, on buses, trains and internal flights, but public transport services in outlying areas tend to be few and far between. Here hitching, safest through agencies, may be your only option.

Regional differences between people are hardly surprising in a country of this size, but Canada is also very much split along national lines going back to the days of direct French and British colonisation. There has always been a degree of tension between British and French Canadians, particularly in

Quebec Province. The 1970s, when the Quebecois separatist movement was at its height, was an explosive time but since the passing of language laws, making French Quebec's official language, relations have been easier. The government is explicitly committed to developing a bilingual national identity, and attempts to do this by emphasising a common cultural heritage, and by regulating foreign, mainly US, influence. Dependence on American investment and technology and the degree to which Canadian culture and lifestyle has been Americanised are a source of continued resentment.

Struggles within national minorities for identity, rights and property have all influenced the **women's movement** and determined its diverse, regional and very active nature. Almost every major town has a women's bookshop, café, feminist theatre, art gallery and local health centre. There are Indian and Inuit (Eskimo) groups, women's causes in national political parties, and active trade union women's groups. The largest national organisation, the *National Action Committee on the Status of Women (NAC)*, is a coalition of just under 6000 groups and represents almost three million women.

Abortion rights, the current rallying call for the American women's movement, is also a key issue in Canada. In January 1989, the Canadian Abortion Law which mandated approval for an abortion by a committee of hospital physicians was ruled unconstitutional. Women's groups hailed this as a major victory for the pro-choice movement. As we enter the 1990s, anti-choice activists are promoting legislation to restrict access to abortions, and, for the women's movement, the struggle now moves to public funding for abortions and equal access for all women, regardless of geography (northern Canada tends to be more conservative on these issues) or financial status.

Canadian feminist groups are facing aggressive opposition from a group called *REAL Women* (Realistic Equal Active for Life), an anti-feminist, anti-choice organisation which borrows the rhetoric of the women's movement to bolster their own traditional family and homophobic agenda. They claim a membership of 20,000 women and have recently been granted funding under a federal programme to promote equality. Feminist groups have yet to find an effective strategy to counterbalance the influence of this sister organisation which in fact opposes most feminist issues.

A Taste of the Great Outdoors

. . . .

Geraldine Brennan spent two months in Canada on the first stage of a year's journey around the world. She stayed with family in Ontario and explored alone in Quebec, British Columbia and Alberta.

When I arrived in Canada I wanted to rest and relish an increase in emotional and physical space. At that early stage in a round-the-world trip, I was not ready for the stimulation and hard slog of immersion into a totally different culture. I have lived all my life on an overcrowded island and for me the chance to watch killer whales playing off Vancouver Island, dodge Pacific rollers as I jogged along a deserted beach, and walk for ten hours with only birds for company was thrilling indeed. I appreciated the Canadians' regard for their environment: relatively clean rivers and streams, no smoking on most transport or in public buildings, bottles and paper collected for recycling with the garbage.

When travelling alone I used buses (with some overnight trips), hitched in emergencies (usually within national parks) and stayed in youth hostels. Attitudes towards me as a woman did not get in the way of many good experiences. Generally, I felt safe – I didn't appreciate how safe until I moved on to the US – with only a few moments of unease in downtown areas at night. The Canadians I met were warm, friendly and accepting. Only one man expressed horror at my travelling alone and asked me what my family thought of it (I'm thirty!). Those with British roots often wanted to talk about the royal family, UK soap operas or their grandparents' home town. It was sometimes hard, but showing interest in these topics paid off and I had many good conversations on long bus journeys.

"The current Canadian ideal is the white nuclear family enjoying the great outdoors"

Early in my visit I spent some weeks in Peterborough, Ontario, a small university town which is also the gateway to the Kawarthas. This network of lakes and canals attracts a stream of weekend and holiday visitors from Toronto and the surrounding area. I passed afternoons watching affluent Canadians at play and it became clear that, while Canada may be multiracial with equal opportunities for women similar to those in the States and Britain, the current Canadian national ideal is the white nuclear family enjoying the great outdoors. This impression was backed up by the Canadian media.

As I watched the lavishly equipped motorised houseboats cruising the canals and scaring away the birdlife, I wondered if the national sport might be collecting expensive leisure equipment in order to relive the pioneer experience. The holiday cabin on a remote lake shore, the camper van with twin mountain bikes or kayaks strapped to the roof and towing a four-wheel drive truck, the roadside picnic tables and barbecue pits are all desirable accessories. My solo attempt to get back to nature without even a car or a tent was often viewed with amusement. Like most Canadian consumer goods, the wilderness is available in neat family-size packages with detailed instructions for use.

I was grateful for the clearly marked trails and helpful information staff found in national and provincial parks. These people offer advice on how to deal with all the natural hazards that equally affect women and men: sudden changes in the weather, potential encounters with bears in some areas or the dangers of a long hike without the right footwear or adequate water. Anyone who chooses to hike alone for more than a day is asked to register, which offers extra protection for women. The park staff can also tell you how to enjoy the landscape and wildlife while making the minimum impact on it.

But it seemed that access to Canada's natural resources is not equally distributed. The country has many well-established ethnic communities: Italians and Asians in Toronto, Ukrainians in the prairie provinces, Chinese and Japanese in Vancouver, Afro-Caribbeans . . . yet I met very few non-white Canadians on my tour of beauty spots and forest-screened campgrounds. This was in obvious contrast to my experience on buses, used by those who can't afford cars, where white faces were in a minority.

Wanting to make contact with North American Indian women, I visited a Kwaitukl reservation in Alert Bay, British Columbia. I was warmly welcomed by a woman running its cultural centre who was only too keen to talk about the past and present life of her people. Museums are a good source of background information on the local Indian bands in whichever part of Canada you find yourself and many have reproduced their own histories in book and video form.

My holiday included a break from any kind of political organising. I noticed active women's organisations within reach of most communities and enormous scope for almost any kind of feminist activity in Toronto, Vancouver and Montreal. Peterborough had a downtown women's centre, two good bookshops and at least one university women's group. Despite all this temptation, my resolve to let the world save itself remained intact.

Canada is a country I could happily live in, preferably in one of the larger cities with greater tolerance for lifestyles outside the nuclear family. I arrived expecting it to be like the United States and found it a much more rational and safe place to be.

Hitching Through the Yukon

. . . .

Kate Pullinger is a Canadian writer living in London. She describes hitch-hiking through the Yukon Territory, a massive area north of British Columbia in western Canada.

The Yukon is basically the "Great Outdoors", and not much else. Exceptionally underpopulated, with less than 25,000 people in an area almost as large as France, it is a mountain-lake-forest-river-lover's dream come true. I think the best way to see it, at least in summer, is to hitchhike. I have always found hitching in the Yukon relatively fast, easy and safe, mainly because towns are far apart and nobody is going to leave anyone standing on the side of the road in the middle of nowhere at -20°C, or, in summer, in all that dust.

Last summer I stood on the side of the road outside the Yukon's capital, Whitehorse. My thumb stuck out, I was heading for Dawson City 333 miles away. The first vehicle to stop was an old Ford truck, bed on back with two extremely large sled dogs hanging out over its sides. They barked at me ferociously. A woman jumped out and asked how far I was going. I told her, and she said she was only going fifty miles, but that was a good start. So I jumped in.

She was young, had long plaited hair, and was wearing men's shorts and a felt hat. Next to her sat a small, dark baby, who looked at me curiously. The woman didn't say anything so neither did I. After a few miles she reached above the windscreen and pulled a cigar from behind the sunshade. She smoked it as she drove, clenching it between her teeth when she changed gear. I looked out of the window over the hills and vast, peopleless landscape.

After fifty miles she pulled off the road on to the dirt track that led to her house and I thanked her and jumped out. I slammed the truck door so it shut properly and she and the baby sped off. The sled dogs barked at me until I was far out of their sight.

I stood again at the side of the road. A small Toyota two-door stopped. I put my pack in the back seat and climbed in front. This driver was also a woman, she wore a skirt and her hair was wet. We began to chat and I learned that she was just driving home from a swimming lesson in Whitehorse – a trip of 200 miles, which she made every Friday. There aren't very many swimming pools in the Yukon. The conversation led to a familiar story: she came up to the Yukon ten years ago to visit a friend and stayed. She said she wouldn't leave for anything, and now her brother lives up here too. I began to think there must be something special about this place.

Where she dropped me it was very quiet. There were trees everywhere I looked. In fact, all I could see was trees. I had to wait here around twenty minutes before I heard what sounded like a truck. I saw the dust before I could see it, great clouds of dirt billowing up into the sky. Then I saw the truck and stood on my tiptoes and tried to make my thumb bigger. The driver saw me and started to slow down. It took him a long time to do so and he went past me. I could no longer see, there was so much dust, and I held my scarf over my mouth. When it settled I walked to the truck – a long way up – and negotiated the lift, another fifty miles.

"I knew about this kind of van: lush interior, shag carpets on the walls, a stereo. They call them sin-bins, glam-vans, or more straightforwardly, fuck-trucks"

After hoisting my pack up I climbed in. The driver started the engine and headed down the road. I smiled to myself, thinking I was in front of the dust now. The truck driver seemed to change gears a hundred times before we were up to the right speed. Steaming along, past the endless lakes and hills, he told me about his children going to school, having babies and

working in Edmonton. I listened and then asked how long he's been here. He said he came for a year thirty years ago. There is something about this place.

Dropped at another turnoff I ran into the bushes for protection from all that dust. When he and his cloud were out of sight, I climbed back to the road. A few more cars went by and then a van stopped. It was a newish van, brown with a sunset painted on the exterior. I knew about this kind of van: lush interior, shag carpets on the walls, a stereo. They call them sin-bins, glam-vans, or more straightforwardly, fuck-trucks. Thinking of my vulnerability, I took a look at the driver. He was male, of course, and looked about forty-five. He was wearing a nylon shirt with bucking broncos on it. He had a skinny black moustache and shiny hair. He asked where I was going and said he was too, he didn't know these parts and would like some company. The voice inside me said he was okay. I got into the van.

The driver was called Dan and came from Fort St John. He talked away about his family and I began to relax. He said he was a professional gambler which made me sit up: gambling is illegal in most of Canada. Dan told me all about the gambling circuit in British Columbia, the late-night games in Trail, Kelowna, Hope, the nights when he'd walked away with $4000 in his pocket. He told me about the cards, the passwords and the bribes to the Mounties. I was astounded; this was a whole new side to "Beautiful But Boring British Columbia". I asked him what he was doing up here. Then I remembered: Dawson City is the only place in Canada where gambling is legal. And Dawson City was where I was headed.

It was evening by the time we arrived and Dan dropped me off at the crossing to the campsite. Satiated with gambling stories, I sat down beside the river and waited for the little ferry to take me across. It was full of other hitchhikers: Germans, Americans, Quebecois. It was 8pm and the sky was as bright as mid-morning. I ate and then took the ferry back across to the town, strolling along the wild west wooden sidewalks, past the false-front saloons, hotels and shops and ending up in front of Diamond Tooth Gerties, the casino. I went in, thinking I wouldn't play, just have a look around. The place was full and everyone was drinking, smoking and gambling. There were dancing girls, and a vaudeville show and card-dealers with waistcoats and bow ties and armbands. I had a drink and wondered if this was what it had looked like in 1905. Standing beside the blackjack table I figured out how to play, and watched as people won and lost. I wasn't going to play, just watch.

"I talked and laughed with all the other gamblers I had met. Feeling rather rich and drunk ..."

Many bottles of Molson Canadian and five hours later, I came out, $10 up. It was 2am, broad daylight; if the sun ever went down, I missed it. Running to catch the ferry back to the campsite, I talked and laughed with all the other gamblers I had met. Feeling rather rich and drunk, I crawled into my tent. Someone had built a campfire and people were milling about doing campfire sorts of things but it didn't seem right, campfire and campsongs in broad daylight. I closed my eyes and thought that perhaps after a few nights of lucrative gambling I would hitch that brief 150 miles up into the Arctic Circle. There is definitely something about this place.

TRAVEL NOTES

Languages English and French; in Quebec, French is the main language.

Transport There are *Greyhound* coaches to most towns, good trains and efficient, fairly inexpensive internal flights. Hitching is possible but not always advisable alone on the open, lonely roads. For long distances, college noticeboards are an excellent source of lifts; they specify people wanting or offering lifts and you get a chance to meet the people beforehand.

Accommodation YWCAs are usually a good bet: full details from the national office in Toronto (571 Jarvis Street, M4Y JJ1 ☎416-921 2117). Universities outside term time are also recommended.

Guides *Canada – A Travel Survival Kit* (Lonely Planet). *Moneywise Guide to North America* (Travelaid) includes a Canada section. Recommended for the Yukon is *The Alaska-Yukon Handbook* (Moon Publications, US).

Contacts
A very good source for addresses and information about the Canadian women's movement is the annual **Everywoman's Almanac** (Women's Press, Canada). Distributed in the UK and available in women's bookshops.

The **National Action Committee on the Status of Women** (NAC) is the political arm and largest national women's movement organisation in Canada, comprising a coalition of just under 6000 groups with a combined membership of close to three million women. Main office: 344 Bloor St.W, Suite 505, Toronto, M5S3A7, ☎922-3246.

Also useful, the **Canadian Women's Mailing List** for up-to-date information of events, publications, services is published by WEB Women's Information Exchange, 9280 Arvida Avenue, Richmond BC, ☎604-274 5335.

Another way of gathering information inside Canada is via the free **networking magazines** available in kiosks in every large city.

These tend to list everything – gay and lesbian groups, ethnic groups, psychodrama, alternative health, ecology groups etc. You could also try phoning the local **New Democratic Party** office, the only political party to seriously consider women's issues on its agenda.

Calgary, Edmonton, Montreal, Quebec, Toronto and Vancouver all have **women's bookshops** and centres. These include:

CALGARY: **Women's Resource Centre-YWCA**, 320-5th Avenue, S.E., Calgary T2G 0E5, Alberta, ☎403-263 1550.

EDMONTON: **Commonwoman Books**, 8210-104 St., Edmonton, Alberta.

MONTREAL: **Androgyny** (gay and women's bookshop), 1217 Crescent, Montreal. Should stock the **Montreal Yellow Pages** which lists resources for women.

TORONTO: **Women's Bookstore**, 73 Harboard St., Toronto.

VANCOUVER: **Vancouver Women's Bookstore**, Cambic St, ☎604-684 052.

Books

Margaret Atwood, *Bluebeard's Egg* (Virago, 1988); ***The Handmaid's Tale*** (Virago, 1987) and earlier novels by Canada's leading novelist and poet.

Joan Barfoot, *Gaining Ground* (The Women's Press, 1980). Novel about a woman who leaves her husband, children and suburban security to live as a hermit deep in the Canadian countryside.

Jane Rule, *The Desert of the Heart* (1964; Pandora, 1986) and ***Memory Board*** (Pandora, 1987) are just two of the books we recommend by one of the country's leading lesbian feminist writers.

Ann Cameron, *Daughters of Copper Woman* (The Women's Press, Canada, 1985). Novel of matriarchal secret legends of Nootka women, off Vancouver island.

Willa Cather, *Shadows on the Rock* (1937; Virago 1984). Classic novel about French settlers in Canada.

Alice Munro, *Beggar Maid* (Penguin, 1981). Best-known book of this Canadian author, again set in rural Ontario and in Toronto.

Susan Crean, *Newsworthy: The Lives of Media Women* (Stoddart, Canada, 1985). Examination of how women have overcome the twin barriers of self-doubt and discrimination and established themselves in print and electronic media.

Peney Kome, *Women of Influence: Canadian Women and Politics* (Doubleday, New York, 1985). Somewhat academic but a useful overview of women's place in political life.

Susanna Moodie, *Roughing it in the Bush: or Forest life in Canada* (Virago, 1985). Sharp, enduring account by an early British settler; new introduction by novelist Margaret Atwood.

Thanks to Anne O'Byrne, Catherine Pepinster and Jo Siedlecka for introductory information and Travel Notes.

Chad

. . . .

Not many travellers go to Chad. The country has suffered badly from years of civil war and horrendous drought; there is virtually no public transport and travel is by pick-up truck or lorry, usually on top of a pile of goods.

Despite the ravages of war, evident everywhere in the ruined buildings, untarred roads and general lack of public services, Chad is reportedly going through a period of revival and optimism. What began as a civil war, only five years after independence from the French, has gradually narrowed into war against Libya. The French, only too willing to support their former colony against Colonel Gaddafi, have piled on military assistance and, by 1990, it looks as if Libya may be losing its stronghold. The economy, largely reliant on cotton production, also appears to be improving, though in reality the country is more or less totally dependent on foreign aid.

After a long period of restriction, it is possible to travel almost anywhere in the country; just don't expect to get there quickly. Hotels are few and far between, but in the more populated south most villages seem to have a mission station where, once people have got over the shock of seeing a lone woman traveller, you will probably receive a warm welcome. Also you will nearly always find yourself among travelling Chadienne women, eager to look after you and help find you a bed for the night. Travel in Chad may be unpredictable and hard going at times, but the absence of tourism and subsequent hustle, coupled with vast stretches of wild and beautiful scenery, make it definitely worth a visit.

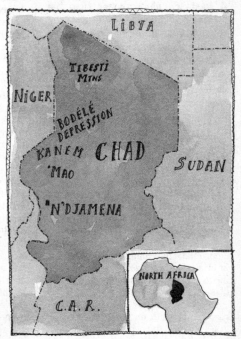

Oxfam and UNICEF focus a proportion of aid on women's income-generating and health projects but, despite an official Department of Women's Affairs, there appears to be little specific concentration on **women's needs** from within the country. Circumstances vary considerably from north to south, but generally women have only limited property rights and bear the brunt of water and wood carrying on top of childcare and general domestic chores. Though village women's groups exist to try to ease the burden, as long as the country remains hampered by war, it will be some time before Chad sees any kind of concerted movement for women's rights.

Days on the Road

. . . .

A freelance photographer from the northeast of England, Chris Johnson spent a year in Africa, researching into the lives of local women and taking photographs for an exhibition. In Chad she travelled much of the time by lorry, hitching lifts wherever she could.

From the capital, N'Djamena, a narrow strip of pot-holed tarmac runs north; we follow alongside on the broad sandy track through the scrub. There are very few paved roads in Chad, and those that are paved are usually in such bad condition that people prefer making their own tracks. It's hot and I'm thirsty. I look longingly at the bottle of water beside me, but it's the second day of Ramadan and as neither of my companions have had anything to eat or drink since sunrise it seems unfair of me to add to their misery by indulging myself.

At 4pm we stop for them to pray. The road continues through sparse red gold grass and past the occasional dusty tree. Half an hour later we reach a village where we stop to rest. The driver sends off for cans of cold orange juice and hands one to me, brushing aside my protests and insisting I drink. It feels like the height of generosity and is typical of my experiences with Muslim men in Africa.

En route again. We've now lost all semblance of tar, and in places there isn't even much semblance of track, just tyre marks in the sand. At 6.30pm we stop again to pray. The ordeal is over for the day and at last they can drink. They tell me the first three days of Ramadan are the worst; after that one gets used to it. The evening is a pearly grey-pink; above is the thin crescent of the moon. All around is vast emptiness. We drive on again, often through thick sand. A man comes by on his camel, our headlights picking out the rich colours of the woven saddle cloth.

We reach Chaddra, our first port of call, at 10pm. The vehicle is unloaded and we stop for a meal. Inside the courtyard, lit by the flicker of oil lamps, a group of white-robed men sit round the large mat. As a visitor, I am accorded the status of honorary man and sit with them to eat. A woman waits on us silently.

Then it's another two hours' rough driving. Exhausted, I keep falling asleep, only to be jolted awake again. At midnight we stop by a cluster of houses. We roll out our mats and the local inhabitants come across the sands to chat and to bring us more mats. I am aware of the faint sound of someone playing a thumb piano, before falling asleep. Sometime in the early morning the cold wakes me and I crawl into my sleeping bag.

"As a visitor, I am accorded the status of honorary man and sit with them to eat. A woman waits on us silently"

Prayers are at dawn and we are off by six. Apart from the occasional tree, the only vegetation is a pale green plant, about three feet tall and with leathery leaves. Mostly there is just sand. An hour later we pass a small group of rectangular houses with flat roofs; then, coming over a rise, see the village of Mao spread out on the hillside ahead. The single-storey houses are built of the local pale coloured earth which is found in bands by the wadis. They are very Arab looking – rectangular in shape, with flat roofs and little turrets at each corner and halfway along the long walls – and are entered through tiny gateways in the street walls.

One of these houses is my home for the next few days. The thick walls and tiny slit windows keep it wonderfully cool, a welcome contrast to the modern houses of the city. Inside the courtyard someone has planted trees and flowers; an awning keeps off the fierce sun and a gentle wind rustles my papers as I try to write.

Mao is the capital of Karem province and an ancient trading centre. As you enter the village the words "Sultanate of Karem" can be seen written in black over the white archway. The weekly market still brings in people from a wide distance and even the daily market is large, though it has little fresh food: most things are dried to preserve them. Especially good are the dried dates.

Along one side of the village runs a wadi. Down in its valley piles of bricks lie baking in the sun and there is constant traffic to and from the wall. A line of women, swathed in long black robes, walk back up the hill to the village carrying heavy earthen water pots on their heads.

At 6.30pm the muezzin calls the faithful again to prayer. Looking out across the walls, there are only four colours: the pinky-beige of the sands, which is split by a gash of white – the same white as the houses; the dusty green of trees; and the pale, pale blue of the sky. Veiled women greet me and laugh at my taking photographs.

Northwest of Mao is Nokou. It's definitely remote: if you travel northwest for about 320 miles you might, if your navigation is good, hit Bihua in Niger; travel northeast about 400 miles and, if you are lucky, you come across Zouar in the Tibesti Mountains; otherwise the nearest habitation is about 800 miles away in Libya.

We set off from Mao as soon as the prayers have finished. The empty landscape sweeps up into hills, nothing very high or steep, but on a grand scale. It's windy and the surface sand blows off like spindrift. Occasionally there's a sparse covering of grass which from a distance lends the hills a yellow-green colour; but as soon as you get close it is clear there's far more sand than grass. From time to time we see a few goats or a woman on a donkey, but mainly it's just camels: some roaming free, others ridden by men dressed in long white robes.

The people I am travelling with are involved in a project helping to cultivate the wadis. The water table in the wadis is very close to the surface and *shadufs* are used to lift water to irrigate. Traditionally some people have always cultivated in this area: it's one of the features that distinguish it from the eastern Sahel. But when the drought came and thousands of nomads lost their entire stock and ended up in camps, someone decided that the answer was increased cultivation.

Nomadic people have always had their own way of dealing with drought. A *Fulani* friend explained how, when drought hit and they lost their stock, some of the tribe would go into the villages and work for the settled people, just for long enough to raise money to restock. Then they'd be off again. Maybe many will use the new aid schemes in the same way. Some, though, say desertification has gone too far, that the land can no longer support so many people in that old lifestyle.

It's my last day in Nokou. I get up very early and climb the nearby hill to watch the sun rise behind the small fortress that looks out over the desert. Slowly the village wakes up. Women climb the hill, pots on heads; a man walks off across the desert, the wind tugging at his white robes; a laughing girl comes by on a donkey.

As I walk down and wander along the sandy streets taking photos I am sad to be leaving, but there is little option. If I don't get today's transport there won't be another vehicle until Tuesday; and my visa expires on Wednesday. My original intention had been to go west from here rather than going back to N'Djamena, but being Ramadan there are no vehicles going that way.

We leave at about 9am. Somewhere in the middle of an area of beige and white sand dunes something goes wrong with the vehicle. But, as always, they manage to fix it; meanwhile I go round taking photos.

As enquiries at Mao reveal no transport going either west to the Lake Chad or south to N'Djamena I decide to go out with the project for the day. If there are any vehicles going south we will see them and if not I'll go back to Mao for the night and try again in the morning. For a long time the only vehicles we see are the French Army, and one very broken-down lorry. Then, in the distance, a cloud of dust, out of which emerges a very old blue Toyota. We flag it down, and its occupants, three turbaned Arabs, agree to take me to Mussokori – for a price.

> *"For a long time the only vehicles we see are the French Army, and one very broken-down lorry. Then, in the distance, a cloud of dust, out of which emerges a very old blue Toyota . . . three turbaned Arabs agree to take me to Mussokori – for a price"*

Ten minutes along the way we get a flat tyre. They change it and we continue, shuddering our way over the rough ground. My companions speak no French and I little Arabic so our conversation is limited. Almost an hour later the next tyre goes. Luckily we are close by a small settlement. The schoolteacher, a slip of a kid who has probably only had a couple of years' secondary schooling himself, comes to greet us and takes me back to one of the huts. I am brought water and Provita – a nutritional supplement in the form of small biscuits, the result of some aid programme.

The hours tick slowly by. Several times I think I hear the sound of a vehicle, but on investigation it is only the wind. It is very hot. Again I think I hear the sound of a vehicle. I go outside and strain my ears; then over the horizon appears a cloud of dust, followed by two very large and very new lorries, each towing a trailer wagon and carrying a handful of passengers. I flag down the first one; the driver is happy to give me a lift and in I climb. It transpires that the lorries are part of a six-truck UNDP convoy returning from delivering food to displaced persons in the war zone.

Such lorries are not fast but they are relatively comfortable and I am well pleased with the lift. The driver has been all over, driving lorries across the Sahara to Tripoli, Algeria, Agadez, Tunis. The only problem with the journey is lack of water – I have stupidly managed to leave my water bottle in the fridge at Mao and by the time we reach Mussokori in the early afternoon I am so thirsty I can hardly speak. In desperation I manage to down 1.5 litres of disgusting Camerounian fizz.

The convoy of UN lorries is staying the night and I should probably stay with them; but I am short of time and anxious to get back to N'Djamena. A pick-up was meant to be leaving "toute de suite" so I decide to take it. At 4pm it still hasn't left. I transfer to another pick-up, we leave, get stuck in the sand, push it out, get stuck again . . . "toute de suite" passes us, we push ours out again and pass them, with much glee.

At 6pm we stop in a village where we are all instructed to dismount while the driver simply wanders off. I try to find out what's going on and am told that he has gone to meet his wife and that we'll be leaving again in an hour. I bet. I sit down on a rug, feeling very tired. Not just physically tired, but tired of the endless waits, of the uncertainty, of travelling on my own. At 7.30pm our driver comes back and we pile in, only to find the Surete suddenly want to see my papers – I have only been sitting outside their office for the last hour-and-a-half! Still, at least they are quick and pleasant.

We set off, stop to pick up wood – everyone off, load the cargo of wood, everyone on again – then, on the outskirts of N'Djamena, a motorbike roars up, overtakes us and demands we stop. Apparently we have failed to stop at a checkpoint. Back we go, off we get, and watch them go through all our baggage. Arriving at N'Djamena market at about 9.30pm, I flag down a taxi to take me to the house and collapse.

TRAVEL NOTES

Languages Largely Arabic in the north and French in the south, plus about 70 local languages.

Transport There are few surfaced roads, no buses and no railways. Your only option is to ask around for a lift. Travel this way is slow and erratic, but generally safe.

Accommodation Hotels are in short supply outside the capital. Again, your best bet is to ask around on arrival in a particular place.

Guide *Central Africa: A Travel Survival Kit* (Lonely Planet) – a reasonable section on Chad.

Contacts

We know of no women's groups currently operating. **Oxfam** and **UNICEF** could put you in touch with development projects including women.

Books

We have not traced any books on Chad. However, Chris Johnson recommends the following academic studies for readers interested in the situation of women in Africa:

Niki Nelson ed., *African Women in the Development Process* (Frank Cass and Co., 1981).

Christine Oppong ed., *Female and Male in West Africa* (Allen and Unwin, 1983).

Margaret Jean Kay and Sharon Stitcher eds., *African Women South of the Sahara* (Longman, 1984).

Thanks to Chris Johnson for supplying much of the information for the introduction and Travel Notes.

Chile

· · · · · · · · · · · · · · · · · · ·

Since General Pinochet seized power in September 1973, Chile has not seen a great many foreign travellers. In the years immediately after Pinochet's military coup, which toppled the elected socialist government of President Salvador Allende, the country became home to one of the most brutally repressive regimes in Latin America. Thousands of Chileans were imprisoned, murdered, tortured or went into exile.

Sixteen years later Pinochet's rule finally came to an end. Unable to resist any longer the mounting pressure to call a free election he took a gamble on "democracy" and lost. Patricio Alwyn, a centrist politician, now heads a broad but tenuous coalition government in charge of making good the transition to democracy and, most urgently, limiting the role of the army (and with it Pinochet) in the political life of the country. Encouraged by these changes exiles are returning and a spirit of cautious optimism hangs in the air.

Visiting Chile, it is hard to forget the widescale political repression that overshadows the nation's recent past. At the same time, overwhelming hospitality and a general lack of crime against tourists make this one of the more relaxing Latin American countries to explore. Even hitching is reported to be relatively safe for women.

Good roads and an efficient bus and rail network make it easy to get around central Chile, where most of the population is concentrated in and around the capital, Santiago, and in the beautiful lake district, home of the Mapuche Indians. Elsewhere, in the northern desert and south towards Patagonia, transport is more erratic and accommodation can be hard to find. Travel in general can be expensive with prices, including bus fares, at their highest in the south and everywhere during the high season of December to March.

Women have always been very active in the struggle for democracy in Chile. *CODEM* (Defence Committee for Women's Rights) co-ordinates a large network of working-class **women's organisations**. Local groups in different parts of the country develop training schemes for women in areas like health and technical skills; they campaign for women's legal rights, for adequate housing, and for the release of political prisoners; and organise soup kitchens, alternative schools, cultural events and protest activities, especially in the shanty towns. There are also a number of action-oriented research groups, such as the *Centro de Estudios de la Mujer* (CEM), based in Santiago, which has carried out projects with peasant women, including the minority Mapuche Indians of whom only around 150,000 remain.

A Nation of Hospitality

· · · · · · · · · · · · · ·

At the age of 26, Barbara Gofton gave up her job as a sub-editor to travel around the world. She spent six months altogether in South America, almost half of the time in Chile where she travelled the whole length of the country with a friend, Louise.

To people throughout the world Chile and its president Pinochet are almost bywords for brutality and repression. Only too familiar with the tales of atrocities that have been committed by the present regime, I was surprised to find that on the surface Chile is a land of calm and order where *carabineros* (armed police) maintain a watchful, though usually unobtrusive, presence. Today's methods are clearly more sophisticated and as a visitor you are unlikely to observe them first hand. I was told that these days the regime works partly through an element of fear. Pinochet is frequently to be seen on television carrying out works for the public good. "He speaks in platitudes," said a friend. "He says the choice is him or chaos" – the latter being depicted in televised images from the USSR.

Initially I was wary of even mentioning politics, but the days of hushed voices are gone. I heard many points of view, from first-hand accounts of violence in response to public protest to insistence that the foreign press convey a false picture of the country. I learned to keep my mouth shut at times. But overall I felt a spirit of optimism in the air. Since losing majority support in the plebiscite of 1988, Pinochet seems to be fading from the political scene, opening up the way for a new era of democracy.

"In a continent where excessive paranoia can so easily ruin your trip, we felt virtually none of the threat of theft experienced elsewhere"

The peace of mind we enjoyed and the straightforwardness of getting from one place to another were not quite what we had expected from South America, least of all a notorious dictatorship. Things seem so easy here, we'd say, half guiltily (weren't we supposed to be roughing it?) and half relieved. And we'd stay a little longer, in no hurry to confront the hazards we were sure lay ahead. After hearing all the horror stories from visitors newly arrived from Peru and Brazil, Chile was beginning to seem like a travellers' paradise. In a continent where excessive paranoia can so easily ruin your trip, we felt virtually none of the threat of theft experienced elsewhere.

We were also struck by an apparent lack of interest in making money out of foreign tourists who, in Chilean terms, must seem incredibly rich. Perhaps this will change in time, especially if a return to democracy helps to revamp the country's image abroad. For now we should appreciate a nation where people with so little show so much hospitality: like the waiter who brought us free drinks with our beautifully served meal and refused to accept a tip, and the off-duty taxi driver who stopped on his way home to give us a lift.

Yet the trip did not have an auspicious start. Our plans to meet at Santiago airport fell apart when I was over 24 hours late in arriving. Being surrounded by loud emotional family reunions provides little comfort when you find yourself alone in a capital city of four million inhabitants with no sign of the friend you've arranged to meet, nor even a clue to her whereabouts. By this time it was late and the airport information offices where I might have found a message were closed. As people flapped around me and I listened in alarm to the fast and clipped variant of the language I thought I knew so well, I was thankful to be taken under the wing of a bus driver and his conductor. They were about to leave for the city centre and said they would find me a place to stay. Half an hour later on a dark and deserted city street, accompanied by a complete stranger, I wondered if I had lost my head entirely. Needless to say there were no problems and I was simply delivered to a reasonably priced hotel, as promised.

Ironically, this potential disaster may well have been the best thing that could have happened, for it obliged us to put our trust in people who, we soon discovered, take great pleasure in offering all kinds of assistance.

"First impressions of Santiago were of a clean, modern, bustling city full of friendly, helpful people"

I was lucky to meet Rosana who was working in an airline office as part of her studies. When I turned up the next morning she was clearly overjoyed to have a lost English girl to look after. Before I'd been there half an hour I had been invited to stay with her in Santiago and to visit her family in their summer house at the beach (offers we later took up). And when Louise and I were finally reunited via the British Embassy later that day, I discovered that she too had been shown considerable help; a Chilean man she met at the airport had not only gone out of his way to make enquiries as to my whereabouts, but found her somewhere to stay and taken her to see some of the sights of the city.

First impressions of Santiago were of a clean, modern, bustling city full of friendly, helpful people. In fact, smog is so dense in the capital that what would otherwise be a spectacular view of the Andes is blotted out most of the time. I remember my surprise on waking up one morning in the apartment in which we were staying to see snowcapped peaks in the distance: I'd been there a week and had not seen them before. By the afternoon they had disappeared again beneath their grey shroud; that same day on the city streets my eyes smarted and the air was thick and choking.

Santiago afforded the anonymity I take for granted in London and long for in Mediterranean cities once the clicking tongue brigade and the hissers get going. Or it almost did. The only sign of interest you are likely to receive is from the money changers on the street, looking out for gringos, male or female, as potential customers. I don't remember experiencing any sexual harassment, in the capital or anywhere else.

For our first couple of weeks in Chile we stayed in hotels and hostels until we discovered the alternative of staying with families in private homes. Cheaper than hotels, this accommodation provides a good opportunity for meeting people and exchanging information, often leading to contacts in other towns. Another attraction of these *casas de familia* was the chance to use a kitchen and prepare our own food, something of a luxury once the novelty of eating out all the time had worn off. It was interesting, too, to be able to observe something of family life, though these were hardly typical households where the children seemed to take for granted the constantly changing faces, foreign tongues and having to step over bodies on the living room floor.

In a country where women are unable to travel without their husbands' permission, we were treated with courtesy, kindness and a great deal of curiosity everywhere. Certain questions cropped up again and again: Were we German? Were we sisters? (the only likenesses we could see were fairness of complexion, blue eyes and permanently sunburnt noses) and – with great incredulity – Were we on our own? We were also asked, sometimes repeatedly, if we liked Chile.

More than in any other South American country, we met and made good friends with people our own age. Socially, we often found ourselves in male company, spending a few weeks in the far south of the country with a group of students from Santiago we met on a boat trip. The women we got to know, all from wealthy homes in the capital – confident, articulate, and speaking excellent English – were hardly representative of the nation's female population. All lived at home with their parents, explaining that though they had jobs, they simply couldn't afford to do otherwise.

"Hitching can be a practical as well as economical and interesting way to travel"

Travelling with our Chilean friends was an education. With strict budgets to stick to they hitched lifts everywhere, searched a town for a free place to stay (they once, to our amazement, were given permission to sleep and cook in an empty room in the local fire station) and bargained their way shamelessly through all situations. We meanwhile rather guiltily swanned around on luxury coaches where attendants opened and closed our curtains, reclined our seats for us and helped us disembark, and ate delicious meals in often empty restaurants.

Travelling by bus was a joy, but as Chile has good roads, hitching can be a practical as well as economical and interesting way to travel. Most important, it feels generally safe and we never heard any bad reports.

Louise and I hitched the 1300 miles from Arica, close to the country's northern border, back down to Santiago. Two-and-a-half days and four lifts later we arrived back in the capital having spent over half the time with one lorry driver who was carrying a huge load of salt. There was little transport other than trucks on that road which stretched through an inhospitable desert, dotted with the ghost towns of old nitrate mining settlements. Our driver shared his food with us, treated us to a meal, ignoring our protests, and let us sleep in the bunks in the truck. His seemed a harsh life, spent mostly on the road, hardly sleeping, and rarely seeing his family, but he never complained. When we stopped in a small settlement I watched him unscrew the radio cassette player to reveal boxes containing electrical equipment. He explained that by selling these on the black market he was able to send his elder daughter to university in Santiago, whom, in true Chilean fashion, he insisted we contact on our arrival.

South of Puerto Montt the only transport is by sea or air. The thought of pressing on and reaching what is almost the end of the earth appealed to our imaginations. But to do this we had to first take a three-day boat trip down Chile's coast, through the calm waters of the islands and, for a short stretch, venture into the wilder waters of the Pacific. Chatting to our fellow passengers with dolphins leading the way, I thought there were few places I would rather be. From Punta Arenas, the world's most southerly city, we took a ferry to Tierra del Fuego where we could look out across the Beagle Channel knowing that nothing lay between ourselves and Antarctica.

The Torres del Paine national park in southern Chile is one of the natural wonders of the continent – an unspoilt area of lakes, glaciers, and needle-sharp peaks. To take the week-long trail round the park we needed camping equipment. Luckily we'd made a friend who had all the essentials. With Assi we squashed into a tiny tent, marvelled at the raw beauty around us and bathed in icy streams. He baked us pitta bread in the ashes of the fire for breakfast and we all dreamt of pizzas and chicken and cans of Coke. Once we'd set off we were truly on our own amidst this spendid landscape, meeting just a few people each day coming from the opposite direction.

"As a woman traveller you will inevitably attract attention, but, in this country anyway, it is usually of the most pleasant sort"

Chile is a country of surprises. In Frutillar where we arrived in the week of the annual classical music festival we were amazed to find a mini 'Proms' in the Chilean lake district. In Valdivia, having missed the boat home from a tiny peninsular settlement we were visiting, we were rescued by four yachtsmen who not only returned us to our hostel, but cooked us a meal on the way back. And one day we climbed the smoking volcano Villarrica, rising above the clouds, to peer into the crater to see the occasionally spurting lava before sliding back down in the snow.

Though I did very little travelling on my own in Chile, I would not hesitate to recommend it to anyone who merely lacks reassurance. As a woman traveller you will inevitably attract attention, but, in this country anyway, it is usually of the most pleasant sort. We often wondered if we were just lucky in our experiences here. I don't think so. Other travellers we met, whether alone or in couples, male or female, shared similar tales of hospitality and welcome. When we finally crossed into Argentina, unsure if we would be returning, I felt sadness, wondering if we would be made to feel as welcome in this new country. Later, when we did go back, it felt almost like coming home.

TRAVEL NOTES

Languages Spanish and some remaining indig- . enous languages.

Transport Buses are many and frequent. Travelling directly from north to south, or vice versa, internal flights are quick and comfortable, but you obviously miss out on much.

Accommodation A wide range of hotels and pensions at all prices can be found throughout the country. There are also quite a few Youth Hostels. Most towns have a tourist information office or it's easy just to ask in the street.

Special Problems Remember to buy Chilean-made products whenever possible. You are usually offered brand-name imported goods at highly inflated prices. Beware of taking part in any overt anti-government activity. A foreign passport doesn't necessarily make you immune to police brutality.

Guides *The South American Handbook* (Trade and Travel) has an excellent chapter on Chile. Also recommended is *Chile and Easter Island: A Travel Survival Kit* (Lonely Planet).

Contacts

For up-to-date information before you leave Britain, contact **Chile Solidarity Campaign Women's Section**, 129 Seven Sisters Rd., London N7 7QG. ☎071-263 8529/272 4298. Or write to **Isis International Women's Information and Communication Service**, Casilla 2067, Correo Central, Santiago, Chile. ☎490 271. Isis has a huge network of contacts, especially in Latin America and the Caribbean, produces publications and houses an excellent resource centre to which visitors are welcome.

Books

Alicia Partnoy, ed., *You Can't Drown the Fire: Latin American Women writing in Exile* (Virago, 1989). Anthology of essays, stories, poetry, letters and songs by 35 Latin American women, including Veronica de Negri, Cecilia Vicuna, Marjorie Agosin and Isabel Morel Letelier from Chile.

Joan Jara, *Victor, An Unfinished Song* (Jonathan Cape, 1983). Moving account of her life with Victor Jara, the legendary Chilean folksinger who was murdered by the military in 1973.

Marjorie Agosin, *Scraps of Life: The Chilean Arpilleras – Chilean Women and the Pinochet Dictatorship* (Red Sea, US 1987). Arpilleras are artisan women who make lacquered cloth wall hangings; this book is an examination, through their accounts and representations in their art, of their sufferings under the dictatorship. Many lost husbands to the military: they tell stories of jail, torture and bureaucracy. Moving, if a little short on analysis.

Isabel Allende, *House of the Spirits* (Black Swan, 1986) and *Of Love and Shadows* (Black Swan, 1988). Two compulsive novels, the first interweaving family saga with political events in an unnamed Latin American country; the second dealing with a passionate love affair against a similar background of violent political turmoil.

Elizabeth Jelin, ed., *Citizenship and Identity: Women and Social Change in Latin America* (Zed Books, 1990). Examines women's roles in Latin American movements for social change from the Mothers of the Disappeared in Argentina to trade union organisations in Chile.

Latin American and Caribbean Women's Collective: *Slaves of Slaves: the Challenge of Latin American Women* (Zed Books, 1980). Portrays women's struggles in eleven different countries, including Chile.

China

Nobody can travel to China any longer without being painfully aware of the politics which grip and strangle this vast and extraordinary country. For a decade, since the much-vaunted "opening" of China by paramount leader Deng Xiaoping, millions of Western tourists have romped throughout China's cities and countryside, marvelling at her ancient wonders and at her more modern accommodation between communism and capitalism. China was the world's communist sweetheart – a safe and unthreatening Marxist/Maoist giant where totalitarian rule could be justified by Confucian tradition and a historically communal culture.

No more. Justifications for China's current leadership no longer ring true after the crushing of the students' pro-democracy movement in the spring of 1989. Out of numerous alternative solutions to their crisis, Chinese leaders chose the most brutal and bloody. To say China's international image has

been tarnished would be a gross understatement. The world was rightly shocked and appalled by the Chinese military's use of brutal force to clean out Tiananmen Square on the night of June 3, and China's international "image" was destroyed. It was revealed to be, in truth, an illusion.

The consequences of the crackdown on students and on a huge segment of the population deemed infected by "bourgeois liberalism" – a euphemism for Western ideology, including market liberalisation, arts and literary freedoms, freedom of the press, civil and human rights – are only now becoming apparent. According to the best estimates, arrests of activists and sympathisers now number in the tens of thousands, and the seemingly unstoppable momentum of China's "opening" to the West has been stalled, if not completely derailed.

This opening had brought prosperity to many segments of society, and had made China more accessible to visitors from the West than ever before. Travelling to China in the Eighties, Westerners could understand and applaud the ever-growing numbers of entrepreneurs who populated street markets and the ever-growing enthusiasm apparent in the general population for change, movement and growth. Yet the opening, the attendant economic reforms, and relaxation of central control, brought with them a host of extraordinary problems. Inflation, running at an estimated thirty percent nationwide, rampant corruption among officials at all levels of the government, an over-taxed and inefficient transportation system that couldn't come close to meeting demand, and a widespread disillusionment with the ideals of communism were just a few of the most obvious problems which accompanied Chinese *perestroika*.

Something had to happen, and it is still a running debate among China watchers whether the democracy movement and its suppression were the victims or the cause of a power struggle between hardliners and reformists within the Chinese government. In any case, the so-called hardliners, orthodox Marxist-Maoists, most definitively won, and China's political and economic future are now careening down a far different path than the one assumed in the early months of 1989.

For tourists and travellers to China, this means a different experience in the Middle Kingdom. For many, and up to this point millions, a vacation or tour through China seems to be in bad taste under current circumstances. Politically, spending one's tourist dollars on a country moving forward, rather than lurching adamantly backwards, is far easier to justify. Yet the people of China remain the same. They are the biggest victims of the crackdown and its economic consequences, of inflation, corruption, and of the disappearance of opportunity and hope. If you travel to China now, the Chinese people may not be able to speak with you honestly, but your presence there will not go unappreciated.

Many people have cancelled their China trips because of the reported violence and out of fear for their own safety. These fears are no longer valid. The pacification of the demonstrators and the wholesale repression across the nation have effectively silenced dissent, for a time. Moments and periods of great tension still occur, especially in occupied Beijing around important anniversary dates, when soldiers jog through the streets in an intimidating show of force. With one frightening exception, the violence that struck the capital in early June was never directed against "foreign friends", but only by Chinese against Chinese. Even the current government, with its seemingly callous disregard for international opinion, realises the importance of safety for Western visitors.

The greatest difference between the China now and the China prior to June is one of mood and climate. The population is, understandably, sullen and far more silent than in the past. On the surface, there are few obvious reminders of the ongoing crackdown and of the campaign against liberalisation. The Chinese people are, as always, polite, welcoming, and even open in expressing their support of the government. In their inner lives, however, nearly impossible to see now, they have different thoughts and different passions, a greater sense of hopelessness than ever before, and a greater fear of speaking honestly with foreigners and of the consequences this can bring right now.

China is as vast and as varied as it ever was, and the further away you travel from Beijing and other large cities the more open and easy your conversations are likely to be. Travelling conditions are greatly eased due to the fact that there are very few Westerners touring China these days. Train and plane tickets are relatively easy to procure, and hotel prices have plummeted as much as fifty percent in the major cities.

If you travel to China these days your presence there will be viewed by the government as an acknowledgement that the situation has returned to "normal". Despite this very uncomfortable impression, there remains much to be learned and explored in this post-Tiananmen China. The repression cannot and should not be ignored, whether you journey to the far edges of the empire in Tibet or Urumqi, or to the centre, Beijing. The traveller under present circumstances must keep in mind that surface impressions of normality are not the true picture, and in fact they never were.

Many of the prominent student leaders during the democracy movement, and some of the most outspoken and brave sympathisers among journalists and intellectuals, were women. Like their male counterparts, most have been arrested and their circumstances are currently unknown. In heralding a new, and as yet unborn China, however, the movement gave voice to a group of women political activists on an equal status with men for the first time. For these women, concern for the future of their nation took precedence over **feminist issues**.

China has always been a patriarchy. The Communist era heralded enormous changes for women, but it institutionalised the problem of dual labour. According to Mao's two zeals, women were expected both to help build the socialist future and fulfil their traditional family role. Many women now have full access to education and employment; contraception is free, abortion legal, and divorce instigated by wives is common. But the traditional view that women are specially suited to certain jobs (childcare and housework) and incapable of others (anything too mentally and physically taxing), as well as the Confucian ideal of the three obediences to father, husband and son, are as strong as ever. The clearest and most frightening demonstration of women's subordinate status has been the increase in female infanticide, associated with the introduction of the one-child-per-family policy.

In Tiananmen Square

. . . .

Alison Munroe, a freelance journalist, writer and television producer, has been a constant visitor to China over the last seven years after living and working in Beijing. In Spring 1989 she returned to report on the progress of the pro-democracy movement for American television. She remained as a witness to its tragic suppression.

I went to China in late April because something was happening. The student demonstrations (of mid and late April following the death of Hu Yaobang) would probably blow over, I reasoned at the time, but their strength and passion were unusual. Gorbachev was coming to China within a few weeks and, given the powerful forces underway in his own country, I believed his visit would make an impact at least in Beijing. His visit and my visit would coincide; we would both see China at a time of change.

What I experienced in China from the end of April through the beginning of July was unlike anything anybody had ever seen in that country before. For a long time China visitor and watcher, it was the most thrilling and the most crushing of experiences, all wrapped up together into one huge convulsion.

Imagine an epidemic of manic depression. Imagine an entire city of twelve million people experiencing mood swings from euphoria and exhilaration to terror, bitter resignation and furious anger, all within the space of a few days, and sometimes in the course of one day.

It seems that, in the West, everybody remembers the "massacre of Tiananmen", but few recall the even more extraordinary events of the weeks before. During that time, most incredi-

bly, Beijing was a city ruled by the emotions and dreams of her people. It had become a People's Republic, arguably for the first time, and everybody was overwhelmed with a sense of mass power, with the narcotic of an uprising. The stereotypically passive Chinese stunned the world – as they have in the past – with their hidden passions, and all participants and observers were blown away by the storm.

It felt like a revolution in Beijing for a time; less like an "awakening" of political consciousness than a sudden explosion of reality. The Chinese people have always had a great deal to gripe about; poverty, corruption, inflation, repression, deception. But few expected such a passionate, peaceful, and determined effort to redress those wrongs.

For me, watching, reporting, interviewing, it was difficult to maintain a semblance of objectivity. In the early days of the hunger strike and massive demonstrations, I was frightened. "Remember," I said to Western friends who were enthusiastically supporting the students, "remember how powerful this government is." By the end, after the tanks rolled into Tiananmen Square, I was reminded by someone that I had warned them early on, and I realised how completely caught up in the movement I had become, how I had forgotten my own warning.

Bits and pieces from my diary and memories of the early days of the movement are more telling, I believe, than a recounting of the terror of the latter days.

May 15: When student broadcasters on Tiananmen Square announced that the welcoming ceremony for visiting Soviet President Mikhail Gorbachev had been moved from the Square to the airport, there was a sense of disappointment, but also of rising jubilation. Students had anticipated a colourful confrontation between protestors and the motorcade, but at the same time many began to realise the power of their occupation of the Square.

Some feared that the government had "lost face" and would retaliate against the students with greater ferocity. Yet the hunger strikers were proud. "The government may lose face," said one student, "but the Chinese people have gained face."

The Square was festooned with incredible banners and slogans. A festival in the making. A hot, sunny, and very happy democratic festival.

May 16: The numbers of supporters who marched to the Square to support the core group of hunger strikers swelled into the hundreds of thousands. Intellectuals from institutes and universities from all over the city marched; journalists from the *People's Daily*, the Communist Party newspaper, marched. An old woman marched, holding up a plate on which was written: "My children are hungry. What are Deng Xiaoping's children eating?"

"All you could hear in the centre of Beijing was the scream of ambulance sirens as they took fainting fasters to the hospital, and the roar and honks of trucks, buses, cars and motorcycles signalling their support"

The students were holding out, and were greatly encouraged by the throngs of supporters. But tension was growing, as was the fear that the government was just going to ignore the millions in the Square. There was talk of suicides. People were frightened that the tinderbox of defiance would explode into massive work strikes and violent rebellion. A rumour spread through the city that two hunger strikers had died. All you could hear in the centre of Beijing was the scream of ambulance sirens as they took fainting fasters to the hospital, and the roar and honks of trucks, buses, cars, and motorcycles signalling their support to the movement. It began to feel eerie.

May 17: At least one million people flooded into Tiananmen. Workers' unions, flight attendants, social scientists, factory labourers, the China Travel Service, the staffs of most newspapers and the central television station. The main street leading to the Square was mobbed for miles. The pedicab purveyors were making a mint. All over Beijing, crowds were singing the Internationale and chanting, "Long Live Democracy". The Square and its immediate environs looked like the scene of a rock concert that had gone on for too long.

Few people in Beijing went to work that day, and after a few hours it became commonplace even miles from the centre of town to see honking brigades of commandeered trucks and buses covered with banners and filled with shouting, laughing, chanting demonstrators. Everywhere they went, people on the street applauded, cheered, and flashed "V" signs of solidarity. The city stopped functioning and the citizens of Beijing just gave in to a new atmosphere of unrestraint.

"This government is corrupt," shouted one hard-hatted construction worker to me, "we need a new one." A factory worker, surrounded by a crowd of gawkers as he talked to me, said, "a man should not act like a slave. It is time Chinese people dared to speak out."

May 18: Another million people marched. Beijing almost resembled those old Cultural Revolution newsreels, every blank place in the city covered with pro-student, pro-freedom, pro-democracy banners. A public bus drove by with the Chinese characters for "support" etched in the dust on the back.

China Central Television, the government-financed and controlled broadcasting network, looked like a revolutionary headquarters. A huge banner swung from its lofty spire, more banners and flags were strewn through the halls inside. Over 1000 employees had marched to the Square that afternoon, and then returned to broadcast footage of the Beijing rebellion to the whole nation. Late that night, they broadcast a dialogue which had taken place earlier in the day between hardline Premier Li Peng and the student hunger strikers. Li was reviled by student leader Wu'er Kaixi, told that he wasn't doing his job. Confucius spun in his grave. The whole nation watched. At the end of the dialogue – at least so went the rumour the next day – Li Peng dismissed the students and thanked them for coming. Wu'er Kaixi turned to the Premier and said, "You didn't invite us, we invited you. And you're late."

May 19: The government had taken no action either for or against the hunger strikers. The workers had joined the movement, Beijing citizens were going into the Square in droves, even Party officials and government functionaries were carrying banners and shouting slogans. In dozens of other Chinese cities, students and citizens were demonstrating. Gorbachev had left China and the centre – China's governmental authority – seemed unable to hold on.

The Square was awake all that night, and so was I. Standing on the monument steps overlooking the tens of thousands of students and their supporters, it seemed impossible that the government could not listen to their demands. We were kept sleepless by continuous broadcasts over the government loudspeakers of a harsh speech by Li Peng warning that the army was coming in to restore order. "It is hopeless," said a female medical student attending the hunger strikers at the square. She was crying as she listened to the speech. "We are really very angry," she said, "We want to kill Li Peng."

May 20: At 10am, as I ran back into the dirty Square, five military helicopters buzzed Tiananmen in formation. It was terrifying, intimidating, and the students awoke shaking their fists at the power and authority of their government. The imposition of martial law was announced over the loudspeakers, and we all looked at each other in fear, knowing the showdown was inevitable.

"Blood was anticipated to flow that night, and the entire city began its 24-hour vigil. Students drove around the city chanting 'Arise, Unite, and Protect the Students'"

The terror had begun, yet the streets and the Square that morning were once again filled with marchers, trucks crammed with flag-waving protesters, honking, screaming in defiance, "V" waving motorcycle brigades, and one huge bulldozer packed to the brim – even its enormous shovel – with banners and people.

Blood was anticipated to flow that night, and the entire city began its 24-hour-a-day vigil. Students drove around the city chanting: "Arise, Unite, and Protect the Students." All through town people were shouting "Down with Li Peng": words that sent chills down my spine. You could be shot for saying that in China. The peoples' barriers went up on every intersection leading into Beijing, and, incredibly, the people stopped the military from advancing on the Square.

After May 20, and the imposition of the "paper tiger" martial law – a martial law that was unenforceable, even laughable – the exhilaration ebbed and flowed, alternating with boredom, fear, and confusion. Slowly, the students grew tired of their dirty, unhealthy vigil in the centre of the city, and the leaders and vanguard, students from Beijing universities, began to filter back to their homes and campuses. There was one major re-swelling of enthusiasm when art students hauled an enormous statue called the "Goddess of Democracy", modelled after the Statue of Liberty in New York, to the Square. Lined up with cosmically appropriate symmetry between Mao's mausoleum and the Gate of Heavenly Peace, it was the last and most extraordinary gesture of brazen independence. Like a statue of Mao Zedong on the White House lawn. It must have driven the Chinese leadership mad.

The "Goddess" stood out like a very sore thumb and people on the street still dared to stand in front of foreign television cameras, denouncing their government's lies. "Tell the truth," they told us, "tell the world. They say they are enforcing martial law to protect us. We don't need their protection."

Of all the things experienced, this bravery was the most unforgettable. On the night of the assault on Beijing, two weeks after martial law was imposed, the shooting began to the west of the Square in a place called Muxudi. As the hundreds of troop trucks, tanks, and armoured personnel carriers moved east, public buses blockaded the road on a bridge just one mile from the Square. The shooting grew closer; machine guns, rifles, tanks crashing, people running, screaming. They raced to the side streets and watched as the buses were set alight; they roared and cheered as the bus blockades burst into great, dramatic balls of flame.

"People ask me if I was afraid. No, I should have been, but like everybody around me that night . . . I was more shocked, numbed, horrified, and – it must be admitted – exhilarated by the struggle"

The troops were shooting into the crowd, killing some, but at every lull thousands more surged forward again to watch in disbelief as the People's Liberation Army launched its assault on the people. The flames roared, the tanks crashed through, and the two-mile-long convoy of assault troops passed across the bridge while all around them people chanted, "Criminals, criminals!" and "Traitors, traitors".

People ask me if I was afraid. No, I should have been, but like everybody around me that night, including many who died, I was more shocked, numb, horrified, and – it must be admitted – exhilarated by the struggle. Exhilaration rotted with horror soon after, however, as we began to comprehend what had happened and what was happening. My own personal horror came one week later.

A few days after the assault, we interviewed a man on the streets of Beijing for American television. Like thousands of others, he was standing on a street corner, shouting out in despair at what he had seen. We asked him to talk to us, and our cameras, and he told us, and the crowd, of the killing he had witnessed, of his hatred for the government. He said, "After what I have seen, I'm not afraid of death anymore." As he spoke, the small crowd cheered and applauded, and his interview with us ended with a fists-in-the-air crowd chant of "down with Li Peng".

We used a few seconds of this interview in a news piece for American television that night, as part of a larger story about the ongoing defiance and horror in the city. A few days later, exactly one week after the assault, the Chinese nightly news – already a nightly barrage of brazen falsehood about the quelling of the "counter-revolutionary rebellion" – ran a tape of the entire raw footage of my interview with this man.

Apparently, they had "pirated" it off a satellite feed from Tokyo to New York. There was no other explanation for how they obtained the raw footage. They ran the tape, identified the man as a "counter-revolutionary rumour mongeror," and asked anybody recognising him to inform the local Public Security Bureau.

The next evening's news included footage of the man, a 42-year-old accountant named Xiao Bin, beaten and contrite, confessing his crimes to security officials after two enthusiastic patriots had turned him in.

"I could no longer do my job in China, could no longer even attempt to interview people or to find out what was going on. I was quelled, silenced, pacified"

This was the final blow for me. I could no longer do my job in China, could no longer even attempt to interview people or to find out what was going on. I was quelled, silenced, pacified. It was easy in those days to give in to the general melodrama surrounding our circumstances, but still I felt that the government's actions in using me to identify its own malcontents was aimed directly at my personal conscience. They made an example out of Xiao Bin, and taught me the worst lesson of my life. I had forgotten, and had never quite believed, how powerful this government was.

Within a week I left China, determined to go back soon and somehow repay my debt to those people – like Xiao Bin – but I left knowing that my own bitterness and sense of personal defeat would only impair my efforts to continue reporting on China, to tell the truth about what was happening and what had happened.

As a foreigner in China, I have never seen the people full of so much hope, so much true patriotism and passion. The movement was a profoundly idealistic quest, with few concrete goals and little realistic appreciation of how this government was likely to react. It was a feeling, an emotion, a yearning, and eventually almost a hysteria. It was a movement that became a mass narcotic – for those watching as well as those participating – and it swelled up in Beijing and across the country into a euphoric and temporary wave of power. We all forgot about the government, and their personal priorities of power preservation. But the events of May and June revealed, for the first time, the true face of the Chinese government, and of its people.

An Eastern Westerner in China

. . . .

Adrienne Su, an American of Chinese descent, completed a year's study at Fudan University in Shanghai in June 1988. Her experiences of being mistaken for a citizen of the PRC forced her to reconsider the privileges foreign travellers routinely depend on.

Not until a customs official at my port of entry into China berated me for speaking halting Chinese did I realise that my Chinese ancestry would exert a powerful influence on all my experiences in this country. My dealings with the Chinese differed from everything I had read in guidebooks. I had never questioned my being an American, but no one in China could tell I was one.

By government policy, a foreigner's dissatisfaction carries more weight than that of a Chinese citizen. If a road accident involves a foreigner, rescue forces arrive efficiently; if only PRC citizens are involved, the ambulance takes its time, if it comes at all. There are not enough ambulances around to accommodate everyone's needs and as a result the Chinese pay for the comfort of foreign guests.

In ticket offices, citizens may have to stand in line for a full day or more, therefore having to take turns with friends and relatives. Foreigners, on the other hand, are free to walk straight to the front. Soft sleepers on trains are available only to an elite few but any foreigner is free to buy a ticket. Large tourist hotels admit Chinese visitors only when accompanied by foreigners and once inside the staff treat the guests of their own nation with contempt while all but kneeling to their foreign companions. Unfortunately this policy is conducted on such a wide scale (the whole country) that it feels more like the privation of the human rights of the Chinese than the extension of hospitality to their visitors.

"I was ashamed of American travellers for riding on their privileges after all their talk about human rights and racial equality"

I detested this policy on arrival, but after a few months became accustomed to it and even grew to expect it. It's not only the expectation of special treatment that changes one's character; the daily observation of the Chinese in a lower position leaves a deep mental image. I was on the verge of thinking myself worth more than the Chinese when I reconsidered my experiences of being mistaken for a local resident. It had been mortifying to be ignored, shouted at, put last in line, and even pushed in favour of white tourists, while fellow Americans enjoyed an attentive service and paid no heed to my abuse. Just as I was appalled by the Chinese acceptance of a secondary status, I was ashamed of American travellers for riding on their privileges after all their talk about human rights and racial equality.

Repeated inhospitable receptions transformed my feelings of sympathy and kinship with the people of my ancestry. Until I made local friends, I found it hard to stay courteous and detached. Acquaintances from Japan, Taiwan, Hong Kong and Korea reported similar difficulties of feeling guilty for using privileges and angry at being denied them. (The black visitors I met faced even more extreme reactions; even in Shanghai, they had to contend with people staring, pointing and drawing away, all of which massively increased the pressures of travelling.) When I came across other white Westerners on the road, their attitude towards me was high-flown and condescending until I spoke English. It wasn't entirely their fault; the environment had deluded them into seeing the Chinese as less than people.

I also, however, found that there was an advantage to blending in, in that I could observe the street scenes without becoming one. Subtle differences in manner made me stand out, even when I dressed inconspicuously, but I could conceal myself in heavy traffic and large crowds, both of which China has in plentiful supply. Most people took me for a citizen of another region in China, or a tourist from another Asian country, and dismissed me as less strange than a Westerner, leaving me at peace to watch and not be watched.

In spite of the inconveniences I faced, I always felt reasonably safe in China. A solo woman is unlikely to encounter violence. Crowded buses make all women (and men) easy prey to wandering hands, and theft is on the increase in touristic cities like Canton

and Guilin. But physical harm to a foreigner invites grave punishment and rarely occurs. It is easy, however, to drop precautions considered routine in the West simply because state media controls keep domestic crime inconspicuous.

Seldom does a Chinese man open a door for a woman, and on trains I have struggled alone to push my bag into a high luggage rack while Chinese men smoked and stared. Their attitude I attribute to the Cultural Revolution (1966–76) and not to Chinese culture itself. In comparison to most Asian cultures, the PRC has made great strides in restoring equal treatment of the sexes. Men and women all receive jobs upon finishing school, with comparable (although scant) salaries. The blue proletarian garb of Mao's China does away with feminine beauty and transforms the visual man and woman into nearly identical units. While many people still wear the old uniform, the streets of Canton and Shanghai boast short skirts, high heels and casual Western-style sportswear for both sexes.

"The sight of a woman on the road by herself evokes concern among the Chinese, who see convenience in numbers, if only to fight the bureaucracy"

Too often, visitors dismiss the Chinese as an homogenous mass of people without considering the many different groups and classes that make up their society. To someone unfamiliar with Chinese ways, general similarities such as black hair, black eyes, plain clothing, and a slighter build than the average Westerner will make people of totally different characteristics seem identical. Until you have developed a sensitivity to cultural differences within China you will blame all Chinese for the offences of a few unhappy encounters. One obstacle is that many who consider themselves well-bred and educated feel it is improper to approach strangers unintroduced, which immediately limits the type of spontaneous contacts you'll make.

An advantage of travelling alone in China is that you do have more opportunities to meet people. The sight of a woman on the road by herself evokes concern among the Chinese, who see convenience in numbers, if only to fight the bureaucracy. Outside large cities, I was invited into homes, given food and escorted around town. One rule to keep in mind is that the Chinese almost always try to pick up the bill even if they haven't the money. Be sure to emphatically resist this and make a genuine effort to pay your share or both; not only is it rude to accept, but most PRC citizens live on minimal salaries that would make one foreign dinner guest a burdensome expense. By tradition a Chinese family gives the best of everything to a guest, even at great personal cost.

"Every Shanghaiese who was there on the eve of the revolution remembers the British sign on the gate of a Shanghai park: 'No Chinese and dogs allowed'"

The extended absence of foreigners has very much increased their mystique, giving rise to rumours about our strange cuisine, etiquette, religions, courtship and rituals. Because no one trusts the government-printed newspapers, reports of the world outside are in high demand. People will treat you as an object in some places, but although you look unusual to them their fascination is more for the world you represent than for your personal peculiarity.

The Chinese conception of the *waiguoren* (foreigner) has been shaped by a dramatic history. Every Shanghaiese who was there on the eve of the revolution remembers the British sign on the gate of a Shanghai

park: "No Chinese and dogs allowed." The European "spheres of influence" and the establishment of the Shanghai International Settlement humbled the Chinese, while foreigners enjoyed immunity from local law. Japanese atrocities in the 1930s left indelible memories.

Today, shortages and an enormous population require the pooling of the best resources in order to house, transport and feed foreign guests comfortably, and, considering past injuries, the Chinese are noble hosts. Most live in overcrowded quarters, whole families to a room, without indoor plumbing, and for everyone south of the Yangzi River, without indoor heating. Winter brings a harsh chill to Shanghai, Hangzhou and other southern cities. The discomforts of visitors, such as inefficient service, limited hot water, and difficulties in transport, are minimal compared to the limitations on the local quality of life. The tendency among foreigners, however, is to blame the Chinese for these inconveniences.

And it's easy to feel angry at China; every bus is early or late, many clerks are hostile, crowds push and clamour, and boarding trains, planes and coaches demands a physical struggle. People stare openly at foreigners, sometimes gathering in small crowds to observe while rash youths follow you around, trying to practise English and get a foreign address. You can quickly become overwhelmed by a language you do not properly comprehend and by customs, hemispheres removed from your own.

But beyond all this, there's no denying the grandeur of China's natural scenery, its position on the world scale and the influence it exerts over the rest of Asia. China requires patience, flexibility and humour. The unpredictability of wandering the Middle Kingdom has its rewards, and for women going it alone, it's bound to feel safer than home.

Striking out Alone

· · · · · · · · · · · · · ·

Caroline Gimbly spent five months (January to June 1988) travelling alone around China, covering the major tourist routes and striking out into the lesser-known territories.

This was the first time I had travelled alone and, not being particularly confident, had to grapple with all sorts of anxieties about how, and whether, I would cope. I couldn't speak a word of Chinese at the outset, but got a huge amount of pleasure from trying. Gaining the basics over the weeks helped enormously with the ordinary logistics of travel, buying train tickets etc, as well as giving me opportunities to make contact with people on the way.

Very few spoke English but a phrasebook and dictionary, alongside my own struggling attempts, enabled surprisingly complex conversation. It also created situations ripe for laughter – I found the Chinese invariably displayed a brilliant sense of humour – a perfect tool for making links with people.

"The words for 'I am a woman' came pretty high on my essential phrases list"

Many of the people I met expressed real surprise at meeting someone who had chosen to travel alone. On top of the open, unaggressive curiosity I encountered almost everywhere and the incessant questions about my income and the cost of my camera, people were constantly trying to puzzle out why I would want to be on my own.

Chinese life, in the most stereotypical way, appears to be so very group-based and their concept of a holiday is no exception – if a holiday photo hasn't got people in it, it isn't worth taking. The only snag I did encounter, being on my own, was that because eating is also a social, group occasion, I lost out when it came to ordering in restaurants – a steamed fish eighteen inches long is something of a struggle for one person.

Being a woman on my own seemed barely comprehensible. Being a tall woman with short hair, usually bundled up in a jacket and jeans, created genuine doubt and confusion. I had a number of female communal shower doors slammed in my face by shocked Chinese women and the words for "I am a woman", came pretty high on my essential phrases list. It's an extremely bizarre statement to find yourself yelling out in echoing corridors or dingy backyards. I spent three days sitting on a bus talking to a young Chinese man, who was only convinced I was a woman when, at the end of the second day, I produced my passport.

I wondered whether this was because of my appearance, or whether it was more socially acceptable to talk to me as "man to man". In Kashgar, I was ambling through the main square when a woman walked up to me and, quite matter-of-factly, placed both hands where she thought she may or may not find my breasts. Somehow, it was impossible to be feel angry because it seemed such an honest gesture and she accepted my mock slap across the face in good humour. I also had problems with very tentative barbers, who evidently thought my hair was quite short enough already and were highly reluctant to remove any more.

I cannot remember a time in China when I felt afraid of being on my own, from the point of view of safety. I walked around freely at night, left bags lying around on trains and never felt worried about being amongst groups of men. In Hohhot, I walked into a restaurant after a long day's cycling and was invited to join a table of four young men. They proceeded to engage me in a drinking contest, brushing aside my moans that I would never be able to cycle home by offering to accompany me.

Several glasses of something disgusting later (they manage to eat, drink and smoke at the same time!) they kept their promise, leaving me at the hotel gate after helping me to return my bike to an incredulous attendant. Obviously I was taking a risk (as were they), but it was one I felt prepared to take after four months in the country. I was wolf-whistled once and touched by a man who offered me a lift on his bike, both in Kashgar. This is possibly because it's a Muslim area; I was certainly not welcome at the mosques and was asked to leave one during prayers.

There were many more occasions when I was not only treated extremely hospitably, but was also shown great kindness and a willingness to help, often in quite a protective way. The more surprising of these involved a bureaucrat. A government official drove me all over Hohhot on his motorbike, looking for the relevant person to extend my visa. It's difficult to say who was the more excited; him, having a foreigner in his sidecar, or me, bouncing over the pavements in his machine. On top of this, once we had tracked the right person to her home and I had handed over my "foreigner's money", she asked me whether I'd prefer to pay in "people's money", which is only obtainable on the black market. Chinese bureaucracy is unpredictable to say the least.

My most unpleasant brush with "the system" occurred on a train journey and involved a Chinese man I had got to know on the bus coming from Kashgar. Teasing and teaching each other, we shared our very limited knowledge of each other's langauge. A young man of 21, he was born in Suzhou, on the east coast and had left two years previously with his brothers to look for work. He had settled in Kashgar, about as far from his home as possible, and was now travelling hundreds of miles to buy tractor parts.

Though committed to the ideals of communism, he believed China would be capitalist in twenty-five years. Continuing our journey on this train together, our friendship was treated warmly by fellow travellers but any display of affection was treated very harshly by the train staff.

"He showed great courage by hugging me at the station when I got off the train, observed closely by what looked like just about every attendant on the train"

My friend was hauled off to the guard's cabin for a lecture, had his (false) name and address taken and, so he told me later, had to make out he was an ignorant peasant and therefore not responsible for his actions. I, in my turn, was asked into the office where I was treated with great courtesy, which made me feel uncomfortable and angry. My friend became so nervous about what might happen to him that he barely dared talk to me whilst staff were around. He showed great courage by hugging me at the station when I got off the train, observed closely by what looked like just about every attendant on the train.

Physical contact in China appears to have laws attached – which, as a foreigner, I was never quite able to grasp. In cramped and seething trains, nobody seemed to mind if you used their shoulder or back for a pillow at night. Touching seems fairly acceptable between same-sex friends; I was sad to see one young man rapidly brush his friend's arm from around him when he saw me approaching, as though Western stigmas were affecting his perception of his own cultural rights and wrongs.

However, very few couples display physical affection, even holding hands, married or not. Conversely, in many hotels I came across assumptions that Western men and women would happily share dorms; if I objected, I was always found another room. Generally, personal space felt like a luxury I couldn't always guarantee, leaving me on occasions feeling irritable and claustrophobic. And, back in England, I still have to check myself, barging my way down crowded main streets.

Hitching to Lhasa

. . . .

Alison Gostling hitched independently and illegally into Tibet with another Western woman whom she had met in central China.

August 1988 found me wandering the bleak corridors of a government hotel in Xining, Central China, trying to find someone willing to attempt a three-thousand-kilometre hitch with me to Lhasa, the capital of Tibet.

Having waited all spring in Kathmandhu without success for the Nepalese/Tibetan border to reopen I had flown to Hong Kong and spent four days crossing China by train. When I arrived in Xining, which despite that distance of three thousand kilometres is considered the "threshold" of Tibet, I was told that individual travel to Lhasa had been banned. Determined not to be cheated, I decided to try and sneak in from the East on long-distance trucks.

Xining was full of disappointed but resigned backpackers. Most thought I was crazy. Then I met a tall French-Canadian woman, Margo, who liked the idea. We checked each other out quite carefully. She still had her child-hood love of dirt and discomfort, had mountain-biked around New Zealand, had a great sense of humour and offered me a pair of Chinese silk boxer shorts (secondhand) as an initiation present. By choice I always travel alone, so it seemed extraordinary luck to meet such a good companion.

We decided we would look less conspicuous in Tibetan clothes and, because we are both nearly 6ft, and local men wear broad-brimmed hats and large baggy coats suited to clandestine journeying, we chose to dress as men. Tibetan women, as happens often in mountain areas, tend to be forceful, independent characters who often hitch long distances. But we would have needed long, straight black hair to pass as one of them, even at a distance.

We did feel fairly stupid to be masquerading as men. In hindsight I doubt if this was necessary; it made local people doubly curious about us. From the harassment point of view it probably made no difference; we were treated with great kindness and respect throughout, even when sleeping in a truck packed like a sardine can with Chinese roadworkers.

"Neither of us had done anything like this before, and couldn't believe we were about to set out"

We prepared ourselves by buying whatever "survival rations" we could find – peanuts, biscuits, boiled sweets and dried apricots – and changed lots of money into the local currency on the black market. Neither of us had done anything like this before, and couldn't quite believe we were about to set out. Our biggest concern was that we might be putting local people at risk by help-ing us – a justifiable fear since security is tight, with as many as eight soldiers to every Tibetan, and many informers.

On the other hand, Eastern Tibet (not only the "Tibetan Autonomous Region" but also a huge area now attached to the Chinese provinces of Qinghai and Sichuan) has always been off-limits to foreigners, and we argued that we might be of some service as outside observers of life under Chinese rule.

Woken up by trumpets calling pilgrims to prayer, we set off precipi-tously one morning before we lost our nerve completely. The suburbs of the town seemed endless as we struggled along in our strange new clothes, our backpacks concealed in unwieldy sacks. A small boy said "hello" (in English!) which was hardly encouraging.

Almost immediately we found ourselves off the beaten track. Sitting in a ditch eating a breakfast of dried apri-cots, we watched hundreds of identi-cally-clad men being marched out of a compound to work in the fields: a tiny proportion of the vast Chinese gulag said to exist in the region. A few hours later, having skirted some checkpoints, we were heading south on our first truck.

Travelling by truck across the high plateau and passes of Tibet is a world apart. Physically the distances are immense; psychologically they are immeasurable. The grasslands stretch away endlessly from the solitary road.

Once a travelling companion jumped down from the truck and set off into a completely featureless horizon, sure of his lone path. Elsewhere horses grazing around a distant cluster of nomadic tents, strung with prayer flags, were the only hint of human habitation.

"Often we slept in the trucks and ate a supper of boiled rice heated with a borrowed blowtorch"

Switchbacks climb for half a day out of the dead-end valleys. From the crest a magical expanse of peaks extend like waves, with snowy froth on their summits. The clear light dazzles, and the thin air makes everything doubly breathtaking.

On and on for hours, then days, with sometimes no sign of movement for a hundred miles at a time. Mind and matter begin to play strange tricks on each other.

We sprawled on grainsacks in the back of an open truck or huddled together with the rest of the passengers from the wind and rain and dust under a tattered tarpaulin. This is how most Tibetans travel, and a special camaraderie developed, with great whoops of triumph at the top of a high pass and rueful laughter at the bumps when freewheeling for hours down the other side.

Once a half-naked man with matted beard climbed in, carrying only an axe and a kettle. A local chieftain in fur-trimmed coat and knee-high boots, he

was armed with both a silver dagger studded with turquoise and a revolver wrapped in red silk. On a windy plateau we paused to pick up two nomads transporting an assortment of sacks to market: each one contained a section of dismembered yak. A very smelly leg of goat swung beside me, splashing blood.

At night the vehicles rolled into truckstops with high walls and gates like medieval fortresses. Often we slept in the trucks and ate a supper of boiled rice heated with a borrowed blowtorch. I played "Grandmother's Footsteps" with children terrified of the two strangers. One evening a cassette player was produced and Margo's Grace Jones tape echoed in the wilderness.

Set in this raw landscape were sinister new towns with huge walled compounds and a heavy military presence, which we guessed to be prison camps. One road passes through them all, disappearing from and into the emptiness, but guarded by frequent roadblocks.

Sometimes the heart of an old Tibetan town had been ripped out, or else there was just a ribbon development of concrete accommodation for the many Chinese immigrants, with loudspeakers blaring state news and music as if to help them ignore their surroundings. The mud houses of the Tibetans have been squeezed out and huddle low on the edge of the villages, beyond any water or electricity supplies.

We were amazed by the sheer numbers of Chinese we saw – as different from Tibetans in appearance, language, diet and customs as the Japanese are from us. We learnt the facts later. Reeling from the devastation wrought by the Red Guards in the 1960s, and the famines of the 1970s in which more than 300,000 died, Tibet now faces the greatest threat of all – a massive population transfer from the overcrowded mainland.

As far back as 1952, even before the Chinese invasion of Tibet, Mao envisaged that these empty plateaux could house a ten-million overspill from China. As Chinese shops and restaurants proliferate, as good jobs are earmarked for Chinese applicants, as higher education is limited to Chinese speakers, as decent healthcare is reserved for Chinese immigrants, the voice of Tibet is silenced. We grew sadder and sadder over the journey.

For two nights we stopped in a village, which, being a prosperous community, was a cheerful exception. The villagers had made money from the rising value of their yak herds (the Chinese are being re-educated to eat yak meat) and from the endless convoys of trucks that pass through, carrying logs out of the newly-deforested environment.

"No ingratiating friendliness or politeness around here. Locals would look strangers slowly up and down, and only then smile if they liked what they saw"

Central China needs Tibetan wood, but the devastation seemed dramatic to the point of lunacy. We saw whole mountainsides shaved bare, the animals and birds gone and erosion taking over. The Tibetans "steal" the logs that get left behind, and the local bar and store were faced with rough-hewn wood like a Wild West filmset.

The place had great style. Fresh yak, a lighter and leaner version of beef, was the only food available for breakfast, lunch or dinner, along with iced gem biscuits which we found in the village store among the socks, stirrups and silks.

The local equivalent of cowboys would ride up and rein in ponies with beautifully plaited tails, tethering them to the telegraph poles. They were Khampa people, famous for their beauty and ferocity. The men wore jade rings and a mass of red silk tassels in their long black hair, the women, chunky ornaments of turquoise, coral and silver.

No ingratiating friendliness or politeness around here. Locals would look strangers slowly up and down, and only then smile if they liked what they saw. Once we were asked back for black salt tea only to find the heavy barred door shut in our faces. The kettle was brought out to us.

We arrived in a small town on the eve of a two-day religious festival. It is a famous monastery town (the main temples razed to the ground during the Cultural Revolution were now being rebuilt by local volunteers), but is also in a strategic position across a river gorge and the streets were heavily patrolled by Chinese soldiers. As it now seemed impossible to avoid being spotted we resigned ourselves to the possibility of being sent back and registered with the police. Incredibly, we were given three days' leave to stay with no questions asked – perhaps because we were now in Sichuan, a province traditionally hostile to Beijing. We'll never know, but it was strange suddenly to be ordinary travellers again, wearing our own clothes and wandering about openly.

We followed the Tibetan crowd, gathered from all over the region, down to a shady field by the river with applique tents all around a rectangular arena. It had the atmosphere of an English country fair. Everyone milled about meeting friends. Families camped around picnics, horses grazed under the trees and in one corner old peddlars crouched over huge hide bags of jewellery, teacups and devotional objects.

But it was so much more colourful than England: rainbow-striped aprons, men wearing silk brocade shirts under their homespun coats, teenage girls with myriad tiny plaits strung with turquoise hair ornaments. Ninety-nine percent of the women wore traditional dress. A few sported cropped hair and Mao suits; I couldn't decide whether they looked sadder than the rest, or whether it was my imagination.

The previous evening a young Tibetan girl had introduced herself to us in English and for the two days of the festival acted as our interpreter. Her family had fled as refugees in the Sixties (along with thousands of others) and she had received a Western education in a Tibetan children's village in India. Recently the family had returned, bringing her back with them, and she now finds herself an over-educated outsider, lonely for like-minded teenage friends, unable to leave China again. We wished we could have offered her some help. Keeping a promise, Margo sent her a Michael Jackson tape from Bangkok.

"Finally we crept out of the town at dusk . . . and set off for the river on foot, sleeping the night under a bridge"

We were now only thirty kilometres from the Yangzi River which forms the border of the Tibetan Autonomous Region, but our prospects of getting to Lhasa had never seemed bleaker. The one bridge was guarded by machine-gun turrets. Soldiers armed with rifles and bayonets searched every vehicle, and it was rumoured that any driver taking us across could be fined 2000Y (over five years' savings) and lose his licence. Two dubious characters offered to ferry us across at night but we declined. Finally we crept out of the town at dusk (the Public Security Police seemed to go home at 6pm) and set off for the river on foot, sleeping the night under a bridge.

The next day a truck full of Chinese roadworkers just drew up and took us on board. Yet another inexplicable piece of luck. We steamed across the dreaded bridge concealed in life-size

sacks a local tailor had stitched for us. One man helpfully sat on me as I crouched in a yoga dog-pose, wedged up against two oil-cans, every muscle and bone aching.

We didn't believe we had succeeded until we climbed another high pass and emerging from our sacks were confronted with a staggering panorama of peaks, stretching endlessly into the horizon. It really did feel like the "Roof of the World".

Our jubilation was short-lived. At the next stop a plain clothes policeman hauled us out of the truck and arrested us – along with our driver.

At the police station we were left in a room while an interpreter was fetched – a Chinese Christian priest who had just been released after twenty years in jail. He pleaded our case, and managed to gain permission for us to continue, along with warnings of bandits on the road ahead. The driver was fined (we paid) and we were handed certificates of arrest.

Later we heard the priest's story. His wife had accompanied him to jail during the Cultural Revolution, and his children were left destitute. His Bible had been confiscated. I gave him the one that I had smuggled in; it was the least I could do.

As we continued west towards Lhasa, the way became more and more treacherous. The dirt road had turned to knee-deep mud in the summer rain bringing us to a standstill every few miles. Adding our muscle to that of our companions, the roadworkers, we repeatedly heaved the truck out of the mud with ropes.

The real crisis of the trip came when the road reached a dead stop on a high pass and we were forced to walk on alone. We were now at over 16,000ft and experiencing the headaches and breathlessness which are the first signs of altitude sickness. Night found us stranded on the barren mountainside freezing cold and soaked through from the constant downpour, with no food or shelter of any sort. Our chances of survival seemed slender.

"Our jubilation was short-lived. At the next stop a plain clothes police-man hauled us out of the truck and arrested us – along with our driver"

Out of the darkness loomed a tent put up by the Chinese labourers. We appeared at the doorway to their utter astonishment. With some protestation that their home was too humble for two Westerners and that it wasn't suitable for women, they invited us in, shared their meagre rations of rice and boiled water and lent us their own bedding for the night. Living for months on end without electricity, a water supply, fresh food, music, books or female company, their life lacked every human comfort. We spent the evening singing.

The strange sound of "Frère Jacques" wafted over the Himalayas.

Twenty-one days later we turned into the Lhasa valley. The sacred pilgrim route to the magnificent Potala Palace, once the home of the Dalai Lama and the very heart of old Tibet, had been desecrated. The famous golden roofs now preside over miles of soulless mili-tary compounds punctuated by waste-lands of rubble and barbed wire.

As we got closer we saw nothing but Chinese people on bicycles. Not surprising since in Lhasa itself the Chinese now outnumber Tibetans three to one. Before our feet could touch the pavement we were besieged by a crowd of Tibetan porters begging our custom. A Western girl walked past in a spotless white sweatshirt. She had just flown in with a tour group and didn't even bother to smile a welcome.

TRAVEL NOTES

Languages Standard Chinese (*putong hua* – "common speech" or Mandarin) is based on Beijing Chinese and understood everywhere to a degree. In addition there are major dialects such as Cantonese and Fujianese, plus distinct minority languages. English and Japanese are the main second languages taught in schools, but English is still spoken mainly in the bigger cities and by younger people. It is essential to learn some basic Chinese words and phrases and recognise the basic place names in characters.

Transport Visas are easily obtained from travel agents in Hong Kong and should cover most of the areas you might want to visit. Otherwise Alien travel permits can be picked up, at nominal cost, from the Public Security Bureau. The situation is however constantly changing, especially as regards travel to Lhasa; contact CITS or the Embassy for the most up-to-date information. Trains and buses are fairly efficient but incredibly cramped (unless you opt for first class travel). Hitching is officially frowned upon although it is possible to get lifts from long-distance lorry drivers. The main risk

you'll face is arrest and a fine from the Chinese patrols – your driver, however, could lose his licence, face crippling fines and continuing suspicion by the authorities. It's important to pay as much as you can for your lift.

Accommodation Tourists are designated specific hotels, generally the more expensive; in practice most hotels put you up in their dormito-ries or cheaper rooms if you are persistent. Men and women are often clumped together but you can insist on a women only room.

Special Problems None which affect women specifically. In general terms you should be sensitive to the political climate and discreet in your dealings with people you meet. The black market for FECs (Foreign Exchange Certificates), especially in the south, is still a going concern. You can exchange your money for "people's money" (*renminbi*) at lucrative rates – but be aware that the authorities are clamping down on this – Chinese can get jailed or shot if caught, tourists deported first class at their own expense. The use of false student cards is also now being cracked down upon by the Chinese.

Health problems include colds, nose and throat infections, caused by the dry atmosphere and industrial pollution. Chemist shops, however, are well stocked and local pills potent.

Special Problems for Tibet Altitude sickness can afflict people quite badly – Lhasa is at 12,000 feet. Don't do anything too energetic for several days after flying in. Outside Lhasa medical facilities are rare and unsophisticated.

Guides *China, A Travel Survival Kit* (Lonely Planet) is a thorough, almost encyclopaedic, 800-page guide, carried by just about every Australian in China. *The Rough Guide: China* (Harrap Columbus) is currently being updated.

Contacts

All China Women's Federation, 50 Deng Shi Hou, Beijing or Box 399, Beijing. Also has branches in most cities, but you will probably need a special introduction by someone at the university or other body of authority in order to meet any representatives. Set up in 1949 under the umbrella of the Communist Party, the federation is often criticised as a Party vehicle, especially as regards the one-child-per-family policies. On the positive side it does provide crucial legal advice and help for women as well as acting as a pressure group to monitor and increase political representation.

Society for Anglo-Chinese Understanding (SACU), 152 Camden High St., London NW1 ☎071-267 9840. A good source of information and also short language courses.

Books

Dympna Cuzak, *Chinese Women Speak* (Century, 1985). Classic, in-depth study of Chinese Women, researched from the 1950s on.

Elizabeth Croll, *Chinese Women since Mao* (Zed Books, 1984). Informed analysis of the effect of Revolutionary policies on the lives of women. Important for understanding the pressures women face in choosing to have children is **Elizabeth Croll, Delia Davin and**

Penny Kane, *China's One Child per Family Policy* (Macmillan, 1985).

Agnus Smedley, *China Correspondent* (1943; Pandora Press, 1985). Compelling account of women's role in the Revolutionary period by one of the US's most unjustly unsung, great, early feminists. Her autobiography, ***Daughter of the Earth*** (Feminist Press, US, 1987) is an inspiring and engaging read.

Jan MacKinnon and Steve MacKinnon, eds., *Agnes Smedley, Portraits of Chinese Women in Revolution* (The Feminist Press, US, 1988). Eighteen of Smedley's pieces on Chinese women written between 1928 and 1941, based on interviews and observations.

Emily Honig, *Sisters and Strangers: Women in the Shanghai Cotton Mills 1919–1949* (Stanford U. Press, US, 1986). A model of good, readable labour history – though academic. Interesting and with masses of evidence, examining family life, workplace tensions, strikes, and the revolutionary period.

Andrew Higgins and Michael Fathers, *Tiananmen: The Rape of Peking* (Doubleday, 1989). As yet, the best researched piece of analysis and reportage covering the events of June 1989.

Fiction

Zhang Jie, *Leaden Wings* (Virago, 1987). One of China's most popular and controversial writers; her absorbing account of life in an industrial town was both praised and condemned as a powerful contemporary satire. Also translated are her short stories, ***As Long as Nothing Happens, Nothing Will*** (Virago, 1988).

Yu Luojin, *A Chinese Winter's Tale* (Renditions, US, 1986). Intensely personal chronicle of life during the Cultural Revolution.

Wang Anyi, *Baotown* (Norton Press, US, 1989). A moving account of village life written in the style of a folktale.

Thanks to Alison Monroe who provided the Introduction to this chapter.

Colombia

· ·

Colombia is a violent country. Robberies and muggings are common and, as centre of Latin America's illicit drug traffic, whole areas of the country have been taken over by the cocaine trade. Smugglers see tourists as an easy target to use as innocent carriers, making them a prime suspect for the police who themselves may not think twice about planting drugs on the unwary traveller. Not surprisingly, despite attractions that include quite overwhelmingly beautiful landscapes and a seductive popular dance culture, European travellers are a comparatively rare sight. Being a woman in a strong *machista* culture makes problems worse, and without a male companion be prepared for continual sexual harassment. Probably more than anywhere in Latin America you will need strong wits and a good knowledge of Spanish to get by!

Political conflict adds to Colombia's dangerous reputation. As recently as 1950, thousands of people were being killed in a long and bloody battle between Liberals and Conservatives. Today there is threat of another civil war, fuelled by the ruling Liberal Party's failure to meet the basic needs of the population, let alone confront well-known complicity between sections of the military and the nation's notoriously powerful drug cartels.

Feminism in Colombia has made a lot of progress since the first groups started up in 1975. Besides being the venue of the successful First Feminist Meeting of Latin America and the Caribbean, the country has witnessed several women's demonstrations, the publication of feminist literature, development of research and the increasing participation of women in cultural events. Even in such a tense political climate several autonomous groups survive – some of the most effective dealing with women's health – as well as others, such as *Mujer en la Lucha*, which are directly linked to political opposition parties.

Reaching women of all backgrounds is a major problem for the Women's Movement in a country where social and economic divisions are so rigid. One of the most progressive groups in Colombia is *Cine Mujer*, a women's film-making collective which has made some headway in gaining access to the all-important mass media of cinema and television. Even the poorest families in Colombia tend to have TV, and cinema is a popular form of entertainment. *Cine Mujer* have made several short films about the position of women in Colombian society, which have been shown up until recently in cinemas throughout the country. As long as they don't openly attack the church or the hallowed concept of the family, the group can use this access to a mass audience to challenge many popular myths. As they take advantage of the increasing use of video, there are hopes of achieving an even wider distribution.

Taking the Rough With the Smooth

. . . .

Janey Mitchell spent a year teaching English at a state university in the Andean market town of Tunja, three hours from the capital, Bogotá. She used her holidays to travel around the country, mostly on buses and occasionally hitching.

I was nervous about going to Colombia, a feeling confirmed by the discovery, on arrival at Bogotá airport, that half the contents of my rucksack had evidently flown in a different direction. However, any doubts I had disappeared in the first weeks and today I look back with amusement at my own and others' exaggerated preconceptions of the country.

I cannot deny that Colombia has multiple and currently insoluble problems and it certainly isn't the safest country for a woman to travel alone. I am writing from the point of view of someone who spoke reasonably fluent Spanish on arrival and picked up a great deal more as the year progressed. This is a huge advantage, but you still cannot help drawing attention to yourself. Clad in poncho, local hat concealing any trace of blondness, and dark glasses, I was no less conspicuous than otherwise. It's in your walk, your height, your demeanour. You can't escape it.

> **"Besides two Moonie missionaries, I was the only so-called alien in the place where I was teaching"**

Conspicuousness brings *piropos*, catcalls, comments – even when you have just crawled out of the house with a hangover at seven in the morning. Whistles and psssts from men, as if calling a dog to heel, are blood-boiling, but they are human and once you show yourself to be human too, the situation becomes far less strained.

Your acute visibility as a foreign woman can even be an advantage.

Besides two Moonie missionaries, I was the only so-called alien in the place where I was teaching and naturally provoked considerable curiosity. Blue eyes, white skin and unjustly magic words like Cambridge open all the doors; I was spoilt with constant companionship, invitations into people's homes, VIP treatment, and paid not one peso of rent. I can't help feeling guilty at the undeserved esteem that British nationality seems to inspire and would like to think that the high regard and interest are mutual. However, I fear that Latins in Britain are, in general, poorly received.

During my first month in Tunja the words "es la gringa" followed me everywhere. "Gringa" is the female version of the term for all Western foreigners, although it essentially refers to North Americans, and, as local people regard the States as a rich, powerful, and envied Big Brother, the word is often used derogatively.

The one conversation when I attempted to clarify the difference between the British and North Americans provoked genuine interest, besides revealing people's far from infallible knowledge of world geography. Many believed England to be a little island off the US coast. By the time a month was up, the words "es la inglesa" echoed in my wake.

Colombian women generally have a raw deal unless they come from affluent families, have perhaps been educated abroad or, for whatever reason, have come to challenge traditional expectations. *Machismo* rules and men with means may have any number of girlfriends. In this respect women simply cannot achieve an equal footing with men, even in the most open of relationships.

In indigenous areas a woman who two-times or is merely seen in public with different men is invariably classified as a whore. Women are a domestic necessity or pastime, yet a pregnant woman, even unmarried, is conceded a level of courtesy. Travelling alone, when I felt most at risk, I sometimes used a small padded rucksack over my stomach and inside a coat as a talisman.

The university environment brought me into contact with a huge range of people. Women were inquisitive and warm, but simultaneously suspicious and envious of my liberty, ability to travel (concomitant with money) and my novelty. I rarely went out with unaccompanied women as most had families and husbands and, for Colombian women, socialising is inseparable from contact with the opposite sex.

Dance is a vital element of social life. *Salsa*, *merengue* and *cumbia* are barely conceivable in a single sex environment. *Merengue* in particular is a fast dance requiring man and woman to swing from side to side with their bodies as close as possible. It wasn't easy to accept that such sudden physical proximity could be less significant than buying someone a drink.

> *"Though I hardly escaped criticism for mixing with as many men as I did, I probably would have been branded a complete slut had I been local"*

I found myself in a unique position in Tunja. Being foreign, I was far less obliged to conform to the unwritten local code of conduct. The vast majority of Colombians are Catholics and in a community rife with gossip and assumed unblemished personal virtue, hypocrisy has the upper hand. Though I hardly escaped criticism for mixing with as many men as I did, I probably would have been branded a complete slut had I been local.

I actually lived with two men for most of the teaching year and was constantly cornered by women demanding to know whether I was sleeping with them both or if just one, which. It was unthinkable that I could be cohabiting with two men without having a relationship with either one. I was incredibly lucky to meet this pair who were like brother-bodyguards to me and unusually lacking in *machismo*. They even cooked and washed up!

Through these two I was initiated not only into the art of dance, but that of drinking *aguardiente*, a sugar-cane based quasi-toxic liquor flavoured with aniseed. It is customarily drunk in liqueur-sized glasses, but don't be misled by the size of the glass. "Fondo blanco", meaning "down in one", becomes a dreaded phrase, but to refuse is impolite and can cause offence.

Women are excused for lacking pride in their stamina for alcohol consumption, but it may take a lot of determination and some strategically placed flowerpots to avoid inebriation. Beware of men using intoxication tactics to try and weaken your will.

As far as travelling in Colombia is concerned, no advice is complete and I can only offer guidelines to bear in mind. A woman alone will inevitably be harassed, but common sense and care go a long way. Thieves and pickpockets riddle bus stations in particular so stick to the obvious precaution of not displaying watch, jewellery or camera in public. Local women have a huge advantage in the Andes in that they wear countless layers of clothing in which to conceal a purse. Most carry notes in their bras.

I wore a money belt and had dollars sewn into the hem of a T-shirt until washing it became a problem and I transferred them to the waistband of a pair of trousers. I once stupidly left the $240 T-shirt in a hotel room (in San Agustin) in a pile of clothes. It disappeared and I still seethe with fury to think of somebody going through every inch of clothing to find my money. Hotel safes are wise but if there was any doubt about the security of money in deposits, I split my cash, wearing half in my clothes.

I would advise women against hitching. I did so rarely, only in daylight and in areas where tourists were few and far between. This may seem to contradict a warning not to wander too far off

the beaten track – lone travellers have been known simply to disappear without trace, especially around guerrilla strongholds and the remote foothills used to cultivate *coca* and marijuana.

"A Colombian woman would rarely travel alone and it is difficult for men to envisage a culture that allows women such independence"

But, where foreigners are rare, local people tend to be less wise to means of ripping you off and more likely to take a genuine interest in the whys and wherefores of a woman travelling alone. Here I found that white lies about my Colombian husband did not go amiss. It's wise to explain the reasons for your solitude, whether it means inventing a partner or honestly trying to outline your position. Just remember that a Colombian woman would rarely travel alone and it is difficult for men to envisage a culture that allows women such independence. Hitching also may require a degree of physical and mental stamina as you crouch, squashed between pumpkins and yams, ears deafened by the sound of squealing piglets.

On one occasion, I leapt over the back of a high-sided lorry to find myself landing on a heap of oranges from the valley, in which a bunch of distinctly pickled pickers lay sprawling or half buried. My instinctive recoil was met with a helping hand which then hesitantly offered a petrol can. It turned out to contain their local *trago*, a distilled sugar-cane hooch. They probably thought they were hallucinating as I appeared. However, a spattering of English was successfully dragged out from somewhere in my honour and I even managed to add to it. I soon discovered that making moves to pay the driver is appreciated, but money seldom changes hands.

There were times in Colombia when I knew I was at risk, but after my first few trouble-free months I had become ridiculously blasé about the whole thing. My sense of invulnerability subsequently took a beating.

"Attempted rape radically altered my attitude to travelling alone"

I advise women not to arm themselves with any kind of weapon as men are likely to act more aggressively under threat. I had taken general self-defence classes at the university before setting off alone during the holidays and when I did find myself under attack my automatic reaction was to aim for the organs most likely to debilitate. I was lucky in that in both cases the attacker was unarmed and my aggression won. The scrotal sac is woman's one concession against male physical strength. I remember little of the actual struggle: yelling, uncontrollable shaking afterwards, curiosity on seeing human hair between my knuckles and a recollection of the jelly-like texture of the eyeball as my fingers lunged.

Attempted rape radically altered my attitude to travelling alone. I was astounded by my own physical strength and mental determination to fight off attack. Full accounts of what happened would entail lengthy explanation; it is sufficient to say that, in each case, I had wrongly trusted my intuition and demonstrated a degree of friendliness.

Travelling unaccompanied and without contacts in an unfamiliar city, it isn't easy to reject all approaches from men and I cannot stress enough that these violent incidents came about through a slackening of caution.

Mine was a conscious choice to travel alone and fluent Spanish made it easy to make friends with Latin Americans. Had I been travelling in company and with a person of less fluency, I would not have become as integrated into the communities I visited or have felt as close to their culture. I was often with people so trustworthy that I became blind to the proportion of the population who regard a Western woman travelling alone as a piece of flesh to be bought or taken by force.

Following these incidents, however, I took a great deal more care, making an effort to team up with fellow travellers and, where possible, share rooms with women. Had my attackers been successful, my attitude towards the whole trip would be drastically altered.

As it is, those experiences have given me a deep spiritual resilience. I know that I'd travel alone again under similar circumstances. The good times – visiting Colombia's lesser-known Caribbean islands, dozing in steaming volcanic pools, exploring prehistoric sites on horseback – far outweigh the bad.

A Lot of Dire Warnings

· · · · · · · · · · ·

As a feminist academic, writer and translator, Susan Bassnett has travelled and lived in a number of countries. With her eight-year-old daughter, she visited Colombia at the invitation of the Universidad de los Andes.

Although I had worked on Latin American Literature for some years and taught courses in Britain on Latin American culture, I hadn't visited a Latin American country until I was invited to go and do some teaching at the Universidad de los Andes, Bogotá, Colombia.

I was given a lot of dire warnings before setting out, many by people who had already visited the country. I was told about the high level of street violence, of areas which are effectively civil-war zones and the dangers of walking anywhere alone. When they learned that I was also proposing to take along my eight-year-old daughter, the warnings increased and I was told horror stories about kidnappings, child prostitution rings and ransom demands. I left Britain in a state of some anxiety. My experiences of the country revealed a lot about the way in which Europeans and North Americans perceive Latin America.

Viewed from afar, the South American continent seems like the final bastion of civilisation: the place to which embezzlers and train robbers flee, the place that harbours undiscovered war criminals and to which people go to lose themselves and change their identities. Seen from the North American fastness, it is source of a steadily creeping communist menace, it is "down below" with all its associations of hellishness and incivility added to the European's image of distance and solitude. And however much we may dismiss these images of another continent, they do exist and consequently colour our own perceptions too. Despite all that I had read, despite the many friends from Latin America that I had made over the years, traces of these negative images remained.

Once I landed in Colombia, after a brief stopover in Caracas, everything changed. The visit remains one of the high points of an extensive travelling life and I can't wait to go back. It is an extraordinarily beautiful country, with a huge range of completely different landscapes, from the high Andes to the glorious Caribbean coast around Cartagena, the great fertile plateau and the Amazonian jungle. It is the only country in Latin America to have a Pacific and a Caribbean coastline, and stands in a unique geographical position, which no doubt is why the conquistadors, the English pirates and later North American profiteers, drug smugglers and the Mafia have always

seen it as a prime target for exploitation.

The history of Colombia is a history of violence and there is no denying that it is a country where you have to take certain precautions. When I arrived, the regular traffic police had been replaced by military units, and on every street corner in Bogotá there seemed to be a nervous teenage soldier clutching a sten gun.

"I was careful not to wear jewellery, not even earrings, or anything that might seem in any way ostentatious"

But it is also a country that makes you face up to what it means to be, in the terms of those millions living in appalling shanty towns, a wealthy foreigner. We may not perceive ourselves as rich; but the boy who held up a British Embassy official at knifepoint the week I arrived and stole his coat, his watch, his wallet and his glasses clearly saw the possession of those things as a sign of wealth. Most people carry small sums of money; if you are held up at knifepoint or gunpoint, it is best to hand over a small sum straight away and the thief will then simply take it and vanish.

Colombia, of course, has abject poverty, and stealing from the rich is a way of surviving. I lost count of the number of times Colombian friends told me about their fears in North American cities such as New York, where their doors were fitted out with more padlocks than a Colombian would ever dream of and where you cannot be assured of safe delivery from a mugger if you simply hand over two dollars or an old watch. This difference illustrates two concepts of social crime that cannot fairly be compared.

I lived in Candelaría, the old part of Bogotá, an area reputedly unsafe. I did not walk on the streets at night, but I did walk the fifteen minutes or so to the place where I was working, and never felt remotely uneasy. My daughter and I used to go shopping, visit some of the magnificent churches in Bogotá and walk around quite happily. I used public transport and the ramshackle Bogotá taxis quite normally. However, I was careful not to wear any jewellery, not even earrings, or anything that might seem in any way ostentatious.

Occasionally a shop assistant would remind me not to let my daughter carry a package, in case anyone snatched it from her as we were walking, but otherwise we behaved as though we were in any European city. Bogotá is an extraordinary city, with some beautiful colonial architecture and one of the finest museums in Latin America, the Museum of Gold. Best to walk quickly past the men who hang around outside the museum, with handkerchiefs full of emeralds for quick sale to tourists: a refusal to buy might easily turn into something unpleasant.

Travelling across the country, it is easiest to fly or, if that proves too expensive, to go by bus. The buses may not look it, but they tend to be very efficient and quite safe. Nevertheless, I never mastered the rationale behind catching an inter-city bus outside a bus station: you go to the outskirts of the city and then leap out into the road at a passing bus – and it stops! When uncertain, it is always best to go to the central bus station and start the journey from there.

"Responses to children were magnificent everywhere"

I did not have enough time to travel down to the Amazonian jungle, which I would dearly love to do in the future. Crucial to any visitor's itinerary is a trip to Cartagena, the magnificent coastal town that was considered the jewel of the Caribbean in the sixteenth century. Northern Colombia, with its hot coastal flatlands, has been made famous by Gabriel García Márquez who was born

and raised there and who contrasts the fertile plains with their brilliant sunlight with the colder, wetter climate of the high Andes. Bogotá is one of the highest capital cities in the world and although close to the equator is rarely hot. In fact the climate of Bogotá is not unlike that of an English summer, and it can be very wet indeed.

A highlight of our visit was a trip to one of the oldest colonial towns in Colombia, Villa de Leyva, about four hours' bus ride from Bogotá. This amazing old town, constructed around the biggest stone-paved plaza I have ever seen or could ever imagine, stands at the edge of the desert, and the hot, dry winds blowing across the barren landscape have produced a geological miracle.

Close to the town are the skeletons of thousands of prehistoric animals, and all the stonework is full of fossils. Eighteenth-century colonial architects with baroque sensibilities played with the raw materials available, and so there are fountains built out of giant ammonites, courtyards paved with the vertebrae of dinosaurs, ornamental stonework in which the patterns are made out of fossilised bones of all sizes. You can wander around and pick up fossils everywhere, or buy rarer examples for very little from local children who roam around the plaza in groups, looking for likely sales.

The combination of whitewashed houses built around little courtyards that are full of red and purple blossom (apparently all the year round) with the grotesque richness of bones and fossils everywhere was truly memorable. My other, strictly personal, memory to cherish from Villa de Leyva is the sight of my daughter running wildly down a hill in her pyjamas in pursuit of a contemptuous llama who had obviously seen too many enthusiastic small girls before.

I learned a great deal, too, from having a child with me. Responses to children were magnificent everywhere, and something of the wonder of a completely new continent can be lost when adults (and intellectual adults at that) exchange experiences. My daughter kept a home-made diary of the trip, collecting postcards and bus tickets and anything else of interest; and she wrote about the things that most impressed her. I felt that only with a child as a companion would I have sat in a colonial building now converted into a restaurant and stared in amazement at the mummified alligators and boa constrictors hanging from the oak beams above our heads. And having a child with me made me acutely aware of the cruelty of social inequality, where boys younger than mine are out at work or begging in gangs in the streets. One disconcerting fact that my daughter drew to my attention was the absence of girl children either as beggars or as child labour. Though no accurate figures exist, the implication of this absence suggests that the route through life for destitute girls, even at a very young age, is the brothel.

As in many Latin American countries, the position of women is profoundly ambiguous. On the one hand, the cult of *machismo* relegates women to low status as sex objects in the eyes of most men; and yet there are also many powerful women in political and business life who exercise a great deal of authority.

As a centre for Latin American publishing, Colombia is also very much a focal point for the region's culture and there are a growing number of women writers whose work is well-known and widely read. Working in a university context, there was not much evidence as yet that the field of women's studies have begun to gain much ground, but there are women keen to promote them.

Montserrat Ordonez, the feminist writer and critic who has spent some time teaching in the United States, was enormously helpful in introducing me to some of the problems of a Latin American feminist movement – the absence of models except those offered by European or North American women, the need to work specifically with the history and culture of women from Colombia, the problems of class and education that are so extreme in such a hierarchical society.

The first feminist conference in Latin America took place in Colombia in the early 1980s, and women are well represented at the Colombian international theatre festivals that have also become a regular feature over the past decade. Plans are under way for a meeting in 1992 of the Magdalena Project, the international women's theatre association based in Cardiff that has held conferences, workshops and performances throughout Europe since 1986, and it is significant that of all the Latin American countries, particularly those such as Argentina and Chile with a tradition of great women playwrights, it should be Colombia that is preparing to host the meeting.

I would like to go back, ideally in time for the proposed Magdalena Project. That will also be the year when the extent of the changes brought about by Latin American women and Colombian women in particular will be apparent, because it will be the 500th anniversary of Columbus' discovery of the Americas that heralded the centuries of colonialism and reaction against colonialism that is still going on today. Latin American nations will be celebrating their own struggles for independence, and Latin American women will feature prominently – not only celebrating the struggles they have shared with their menfolk, but marking the progress made in their fight for equal rights and status in a *machista* culture.

TRAVEL NOTES

Language Spanish.

Transport Buses are cheap and frequent. All long-distance routes are covered by coaches – comfortable but a bit more expensive. There are few passenger trains. Never travel in a taxi without a meter as you'll be overcharged.

Accommodation The poor exchange rate on the peso makes Colombia one of the most expensive South American countries. However, hotels outside the main cities can be very cheap. Camping isn't advised.

Special Problems Thieves and pickpockets are rife – hang on to your luggage at all times, watch your pockets and don't wear a watch or jewellery. Expect harassment from all kinds of men, including the police and the military. Colombia is perhaps the worst country in South America for *machismo*. Bus stations can be particularly frightening places for harassment of all kinds. The drug scene is very heavy. Buses are periodically searched by the police and it's common for drug pushers to set people up. Never carry packages for other people without checking the contents. Sentences for possession can be very long.

Guides *The South American Handbook* (Trade and Travel Publications) includes 100 pages on Colombia. *Colombia – A Travel Survival Kit* (Lonely Planet) is more in-depth.

Contacts

Casa de la Mujer, Carrera 18, No. 59–60, Bogotá, ☎2496317. Women's centre run by a long-standing collective.

Centro de Informacíon y Recursos para la Mujer, C1 36 17-44, Bogotá; ☎2454266. Rape crisis counselling, family planning etc.

Cine Mujer, Av. 25c 49-24, Apartado 202, Bogotá, ☎2426184. Women's film collective.

Books

Alicia Partnoy, ed., *You Can't Drown the Fire: Latin American Women Writing in Exile* (Virago, 1989). Moving collection of essays, stories, poetry, letters and song, including several contributions from Colombia.

Starting with arguably his best novel, ***One Hundred Years of Solitude*** (Picador, 1978) it's worth reading any books by **Gabriel García Márquez**. Colombia's most famous contemporary writer brilliantly captures the magic, beauty and madness of his country.

Lyll Becerra de Jenkins, *The Honourable Prison* (Virago, 1989). Part of Virago's teenage list, this extraordinary tale of political intrigue is based on the author's own life in Colombia.

Charlotte Méndez, *Condor and Hummingbird* (The Women's Press, 1987). Passionate novel around North American woman's visiti to Bogotá with her Colombian husband.

Cuba

· · · · · · · · · · · · · · · · · ·

In the face of a continuing US trade embargo, Cuba is turning to mass tourism as the most obvious means of importing dollars. Luxury resorts, such as Cayo Largo, have sprung up along its coastline, offering exclusive sun-sea-and-sand holidays for a new, privileged class of hard-currency tourists from Europe and Canada – North Americans still have problems getting visas. Politically motivated tours are also organised (with visits to factories, schools, hospitals and prisons or to pursue special cultural interests) but the impetus to demonstrate the achievements of the Revolution is gradually giving way to the demands of a more mainstream holiday industry.

For the average Cuban, denied the facilities freely available to dollar-wielding foreigners, resentments are beginning to surface. Cuba has long had a reputation as a safe haven for travellers and for many years street violence was almost unheard of. Tourist muggings are now on the increase, and although the numbers are neglible compared with other South American or Caribbean countries, it's a continuing trend. Travelling independently, you're bound to experience some degree of street hassle from illegal money-changers. Sexual violence, however, is incredibly rare. Cuban men can seem as steeped in *machismo* as their Latin American counterparts, but the propositions and comments you face seldom seem aggressive. If you feel at all uncertain, take stock of the cursory way that Cuban women deal with unsolicited approaches. Despite the tensions caused by tourist privilege, the large majority of Cubans tend to be friendly, helpful and interested in making contact with foreign visitors.

With so much of the Eastern bloc embracing wide-sweeping reforms, the Cuban regime no longer seems the showpiece of progressive socialism that it used to be. Thirty years after the Revolution dissatisfaction is setting in at the apparent unwillingness of Fidel Castro to open up and further democratise the country. A new generation has emerged who can now take for granted the massive advances in health, education and housing. Living with the continual and widespread problems of shortages and bureaucratic restrictions, change, for them, can seem frustratingly slow.

There's no doubt that the **status of women** has improved markedly in the post-revolutionary period. Successful efforts have been made to ensure equal access to education and job opportunities and women have played a leading role in health and literacy campaigns. Most of this work is carried out through the Federation of Cuban Women which was set up by the government in 1960. With well over two million members, the Federation has the ability to organise and change women's lives on an unprecedented scale. Its achievements are impressive, but the fact remains that few, if any, Cuban women hold any high position of power in the government. And "The Family Code", for all its radical stipulations that men should share housework and childcare, has brought about little change in the balance of labour at home.

Just Another Resort?

. . . .

Jane Drinkwater is a professional researcher, formerly in the Trade Union Movement and now in television. She has visited Cuba twice, travelling with a mixed group of friends and occasionally striking out alone.

I first went to Cuba on an unexpected windfall, for what I thought would be the holiday of a lifetime. It wasn't. I liked it so much that I borrowed the money and went back again the following year . . . and as soon as I can afford it, I'll be off again.

British holidaymakers, about two thousand every year, still tend to visit Cuba on group tours organised to meet trade unionists, healthworkers, women's organisations, or attend the cinema or jazz festivals. There's a grow-

ing trade from Italian and Canadian tour operators too – though the good time they offer is more usually geared to the traditional, if up-market, holidaymaker. Most of their time seems to be spent at the classier beach resorts, with occasional air-conditioned and fully guided coach trips into Havana for shopping, sightseeing and entertainments. The British tours offer a more rounded view. Visits to factories, schools and hospitals are combined with a trip to the popular Varadero beach resort, with a chance to travel alone from time to time as well.

I went with a small group of friends, both men and women. None of us wanted to be part of a formal tour, so we thought we'd try it the other way around: "buying-in" to the official sightseeing visits, but organising our own timetable and itinerary. This is relatively new in Cuba, but it proved unexpectedly easy – and rewarding. We had to book five nights' accommodation in Havana through the travel agent and after that could set off on our own.

Although Cuba is a big island, travelling its length and breadth isn't as daunting as it sounds. To get to Santiago de Cuba (the hot, very Caribbean "second capital" at the eastern end of the island), we travelled cheaply overnight from Havana on a Russian plane. Pinar Del Rio, to the west of Havana at the heart of the island's tobacco-growing region, we saw from a more expensive hired car. Travelling south, we flew again, this time on a "mini-package", booked from Havana, to Cayo Largo.

"The Bay of Pigs is now a flashy tourist resort with bamboo beach bars that happily accept dollars or travellers' cheques"

Cayo Largo is a tiny island which has been reclaimed from the mosquitoes and cleared of the debris which dropped and drifted on to its beaches in the American-backed invasion of 1961. It is now Cuba's most exclusive tourist resort and offers horse riding, snorkelling, and some of the most spectacular and safest scuba diving in the Caribbean. Exclusive, because it is strictly reserved for travellers in possession of the all-important hard currency, catering for neither Cuban nor Eastern-bloc holidaymakers.

Most of the Cubans working there were on secondment from their regular jobs (we met computer programmers, university professors and Havana hotel porters) and regretted that their only access to the island's attractions was on a working holiday. English visitors were something of a rarity there too. Most of the other guests came from Italy and some from Canada, stopping at Havana only in transit or for an evening's excursion by plane to the famous Tropicana nightclub. They were keen to find out from us what the "real Cuba" was like.

It was much more interesting to explore the mainland by cheaper and more Cuban means – on the network of coaches linking main towns and cities, and by the unofficial collective taxis. You can catch a ride in these *carrios* at most coach stations, where their drivers advertise their preferred destination with a handpainted cardboard sign.

Usually you'll find yourself travelling in a souped-up pre-revolutionary American classic car (a Zodiac, Chevy or Buick). These days they come handpainted, patched, welded and wired together and running on sickly-smelling Russian fuel, with engines that sound more like they belong in an aeroplane. These rides seem to involve any number of ever-changing passengers and can take the most unexpected routes (which on more than one occasion included the driver's home for a cup of coffee laced with rum). The charge is individually negotiated before you set off – but it can alter along the way.

Aiming south and east from Havana we eventually arrived – via any number of small-town suburbs, delivering and collecting passengers on the way – at the Bay of Pigs, America's tried and failed stop-off point in 1961. The area is now a flashy tourist resort with bamboo beach bars that happily accept dollars or travellers' cheques. Many Cubans died fighting off the counter-revolution and the local museum is dedicated to commemorating (movingly) those who fell; beach hoardings proudly proclaim this the site of "the first great blow to imperialism in Latin America".

Much of the land around the Bay of Pigs has also been developed for tourism. Just along the coast is a Butlins-type beach camp, Playa Larga, where Fidel himself holidayed in the early years after the Revolution. It is now used mainly by tourists from the Soviet Union and we joined them there – again the only English tourists – for a few days. The Russians travel in packs, and seemed to be regarded with wry amusement by many of the Cubans I met.

The Soviet Union's relationship and attitude to Cuba is peculiar (although "special" is the usual description given in political circles). That's to be expected: Cuba is the smaller, black and more recently socialist country, with a growing economic dependence on the huge, powerful, and largely white "mother" of socialism. The *Sovietikas* seemed more concerned with their own travelling companions and getting some sun whilst they could, than with exploring Cuban life (they know about it from school, they explained). But they were not disdainful: they protested a real sense of solidarity with Cuba's youthful revolution and respect for its achievements.

Cubans, for their part, seemed open and interested in talking to all tourists – especially to those like ourselves from England, who are still something of a rarity. I enjoyed scores of acquaintances struck up easily over my two trips with many very different people: from the mother who wanted to explain to me what Cubans thought of Margaret Thatcher; to the "revolutionary policeman" who just wanted to share a beer; to the Havana hotel lift attendant (by no means the only Cuban critic I met), who recounted tales from the good old days before the Revolution when he was a casino croupier and mixed with America's rich and famous.

"Cuban women seemed quite confident walking home late"

As in many other relatively poor countries hosting an influx of richer holidaymakers looking for a bargain, there's a brisk currency trade on what seems to be a highly developed informal and illegal economy. This trade brings many tourists' first (and most persistent) contact with the Cubans. It's typically a trade pursued by inner city youths, and because in the main they're young men (sometimes with drugs and prostitution connections, too), their approaches can feel like harassment with a sexist edge.

There were times in Cuba when, on beaches or walking though Havana on my own, I felt uncomfortable, but never more than in any other capital; and I never felt actually threatened. Cuban society generally, even in downtown Havana, is striking for its non-violent atmosphere. Streets in cities may be busy but never, I felt, dangerous. Cuban women seemed quite confident walking home late, and some worked in jobs (like car park attendants or guarding buildings) which left them alone at night in dark, secluded parts of the city – something you would never see in London, for example.

I shared the observations, too, of a black travelling companion, that many of the everyday tensions of racism found in so many other countries seemed curiously absent. It is still nevertheless the case that the higher status the jobs, the whiter the workforce. Life for Cuba's black population, as for its women, seems to be improving – with effort.

We started and finished our holidays both times in Havana, and returned there as a base in between our exploratory journeys. I always left the city needing to slow down and relax, but looking forward to another chance to get to know it better. It is big and busy, but easy to get around, since it's covered by a criss-cross of frequent, if overcrowded, buses.

Shopping – and contrary to popular expectations there is plenty of it – is an experience. Many of the shops in Old Havana are abandoned American Fifties department stores, still sporting original neon signs and laid out to the archetypal Woolworth's formula, some complete with functioning lunch counters. I couldn't resist the Cuban records, and ended up buying far too many to carry.

Unfortunately, it's easy to get a bad impression of Cuban music if you stick to the hotel cabaret circuit. Bands come complete with sparkling bikinis, coconuts, lots of dirty jokes and can be unbelievably tacky. (Strangely, there's a resurgence of interest in this sort of entertainment.) But when the cabaret bands knock off for the night from the hotels, some of them re-appear in the odd jazz club dotted around the suburbs, singing and playing the real thing. Concerts which feature a stream of female ballad singers (sporting ever more impressive ballgowns as you get higher up the bill) are popular. So too, on our first visit, were competitions for the best Madonna look-alikes which every girl under twelve in Havana seemed to have entered. They mimed collectively on the Teatro Karl Marx stage to "Material Girl" and a minor celebrity chose the winner.

On each trip I took some time off on my own. Cuba struck me as a very safe country to travel around; hotels are generally secure, with plenty of staff to call on and the people can be very helpful. You can also use the state tourist office in every major city to book your travel and accommodation ahead as you go, and, of course, living is cheap if you have the right currency.

Needless to say, there are frustrations; some things seem to take forever to sort out, and queueing is practically an art form. The British, proud of their reputation as queuers, have nothing on the Cubans, who go out of their way to find out who is last and then take their place behind them. On any journey it helps to have someone to share the chores and moans with. In a place where seemingly simple tasks can take on epic proportions, travelling alone in Cuba can sometimes be a real strain. But it's undoubtedly worth it.

Framing Cuba

. . . .

Geraldine Ellis, a film-maker and journalist based in London, first went to Havana as a delegate at the International Film Festival. She returned to make a film about the position of women working in the arts and media.

The first time I went to Cuba was for the Annual Festival of Third World Cinema held in Havana. It was easy to get caught up in the Festival and forget to take any account of the host city, but even the most cursory tourist jaunt confirms it as a place rich in character. The architecture bears the stamp of Spanish and American colonisation but the most obvious reminder of the historical rupture with US interests are the cars. You still see vintage American cars of the Fifties, miraculously roadworthy and often eyed with envy by drivers of modern Ladas. Another high-profile American legacy is the *Capitolio*, a sort of mini-White House in the centre of Old Havana, surrounded by parks graced with tall palm trees and benches where the old men sit.

At around 4pm clusters of schoolchildren in maroon or gold uniforms swarm around the bus stops along the central square. The churches, the Plaza de Alma, the *Bodeguita del Medio*, rub shoulders with community centres, light industry, shops and housing. The rattle of industrial sewing machines can be heard from early morning in a side street which also serves as a playground and baseball pitch. People sit and chat in doorways and washing is pegged out on balconies.

Turn a corner and you find yourself on a building site. Women and men are mixing concrete, loading timber into the open lift, and grinning for the tourist with a camera. These construction teams, or *microbrigadas*, are at work on a variety of sites all over Havana, many of them taking a day off while their comrades cover for them. Some are working on accommodation they will themselves inhabit, and their labour is counted as future rent.

This lively and attractive part of Havana is being refurbished with help from UNESCO; inevitably with an eye to the tourist trade. But there are fears that foreign currency bars would replace residents who would find themselves moved to estates on the outskirts of the city. Like many "Third World" countries, developing the tourist industry is a way of bringing much needed hard currency into Cuba – for instance to buy the building materials essential for solving Havana's acute housing shortage. But ironically it means once again a privileged class emerging – the tourist.

"You can have problems trying to enter a hotel bar with a Cuban friend – it's immediately assumed that illegal money changing will occur"

For instance, two types of taxi operate in Havana: those licenced to deal in dollars, and peso taxis which often collect extra passengers en route.

For Cubans, food produce is rationed, and this can entail several hours queueing for something like yoghurt or bread. But this doesn't affect its availability in the hotels. Fruits produced solely for export are sold to tourists yet never reach Cuban tables. Hotel shops are full of unlikely souvenirs like pressure cookers, electric fans, Walkmans, televisions and running shoes – goods which can only be bought with hard currency. Cubans can be imprisoned for possession of dollars but some still wait by hotels to "ride tourists" and change money. They are known as *jenetes*, or *jockeys*, although unfortunately the term often

sticks to any Cuban who develops a relationship with a foreigner.

Because of this you can have problems trying to enter a hotel bar with a Cuban friend – it's immediately assumed that illegal money changing will occur. I met one dissident who, having been caught trying to leave for Miami, claimed to be permanently barred from finding work. He explained that he wanted to leave because, "why is it that you as a tourist have more rights in my country than I do?"

Not surprisingly the US exploits dissent like this for all it's worth. *Radio José Martí*, cynically named after the great Cuban fighter for national liberation, is broadcast from Washington by "Voice of America", with music and politics from Cuban exiles. However most of the Cubans I met regarded the station as a bit of a joke and countered the propaganda with a high degree of political awareness and an impressively internationalist outlook.

On my second visit to Cuba I went with a 16mm camera, one crew member and a Thames TV student bursary to gather material on the position of women in the arts.

Cuba had aroused my curiosity on several counts. Despite the fact that the mainstream British media ignore it as far as possible, everyone seems to have an attitude about it. Take a holiday in Turkey or Tenerife, and people rarely question the politics or human rights record of the country, but go to Cuba and they do. It's almost as if we've subliminally absorbed trace elements of US foreign policy along with Hollywood, TV soaps and chat shows. I spent seven weeks in Havana researching and shooting but had barely enough time to scratch the surface.

For all the economic hardships imposed by the longstanding US embargo, it is clear that irreversible gains have been made. Illiteracy has been almost eradicated in just thirty years and the opportunities available to women, in education, career, and reproductive rights, certainly compares well with more affluent and "developed" countries. The arts are considered the "second wave" of the literacy programme, and concerts, cinema and theatre are very cheap. There are no Cubans who could not afford them. During the 1980s it has become increasingly possible for the photographer, jeweller, or clothes designer to work independently with their home doubling as a studio.

One of the painters I met, Zaida del Rio, earned a monthly salary for which she was obliged to produce three paintings per month to be sold through a government organisation. Anything else she made, she could sell privately. Her work was very popular and she was one of the few who could make a living from it. She works from a small unlit table in her bedroom. Her ten-year-old son has an adjacent room and they share a living room and tiny kitchen.

Caridad Martinez studied at one of the first schools of art to be opened after the Revolution. A dancer and choreographer, she had been with the Cuban National Ballet for eighteen years but in 1987 left to form her own contemporary dance group in conjunction with actors. This break was without precedent and was initially frowned upon by the Ministry of Culture, but they continued to draw salaries as dancers and gained a fair degree of success and recognition.

Many other women have taken advantage of the educational opportunities provided by the Revolution and universities currently have a higher intake of women in nearly all the subjects, not just the arts but also science, engineering, economics and philosophy (so much so, that there was talk of introducing positive discrimination for men). But, whilst women have equal rights, and a strong presence in the workforce, they still face the problem of the double shift.

A few years ago a comprehensive piece of legislation, "The Family Code", was passed, which underlined the principle that all domestic tasks should be shared if both partners work. In other words, men are legally bound to do fifty percent of the housework. Although difficult to enforce, it's reckoned to at best alleviate the shock of embarrassment experienced by the *machista* when he dons an apron. Every woman can choose, under the terms of the Family Code, whether to continue or terminate pregnancy, and equal support is available for either course of action regardless of whether she is married or single, employed or not.

"I used to take the bus back to the Hotel Caribbean in Old Havana, often in the early hours of the morning, without any sense of threat"

Although I couldn't verify the claim that neither rape nor domestic violence are common in Cuba, I used to take a bus back to the Hotel Caribbean in Old Havana, often in the early hours of the morning, without any sense of threat, and in fact many Cuban women were travelling alone at this hour, their activities unrestricted by fear of sexual harassment. This may be due to the self-defence women learn in military training, or to the discreet policing of the CDRs (Committee for the Defence of the Revolution), a sort of neighbourhood watch scheme which governs local affairs.

Even though the past few years have seen an increase in tourist muggings, they're still counted in tens rather than the hundreds that occur in so many capital cities, and the vast majority of Cubans would step in and help if they saw anything happening.

Most of the Cubans I met were open and friendly and it was the contact with people that formed my most enduring memories. Ana, for instance, seemed to have been nearer than most to the hub of Cuba's turbulent history. She brought out photos of herself as a young woman, in light blouse and slacks, crouched with a rifle on the steps of the university and another in army fatigues addressing a large audience of women recruits. She fought at Playa Giron and the Sierra Maestra but is now disillusioned. "No es socialismo," she said, "es Fidelismo." "What will happen when Fidel dies?" I asked. She grabbed the bottle of rum; "There'll be no more of this in the shops, there'll be dancing in the streets!"

The Revolution has its share of successes and failures, and most people dwell on whichever aspect suits their temperament and ideology. Their answer is likely to tell you more about the person than the place. If you're looking for betrayal, blind dogma and the dead hand of bureaucracy, you can find it. And equally if you want to find a triumphant revolution, there's the free and abundant healthcare and education for all. You can be suitably inspired by rent levels fixed at ten percent of income, with transport and food together at about fifteen percent. While for some the experiment has already ended in failure, for others, it's scarcely begun.

TRAVEL NOTES

Language Spanish. Few Cubans speak any English.

Transport Bus and train services are extensive but tend to be slow and generally inefficient. Theoretically, hitching is illegal, but in practice it works quite well.

Accommodation Travelling independently, you're obliged to book five days' accommodation in advance; from then on it's still advisable to book through the official *Cubatur* office, Calle 23, No 156, Velado, Havana, ☎32-4521, as the cheaper hotels tend to fill up quickly, especially in the provinces.

Special Problems You may well be hassled by money-changers, especially outside the main hotels; it's best to steer clear. Shorts and skirts are very rarely worn by adults except on the beach. Many rich Western tourists break the rule but it's frowned upon and will incite critical comment.

Guides *Hildebrand's Travel Guide: Cuba* (Harrap Columbus) is a good short guide with an excellent map of the island. *The Caribbean Handbook* (Trade and Travel Publications) also has a useful chapter. Paula DiPerna's *The Complete Guide to Cuba* (St Martin's Press, New York), though outdated, is still highly recommended.

Contacts

Federation of Cuban Women, Calle 11 No 214, La Habana, Cuba. Central organisation for making contact with women's groups throughout the country.

Britain-Cuba Resource Centre, Latin America House, Kingsgate Road, London NW6. Organise places on work brigades.

Books

Jean Stubbs, *Cuba, the Test of Time* (Latin American Bureau, 1989). An illuminating, well researched look at contemporary Cuban life.

Elizabeth Stone, ed., *Women and the Cuban Revolution* (Pathfinder Press, New York, 1981). Collection of speeches and documents, including the thoughts of Fidel Castro.

Inger Holt-Seeland, *Women of Cuba* (Lawrence Hill, US, 1981). Interviews with six women, from farm worker to university teacher.

Margaret Randall, *Women in Cuba: Twenty Years Later* (Smyrna, US, 1981). Good if slightly dated socialist-feminist analysis of women's gains in Cuba in the first two decades of the Revolution. Offers a positive view of advances in legal, political and workplace rights and positions, and in particular gains made by women against *machismo* in family life.

Ecuador

· ·

Ecuador, one of the smallest
and richest countries in South
America, is commonly considered
the most beautiful. It also has a
reputation for political stability in
spite of a noticeable military
presence.

The country is divided into two
main areas: coast and *sierra*, the
latter dominated by the Andes
mountains. The majority of
Ecuador's large Indian population
eke out a living from working on
the land of the *sierra*. Despite
certain progressive agricultural
policies, both here and along the
more developed coast, a growing
number of people flock to the
towns for work. More than half of
them are women.

For the last two decades, Ecuador has been able to rely on oil resources to
bolster its economy – as the saying goes: "We may be poor, but down there
(Peru) they're dying of hunger." But the crash in world oil prices, followed by
recent earthquake damage to key installations has very much undermined
this financial security. This, together with widespread disillusionment with
the free-market policies of the conservative government contributed to the
election of the centre-left Izquierda Democratica, currently in power. Despite
signs of improvement in the overall state of the economy, political dissent
continues to be fuelled by unemployment, rising prices and the need for
more radical social reform.

Theft is said to be on the increase in Quito and the steamy port of
Guayaquil; otherwise travel in Ecuador is generally hassle-free with few of
the grounds for paranoia experienced in, say, Colombia or Peru. Ecuador has
a gradually awakening **women's movement**, the core of which is dedicated
to developing and working with grass-roots women's organisations. An important group is *CEPAM* (Centre for the Promotion and Action of Ecuadorean
women), whose work led to the opening of the country's first women's centre
in the capital, Quito, in 1983. *CEPAM* runs various training programmes for

rural and urban women; publishes resources on issues such as health and women's legal rights; and helps to co-ordinate most of the twenty or so other women's groups active in and around Quito. The centre is keen to make contact with feminist groups from other countries in order to exchange ideas and promote understanding about the situation and activities of Ecuadorean women.

A Village Film Project

· · · · · · · · · · · ·

Zuleika Kingdon travelled to Ecuador with an anthropologist friend, Harriet Skinner. They spent six months living in an indigenous highland community in Chimborazo Province, where Zuleika was making a film in support of Harriet's field research.

Arriving in Quito with little knowledge of Ecuador and very poor Spanish, our first task was to get to know the country, to travel and make contacts before deciding where to establish our project. A development worker we met through the British Embassy provided useful information about the communities he had worked in, but wherever we went we also encountered Ecuadoreans who were only too happy to pass on the addresses of helpful friends and relatives all over the country, from teachers, university professors and filmmakers, to priests, nuns and community workers. Barely two weeks had gone by when we heard about Cacha.

Situated in the beautiful mountainous province of Chimborazo, Cacha is a small traditional community which, through the help of a certain radical priest, is undergoing great social changes. True to the spirit of liberation theology, this man has spoken out

strongly against the oppression within his own church and supports the need for Cacha's self-sufficiency, brought about through the implementation of self-help development projects. Inspired, we decided to contact the priest who, after a hasty breakfast meeting, consented to give us a lift up the rough, dusty road that leads to Cacha's main village.

Preoccupied with having to take a funeral service, the priest was uncommunicative as we bumped and rattled along in his battered old car. Suddenly without warning he stopped at a crossroads: "I'll leave you here," he said,"Walk up to the village and speak to the community leaders." He drove off and we stood coughing in his dust trail, somewhat daunted by the hike ahead. The spot commanded a fine view of the city of Riobamba far down in the valley but, despite its peaceful stillness, the landscape was far from welcoming: hillsides crumbled into gorges, small cultivated patches bore weak and dying crops, and the hard packed ground was punctured only by eucalyptus trees.

In the village we met a young woman who worked in the local health centre though she lived in Riobamba. She was aghast that we should want to live in Cacha. "What will you eat?" she asked, revealing an attitude we had come across before, namely that women like us (in her mind the daughters of rich *mestizo*, mixed-race, families) grow up with servants and simply do not learn to cook. Nevertheless she introduced us to the council secretary and so the process of being accepted into village life began.

Following decades of acute exploitation and oppression, Cacha's population is now among the poorest in Ecuador. Denied self-sufficiency through the exploitative *hacienda* system, which appropriated the most fertile valley land, these indigenous people were left to make the best of poor arid terrains. The ground was consequently overcultivated, helping to precipitate the landslides and soil erosion we could see all around. Dependency on the richer Spanish communities inevitably limited their economic growth and social advancement, leaving a people understandably sceptical of foreigners. It was therefore very important to all of us that our project should be of benefit to the people of Cacha themselves.

The secretary asked us to submit a written proposal, to be circulated around various village meetings in order for the matter to be discussed outside our presence. Our main contribution was to offer a copy of the film (viewable on equipment supplied by a local development worker) as a resource for popular education campaigns. Likewise we hoped that Harriet's thesis would prove helpful as a historical record of changes taking place in the community.

"The villagers seemed pleased that two young women should be so keen to learn about their community"

This preliminary discussion with the council secretary unexpectedly led to our first encounter with some of the reality of village existence. We were standing explaining our mission in faltering Spanish when a man appeared calling everyone to follow him. The invitation extended to us and we climbed up a steep bank through a maize and *quinua* plantation to arrive at a tiny

mud-brick house that, had it had any windows, would have overlooked the beautiful valley to communities on the opposite sides.

Inside was pitch black save for a solitary candle, the light of which revealed hundreds of little guinea pigs running around the fireplace. On the bed lay a man who had just died, aged 102. I couldn't help being shocked. Women and children gathered around to have a look and then equally nonchalantly wandered out as we learned how, traditionally, villagers must all pay their respects before the body is moved in order for him to leave in peace. They said he had died from loneliness.

The villagers seemed pleased that two young women from a distant foreign country should be so keen to learn about their community, accustomed as they were to having their culture devalued, and I was impressed by the serious consideration they gave to our project. Our obvious sincerity was demonstrated by the fact that we wanted to live in Cacha as opposed to the comfort of digs in the nearest town of Riobamba.

Children were our first visitors when we were finally allotted a little house. Dark-eyed, curious and cheerful, they would come bringing us presents of sweetcorn or invite us to accompany them while they pastured the sheep. The women, being more shy, were harder to get to know. Initially the girls working in the crafts workshop would sit giggling and joking in Quichua, making these encounters far more intimidating than the formal introductions we had to face in village reunions.

Soon, however, one girl was appointed general spokeswoman and translated their questions for us: "Why did we wear trousers? Were we married? Why not? How far from home were we? Why did we leave our families?" They gradually became more relaxed and conversational, wanting to know most what our country looked like and what crops we grew, comparing prices of potatoes and other fruit with wonderment.

Our friendships were further reinforced the day we presented these girls with the photos we had been taking. They were thrilled and, as if it had been proof of our honesty, we were now able to sit among them without being ridiculed; we found ourselves invited to events, music rehearsals, or simply to their houses; talk was less reserved and we were shown how to crochet the brightly patterned *shigras*, bags made to sell in the markets.

I set about crocheting a bag to carry the tripod for my camera. There was plenty of time for I didn't want to start filming until our relations with people had been well established. We had to learn to pace ourselves to a new tempo – the Ecuadorean hour is invariably slower to arrive – and adapt to a very simple, basic daily routine that included new and unfamiliar foods. The local delicacy is roast guinea pig which, though well skinned and gutted, comes complete with head and eyes. Served with potatoes cooked in a delicious peanut sauce, this dish is offered to guests as a great honour, so to refuse it would cause deep offence. Fortunately, we quickly got over our squeamishness.

More important than adapting to local food was the need to pick up basic Quichua, as well as to improve our Spanish. The former is very similar to Peruvian Quechua, with just three vowels: i,u and a. Words are given different meanings by adding different structures to the beginning and/or end. As everyone speaks with lightning speed it is far from easy to learn, but when we enrolled for a week's intensive course run by the Church in a nearby community we found that villagers responded very keenly. People greatly enjoyed testing us with phrases, shaking our hands with enthusiastic laughter when we managed to deliver the correct replies. News of our lessons spread and attracted people to join in

and allow opportunities for us to practise. Spanish, however, remained our main language.

Our accommodation turned out to be needed for a student doctor from Quito, who had come to help immunise the children, so we moved on by invitation to share a traditional three-roomed home with a family. Harriet and I were given the largest wooden bed where we slept in our sleeping bags on reed mats in place of a mattress. Washing facilities were very basic: we heated up water in large saucepans and washed out of a huge bucket in the "shower room" outside. Clothes were scrubbed on the block by the water tank in the yard. As in the other house, drinking water had to be boiled for twenty minutes to ensure its safety.

The family offered us food whenever they cooked and so we adopted the same principle. To begin with the children were too shy to eat what we gave them in our presence and would run off with it to their bedroom, but their hesitancy gradually wore off and we became good friends. Despite being fascinated by our possessions, they never demanded anything. They were extremely capable, much of the time having to fend for themselves and take care of the animals while the parents spent most days in another house in the village across the gorge.

"In Cacha it could never be said that women are the weaker sex"

Our offers to help out with daily duties were always accepted, but our clumsiness would invariably cause great hilarity. On one occasion I walked down the hill with Rosa, the mother, to join Harriet who had gone down to help the children cut alfalfa for the animals. In the distance we caught sight of her little figure struggling to load a large bundle on to her back, bent double to prevent it constantly slipping down to her backside. Rosa giggled all the way down the hill, unable to understand the difficulty of doing something that every local child is expected to learn from an early age. Having got this far, Harriet was keen to hand over the load for me to carry back up the steep hill. It was my turn to gasp for breath as I eventually staggered up to the house.

In Cacha it could never be said that women are the weaker sex. Among others, we were constantly impressed by Luz Maria, a mother of five children and the only female full-time worker on the village building site. She seemed burdened with all the labour of fetching and stacking piles of bricks, carrying them in a sling on her back to cart up to the top of the new federation house. She didn't appear to receive any harassment from the men on the site (nor was harassment ever an issue for us), but she had enough problems with her husband who rarely came home and was then invariably dead drunk.

Filming, when it at last began, brought with it many practical and technical challenges, not least of which was carrying around twenty kilos of camera gear at an altitude of over 3000 metres. Fine wind-blown dust also proved a constant nightmare. Yet these problems dwindled in the face of enthusiastic co-operation from the villagers, eager to document the fact that they were taking the future into their own hands, lobbying government and foreign organisations alike to raise the major funds needed for their projects – to bring water supplies to the community; to combat malnutrition; improve education opportunities and generally better the quality of life for the people in the region.

TRAVEL NOTES

Languages Spanish, Quichua, Jivaroa.

Transport Buses are plentiful and very cheap. Trains are also cheap, but erratic.

Accommodation Hotels too are inexpensive, especially outside the main cities, but always ask to see the room.

Special Problems No particular problems for women, but all travellers must carry a passport at all times.

Guides *Ecuador – A Travel Survival Kit* (Lonely Planet) is solid on practicalities. *Climbing and Hiking in Ecuador* (Bradt Enterprises), by the same author, is a good adventure supplement.

Contacts

CEPAM, Los Rios y Gandara, Quito (see introduction); and **Centro Accion de las Mujeres**, Casilla 10201, Guayaquil. Activities include organising literacy campaigns, healthcare, producing audiovisual resources and running a women's bookshop.

A good general bookshop in Quito is **Libri Mundi**, Juan Leon Mera 851 y Veintemilia. The proprietor is European (married to an Ecuadorean Indian) and has information in almost any language. He also keeps a notice-board for "what's On in Quito".

Books

Audrey Bronstein, ed., The Triple Struggle: Latin American Peasant Women (War on Want Campaigns, London, 1982). A collection of interviews including discussion about the lives of Ecuadorean peasant women.

Egypt

. . . .

Egypt is well used to tourism, with a long-established and well-organised holiday industry, geared for the most part towards shunting visitors along the Nile to Cairo, round the Pyramids and on to Luxor and Aswan. If you want to travel independently, it's best to go around February or October when the crowds thin out.

The country, and in particular the capital, Cairo, can seem initially confusing and intimidating. In all the main tourist areas you'll be approached frequently by hustlers and guides, many of them incredibly skilled and persistent in their dealings with foreigners. It can take a while to come to terms with being a symbol of affluence (to some people, the only viable source of income) in a country where unemployment is high and poverty intense. Egyptians routinely give money to beggars and won't easily understand why a wealthy and privileged tourist should refuse. Added to this there are all the prevailing myths and stereotypes of Western women to contend with.

As with any predominantly Muslim country your independence and freedom to travel can be misinterpreted as a sign of immodesty. Much of the attention you'll inevitably attract will have sexual overtones and coupled with more general hustling, this can become quite oppressive. It helps to dress inconspicuously, taking your lead from more Westernised Egyptian women. As ever, these problems become much less intense as you grow more used to travel, or live for a while in one place.

Politically, Egypt's "open door" economic policy has attracted an enormous proliferation of multinational enterprises and their effect has been to widen the already extreme poverty gap. Unemployment and homelessness are approaching ever more critical proportions. Over the last one-and-a-half decades, partly in reaction to these rising encroachments of Western capitalism, and partly due to the influence of Iran, there has been a powerful swing towards Islamic fundamentalism. The government, whilst attempting to subdue fundamentalism as a political movement, has, socially, made concessions.

Women are returning, sometimes voluntarily, but also under considerable social pressure, to traditional roles. The familiar scapegoating of women who attempt to retain their positions in the workplace during a climate of economic recession and high unemployment is particularly strong in Egypt. In rural areas women continue to labour for long hours under arduous conditions to maintain a subsistence living. The **women's movement**, as such, exists only underground. A small number of women have distinguished themselves through feminist writing – Nawaal El Saadawi (see booklist) has perhaps been the most influential, but the development of an autonomous feminist movement appears a distant prospect.

An Instinctive Kind of Care

. . . .

Kate Baillie, a freelance writer, lived in Cairo for two-and-a-half months, teaching English and learning Arabic.

Egypt is the West's pet Arabic country, "moderate" being the favourite adjective. It's important to know that this reflects little of the internal situation, but is simply Egypt's pro-Western economic and diplomatic policy. In reality, Egyptians are imprisoned for criticising the government; censorship of the arts and media is commonplace; political parties are suppressed, and Cairo and the provincial capitals are infested with armed police and soldiers. In the Cairo press and television centre, levelled rifles greet employees from a sandbag emplacement inside the foyer. The oppression is not quite as bad now as it was under President Sadat, but while a few political prisoners are released and the odd paper is

allowed to publish again, American enterprise continues to prise apart Egyptian culture, values and economy.

A new polarisation has appeared above the basic division of peasant and bourgeois, villager and Cairean. Those in the pay of the multinationals form their own super class. Speaking only English, adopting Sindy-Doll and grey-suited dress, their living standards leap while their lives become subservient to work patterns evolved for a very alien climate and culture. Speed, greed, glamour and competitiveness are the requisite values. Meanwhile, the majority, who don't or can't choose that rat race, remain in their desert robes and poverty, upholding values and a vision of society derived from a history much older than the West now knows.

The re-emerging strength of Islamic fundamentalism has to be appreciated in this context. An apparently fanatical religious social movement is hard for us to comprehend. What has to be grasped is that Islamic fundamentalism is both political and religious and there is no distinction because of the nature of Islam. The Muslim faith is a set of rules for a state, not just for individuals and it is in this that it differs so much from Christianity. Inevitably, the religious text, the Koran, is open to all manner of conflicting interpretations.

It can be argued – contrary to actual practice in Egypt – that the Koran stipulates the right of women to choose their husbands and to leave them. The financial rights it lays down for women were not achieved by European women until the nineteenth and twentieth centuries. Its banking policy would make you open an account tomorrow. Its precepts on virginity and menstruation would make you run a mile. During the Prophet's lifetime, some women complained that only men were being addressed. From then on, the two words for male believers and female believers appear. There is nothing in the Koran about female circumcision.

"There is a communion between women that our Western conception of sisterhood could never emulate"

Leaving behind the fifth and sixth centuries, the struggle for emancipation was started by Egyptian women at the end of the last century. In 1962, under Nasser, they obtained the vote, access to free education at all levels, and a woman minister for social affairs was appointed. In the last twenty years, women have entered the professions, factories, the civil service and business, though they are not allowed to be judges. In the public sector, equal pay is legally enforceable. Women now comprise almost fifty percent of the workforce though nearly half of those are peasant women working in the fields with their men as they have done for centuries. Abortion remains illegal and clitoridectomy, proving virginity on the wedding night and the punishment of adultery are still practised.

Sadat created an official Women's Movement with his Madison Avenue-bedecked wife Jihan as president.

Although they managed to push through certain reforms, such as allowing women the right to instigate divorce, the movement had little popular support. It was seen as little more than a tea party circle of her friends enjoying the freedoms of power and riches. The real Women's Movement, though inevitably made up of educated urban women, is pan-Arab and takes its position from Arab history and experience, not American or European feminist texts.

In the villages and amongst the urban poor, where feminism is unheard of, there is a communion between women who share work in and outside the home, in ways that our Western conception of sisterhood could never emulate. In Cairo, I experienced from women this almost instinctive kind of care and protectiveness. On several occasions women who were strangers to me and spoke no English rescued me from situations in which I was unwittingly at risk. Wandering, heat-dazed and lost, in a slum behind the Citadel, a woman took my arm, smiled at me and led me out of the maze, shooing away the men and little boys who approached us. A few days later I tried sleeping in Al Azhar mosque, unaware that this is forbidden to women, let alone infidels. A soldier appeared with the intention of arresting me, but I was saved by a woman who sat me behind her and talked at length to what were by now five soldiers and seven other men grouped around. Presumably she explained my ignorance: the only words I could catch from the men were "Police" and "Koran". But she succeeded, the men left and the woman smiled at me and patted the ground to show I could stay.

Aside from the pyramids, the mosques are the sights to see in Cairo, both from the "gaping at beautiful buildings" point of view and to experience the use Muslims make of their places of worship. A note on dress – you always have to take your shoes off and in the more tourist-frequented mosques you may have to pay to get them back. Though not usually enforced, I'd advise wearing a scarf, out of courtesy if nothing else. As for shorts, short skirts, punk hair styles and bra-lessness with clinging clothes, forget it, whether in mosques or in the street.

"I learned to avoid any words the dictionary gave for 'atheist' which carry the same connotations as saying you eat babies"

Mosques can also be the best places to meet Egyptian women – especially where a women's area is curtained off. Not long after the incident in Al Azhar, I was very comforted to be separated from the men. But I still wasn't sure about the sleeping rules, so I gestured an enquiry to a woman, in her fifties I supposed, veiled and gowned to the floor in black. She immediately bounced up to me, talking nineteen to the dozen and then went off to fetch two friends who spoke some English. With their fifty odd words and my fifteen of Arabic, gestures, pictures and a dictionary, and joined by two more women, we passed several hours together in enthusiastic discussion. They asked me the two standard questions that had opened every conversation I had had in Cairo with men or women: "What's your religion?" and "Are you married?" the latter, once answered negatively, would be replaced by "Where's your friend?".

The first question had involved me in metaphysical arguments I had long forgotten, and I learned to avoid any words the dictionary gave for "atheist" which carry the same moral connotations as saying you eat babies. I don't know what these women understood about my religion or lack of it, but they burst into delighted laughter at the fact of my having not one "friend" but lots.

They removed my scarf, combed my hair, called me *halwe* (sweet, pretty) and invited me to eat with them later.

Egyptians are renowned for their kindness, humour and generosity. It was these qualities that I appreciated in the Egyptian men I became friends with. I was treated with great respect and my views were listened to without having to force a space to speak. But when it came to anything to do with sex, they were pathological. One group of colleagues assumed, on zero evidence, that I was having an affair with one of them. They persuaded his wife that I was, expected their turn to be next, and were baffled by my astounded refusals. Their image of Western women and their idea of American companies are similar illusions: free sex and fast money. What I found again and again after similar and worse experiences, was a childlike shame, profuse apologies and misconception of my attitude when I taxed them with their behaviour. These men were all liberals or socialists and well-educated.

However, don't let this put you off getting into conversation with Egyptian men. Though I don't know the statistics for rape and assault, I'd stake a lot on Cairo being a safer place than London for a woman on her own. But even if you encounter no unmanageable difficulties, Cairo is an exhausting experience. Oxford Street during the sales has nothing on every street in the centre of the city all day and most of the night. Crossing roads is like trying to fly a kite at Heathrow. The fumes, heat and dust, the noise of car horns and shouting, and the spilling, squashing buses are a nightmare. And manoeuvering through this you have to contend with constant pestering, mostly verbal, from the passing male masses. There are times when you feel very exposed and wish you were robed and veiled.

A Student in Alexandria

· · · · · · · · · · · ·

Caroline Bullough has travelled extensively around the Middle East. After completing a degree in Arabic and Persian, she moved to the University of Alexandria to spend a year studying Arabic.

The arrival of thirty British students of Arabic (half of them female) caused quite a stir on Alexandria University's dusty concrete campus. I was lodged, along with three other women, in a newly built hut (already falling down) in a far corner of the campus and it was soon surrounded by a gaggle of curious onlookers. For the first few weeks we were showered with invitations and accosted by students eager to practise their English.

Most of these were men. The female students were initially shy and perhaps a little wary of us. Those who did approach us were obviously considered "forward" and therefore disapproved of. It was also clear that many parents disliked the idea of us associating with their daughters – friendships were suddenly broken off or invitations withdrawn without warning. The very fact that we were four girls living in a flat of our own without parents or guardians was enough to guarantee their disapproval. As foreign women it was frustratingly difficult to maintain platonic friendships with Egyptian men as at some stage it was always made clear that more was expected.

Foreign women are well-known as "easy game". Every Egyptian man claims to have at least one friend who can testify to the willingness of a foreign woman he once met. In a society in which pre-marital sex is officially taboo and a complex set of rules govern even informal relations between the sexes, the freedom enjoyed by most Western women is easily misinterpreted. I was asked constantly what my relationship was with the male students on the course. That they should be my close friends and no more seemed beyond comprehension. Those Egyptians who had begged for invitations to our parties, with the expectation of witnessing orgiastic mass coupling, were disappointed.

> *"To live each day facing a barrage of comments, whispered or shouted, humorous or insulting, can be a strain"*

We could do little to dispel the myths which abound about foreign women (probably fuelled by imported American films and television programmes). However hard I tried to adopt an appropriately decorous way of life, I could not escape the fact that I was foreign and all that it implied. I was evicted from my first flat for having my fellow students (some male) to tea!

To live each day facing a barrage of comments, whispered or shouted, humorous or insulting, can be a strain. I became increasingly adept at avoiding particularly difficult situations, such as passing groups of young boys, who learnt at an early stage to imitate their elders' attitude to foreign women, or crowded pavement cafés. I learnt to ignore, and sometimes not even hear, the comments and asides. I learnt to stride purposefully through the milling crowds, defying passers-by to challenge me. The hassle was often at its worst when we were in groups of girls or pairs, but seldom did I actually feel under any physical danger. I was followed on several occasions both in Cairo and Alexandria but this never happened when I was alone and because we were familiar with the area, it was less frightening than it might have been.

I often went out alone and found a café where I was able to sit undisturbed, my back to the road. I longed to be able to wander at will but it was only when I was with someone else that I felt confident enough to look around me. Alone, it was easier to walk head bowed, ears closed rather than risk attracting anyone's attention. This was the stance adopted by many Egyptian women who are themselves the object of unwanted attention.

Nowhere are wandering hands or, for that matter, wandering bodies, quite such a problem as on crowded buses and trams. Morning tram rides to the university were a constant nightmare of sweaty bodies, grinding hips and whispered comments. However, if you find yourself seriously cornered you should make a fuss, and other passengers will invariably help you out.

"A woman covered from head to foot in a black, Iranian style chador is an unnerving sight"

Egyptian students seemed to pay far more attention to appearance than their British counterparts. Most were dressed in smart Western clothes. Growing support for Muslim fundamentalism with its restrictions on dress was, however, clear. During my last months at the university, there was a student election in which a large number of known members of the Muslim Brotherhood were elected. During the week of the election the walls of the university were plastered with banners exhorting all female students to dress in the prescribed Muslim manners. Bizarre fashion shows were organised on the university campus to demonstrate suitable garb.

Few women in Egypt have returned to full Islamic dress but a woman covered from head to foot in a black, Iranian style *chador* is an unnerving sight. The voluminous garments and thick veils rob her of human shape or form. Her feet are carefully concealed under the floor length folds of her skirt and her hands are covered by thick

black gloves. Once, leaving a crowded bus (all public transport in Egypt is crowded), I was prodded from behind and shouted at by a woman concealed by a thin black veil and cape. Her strident tone of voice and colourful language astonished me and seemed at odds with her devoutly religious appearance. The force of her impatient curses was undoubtedly increased by her anonymity.

Alexandria is more Mediterranean than Arab with its elegant colonial buildings and pavement cafés. The Alexandrians are proud of their city and "Welcome In Alexandria" or "Welcome In Egypt" is on everyone's lips. At night the city is bright and vibrant, the streets teeming. Because of terrible overcrowding at home and particularly in hot weather, most Egyptians spend a large part of their lives on the streets. Coffee houses are exclusively male preserves but respectable restaurants and cake shops are full of women and families tucking into large platters of *ful medames* (a stewed bean dish) and small cakes oozing with honey.

The city is famous for its beaches which attract visitors from throughout the Middle East. In fact they are overcrowded during the summer and rather windswept in winter. Most Egyptian women remain fully clothed on the beach and even in the sea. Hassle is inevitable – Alexandria has its share of rather overweight "beach bums" – but not unbearable. Swimsuits are even now sufficiently rare to arouse interest in all who pass. There's a private beach in the grounds of the Montazeh Palace on the outskirts of Alexandria where we were able to swim and sunbathe almost undisturbed but bikinis are rarely seen even there.

Standards of medical care in urban Egypt are generally high, at least if you are rich or a foreigner. However, although many Egyptian doctors have been trained abroad, there seems to be considerable ignorance of specifically female ailments. Suffering badly from thrush, I visited a doctor associated with the university with whom I had been registered on arrival. Most drugs are available over the counter in any pharmacy so, had I known, I could probably have treated myself. Instead I was subjected to a rather ham-fisted internal examination and a long series of questions. It was clear that the doctor assumed that I must be suffering from a sexually transmitted disease and seemed only partially convinced by my protestations. To be fair, though, the medication I was prescribed, made in Egypt under licence, was extremely effective.

A Camel Ride in Sinai

. . . .

Laura Fraser, an American freelance writer, crossed into Sinai from Israel with two female friends. They took up the offer of joining two Bedouin men on a camel trek into the desert.

My trek into the vast, magical mountains of the Sinai peninsula began when I asked a Bedouin man, Iash, if I could ride his camel.

By that time I felt as if I knew him well enough to ask. I had arrived at his village, Nueva, the previous day with two friends (we had been working together as fisherwomen on a kibbutz). The village, on the coast of Sinai, looked almost medieval, with broken stone structures and makeshift shacks. It appeared to be a common way station however, and we went to a hut near the beach where other travellers were camping. Before long, a couple of Bedouin men, in their cotton djellabas, came over, built a fire, and offered us tea.

Drinking tea with the Bedouins made me realise that as impoverished and primitive as their huts made of cardboard and spiky ferns seemed to me, theirs was a culture with a highly refined sense of etiquette. When Iash poured the tea and gave me a cup, I drank some and passed it along to my friend. Iash told us no, it is the Bedouin custom that each has his own cup of tea, then the other has his, "slowly, slowly". Slowness, relaxation, and calm are highly valued virtues here, which is surely another sign of real "civilisation". We sat by the campfire, quietly, and watched the moon rise orange over the red sea.

After nightfall, one of the men brought out a Bedouin guitar, playing a vibrating, metallic melody, while the others laughed and sang. I noticed how the men all play with their head scarves the way American women play with their hair, arranging them in soft folds accentuating their faces. I felt a flash of resentment; it seemed the men have all the privileges, even of being beautiful and vain. "Why aren't the women sitting here, too ?" a German man asked one of the Bedouins. The Bedouin put his scarf over his moustache, covering his face like a veil, and tittered like a Bedouin woman. "The women, they are shy. She doesn't want anyone to see her," he explained. Our only glimpse of Bedouin women so far had been from a distance; one was wading in the sea in her long black garb, catching an octopus with her hands and twisting its head off. We asked whether Bedouin women are ever allowed to sit with the men. "Men here, women there", he replied.

We all went inside an abandoned blue bus, and the Bedouins passed around cans of grapefruit juice, big spliffs, and a booklet of pictures of the Egyptian president. One played music, and the rest clapped. Another got up to dance, imitating a Bedouin woman. The men laughed, not so much at his performance, as at woman in general. He was very funny, but the laughter still rankled.

The next morning, after tea, I asked Iash if I could ride the camel. He seemed quite happy to let me ride, but then he disappeared for a long time. Slowly, slowly, I thought, and then forgot about it. After about three hours, he came back with three camels, loaded with blankets and bags. "What's this?" I asked him, and he told me the camels were ready for the ride. I asked him where. He pointed to the mountains rising out of the desert. I glanced at my two companions. I asked him how long. "Four, five days, maybe a week," he said, smiling. "Ten dollars a day, meals included". We settled on four days.

"Even with our sleeping bags covering the Bedouins' wooden saddles, we were sore from the start"

Camels are as nasty as their reputation. The camel I rode, behind a Bedouin named Psalem, had a tricky habit of calmly letting someone get up three-quarters of the way, and then lurching up violently so the rider had to hang on tight and scramble up the last bit. They are bony beasts; even with our sleeping bags covering the Bedouins' wooden saddles, we were sore from the start.

Before setting off into the mountains, we stopped at a checkpoint run by the multinational peace keeping force, where swarms of military men came to photograph the camels. One man in a helicopter asked Iash for a photo on the camel; Iash insisted he would only let the man sit on the camel if he could sit on the helicopter. After several bits of form-filling and arrangements, we set

off into the mountains. We started up a *wadi*, and a man in military garb chased after us with a sabre-tipped gun. He argued with Iash, who finally gave him cigarettes, and let us go. I was happy to get away from the settlements and into the mountains.

The *wadi* ran through creviced rock, a stream of dust, empty except for an occasional scrub tree, or a group of black-clothed women huddled around the goats. The sun and the camels and the slowly swirling rock were hypnotising as we swayed up into the canyon. The camels showed their spite every so often, frothing and gurgling up a red sac that lolled out of their mouths like a bladder. Soon we didn't care if we never rode a camel again, and were glad to reach a camping place by a small water hole and sheltering rock.

We gathered twigs across a rocky bed, hardly enough in the canyon for a fire. Then we climbed some smooth pink rocks to gaze around us in the evening light. The stillness was complete, except for the noisy crunching of our shoes echoing off the canyon walls. It was so silent and barren we could almost hear the rocks growing.

For dinner, we sat on our saddle blankets (the ones we would sleep under later) and drank tea, then baked bread in the cinders and ate it with sardines. The Bedouins asked us to tell them stories of the world they would never travel. Linda described man-eating grizzly bears, and we compared the southwestern United States with their land. As it grew colder we crowded together and waited for the moon. "She comes", Psalam said, as the sky gradually dimmed. The moon tipped up from the rocks and Iash taught us some Arab words we didn't remember later.

The next day, we rode up the *wadi* to an oasis – a bunch of palm trees and shacks where Iash and Psalam's relatives lived. It seemed more relaxed than on the coast. We sat in a house made of burlap and thin wood, with a dirt floor and fire, drinking tea with the Bedouin women. Their kohl-rimmed eyes smiled at us above their black veils. They admired our jewellery, which we parted with for strings of beads. They smoked our Israeli cigarettes, puffing through the black gauze. A green-bonneted daughter laughed and brought us match covers and bits of plastic as gifts. The women didn't speak much English, but one ventured to ask us how old we were, and whether we were married or had any babies. When they learned we were in our twenties and had no husbands or family, they clucked in sympathy. Then one woman put kohl on our eyes, circling them with dark rims, to improve our luck.

> **"When they learned we were in our twenties and had no husbands or family, they clucked in sympathy. Then one woman put kohl on our eyes . . . to improve our luck"**

We rode to another *wadi*, where we encountered other travellers from the camp. We listened to an international radio station around the fire, passing spliffs around and talking in the firelight, which now and then flared into a blaze as the dried palm fronds burned. The Bedouin men went from fire to fire; the women never really met the visitors. The men spoke in easy Western slang, "sure, sure", while the women remained hidden and silent, although occasionally we would hear one of them screeching at the goats. It seemed like the men and women were from two different ages. We drank teacup after teacup. Always we must drink first if they will drink. Always they rinse the leaves with water and swish the rim with their thumb before another drink.

By the end of the trip, I was quite ready to get back. I had never been so saddlesore. On the last stretch, all I could think about was swimming, shitting, and cleaning the camel piss off my jacket. And then my camel started to run, and I lost all thought as I marvelled at the swiftness, the smoothness of this beast I had wanted to sit on to have my picture taken.

The camels slowed as we reached some fences and settlements. Iash sputtered with indignation at the fences. "Why do they say this land is theirs?" he said. "Are they crazy that they think they can put fences on the land and make it theirs?" The Bedouin men have adapted to the world as they have had to, whilst resisting anything that has kept them from living on and with the land. The Bedouin women, however, are allowed no such compromise; their lifestyle remains much the same as in ancient times.

TRAVEL NOTES

Languages Arabic. English is spoken in the tourist areas but it's useful at least to be able to read Arabic numerals.

Transport Buses and trains are cheap, but very crowded. Egyptian women would avoid sitting next to a strange man, which is how prostitutes solicit customers. All women, Egyptian and foreign, are subjected to being groped and pinched in the crush. You should make a fuss and enlist the help of women nearby. Efforts have been made to assign sleeper compartments on trains by sex (and complaints are honoured in case of mistakes). Second class cars are not segregated and women have been hassled on overnight journeys. Most Egyptian women travel second class during daylight. Taxis are readily available in the cities and main towns.

Accommodation There are hotels at all prices. In the high season (Oct–March) the expensive places tend to be fully booked, but finding a cheap room is rarely a problem. If you end up late at night booking into a hotel that makes you feel uneasy or unsafe, move on the next day – there are always plenty of alternatives.

Special Problems Harassment – particularly if you're on your own. Though many tourists do wander about in shorts and sleeveless T-shirts, this is considered both offensive and provocative. It's best to keep arms, legs and shoulders covered. It's a good idea to carry coins with you for *Baksheesh*.

Other Information Along the Mediterranean coastline there are both private and public beaches. On public beaches there are few foreign tourists and almost all Egyptian women swim in their clothes. Private beaches do not cost much and you'll feel far less self-conscious as you'll be amongst other women (both tourists and Egyptians) who will be wearing swimming gear.

Guides *Guide to Egypt* (Michael Haag) is well-informed and practical (if not always too helpful for the cheaper hotels). A *Rough Guide: Egypt* (Harrap Columbus) is forthcoming.

Contacts

Arab Women's Solidarity Association, 25 Murad St., Giza, Egypt, ☎Cairo 723976. Strongly supported by Nawal El Saadawi, **AWSA** is an international, non-governmental organisation aimed at "promoting and developing the social, cultural and educational status of Arab women".

Books

Nawal El Saadawi, *The Hidden Face of Eve* (Zed Books, 1980). Covering a wide range of topics – sexual aggression, female circumcision, prostitution, marriage, divorce and sexual relationships – Saadawi provides a personal and often disturbing account of what it's like to grow up as a woman in the Islamic world of the Middle East. Also recommended are Saadawi's novels, ***Woman at Point Zero*** (Zed Books, 1983), a powerful and moving story of a young Egyptian woman condemned to death for killing a pimp, and ***God Dies by the Nile*** (Zed Books, 1985), the story of the tyranny and corruption of a small town mayor in Egypt and the illiterate peasant woman who kills him.

Alifa Rifaat, *Distant View of a Minaret* (Heinemann, 1985). Well-known Egyptian writer in her fifties. She expresses her revolt against male domination and suggests solutions within the orthodox Koranic framework.

Nayra Atiya, *Khul-Khaal Five Egyptian Women Tell Their Stories* (Virago Press, 1988). A fascinating collection of oral histories, recorded over three years, which reveal the lives and aspirations of working-class women in contemporary Egypt.

Huda Sha'rawi, *Harem Years: The Memoirs of an Egyptian Feminist* (Virago, 1986). A unique document from the last generation of upper-class Egyptian women who spent their childhood and married life in the segregated world of the harem.

An excellent article on Egypt by Angela Davis can be found in ***Women: a World Report*** (see General Bibliography).

Thanks to Dana Denniston and Beverley Milton-Edwards for help with the introduction and Travel Notes.

Finland

· · · · · · · · · · · · · · ·

Despite the obvious attractions of a wilderness of lakes and forests, a stunningly modern capital city, and easy access to neighbouring USSR, Finland tends to be overlooked as just a little too remote, obscure and expensive for most ordinary travellers. For those who can afford it, however, the tranquility and architectural fascination of the towns and cities, and the sheer natural beauty of the countryside, hold an enduring appeal.

Finland is an easy country to visit alone or with other women. Besides the expense, your biggest problem will be coping with the isolation of travel; people will offer help if needed but for the most part leave you to yourself and, in the more remote countryside, you might well get a frosty and suspicious reception from older Finns. It is much easier to break down barriers of reserve in Helsinki, a cosmopolitan and progressive city with a lively alternative culture.

Since gaining independence from Russia at the beginning of this century, Finland has struggled to assert its neutrality (and revive its unique culture and traditions) against the competing claims of the USSR and Western Europe. Threats of annexation and foreign interference loomed over much of the post-war period and although these now, in the light of Gorbachev's reforms, seem far-fetched, the memory of a recent beleaguered period still rankles.

The younger generation tend to be open and confident about their country's security and future. Relations with the USSR are good and travel across the Soviet border for short trips to Leningrad is fairly routine. With alcohol heavily restricted, many Finns use the boat and rail crossings to go on drinking sprees; and for this reason it's a good idea to avoid late-night crossings (and also night ferries to Sweden). Daytime trips are considerably more sober and sedate.

Finland was the second country in the world (after New Zealand) in which women gained political rights and the current parliament has over 25 percent women representatives. Progressive equal opportunities legislation (backed up by good childcare facilities and maternity leave) has ensured that women retain a high profile in all aspects of public life. Younger women, especially, seem aware of, and confident of, their rights to equality. Sexual harassment and violence towards women are relatively rare (interestingly, in the case of prostitution it is the punters not the women who face prosecution under the law).

The contemporary **women's movement** is now fairly small and centred in Helsinki. Women who were active in the early Seventies tend to have moved into more mainstream politics or joined the various peace, environmental and anti-nuclear organisations and campaigns that have flourished in the post-Chernobyl age. There are a few autonomous lesbian organisations which also operate in the capital (attitudes tend to become more conservative as you move further away from Helsinki), the largest being a group called *Akanat*.

A Halcyon Summer

. . . .

Penny Windsor has worked as a teacher, youth worker, freelance writer and performance poet. She spent a month travelling with her partner around the south of Finland.

All journeys are, of course, personal journeys, but my journey to Finland last summer was a peculiarly emotional one. I was three months pregnant and, at the age of 41, with an eighteen year-old daughter, felt deeply uncertain about my future. My travelling companion had studied Finnish literature and history for many years and had shared his dreams with me of visiting the country. At the end of June, when we had earned enough money to pay the price of the air fare to Helsinki – measured out in potatoes picked in the fields of Pembrokeshire – we began our trip.

Without doubt it was the right country to visit at the time. We had weathered the many curious questions of friends and acquaintances, "Why Finland?", "Where is Finland", "Won't it be cold?", insisting Finland was indeed a European country of considerable interest and beauty and the summers were often warmer than our own.

In bald terms Finland is one of the Scandinavian countries, bordering Norway to the far north and having a long frontier with the USSR in the east. It has a population of about five million people, many of them living in the major cities of Helsinki, Tampere, Turku, Lahti and Oulu. Although a small proportion of the people speak Swedish as a first language and Swedish is the official second language, the overwhelming majority of people speak Finnish, a strange and unique language with affinities only to Hungarian (and a language making no distinction between "she" and "he" – the pronoun for both sexes being *hän*). English is widely spoken but my companion's efforts to speak Finnish at every opportunity were greeted with surprise and delight.

Other than these facts . . . Well, Finland is an independent, democratic republic, the first European country to give women the vote (in 1906), has an excellent record in human rights, and a long history of fighting for national independence from Sweden and from its giant neighbouring Russia. (Finnish history makes fascinating reading, a spellbinding account of a David surviving the onslaught of a Goliath.)

We arrived in Helsinki at midnight and put up our small mountaineering tent in Hesperia Park, in the middle of the city, next door to Finlandia House, the international conference centre. It was our first experience of the Finns' "laissez-faire" attitude to all except those who flagrantly break the laws. At no time during our three weeks in the country were we told *not* to do anything. Rules were kept to a minimum and the country seemed to run on the assumption that people would behave well if left to go quietly about their business.

For the rest of our time in Helsinki we camped between fir trees on the island of Seurasaari, a few miles from the city centre. The island is an open-air museum full of historic buildings from all over Finland – a fact we didn't realise until we saw the place in daylight. The red squirrels and even the hares that live there seemed unafraid of people.

From this secluded camping place we explored the city – the National Museum where grand scenes from the Finnish national folk epic, the *Kalevala*, were displayed; the monument to the famous and much-loved musician Sibelius, a vast organ of silver pipes; the island fortress of Soumenlinna, built originally by the Swedes to fight off the Russians; the markets on the harbour fronts; the Academic Bookshop in the main shopping street, which has the largest selection of titles in Europe.

Sometimes I explored the city with my companion, at other times alone. I was never hassled in any way, whether I was wandering about the city centre after dark, whiling away a sunny afternoon reading in the park, or sitting drinking coffee in the green-draped, elegant waiting room in Helsinki station. There were a few drunks, predominantly men, at Helsinki station and various inland stations, but I never felt under any sort of threat from them. Alcohol is expensive and only light lager is easily available, other drinks being sold at state-run stores, called *Alkos*, with mysterious opening hours. Drinking trips are often made to Sweden and across the border to Leningrad where alcohol is cheaper and more readily available.

"Sometimes it (Helsinki) can be too much like the perfect, suburban dream. Full of rosy, stable nuclear families"

Helsinki is a pleasant, restful uncity-city – an orderly place where things work well, people appear prosperous and healthy. Sometimes, perhaps, it can be too much like the perfect, suburban dream. Full of rosy, stable, nuclear families, it rocks along gently with its well-dressed people, nicely displayed museums, beautiful parks and buildings and lovely harbour views. If it lacks altogether that dynamic, volatile, wicked quality of many other capital cities, I can only say it was the perfect place for me last summer, a place where nothing I saw was ugly or violent or dirty, where I could wander freely by myself, thinking and writing.

Leaving Helsinki we travelled north to Hameenlinna, birthplace of Sibelius, then east through the cities of Lahti and Imatra to the province of Karelia, near the Russian border and in a wide loop back to Hameenlinna by way of the industrial cities of Varkhaus and Tampere. We travelled by a mixture of train, bus and hitchhiking.

By our standards all prices were high in Finland, particularly the food, but train travel is marginally cheaper than travelling by bus. As with all public places, trains are comfortable and clean and the waiting rooms provide toys which don't appear to get either vandalised or stolen. The toilets have baby-changing rooms and potties, in some cases in the men's as well as the women's sections. This last seemed to me a litmus test of equality – I was truly impressed.

Hitchhiking is difficult. We had a number of short lifts but had to wait long hours for them, even on the main road between towns. We came to the conclusion that this was in tune with the national Finnish character – they are, after all, a nation renowned for their reserve and insularity, wanting, it seems, little to do with an outside world which knows and cares little about them. They treasure the quality of *sisu* – youthfulness, independence of thought, "guts", embodied in the characters of the life-giving, daring Lemminkëinen and the dour, brave Kullervo, the adventurers in the *Kalevala*.

As far as national characteristics can be true, yes, the Finns did seem to be reserved people but, once approached, they proved almost overwhelmingly courteous and helpful. I hold warm memories of the family who gave us supper and breakfast and asked us to camp in their garden outside Lahti, when we stopped to ask the way; the man on the bicycle in Hameenlinna who went off to photocopy a street map of the town for us; the guard who scrupulously looked after our interests on our strange circular journey across the country when we had taken the wrong train.

"We sometimes breakfasted on mustard and onion sandwiches and windfall apples"

We did not use official campsites, preferring to put up our tent in the forest and by the side of lakes. However, the campsites we saw were, like everything else, well organised and clean.

Our biggest problem was money – basic items of food, even in large supermarkets, often cost double the price charged in Britain. Hence we sometimes breakfasted on mustard and onion sandwiches and windfall apples. On the other hand, nobody bothered us in the remote forests where we camped, unless you count the restless midnight mole in the glade above the Aulanko Lake and the early morning woodpecker. Bathing naked in the great quiet lakes of Aulanko Forest and Karelia we were similarly undisturbed. And the sunsets on the lake marshes as we watched the short summer turn to autumn at the end of August were brief, dramatic and perfect.

In those weeks I spent in Finland, I grew accustomed to the gentleness of the country, the mild intimacy of the wilderness forests and the sudden openness of the lakes. It was restful to be in a country which did not seem to deal in unnecessary rules, but where the streets were free of litter, where factories and houses were hidden by trees, lakes and rivers clear and full of plants and bird life.

For me, it was definitely the right country to visit that particular summer, but also the right country for any woman traveller who just wants to sit or wander, reflect and daydream, without comment or interference.

TRAVEL NOTES

Languages Finnish. Swedish is the official second language although many people also speak English.

Transport There are plenty of highly efficient and speedy options – both trains and planes are comparatively cheap (in Finnish terms). It's wise not to join the overnight ferries or train trips to Sweden or Leningrad which tend to be used as cheap boozers and. can develop an obnoxiously sexist atmosphere. Hitching is perfectly acceptable and (as much as it can ever be) quite safe, although you'll have to wait a while for lifts.

Accommodation Again the various options are expensive. Many women camp on their own. (See contact listings for the Women's Summer Camp.)

Special Problems None beyond the already mentioned problems of expense and men using boat and train trips for rowdy drinking sprees.

Other Information It's fairly common to find *Naistentanssit* dances organised specifically for women on their way home from the office, usually from 4pm. Women rather than men take their pick of partners. Some mainstream discos also arrange evenings for women (*Sekahaku*), where men and women choose partners freely.

Guide *The Rough Guide: Scandinavia* (Harrap Columbus) has a useful and concise section on Finland.

Contacts

The Women's Movement Union (or Naisasialitto Unioni), Bulevardi 11a, Helsinki, ☎90.64.3158. The oldest and largest of the women's organisations. It's worth dropping by to get information about the range of groups currently operating. The Unioni owns **Ida Salin's Summer Home** which houses the Open Women's University. As well as various consciousness-raising courses a Women's Summer Camp is held in the grounds once a year. There are plans to open a "book café" and reading room.

The Organisation for Sexual Equality (SETA), P.O. Box 55, 00531, Helsinki, ☎76.96.42 and 76.96.32. Has information about current lesbian groups and provisions.

Akanat, PL 55, 00551 Helsinki, ☎76.96.41. A lesbian collective that publishes a campaigning and listings magazine, **Torajvva**.

Books

We've been unable to track down any translations of books specifically by or about women. Of the others, **Christer Kilman, *The Downfall of Gerdt Bladh*** (P Owen, 1989) gives you a flavour of Helsinki life. It's about a businessman unable to come to terms with his wife's infidelity.

Thanks to Penny Mote and Helen Prescott for help with the Travel Notes.

France

By far the most visited country in Northern Europe, France draws more or less every kind of tourist and traveller. Yet despite the obvious appeal of its food, landscape and city life, it can be a hard place to get to know. An image of exclusive *chic* permeates the centre of Paris, the much glamourised Côte d'Azur and the Alpine ski resorts, and the country as a whole has a reputation for cliquishness. Without educational, business or social connections you may find it hard to slot in, no matter how good your French might be. Regional affiliations are very strong and local communities tend to be tightly knit. If you do manage to break down the barriers, however, the rich culture of France, the appreciation of the qualities of life and zest for politics may well have you hooked.

Travelling around is generally straightforward, although in Paris you can come up against a fairly low-key, but persistent harassment – usually running commentaries from men who overtly size you up as you walk past. It's irritating but probably no more prevalent or threatening than street harassment in London or New York. The main difficulties are where sexism merges with racism. French people, and particularly Parisians, will warn you against "les Arabes". If you come from an Arab or North African state, or look as if you do, you may have to contend with some pretty blatant discrimination. (Hotels are suddenly fully booked, etc.) The same applies if you're black (whatever your nationality), and you might find obstacles in gaining entry.

Besides the occasional, often poorly attended, demonstration there's little sign of a resurgence of the **women's movement** in France. The *MLF* (*Mouvement de Libération des Femmes*) which flourished throughout the Sixties and Seventies was declared by the national media to be dead and buried in 1982. Since then, feminist bookshops and cafés have been closing, feminist publications have reached their last issue, and International Women's Day has come and gone without noticeable commemoration. Women have, however, remained active, but in localised areas – running battered wives' hostels, rape crisis centres and organising within the Communist and Socialist Parties, the Trade Unions, or within the wider anti-racism movement.

Yvette Roudy and Hugeuette Bouchardeau, France's two most prominent feminist politicians, have continued to highlight women's issues but with the fluctuating popularity of the Socialists and little outside support, this has proved a determinedly uphill struggle. Although they were able to initiate legislation on equal pay, a motion to change the law against degrading, discriminatory or violent images of women in the media was thrown out of the Assembly. The constant barrage of exploitative images in advertising remains one of the more disturbing aspects of a first-time visit to the country.

Afloat in Paris

. . . .

Louise Hume spent a year studying in Paris. She returned shortly after and, unable to get a job, stretched out her savings by living for nine months on an abandoned barge on the Seine. She is currently back in Paris working as a guide for a British tour company.

My ambition to find out what lay behind the more obvious clichés of Paris began on day one of my first ever school trip. It was a dire holiday with the city lying flat and lifeless outside a steamy school coach window, squashed by endless lists of historical dates and the exploits of Louis-whoever-he-was. But on the final night the school coach accidently tootled into the middle of a spectacular car chase on the Champs-Elysées where a band of criminals were trying to make off with the contents of a jeweller's shop. I decided the place could be worth getting to know after all.

I next returned under the safe and secure umbrella of studentdom, with a grant cheque, accommodation and a relatively respected identity. Equipped in this way it was all too easy to slip into the role of a spectator, "ooohing and aaahing" at the city in full intoxicating action but hardly experiencing it from within. It was only after I'd lived there for a while as an unemployed foreigner, with next to no money, that I started to break through the glitzy veneer of the place.

I had been lured back to Paris by an old friend with promises of a place to stay and a never-ending succession of occasional work should I need it. I arrived to find that he had left his flat to live on a very bare and very cold barge that he had found abandoned on the Seine – a great and exciting idea if occasionally marred by the pungent reek of boat oil and the wild pitching and tossing whenever a tourist *bateau mouche* swanned past.

The first few days were taken up with furnishing the boat, using discarded bits and pieces Parisians seem to routinely fling on to their streets. After that I set about finding a job. The most obvious place to look is at the *Centre d'Information et de Documentation de Jeunesse* next to the

Eiffel Tower on the Quai Branly where scores of jobs for mainly young people are displayed on huge noticeboards. It took a while for me to realise just how many of the crowd that gathered around the notices were chasing the same jobs as myself and, after a week of scrambling in and out of a grimy trapdoor that seemed designed to rip off buttons and tear skirts, I was becoming less and less able to compete. I eventually gave up, deciding that for the time being at least I would accept the label "unemployable".

Parisians are considered a cold, unfriendly lot by the rest of France as well as foreign visitors. This I found nowhere so obvious as by their blatant discrimination by appearance. The conventions of neatness, tidiness and feminine prettiness are rigidly upheld. It seems if you can't or don't wish to conform to the high-heeled, well groomed, perfumed and decorated image, then you must expect to meet the sharp end of snubbery and snobbery.

"'Why do you want to go there?', he asked, 'It stinks, it's dirty, It's full of Arabs.'"

In the mornings when I loped along to the local *boulangerie* for bread, the hoards of workpeople dashing to their offices, crisp, white raincoats swishing behind, would often eye me with distaste. If one of them accidentally bumped into me the usual reaction would be to look me up and down, decide I wasn't worth the effort of an "excusez-moi" and stride forcefully on. I was after all living in the richest square kilometre in Paris, where the glut of elegance and glamour could intimidate women and men many times smarter than myself and where the wonderful-smelling restaurants made my bread-and-nothing lunch seem pitifully unappetising.

Of course Paris isn't so restrictively wealthy everywhere. I used to buy vegetables from the comparatively cheap greengrocer shops around the Belleville and Barbès Rochechouart metro stations in the northeast. Both areas are inhabited mainly by new immigrants and, wandering down the narrow sloping streets into the alleyways, you find tiny cafés selling Tunisian sweets – all the more tempting when lit by neon strips – and Arabic music chanting from wide open windows strung with washing. These parts of the city tend to be neglected and cold-shouldered by other Parisians, and trenchant suspicion is shown towards people of Maghrebian origin and expressed in racist graffiti. Once, on one of my vegetable trips, an oldish man, assuming I was a stray tourist, advised me against going further. "Why do you want to go there?" he asked, "It stinks, it's dirty, it's full of Arabs, you'll be pickpocketed." Belleville can seem an intimidating place to wander alone at night, but this is mainly because it is so quiet.

Food is expensive in Paris and prices vary drastically from one shop to another. At the beginning I could still afford to eat in the many student cafeterias (*Restau-U's*) where they don't insist on student identity, although looking the part is an advantage. The countless plates of lentils, ice cream and as much bread as I could sneak kept hunger out of my head even if it didn't supply much in the way of vitamins.

Being vegan and vegetarian is a problem – reasonably priced food co-operatives seemed to exist only as rumours or unfindable addresses on scraps of paper and requests for something without meat were treated with wide-eyed misunderstanding by ordinary shopkeepers or café attendants. Worst of all was when they would look at me and say "Oh, you young girls, always concerned about your figures!". Compassionate eating hasn't made much headway in the tightly guarded bastion of French gastronomy.

In general terms I found that having an entertainment budget of nil helped to emancipate me from the celebrated equation of money equals entertainment equals fun. Some of the sights and monuments are free to the public on certain days, such as Sunday at the Louvre and Sunday morning at the Beaubourg Modern Art Gallery and there were always those spontaneous moments of silence and stillness that form such a memorable part of Parisian life – like sitting on the steps of the white dome of the Sacré Coeur watching the invariably pink evening sky settle the dirt and dust on the rooftops below, or the intensity of the incense-filled darkness inside Notre Dame.

I gradually stopped wistfully eyeing the entrances to cinemas, jazz clubs and lively bars and settled down to more thoughtful activities, sitting on the roof of the barge, wrapped in blankets talking and laughing with the odd passer-by.

"There's a special kind of creep which seems to thrive in Paris which the French call a drageur"

The adventure of our floating home ended when reality produced an owner demanding rent. Even though I had failed to get a job I felt I had at least absorbed Paris. It seemed to me now like a succession of country villages spiralling out from the centre all living on top of each other. I was once told, by a woman I happened to share a bench with, that it was a "woman's city". She was an architect and a staunch believer that the small, curvy streets and light-coloured, soft-edged buildings which lined them, plus the general lack of intimidating high-rise skyscrapers were conducive to female well-being. "It's just the whole irrationality of it all," she enthused, pointing into a direction where the few narrow streets were promising to lurk into obscurity. I knew what she meant and yet it made it all the more disheartening that almost every woman I met swopped tales with me of being threatened and insulted when wandering about this city.

There's a special kind of creep which seems to thrive in Paris which the French call a *drageur*; he smiles, greets, and follows you, pays you the most banal and condescending compliments and then launches into a speech about "love at first sight". Usually *drageurs* concentrate on the most obvious tourist, cashing in on the "nothing-can-happen-to-me-I'm-on-holiday" mood. It could be on any street, regardless of the business, the area, the time of day. If you sit, so much the better, you're no longer a moving target. I have found myself instinctively on the defensive, which I consider an unhealthy state of mind, but unless you are obviously unavailable, say, hanging off a man's arm, it's necessary.

For a long time I would wander around alone at all hours of the day or night, even in the far northern districts which other women had warned me against (it gets more risky the further you are away from the centre). I foolishly believed that my confident stride and air of being able to look after myself would psychologically deter any potential hassler. I was made to think again after an incident in the metro station when an old man, obviously very drunk, began to insult me, push me around and then tried to throw me against a wall. It happened quickly and the train came just in time. I did learn, however, that you can't rely on passers-by to help you – there were five people all watching open-mouthed.

"As in London you're assailed on the streets by advertising images portraying women as glamorous, usable, disposable and weak"

I also learnt that the metro is at its most dangerous, not around midnight when the theatres and restaurants are emptying, but between nine and eleven at night. At these times most people have already got to where they are going and the stations are left to people on the look-out for trouble. Once on the platform you should hang around the exit rather than straying to the deserted ends as one does in vacant moments of waiting.

As in London you're assailed on the streets by advertising images portraying women as glamorous, usable, disposable and weak. Somehow these seemed more offensive and degrading – I think mainly because they seem to come and go without anyone trying to deface or subvert them. I was surprised by how few of the women I met considered these images a problem. When I expressed my own indignation I was accused of showing an unwelcome intolerance amidst another country's culture.

All of which served to bolster a general feeling that there is less feminist sensitivity in Paris. I learnt to attribute this to the intellectualisation and inaccessibility of the feminist movement. It's the same story for the low-profile ecology and peace movements; in fact anything "alternative" seems to live in books and journals rather than as a grass-roots organisation. It was disappointing to find only one haven of female solidarity, although a good one, at *La Maison des Femmes*, Cité Prost. There was always a friendly atmosphere, someone to talk to in English, and feminist publications from all over Europe. On Friday night there is a café run by *MIEL*, the lesbian group and the

Maison puts out a fortnightly magazine "*Paris Féministe*" which contains information on feminist actions all over France as well as the other groups that currently meet there, such as a women against racism and a Maghrebian women's group. There are also noticeboards advertising self-defence courses, holidays and accommodation. Women from all over the world seem to drop by while staying in Paris.

Although I finally had to shrug my shoulders and admit that as I could no longer support myself I would have to leave Paris; within a year I was back.

This time I came with suitcases, strategies, and a series of carefully worded job requests to install in shop windows. Domestic work, cleaning homes in the affluent western suburbs, more than paid my way until, by a combination of timing and great good luck, I landed a job as a guide with a British tour company. At last I can communicate my enthusiasm for this city to over 250 willing ears per week. Paris seems almost a different place from the occupied-and-earning perspective. I'm still here, well-nourished, smartly clothed and securely housed between four wonderfully solid walls.

But even now, as I take a coachload of tourists over the Concorde Bridge, and point them towards the river where my old barge still bobs up and down, I can't resist my private bit of irony; ". . . and here are the houseboats where many people still, in fact, live!"

TRAVEL NOTES

Languages French. Basque and Breton, as well as regional dialects, are still spoken but losing way. Perhaps more important today are immigrant/migrant languages – Maghrebi Arabic, Portuguese, etc. English is spoken reasonably widely but you'll find it frustrating to depend on.

Transport The French rail network is the best in Europe – efficient and extensive; bus services play a relatively minor role. Cycling is big and you can rent bikes from most train stations and in all towns of any size. Few French women would consider hitching, although reports are that it's no more/less safe than Britain. If you have to hitch it's best to make use of *Allostop*, an organisation for drivers and hitchers to register for shared journeys.

Accommodation Plentiful, though if your money is tight you'll need to depend on the numerous Youth Hostels and campsites. There are also a few women's holiday camps (see listings below).

Guides *The Rough Guide: France* (Harrap Columbus) gives a refreshing alternative perspective while also covering all the traditional tourist interests. *Gaia's Guide* (Gaia's Guide, UK) has a good, up-to-date, listings section for lesbian and feminist venues throughout France.

Contacts

French **women's centres**, particularly in Paris, continue in a state of flux. The following are reasonably established and should be able to provide full and up-to-date contacts for other French cities.

Paris

Maison des Femmes, 8 cité Prost, 11e, ☎93.48.24.91. The capital's best-known feminist centre. They publish a fortnightly bulletin, *Paris Féministe*, run a cinema club and radio station, *Les Nanas Radioteuses* (101.6Mhz; Wed 6pm-midnight), and provide a meeting place for most Paris groups including *MIEL*, a lesbian organisation group which runs the centre's café – *L'Hydromel*.

Feminist Bookshops, all of which stock the French **feminist calendar/guide** and *Lesbia*, a monthly lesbian listings and events magazine

can be found at: **Librairie des Femmes,** 74 rue de Seine, 6, ☎43.29.50.75; **Librairie Pluriel** 58 rue de la Roquette, ☎47.00.13.06; **Marguerite Durand Library**, 21 Place du Pantheon, 75005, ☎43.78.88.30.

Lesbian/feminist bars: **La Champmesle** 4 rue Chabanais, ☎42.96.85.20; 6pm-2am; a popular bar, the front is mixed, the back is women-only: **Katmandou** 21 rue de Vieux Colombier, ☎45.48.12.96; 11pm-dawn; best-known and most up-market of the lesbian nightclubs, with Afro-Latino and international atmosphere.

Restaurant and Coffee Shops: **Le Mansouria**, 11 rue Faidherbe and **Central**, 3 rue Ste. Croix de la Bretonnerie, ☎274.71.52, are both owned and run by women.

Elsewhere

MARSEILLE: **Maison des Femmes**, 95 rue Benoit Malon, 5. Again a meeting place for all groups, with people around on Tuesday and Thursday 6-10.30 pm. **La Douce Amère**, a lesbian campaigning group, can be contacted at the bar *La Boulangerie Gay*, 48 rue de Bruys; There's also a feminist bookshop, **La Librairie des Femmes**, on rue Pavillion.

NICE: **Le Papier Maché**, 3 rue Benoit Bunico. Co-op bookshop, restaurant and arts centre – a friendly leftist haven and meeting place for feminist, ecology and radical groups.

Holidays

Women's/lesbian holiday houses and campsites. Write first for a prospectus to: **Barriare, Les Essades** (holiday camp), 16210 Chalais, ☎045.98.62.37;

R.V.D. Plasse (holiday camp), Les Grezes, St. Aubin des Nabirat, 24250 Domme, ☎053.28.50.28.

Chez Jacqueline Boudillet (guesthouse), Langerau à cere la Ronde, 37460 Montresor, ☎16.47.94.34.63.

Saouis (guesthouse with camping), Cravenceres, 32110 Nogaro, ☎0033.62.08.56.06.

Women's Holiday Centre (Pyrenees holidays), c/o Jean Ginoux Déu Bas, 09 Artigat, Arigée.

Books

Simone de Beauvoir, *The Second Sex* (1949), ***The Woman Destroyed*** (1967). Both published by Flamingo in translation. One of the founders of French feminism – and existentialism, **Judith Okeley's** *Simone de Beauvoir* (Virago, 1986) provides an illuminating revaluation of her life and work.

Claire Duchen, *Feminism in France* (RKP, 1986). Chronicles the evolution of the women's movement in France from its emergence in 1968 to the present. Highly recommended.

Marguerite Duras, *The Lover* (Flamingo, 1985). Autobiographical novel by influential avant-garde writer.

Marguerite Yourcenar, *Coup de Grace* (1957, Corgi, 1983). The first woman to be elected to the Académie Française, Marguerite Yourcenar's novels show an incredible breadth of scholarship and experience.

Eveline Mahyère, *I Will Not Serve* (1958; Virago, 1988). Powerful lesbian fiction set in Paris in the 1950s.

Shari Benstock, *Women of the Left Bank: Paris 1900–1940* (Virago, 1987). Somewhat dry and academic but full of information about women's contribution to the expatriate literary scene and the founding of literary modernism.

Elaine Marks, *New French Feminism* (Harvester, 1981). A part of the continuing debate that divides French feminists – Beauvoir describes Elaine Marks' book as "totally distorted".

Look out for **cartoons by Claire Brétècher and Catherine Rihoit.**

Thanks to Kate Baillie who provided information used in the introduction.

West Germany

At the time of publication, elections are due in both Germanies. Their result, it seems almost inevitably, will be reunification of the states that have existed, since the last war, split between Eastern and Western orbits. Clearly, very great changes lie ahead for the East (the GDR), as its economy and orientation becomes integrated into the European Community and Western free market system. Many Germans in the West (the Federal Republic, or FDR), however, are equally apprehensive as their nation, Europe's wealthiest, absorbs the crisis-ridden and formerly Communist-run territories.

Such an agenda reduces all previous West German politics to a bizarrely minor role. Yet the Federal Republic's post-war years, in which rapid industrialisation and rampant consumerism have characterised its "miracle" economic recovery, have not been without challenge or dissent. Indeed, in terms of political attitudes, the Republic was – in itself – the most divided European nation. Feminist, environmental, civil liberty, and various other left and radical groups, forged over the last two decades, form a full and organised political stratum, continually at odds with the state. They draw support from an extensive city network of housing and workers co-operatives, alternative schools, cafés and bookshops and a flourishing free press – and also from an increasing section of conventional German society, concerned about ecological problems like the acid rain that is destroying the Black Forest. It was from this social fabric that the Green Party was forged and became in 1983 the first ecology party to gain seats in a European national parliament.

More recently, there have been worrying political trends on the right, with the emergence and subsequent election successes of the neo-Nazi Republikaner party. They have capitalised on the already entrenched racism shown towards the country's large migrant worker population, particularly towards Turks. The problems likely to be created by a future absorption of the East German economy are likely only to inflame the situation.

As far as the realities of travel go, if you're Turkish, or look as if you might be, you may well experience some degree of hassle. For any other visitors, sexual harassment is uncommon and money is usually the biggest problem. To take advantage of conventional attractions – and Germany has superb galleries, music festivals and scenery – you'll need to be prepared to spend. On the plus side, there is a well developed network of women's cafés, holiday houses and lift agencies that you can tap into, and some cities run free bus or taxi services for women travelling at night.

The current wave of **feminism** derives from the recent history of alternative politics. Feminist publications (*Courage* and *Emma* are the most widely distributed) proliferated during the 1970s and remain. So too do women's centres, bookshops, and groups, including a large number of lesbian collectives. Many of these, however, are part of an established local scene and are not necessarily open to casual travellers. Activist campaigns – such as organising against pornography and violence against women, "Reclaim the night" demonstrations, etc – continue, but tend to be incorporated in "wider issue" demonstrations led by *Bügerinitiativen* (Citizens' initiatives) or ecology groups. Women have retained a high profile in the Green Party, and not only through Petra Kelly, their best known international spokeswoman. Both the Green Party and Social Democrats operate a quota system to ensure that women are represented on both a local and national level.

Staying on in Hamburg

· · · · · · · · · ·

Jane Basden left Australia after finishing university to travel to southeast Asia, China, Russia and Europe. She ended her five-month journey in West Germany where she lived and worked for eighteen months. She has since returned a number of times in her work as a freelance radio journalist.

My decision to go to Germany was partly due to geography – that's where the Trans-Siberian took me; partly due to economics. I'd run out of money, desperately needed work and it happened to be my first EC port of call. But most importantly it was due to an inexplicable feeling that I ought to understand this country and the people who lived there.

Having said that, I had no real expectation of what Germany would actually be like. There were images of *lederhosen* and Bavarian landscapes, gleaned from uninspired high school language classes. And there were images of Baader-Meinhof news reports, and the ubiquitous American war films. But none of them prepared me for the reality which was at once very normal, very familiar, and yet totally unlike what I'd grown up with in urban Australia.

I arrived in Hamburg on a warm, drizzly summer evening, with very little money, less German, and totally without guidebooks or acquaintances of any kind. It's not the way I'd suggest arriving, although there is something to be said for having to talk to, and depend on, local people for information and directions.

Unlike many other countries I'd travelled in, where contact with local women was limited if not almost impossible, West Germany was an utter relief. When I needed directions on the street I could always find a woman who, hearing my appalling attempts at German, would switch the conversation to English and tell me what I needed to know. (Later experience showed me that many, though undoubtedly fewer, would just as quickly swap to French or Spanish.) A few times these footpath contacts resulted in phone numbers being given, café invitations and, in one case, tips about where to find work. All these offers were genuine, and over the following months I began to realise there was something very German about that.

Hamburg was the first place I'd had time to stop and really observe people since leaving Asia. I felt starved of contact with women, and especially with feminist and lesbian women. One of my first joys was walking through the city squares taking in the sheer numbers of women, walking arm in arm, having animated if incomprehensible conversations, sitting around tables in outdoor cafés . . . women who simply looked like the kind of strong, independent women I knew at home.

I began to sense a feeling of tolerance or at least awareness amongst younger Germans (by that I mean people born after the War). It was a difficult thing to put my finger on, and I wasn't sure whether the few people I'd met were representative, but I kept the thought at the back of my mind for future reference.

"German women, if I can generalise, have a certain outward independence about them"

The other thing I very soon noticed was that, as a single white woman walking alone around Hamburg, I didn't feel openly harassed by men. In eighteen months there, I can recall only a few minor incidents. Sexism certainly exists, but it seemed to me that the men I met were more subtle and more anxious to please than their brethren in Australia or England. Nevertheless, for women travelling alone, the absence of overt harassment can often make the difference between a lousy time and an interesting, enjoyable one.

Also, German women, if I can generalise, have a certain outward independence about them. They tend to stand up for themselves and their rights, at least in public. West Germany has a very active women's movement, and if nothing else, "liberated women" are now accepted there. I suppose the point is, if you're a woman travelling alone in West Germany, you won't stick out like a sore thumb from the bulk of women who live there.

And on the question of tolerance: most young people in Hamburg – and I met a wide cross-section eventually, through teaching English – seem to be very tolerant on the question of sexuality; are in favour of the rights of refugees and migrants to live and work in their country as equals; do not seem racist or anti-semitic in any way; and are not prudish or titillated by topless or nude sunbathing. I added this last slightly odd measure of tolerance because, on my "tolerance gauge" of "would this happen in the same situation in Australia?", the ability to sunbathe naked and unharassed with a girlfriend on the banks of Hamburg's many small lakes broke the record.

I wouldn't, however, suggest doing this in Bavaria, nor in fact anywhere outside the more liberal big cities, Hamburg and Berlin being the most notable. My rather limited experience of the south of Germany gave me the distinct impression that, whilst people there were friendly and in some ways less "ordered" than in the north, they were definitely less tolerant of non-white foreigners, people of "dubious" sexual, political or moral persuasions, and so on.

Making the decision to actually live in Germany as opposed to travelling through wasn't easy. On top of all the personal feelings of doubt, insecurity and isolation that typifies culture shock, my decision to stay meant that I had to deal with the immense German bureaucracy. Applying for a residency permit; registering with the area housing office; the foreign police and the tax office . . . there seemed an office for everything, with a language, and a formality, unto itself. As with any government department, the way I was treated depended largely on the personal whim of the official who dealt with me.

In the end, dealing with this red tape wasn't really as bad as I'd anticipated, and in fact, because I had an EC passport, I quite easily became eligible for social security assistance, housing benefit and so on. The hardest part was finding out about these possibilities in the first place. It's definitely worth a trip to an *"Auslanderberatungstelle"* (foreigners advice centre) if you're unsure of your rights.

Having said all of that, living in Hamburg was a mixture of a huge range of experiences, some pleasant, some inspiring, difficult, or even disturbing. In retrospect, it all seemed extremely worthwhile.

As a feminist there were constant opportunities to become involved in active political projects and take part in cultural, craft, academic or manual trade courses, workshops and discussions. There are women's bookshops (*Frauenbuchladen*), holiday houses, cafes, education centres, pubs, advice and support centres all over Germany.

A good place to begin in the search for any or all of these are the bookshops, or backs of the women's, lesbians' and alternative diaries.

"Lesbian households will usually make it clear on the notice"

If you've got the time, inclination and money, the women's education centres and country holiday houses are well worth a visit. Most of the large cities have women's education centres which run courses throughout the year in everything from plumbing and car maintenance, to theoretical analyses of the future of feminism to African music and dance. Many of the country houses like *Osteresch* and *Anraff* run intensive weekend and week-long residential courses along the same lines. The courses aren't all that cheap, though they're usually run on a sliding scale according to means, and the residential ones include all meals and accommodation. When I got sick of the cement and noise of the city, it was good to know that there were places I could escape to.

These courses are a good way of making friends, a difficult thing in any strange city, and also finding out more about what's going on both within and outside the women's movement. Köln, for example, holds a women's film festival every year around October; Hamburg has a *Frauenwoche* (Women's week) each year in February/March; Berlin has a *Lesbenwoche* (Lesbian week) in September/October. There are lots more, so try to find out about them.

The women's bookshops and education centres are also handy for "rooms vacant" notices – for women's, lesbians' or mixed "WGs" (*Wohngemeinschaften* – literally "living communities", or group houses). Other good places to look are university noticeboards, alternative cafés, and the back pages of the left-wing daily *"Die Tageszeitung"* (commonly called *"Die Taz"*). Housing shortages have become quite severe in West Germany in the last couple of years, especially in the big cities like Berlin, Hamburg and Munich, forcing up prices and competition for vacant apartments. Unless you've got lots of money and glowing references about your financial means, you'll probably be better off trying to find a vacant room in an already established household.

If you're looking specifically for a lesbian household, it's worth remembering that *"Frauen WG"* (women's household) usually means that the women are not lesbian, and probably have boyfriends and other male guests staying over. Lesbian households will usually make it clear on the notice. If you're in any doubt, just ask. Even comparatively straight German women don't seem shocked by such questions.

Despite being white, middle-class and speaking English (the language of the tourists opens a lot of doors to work), the pay and conditions in the first two jobs I found were incredibly grim. They were kitchen jobs where migrant workers who, like myself, couldn't speak German were treated as deaf, dumb or stupid and given the dirtiest, heaviest work. Trade unions are fairly inactive in these areas, and workers' rights seem to be explained only in the longest words and the finest print. In one job I was really shocked to find I'd been working an hour per day extra for over three months, and no one had bothered to tell me. The manager and most of the other workers, as it turned out, had known all along . . . and I was one of the privileged workers who could get a legal job with a written contract!

Very little money meant very little choice about which neighbourhood I could live in. But, in my experience, warnings not to live in "the rougher quarters" of the big cities – Kreuzberg in Berlin, Altona or St Pauli in Hamburg – are a bit exaggerated. I lived in and near St Pauli for eighteen months. Despite being Hamburg's notorious red light district, supposedly teeming with pimps, dealers and racketeers, I never felt directly threatened. I was maddened by the whole industry of prostitution and pornography, and often sorely tempted to lob a few bricks through windows, but it seemed to me like you were either involved in it all or not, and the different communities simply moved around each other and rarely met.

Besides, these areas also have the highest concentration of alternative political, social and cultural projects, cafés and so on, with quite a strong feeling of community.

Because cafés, bars and clubs tend to stay open to the smallish hours in West German cities, I found that my waking hours started and finished later than normal. It wasn't unusual to go out for dinner at 10 or 11pm, or to go for a coffee at 1am. So the issue of transport was pretty important.

"For longer journeys elsewhere in Germany, I usually hitched"

German cities are quite compact, and often it's only a matter of a few blocks' walk to a whole night's entertainment. Generally speaking, I felt safer walking around after dark in Hamburg than almost anywhere else I've been, even quite late at night, and especially in the inner city suburbs. That's mainly because the streets were always busy. Walking with a friend, female or male, was usually enough to feel totally comfortable. For slightly longer journeys, or if you feel a bit nervous after dark, bicycles are an excellent means of transport, and one that is completely catered for in all areas of Germany. There are cycle ways on all main roads around Hamburg, and you'll save a packet on the relatively expensive though efficient public transport.

For longer journeys elsewhere in Germany, I usually hitched, though if I wanted to get somewhere by a definite time I often tried the *Mitfahrzentralen*, (lift centres). Most major cities have at least one just for women – drivers and passengers – and the staff can usually cope with English and French. You just ring up and ask if they've got someone going your way and the day/time you want. There's a small fee (roughly half the equivalent train fare), part of which goes to the centre and part pays for your share of the petrol. It's a good compromise between hitching and public transport.

If you do decide to hitch, it's best to start at the Rest Stations on the *Autobahns*, or, in Berlin, at the border crossings on the *Autobahn*.

My rule of thumb was always to trust my gut feeling, err on the side of caution, and never get in with two or more men if alone. Long-distance truck drivers were good because they were usually intent on getting to their destination as fast as they could, to make as much money as they could, which left little time to chat up women passengers. Mostly they were just bored out of their brains and welcomed the company. Some were surprisingly helpful and friendly, even arranging the next stage of a lift with fellow drivers.

I had a couple of minor irritating lifts with private drivers, but never one where I felt in any danger. It was much easier and more pleasant, and a much more accepted mode of transport, than in other countries where I've hitched. Despite that, it's not unknown for hitchers to be attacked, in fact, there's a rather unnerving sign at the hitching point out of Berlin which warns you of the dangers and, to add impact, displays the number of people killed whilst hitching for each of the last few years. So, if you're travelling alone and feel uneasy about hitching, don't do it.

Politically speaking, West Germany is a very intense country, and has been for centuries. There's a very entrenched conservative and wealthy stratum, a great many liberal "free thinkers", and a lot of politically radical

groups on the left, far greater in numbers, support and activity than anything similar in, say, Britain or Australia. The effect of this is a serious and long-running struggle for political power – whether parliamentary or not – with huge and sometimes violent demonstrations on the one hand, and stringent, all encompassing police surveillance and muscle flexing on the other (and all manner of things in the middle).

"I found out later that at least a couple of women suspected me of being a police plant"

I had my first taste of this in week one. I met a few women at the women's pub, and after talking to them all evening, one of them suggested I could stay in her flatmate's room for a couple of days while I looked for a room of my own. As I was otherwise doomed to the youth hostel, I eagerly accepted, and said, by way of a "Thank you", that I'd make breakfast in the morning and she could sit down and tell me all about the women's scene in Hamburg. With that, one of the other women at the table stood up, made some obviously scathing comment to my temporary host, and left. "A lovers' tiff?", I thought.

Unfortunately, nothing so easy. I found out later that at least a couple of women now suspected me of being a "police plant" who was going to dig up names and addresses of all the active feminists in Hamburg. At the time I thought this was just a bad case of paranoia, but I soon learnt of instances where exactly that had happened, with an apparent friend, even an apparent lover, suddenly turning out to be a member of the secret service and leaving behind her a string of arrests, questionings, house searches, and the knowledge that files somewhere were being fattened for the kill.

Whether you're politically active or interested or not, even the most inane situations force you to deal with the political realities of West Germany. Proving you're not a police spy is about as easy as convincing the inquisition that you're not a witch, though the result isn't quite as bad. Events in West Germany in the last couple of years, especially raids against over thirty women active in the areas of genetic engineering and population control, have made feminists more wary of police surveillance, and therefore more suspicious of strangers.

Don't go to Germany expecting the warm welcome of sisterhood . . . you may not get it, at least, not straight away.

TRAVEL NOTES

Language German. English is taught in most schools and widely spoken.

Transport Hitching, there are around fifty agencies which arrange lifts – specific agencies for women are *Frauen-Mitfahrzentrale*, in Berlin (Potsdamerstrasse 139), Hamburg (Rappstrasse 4) and Munich (Baidestrasse 8). Ask at the local women's café (*Frauencafé*) for information on free transport at night.

Accommodation Besides hotels, Youth Hostels and campsites there's a fair number of women's holiday houses, some of which offer a range of feminist workshops and courses. (See Contacts listings).

Guides *The Rough Guide: West Germany* (Harrap Columbus) is useful; *Gaia's Guide* (Gaia's Guide, UK) has a wealth of listings.

Contacts

The **Frauen Adressbuch** (Courage, Berlin) lists all women's centres, cafés, bars, bookshops, etc; there are also more detailed *Frauenstadtbuchs* for Berlin, Dusseldorf and Munich. Below is a small selection.

BERLIN: **Infothek für Frauen** (Women's Information Desk), Goldrausch e.V., Potsdamer Strasse. 139, 1000 Berlin 30, ☎215.75.54. Provides tourist information for women.

Die Begine, Potsdamer Strasse 139, 1000 Berlin 30. ☎215.43.25. Women's multicultural centre, with café, theatre, cinema and bar.

BONN: **Nora-Frauenbuchladen** (Feminist bookshop and information centre), Wolfstr. 30, 5300 Bonn 1, ☎65.47.67.

Frauenmuseum (Women's Museum), Im Krausfeld 10, ☎69.13.44.

HAMBURG: **Von Heute An** (Feminist bookshop and café), Bismarckstr. 98, ☎420. 47. 48.

MUNICH: **Lillemor's Frauenbuchladen** (Feminist bookshop and information centre) Arcisstrasse 57, ☎272.12.05.

Frauen Kultürhaus (Women's cultural centre, gallery and café), Richard Strauss-Strasse 21 ☎470.52.12.

Women-only holidays,

Frauenreisen, c/o Gabi Bernhard, Kaiserdamm 6, 1000 Berlin 19, run skiing, hiking, historic trips with the intention of promoting contact between European women.

There is also a network of **holiday houses** with courses and cultural activities. For prospectuses write to: **Frauenbildungsstatte Anraff-Edertal**, Königsbergerstrasse 6, 3593 Anraff-Edertal, ☎0.56.21.3218.

Frauenlandhaus Charlottenberg, Holzappelerstrasse 3, 5409 Charlottenberg, ☎0.64.39. 75.31.

Frauenferienhauser Hasenfleet, Hasenfleet 4, 2171 Oberndorf, ☎04.772.206.

Frauenbildungsstatte Osteresch, Zum Osteresch 1, 4447 Hopsten-Schale, ☎0.54.57.1513.

Frauenbildungszentrum Zulpich, Pralat-Franken-Strasse 13, 5352 Zulpich-Lovenich, ☎0.22.52.6577.

Frauenfrienhaus Tiefenbach, Hammer 22, 8491 Tiefenbach, ☎0.96.73.499.

Books

Petra Kelly, *Fighting for Hope* (Chatto, 1984). Petra Kelly was unhappy about the editing of this, touted as her "personal manifesto". Inspiring ideas nonetheless and good background on the Greens.

Gisela Elsner, *Offside* (Virago, 1985). Revealing portrait of women's life in middle-class Germany.

Paul Frolich, *Rosa Luxembourg* (1939; Pluto, 1983). Original, revolutionary thinker at forefront of working-class struggle and Communist Party of Germany founder. Definitive biography by revolutionary contemporary.

Günther Wallraff, *Lowest of the Low* (Methuen, 1987). An inside view of the cynical (and criminal) exploitation of Turkish migrant workers by one of Germany's most controversial journalists. A political bombshell when released in Germany in the mid-Eighties.

From **East Germany**

Five novels by **Christa Wolf** have been published in England by Virago. A committed socialist, described as East Germany's most formidable woman of letters; her books examine the post-war conditions of Germany as well as evoking life under the Nazis.

Thanks to Dörte Haarhaus for help with the introduction.

Ghana

For many years travellers steered clear of Ghana, deterred by its reputation as one of the most economically distressed countries in the region. Its wealth and resources, amassed during a period of remarkable growth in the Fifties and Sixties, had all but collapsed, leaving an economy floundering in massive foreign debt, political conflict, corruption and famine. Slowly, under the revolutionary council of Flight-Lieutenant Jerry Rawlings things have started to improve. The worst of the poverty has eased, food is again readily available, and although there are few tourists, Ghana is beginning to feature again as part of a West African tour.

Getting around Ghana can be arduous – roads are poor and accommodation limited – but there's a good bus network, and, compared with many nearby countries, it is a relaxed and easy place to travel alone. Ghanaians are renowned for their incredible warmth and openness, and even in the predominantly Muslim area in the north, where travellers are very rare, you're unlikely to face more than a few curious comments. In terms of dress it's worth remembering that, outside of the main towns and the Christian areas along the coast, legs are more taboo than breasts and should be covered. In general, however, the atmosphere is tolerant and very few local customs are imposed on travellers.

Traditionally, **women** have been active in Ghana's economy as subsistence farmers and market traders. The market women's associations continue to wield considerable power over local trade and transport and, under the new regime of the People's National Defence Council (*PNDC*), a small minority of educated women are gaining greater access to the professions and to government posts. It is still, however, a strongly male dominated society with the burdens of child rearing and heavy domestic work falling squarely on women's shoulders. Polygamy is common (usually involving a wife and several "girlfriends"), with women often being left to provide for large families. Even within the semi-matriarchal Ashanti region, where inheritance passes from a man to his sister's son, the secondary status of women holds firm. Mrs Rawlings, who is head of the women's section of the *PNDC*, has toured the country to form local branches. There are also a number of women's development groups geared towards healthcare and helping to set up income-generating projects.

A "Foreign Expert"
. . . .

Naomi Roberts, an English woman in her forties, spent eight months working as a volunteer in a Ghanaian village.

Only a few parts of West Africa have opened up to tourists – little strips of beach backed by new hotels – and even here the slightly adventurous traveller has only to walk past the barbed wire inland for a few hundred yards to discover a very different continent. If you want to you can stick to a life on the fringes – or you can try, with some difficulty, to penetrate the less glamorous and more struggling daily life.

I lived for eight months in a village in the coastal forested region, about 120 miles from Accra. I had been brought out by a British volunteer agency to assist in setting up primary healthcare programmes. I stayed only eight months because I became uncomfortable in my role as "foreign expert". The undue respect I received seemed to be based on little more than my being English and therefore seemed demeaning to the people who gave it. My job had been worked out between the British agency and a Ghanaian central government department and no one locally had been properly consulted. No effort had been made to see if a Ghanaian could have done my job.

> *"The job . . . gave me an entry into a shared way of life that will forever make our boxed British existence seem thin"*

However, putting these deep objections to the work aside, my time in Ghana was full of interest. I lived with people who were unused to tourists and entirely generous and accepting. They welcomed me into their homes so uncritically that even in such a short time I felt I had gained a new family.

The job, although not working out, gave me an entry into a shared way of life that will forever make our boxed British existence seem thin.

My stay began with a few weeks training, after which I was taken out to the district where I was to work. A truck had been laid on, and loaded up with a bed, a table and two chairs, a few buckets and saucepans, a kerosene stove and lamp and a water filter, as well as my suitcases from England. The journey, although only 25 miles, took about six hours. The truck came at dusk and we drove out into the bush as night fell, over roads which were almost continuous pot holes with vast puddles shining in the moonlight. The towering forest trees and the thick, jungly growth beneath them lined both sides of the road. Occasionally we passed through small villages, crowded and tumbledown, their only signs of life a scattering of roadside stalls, lit by small points of light from oil-lamps. There were dogs tearing along the roadside in the light from our head-lamps and strange birds which crouched on the road waiting to streak off, striped plumage flashing, into the forest darkness.

We arrived in the village at about one in the morning and drove off the road up to a large, low house with its door locked and wooden shutters closed. After pounding on the shutters around the back, the door was pulled back with a great scrape. There was a young woman, a man and a small child, smiling but shy, holding back except to help with carrying my belongings. I didn't know yet just how extraordinary it must have seemed to them, so much stuff arriving with just one person.

I had come to live in a compound house of the chief of the village. It was five miles away from the small district capital where I was to work but no one had been able to find a room for me there. One of my future Ghanaian colleagues, Tony, had found me the room. He lived in the house, too, and

that first night he helped me place my things in my room, hiding them as far from view as he could and warning me to keep my shutters closed at all times. He was a city dweller and convinced that all my belongings would be stolen by these ignorant villagers. When I later stopped following his advice, nothing was ever taken from my room.

Next morning the household was awake well before 6am; banging, chopping, sweeping, talking. As soon as I emerged from my room there were many, many introductions, as half the village had come to see the new arrival. Everyone shook hands and, as I had learned a very few phrases in the local language – "How are you?", "I am well – how about you?" – there was a great deal of laughter.

"It was clear that I could become an honorary man in this household"

The Chief was referred to as Nana (the name for all chiefs) and was about 65 years old, very tall and erect. He looked benign and wise. I felt that he was pleased and proud that I had come to his house, although very shy and embarrassed too. Through an interpreter he welcomed me and told me that the women would do everything for me that I needed doing – cooking, washing, sweeping. I could go to work and then relax in the evenings with him. It was clear that I could become an honorary man in this household. The other men in the house were Nana's younger brother, called Teacher, because that was what he was, and another lodger – an unattached man whose wife, I later learned, had left him and who was visited by his little daughter who lived elsewhere in the village.

There were many more women. The Chief had four wives, although only two lived in the compound. His senior wife lived in the next village, looking after her ageing mother. The next lived in the compound and so did the youngest wife, who was in her early twenties. Teacher's wife, Beatrice, who was herself also a teacher, became my closest friend. There were three single women relatives and about ten children. Round the back of the compound lived several teenage boys and young men. They did not have much to do with the rest of us.

Over the next few days I began to learn about the first basic, practical problems of everyday life: how to light a kerosene stove and lamp, how to wash myself in a bucket of water, how to get to the wash house at night carrying my bucket, lamp, soap and towel, how to wash my clothes and how to cook. But whatever I did, someone immediately came to help, took over, carried my bucket or washed my clothes for me. I had very mixed feelings about this. I did not want the people I lived with to think that I took them for granted and thought of them as servants, and I really wanted to learn how to do things for myself. Nevertheless I was so slow and clumsy at these tasks, making all sorts of mistakes and having accidents like scalding my hands all over with boiling water when I tried to sterilise my water filter. The young children were much more efficient at so many things: at stripping the skin off plantains and at washing clothes and even sweeping the floor.

I shopped in the local market and bought the same ingredients as the Ghanaians that I lived with: mainly vegetables and dried and smoked fish. But I used to cook them the way I would at home – omelettes when I could get eggs, and stews with large lumps of vegetables and fish, ten times as much fish as any Ghanaian would get to eat. The results were looked on with horror and only a few brave people wanted to try some of my mixtures. Nana was sure that my food would make me ill and urged me again and again to let his wives look after me.

Proper Ghanaian food took hours to prepare. At about 3pm every day the women started to prepare the vegetables for the evening meal: mainly plantains and cassava. After boiling in big pans on wood fires, the vegetables were smashed and mixed together in a large wooden bowl, the children taking turns to pound with a long heavy pole. A steady thud of regular pounding was a late-afternoon sound wherever you went in Ghana. The sticky mixture produced was called *fufu*, and had a texture like uncooked bread dough. This would be eaten in bits torn off by hand and dipped into a very peppery soup made of ground vegetables and fish.

"I attempted nearly everything at least once, including great land snails, though I did baulk at a roasted bat"

The women and children ate together while the largest portions would be taken to the men, who ate alone. I used to prepare my English-style meals over my own kerosene stove and take them over to eat, sitting with the women. We would try bits and pieces from each others' plates. I attempted nearly everything at least once, including great land snails, though I did baulk at a roasted bat. The fruit, however, was wonderful – oranges, avocados, paw-paws, pineapples, mangoes and bananas so good that I haven't been able to enjoy the hard, bright yellow ones in English shops since.

On weekdays I went to work in the "office", sometimes biking there, sometimes catching the passenger lorry or *tro-tro*. Some days of the week all the family went to their farm, which was a good hour's walk out into the forest. They came home at the end of the day laden with plantain, yam, fruit and firewood. On one of my first days off I went with them. At the end of a hot and exhausting walk all I could do was sit on the ground and watch them work: which, at that time of the year (November), involved cutting down the plantain and cassava crops. Women and children worked together and carried the great loads on their heads. Men also went to the farm to work and, on our farm, were involved in tapping palm wine and distilling it in a little dark shed in the forest. But men never carried anything back home. It seems that once a man is old enough to have a wife it is considered improper for him to be seen carrying anything on his head. I had offered to carry a basket of oranges but was defeated by the head carrying; the basket slithered every way on my head and my neck started to ache after a very short while. A little seven-year-old girl took the basket from me, put it on her head and jauntily walked ahead all the way home.

When we were not working, we relaxed together; mainly just sitting and chatting. I loved to be outdoors day and night. My room, despite my attempts to decorate it with a batik tablecloth and postcards and photos of my family stuck to my wall, seemed dark and enclosed. In the evenings we would sit in the courtyard of the compound, an outdoor "drawing room", brilliantly lit on nights with a full moon. Luckily there were few mosquitoes where I lived. Nana would be visited by a stream of people coming up from the village, often consulting him on business or about disputes that he would be asked to settle. They would talk in a little group on one side of the courtyard and drink the palm wine brought home from the farm. The women and the children and I would sit in another group. I could only understand little bits of the language and to learn more I would write down words and phrases in an exercise book. Although my language skills improved, I remained dependent on those people who were able to speak English to me.

"In the evenings Beatrice and I would talk together, sometimes about her life, sometimes about mine"

Beatrice and I soon became friends. At first she must have felt a dutiful concern for me and took responsibility for showing me how to do things and for seeing that I was not lonely, for saying goodnight to me and for enquiring how I felt each morning. If I went for a walk, she would find out and send her nine-year-old son, Kofi, to accompany me.

In the evenings Beatrice and I would talk together, sometimes about her life, sometimes about mine. She asked me questions: what did it feel like to be cold, how did we carry our babies, were there tall mountains in England, which were the biggest towns, what did we export, what did we import? Some of these facts, the sort that must have been in the geography textbooks of her schooldays, really interested her. After a while we talked more intimately. I told her about my frustrations at work and if I was feeling homesick and she gradually and very discreetly began to tell me about Teacher and his other wife, an older woman who lived with her aged mother in the village. I had begun to notice that Teacher was often away at supper time and later on in the evening. On those evenings Beatrice was much more ready to come and talk to me.

Her reaction to the whole affair was mixed in just the same way as an English wife's might be, although she said in a rather defiant sort of way "I don't mind as I don't want to bear any more children". She had five already. As Teacher left the house in the evening, Beatrice would call out "ochina" ("till tomorrow"), embarrassing him by her openness. If I called out "ochina", too, Beatrice and I would laugh together, aware of causing discomfort. When Teacher did spend an evening at home, though, Beatrice was very keen to be with him, leaving me to read my airmail *Guardian Weekly*.

I had other companions, though I could talk less easily to them. Kofi would come into my room to see me in the evenings. He would draw pictures with my coloured crayons and especially liked me to set him rows of sums to do. Nana had a sister who told me that she was adopting me as a daughter. She used to come and sit in my room, smiling at me and holding my hand. She was an old lady whose children had all left the village and who lived with just one grandchild, a little boy of about six. He would be sent up to see me with presents – some mangoes or some beans that she had cooked.

Being in my middle forties, I did not naturally become part of the village courting and coupling activities which took place in the main street after dark. Many of Nana's friends told me that they wanted to marry me and there were lots of jokes with Nana telling them that they would have to apply to him as he was my father now. I did have a more serious suitor, who used to come and talk to me in the evenings and made it very clear that he wanted me to come with him to his room. I did once, but I didn't want to again and he put no pressure on me.

Generally I think women travelling are relatively safe with men in Ghana. I felt no danger from harassment wandering about in the village or in towns day or night. Obviously one should be careful about physical relationships, as aware of the problems of AIDS as you would be in England or America.

Over the months that I lived in the village the family became more and more aware of my frustrations at work and my homesickness. In the spring my plans to return began to shape and

there was genuine sadness – plus, I felt, a bewilderment that I was such a free agent, that I alone decided whether I came or went. Didn't my boss in Accra have to give me permission to go home?

"I questioned the luxury we have as Westerners to pop in and out of other people's lives"

On my last evening we had a party. Earlier in the week I had brought five live chickens and lots of vegetables and that day the women prepared a vast quantity of chicken stew. Even so, Nana had invited so many important men from the village that my friends in the compound stood at the edge of the crush and never got any party food. There was dancing and I tried to get Kofi to dance with me. Like many boys at an age just before growing into manly confidence he hated to show off. He looked on and seemed lost in sadness. That night he just came and slept in my room. After I had left next morning with goodbyes all round the village and was driven off towards Accra, I questioned the luxury we have as Westerners to pop in and out of other people's lives.

If you do manage to stay for a while in a village, there are basic courtesies to observe. Take presents; it is unlikely that anyone will let you pay any rent. Once in a village you must, first and foremost, pay a call on the Chief. He may be able to find you somewhere to stay or will introduce you to the "Queen Mother", the head of women's affairs in every village. If my experience is anything to go by you will be treated with great kindness and generosity as well as being a source of excitement and curiosity. Both sides can give a lot to the other, so much more than when a tourist sticks to a hotel by the beach, getting impatient because of the time it takes to bring the beer.

This Lady, She Takes Time

. . . .

Helen Scadding has been living in Tamale in the north of Ghana for the last year and a half. Her job, running in-service courses for teachers of the Ghana Education Service, involves a fair amount of travelling, usually by motorbike, around the northern region.

If your first impressions of Ghana are – as mine were – of the airport and the capital, Accra, you're likely to be a little unnerved. Both are frenetic places, with people insistently competing for your custom: taxi-drivers, hawkers and porters, and once in Accra, dozens of hawkers for stalls, markets and street food (*chop*). None of this is typical of Ghana, as you quickly realise once you're out in the villages of the countryside.

I came to Ghana in 1987 to work in the northern region, and currently spend much of my time travelling around different districts, running train-ing courses for teachers. During my stay here I have met with a hospitality and warmth that are hard to credit. English is widely spoken and Ghanaians tend to be eager to meet and discuss issues with strangers. The few travellers I've come across, couples and single men and women, were almost all visiting the country as part of a general West Africa trip. They viewed Ghana as a pleasant respite from the tourist traps of Togo, Mali and the Ivory Coast and the more difficult trav-elling conditions of Sierra Leone and Burkina Faso.

Travelling in Ghana, I have person-ally felt safer than in any other country (including my own). A single woman, although likely to arouse curiosity and the odd proposal of marriage, will be welcomed, entertained, cared for and protected (especially, I'm afraid to say,

if you are white). It is wise however, as anywhere, to avoid walking aimlessly around in the capital at night, especially near the beach.

Ghanaian women are independent and powerful and many of them are challenging and achieving high status positions in "a man's world". Nevertheless there are very rigidly imposed male and female roles which, even in the strongly matriarchal Ashanti region, are upheld. White women are generally viewed as "differ-ent". The men and women that I meet tend to expect and accept that my ideas about relationships and my experiences of life and work will be different to theirs. From my discussions with black female colleagues who visit Ghana, they may feel more pressurised to conform to the image of the ideal Ghanaian woman: a good wife and mother.

> *"A single woman, although likely to arouse curiosity and the odd propo-sal of marriage, will be welcomed, entertained, cared for and protected"*

However, travelling in Ghana is still quite a challenge. Outside of Accra there are few hotels (although you will find government rest houses), hesitant electricity and water supplies, and some terrible roads. Food, however, is plentiful, healthy and tasty, if a little monotonous. There are also constant improvements and changes in all the infrastructures as Ghana tries to claw her way into the "developed" world. Dehydration and malaria need to be carefully avoided – so come prepared.

My impressions of travelling in Ghana all revolve around one factor – the mode of transport used. At first this was by bus, for the long journey from Accra to Tamale in the north. As with all bus journeys you begin the long, frustrating wait at dawn. It's quite possi-ble that the bus will eventually leave in the early afternoon, after a panic-stricken rush to get aboard (it may even be cancelled altogether). You quickly learn that "take time", "in God we trust", and "no condition is permanent" are well deserved Ghanaian mottoes. Usually you will get where you want to go but there's no way of estimating when. A relatively simple journey of three or four hours can turn into a nightmare of dust, punctures, breakdowns and hours of waiting by the roadside. You learn to save yourself a lot of nervous energy by expecting to be a day late and by always carrying something to read. Still, the dust, sweat and jarring of the bus bumping along the road can take all your concentration. It's nice when you arrive.

One memorable journey from Tamale to Nalerigu started, as usual, after a few hours' wait. As the bus finally swerved into the lorry park men literally leapt for the two open doors, clinging on and fighting other hopeful travellers struggling to reserve one of the few seats. I managed to squeeze on to the edge of a seat, already carrying two others. In front of me, a friend did likewise only to suddenly find his lap, and the others on the seat, occupied by a large woman. Crying out grumpily at everyone in the bus and the bread sellers outside to witness her plight, she continued a jocular tirade against everyone for twenty minutes. Finally my friend moved and she edged her way on to the seat, only to give way seconds later to her friend who had been waiting in the wings.

At last we got going, stopping at every village to let off market women. At each stop the bus became surrounded by small children selling bread, yams, doughnuts, fish and oranges, always amid the clamour of "Ice-water! Ice-water!" At the outskirts of Diare the bus stopped. A large tree trunk lay across the road and on each side there were crowds of men, women and children carrying large sticks, hoes, cutlasses, knives and guns. Men walked up and down the bus, banging on the side and shouting at the driver. Eventually we

were allowed through and discovered that the villagers were searching for their chief, who was now banned from the village. All vehicles were being stopped and searched. It took us seven hours to reach our destination, only a hundred miles from Tamale. But not all journeys are so eventful.

Later I bought a motorbike and started using it for most of my travel – both locally and exploring the country. The bike provided a mixture of exhilaration, exhaustion and risk. I once got a puncture on a very isolated road and had to push the bike at noon, with a high sun and no water. I was lucky. It was little more than a mile before I came to a village, where the children rushed to greet me and help haul the bike to the local vulcaniser (puncture-menders). The expertise of mechanics in Ghana is an inspiration in improvisation. Even the most tattered inner tube, sealed over and over again, can be repaired by melting small pieces of rubber over the tube. Bicycles are welded together, plastic bits sewn up, huge tractor tyres held fast with nuts and bolts, anything that will keep the wheels moving. After over 12,000 miles and eleven punctures I have learnt to respect village bike-menders in a way I would never trust my local mechanic at home.

"Returning, I hit a large bush fire, the smoke visible in the sky several miles away, with orange flames burning ominously across the track. There seemed nothing else to do but accelerate . . . and pray"

The most interesting journey I made was to a small village called Kubori in an area known as "Overseas". This was during the wet season when the many tributaries of the Volta flood, making the roads impassable. Arriving at the river I drove down a steep bank and waited for a fisherman to bring his dugout to the shore. We then lugged the bike onto it and paddled cautiously across the muddy water sitting very still. You try not to think about the "what ifs" when doing this. Once over, I rode along thin ribbons of dust, curtained on either side by six-foot-high bush grass. Not being able to see where you are going, collecting grass in your helmet, shoes, gloves and spokes and knowing you could be lost forever, can be a little unnerving. At every small village I breathed a sigh of relief and greeted the elders who pointed me in the direction of the next thin track. Returning, I hit a large bush fire, the smoke visible in the sky several miles away, with orange flames burning ominously across the track. There seemed nothing else to do but accelerate brazenly through and pray.

Basically, "getting there" is what it all seems to be about. A bucket of water and a plate of T.2 (millet flour and water) can seem like a feast. Arriving with dusk in small towns or villages, stopping at a street stall to drink sweet milo or tea and eat a hunk of bread and egg, while listening to the drumming and high-life music from a tinny tape recorder, is a real pleasure after hours on a dusty road. This is nightlife in Ghana. There is little to do but feel the night breeze, avoid the mosquitoes, wander among the street stalls with their flickering hurricane lamps, read, or, if your luck is in, drink a warm beer in a small bar.

These dry, never changing savannah roads of the north are worlds apart from the cooling sea breeze and easy tarred road of the southern coastal route. Heading out from Accra to Winneba, Cape Coast and Elmina, you meet the beginnings of the confusions and contradictions of Ghana. The coastal towns are very beautiful, with palm-lined beaches and lively fishing ports, but they all carry reminders of the past savagery of the slave trade. Every major town is dominated by a castle or fort built by the British, Dutch, Danish, or Portuguese slavers. "Touring" Elmina Castle with Ghanaians and reading the mixture of tolerance, sadness and bitterness of people's comments in the visitors' book was one of the most poignant experiences I have had in Ghana. Some of this southern route has been developed for tourism with one or two well-known motels and beach villa complexes, but mostly these are used by wealthy Ghanaian business families on a visit to the coast, or development and expatriate workers on holiday.

My memories of Ghana will be mainly of the people who so kindly welcomed me into their homes; of the many hundreds of conversations struck up on buses, in queues and in bars; and of the strength and humour of the women I have met. I will probably even remember those long, red, dusty roads with affection. The biggest compliment I have received in Ghana came from a fellow teacher, "This lady, well, she takes time."

TRAVEL NOTES

Languages English is widely spoken, especially in the towns. Twi, the language of the Ashanti region, is also used in the south, whilst in the north there are many different languages – Dagbani, Mampruli and Wala, to name but three.

Transport State-run buses operate between the major towns. In the towns there are small buses (*moto-way*) and minibuses (*tro-tro*) but these, like the wooden trucks (*mammywagons*), are massively overcrowded.

Accommodation There are a few hotels in Accra and in all the state capitals, otherwise you are dependent on fairly basic, but quite safe, guesthouses. It's very likely that you'll be invited to stay at someone's house – be conscientious about the expense this imposes on your hosts, by taking gifts and paying for food and entertainment.

Special Problems Take any health provisions (contraceptives, tampons, etc) you may need – little is available.

Guide The Rough Guide: West Africa (Harrap Columbus) has a good section on Ghana.

Contacts

Ghana Assembly of Women, PO Box 459, Accra. Contact Evelyn Amartejio or Mildred Kwatchney.

Federation of Ghanaian Women, PO Box 6236, Accra.

African Women's Association for Science & Technological Development, Pecorudos, PO Box 6828, Accra. Promotes self-help projects and is active in education, healthcare and environmental projects.

Books

Ama Ata Aidou, *Our Sister Killjoy* (Longman, 1988). Noted Ghanaian playwright explores the thoughts and experiences of a Ghanaian girl on a voyage of self-discovery in Europe.

Kurei Armah Ayi, *The Beautiful Ones are Not Yet Born* (Heinemann, 1988). Realistic portrayal of a man's struggle against endemic corruption.

Asiedu Yirenkyi, *Kivuli and other Plays* (Heinemann, 1980). One of Ghana's best-known playwrights. *Kivuli* is about the break-up of a family strained by inter-generational conflict.

Greece

• • • • • • • • • • • • • • • • • • •

Literally millions of independent travellers go to Greece, attracted by the easy-going Mediterranean culture, the islands, legendary ancient sites and relatively low costs. The country seems to get into people's blood, and many return year after year, exploring a different circuit of islands, perhaps, or – increasingly popular – walking in the mountainous countryside of Epirus, in the north. Foreign women also have a strong work presence in Greece, most often as teachers in one of the hundreds of language schools. If you want to spend a year in the country, and to learn Greek, this is by far the most promising possibility.

Travelling about the country is pretty straightforward, with good transport (by bus and ferry) and a pleasingly low-key network of campsites, rooms and hotels. Harassment – from Greek men picking on "easy" tourists – can dampen experiences, though it's more on the persistent, nuisance level than anything more threatening. Even in Athens you rarely feel unsafe. A bigger problem perhaps is the low public presence of women. Off the tourist track, in the villages, you'll find the local *kafenion* (café) is often the only place to get a drink – and that it's completely male territory. As a foreign woman your presence will be politely tolerated, but, travelling alone, you won't always feel comfortable. The major concern for most travellers, though, lies in escaping your fellow tourists. Greece has seen some of the Mediterranean's most rapid development over the last decade and places that one year had character and charm are too often covered in concrete villas the next.

Socially, Greece remains a distinctly conservative country, though one of the few conspicuous achievements of the socialist government (which held power for the best part of the decade until disintegrating in a sea of scandal in

1989) has been a theoretical advance in **women's equality**. The *Women's Union of Greece*, closely identified with the *PASOK* government party, helped to push through legislative reforms on family law – dowry was prohibited, civil marriage recognised, and equal status and shared property rights stipulated. The reforms may have had limited impact in the rural areas, but they at least exist. Another positive, if small-scale, achievement of the socialists was the setting up of Women's Co-operatives in rural communities; these provide loans for women to run guesthouses, and an opportunity for visitors to experience local village life.

In addition to the *Women's Union*, whose influence is uncertain now that the socialists are out of power, several autonomous feminist groups are active in widening public debate around such issues as sexuality, violence and the representation of women by the media.

A Lasting Idyll
. . . .

Janet Zoro has long held a passion for Greece. Sparked off by an initial visit in the late Sixties, she now makes a habit of returning twice a year, travelling alone to wherever she can get the cheapest last-minute flight.

I fell in love with Greece on my first trip, twenty years ago. I was a student then, surprisingly politically naive at a time when others were sitting down in Grosvenor Square. The Colonels were in power and I should not have gone, but I did and I discovered an almost instant affinity for the place. The affair continued intermittently but it was in 1986, when I made my first solo trip, that the flame rekindled. Now I go in spring and autumn, usually for two weeks, but for longer if I can get a flight.

What is it about Greece? The country is so full of clichés: the perfect blue harbour, the white-cubed houses climbing the harbour slopes, the sunsets and moonrises, smell of oregano and grilling fish, cool, shaded waterside bars, white beaches and brilliant glass-green water; but the clichés work every time. Whenever I arrive and cross the burning tarmac of the island runway, fight through the tin customs shed and head off to yet another idyllic fishing village, my heart beats faster and my spirits lift; I feel as if I am coming home. Familiarity breeds a warm and ever deepening affection.

I am not attracted by the archaeology. I go to Greece to swim and walk and paint and recharge my batteries. I do not want discos or bars or water-skis or umbrella-covered beaches. I want my own vision of Greece: a perfect place to travel alone; no one bothers me if I do not wish to be bothered.

I can sit for hours in solitude over a drink, writing postcards, watching the harbour lights, listening to other tourists talk, or I can strike up conversation with the waiter or a fellow diner. The odd occasions for evasive action inevitably arise: the elderly gentleman from the tailors-cum-shipping agency who presses dinner invitations; the bored boy soldier who ignores my protestations that I am old enough to be his mother; the sailor on the little inter-island steamer who cannot understand that I should choose to be alone, but I would never call it harassment. I find I can accept lifts, drinks or compliments from Greek men and when I smilingly say "no" they shrug and smile and buy me a drink anyway. I never feel worried or lonely.

The Greeks generally welcome foreigners and, though an obvious curiosity as a lone traveller, I feel easily accepted. I have picked up enough words to gather the gist of basic questions and in signs and single words explain that my husband is in England, I am travelling alone, I like to paint and walk, and I have no children. Sitting in the shade of some village square, the old men express amazement while the women offer congratulations. Greek women are slaves to their boy children who, as far as I can see, are allowed to do anything they like as soon as they are mobile enough to elude the maternal embrace.

I wish I knew more Greek. I want to talk to them, the women who run shops from dawn until late, let rooms upstairs, hang out hand-washed sheets each day and still have time to water and weed their miraculous polychrome jam-packed gardens; the women who call to me from balconies as I sit and paint in some un-tourist-frequented hill village, who speak no English at all, but smile and admire my picture and give me apples; the old women who let white cool shuttered rooms with makeshift plumbing and give me coffee and figs for breakfast.

In the Dodecanese, some people speak Italian (compulsory in schools during the Italian occupation), and anywhere in Greece you'll often find men who have picked up a bit of English on their travels as merchant seamen.

Others have Australian connections. In Ithaca a very old woman hailed me as I wandered into a village: "G'day, are you looking for the beach?", and so on. It turned out she had left Australia when she was twelve, but reckoned

she'd kept a bit of the accent! In Limnos I was sitting in a tiny bar-cum-shop, slaking my thirst with cold beer, when a woman came in to fetch one of the men for Sunday lunch. Glimpsing me on my perch behind a sack of onions, she immediately burst into delighted conversation; home from Australia, she was going to lunch with her cousin and invited me to join them for tea. The cousin was about to make her first trip out to visit a son she hadn't seen for twenty years and, over sweet Greek coffee and even sweeter honey pastries, my help was enlisted to try and teach her a few words of English. I struggled home hours later, laden down with bags of grapes and peaches.

"There is a new kind of young Greek woman . . . Here, in her tourist empire, the daughter is in charge"

Now that tourism is big money and English taught in all schools, the family pattern is changing. There is a new kind of young Greek woman. Increasingly in small villages I find the local restaurant tends to be run by the daughter of perhaps nineteen or twenty. She speaks good English and/or German, takes the orders, does a lot of the cooking and will talk to the customers about anything: life, politics, tourists, Greece.

She is the pet of her regulars, the English, German and Australian captains of sailing holiday yachts who bring their passengers to eat there throughout the summer. They hug her; she hugs them. They joke and laugh throughout dinner. If she has a husband, he probably builds apartments over the winter, helps in the restaurant during the tourist season or catches fish for her to cook. He may add up the bills. There may be a baby who toddles round the café, harnessed on a long string, tying tables, chairs and tourists into knots. And all the while, in the background, are the parents who, with little grasp of English, cook, carry and watch.

Here, in her tourist empire, the daughter is in charge. At the same time, her education is limited and she has little chance of breaking away. Nor can she escape Greek mores. She can laugh and joke with foreigners, but spend half an hour alone with a village boy whom she has known since birth and there would be hell to pay. No doubt this too will change. Ten years ago these bright, tough girls were with their mothers at the kitchen sink. Learning languages has given them a kind of freedom which in itself has become an economic necessity.

The actual physical business of getting around in Greece is part of the pleasure. Best of all are the boats. They are a sort of game. First, you go to one of the shipping offices which cluster round the harbour. Often these deal with only one line, so you ask for some island and they shake their heads: "Ah no, not there. Try the office next door!" Then there is the timetable; no office will ever admit to its fallibility, though I soon found out that a bit of a gale might well delay a boat for as much as one or two days. However, if you have asked around you will have found a man in the grocery shop who *knows*. He is in actual telephonic communication with the next island and knows that the ferry is running six hours late. Thus the man who sells you the ticket will say 3am, absolutely definitely; the man in the shop will say 9.30am. It makes a difference.

Although it takes a while to get the hang of ferries, the effort is rewarded by the sheer joy of racing through that dark blue sea beneath a cloudless sky, watching for the shadowy shapes of islands in the distance and sometimes, if you are very lucky, seeing a school of dolphins racing and jumping alongside in the creamy wake. Boats are good for sunbathing. They can also be useful for exchanging travellers' information: you'll nearly always meet island-

hoppers with news of elsewhere, or someone to team up with in the search for the perfect place to stay.

"I walk miles in totally unsuitable shoes ... And I take lifts if someone stops, as they generally do."

I love to walk in Greece. There is something about the dry, blue, herb-scented heat that invigorates me. I walk miles in totally unsuitable shoes, armed with my paints and my swimsuit and a beer in case I don't reach a village. And I take lifts if someone stops, as they generally do. Usually, even if I am not thumbing, passing vehicles – anything from German tourists in Mercedes to those rickety three-wheeled trucks full of potatoes – will stop and offer a ride. Again, I've never encountered any problems. Because there are relatively few vehicles in country areas it is the natural thing to do, as it used to be in rural parts of England. I even take lifts at night.

I think what I love about being in Greece is that it is closer to how I feel life should be. I should be able to sit on a balcony overlooking the sea for my early morning coffee and late night brandy; I should be able to go out for a whole day leaving my door unlocked and knowing that nothing unpleasant will happen. The sky should always be blue and the sea transparent.

Greece for its people, though, is not heaven. The Greeks work very hard, particularly the women. Where there are a lot of tourists, the country's character is being sadly eroded by English-style pubs, bars and big hotels. But it is extraordinary how slow this erosion is and I am somehow confident that the Greeks will weather the onslaught of mass tourism: they are intrinsically so much themselves.

I have of course considered living there, but I really think Greece is a hard place for a foreign woman to settle in. I have come across quite a few women who have gone out and simply stayed on; they have a wonderful time, picking up work and drinking with the men in the bars. I met a German girl who stayed just one winter and said she would never do it again, as once the tourists had gone there was really no place for her in society. She could neither drink with the men, nor sit and crochet and talk babies with the women. And the few women I have encountered who have married Greeks don't seem very content, having little choice but to fit into their husbands' life-style, the extended family, the cooking, sewing, gardening, washing and having babies way of life that Greek women lead. As far as I am concerned my spring and autumn visits are perfect.

A Part of My Life
· · · · · · · · · · · ·

Mary Castelborg-Koulma is half-Greek and visited Greece on and off as a child and later as a student. She went for a longer stay in 1974 – and remained for the next thirteen years.

I first went to live in Greece in 1974, the year the dictatorship fell. After a year of teaching in England, I'd had more than enough – and I had always promised myself a long stay in my mother's country.

Although I was brought up in England, I had gained at least a part knowledge of Greek culture, from trips as a child with my family, and later as a student. I was also reasonably at home with the language, which confers an immediate and vast advantage on any visitor. However, I had no idea that I would end up living in the country for the next decade and a bit – nor that it would become so much a part of me, my growth and development.

Like most graduates in Greece, I began life in Athens, working in one of the innumerable language schools, or *frontisteria*, that provide jobs, if not much money, for anyone with a degree and enthusiasm. My school was sited in one of the suburbs, a fact I was thankful for in the light of the city's ever-worsening pollution.

Living in this quarter also provided me with an escape route to the sea and the surrounding countryside, and made me feel I had made a wise decision in bringing over my British registration car (an old banger even then), despite endless hassles with the customs. I would never have been able to buy a car in Greece, where prices are about double those in Britain. Driving in Greece was at first a bit nerve-racking, though the necessary survival tactics didn't take too long to acquire.

The mid-Seventies and early Eighties were a good time to be in Greece, as the country basked in the revival of democracy after the oppressive years of the Colonels' dictatorship. When in 1981 the PanHellenic Socialist Party (PASOK) won the elections, the country seemed full of optimism and hope. These years also saw an incredible surge in tourism, which changed from small-scale to mass status in under a decade. Both factors coloured my experience.

On my trips out of Athens, I found myself growing more discriminating about where I chose to visit, listening to the advice of Greek friends in Athens about rural areas as yet unaffected by the tourist boom. Such advice was offered frequently and generously. An incredible proportion of the capital's population are recent emigrants from the countryside. Almost everyone has their "home village", with which they continue to identify, even if they visit just once a year for Easter or the local festival.

Some of my strongest memories are of trips I made in the winter months, when tourism was in virtual hibernation, and naturalness and quietness reigned. I will never forget the swans flying over the near-frozen lake of Ioannina, highlighted against a dark red sky; the gaunt old woman carrying a mountain of wood and sticks on her back, walking unsteadily through the snow on the outskirts of Florina; the night spent sleeping under a huge *flocati* rug near Vergia, when the roads were cut off. The winter was a time for roughing it. Accommodation often had little or no heating, and in these remote parts of the country – the region of Epirus kept drawing me – wolves were known to be on the prowl outside villages.

At Easter I joined up with Athenians returning to their villages for the festivities. The countryside was bursting with spring flowers and the scent of orange blossom filled the air. One of my best experiences was in the beautiful peninsula of Mount Pilion, drinking warm goat's milk for breakfast and helping to roast the Easter lamb on the spit.

"Harassment in Greece takes on a highly predictable and organised form"

In summer I headed for the islands, trying to figure out the least crowded and the least spoilt. One year, with a woman friend, I tried the island of Karpathos in the Dodecanese – then very remote, though changing now with the arrival of an airport. It was a stark insight into the differences between urban and island-rural Greek life. People there asked us why we didn't paint our fingernails or wear

make-up – we lived in Athens, after all. I was learning what rural unworldliness meant.

The tourist resorts certainly lost their appeal for me. Travelling through Rhodes in midsummer was unbearable. If I spoke in Greek, the answer came back in English. Nothing was authentic. Harassment, too, was a problem. In Greece, it takes on a highly predictable and organised form: so much so, in fact, that its practitioners have a group name – *kamakia*. A *kamaki* means a harpoon and "to make *kamaki*" means "to fish"; the woman's role in this analogy is, of course, the fish.

Most Greek males have indulged in this practice at one time or another and *kamakia* are to be found more or less anywhere where there are tourists. They can be local, or on holiday from the cities, and their ages run from sixteen to sixty. Motives are varied. Some just want to spend a summer being treated by tourist women. Others might be looking for a prosperous foreign marriage, or even just a way into the woman's country for work or study. They are not often dangerous, though their techniques and persistence – "playing hard to get" is part of the bargaining culture – can be tedious. An indirect result of the phenomenon are the semi-pornographic postcards on sale throughout Greek resorts; depicting "sexually available" women, they probably perpetuate the practice of *kamakia*, too.

Later my experiences of this phenomenon – and my status, generally – changed, as I married a Greek and gave birth to a son. Travelling as a mother, with a child, puts you in a privileged position. Greece is a child-centred society and people go out of their way to give attention and show appreciation to children. It can take the edge off your exhaustion when someone comes up and offers to hold or play with the baby – and you can confidently accept. And a baby lets you off the hook of the *kamakia*, too.

"A positive development, if you actively want to make contact, are the Women's Agro-Tourist Co-operatives"

Greek women often appear peripheral bystanders from the viewpoint of a holiday experience. Yet they play a key role in providing the services that tourism requires in the typical small-scale family enterprise.

Because these jobs are home-bound, however, it can be hard to have any real interaction as a visitor. A positive development, if you actively want to make contact, are the Women's Agro-Tourist Co-operatives that have been set up in various areas of the country. These have been sponsored by the government Sexual Equality Secretariat and are intended to help rural women earn their own livelihood. The co-ops have been geared towards fairly remote communities – and towards local women who are often illiterate or semi-literate and may never have left their village. The women are given a bank loan to fix up a guestroom in their house in traditional style and are asked to provide bed and breakfast for visi-

tors. The co-op arranges stays and keeps a five percent commission on the charges.

Curious to see how the project was faring, I chose to visit the co-op at Ambelakia, a mountain village in Macedonia, five hours' drive from Athens. Most of the co-op rooms had been taken by a large party of Germans, but a widow in her sixties was found, who had space for my family. We checked in and then set off for the huge café-restaurant in the main square, which was also associated with the co-op. I was surprised by the presence of so many local women, the co-op members, who were celebrating with their German guests, whose last evening it was. The women seemed to mingle easily, eating and drinking, and even leading the dancing; the men, by contrast, maintained a low profile. There was a lightness about the whole setting that seemed to confirm what I had been told by one of the co-op organisers in Athens, that the co-ops had "opened the women's spirits". It is a cheering thought, too, to leave the village and know that what you are paying goes directly into the women's pockets.

What the Chambermaid Saw

. . . .

Juliet Martin witnessed another side of tourism, working as a chambermaid on Crete. She explored the island in her spare time, mainly by hitching.

Having spent the first week of a vacation working as a waitress in a pub, I took a one-way plane ticket to Crete to search for similar work in the sun. It is not easy to find. I spent the first week unemployed in Heraklion spending what little money I had. You need a work permit to work there – too many tourist police about.

I ended up getting a job, by word of mouth, in a small resort outside Malia. In return for food and a small room shared with the laundry and cleaning materials I was to work three hours cleaning, occasionally taking the children swimming and doing other odd jobs. The work was tiring in that it took place when the sun was up. Although I was to start at 10am it was often later by the time the rooms were vacated. By midday the humidity made for exhaustion. Weekly, I had to travel up the mountain to clean some villas. For this I was given a moped, which often broke down. Pushing it loaded with linen and cleaning materials was more than tiring, and the mess left was often unpleasant, too. A kitchen table covered with brown sticky glue-like stuff proved a minor challenge. It was hot chocolate. On another occasion my employer's husband shouted at me for failing to remove the shit on the outside of a toilet. Somehow it had escaped my attention.

My boss was English. She'd come to Crete as a courier, "fallen in love with everything" (her words) and stayed to marry. Many of her women friends, also foreign, had fallen for the apparent dream-like existence on the island, married and become disillusioned. They would sit drinking gin and lemonade, discussing their unease. Many husbands were unfaithful, continuing their bachelor existence despite marriage. Nikos took off with a tourist "for dinner" the evening after his Dutch wife gave birth. This was "to celebrate". Such marriages can also cause division in the Greek family who may not accept the foreigner, since she has no dowry. Although it is accepted that men "play around" with tourists, it is still expected that their wives will be virgin locals.

"From the wings I witnessed the Greek beach bums picking out new tourists"

The foreign chambermaid is caught in the middle, neither part of the family/local scene nor a tourist. Many tourists used me to tell their life stories, though, and some included me in their socialising and on their trips around the island. The family frequently entertained relatives and friends for barbecue fish suppers. Although I was welcomed, language was often a barrier to full participation.

From the wings I witnessed the Greek beach bums picking out new tourists fortnightly, declaring unending passion for them, only to find a replacement from the next plane in from Scandinavia. These young men don't work; their mothers do. They are involved in servicing the hotels, usually as cleaners. One woman stood ironing bed linen all day for a hotel, her calves purple-knotted with veins. Such labour supported her son's endeavours to "get to know other cultures" – well, the female side anyway.

Theoretically I worked only mornings so there was plenty of time to see the island, mainly by hitching. Although the buses are cheap and frequent, this is a good option if you're broke. As a woman alone I felt confident hitching by day. Lifts are easy and can be fun if you don't mind the ridiculous conversations in simple English/Greek. Often I'd hitch into Heraklion to walk around the harbour or market or just to sit in the main square with a coffee. It's a big, dusty city relative to the rest of the island, but has its own charm.

Men in the towns or those who give you lifts may ask you for a drink or to meet them later. Refusals are quietly accepted. My trickiest situation was being driven to a deserted beach "to swim". He stripped off; I looked bored. No, I wasn't joining him. He could go ahead. He didn't. We drove on in silence to Ierapetra.

Mopeds and cars are easily hired for those with a bit more cash. Mopeds have a reputation for breaking down, but some places are only accessible in this way. I got to Lassithi Plateau in a tourist's hire car. It's well worth it, to see the thousands of white-sailed windpumps that serve to irrigate the region.

The views are incredible, but take a jumper – it gets blowy.

The most challenging day was spent walking the Samaria Gorge, the longest in Europe. The cheapest way of doing this excursion is to stay in Hania overnight and get the 6am bus to Omalos where the six-hour descent begins. On the way you'll see 1000ft drops, beautiful woodland and springs as well as wild goats. Halfway through is the deserted village of Samaria. At the end in Ayia Roumeli is a restaurant (not too pricey considering its position) and a boat which heads along the coast to Hora Sfakion. There a bus takes you back to Hania; it's a long day but well worth the effort.

Anyone wanting to combine work with travel in this way should take enough cash to get home and to spend during your stay. You may earn a little but not enough to get home. One-way flights from Crete are very expensive. The cheapest way is to get a deckclass ticket on an overnight boat from Heraklion or Hania to Piraeus, the port of Athens. From Athens you may be lucky to get a cheap flight or, failing that, the bus or train.

TRAVEL NOTES

Languages Greek. It's worth at least learning the alphabet to work out bus destinations and timetables. English (if only tourist essentials) is fairly widely understood, as many Greeks have worked abroad and there's a current proliferation of English language schools.

Transport An efficient, reasonably cheap bus service connects main towns and major resorts. Hitching – relatively safe – is accepted, if slow, in the isolated regions where buses do a daily round trip, if at all. Be careful of mopeds, hired out on most islands. Maintenance is a joke and accidents common on the dirt tracks. Island ferries get crowded so arrive early and leave time to get back for your flight – bad weather, strikes and out-of-date timetables make them unreliable.

Accommodation Plenty of cheap hotels, rooms in private houses and reasonably good campsites. Camping wild is illegal but often tolerated (police attitudes vary). On islands you'll be offered rooms as you get off the ferry – usually a good option for a first night.

Special Problems *Kafeneia* (cafés) are traditionally male territory; *kamakia* are a pain. See introduction and articles.

Guide *The Rough Guide: Greece* (Harrap-Columbus). A practical and honest guide, good on background, and which doesn't romanticise islands that are sometimes thoroughly spoilt.

Other Information The Greek Council for Equality in combination with the Greek National Tourist Organisation and Greek Productivity Centre have organised holidays with **Women's Agro-tourist Co-operatives**. Contact addresses are: LESVOS – Petra, Mitilini, ☎0253/41238; HIOS – c/o The Prefecture of Hios, ☎0271/25901; AMBELAKIA (near Larissa, central Greece) – ☎0495/93296; ARAHOVA (near Delphi) – ☎0267/31519; MARONIA (near Komotini, Thrace) – ☎0533/41258.

Contacts

Comprehensive **listings** for all feminist groups and centres in Greece appear in the women's *Imerologio* (diary) published in Athens by Eyrotyp (Kolonou 12-24), and meetings are often advertised in the English-language magazine, *The Athenian* (monthly from news stands). Those groups listed below are the more accessible contacts, particularly if you don't have good command of Greek.

Athens

Women's Bookstore, Massalias 20 at Skoufa; **Selana Bookstore**, Sina 38. The capital's two feminist bookshops are useful starting points for all contacts.

Genovefa "Our Ouzeri", 17 Novembriou 71, ☎653-2613. Women's café-bar.

Woman's House, Romanou Melodou 4 (entrance on a side street of Odos Dafnomili), Likavitos, ☎281-4823. The city's main feminist meeting point.

Xen, Amerikis 11. The Greek YWCA offer language courses for women and maintain a library and archive on feminism and women's issues.

Autonomous Women's Movement Contact Marika, ☎363-1224.

European Women's Network, Portaria 22–24, ☎691-3100.

Federation of Greek Women (*Omospondia Gynaekon Elladas*). Focuses on discrimination at work and disparities in pay; active in the peace movement. Main Athens branch at Akademias 52, ☎361-5565.

Union of Greek Women (*Enosis Gynaekon Elladas*). Emphasises the oppression of women in rural areas and Mediterranean women in general. It is responsible for forming the Council of Equality which has branches in all major towns – in Athens at Enianon 8, ☎823-4937.

Outside Athens

Thessaloniki: *Autonomous Women's Group*, Vass Irakliou 19; *Spiti Gynaekon* (women's bookshop), Yermanou 22.

Ioannina: *Steki Gynaekon* (women's bookshop), M. Kakara 25.

Books

Ursule Molinaro, *The New Moon with the Old Moon in her Arms* (The Women's Press, 1990). Witty and passionate novel, set in Ancient Athens, about a young poet who interprets the waning of the Moon Goddess, Circe, as an omen that women's position in society must be strengthened.

Katerina Anghelaki-Rooke, *Beings and Things on Their Own* (BOA editions, US, 1980). Powerful erotic poetry, full of sexual metaphor and sensuality.

Sheelagh Kanelli, *Nets* (The Women's Press, 1983). A short, lucid novel that reconstructs the events leading up to a disaster in a small Greek coastal village. Though British herself, Kanelli is married to a Greek and has lived there for some years.

Dido Sotiriou (author of *Endoli* and others) is perhaps the best known and most respected Greek woman novelist but none of her books have as yet been translated into English.

Journals

Feminist journals include *Dini* (Zoodohou Pigis 95–97, Athens), *Hypatia* (Piliou 1, Athens), and *Katina* (Vass. Irakliou 19, Thessaloniki).

Haiti

· · · · · · · · · · · · · · · · · ·

Haiti, covering one third of the Caribbean island of Hispaniola, is the poorest country in the Western hemisphere. Despite the achievement of early independence from the French in 1804, when a successful slave rebellion made Haiti the first independent black republic in the world, little has changed in terms of the exploitation of the mass of people by those in power.

From once being the richest colony in the Caribbean, Haiti has become entirely dependent on international foreign aid. Low agricultural productivity, over-population, political instability and the negative effects of deforestation have all contributed to a state of economic chaos which shows few signs of letting up. Any optimism inspired by the comparatively recent forced departure of Jean-Claude "Baby Doc" Duvalier, "President for Life" (a title inherited from his notorious father, "Papa Doc"), in 1986, has since reverted to despair in the face of persistent repression, corruption and a series of military coups. The main issue for Haiti's predominantly rural population is simply survival.

Besides Carnival, which draws hordes of tourists every year, the combination of political turmoil and shocking poverty has prevented Haiti from becoming a large-scale holiday haven for foreign visitors. There's certainly plenty of scope for adventure, though you may well feel better going with a more helpful purpose, for instance to work in some way with a relief agency. Theft is rife in and around the capital Port-au-Prince but elsewhere, provided you treat people with warmth and respect, you will find the atmosphere surprisingly relaxed. Sexual harassment does not appear to be a particular problem.

There are a great many grass-roots organisations in Haiti, working largely on popular education projects with the urban and rural poor. Most of them are affiliated to the church, the only place where people could get together to share their feelings under the Duvalier dictatorship. **Women's groups**, in particular, have multiplied since the departure of "Baby Doc" as women discover themselves gaining far more confidence in separate meetings. Despite some resistance, according to Claudette Werleigh, a leading Haitian educationalist, "the men are very aggressive and sometimes throw stones at them or the places they meet . . . the men think that the women are getting together just to criticise them." These meetings have formed the basis for a growing movement to campaign for women's issues within the framework of fighting for a better society.

A Fact-Finding Mission

. . . .

Worth Cooley-Prost is an American medical writer from Arlington, Virginia. She travelled to Haiti with a group of people from her local parish on a fact-finding visit to their sister parish in the small town of Cavaillon.

The four women in our group included a student in her late fifties, a widely-travelled secretary, a nun with a doctorate in counselling and myself, a medical writer. Our male traveller, a school guidance counsellor, had been to Haiti the previous spring with our parish priest.

Our visit began with a brief but unnerving exchange with the Haitian immigration officer. On seeing from our entry cards that we were going straight to Cavaillon rather than to Port-au-Prince, he became immediately interested and somewhat suspicious, questioning us at length about who we were going to visit and exactly what we were doing in Haiti. He finally proclaimed us "missionaries" and let us go through. It was a good early remin

der that we were visiting a military dictatorship where anything perceived as unusual was considered potentially threatening.

Once outside the airport, we were immediately overwhelmed by the sea of people, riotous traffic, including small herds of cows, and waves of smells – charcoal, garbage, incense, sewage, cooking. The road was lined with tiny store-fronts and everywhere there were groups of people gathered around small fires and women carrying whole tables of food and other objects on their heads. Added to the visual and olfactory riot was noise: people singing, dogs barking, children screaming, horns blowing and music blaring from *tap taps*, the small brightly painted covered pick-up trucks, always jammed with people, that serve as public transport throughout Haiti. We were grateful that the Cavaillon priest had arrived to act as our translator and guide.

Beyond the city the traffic quickly thinned to nothing. We would drive for miles in absolute darkness, then suddenly come upon a busy late-night throng of people around fires at the side of the road. Twice we encountered *rah-rah* bands, rowdy groups of men and boys dancing in the road with drums and rum late at night. The first simply opened ranks to let us pass, but the second had a hostile air and the priest had to pay them to let us go on. Without his Creole, we'd have been lost in that situation, unable to interpret what was going on and thus unable to gauge the response.

Cavaillon is a town of about 1000 people, some three hours' drive west of Port-au-Prince. Electricity is on for four hours each evening, but few houses are wired; virtually none have running water or refrigeration. With the exception of some military jeeps and our own car, about the only motor vehicles we saw were *tap taps* passing through.

We stayed in the rectory, a castle-like concrete hulk towering on a hill at the edge of town, with a distinctly medieval feel. Cold running water, indoor toilets and showers, all extremely unusual in this area, had been added only in the past year. The system was very rudimentary: when our toilet flushed, our shower responded in kind. The "kitchen house", a free-standing concrete room in the backyard, held the cooking utensils and three big wood fires. Meals were prepared on a table outdoors and whatever animal was destined to be eaten that day (during our stay, a turkey, several chickens, and a goat) was slaughtered behind the house. A couple of skinny dogs haunted this area. Unconsumed garbage and plain trash got dumped in a pile a little way up the hill behind the yard, left for the elements to dispatch over time.

Visitors were clearly a burden for the three women who lived and worked at the rectory; in addition to having to prepare meals for five extra people, all water used for our coffee and cooking had to be boiled. The women, in their mid-twenties, shared one bedroom and by all appearances functioned as house servants. They were up at six each morning to start the kitchen fires, mop the house and porches, and sweep the yard before breakfast was laid out. The rest of their day consisted of more cooking, cleaning, and doing laundry in the yard. When the electricity came on each night, one of them would immediately spread a sheet on the floor of the meeting room and begin ironing. Later, they would wait for everyone to retire, before locking every bedroom door from the outside – a distinctly eerie feeling.

"Attempts to help with any of the chores seemed to be inappropriate, even mildly alarming"

Only the educated minority in Haiti speak French, while everyone speaks Creole. Language serves as a social barrier within the culture as well as to visitors – all government pronouncements, laws and court proceedings are in French. Our absolute inability to talk to the women in the rectory made us feel very uncomfortable and attempts to help with any of the chores seemed to be inappropriate, even mildly alarming to them.

Every morning I'd wake about six, realise I could sleep another hour or two, then remember where I was and be up for the day. None of the other visitors woke up that early and I used to treasure my time alone on the balcony just watching and listening. Country or city, roosters crowed and dogs barked around the clock. A typical house in Cavaillon consists of a one-room concrete hut without kitchen, water or toilet facilities. Four families, including ten children, lived in the little house below the rectory which can't have been more than ten feet square. Soon after dawn one or two of the children would head down to the river to bring back water in big plastic pails. These stayed in the yard and people gradually came out one at a time to wash, while the younger children sat quietly on a stump in the yard and fixed each other's hair. The process looked so calm and measured in the early light.

Soon trucks began passing on the way to and from the mountains, cows were led down the road toward the riverside marketplace, and hordes of children in various coloured uniforms gathered for school. One morning we visited the priest's school, taking some notebooks and posters we had brought from home. (Paper is very expensive in Haiti; at one mountain school we saw, the children use nothing but slates and chalk.) About 200 children attended, at a cost of around six dollars a month for tuition and supplies. Since the average annual income for a Cavaillon family is only a hundred dollars, many cannot afford to send their children at all.

It was upsetting to see ninety children, crowded three to a rickety desk, shiny little faces reciting in French to one single teacher. These few years of elementary school – no more than three percent of children in rural areas advance any further – are achieved through great family struggle and yet have virtually nothing to do with the everyday reality of people's lives. The illiteracy rate in Haiti is eighty percent – and for women, ninety percent. In 1980 a national adult literacy campaign, Missyon Alfa, was launched by the Catholic Church. Individuals from each community were trained in basic literacy and community organising skills, then sent back to work with their people around local issues.

The programme's popularity quickly led to threats, arrests and even murders. While an educational system that involves a few years of rote drills in French does not threaten any military dictatorship, Missyon Alfa was quite another matter. We were told of a meeting between one of the Missyon Alfa founders and the government Minister of Education. "It's all very well," said the latter, "to teach a peasant to write 'The sun is rising and the day is beautiful', but if you teach that, then he can also write, 'I am poor and I know the reasons'." The violence against Missyon Alfa grew such that the programme was suspended in early 1988.

One Sunday we drove into the mountains. In parts this country is unbelievably beautiful, with primeval forest at every other turn, and, at the beach of Port Salud, the Caribbean a shimmer of unearthly green and blues, the mountains rising right at the edge of the sea. Everywhere, the people showed a friendly interest in us, though language beyond "hello" remained a real barrier. Open markets at crossroads were full of women squatting by baskets of grain, fruits, and an amazing array of plastics from Taiwan.

"The boys either roam around town in small groups or tend cows or goats; only girls under about three years old seemed to be free to play"

We attended a mass with about a hundred Haitians in a tiny mountain chapel. The service lasted almost two hours, with a lot of singing and talking back and forth between the priest and the people. The music was accompanied by drums, wood pipes and rhythm produced by scratching a sort of wand along a metal tube. We could understand none of the words, of course, but were struck by how universal the mass itself is. Without any language, we felt full participants in the service and a bond with people that simply wasn't possible in other settings.

In Port-au-Prince, we stayed in a guesthouse run by a Canadian who moved to Haiti twenty-eight years ago to do quickie divorces. Our rooms were rather seedy by American standards and had neither air conditioning nor hot water, but we were comfortable. The proprietor told us that women were unquestionably the backbone of the country, functioning as the planners, administrators, and marketers. Overtly, the culture is male dominated. When the school day ended in Cavaillon, boys played outside while the girls disappeared to do chores. Among children who don't go to school at all, the boys either roam around town in small groups or tend cows or goats; only girls under about three years old seemed to be free to play. We saw no men cooking, cleaning or washing clothes, although perhaps a tenth of those selling at countryside marketplaces were men.

The degree of poverty everywhere in Haiti is difficult to express. In the huge city slums it is shocking; one of our group commented that even Calcutta was benign in comparison to City Soleil, the largest of the Port-au-Prince slums. Tens of thousands of people live, somehow, in a filthy concrete rabbit warren of tiny rooms and tinier alleys, all connected like a giant maze except for open areas where the sewer trenches serve also as washing and water gathering places. Even so, the people we greeted were usually openly friendly. My most lasting impression of City Soleil was the endurance of the impossible with genuine dignity. Until drawn to the city by promises of factory jobs over the past decade, many of these people lived as subsistence farmers in the countryside, where at least they fed their children: in the city, their apparent powerlessness is overwhelming.

In the countryside, a marketplace appears wherever a river meets a road. In the city, the street itself is the river: everywhere we went, sidewalks and the edges of the street were crowded with people, mostly women and girls, minding a dizzying array of vegetables, clothes, plastics. Much of the food consisted of cans and boxes, mostly American brands, some of it clearly marked as donated by CARE or some other relief agency. Food, especially US food, has a great deal to do with the poverty in Haiti. American policy toward developing nations stresses "food security", the argument being that modern production methods provide more, better and cheaper food. Therefore, instead of growing their own food, these countries should buy food from the US, and in order to have money to buy that food, the people should work in foreign-owned assembly industries.

Haitian friends had counselled us against responding to street children begging, since giving even small change would accomplish little for the child and would result in our being besieged by hundreds of other children. They advised us to say "Later" and keep walking. We also found that persistent vendors generally withdrew when we said "Finis"; otherwise, at times we were unable to walk a block in less than fifteen minutes. Efforts to politely decline an article for sale were invariably interpreted as an invitation to bargain, leaving us feeling confused and hassled and the vendor angry.

"Riding a tap tap would have felt like a tourist lark of some sort"

In terms of getting around, I saw no non-Haitian hitchhiking and wouldn't recommend it. Communicating about such simple things as bottled water is hard enough. You could ride a *tap tap*, but we were uncomfortable, as white foreigners, about being granted a markedly different status than the Haitian women. Riding a *tap tap* would have felt like a tourist lark of some sort and an insult to the local women who are forced to sit on the floor if a man wants a seat. Sexual harassment was not an issue, perhaps in part again because we had no earthly idea what was being said in Creole and because we were rarely out alone. I also thought that, given such complete poverty, if a woman went out stark naked except for a purse, it would be the purse that drew the attention.

Ironies abounded throughout our trip. In the city, with its garbage-filled gutters and people struggling to sell scraps of something to another poor person, we saw beauty shops on every other corner. Advertisements for pain pills were epidemic. Most of all, I was struck with the juxtaposition of beauty and ugliness.

The people themselves have a gracefulness I've never seen anywhere else – the curve of a jaw, the fluid elegance tossed off by a woman swatting a fly, the beautiful open faces. Haitians also impressed me as vibrant, creative and powerful. This grace and power exist within a culture marked from its beginnings by restriction and brutality, both foreign and domestic, whose proverbs observe that laws are made of paper while machetes are made of steel.

TRAVEL NOTES

Languages All Haitians speak Creole, derived from French and African dialects. The fifteen percent or so who have had schooling also speak French and often some English.

Transport Collective taxis, known as *publiques*, and *tap taps* run between all main towns, usually leaving whenever they are full.

Accommodation Low-cost rooms, often including one or two meals, can be arranged through various religious missions. Port-au-Prince also has a few major hotels, but lodging in the countryside is best arranged in advance.

Guides *The South American Handbook* (Trade and Travel Publications) has a small but useful section on Haiti.

Contacts

There are a number of **missions and human rights groups** in Haiti. Worth Cooley-Prost recommends first getting in touch with the Holy Ghost Fathers in Port-au-Prince or Mission Wallace outside Petionville.

We have been unable to locate any women's groups. However, it may be worth writing to the **Caribbean Association for Feminist Research and Action**, PO Box 442, Tuniapuna PO, Tuniapuna, Trinidad and Tobago, which is dedicated to developing the women's movement throughout the Caribbean.

Books

Mary Evelyn Jegen, *Haiti: The Struggle Continues* (Pax Christi, US). Excellent 58-page booklet providing an overview of the recent situation in Haiti with an emphasis on the status of women. Available (for US$2 plus postage) from Pax Christi USA, 348 E. 10th St., Erie, PA 16503.

Claudette Werleigh, *Working for Change in Haiti* (CIIR, 1989). This short booklet, published by the Catholic Institute for International Relations, describes the work of Haiti's popular education movement.

James Ferguson, *Papa Doc, Baby Doc: Haiti and the Duvaliers* (Basil Blackwell, 1987). Lively and accurate account of the rise and fall of the country's notorious dictatorship.

Alejo Carpentier, *The Kingdom of this World* (Penguin, 1980). Powerful novel, based on the slave revolt that first created the black republic of Haiti. Out of print, but worth tracking it down in a library.

Hong Kong

ong Kong is in the grips of a deepening crisis of confidence about its future. Since the signing of the Sino-British agreement to return the colony to Chinese sovereignty in 1997, a steady stream of citizens have been leaving the country.

It has now become a flood. The June 4th massacre in Tiananmen Square effectively erased hopes that China will keep to its bargain and allow Hong Kong's economic freedoms to continue for the next half century. For the vast majority who have neither money nor connections enough to emigrate, anger is mounting at the British colonial government's continuing concessions to China and refusal to grant citizens the right of abode in Britain. On top of this there are considerable tensions over the daily influx of Vietnamese refugees, housed in crowded island refugee camps. With space already at a premium, pressure is growing to launch a programme of forced repatriation.

Ironically, Hong Kong remains a land of opportunity for Western expatriate workers, who are offered increasing incentives (low taxes and few currency restrictions) to fill the rapidly dwindling professional class. The cost of living is high but then so are the wages, and many women with British qualifications come here on two- to three-year contracts to boost savings. Luxury hotels, apartment blocks, an amazing range of restaurants and clubs, and the much-touted shopping areas of Kowloon and Hong Kong Island reflect the lavish lifestyle of the multinational business community, as well as catering for nearly three million visitors a year.

Whilst you might well feel bewildered and overwhelmed by the rampant consumerism, crowded streets and the hectic pace of Hong Kong life you're unlikely to feel under any personal threat. Harassment and violent crime certainly occur but they tend to be contained within the different communities. You can expect far more trouble from sexist foreign residents than the Hong Kong Chinese. It can, however, take a while to adjust to being an outsider in this country. The well established ex-pat scene has all the distasteful elements of colonialism and commercial opportunism – creating an independent social network can be a slow and isolating process.

Within the Chinese community women are expected to take on the full burden of domestic work and also to help ensure the family's survival in the economic rat race by working long, hard hours in family businesses, sweatshops etc. For middle-class women these pressures are eased by the use of migrant labour – mainly Filipina maids or Chinese *amahs*. The majority, however, have to rely on support from extended family networks, a resource which is gradually being eroded by the continuing waves of emigration and the move towards living in tiny multistorey flats. With few welfare provisions, no unemployment benefits, costly health and education services, and intense overcrowding, life for most women is fundamentally insecure and stressful. There is little by way of a co-ordinated **women's movement** in Hong Kong and, in general, little interest is shown in feminist debate. The largest and most influential women's organisation, the *Hong Kong Council of Women*, is heavily dominated by ex-pats and, as such, is criticised for being elitist and out of step with the priorities of the Hong Kong Chinese. Its attempts to launch overtly feminist campaigns, against sexual discrimination and harassment, have floundered through lack of support. Much more popular are the grassroots groups (*ying ngai*) based in the larger estates, that offer practical support, communal activities and classes (anything from childrearing to international currency exchange).

An Uneasy Path

. . . .

Alison Saheed travelled to Hong Kong in 1974 to work for a while before journeying across Asia. She stayed thirteen years, worked in various jobs, married and had two children. She eventually had to return to Britain with her family in order to escape the restrictions of the new nationality laws.

Arriving in Hong Kong in the post-summer heat of autumn 1974 knowing no one and with no preconceptions about the place, I little realised that it would be my home for the next thirteen years. Those years threw up dramatic changes for Hong Kong both politically and socially; a shift in attitudes, the emergence of a burgeoning Chinese middle class, Mao Tse Tung's death and the doors opening to China. It also finally became clear that its time as a freewheeling, often exploited entrepot was running out as 1997 crept closer. In that time, I too experienced changes; having arrived young, free and single I left wiser, married, a mother twice over, and with three career switches behind me.

"Above all, I suddenly felt very large and ungainly next to people of much slighter build"

Initial impressions were not favourable; Hong Kong struck me as a hard, harsh place without any softness, its neon-lit buildings perched on the waterfronts, impersonal. The population, all distinctly Chinese as far as I could see, seemed brusque, forever busy, and, contrary to tourist pamphlets, emphatically did not speak English. Humidity, something I had never encountered, seeped from every crevice, interrupted only by blasts of icy cold air conditioning from inside the angular buildings. The smells of cooked food stalls in the streets, and the sights of fresh food in open air markets, so intrinsic a part of life in Asia, were new to me and initially sometimes overwhelming. Above all, I suddenly felt very large and ungainly next to people of much slighter build.

Arriving fresh from an easygoing southern European lifestyle, I was unprepared for the division that appeared to exist between the local populace and the foreign elements. I was shocked by the attitudes of the Europeans I was to meet initially; elitist, racist and snobbish, to me like creatures dragged out of a Somerset Maugham story – characteristics I would later learn were more than equalled by many Chinese.

I met no other European women at that time and to this day cannot fathom where they were. Consequently, the only English speakers I came across were men whom I found to be chauvinistic to extremes. To compound it all, everyone, it seemed, had been in Asia for a very long time. Life, apparently, simply did not exist outside and I grew tired of the catch phrase "You don't

understand, this is Hong Kong/Asia", whenever I queried something unfathomable. All in all, I felt I had inadvertently wandered into the wrong party.

Retreating from this chilly reception, I decided to get on with my life and set about looking for a place to stay and work. The first proved to be easy and I ended up sharing a flat with three Asian career women, two Overseas Chinese women who had grown up in other parts of Asia and had come to Hong Kong to link up with their roots, and a locally born Eurasian woman. I didn't realise then that it was extremely rare for a European woman to live with Asians, nor that the assumption, on the Chinese side, was that only women of loose morals would live away from home. As it turned out, my flatmates saved my sanity through those bleak early times with a sensitive blend of loyalty, tolerance and patience and we remain firm friends today. They also unknowingly taught me a great deal about the Chinese way of thinking and introduced me to aspects which could have taken me years to discover.

Not being particularly career oriented at that time, I continued on the path I had been on in Europe and found a job teaching English in a Chinese-run language school. Here I confronted an impenetrable mask of "no response". I did not know that schools taught by rote method, that the teacher was highly regarded and would be listened to unquestioningly, and that a blank "no" to a question could mask any number of conflicting emotions, ranging from an unwillingness to give the wrong answer and thus lose face or an equal unwillingness to admit that the question had not been understood.

My students were extremely polite, and in casual chats showed great charm and interest, but I was initially baffled by their attitudes. Culture shock by now had well set in. I muddled through, not even realising what it was. Today, there are counselling services available for precisely that in Hong Kong.

"Gaining or losing face" is a concept bandied around a great deal with regard to the Chinese, as if, for some reason, it was unimportant to anyone else. Simply put, it is akin to maintaining your pride but it is much more extensive than that, encompassing many aspects of life whether through openly grandiose gestures or small seemingly insignificant ones. It runs through controlling one's emotions to the meaning behind the spoken word. It has something to do with how you are perceived by those around you and verges almost on a power trip rather than internalised values. I never really came to terms with it.

Breaking through language barriers is also difficult. Cantonese is mastered by few foreigners and is fraught with tonal disasters for the novice. Cantonese love to play with words, much like the English, and words can be changed easily by altering the tones. At one time I lived at an address which, if pronounced incorrectly, equalled a proposition and amused many a taxi driver as I grappled with my "tones". Just a few words of Cantonese can generally evoke a very different open response, particularly in the marketplace if only you can follow the flow of Cantonese that you elicit. I did not manage to learn much though I eventually came to understand a lot of what was being said around me.

But one sure way to crash all barriers is to have a child. I had my elder son in a charity-run hospital in a poor part of town because it was recommended to me. Not having had a child before, I didn't know quite what to expect, but when the time came, it seemed to me to be perfectly adequate. The hospital was run by nuns and men were kept well away while they got on with "women's business". I went into labour, was given a ghastly enema and then sent to lie down in the equivalent of a "waiting room" staffed by an old *amah* who wandered around checking on dilation. I felt very alone and scared

as labour progressed. I was then wheeled into the delivery room where two midwives attached my legs to stirrups and told me in schoolteacherly tones to push. An obstruction in my son's throat after his birth was dealt with briskly and efficiently and he was carried off to be bathed. I was not however, prepared for the painful stitches and more than once was told to behave myself.

Afterwards the staff couldn't have been kinder and I was given all sorts of concessions, including open visiting hours, partly, I believe, because I was the first European to have a baby in that hospital. Although they were at that time promoting bottle feeding, when I explained my preference to breast, they complied.

"I was bewildered when I took my newborn baby to the shops with me as everyone stared at us"

Post-natal care was excellent and when I did develop an infection, they kept me in until they were satisfied and then released me only on condition that I be seen three times a week at home by a nurse, which they arranged. I was in an open ward filled with new mothers whom I shocked by taking a shower and washing my hair after giving birth. Chinese tradition dictates that post-natal mothers do neither until one month after delivery. Special foods, too, are prepared for the mothers and brought to them by visiting relatives. Often soups, they contain vegetables and ingredients to cleanse the blood and act as tonics. After being discharged from hospital, my ex-flatmate very kindly brought me those dishes prepared by her mother.

Superstition runs parallel with tradition regarding newborns and great care is taken to follow the rigid procedures. I was bewildered when I took my newborn baby to the shops with me as everyone stared at us. I was to discover that, according to Chinese custom, a baby should never be taken outside so young for he/she will fall prey to evil elements.

Children are all important to the Chinese family; they secure the lineage and ensure, in turn, that their parents will be looked after when they are old. They are welcomed, protected with a vengeance, and are accepted as a part of life. You will find, in any restaurant, large families including babies and toddlers eating together. Waiters often play with them. They are picked up, cuddled, played with, admired in public wherever you happen to be.

Consequently, I never felt trapped by my child. I took him everywhere with me and never once felt we were intruding. Returning to part-time work shortly after his birth I found, through a friend, a large gregarious Portuguese family who simply absorbed him into their den until I picked him up after work. This is one of the most positive aspects of life in Hong Kong for working mothers; help is available. You pay for it but it is worth it if, like me, you need to work.

This childcare freed me to search for a more satisfying form of employment. This to me is another plus about the place. If you are willing to try, you can break into new fields. Hong Kong pivots on the axle of rapid change so it makes sense to go along with it. You don't have to stay stuck in a rut. Entrepreneurial flair helps too. I am not talking about the white collar professions so much as the person who is vaguely dissatisfied with his or her chosen occupation and wants to venture into something completely different.

At one time I was teaching alongside three female colleagues and all of us knew we wanted out. We each struck out on our own paths. One took up Asian studies at the university, then joined a magazine which concentrated on the politics of the region, was then posted to the Bangkok bureau for a couple of years before returning, with

the same magazine, to Hong Kong. Another did management studies and was hired by an international hotel group to teach her subject in Bali. The third is now near the top notch in an educational publishing house. I worked at a radio station as assistant producer, learning the ropes for three years, while tentatively trying to write articles, had a bash at PR, then freelance writing with a bit of broadcasting thrown in, and finally ended up co-ordinating a new weekly lifestyle publication for one of the English-language newspapers.

For all of us, the transitions and stumbling around in new areas took a long time and lots of hard work, but we found it could be done. The momentum of Hong Kong tends to carry you along and you have the added pressure of not being able to give up because of the very real financial burdens.

"Sexism from Western men is still strong and Asia, with its tradition of submissive women, promotes it"

Money is at the root of the zeal. "No money, no life" goes the Cantonese saying and it is based on reality. There is, after all, no welfare state and no subsidised study. You pay for what you get. Consequently, if you have the fortune, you flaunt it and if you don't then you try to dress as if you do. People in Hong Kong are well-dressed, even if it's casual wear. And there is no excuse for being sloppily dressed because ultra cheap bargains abound on the market stalls. Salaries are wildly fluctuating and uncontrolled with massive disparities of income. This imbalance means a lot of sniping by everyone and you are constantly reminded of the inequality wherever you go. Socialising is to a great degree an extension of work and as such tends to take place outside the home. Needless to say, it places a great strain on personal relationships.

While a fair number of Chinese women marry foreign men, the reverse is not so. In general, Chinese men are not particularly attracted to European women, which leaves you free from any harassment at the office or in the street. It also enables you to function freely at work, deemed as you are as sort of sexless. Sexism from Western men is still strong and Asia, with its tradition of "submissive women", promotes it. Most Chinese women have jobs and those who manage to clamber up the corporate ladder have had to fight tooth and nail for it in hailstorms of Chinese male chauvinism.

"To be British in Hong Kong, if you are remotely sensitive, is to tread an uneasy path fraught with conflicting emotions"

Hence the "dragon lady" syndrome – a fiercely neurotic holder of power, whose tactics in maintaining it make her Western counterparts look like puffballs. Not surprisingly, many of the high flyers are unmarried as the balancing act between being very successful in the workplace, while giving your husband face by being submissive at home, must be a nightmare.

To be British in Hong Kong, if you are remotely sensitive, is to tread an uneasy path fraught with conflicting emotions. It has been, after all, a British colony, ruled by a government which receives its instructions from Britain and as such is terminally out of touch with the population it is supposed to be governing. The Sino-British Treaty regarding the handover of Hong Kong in 1997; the ensuing wrangles over the Basic Law drafting; and the resulting loss of nationality for Hong Kong British passport holders has done little to aid race relations. And the British government's current policy on kowtowing to China for future trade while ignoring the fate of some six million people is impossible to justify.

No one knows what will happen in Hong Kong, one can only go on indicators. What to me is tragic is that the people the place needs, mainly the expanding middle class, well educated, bright and responsible are leaving in droves. The very rich have already set up their families in Australia, Canada or the USA and return to Hong Kong for business, their boltholes secured. The rest are either left there or are desperately trying to figure out where else they can go. No one really wants to leave. With regard to Hong Kong's future, money may well win out. Chinese millionaires have for years now been pouring money into the mainland in the form of hotels, factories and leisure centres. They have smoothed their path and their way of doing it may well prove to be a great deal more successful than the fumblings of the British government.

A year or two ago, I would have advised anyone going to Hong Kong that the localisation policies had tightened up the job market for non-Chinese. Today, I understand this has gone into reverse due to the large numbers of people leaving. It was hinted at recently that Hong Kong will soon have to recruit foreigners again to fill the burgeoning middle management vacancies that are growing daily.

TRAVEL NOTES

Languages Cantonese. English is widely spoken in the main tourist areas.

Transport Easy and cheap by bus, ferry, tram and train.

Accommodation There's plenty of it but it tends to be expensive. Cheapest are probably the YMCAs (Salisbury Rd., Kowloon, ☎3-692-211, and overspill, 23 Waterloo Rd. (Yaumatei), Kowloon, ☎3-319-111), which admit both women and men.

Guides *The Rough Guide: China* (Harrap Columbus). Look out for the forthcoming *Rough Guide: Hong Kong* (Harrap Columbus). The local tourist board supply reams of information at points of arrival.

Contacts

Association for the Advancement of Feminism in Hong Kong, Room 1202, Yam Tze Commercial Building, 17-23 Thomson Rd., Wanchai, ☎05 282510. Created in 1984 by local Chinese women, the group collects information on women's social and political participation. They produce a news digest on women in Hong Kong and China.

Hong Kong Council of Women, S 82/F Lai Kwai House, Lai Kok Estate, Kowloon, ☎3 866256. Originally set up by Chinese women to fight for the abolition of concubinage. Now a fully-fledged feminist group, with resource library and telephone information service.

Asian Students Association (ASA), 511 Nathan Rd, 1/F, Kowloon, Hong Kong. The ASA takes a strong anti-imperialist, anti-colonialist and anti-racist stand. Its **Women's Commission**, set up in 1975, is currently chaired by the League of Filipino Students (LFS) and promotes the emancipation of women and encourages the formation of national women's groups. ASA publishes a bi-monthly *Asian Students News* which includes regular information about women's struggles in Asia.

Books

J W Salaff, *Working Daughters of Hong Kong: Filial Piety or Power in the Family* (Cambridge University Press, 1981). In-depth study of working women in Hong Kong and the effects of industrialisation upon family life.

Xi Xi, *A Girl Like Me* (Renditions, Washington UP, 1986). A collection of short stories drawing on the traditional Chinese and modern Western experience of Hong Kong.

Thanks to Deborah Singerman for help with the introduction and Travel Details.

Hungary

. . . .

After years of experimenting with political and economic reforms, Hungary has now launched itself as an entirely new entity in Europe, a multiparty Socialist state. Yet the outcome and implications of such a vast and rapid change (including dismantling the border with Austria, transforming the Communist Party and instituting the first "free" elections in the

Eastern bloc) remains deeply uncertain. A critical issue seems to be how far the West will back up its supportive rhetoric with large and timely foreign loans. This sudden opening up is providing a boost to an already very well established tourist industry – in the summer months there are said to be more foreign visitors than Hungarians in the country. Most are from neighbouring Austria and West Germany, lured by cheap holidays in the resorts around Lake Balaton or in Budapest. But in recent years there have been an increasing number, too, from Britain, The Netherlands and the US.

Arriving in Hungary it can take a while to register that you've crossed into an Eastern bloc country; there are no minimum currency change requirements, few restrictions on where you can stay (many people rent out rooms in their homes), few hassles with black marketeers and a surprising degree of Western-style consumerism. Budapest especially is a highly cosmopolitan city with a lively café scene and numerous hotels, shops, restaurants and bars competing for the tourist trade. Yet unlike its Western counterparts, the capital has a reputation for safety. There are few problems in wandering around alone, even at night, although taxis are cheap enough to make this unnecessary. Outside of the main cities people may seem curious about you or concerned for your safety – old notions of "gallantry" towards women have been slow to fade and although this can seem intrusive at times it's rarely threatening.

Amongst the plethora of oppositional parties that have sprung up over the last few years, there are as yet no autonomous **women's groups** or organisations. In fact "feminism" tends to have negative connotations in Hungary, as an old piece of Communist propaganda, and a distraction from the main business of gaining democratic rights. The state-organised *National Alliance of Hungarian Women*, which campaigns around issues such as equal pay for equal work, is too clearly a party vehicle to gain much support. In many ways the political climate carries echoes of Britain in the Sixties. Pornography, which has long been the cornerstone of Hungary's booming advertising industry, is widely used to express sexual liberation, with little debate as to how such images exploit and degrade women.

Teaching in Pest
. . . .

Victoria Clark, a teacher and free-lance writer based in London, spent two years teaching English in Budapest. She lived alone in a rented flat for much of this time and travelled widely around the country. Since her contract finished she has returned to Budapest for holidays.

How can I explain a relentless pull towards Eastern Europe? I arrived in Budapest pretending to myself that I would stay there long enough to learn a Slav language and would then set off across the Eastern bloc. In fact, as soon as I stepped off the train from Vienna, I had a feeling that I had come home and that night made up my mind to stay on for as long as I could. My vague plans would anyway have proved impossible; Hungarian is of Finno-Urgic not Slavonic origin and is famously impene-trable, spiked as it is with accents, prefixes and suffixes. Also, being employed by one of the privately formed teaching co-operatives, I was paid in non-convertible Hungarian currency which I could not, as a Westerner, spend on travel outside the country.

I was, however, delighted by the astonishing beauty of the city in autumn; by the feverish entrepreneurial energy of a people beginning to shake off the effects of forty years of totalitar-ian rule; by the Chinese toothpaste, Albanian eels and Vietnamese lychees in the shops. It was easy to ignore the fact that I would surely be leaving Hungary poorer than when I arrived.

After two years of luxurious living in Barcelona, it took a while for my system to adjust to Budapest. I was housed in a ten-storey concrete block on the road out to the airport. My first evening, I emerged from the nearest metro (whose name translates as Spotty Street) to find myself lost in a dark forest of identical concrete blocks, any one of which might have been mine. An elderly gentleman with a rusty command of Hapsburg Empire German called me "Dear Lady", directed me to my flat and clicked his heels before bidding me goodnight. For the first three months I lived off bread and imitation brie, expensive cans of Israeli orange juice and quick-souring milk in bursting plastic bags. Not because there was nothing else to eat, but because I couldn't read the labels on the packages.

My students at the language school were an uneasy but interesting mix. Many were the children of the nouveau riche who lived in new villas on the verdant slopes of the Buda Hills, built from the profits of a greengrocery or Barbie Doll importing business; others were from the tired remnants of the intelligentsia. Even if there were not enough pens, textbooks or classroom space, even if thirty and not fifteen non-English-speaking children turned up for my first class in the living room of a sixth-floor flat, my work was extremely enjoyable. Most of my colleagues were Hungarian women who also worked at the university or in grammar schools and were fantastically committed teachers in a society which respects the profession.

When a private student kindly offered me his flat rent-free for the following year, I had nothing more to ask for. Having a flat all to yourself is an almost unthinkable privilege in this overcrowded capital. I knew of large families who had to make do with a few rooms, and divorced couples who led completely separate lives but remained under the same roof for want of anywhere else to stay.

"The old woman had soon gained enough information about me to conclude that I was a foreign prostitute"

Number 3 Garibaldi utca, its roof graced by three crumbling stone muses, was supported by sturdy wooden scaffolding. Like many buildings in downtown Pest it was due for renovation and had a hallway strewn with dust and rubble and broken glass. On the concierge's door by the wrought-iron lift was a sign which read "House Supervisor" – a tatty relic of the terror-stricken Fifties. Flicking at the greasy curtain over the window in her door, the old woman had soon gained enough information about me to conclude that I was a foreign prostitute and before long I had a visit from a forlorn plainclothes policeman in a bomber jacket. I shouldn't have been surprised that she'd interpret my visits from students in this way. It seemed to me that, much like Britain in the Sixties, sex had become a popular obsession.

I was very happy in that dingy second-floor flat with its high ceilings

and badly appointed rooms, and would often just sit there watching street scenes from the window. At one end of the narrow street stood a caravan selling the chocolate pastries I bought for my breakfast. At the other end I could catch glorious sunlit glimpses of the steeples and domes of Buda across the River Danube. The fairy-tale Gothic parliament was just around the corner, my school five minutes' walk away, my favourite cheap restaurant closer still. On March 15th I marched around the city all afternoon to commemorate the Revolution of 1948 and challenge the restrictions of the present day. This was the thick of it!

I never moved across the river to live in Buda. Pest, with its long tree-lined avenues and extravagant Art Nouveau, was the real hub of the city. Like a mini-Vienna, Pest has its opera house and parks and austerely grandiose government buildings, where Buda strikes me as altogether less civilised, more medieval, with its castle, Turkish bath-houses and pattern-roofed churches clustered around the hills. Buda is for the tourists and elegant relaxation; Pest is for the serious business of living and working in the city.

I found Hungarians a serious people – overworked, intense, sceptical and often alarmingly intellectual. It was only in the summer months at the resorts around Lake Balaton that I had a glimpse of a more happy-go-lucky and relaxed approach to life. Staying at a friend's lakeside villa one August weekend, it was refreshing to see my hosts rising late and downing a thimbleful of brandy before tucking into a healthy breakfast of spring onions, green peppers, cream cheese and coffee.

Another summer I stayed at Szigliget, in a country mansion confiscated by the Communists after the war and used as a holiday home for the Writers' Union, where I watched eminent writers in shorts discussing "literature" until the small hours of the morning. I would sometimes retreat to the lake with Agota, a teaching colleague whose mother had a cottage on the northern bank. It had been her grandfather's property before the war and she had spent all the summers of her childhood there. The Communists had confiscated most of the land but there was still a little vineyard and some grassy slopes which they kept up with the help of an old friend of the family, who would turn up with his lawnmower, improvised from a pram and a washing machine motor, and share a glass of wine.

Hungary is changing every day. I hear Agota's mother is confused and not sure that things are improving. Taxes on most commodities are hitting hard. An architect friend tells me no politician has a clean enough record to be entrusted with the awesome task of restructuring Hungary. West Germans are cashing in on property around Lake Balaton; Austrians nip across the border for cheap dental treatment. In Budapest's main shopping street there is now an Adidas shop, a Benetton and a McDonalds. In Gyor there is a Marks and Spencer.

I imagine, though, that for most people life will improve. Hungary's provincial towns will be beautified and upgraded with the help of foreign loans. High speed trains will replace the old blue ones which took the best part of a day to reach anywhere in the small country. I expect the trams in Budapest will be gradually phased out and the cobbled streets, scored with tramlines, replaced with tarmac. They are already renaming the Moscow and Marx squares. A Westerner still, I am already allowing myself the luxury of nostalgia for the "old" Hungary.

In Search of Magyar Feminism

· · · · · · · · · · · ·

Emma Roper-Evans spent four years living and working in Hungary. During this time she had her first child and continued as a single mother working as a freelance proof-reader.

When I first arrived in Hungary in September 1984 I was impressed by a number of things; childcare facilities were free and took children from the age of six months; the streets of Budapest were so unthreatening that I could actually enjoy walking across the city at three in the morning; there was very little pornography of any kind; and virtually all women worked and contributed to the family income. Since then I have come to the conclusion that these advantages (which we in the West are still struggling for) are eroded by the fact that women have no arena in which they can speak for and about themselves, and that they have no access to real power.

Today Hungary is in flux. It seems as if a pluralist doctrine may replace monolithic Communist dogma. Yet out of the 200 independent groups and movements that now exist, no powerful women's voices have emerged. Reform is the word on everyone's lips and yet the only reform affecting women appears to be the one that collapses the traditional image of the courageous, fertile socialist mother into that of the allegedly "liberated" sex bomb, who was displayed pouting and topless in the first Hungarian tabloid of that name, *Reform*. Avant-garde artists and performers, keen to push the limits of censorship as far as they can, also rely heavily on pornography, with women performers using fetishistic gear in their shows.

The family has always been held sacred by the state, especially in a country where the birth rate is lower than the death rate and women are actively encouraged to have as many children as possible. For example, it is much easier to get a prized state flat if you have three or more children. The other side of this is that abortion involves going before a board of doctors, sociologists and psychologists and answering questions about sexual history, financial security and so on, before your case is even considered.

Women might work but when they return home they have the full responsibility of all the household chores. The division of labour in the home is rarely questioned, even though women have been working alongside their male counterparts a good deal longer than we have and Hungary's workforce would not survive without them.

I must explain at this point that my position was considerably better than most men and women in Hungary. I arrived on a tourist visa hoping that I would somehow be able to work. After the initial difficulties of persuading the authorities to give me a work permit, a process which took three months of dealing with bureaucrats and filling in forms, getting a job was relatively easy. English speakers are in great demand, and as soon as I put up notices around the city advertising myself as an English conversation teacher, students flooded in, willing to pay high prices for the dubious pleasure of talking to me in English for an hour or two each week.

Later I taught at International House in Budapest, despite the fact that I have no teaching qualification and my degree was not in English. Budapest is also a great centre for publishing and so I was able to get an official position (written in my identity card which everyone must carry) as a proof-reader of English texts in one of the big state publishing houses. My work was of a freelance nature, with much shorter hours than the usual nine-to-five and earning about twice the average wage. I also found I had access to all sorts of high-powered circles, meeting academics, writers and intellectuals, simply because I was English. They were all intrigued by the fact that I had come to Hungary to work and to learn their language and therefore took me seriously even though I was a graduate still wet behind the ears from university.

"They could not understand the idea of women meeting and speaking about themselves and saw it as very anti-democratic"

My interest in women's issues was, however, met with scepticism and amusement. When I proposed starting a women's group to some of my female friends, work colleagues and acquaintances, many of them said, "but why no men?" They could not understand the idea of women meeting and speaking about themselves, and saw it as very anti-democratic. I think this is partly because the Communist Party has for years issued great tracts on equality and heroised certain women who took part in the struggle for communism between the wars, but nothing was done and nobody believed it was anything but a propaganda ploy. Feminism tends to be viewed as something the West can afford to dabble in but which has no place in Hungary.

Women are of course involved in political activity, either as part of the ruling Communist Party or in dissident circles. The Party has a Women's Section which is run along the lines of a Stalinist Women's Institute, all thick tweed skirts and pamphlets on breast-feeding in which the young mothers are addressed as "comrade", a very disconcerting experience.

Among independent groups I have mentioned a few have women on their executives. One of the best-known women activists is Ottilia Solt, a prominent dissident during the Kadar years. When I went to talk to her she stressed very emphatically that she was not a feminist, saying that there were far more important issues on her agenda to start worrying about whether women have equal rights or not. In a country where everybody is a second-class citizen, why should women receive special treatment? The idea that a struggle for a democratic constitutional state is of paramount importance and that other freedoms will necessarily follow is an old one. Women are co-opted into the radical movements where they must be content to share platforms with angry young men, old revolutionaries and power seekers.

The notion that the personal is political, which has been so central to feminists in the West, does not exist in Hungary. The private sphere is subordinated to the public domain which is concerned with more concrete reforms such as the economy, the political system and environmental policy. This not only affects women but the homosexual community too. There is no concept of being gay, of creating a forum where people can speak openly about sexuality and oppression. Your sexual proclivity is considered a private matter that should not be discussed in public.

The one place you can be sure of women-only company is at the Turkish baths. There you can luxuriate in the warm pools after being pummelled and massaged by middle-aged amazons, wearing amazing, medieval-looking bras. The baths are a traditional meeting place, the last remnant of the Turkish occupation which lasted about 150 years, into the late seventeenth century. Women of all ages sit about in a series of hot pools and saunas, chatting, playing chess and reading the papers. I found them the best cure for a hangover after too much *alinka* (fruit brandy), and the best way of reviving after having to go to work at an unearthly hour in the morning.

One of my jobs was teaching women textile workers in a factory on the edge of the city. This involved getting up at about 5.30am in order to be there at 7am when work started. The hours were arranged so that the women could get home in time to collect their children from school. There were about ten women, mainly in their late thirties, who had arranged special English lessons during work hours. I had to have permission to enter the factory, which is a restricted area for foreigners, although I suspect industrial espionage is hardly rife in a country where manufacture is in crisis.

We had many discussions about the role of women in Hungary; they all agreed that they did too much housework and childcare, but that change would only come about in the next generation and that women are anyway more caring than men. I liked them all and even went on holiday with them to the factory guest house on Lake Balaton. The very funny, but also indulgent, anecdotes they told me about their husbands and boyfriends reminded me of the stories I used to hear from women of my mother's generation.

"All the women on the ward were amazed that not only was I unmarried but I did not even claim a father for her"

I encountered a good deal of conservatism when dealing with such issues as marriage, child-rearing and sexual behaviour. This is perhaps partly due to economic pressures – to support children and have a reasonable chance of getting your own flat you virtually have to be married. There is state child benefit but it is minimal and impossible to live on without an additional income. It would be incredibly difficult to bring up children as a single parent, and I met no women who were doing so.

When my daughter was born in Budapest in July 1986 all the women on my ward were amazed that not only was I unmarried but I did not even claim a father for her. They were all married and were looking forward to a welcome break at home bringing up their children (the state allows up to two years off, with a job guaranteed at the end of this period). All of them had been married in church, as well as the obligatory registry office ceremony.

The only other patient who caused more of a sensation than I did was a middle-aged gypsy woman having her fifth child. The other women were completely unabashed about expressing their racist views. Out came the old platitudes: gypsies are dirty, they steal, are dishonest, abuse their children and so on. Gypsies have lived in Hungary for centuries (and currently make up three percent of the population) but because they look different, speak a different language and refuse assimilation into the state socialist system they have become the nation's scapegoats.

Many of them live in abject poverty in rural areas, especially in the east of the country where I saw gypsy encampments of unbelievable deprivation and squalor. The men tend to gravitate towards the towns to find work. Once there, they live in overcrowded workers hostels, while the women stay behind in the villages working on the collective farms and bringing up their families. I often heard the complaint that the state had allocated a flat to an urban gypsy family, who would only "sell" it (transfer it for a great deal of money – a standard practice) a few months later, rather than to a worker's family who had been on the council list for years.

Hungary is not a classless society at all; gypsies, peasants, workers, professional and Party functionaries are all ruthlessly divided. The urban middle class may have lost everything during the country's wars and revolutions but their manners, attitudes and aspirations have barely changed and they still tell jokes about the peasant politicians and their coarse ways. Interestingly, the few immigrants, some Cuban guest workers and African and Arab students, were usually treated with great courtesy.

TRAVEL NOTES

Languages Hungarian – an incredibly difficult language to pick up. German is widely understood, but English is only spoken in the more heavily touristed parts of Budapest.

Transport Visas are necessary but are issued routinely on entering the country. Travel within the country is fairly straightforward by bus and train and you can go wherever you want. Few Hungarian women hitch – it seems the risks are much the same as in most Western countries.

Accommodation The few cheap hotels in Budapest are usually full but the tourist organisation, *Ibusz*, arranges private rooms. Around the country, *Turistahaza* dormitory hostels are useful and campsites plentiful, as well as the conventional hotel network.

Guides *The Rough Guide: Hungary* (Harrap Columbus). An excellent book – informative, insightful and a gripping read.

Contacts

Hungary Women's Council, Nepkoztarsasag Utca 124, Budapest 5, was set up by the Communist Party. We know of no autonomous women's groups.

Books

Volgyes, Ivan and Nancy, *The Liberated Female: Life, Work and Sex in Socialist Hungary* (Westview Press, US, 1977). Looks at the position of women in Hungarian society from feudal times up to the Seventies.

Iceland

*L*ong popular with geologists and birdwatchers for its weirdly beautiful volcanic landscapes, glaciers and migration grounds, Iceland is now beginning to attract more mainstream travellers. Since the 1986 superpower summit in Reykjavik effectively relaunched the country as a tourist destination there's been a growing trade in package/hiking tours with new hotels opening in and around the capital.

Outside of Reykjavik, however, facilities are very thinly spread. The country's tiny population is centred on the capital and a few small fishing settlements around the coast, which makes travelling further afield a lonely and arduous business. Transport is infrequent, with many roads impassable much of the year, costs can be exorbitantly high, and the weather unpredictable – a sudden downfall cutting off your chances of getting your next supplies. Added to this, Icelandic communities have a reputation for being insular and self-reliant, and though ready to give help when needed, people generally seem uninterested in making contact with visitors. It is however, a very safe place to travel (there are few problems with camping or hitching) and, provided you like the hardy outdoor life, you'll find ample rewards in strange and wild scenery, unlike anything else in this part of the world.

The Icelandic **women's movement** has long had a powerful impact at the centre of mainstream politics. *Kvennalistur*, the "Women's Alliance" was the world's first feminist party to win seats in a national parliament. They currently hold six out of 63 seats and are predicted to take the balance of power after the next election. Ten years ago the Movement demonstrated its full collective strength by calling a one-day women's strike for equality in the workplace and parity of wages. In 1985 the action was repeated – again, in protest against discrimination at work. With the unequivocal support of Iceland's first woman president, Vigdis Finnbogadottir, thousands of women walked off their jobs, closing down schools, shops and government offices. More recently the Alliance has become linked to anti-NATO campaigns, and leads the mounting opposition to the US airbase at Keflavik.

Cod Row

. . . .

Cathryn Evans spent ten months working in a fish factory in the northwest fjords before setting off alone on a tour of the country.

I'd spent a few weeks' holiday in and around Reykjavik in the summer and really wanted an extended stay. After searching unsuccessfully for a job and a work visa I decided to try and join the quota of overseas women employed in the fish factories on the coast. Unfortunately the jobs are set up by agents in England who insisted that I return to London for an interview.

They offered me an eight-month contract, with a free return flight thrown in if I lasted the course, and within a fortnight I was flying back to Iceland, heading for the village of Flateyri in the northwest fjords with ten other women. Some were travellers, from Australia, New Zealand and Europe, lured by the chance to fund their fare home in a short time while others from the Southern hemisphere came out of curiosity, knowing only that they were guaranteed a white Christmas.

> *"Salla, the quality controller, showed us how to sheer the backbone away from the meat, pluck out live worms . . . and cut out some nauseating blemishes"*

Before leaving, most of the people I met seemed to think of Iceland as a snow-covered wasteland populated by Eskimos fishing through holes in the ice and living in igloos. They certainly couldn't imagine a socially and technologically advanced nation with a very high standard of living.

The northwest coast is one of the best fishing grounds and, consequently, Flateyri one of the country's wealthiest and best equipped villages. As with most of the settlements outside Reykjavik, the village only existed because of the fishing industry. The factory was run on a co-operative basis, its profits servicing the community of 425 with a swimming pool, sauna, shop, snack bar, library, surgery, school and guesthouse – outstanding amenities for a place of its size. We were given a large house next door to the factory – an instant introduction to the all pervasive smell of fish.

The day after our arrival we were plunged into work. Donning aprons, gumboots, baseball hats and layers of warm clothes we watched apprehensively as Salla, the quality controller, showed us how to sheer the backbone away from the meat, pluck out live worms with a deft flick of the wrist and cut out some nauseating blemishes. It was best not to think too hard about what we were doing and switch to automatic. The hours were long and hard in cold, wet conditions and by the end of the first week we ached all over. Some of the women were already plotting escape plans during the coffee breaks.

I was a little surprised by how clearly the labour was divided, filleting and packing were termed "women's work" while the men unloaded crates, watched over the gutting machines and loaded trays into the freezer. It was a highly mechanised factory but there was no getting round the sheer monotony of packing, alleviated only by the prospect of different fish to work on. Nevertheless it was a comforting routine and very much the focus of life in the village. At the end of the week there was always a rush to finish the week's catch and if there was a particularly big haul at the height of the season the whole village would turn out to help. There was a tremendous community spirit and, as part of the workforce, we gradually felt accepted within it.

At first, of course, we were viewed with what seemed like cold indifference. Foreign workers had been coming to the village for twenty years and we were just another batch. The village mentality, which thrived on gossip and newcomers, focused on us. But they were also shy people and their reticence was taken by some of the foreign women as very inhospitable. There was certainly no great reason for them to be especially welcoming. The younger women, in particular, saw us as coming to their country merely for the money and as potential rivals for affections of the men. Obviously, there was a precedent to this as it was something of a status symbol to go out with a foreign girl and the trawlermen with money to burn would often shower visitors with gifts, adding to the money-grabber image.

On an individual level the people were very friendly and hospitable and it was a pleasure to share with them their great passion for their country and community. I became closest to a woman called Hjordis, the headmistress of a tiny school. She had represented Iceland at the United Nations and travelled a great deal but had settled on her own in a house at the far side of the fjord from Flateyri. She spent the summer charting the different migratory birds and was dedicated to nurturing a forest in the harsh climate and thin soil. Another good friend was Stina, an imposing figure who had the dubious task of counting the number of worms in the crates of fish and calculating how long it would take us to pluck them out. With a family of three to raise on her own, she supplemented her income by running the swimming pool and gathering expensive eider duck feathers from her farm in summer. She would patiently help me to grasp Icelandic, a language that has changed little from the time the great sagas were written.

The villagers always made sure that we joined in the celebrations of major festivals and would explain to us the different feasts and rituals such as the

pancake feast to mark the last glimpse of the sun before the dark winter days. Men, women and children had their own festivals dating back to the gods Odin and Thor. The feast of Thorrablot, for the single men of the village, was a memorable trial for the tastebuds. Traditional fare such as braised sheep head, rotten shark, rotten eggs and sour ram's testicles was served. The only thing I really acquired a taste for was *skyr*, a sour yoghurt-like liquid mixed with sugar. Most food is bought in from Denmark and is very basic. The tiny store often looked like it was operating food rationing, especially in winter when supplies often couldn't get through by road, air or sea.

"The women I worked with who were not great nature lovers and were used to big city life found it hard going"

Boredom seemed to be a big problem in Flateyri, especially among the younger people; they spent hours cruising round and round the village or burning rubber up and down the road. The women I worked with who were not great nature lovers and were used to big city life found it hard going as well. Dances with live bands were held every fortnight in summer but less frequently in winter.

Being the largest house in the village, our quarters became the party house at weekends and we would often get impromptu visits from people in neighbouring villages. Icelanders are by nature self-contained and undemonstrative and many relied too heavily on alcohol to let their hair down. Sadly, drink problems were common – even in such a small place, there was a regular "Alcoholics Anonymous" meeting. The sale of beer had, until very recently, been illegal, but as fourteen-year-olds would down a bottle of spirits at a time, this, like the high prices, seemed a futile measure. Icelanders put this heavy drinking down to boredom and depression in the winter months.

The whole country had an air of being untouched by commercialism, although it was clear that this was changing. Even Reykjavik, which since the Superpower summit of 1986 became increasingly aggressively marketed to attract foreign investment, had none of the big city atmosphere, not even the usual neon lights. It was striking at Christmas that most adverts were for books. As a legacy of the long, dark winters, writing, poetry, music and chess are still very popular pursuits, with a high number of experts for such a tiny country. However, videos are set to supplant this and mail order mania has taken grip in the villages. Keeping up-to-date with fashions has become increasingly important for both sexes and it's a matter of pride among the free-spending trawlermen to have the latest hi-fi and cars.

Although winter, with only three or four hours of daylight and snowfall cutting off the village for many weeks, seemed a bleak prospect to most of the villagers and foreign workers, its novelty made it the most magical time for me. Every clear winter night there was a fantastic display of the Northern Lights, with whirling, flickering bursts of colour covering the sky. I enjoyed trekking on the mountain slopes on skis and whizzing across acres of snow on a snowmobile, stopping on a ledge and looking out on to the village below.

Flateyri had many houses hugging the sides of the mountains so there was real danger of damage from an avalanche. Sometimes even a walk up the road was too risky. This was brought home dramatically one day, when with a great roar a cloud of snow and dirt subsided leaving a vast mound of snow just short of a row of houses. The risks of making a living by the sea were also made clear as three fishing boats in the region were lost within the space of one stormy week.

"One of the best moments was climbing up the steep mountainsides and crossing the still snow-covered plateau to watch the Midnight Sun"

"Gyllir" was the name of our trawler. A crew of fifteen would go out on voyages of seven to ten days. It was fitted with the latest computerised instruments as well as the comforts of a sauna and videos. For all this the conditions at sea were arduous. When taken on a trip we had to stay below deck while the men struggled above with the nets in fierce winds. The catch was gutted on board, a very tiring process, and the six-hour shifts seemed an eternity. It was a great feeling, however, to sail back into harbour with a large haul which would be turned into neat packets of fillets during the next week. It's strange to think what a high level of job satisfaction there was working in the factory, singing along to the Icelandic pop songs on the radio and picking up pidgin Icelandic, even though this largely consisted of the different names of fish.

After my contract finished I found it hard to break away from the cosy routine of the community, and especially from the beautiful, peaceful environment. It was a total retreat from the hassles of city life and as the summer approached I would spend long evenings walking at the edge of the fjord watching the boats turn into the harbour, seals and eider ducks on the beaches and the snow thawing to create cascading waterfalls. The endless daylight made it hard to stay indoors and, much as I enjoyed the winter, I could see why the villagers were so cheered by the summer sunlight. One of the best moments was climbing up the steep mountainsides and crossing the still snow-covered plateau to watch the Midnight Sun.

However, I had spent ten months hardly leaving the confines of the village, so excitement slowly overtook my regret at leaving Flateyri, as I took off for Reykjavik to begin a tour of the rest of the country. I travelled mainly by bus and hitched to the less accessible spots. Taking advantage of the six weeks in the year when it is possible to travel across the interior, I joined a sturdy bus which was to cross the Spredgisandur route. The whole journey only took a day but it was a battle to keep the bus moving through the glacial desert wasteland of sludge, sand, and ice-cold rivers. Crashing waterfalls, dark volcanic peaks and imposing glaciers contrasted with slabs of multicoloured rocks and steaming hot pools. Only a handful of drivers were qualified to take this route and we had to help out several stranded cars along the way.

"Iceland is not the place to spend time if you don't like the great outdoors"

Hitching can be quite difficult in Iceland. The most interesting places are often off the main road and there may only be a few cars passing. Trudging wearily along in enigmatic weather was quite demoralising, but I never felt at risk and the lack of cars meant that if one did pass me, it would invariably stop. I spent many days exploring Lake Myvatn in the north-east, fortunately picking a time when the midges were taking a breather. This area has always been a magnet for bird watchers as it attracts a huge variety of migrating ducks in the summer. Great geological turbulence has produced many strange features – the barren volcanic cratered areas were used to train the American astronauts.

Close to this is a sulphurous plain with bright yellow crystals and bubbling pools of grey mud. The twisted statues of lava, called *Dimmuborgir* (dark castles), have still not been satisfactorily explained. There is still a suspicion that they might be sleeping trolls. It is usual for any giant boulder to be attributed to these mythical creatures, and often the course of roads has been altered to avoid disturbing them.

The geothermal activity in this area has some unusual spin-offs. In Hveragerdi the hot earth has been used as the basis of a greenhouse centre where exotic flowers and even bananas are grown. It also acts as an oven to bake delicious sourbread. In Svartsengi, the run-off from the heating plant has created a mineral-rich hot pool. It was a real luxury to bathe in the steam rising from bright turquoise water surrounded by craggy black lava. Throughout this time I stayed at Youth Hostels which were always well equipped and sited around the main routes. They ranged from farm outhouses to school halls and were friendly, relatively cheap places to spend the night. Camping was even better as the level of tourism means that there are few restrictions on where you can pitch a tent.

Iceland is not the place to spend time if you don't like the great outdoors and are expecting a bustling nightlife, as outside Reykjavik there are few entertainments laid on. But the spectacular unspoilt landscape and relaxed lifestyle are reasons alone for taking a trip. It will hopefully be some time before the aggressive tourist and business drive now beginning to operate in the capital spreads to the rest of the country.

TRAVEL NOTES

Languages Icelandic and Danish, but most people speak some English.

Transport No particular problems for women; hitching is probably as safe as it can ever be, but be prepared for long waits between lifts.

Accommodation Again, no particular problems for women. Many Icelandic women camp and hike alone. There's a good network of Youth Hostels.

Special Problems Costs can be devastatingly high. Don't underestimate the dangers of hiking or driving into the interior; the terrain can be treacherous and your chances of being found if you have an accident are alarmingly slim.

Guides There's a good section on Iceland in *The Rough Guide: Scandinavia* (Harrap Columbus).

Contacts

Kvennaframbodid, Gamia Hotel Vik, Adalstraeti, 101 Reykjavik. Main office of the Women's Movement, used as a meeting place for various groups and for advice sessions on legal, social and health matters. They also publish a magazine, *Era*, bi-monthly.

Books

We've been unable to find any books in translation by Icelandic women. Any suggestions would be welcome.

India

I ndia provokes intense reactions among travellers. However much you read, or are told, little prepares you for the differences and richness of the various cultures, the unbelievable poverty or the sheer pressure of people. In many ways it is misleading to talk about India as one country. With its six major religious groups, its differing stages of development, its widely varying landscape and proliferation of local cultures and languages, it is a collection of states easily as diverse as Europe. For a traveller on a short trip, one or two areas are more than enough to take in.

Countless women travel the country alone, and have done so from the days of the Raj through to the hippy era. The lingering hippy stereotype can be burdensome at times, connoting scruffiness, promiscuity and drug abuse, but it also has its positive side in an established trail and a legacy of cheap accommodation. Sexual harassment tends not to be a great problem. This is not to say it doesn't occur; in strongly Muslim areas, wandering around on your own is considered a provocation in itself, inviting comments and jeers, and all women in India face the problem of being groped in crowded buses and trains. Actual sexual violence, however, (at least towards foreign visitors) is very rare and dangerous situations can mostly be avoided by making a public outcry – passers-by or fellow travellers are bound to help you.

Much harder to contend with is the constant experience of being in a crowd, the unremitting poverty and the numbers of hustlers and beggars. (Begging carries none of the social stigma that it does in Western societies and Indian people routinely give something.) How you cope with the outrageous disparities of wealth is up to your own personal politics. But whatever you do, or don't do, you'll need to come to terms with your comparative affluence and outsider status – and the attention this inevitably attracts.

The **feminist movement** in India has become established in recent years, though it remains concentrated in the cities and the women involved are predominantly highly educated and middle class. But many women's centres and action groups have been set up and with women's magazines such as *Manushi* and the feminist publishing company *Kali for Women*, the network is widening daily. Local actions like the organisation of lower-caste street workers in Ahmedabad into collectives as a means of protecting themselves from police harassment, and the exploitation of money-lenders (see Una Flett's piece) have been both creative and diverse. One of the chief concerns of the feminist movement is to involve more rural and urban-poor women in various broad-based campaigns – against dowry (the number of dowry deaths remains alarmingly high), discrimination in the workplace and disparities in pay and education.

"Lonely you Come?"

. . . .

Una Flett was born in India but left at the age of five. She has since twice returned as an adult, most recently for a four-month visit.

Somehow, oscillating between resilience and fatalism, India keeps going – keeps going in spite of her 714 million, nearly half of whom are unemployed. This is the enduring image of India, the crowds upon crowds of people everywhere. Most of the population live in rural villages but increasingly they migrate to cities to live in the great sprawls of shanty towns (*bhastis*). The sight of pavement sleepers, beggars and hustlers, tearful young graduates telling you of their destitution, not enough space on buses, queues like insurrecting armies; these are all part of the day-to-day experience. Everything, from buying a stamp to boarding a train, will be done against the pressure of competing hundreds.

"The first thing to learn is to economise in anger. It gets you nowhere and is exhausting"

As a foreigner, particularly a woman travelling alone, the first thing you encounter is the stare, the open curious gaze, followed usually by the open curious question. Indians are avid "collectors" of foreigners, not by any means always in a predatory spirit. To the crowds of unemployed young men who hang around every public place, the foreigner is entertainment, also – my personal theory – a kind of token substitute for travel. Most of them will never "go foreign" but, because the

West still represents much that is desirable and prestigious, any kind of contact is prized.

There is a difficult ambiguity in these encounters. Are you being chatted up by a hustler or not? I have been enraged by an attempted rip-off – though the first thing to learn is to economise in anger. It gets you nowhere and is exhausting. But there is a long and pushy list of people trying to engage your attention for money; offering to be your guide, find accommodation, rent you a houseboat in Kashmir, or show you the local handicrafts, besides the shoal of aggressive sellers of all kinds of pitiful junk.

In big cities the likelihood of outright harassment is much higher than on trains or in smaller places. "Eve-teasing", the term coined by the Indian press for groping, provokes long, scandalised articles in the "dailies" and is for Indian women as much as foreigners a hazard of city life, particularly on buses (so is pickpocketing and jewellery snatching). Sikh and Muslim men are on the whole much more sexually aggressive than Hindus. A memorably unpleasant experience was being pulled around Lucknow (a predominantly Muslim city) in an open rickshaw, a sight that triggered off shouts, solicitations, jeers and cheers from every man I passed. It was the one place where I chose to go hungry rather than look for somewhere to eat on my own.

I travelled clockwise around India by train, a slow and tiring kind of journeying but a certain way of getting the flavour of the country and above all of the people. For all life takes place in stations. Travelling is endemic among Indians – to visit relatives, to take produce to markets, to make pilgrimages, to look for work. Besides travellers, stations have their quota (sometimes enormous, as in Howrah station in Calcutta) of permanent residents, homeless families who have settled in with their cooking pots and babies and cloth bundles. There is an amazing sense of private family life being lived in the open, among travellers and others. It is, after a little practice, curiously relaxing. You lose the sense of a rigid self-conscious boundary between "public" and "private", as it exists in a Western society. The small space occupied by your bags in the middle of the waiting crowd becomes a sort of privacy. I ended up quite naturally unpacking and repacking my possessions on platforms, settling in to write up notes and generally behaving in a "domestic" manner.

"Both men and women found the fact that I travelled alone quite extraordinary"

I grew to love stations as much as I dreaded them in the early stages. They seem bewildering ant-heaps until you find your way around, but you can always get help from coolies (wearing red waistcoats for identification) who know platforms and departure times rather better than the station staff. Fellow travellers, too, are infinitely helpful. Indians are well aware of the impenetrability of their booking system for foreigners and love to help out. Above all, there is the fun of eating in stations where there are all sorts of oily cooked food snacks, fruit, and hot, sweet tea served in little clay cups which give the tea a slightly earthy taste and which one smashes to shards on the railway lines after drinking.

Both men and women found the fact that I travelled alone quite extraordinary. "Lonely you come?" they would ask, incredulous. Although by their standards bizarre, my choice was entirely tolerated. In some states I found separate compartments on trains for women – good places for conversations. I was asked about our marital system, or lack of it, and asked in turn about theirs. Although love matches do occur across caste and religion (disasters in the eyes of most families), the system of arranged marriages has not been seriously challenged; freedom of contact between the sexes is rigorously proscribed and in many areas college students lead segregated lives and there is no mixing among the young in public.

"To do exactly as it was done before is an axiom of life in India"

Women are still seriously hampered at all levels except at the very top by their subordinate and dependent status. Apart from the small group of highly educated and very able women in academic, professional and commercial jobs – a Westernised elite – the rest of the country's women are restrained either by tradition or poverty or both. The dowry system, though made officially illegal some years ago, persists with all its iniquities. Higher education for girls is more a selling point in the marriage market (read the personal ads column in any English-language newspaper) than a means of entering employment. The large bulk of Indian women do not work after marriage, for that reflects poorly on the husband. Only those at the top and those at the very bottom do so.

However, among women at the desperate bottom of the heap an amazing potential for self-help can be tapped. In Ahmedabad, a union for self-employed women – rag and scrap sellers, quilt-makers, joss-stick rollers and market women of all kinds – was started in the early 1970s. By setting up banking and credit facilities, training schemes and protest groups *SEWA* (Self-Employed Women's Association) has managed to rescue its members from the hold of money-lenders, make an effective case against harassment by police, and to develop – from a baseline of total ignorance – a remarkable degree of financial competence. Women have also asserted themselves in ecological issues, most notably in the Chipko movement to save the deforestation of the Himalayan slopes. However, the power of tradition is vast, a force that locks people into a sense of preordained order. To do exactly as it was done before is an axiom of life in India.

If you visit, don't try to do too much. Your senses will be at full stretch all the time because there is so much to take in. The stimulation is tremendous. So is the exhaustion.

A Bengali Retreat
. . . .

Peggy Gregory spent nearly two years travelling around India. She stayed for three months in an *ashram* and spent six months living alone in a rented house in Bengal.

Before I left for India I talked to people who had already been, attempting to grasp what it would be like, and to gain more confidence about going. Talking helped, but I still had doubts – maybe these other people were simply better travellers, stronger, more open and more resilient than I was.

I had managed through a connection in England to arrange a room with a family in Delhi to cover my first few days. That way the initial shock was softened, as I could make forays out into the hustle for short periods and then retreat into the warmth of a family atmosphere.

It was colder than I'd anticipated (in December) and the city seemed surprisingly pleasant, almost sedate. The old part of the city, however, is less congenial, crowded with people and vehicles, very dusty and chaotic; it was enticing, but I felt too raw, too intimidated by the constant staring, comments and questions that assailed me as I walked around or sat resting for a while. I wanted to merge in with the crowds and observe everything unnoticed.

When I started travelling I compensated for my lack of experience by finding other single women to travel with – either another recent arrival with whom I could share my uncertainties, or people who had been in India for a longer time from whom I could gain confidence. From one woman I learnt to speak some Hindi and to read the alphabet, particularly useful for reading timetables at bus stations. Generally just talking to other travellers was helpful, to find out which places were interesting to visit, how they approached travelling and what they had learnt from their experiences.

There are a lot of foreign travellers all over India, especially in main towns and cities or, in fact, any place mentioned in the guidebooks. I too had set out with a guidebook, which was useful for general hints and finding hotels but soon became redundant. I usually stayed in dormitories in cheap hotels, which are less expensive than rooms, and good places to find companions, although you don't have any privacy. I spent the first month travelling around Rajasthan, an increasingly popular state with tourists.

My confidence grew quickly. With it came the realisation that I wouldn't learn much by confining myself to the tourist route or by hanging around with other Westerners simply for the sake of emotional security. The most important thing I learnt during that time was to judge a situation by its atmosphere and to promote an atmosphere myself of being open to unexpected events or

meetings – but not to jump feet first into any situation I was unsure of.

"As a buffer between me and the outside world I developed the persona of a 'nice girl' – strong but odd"

For the next four or five months I stayed in cheap hotels, occasionally with families and once in an *ashram* or sleeping on station platforms or trains when in transit; a passive observer to the life and activity around me. I was gradually changing, relating to things with regard to where I was the month before rather than to England, which began to feel a long way away. The persona I developed was of a "nice girl" – strong but "odd" – as a buffer between me and the world outside: one which both allowed me to communicate and also protected me.

I felt safe, even when walking around at night, travelling in trains or staying in hotels. In cities at night, for instance, many people shop until quite late, and there are women and children on the streets. However, I tried to stay clear of the predominantly Muslim areas at night as the total absence of women made me uneasy. In the countryside it's also not so safe, but when staying in these areas I was often with someone or could use a bicycle. Anyhow, whenever in doubt you can always catch a rickshaw.

I was rarely sexually harassed and never in any sort of aggressive or threatening way, but I did get my share of the street hustlers. Stallholders in the market often pick on foreigners, and leaving a train or bus station with luggage almost invariably brings a rush of rickshaw cyclists and touts insisting on taking you to the "cheapest" hotel in town.

If I felt slightly battered after a journey I'd then hang around for a while and leave the station to look for somewhere to stay, collecting my luggage later. Most situations, however, depend on your reaction and state of mind; if you're feeling bad any hitches or hassles are irritating, but if you're feeling good it is fun. Generally I felt I was hassled less as time went on, partly I think because I had learnt to dress and move around in a less conspicuous manner.

I worked my way southwards over a period of six months. By the time I arrived in Tamil Nadu I began to feel ill. So much so that I had to retreat to a hotel room where I spent a lonely and painful week unable to sleep, eat or do more than shuffle to the toilet twice a day. I had hepatitis. I knew it as soon as I caught sight of my yellow eyes and skin. Gathering the little strength I had, I moved to a local Christian *ashram* at Shantivanam, where I spent a week until they sent me back to Tiruchi to a hospital. *Ashrams* don't usually like people visiting if they are ill but when my symptoms disappeared (after a week) I was welcomed back. I was lucky to have gone to that particular *ashram* as they did genuinely seem to care. They even sent someone to visit me every day while I was in hospital.

Illness of some sort is almost inevitable if you spend any time in India. I was, however, unlucky to catch both hepatitis and later amoebic dysentery, both through contaminated water. I took the usual precautions for the first three months but drinking only sweet tea and soft drinks is expensive and anyway it's extremely difficult if you're staying in rural areas – I lapsed, accepting the possibility that I might get ill.

With a fairly poor diet it took a long time to regain strength so I was at the *ashram* for about three months. Looking back, I realise it was the best place to have convalesced. There was a ready-made structure to the day which I appreciated after so long on the road; and a gentle and open approach to life and "spirituality". I had gone there rather uncertain as to how a casual and unconvinced visitor might be welcomed. The only other *ashram* I'd

been to was a Buddhist one in the north (Igatpur) where I'd gone specifically to do a meditation course. I discovered later that *ashrams* are usually open to anyone as long as they approach with a genuinely sympathetic attitude. Some, however, have become wary as they've been abused in the past for free accommodation – it is often best to write in advance to say you are arriving.

"You can't expect people to become suddenly calm and open the minute they walk through an *ashram* gate"

Most people I met had been disappointed by the lack of harmony they encountered in *ashrams*. It's something I felt myself when I stayed in Igatpur. Everything had been fine during the meditation course, perhaps because we were under a vow of silence and concentrating solely on meditation. Staying on to do some voluntary work (which everyone was asked to do, although this is not so in all *ashrams* – rules vary), I became disheartened by obvious rivalries that emerged between people. Their frustrations and antagonisms weren't particularly new but they seemed out of place. This was true also to a lesser extent in Shantivanam, but by then I was less naive – you can't expect people to become suddenly calm and open the minute they walk through an *ashram* gate. Often the process of introversion and introspection that people enter into can have paradoxical effects, bringing out hidden aspects of the personality.

Moving on, I began to feel more and more the need for some sort of structure – I wanted to become more involved in learning about Indian culture. In Pondicherry I started to learn *tabla*, the percussion accompaniment to classical Indian music, and for the following nine months was completely involved in learning the technique. I eventually settled down in Bengal in a small town called

Shantiniketan, which has built up around an *ashram*, school and university set up by the renowned poet Rabindranath Tagore. It's an extraordinary, peaceful place. I felt at ease immediately, found a music teacher and rented a room. I also started to learn Bengali and taught English privately. I was extremely happy there, and even when the time came when I wanted to return to England I found it hard to wrench myself away from what had become my home in India.

I could have remained in India, and if I had done so it would probably have been for a long time. Yet I was tired of making the compromises necessary to live in a country as a foreigner; and it was that which eventually made me decide to return.

Returning to England and having to adjust to a more complex lifestyle, having lived so simply for such a long time, was very difficult. I felt disorientated for several months, not sure that I had made the right decision. Looking back, it was a good decision, for what I had learnt there had to be put to the test in another environment; much of it has fallen down and much remained.

Between Two Cultures

. . . .

Smita Patel, a British Asian woman, took five months off from her job at a feminist publishing house to travel with her boyfriend to India and South East Asia.

This was not my first visit to India. Like most second generation Indians I had been taken to India as a child and young teenager. But these journeys had always been considered as a duty or "family visit", not as a means of exploring the country or even mixing with the community at large. I had always been aware that as an Indian girl my role was to accept the guidance and protection of my relatives. Returning as an adult independent woman, I knew that I would face problems and dilemmas, and even more so travelling with a white boyfriend.

Our trip had been planned as part of wider travels to the East spanning over five months. I was fairly confident about travelling independently (having done so alone and with friends to Europe and Africa) but the warnings of other Asian women surprised and disturbed me. India, I was told, would be different and travelling with a white partner I should expect much more harassment and abuse. My mind was becoming full of doubts and prejudgements but I drew comfort from the fact that India was a country which has witnessed hordes of travellers of almost every race and nationality, exploring every inch of its land.

I remember arriving at Delhi airport at 3am, feeling apprehensive and excited. I was really no more knowledgeable about what to expect than any other Western traveller. After waiting hours for our baggage we ventured out into "independent" travelling. It was now 6am and though the sun had barely risen we were shocked by the sheer volume of people – the first thing you notice about India is how densely populated it is. The whole area outside the airport was packed with families, beggars, police, rickshaw wallahs, fruit vendors, taxi men, and of course the famed hotel sellers, relentlessly directing us to the "best room in town", as well as countless others trying to attract our attention to sell, buy or give advice. Luckily we had met an American woman on the plane who was being met by her brother who had been living in India for three years, and despite being heavily jet-lagged we managed to struggle out of the chaos and find them. As Ben had been living on a low budget for a year we were soon jostled towards India's cheapest mode of transport, the local bus. It looked ancient and decrepit and I was convinced it would never manage the long ride into Delhi city.

"Even though I had witnessed such scenes as a child and heard of India's poverty, I was still bewildered at the extreme deprivation we came across during our stay"

In India there are no such things as queues and you learn quickly how to push and shove to get to the front. We piled on to the bus with what seemed like hundreds of others, all Indian, and I gratefully noticed that as a female traveller and a new arrival people would give up their seats to me. Our first impressions were of the sharp images of life glimpsed through the bus window. It took about an hour to reach the city along a road marked by small dwellings and shanty towns made out of paper, cardboard, rubber, tin, in fact anything that the poor could get their hands on. Even though I had witnessed such scenes as a child and heard of India's poverty, I was still bewildered at the extreme deprivation we were to come across during our stay.

Our first week in Delhi was just as I had visualised it and childhood memories suddenly flooded back. We were

staying in the Main Bazaar area of Delhi, near the railway station. This is an old marketplace, full of tiny shops selling everything you could ever need. It's an amazing spectacle of colour and smell, with the persistent noise of fruit and vegetable sellers bargaining over the prices for the day, and rickshaws and bikes swerving through the streets, avoiding the sacred cows that amble in their path. At that stage we were using other travellers' tips and living on a very tight budget. Like most backpackers we tended to be attracted to hotels and eating places where white travellers would meet or end up. To begin with I was unaware that my presence among mostly white men would be seen as strange and immoral behaviour by the Indian men who ran the hotels and eating places.

From the moment of our arrival both Max and I had taken care to dress and act according to Indian customs. At no time did we publicly show affection towards each other such as holding hands, kissing or even being physically close. In England I had been brought up to dress "respectfully" in the presence of family and community so this was not new to me. However, despite our attempts to merge in I soon discovered that being an Asian woman travelling among independent travellers I was perceived very differently by Indian men. People didn't always notice that I was with a white man, especially if Max and I were looking at different things, but as soon as we were together the stares intensified and men would start making comments and even touching me as they walked past. Understanding Hindi made me aware of all the derogatory comments being made about me.

Sometimes this would lead to more direct harassment, with men changing seats so they could touch me in full view of Max. On one occasion, six men got into the compartment and all took turns to insult me, including trying to sit on my lap. I also often heard men describing white women as loose and sexually available. It was clear that to them I was a "white product", a British-born woman doing what mostly white women do, flaunting my independence by travelling around with a white man.

> *"It was clear that to them I was a 'white product', a British-born woman doing what mostly white women do, flaunting my independence"*

We also experienced men approaching Max and talking about me as though I was invisible and had no mind of my own. I was made to feel like an appendage, passive and speaking only through him. Towards the end of our travels I had given up trying to explain my own point of view and simply let Max do all the talking. I felt caught between differing values, having to play an uneasy shifting game of what was expected from an Indian woman. As a child growing up in an Indian family I had experienced a similar "balancing out" of values and had learnt intuitively when to be silent. In India I was silent again, superficially accepting men's behaviour towards me simply to get through a hassle-free day of travelling. But this passivity became much harder as time wore on. Things came to a head in Varanasi, where after only three days I had been subjected to so much abuse and harassment that I retreated to my hotel room and wept. I knew this was not an overreaction or paranoia as white travellers had noticed and commented on how differently I was being treated.

I was left with the feeling that perhaps the two different sides of me just did not fit into Indian life. My attempts to cover up my feminism and, by taking a passive role, to try and gain the approval of Indian men, soon gave way to overwhelming feelings of resentment. It was mortifying when I realised that I was dismissing part of my own culture in a way that can only be described as racist. Unfortunately, being so isolated from other Indian women – I experienced little or no contact with them – my experiences in India were very much male dominated.

These extremely harassing times were also contrasted with some blissfully relaxed moments. After leaving India to spend a while trekking in the Himalayas we returned to spend our last three weeks in Kashmir and Ladakh. Kashmir is known as a tourist attraction and in the month of June many Indians themselves leave the hot plains to cool off in the Kashmir hills. We headed for Dal lake and found a house run by an old Kashmiri man who was obviously respected in the community. We were taken under his family's wing and I experienced no sexual harassment during the stay; due mainly, I am sure, to the fact that his many relatives acknowledged and therefore protected us.

Travelling around India I learnt what it felt like to be an outsider in a culture which I regard as my roots. My experiences, however, were very much my own and I really couldn't say how much they'd apply to other British Asian women travellers. Certainly, the prejudice we encountered as a mixed race couple is not confined to India alone. Returning to England left me in complete culture shock and finding my bearings in British society has again taken time.

Trekking from Kashmir

. . . .

Liz Maudslay made her first trip to India as a student in 1968. Since then she has repeatedly returned, often for several months, and has worked and travelled in many different regions. Her most recent trips have been to the Himalayas for walking and climbing holidays.

"You want houseboat? Five star deluxe. Bathroom attached. Very good houseboat. Very cheap." Arrival in Srinigar can seem the antithesis of the imagined Shangri-la where delicately carved boats rest on tranquil lakes surrounded by snow-peaked mountains. The boats and lakes and mountains are all there. So is the hassling. Tourism has created it; generations of tourists, Indian and Western. And then, unjust but inevitable, it is the tourists who most resent it. However, far from all Kashmiris are the unscrupulous grabbers they are made out to be by the generalising, besieged traveller.

On recent visits I have stayed on a houseboat owned by one of the kindest and most honest families I have ever met. The son, Rashid, also shares my passion for walking and climbing. He regularly takes tourists for short treks and it was while we were talking about these that we developed the plan of sharing a much longer and less frequented trek. We both needed each other for this. I would finance the expedition, paying for the pony men whom he could not otherwise afford, while he would be able to act as guide and translator.

A rich variety of treks can begin in Kashmir, including those which go on into the barer regions of Ladakh and Zanskar. This time we decided to stay in Kashmir and walk from Sonamarg in the north to Bandipur in the west, near the Pakistan border. We estimated this would take us about three weeks.

Unlike Nepal, Kashmir does not have the same small villages where you can find board and lodging; hence you need to take a tent and all your food, and on a longer trek this means pack ponies. Rashid's father, Habib, has been walking in the mountains since he was a boy and knew exactly how much of everything we would need. The whole family joined us in packing up gunny bags full of rice, lentils, tea, oats, sugar and salt and measuring out bottles of kerosene. The next day we caught a bus to Sonamarg where we negotiated with two pony men.

It rained solidly for three days in Sonamarg. Three days of waiting in the tent with only occasional drenched sorties splashing through the mud river of the one main street to buy bread or milk. This can be a problem with Kashmiri treks. The months when the high passes are open are July to September but these are by no means the driest. However, on the fourth day a watery sun emerged and we set off along slippery paths. As we climbed up through the steaming green forest I began to get to know the pony men.

"Why was I wanting to walk in the mountains at all, especially on a route which no one was quite sure of and which no one they knew had ever walked before?"

Manikar was elderly with a grizzled face, very bright eyes, and a thin body which I soon realised would be able to outwalk any of us. He had been on numerous treks and this, along with his age, gave him a licence to tease and play. Aziz was younger and shyer. He had black curly hair and incredibly gentle large brown eyes which would flow through expressions ranging from enjoyment, to bewilderment, embarrassment and shock at Manikar's excesses. Those were my impressions of them but what were theirs of me?

Manikar's previous treks had all been with groups of foreigners. Why was I a woman alone? Where were my husband or brother? Why was I wanting to walk in the mountains at all, especially on a route which no one was quite sure of and which no one they knew had ever walked before? Their way of coping with the situation was for Manikar to become my "father", Aziz my "brother" while Rashid could be the "guide". I accepted my role as daughter and sister. I knew it was the only way which would allow us to become close.

We walked through the forest which smelled of damp pine and up above the treeline to where the grass changed into the dirty snow edge of a glacier. Kashmiri shepherd villages comprise just one or two huts made up of pine trunks and built into the mountainside so that they are six or seven feet high at the front and three or four feet at the back. There are no windows, only a space for a door, and the dank inside smells of the sweet pine needles which make up the floor. The roof is pressed earth where the goats are herded at night. They are inhabited in the summer months by Gujar shepherds who come up from the plains.

This village had only one hut, inhabited by a shepherd, his wife and daughter. As we pitched our tents he came up to talk and asked if I had any medicines for his daughter. This was the first of many such requests and I always felt uneasy and inadequate with the role of the Western omnipotent doctor. But it was also one way in which I could talk easily to the women who otherwise tended to hide shyly as their husbands approached. The daughter was about twelve years old and did look pale and listless. While the summer months give plenty of fresh air and exercise, the diet is a monotonous repetition of *chapati*, made from flour carried up the mountain, washed down with endless cups of *Nun chai* or Kashmiri tea – a reddish liquid made from handfuls of green tea, a little soda and a lot of salt and goat's milk. Both are delicious after a long day's walk, but not a very balanced diet for months on end. In the end I gave her a supply of vitamin pills which usually seemed the best "medicine" to distribute.

"This was the first time the pass had been crossed for thirteen years"

Each summer shepherds come up with their goats to their own *nai* or meadow. They know every step of the way to their own grazing place (however many days' walk it is) but seldom travel from *nai* to *nai*. Walking for pleasure is a luxury of the rich. When we said we were thinking of going over the pass to Vishnesar the shepherd's first response was "impossible". We had expected this and, several cups of *nun chai* later, the impossible had become merely a strange thing to do. As time went on the adventure began to appeal to him and he volunteered to come with us. We set off the next morning, five of us instead of four.

Although nowhere near "impossible" it proved a very hard walk; a long slog across a permanently frozen glacier followed by a sustained and strenuous rock scramble. It was longer still for the ponies who could not scramble but had to toil up in endless diagonal lines. A few eagles made sudden black shadows; two marmots whistled to each other standing up on their hind legs; a lone bear lurched away in the distance. By the time we reached the top of the pass the sky was midday blue and deep copper-coloured rocks made jagged silhouettes against it. We collapsed on the summit before starting the deep descent. Calculating for a minute, the shepherd announced with indisputable authority that this was the first time the pass had been crossed for thirteen years and the first time ever that it had been crossed by ponies. He said it had no name so we called it Manikar pass. The achievement of a pass which was new to all of us cemented the sense of solidarity between Rashid, the pony men and myself.

The shepherd left us the next morning and we walked the easy few miles to Vishnasar, which is on a route travelled not just by shepherds but also by tourists walking the Vishnesar circle trek. Vishnesar (Vishnu's Lake) is a large lake surrounded by crags. It is incredibly large and deep (considering its altitude) and frozen for most of the year but when we arrived its clear green water reflected the rocks around it. It was tempting, but far too cold for a swim and even a quick splash wash took my breath away.

We set off before sunrise past another lake, Krishnasar, and up the steep Krishnasar pass. From the top you could see Parbat shining in the distance. The route then dropped down to a hidden valley. Entering it was like going into a vision of a biblical Galilee: wild lilies, anemones, little crimson cyclamen, edelweiss, and so many flowers whose names I did not know, speckled the grass. A few tall, silky goats crossed our path and, further away, small lakes shone blue against the grey blue rock. The lakes still had islands of ice although the sun was easily hot enough to walk with bare arms.

"Maybe it was the altitude, but we all seemed touched by the Nil Nai magic. I felt incredibly happy"

We did not run south along the Vishnesar circle route but continued west a few miles when a group of staring and laughing children heralded a village. Zhaudoor was not a Gujar village but inhabited by Telaili people who do not come to the mountains just for the summer months but live here all the year round. Physically they are different from the Kashmiris – broader faced, sturdier and fair. Their houses are two-storeyed, wooden and very solid. They need to be; for seven months the village is covered with snow. Even the river, that wide, leaping torrent where we had pitched our tent, freezes solid.   *Zhaudoor* means barley and a few acres of it grew around the houses to be stored for winter. We stayed there for three days and were greeted with much excitement. The children danced and sang for us at night and led us through the one village street where every door was opened to us and every family gave us *nun chai* and *chapati*.

For me, from the outside, it appeared like a self-contained pastoral idyll, but how could I begin to understand what it is like to live there twelve months a year for all of one's life? The men will sometimes walk the two or three days' journey to a road then catch a bus to Srinigar to sell goat meat, eggs, or the socks that were knitted through the winter. Meanwhile the women look after the flocks and do the knitting.

There were two young girls, incredibly beautiful in their bright coloured baggy trousers and long tunics belted with woven shawls. They were poised between childhood and adulthood, not quite old enough to have taken on the shyness of the women. In a year or two they will walk the three or four days to the next Telaili village to be married and continue the same tasks. "Does a teacher ever come?" I asked. "Sometimes. But they find it too lonely here and soon they leave." "And a doctor?" "He should, but doesn't." Sick people can only get treatment if they can manage to walk to the road and, from there, be taken to hospital. One man told me that his wife had died last winter leaving him with four children. I asked him what had been wrong with her. He shrugged. It was a typically Western question; diagnosis is not an option for these villagers.

The route from Zhaudoor went higher still and even further from a road. The highest village, Nil Nai, was not a village at all, just one family living in their hut surrounded by a blue vista of mountains stretching far into Pakistan. The two young shepherd boys were amazed at our offerings of chocolate and balloons, staring at them with as much entranced delight as I kept staring at their mountain view. Maybe it was the altitude but we all seemed touched by the Nil Nai magic. I felt incredibly happy and Manikar teased even more than usual. None of us could sleep that night and from his tent we heard Manikar singing loudly, beginning with traditional prayers to Allah but, as time went on, making up his own words, singing our trek back to us and incorporating all of us into the refrain.

From Nil Nai there was a long descent when we had to jump endlessly over miles of boulders until at last we reached the river we had hoped to find. It was late to find it. The melting snows had made it much fuller than it would have been in early morning. But we locked arms and staggered across. A few miles along the bank on the other side we had been told there was a village called Tressingham.

Tressingham. To me the name seemed more fitting to the southeast of England than to the northwest of Kashmir. A narrow bridge separated us from the six or seven Gujar huts and, as we unpacked the ponies and pitched our tents, people crossed over. The men first, mostly tall, all thin and wiry, wearing long *kurta* and baggy Kashmiri trousers. Then the children, tangle-haired and huge-eyed, and finally, hovering on the outer circle, the women, with their straight hair plaited back from high cheekbones and held under small delicately woven hats.

One woman came through the circle of men. She was older, her body like a rope, her hair grey twine. She cradled a lump of salt brought up from below. She stood erect, too old to have to put on the protection of shyness and with-drawal. Her voice was like a single string of wire. "I want to say as the first foreigner to enter our village you are welcome." British immigration laws came into my mind: Bangladeshis

denied a house because they already had a home in Bangladesh; Sri Lankans moored on a boat; virginity tests. What welcome would she receive as the first foreigner from Tressingham to come to my country? Boundaries may be common to all countries but barriers are not reciprocal.

"'I want to say as the first foreigner to enter our village you are welcome'"

We collected wood and lit a fire. People brought milk, yoghurt and hot *chapati*. We brewed *nun chai*. As it grew dark the men started to sing. Rich praising of Allah simultaneously joyful and soulful. "And this song," said the young man, whose serious air and glasses made him look more like an undergraduate than a shepherd, "is in praise of Benazir Bhutto." Pakistan was only a walk and a border away and far more home for these Gujars than the India which had been thrust upon them. After the singing the dancing began – men squatting, Cossack-style, on their haunches flashing long sticks. Another country linked; another border eroded.

Tressingham was the last of the real magic. Now we were nearing roads on the other side. Already what was almost a path appeared as we dropped down to the next night's village, Kindapani (Rock-Water). This was a much larger affair. Two groups of ten or twelve huts each and what, after the last few weeks, seemed like a mass of people. It was the Muslim festival *BoroId* and we stayed two days to celebrate it, giving away what was left of our sweets and balloons and being pressed with goat's meat in return.

Two days later the path became a track and, as if an invisible but definitive line had been drawn, the mountains ended. Paddy fields emerged and proper large houses with farmyards. One by one, signs of civilisation closed in on us: a bicycle, a truck, a small shop. The trek was over. It was in Erin that Manikar and Aziz left us and we said sad goodbyes with promises of photos, letters and more treks. We had shared little actual language but had communicated more than I have with people I have talked with for hours.

Rashid was ill when we stayed at Erin. Kashmiri men, I found out, were no different from English ones when it came to illness. He refused the tea I made him and then insisted on making his own; he grumbled incessantly at the heat and the flies of the apple orchard where we were camping; and he was sure he was dying. "It is always like this," he said "always when I leave the mountains I am sick." I could empathise with that. I too felt an ache at leaving behind the mountains.

When he had recovered we went down to the town of Bandipur and caught a rickety bus to Srinigar. By now the trek had become something different – an adventure to talk and laugh about together, to boast about, and, in my case, to write about. But something of the specialness had to be left behind.

TRAVEL NOTES

Languages Hindi is the official national language but it is by no means universally spoken and there are hundreds of other regional languages and dialects. English is widely spoken.

Transport Trains are the main form of transport. Most tourists use second class reserved seats (second class unreserved gets ludicrously crowded and is best avoided). Some trains also have compartments reserved exclusively for women. Buying and reserving your tickets can take hours; sometimes there are separate queues for women – worth taking advantage of since they massively cut down time. If you've got money you can fly between major cities but there are frequent delays and booking difficulties.

Accommodation A whole range of hotels from expensive luxury palace-style accommodation to bug-ridden cells. There is no shortage of cheap, clean and perfectly safe places to stay. A government tourist bungalow (middling price range) is usually a safe bet. With so much choice there's never any need to stay in a hotel if you feel uneasy there.

Special Problems You're quite likely to get ill in India. Various kinds of dysentery and infective hepatitis are real hazards, though you might get away with just a dose of "Delhi belly". It makes sense not to drink unboiled water or to eat unpeeled fruit.

Theft is common and you should always keep your money and valuables securely on your person, preferably in a money belt. It's a good idea to carry small change to give to beggars, or a little food to share with children. You will also find hundreds of hustlers fighting for your attention. You need to learn quickly how to stay calm and clearheaded.

Guides *India – A Travel Survival Kit* (Lonely Planet) is invaluable, at least to begin with; later you may feel you need to break out of "the circuit". Lonely Planet also publish a regional guide to *Kashmir, Ladakh and Zanskar* and a *Trekking Guide to the Indian Himalayas*. For cultural detail the *Murray's Handbook to India* (John Murray), though originally published half a century ago, remains in a class of its own.

Contacts

AHMEDABAD: **SEWA (Self-Employed Women's Association)**, Textile Worker's Union Building, Ahmedabad (see introduction for more details).

BANGALORE: **Streelekha** (International Feminist Bookshop and Information Centre), 67, 2nd floor, Blumoan Complex, Mahatma Ghandi Road, Bangalore 560 011, Katnataka. Stocks all manner of feminist literature, journals, posters etc and provides space for women to meet.

BOMBAY: **Feminist Resource Centre (FRD)**, 13 Carol Mansion, 35 Sitladevi Temple Rd., Mahim, Bombay 400016. Carries out action-oriented research from a feminist perspective on a range of issues: health, sexuality, violence against women, discrimination at work.

Women's Centre, 307 Yasmeen Apartments, Yashwant Nagar, Vakola, Santa Cruz East, Bombay.

Research Unit on Women's Studies SNDT Women's University; 1 Nathibai Thackersey Rd., Bombay 400 020. Publishes a quarterly newsletter of the Research Unit on Women's Studies – useful resource about organisations and institutions in India involved in research and projects on women and development.

BORIVILI: **Forum Against the Oppression of Women**, c/o Vibhuti Patel, K 8 Nensey Colony, Express Highway, Borivili East 400066.

NEW DELHI: **Institute of Social Studies (ISS)**, 5 Deen Dayal Upadhyaya Marg, New Delhi 2. Voluntary, non-profit research organisation – concentrates on women's access to employment and role in development, also on strengthening women's organisations. The group publishes a newsletter.

Centre for Women's Development Studies, B-43, Panchsheel Enclave, New Delhi 110017. Undertakes research on women and development, and is currently developing a clearing house of information and ideas.

Indian Social Institute (ISI) Programme for Women's Development, Lodi Rd., New Delhi 110003. Aims to increase the participation of women at different levels in the development process through training courses for community organisers.

Indian Council of Social Science Research (ICSSR), 11PA Hostel, Indraprastha Estate, Ring Rd., New Delhi, 110002. Runs a women's studies programme and carries out wide-ranging research. They also organise numerous workshops and symposia on feminist themes.

Manushi, c/202 Lajpat Nagar, New Delhi 110024. Publishes the monthly journal Manushi – an excellent source of information on news and analysis of women's situation and struggle in India. Written in English and Hindi.

Kali for Women (feminist publishers), N 84 Panchshila Park, New Delhi, 110017.

The journal, **Manushi**, can be obtained in the UK from Manushi c/o Colworth Rd., London E11; in the US from Manushi, c/o 5008 Erringer Place, Philadelphia, PA 19144.

Books

Madhu Kishwar and Ruth Vanita, eds., *In Search of Answers: Indian Women's Voices* (Zed Books, 1984). Collection of articles from Manushi which provides a comprehensive, powerful and lucid account of women in Indian society.

Jeniffer Sebstad, *Women and Self-Reliance in India: the SEWA story* (Zed Books, 1985). Account of the formation and achievements of SEWA (see introduction).

Joanna Liddle and Rama Joshi, *Daughters of Independence – Gender, Caste and Class in India* (Zed Books, 1985). Reveals the extent to which class and caste define and limit Indian women's lives.

Gail Omvedt, *We Will Smash This Prison! Indian Women in Struggle* (Zed Books, 1980). A compelling account of women's struggles in western India in the 1970s.

Gita Mehta, *Karma Cola* (Fontana, 1979). Still in print, though now slightly dated. This is a sharp and cynical look at the way Indian spirituality is marketed for Western devotees.

Dervla Murphy, *On a Shoestring to Coorg: An experience of Southern India* (1976; Century 1985). More classic adventures by the well-known contemporary traveller, this time with her five-year-old daughter.

There are interesting contributions on India by **Marilyn French** in *Women: A World Report* (Methuen, 1985), by **Devaki Jain** in *Sisterhood is Global* (Penguin, 1985), and by the Manushi collective and an Indian Women's Anti-Rape Group in *Third World: Second Sex 1 and 2* (Zed Books, 1983 and 1987). See the general bibliography for details.

Minority Rights Group, *India the Nagas and the North-East* (MRG No. 17), ***The Untouchables of India*** (MRG No. 26) and ***The Sikhs*** (MRG No. 65). An exceptionally high standard of research and analysis, the MRG pamphlets will give you a quick and clear overview of the very deep divisions in Indian society.

Fiction

Anita Desai, *Clear Light of Day* (Penguin, 1980), ***Baumgartner's Bombay*** (Penguin, 1981). The best known titles from a widely acclaimed and prolific writer. Her books chart the changing position of women in a rapidly developing society.

Truth-tales: Contemporary Writing by Indian Women (The Women's Press, 1986). A collection of stories, many of them translated into English for the first time, by contemporary Indian women writers.

Attia Housain, *Sunlight on a Broken Column* (Virago, 1989). Set against the backdrop of Indian Independence this centres on the life of an orphaned girl growing up in a fundamentalist Muslim community.

Padma Perera, *Birthday, Deathday* (The Women's Press, 1985). Short stories, mainly exploring the contradictions for an Indian woman educated in the West on returning to her homeland.

Leena Dhingra, *Amritvela* (The Women's Press, 1988). Stylish account of a middle-aged woman's return to her native India after a life in England.

Sharan-Jat Shar, *In My Own Name* (The Women's Press, 1985). Autobiographical account of growing up in the Punjab, a life that includes forced marriage and emigration.

Shashi Deshpande, *That Long Silence* (Virago, 1988). A middle-class woman retreats to the country around Bombay and reconsiders her past.

Ruth Prawer Jhabvala, *Heat and Dust* (Futura, 1976), ***A Backward Place*** (Penguin, 1979), and others. Famous as a Booker prize-winner and long-time collaborator on Merchant/Ivory films, her writing charts the more irrational responses to Indian life.

Indonesia

. . . .

Indonesia extends over a vast chain of more than ten thousand islands. Though remote and exotic by European or American standards, for millions of Australians and New Zealanders this island nation constitutes the nearest form of abroad. Consequently, at least on better known islands, Indonesians are well used to independent travellers and, alongside the thriving package-tour industry (with developments particularly along the beaches of Bali), there is plenty of cheap, basic accommodation.

Despite being rich in resources, the general standard of living in Indonesia is very low, exacerbated by a rapid growth in population. This is most evident on the island of Java which now holds over 160 million people – most of whom are crammed into its polluted, chaotic, and heavily policed capital, Jakarta. As the nation's administrative centre, Java's influence, known as "System Jakarta", is widely resented and often disparaged as the successor to Dutch colonial rule.

In a nation of so many cultures, religions and languages, it is perhaps surprising that different groups manage to coexist and that the country as a whole has an image of stability. But the underside of this is the harsh, swift, and often brutal suppression of any opposition to General Suharto's regime, that has included the forced resettlement of islanders and the brutal military occupation of East Timor and West Irian. The people of Indonesia are predominantly Muslim but tend to be tolerant towards the different habits of Westerners, and provided you are careful to respect local customs you are unlikely to encounter the sort of aggressive sexual harassment reported by

women travellers in, say, Malaysia. You will however attract a fair amount of attention (often just friendly curiosity) which can feel oppressive at times. Indonesians neither share, nor sympathise with, the Western preoccupation with personal space, and privacy is something you have to learn quickly to do without.

Indonesian women certainly seem more independent and visible than in most Islamic countries. The islands' interpretation of Islam does not demand that women are veiled, government schools are co-educational, and there is relatively little discrimination between the sexes with respect to subjects studied and the number of years spent studying. Whether this will endure is uncertain. Despite government curbs, Islamic fundamentalism has recently gained ground, attempting to reaffirm Malay culture in opposition to Western influence.

There is a long tradition of organisation among Indonesian women. Voluntary women's groups have played an increasingly important role in the provision and delivery of social welfare services throughout the country. The Indonesian Women's Congress (*KOWANI*), a federation of the main **women's organisations** set up in 1928, runs a "legal literacy" programme and helps rural women to understand legal rights. It is campaigning for a more uniform marriage law to prohibit polygyny, child marriage and arbitrary male-initiated divorce, is lobbying for equal inheritance laws, and has autonomous groups focusing on a range of issues including reform of the abortion laws. In some areas these groups have to operate amidst considerable (and escalating) harassment from the emerging Islamic fundamentalist movement.

A Plant Collector's Dream

. . . .

After spending four weeks in the well-travelled islands of Java, Lombok and Bali, Janet Bell spent six months collecting medicinal plants on Seram, a small island in the Moluccas in the far east of Indonesia.

Joseph and Meli were transfixed by the tea bag I had produced from my pack. It wasn't until we lit a fire and made a brew that they were fully satisfied that its contents were what I'd promised.

What delight! Joseph's face lit up at the taste and he chuckled quietly.

The light was fading and the almost saturated mist had become quite chill. I still couldn't believe that we were only two degrees south of the equator and I was craving a woolly sweater. The drop in temperature associated with altitude seemed more pronounced than I was used to, but by now the only too familiar mountainous terrain had also modified my attitude to height, when I considered that we were already about the same height as Ben Nevis.

Indonesia's dramatic and varied scenery continued to amaze me. Seram was completely different from the fertile, highly-populated, volcanic islands of Java, Bali and Lombok, which had served as my introduction to this huge and diverse country.

While I cooked some food for our demanding stomachs, Joseph and Meli collected ferns and made a mattress under the overhang, our shelter for the night. Little did I realise at the time that it was for my benefit, not theirs. We ate our rice with some dried spiced fish from the coastal village we'd left that morning. Rice was something of a treat for all of us since, unlike most of Indonesia, sago was the staple diet in the Moluccas. However, its wallpaper-paste-like consistency scarcely lent it the characteristics of good hiking fodder, and neither did the flavour.

Joseph and Meli experimented with a tea bag themselves while I dealt with my pack. Everything I produced was questioned – "apa ini?" (what is it?), "untuk apa?" (what's it for?); my torch, my knife, my first-aid kit, even my loo roll, for which I could provide no explanation. The things I considered essential seemed trivial, when all my companions' needs fitted into a small pouch. Still, they seemed grateful for the odd garment I offered for the night.

I snuggled down on my temporary bed and contemplated the sky above me. It was rare to have the opportunity to sleep under the stars without fear of a night-time downpour. The overhang would protect me sufficiently without blocking my view. I looked up the steep gorge, which was strongly illuminated by the moon, despite the night being somewhat overcast. I thought that if I were to awake during the night once the clouds had cleared, I would probably think it was morning. Already a long way beneath us, I heard the Wai Lala rushing down from the ridge we were heading over, its swirling blue waters ricocheting relentlessly against the sides of the gorge as it plummeted to the south coast.

The morning was chilly. Meli prepared himself for the climb by viciously rubbing *daun sila* leaves all over his legs and producing huge red welts similar to nettle stings, but far more painful. The locals used the leaves whenever they undertook a long trip to ease weariness in their limbs and to ward off cold at higher altitudes. It seemed more like shock treatment to me. Still, I made a note in my book to add to my ever-increasing list of plants used by the local people.

"The women were surprisingly uninhibited in their approach; touching me, playing with my hair, and patting my bottom and thighs in sheer disbelief"

That was, after all, my reason for being on this rugged, paradisical island, 1500 miles from Jakarta. This particular trip was taking me inland over an 1800m pass, one of the lowest points in the dramatic ridge that separated the interior villages from the coast, a formidable barrier that still isolates them from the fingers of commercialism which have encroached upon the coastal villages. The ridge, I learnt, is much more than a physical barrier, but has a significant role in the history and mythology related to the Seramese culture. It also represents the division between the northern and southern tribes on Seram, the Manusela and the Nuaulu.

Further to our west the ridge climaxed in the stark limestone outcrop of Gunung Binaia, the "mother mountain", the greatest spirit force in the eyes of the people and the foundation for the matriarchal lineage that characterises the whole island. This association, coupled with the fact that Islam has no great hold on the island, has meant that the women have rather more of a respected position in society than might be expected. Even in the parts of Indonesia where Islam dominates, women have a better position than in the more fundamentalist areas of the Islamic world. This is the reflection of a culture that has evolved by picking up, adapting and modifying the various religious and cultural waves that have swept through its land over the centuries. As a fulcrum of the Indo-China trading axis, Indonesia has distilled diverse influences to create an identity of its own.

Our hike took us up steeply into the mysterious serenity of the moss forest. There was an uncharacteristic calm and quiet at this height, in sharp contrast to the riotous noises of the lowland rainforest. Misty epiphytes hung from moss-covered trees, beards of soft pastel-coloured lichen draped themselves between the branches, the scenery black and white in soft focus; all my senses were muffled by the mist. My feet sank silently into the spongy moss beneath us, giving life and a new spring to my stride. But this was a false paradise; from time to time my legs would crash straight through the luxurious covering, taking me thigh-deep into a limestone gully.

"Taller and broader than most of the men in the village, let alone the women, white-skinned and Western, I obviously didn't go unnoticed"

A rapid descent led us to Manusela, where we received an extraordinary welcome. Taller and broader than most of the men in the village, let alone the women, white-skinned and Western, I obviously didn't go unnoticed. Joseph and Meli had evidently found our little trip together as amusing and curious as I had, and I was frustrated that my Indonesian didn't stretch to interpreting their breakneck account of the hike.

We had attracted quite a gathering of tiny, smiling people. The women were surprisingly uninhibited in their approach; touching me, playing with my hair, and patting my bottom and thighs in sheer disbelief. "Kaki besar!" (big legs), the Bapak Raja's wife had exclaimed. But, for once it wasn't an insult, simply an observation.

The villagers in the interior were even tinier than their coastal counterparts, which is partly accounted for by their more impoverished diet. The creation of a National Park whose boundaries had encroached into their hunting grounds had resulted in dependence on their gardens, a few domestic chickens (which never seemed to be eaten), and a few tiny fish and prawns from the rivers. Where hunting was still permitted, it was generally the man's job, but out of the hunting season they would tend the gardens with the women; these were often situated at least an hour's walk away from the village. It was also a common sight to see a man cradling an infant and looking after the small children.

We were invited to stay in the house of the Bapak Raja, the village leader, literally the "father king". In Manusela the Bapak Raja not only acted as the father figure and the law, but appeared in church on Sunday morning as the pastor, preaching from the pulpit, his head emerging from underneath the festoons of glittering streamers that I usually associated with Christmas. It was a rare sight in that simple wooden building with magnificent views up towards the heavy rounded form of Merkele Besar and its smaller and more elegant partner, the pyramidal Merkele Kecil. No organ here, just a choir of simple pipes and the rich sounds of what are reputedly the best voices in Indonesia.

Despite Seram's geographical isolation and inaccessibility, it didn't survive the invasion of the missionaries. Most of the villages were at least nominally Muslim or Christian. In the interior they were predominantly Christian, although it soon became obvious that the traditional animist beliefs remained very strong. I was told a story about the history of the island by a man who lived in a neighbouring village. Noah's Ark apparently came to rest on the top of Binaia's neighbour, Merkele Besar, the paternal mountain. The villagers in the interior believe that the whole of the human race diversified from Manusela; their Bible stories all seemed to incorporate this strange blend of Christianity and local mythology.

"Plants were such an integral part of their lives that they couldn't look on them objectively or in isolation, as I did"

I had the good fortune to spend a few days in one of a very few villages to fully maintain its animist traditions. The villagers were proud of their culture and looked down on the rest of the island for having succumbed to other religions. They did not travel out of their territorial areas to any great extent and spoke a dialect which was difficult for even my Indonesian companions to understand. On our way to Houalu we stopped a night at another village on the coast where we came across a huge timbered monstrosity amongst the bamboo huts.

This, it transpired, was a missionary house, and its residents were focusing on the last bastion of traditional Seramese culture: Houalu. I couldn't help but smile inwardly when we learnt that although the missionaries had been there for over three years and were constantly trying to gain approval from the animists to build their house in Houalu, so far no permission had been or seemed likely to be granted. So far there were no converts either.

The day began in the same ways every day while I was staying in these villages. I would wake up to the sound of cocks crowing, babies crying and people coughing. At dawn the river was a hive of activity as the children filled the bamboo poles which served as elegant water carriers. The adults would make off for the gardens as soon as it was light to avoid the heat of the day. Sometimes I went with them, picking up endless plants along the way and inquiring about their uses. I soon learnt that direct questions about the way they used plants for food, medicines or

construction materials yielded precious little information, simply because they didn't understand the question. Plants were such an integral part of their lives that they couldn't look on them objectively or in isolation, as I did. Most of my records were derived from direct observation or pointing out a plant and questioning its use.

During my stay I collected over 300 plants which served some useful purpose, but I had the feeling even then that I was only scraping the surface. Many of these had medicinal value, but others served quite curious purposes. For example, mashed young pineapple served as a DIY perming kit and the serrated and corrugated leaves of one creeping plant were used as toothbrushes.

The use of medicinal plants is not limited to isolated parts of Indonesia though, for in Java there are small factories which have been set up to produce "Jamu", as traditional medicine is known there. This small but profitable industry is run almost entirely by women and is regaining popularity as the preferred form of treatment, even where Western drugs are readily available.

It was very hard to leave Seram and its peaceful way of life, and I wondered what the next few years would bring; how far the logging road will penetrate into the interior, whether the missionaries will achieve their goals in Houalu, how long it will be before Manusela sees its first shop and the dawn of consumerism, how long before Coke cans clutter the pristeen pathways between the bamboo houses in Manusela. Jakarta brought me down to earth with a bump, the city of the great hypocrisy, attempting to unify and represent a country as diverse in culture and ideology as they come. "Do they hunt with bows and arrows in England?", one Bapak Raja had asked me on Seram. His country's capital would have presented him with as many surprises as a trip to London.

TRAVEL NOTES

Languages The national language is Bahasa Indonesian, relatively easy to learn at a basic level. There are over 200 languages and dialects among ethnic groups. Younger people and those working in the tourist industry generally speak some English.

Transport Boats and *bemos* (buses) are plentiful and cheap; hitching is uncommon but possible and relatively safe.

Accommodation Wide range – from luxury hotels to beach huts.

Guides *Indonesia Handbook* (Moon Publications, US) is a classic guide, so fascinating that it has been banned for sale in Indonesia – though you can carry it in.

Contacts

Organisan Wanita Jakarta Raya *(KOWANI)*, Jalan Diponegoro 26, Jakarta, Pusat. See introduction.

Books

Raden Adjeng Kartini, *Letters of a Javanese Princess* (Heinemann, Asia, 1983). Letters of a nineteenth-century Indonesian feminist and national heroine.

Nina Epton, *Magic and Mystics of Java* (Octagon Press, 1975). Interesting travelogue with anthropological slant.

Hamish McDonald, *Suharto's Indonesia* (Fontana, 1980). Thorough political account of events since 1965.

Minority Rights Group, *Women in Asia* (MRG, 1982). Contains an interesting section on Indonesian women.

A chapter on the rise of the Indonesian women's rights movement is included in **Kumari Jayawardena,** *Feminism and Nationalism in the Third World* (Zed Books, 1986).

Iran

· · · · · · · · · · · · · · · · · · · ·

Whilst it is still possible to get into Iran on a two-week transit visa, it is difficult to contemplate travelling through this country with any degree of sanguinity or ease. In ten years of rule, the Ayatollah Khomeini created a climate of oppression unrivalled by even the excesses of the Shah. His successor, President Rafsanjani, has a reputation for pragmatism and a less rigidly anti-Western line, but seems unlikely to significantly challenge the more radically fundamentalist factions. Arbitrary arrests, torture and harassment by the Revolutionary Guards may have slightly abated but still

continue as a day-to-day reality while women, who bear the brunt of the nation's poverty, remain restricted and relatively powerless under Khomeini's interpretations of Shi'ite Islamic Law.

The most obvious laws that affect you as a traveller are those concerning dress – your whole body must be covered and hair hidden beneath a veil. Iranian women who refuse the veil, often as a spontaneous form of protest, run risks of flogging and imprisonment (as a foreigner you're more likely to be severely cautioned and forced to cover up). But however modestly you dress, you are bound to feel conspicuous and vulnerable; asserting your freedom to wander about independently places you in much the same category as a prostitute and you may well be harassed as such.

Against this, however, you can encounter incredible warmth and hospitality. In public, people tend to be constrained from approaching you by the omnipresent Revolutionary Guards, but in the privacy of their homes, Iranians often show traditional generosity and consideration for strangers, welcoming the chance to air their hopes and concerns about the future of their country. You have to be very careful not to compromise your hosts – it's actually illegal for an Iranian man to spend time alone with a woman who is not a relative. Despite these very real deterrents women do still make the journey across Iran. The undeniable beauty of the country and the nostalgic romance of the overland route to India provide the main incentives. Also, in purely practical terms travel is fairly easy. There are good roads and bus networks and plentiful budget hotels.

Whilst the rise of fundamentalism and the re-introduction of Islamic Law has affected the **status of women** throughout the Muslim world, Iran provides perhaps the most extreme example of women's repression under, and resistance to, this trend.

Women had been at the forefront of the revolution that toppled the Shah in 1979. Within the first few days of Khomeini's regime 25,000 women took to the streets of Teheran to protest their rights against pronouncements that women should veil in public. They were beaten and imprisoned. Since then wave after wave of legislation in accordance with Shi'ite interpretations of the Koran has been passed, effectively denying women any economic role, and relegating their status to that of "absolute property" of the man at the head of the family.

With a woman's testimony legally defined as worth half that of a man's, the dangers of being denounced to a popular court (usually for crimes of sexual immorality) are extreme; lengthy imprisonment, flogging and stoning are standard punishments, particularly for working-class women who have no recourse to bribes. Women have continued to oppose these laws, which are seen as threatening their security at the heart of the family and society. Besides mass demonstrations and spontaneous acts of defiance (anything from going unveiled to assassination attempts on Ayatollahs), large numbers of women have supported oppositional parties such as the People's Mujahideen and staged public protests against the Iran/Iraq war.

By the mid-Eighties over 20,000 women had been executed for "counter-revolutionary" or "anti-Islamic" activity. (Holland has been one of the few countries to accept Iranian women as political refugees overtly because of the sexual discrimination they face.) Whilst feminist groups in Iran have been forced underground, many still operate in exile.

A Lonely Journey

· · · · · · · · · · · · ·

Wendy Dison has been travelling for the last eight years. Deciding that a career in administration was not for her, she set off first around Europe and Africa and then on to Asia, crossing Iran alone on her way to the Himalayas.

"Salaam, Salaam." The face of the Iranian immigration officer at the border creased with pleasure when I greeted him in Farsi. Over his desk hung a sign which read "No East. No West. Islamic Republic.", and next to it a portrait of Khomeini glared at me.

As the official inspected my passport, looking from my face to the photo and back again, the smile was replaced by a frown. "Monsieur? Madame?" he asked. My short hair confused him and when he realised that I wasn't a man he made urgent gestures that I must cover my head.

I put on a woollen bobble hat which satisfied him, though the young men I talked to on the bus to Tabriz advised me kindly that to comply with Islamic law I must wear a scarf covering my hair and neck. They were students returning from Izmir university and had brought Turkish scarves, prettier than Iranian, for their mothers and sisters and they generously gave one to me. I must wear a knee-length coat too, they said, to hide the shape of my body.

The February sun was warm and the discomfort of wearing a scarf and long jacket increased my resentment. As we travelled through the pale, stony landscape the students talked to me of the repression and cruelty suffered in Iran since the Shah was overthrown in 1979 and Khomeini created his Islamic Republic. Never before had I felt such foreboding on entering a country.

"At one spot we were ordered off the bus and herded behind a wall under spotlights"

Between the border and Tabriz, a distance of 300 kilometres, we were stopped six times. Sometimes the police wanted to check our passports, other times Revolutionary Guards, wearing military-style uniforms, stopped us. Their job was to enforce the strict Islamic code and they searched our bus for drugs, arms and alcohol, forbidden foreign music and indecent pictures. They emptied handbags, confiscated cassettes, and ripped pictures of women with bare arms – or worse – from magazines.

We were treated with contempt and I was taut with resentment while photos of my family were inspected and my journal read. Probably few of them could read English but after this I kept separate notes, buried deep in my rucksack, of anything likely to cause trouble. At one stop we were ordered off the bus and herded behind a wall under spotlights. The guards bullied us and an old woman was crying. I was taken with the women into a hut where we were body-searched by a female guard, all but invisible under a black enveloping *chador*.

It was dark when we arrived in Tabriz; night is a bad time to arrive in a city and the darkness made me more than unusually aware of the security I was leaving. A man I'd talked to on the bus also got off here. He told me he was visiting his sister and when he learnt that I had no plans he invited me to her house. "She will be happy if you stay with her," he said.

In a modern suburb of the city his sister, Eshrat, lived with her two young children and sister-in-law, Parvin. The women were delighted to see their brother and they fussed happily round both of us. They displayed a talent not rare in the East; that of making me feel at once a special guest yet very much at home. We sat drinking tea around a tall wood stove on Persian rugs, their half-forgotten English slowly returning as we talked.

Parvin and Eshrat were married to brothers who had been imprisoned for "being intelligent and lacking sympathy with the government". With bitterness they talked of life before the Revolution, when the Shah's policies of Westernisation and the new wealth from oil had brought a flood of nightclubs, dance halls, cinemas and bars to the cities.

Religion and politics have always been closely interwoven in Iran and with the overthrow of the Shah the religious leaders, angered by the growing materialism, banned these trappings of decadent Western culture. Only religious or classical Persian music was permitted, fashionable imported goods disappeared from the shops, and the menus in restaurants were restricted so much that people no longer ate out for pleasure. For those who weren't religious there was little joy in life.

Far more invidious was the position of women, who had been forced to return to their traditional role in society, denied freedom, further education and the opportunity to work. Parvin's medical training had been curtailed. Because female staff are needed in girls' schools, Eshrat was able to keep her job as a teacher, one of the few occupations still open to women.

Her uniform was a loose, dark tunic and a cowl that left only a circle of her face exposed. Most women wore the *chador*, a black sheet draped over the head and hanging shapelessly to the feet, worn over indoor clothes when outside the house. Those against the regime could keep within the law – though earn disapproval – by wearing a loose knee-length coat and headscarf pulled well forward to cover the hair. I hoped my jacket, which reached mid-thigh, was sufficiently modest, for I was warned that the Revolutionary Guards who patrolled the streets would stop any woman not considered decently dressed.

"All I could see of the women around me were the triangles of eyes and nose visible under the chadors"

The Iranians I met hated the regime they were forced to live under and all talked of leaving Iran. They dreamed of living in Britain or the USA but passports were not being issued and the few people who left the country did so illegally. Demand for hard currency by those planning to leave has resulted in a thriving black market. Of course, because Khomeini's supporters would disapprove of a veil-less woman, I met only pro-Western Iranians and my impressions were necessarily one-sided.

Next day Parvin and I dressed in our street clothes and caught a bus to the bazaar in the city. I was shocked to find separate entrances on the bus for men and women and that inside we sat segregated by metal bars. All I could see of the women around me were the triangles of eyes and nose visible under the *chadors*. When they struggled on and off the bus with a baby and a shopping bag they had difficulty remaining covered and most of them habitually used their teeth to trap the *chador* tightly round their faces. I felt revulsion against a society that treated women like this.

Women took advantage of one area where they could show their individuality. Though they were always black, the fabric of *chadors* varied from plain nylon to finely embroidered silk – reflecting the taste and social standing of their owners. Other clues to identity were given by elegant high-heeled shoes peeping below a hem, the flash of gold rings on well manicured fingers or a hennaed pattern painted on the back of a hand. Except for the odd turban and the popularity of beards, the men, in trousers and cotton jackets, looked like Europeans.

When I left Tabriz, Parvin guided me through the jungle of Persian script at the bus station and wouldn't let me pay for my ticket. We hugged goodbye, both sorry that I couldn't stay longer, but my visa barely gave me enough time to cross the country. We hoped we might meet again in England. As a result of the Iran/Iraq war doctors were in demand and Parvin was to be allowed to complete her training, possibly in London.

The journey to Teheran began with prayers led by the driver, who possibly had his erratic driving in mind. Frilled curtains hung at the windows and an elaborate arrangement of silk flowers obstructed the driver's view. This was a deluxe bus but there was no air conditioning nor did the windows open. As the sun rose so did the temperature inside the bus, and I suffered in my jacket and scarf. On the back of the ticket was printed "Please observe regulations as to the Islamic covering", which seemed unfair under the circumstances.

The restaurant where we stopped for lunch was a large isolated building in the desert – functional and soulless. As in all Iranian restaurants we paid on entry, a procedure simplified by limiting the menu to one item, invariably *chello kebab*, a bland dish of rice and grilled meat. Meal stops were short and people ate rapidly, leaning over their plates. This time I only wanted tea and was directed to the kitchen where, in the dark and confusion, a man beckoned to me. He gave me tea but held my arm to prevent my leaving while another man thrust a hand up under my jacket.

For a long moment I wanted to throw my tea over them, but they laughed at my anger and I fled. I found a seat and sipped my tea, trying to look calm. A woman sat at my table and we exchanged smiles, allies in a man's world. Back on the bus I wanted to share a bag of pistachio nuts with my neighbour but her *chador* enveloped her so completely that I couldn't talk to her. My feeling of isolation was acute.

Apart from the incident in the kitchen I wasn't bothered by men. The stares I often attracted were curious rather than lecherous. Though I received much Muslim hospitality and people were kind and helpful, I didn't relax in Iran. People seemed afraid to show too much friendliness and usually remained distant and guarded. I was nervous too, not knowing the power of the various authorities. In Teheran when I was taken by police to the station for questioning, even though they were courteous I thought anything could happen and I was worried.

With a two-week visa I hadn't time for more than a superficial look at the cities I passed through, and I only saw the countryside through a bus window. Yet I was left with vivid impressions: mud villages that appeared to grow out of the earth, high snow-topped mountains forming a background to arid plains, goats foraging around the black felt tents of tribal nomads, ancient bazaars with lofty brick-vaulted roofs, tombs of medieval poets in rose-filled gardens and, in every village and corner of the city, the graceful turquoise domes of the mosques. I remember in particular the splendid Royal Mosque at Isfahan, decorated inside and out with intricate patterns of rich blue and gold mosaic tiles which completely cover the walls and domes.

"Once we got in his car, his nervousness showed that he knew the risk he was taking"

The beauty of Isfahan was marred, however, by giant paintings of Khomeini which hung in prominent sites. The heavy brows, hard staring eyes and thick lips appeared merciless. Because of the association with this cruel face I no longer enjoyed the singing of the muezzin calling the faithful to prayer. The chant now sounded menacing.

In Shiraaz I became friendly with a man staying at the same hotel as me and accepted his offer to drive me to see Persepolis, the sixth-century capital of Persia. Once we got in his car his nervousness showed that he knew the risk he was taking – Islamic law forbids an unchaperoned woman to be with a man who isn't a relative. "If we are stopped you must say I am your guide and that you are paying me," he said.

Away from the city he relaxed. We explored the ruins, stopped in a village where the best halva in Iran comes from, and had lunch of kebabs and grape juice at a roadside café. It was good to be out in the sunshine even though I couldn't take off my jacket and scarf. My hotel room was the only place I could remove them; even crossing the landing to the bathroom was considered public.

Checking out of the hotel the next day I discovered that my passport, left at reception, was missing. The next 24 hours were a nightmare. The British Consul in Teheran said he couldn't replace the passport but would issue me with papers to enable me to fly back to England. I wept with frustration. The hotel owner suspected my friend. Wasn't he desperate enough to leave Iran? The idea appalled me that the thief could be someone I trusted.

The police were very concerned and treated me kindly. That night they came to the hotel to question the staff and evidently frightened the thief so much that he jettisoned my passport. I found it lying on the stairs next morning and cried with relief. The hotel owner put an arm of comfort round my shoulder but as soon as he realised his indiscretion he pulled away quickly. "What a bloody country" I thought, smiling at him through my tears. I caught the next bus to Zahedan on the Pakistan border.

TRAVEL NOTES

Languages Farsi, Turkish, Kurdish, Arabic. In the main towns and cities quite a number of people speak some English.

Transport Both trains and buses are relatively cheap and efficient. In the former there are women's compartments which provide a welcome feeling of comfort and security. The bus system however is more extensive and generally quite comfortable and efficient. In some cities the buses are segregated, with women seated at the front.

Accommodation Plenty of reasonably priced hotels remain in the medium-sized towns. For your own peace of mind it's best to carry your own padlock.

Special Problems The most obvious one is gaining entry to the country at a time of fluctuating diplomatic relations. The best bet is to apply for transit visas at the Iranian Embassy in Turkey.

There's no option about dress: you need to cover yourself completely, preferably in sombre clothing. This must include a scarf that covers all your hair.

Security is stringent and Revolutionary Guards will stop and search coaches fairly frequently. You might also be body-searched when you cross over the border into Iran.

Guides There are no specific guidebooks to Iran. For limited coverage of the country as part of the overland route to India, there are reasonable sections in *Traveller's Survival Kit to the East* (Vacation Work) and *West Asia on a Shoestring* (Lonely Planet).

Contacts

Committee for Defence of Women's Rights in Iran, c/o London Women's Centre, Wesley House, 70 Great Queen St., London WC2B 5AX. A broad-based solidarity group geared towards publicising women's struggles in Iran and co-ordinating international campaigns to protest the conditions faced by women. They produce an occasional bulletin in English.

Iranian Community Centre (Women's Section), 465a Green Lanes, London N4, ☎081-341 5005. Resource centre producing a women's newsletter in Farsi.

Women & Struggle in Iran. Quarterly publication produced by the Women's Commission of the Iranian Students Association in the USA. Copies available from ISA, (WC-ISA), PO Box 5642, Chicago, Illinois 60680, USA.

Books

Tabari Azar, et al., eds., *In the Shadow of Islam: The Women's Movement in Iran* (Zed Books, 1982). Written by three Iranian women, this book covers the Women's Movement in Iran since the Revolution, focusing on the relation between Islam and the struggle for women's emancipation.

Guity Nashat, *Women in Revolution in Iran* (Westview, US, 1983). Study focusing on the central paradox of women's participation in a revolution that deprived them of many rights. Analysis of the pre- and post-revolutionary periods as well as the revolution itself.

Farah Azari, ed., *Women of Iran* (Ithaca Press, 1983). A collection of papers by social-ist-feminist Iranian women which bring a fresh approach to the political debates surrounding the Revolution.

Manny Sharazi, *Javady Alley* (The Women's Press, 1984). An outstanding novel set in Iran in 1953, and seen through the eyes of a seven-year-old girl whose childhood certainties are coming under threat.

Freya Stark, *The Valleys of the Assassins* (1934; Century, 1984). Another world – and another classic piece of travel.

Sousan Azadi and Angela Ferrante, *Out of Iran: One Woman's Escape from the Ayatollahs* (Futura, 1988). Harrowing account of a refugee's flight from her country.

Shusha Guppy, *The Blindfold Horse* (Penguin, 1988). Memoirs of a childhood life amid the intellectual aristocracy in pre-Khomeini Iran.

Miranda Davies, ed., *Third World – Second Sex 2* (Zed Books, 1987). Includes part of a study on crimes against women in Iran by Simin Ahmady.

Ireland

Ireland is divided: twenty-six predominantly Catholic counties make up the independent **Republic of Ireland** (Eire), while the six largely Protestant counties of **Northern Ireland** (The North) comprise a separate state, ruled by Britain and, for the last two decades, occupied by the British army.

Although attempts have been made to promote **Northern Ireland** as a holiday destination and centre for commerce, few British travellers without relatives or connections would consider going there. The British media's insistence on portraying an area gripped by sectarian "troubles" and defining its population as either the villains or victims of "terrorist"

attack is a strong deterrent. But there's also the more rational fear that resentment of the British army will extend to visitors.

Since it was drafted into the north in 1969 (ostensibly to protect the Catholic minority from escalating Protestant sectarian violence), the army has been responsible for a continuing catalogue of civil rights abuses, including arbitrary searches and arrests, detention without trial, the coercion and torture of suspects and the lethal use of plastic bullets. And the partisan nature of the occupation has been powerfully revealed by the obvious targetting of Catholic communities.

British travellers may, justifiably, feel uneasy about travel in such a context, yet, with the exception of the Republican bars of Belfast or Derry, little antagonism is shown. The Irish, on both sides of the border, have an unrivalled reputation for hospitality and, unfettered by British propaganda and censorship, a fair number of American, German and Scandinavian women visit the region.

By contrast, the Irish Republic has a well established tourist industry, based mainly on its rural attractions – the miles of green, empty landscape and beautiful, largely undeveloped coastline. Many women return year after year for this, the clichéd (but true) charm of the place, and the relaxed atmosphere you find even when travelling alone. Sexist attitudes certainly prevail but are much more likely to take the form of an old-fashioned male courtesy and genuine bewilderment as to why you should choose to travel alone, than any overt sexual harassment. The cost of living, which is at least 25 percent higher than in Britain, can be an initial shock, but it is alleviated in part by the fact that this is a perfect country for cycling and camping.

Women have played a significant part in Ireland's struggles for self-determination, though the movement for national liberation has not necessarily gone hand in hand with that for women's liberation. Votes for women were introduced into the Republic six years ahead of Northern Ireland and Britain, but women's rights were, and continue to be, severely restricted by a constitution that enshrines many Catholic values. In Northern Ireland, women are, in strictly legal and economic terms, better off, but their rights have always lagged behind those gained for women in Britain.

Northern Irish women played a prominent role in the civil rights movement of the 1960s, and in the 1970s a small but articulate feminist movement emerged, made up mostly of middle-class women. They attempted to operate across the sectarian divide, dealing with issues such as childcare provisions, wife-battering, contraception and abortion (still an imprisonable offence throughout Ireland). They argued that Northern Ireland should be brought in line with British legislation on these issues. At the same time, the Catholic community was facing the introduction of internment without trial. Women as well as men were being arbitrarily detained, more were becoming drawn into direct Republican activism, and women prisoners in Armagh jail were beginning a series of protests for political status, culminating in the "dirty protest" and hunger strikes.

A division arose between those feminists who looked for emancipation through operating within the British government system, and those who saw it proceeding from British withdrawal. The divide still persists today, although notable campaigns – such as that against the strip-searching of women political prisoners and the setting up of the Belfast Well Women's Centre and Rape Crisis Centre – have received widespread support.

Many similar developments were occurring in the Republic, as women began to meet to discuss and act upon the need for specific women's rights. These included access to contraception (at the time banned even for married couples), equal pay for equal work, state benefits for unmarried mothers and legislation for divorce. Twenty years later there has been a slight slackening in the laws against birth control but divorce remains outlawed by the constitution, as does abortion. Since a 1986 court ruling, it has become illegal for agencies even to offer abortion counselling or advice to women.

Lesbians, on both sides of the border, have long had to struggle against entrenched homophobia. It took a ruling by the European Court of Human Rights in 1982 to bring Northern Ireland's homosexuality laws into line with Britain, and gay sex between consenting adults is still illegal in the South. There is, however, a very small but well established network of lesbian groups, and many active gay rights organisations operate within the country.

Behind the Picture Postcards

· · · · · · · · · · · · · · ·

Hilary Robinson has often visited the Republic of Ireland. In particular, she tries to go every summer to County Clare where she travels with fiddle to the annual music summer school at Miltown Malbay.

It is all too easy to be utterly romantic about the Republic of Ireland. The beauty of the landscape, the numbers of people who still live on a small scale close to the land, and the generosity of spirit of so many of the people that you meet: all combine to encourage an idyllic view. Add to this an almost universal ignorance of Irish history on the part of the British (can you remember being taught any at school?) and the notion of a "Real Ireland" encouraged by the tourist trade and you have the stuff of all romantic dreams – a place with an immutable essence where you can put aside the aspects of the twentieth century that you want to escape

Now, I've spent some of my happiest times in recent years in Ireland, but I feel very strongly that the romanticised "Real Ireland" does not exist, not generally and especially not for women. There are elements, of course, on the visual level. It's very easy to clamber up some hillside in Kerry or Connemara and to sit, breathing in the clean air, and gaze out at the beautiful landscape with its fields of luscious green, the Atlantic in the distance, perhaps a whitewashed cottage with a couple of children out in the yard, a smallholding, a man driving his eight cows home for milking . . . This is when the fantasies start about giving everything up to come and live here on the land, where the children can grow up healthily.

However, each time I go and get to know the country better, the mismatch between the picturesque image of the

Tourist Board and the differing realities for the various people I meet seems to become more pronounced.

The parts of Ireland I know best are Dublin, Galway and County Clare, though I have made occasional trips into Connemara and Westport, to Kerry and Kilkenny. I've travelled there for various reasons, but mainly because of Irish music. I play the fiddle a little and try to get to Miltown Malbay in County Clare each summer for a music summer school. It's great fun and draws people from all over the world, even as far as India and Australia, to play and listen. Although most of the traditional musicians who have made recordings are men, and some of the playing in some of the bars is competitively macho, a large number of women also play and attend the school. I found many of the older Irish people, in particular, to be delighted that a non-Irish person should show such an interest in their culture – quite a humbling experience as an Englishwoman.

> **"It's not uncommon for Irishmen to assume that if you're not Irish you must be on the pill and therefore have no good reason to refuse their advances!"**

One of my trips to Ireland was to research part of a thesis about contemporary women artists, when I went to speak to women (mainly in the Dublin area) about their work; another time I went cycling with a boyfriend around Clare, Galway and Connemara, with a tent strapped to the back of a bike.

I have several times had heated arguments with Irishmen who insist that Ireland is a matriarchal society. Their reasoning was based on the romantic ideal that women should be respected simply for being women, mixed with a dollop of mythology about motherhood and strong female figures; I felt it left out any appreciation of the day-to-day realities for their own mothers and sisters, and of the links between

Catholicism and the State in Ireland. The recent divorce and abortion referendums (both won by the church and conservatives) would be a case in point.

The Irish population is nowhere near as dense as in Britain, but it is much more evenly spread across rural areas. Farms are handed down through families and have been important in the past in the support by families of prospective marriages. One of the arguments in the divorce referendum was that women would not only split families but farms, many of which survive only just above subsistence level. Ireland remains the only European country besides Malta to forbid divorce. Not surprisingly, a Dutch friend marrying an Irishman and going to live in Ireland deliberately chose to marry in Holland.

On a practical level, motherhood is held in more esteem than it is in England, something I noticed in little things like the sympathetic attitude of shop assistants to women with children in tow. With regards to sex, it's not uncommon for Irishmen to assume that if you're not Irish you must be on the pill and therefore have no good reason to refuse their advances! On one occasion I realised that a discussion of sexual politics was almost like "talking dirty" to the man I was in conversation with.

In some ways attitudes are similar to those of the British in the Seventies, but for different reasons. The laws around contraception may not be as extreme as they used to be, but the moral climate of Ireland is still a far cry from the so-called permissive era we experienced in Britain. In theory you can buy condoms across the counter in chemist shops; in practice I found it to be a lot more difficult, since many chemists, even in the centre of Dublin, refuse to sell them "on moral grounds". Another difference is that in Britain in the Seventies, men expected sex in the name of "free love". In contrast, the Irishmen that I have met are far more likely to be romantic,

to talk about falling in love, to want to take me across the country for the weekend to meet their parents, to demonstrate a level of romantic seriousness, despite the fact that I am only visiting – in short, to "court".

"This is the only European country I have visited where I've felt happy to hitch alone"

I have heard non-Irish women say that there's a vulnerability in this attitude that can be refreshing after the horribly repressed emotional life of British men. Personally, I've found the "back on top of a pedestal" position, although intended as flattering, deeply uncomfortable. Furthermore, for me to relax into it in a kind of "holiday romance" mode would only end up abusing the man concerned. I learned this the hard way, causing pain on all sides. Irish women would, of course, say something else again; one spoke to me very persuasively of what she called the deep conservatism of Irishmen's notions about women. On looking around a crowded bar in Doolin, County Clare, which every summer is filled with people chasing Irish music, and today seemed mainly to consist of Irish men and German women, she said she was waiting for the first case of herpes to be heard of in the village: then "all the men would soon go home".

There are two aspects of travelling as a woman in Ireland that I especially appreciate. The first, and most practical, is that this is the only European country that I have visited where I've felt happy about hitching alone. Obviously, I got offered lifts on my own more easily than when I was one of a couple, either with another woman or with a man; and I am not denying that things can go wrong. But I've never once had cause to feel threatened and, compared to many countries, hitching in Ireland is much more accepted as a way of getting about. Train fares are high, car insurance astronomical, and buses rare out in the country. Consequently you see all sorts of people at the sides of the road, from old men cadging lifts to teenagers trying to get into town.

A number of people said they'd stopped for me because they saw the fiddle case, and was I sure I wasn't Irish? Sometimes families would stop and once I got a lift all the way across the country from a soldier in the Irish army – we shared a similar dislike of Margaret Thatcher, so that was okay. I once got a lift from a single woman driver who told me she always offered lifts to women because she used to hitch herself, and had once or twice been in awkward situations. She never offered lifts to men.

The funniest time was a few miles outside Miltown, the day the summer school ended. It was tipping down, my friend and I were miles from anywhere, had been walking for an hour and were soaked to the skin. A car finally stopped; the man driving had seen the fiddle cases and took pity on us. He'd stopped for another woman (plus fiddle) earlier, and stopped again for another (plus guitar) a few miles further on.

The second thing I'm grateful for in Ireland took a bit of time to notice and that's the absence of pornography. No doubt it's around somewhere in some form, and no doubt it's missing for all the wrong reasons – repressive attitudes towards sexuality in general, rather than radical attitudes towards the representation of women. But it's just not there when you go to buy a newspaper; which is a holiday in itself.

TRAVEL NOTES

Language English and Gaelic.

Transport Buses and trains are very expensive. A good cheap way of exploring the countryside is to hire a bicycle. Hitching is relatively easy and safe, perhaps the greatest problem being lack of cars. Sunday traffic is usually the worst, either cars are packed with families or you get single men with time on their hands looking for some "fun".

Accommodation You can camp more or less anywhere in the countryside, as long as you ask permission of the landowner. Youth Hostels get booked up in the summer so it's wise to book in advance. Bed and Breakfasts are usually relaxed and comfortable.

Special Problems Travelling in the North you may well be stopped by British Army or RUC patrols, and asked for your name, address, date of birth and immediate destination. Whatever your feelings or politics it's best to be civil and to the point.

It is now legal to sell contraception, although some chemists refuse to stock condoms.

Ireland is notorious for its continuing abuse of gay rights. It's a good idea to get advice from a gay group about the local scene.

Guides *The Rough Guide: Ireland* (Harrap Columbus) is easily the most informative.

Contacts

The yearly **Irish Women's Guidebook and Diary** provides a comprehensive list of addresses for individual women's/lesbian groups throughout Ireland. It is available from feminist bookshops in Britain and Ireland or direct from Attic Press, 44 East Sussex Street, Dublin 2.

Below are a small selection of **groups**:

BELFAST: **Women's Centre**, 18 Donegal Street, Belfast BT1 2GP, ☎0232 243363, and **Just Books**, 7 Winetavern St., Smithfield, ☎225426, are good for contacts. You could also try **Lesbian Line**, ☎0232 222023; Mon–Thurs, 7.30–10pm.

DUBLIN: **Dublin Resource Centre**, 6 Crowe St., ☎771974, and **Women's Centre**, 53 Dame St., Dublin 2, ☎710088, will provide you with information about local groups and campaigns. The **Hirschfeld Centre**, 10 Fownes St., ☎910139, is a recommended gay/lesbian meeting place. **Women's Centre Shop**, 27 Temple Lane, ☎710088; **Books Uptairs**, Market Arcade, off South Great Georges St., ☎710064, and **Spellbound Books**, City Centre, 23/25 Moss St., ☎712149, all have a good selection of feminist and lesbian literature and stock.

Holidays

The **Southern Ireland Wimmin's Holiday Centre**, "Amcotts", Clonmore, Piltown, County Kilkenny, Eire, ☎Waterford 43371, offers luxury accommodation in a tranquil rural setting, plus good food, a library, cycles for hire and a convivial, hospitable atmosphere.

Magazines

The entertainments guide, *In Dublin*, and the gay magazine, *Out*, both have listings on women's groups.

Books

Eileen Fairweather, ed., *Only the Rivers Run Free: Northern Ireland, the Women's War* (Pluto Press, 1984). A selection of women describe the everyday realities of life in the North.

Eilean Ni Chuilleanain, ed., *Irish Women: Image and Achievement* (Arlen House, Ireland, 1986). Ten essays by specialist authors trace the position of women in Irish society from ancient to modern times.

Nell McCafferty, *A Woman to Blame* (Attic Press, Ireland, 1986). Brilliant study by one of Ireland's most acclaimed journalists of the "Kerry Babies Case". It examines the grip on Irish women by the Church, patriarchy and culture. Also look out for McCafferty's selec-tion of articles and essays, **The Best of Nell** (Attic Press, Ireland, 1987).

Liz Curtis, *Ireland: the Propaganda War* (Pluto Press, 1984). An excellently researched, clear and unanswerable indictment of the British media's campaign against Irish Republicanism.

Fiction

Frances Molloy, *No Mate for a Magpie* (Virago, 1985). Tragi-comic tale of a Catholic girlhood in Ireland.

Emma Cooke, *Eve's Apple* (Blackstaff, 1985). Set against the 1983 Irish abortion referendum campaign, this novel describes a woman's isolation and desperation with middle-class provincialism and the hypocrisy of religious values.

Edna O'Brien, *Johnnie I Hardly Knew You* (Penguin, 1977), and *The Country Girls* (Penguin, 1960). Accomplished novels from a popular and prolific author. Both explore issues of emerging female sensuality within the repressive social climate of rural Ireland.

Mary Lavin, *Mary O'Grady* (Virago, 1987). Best-known work by a prestigious Irish writer about a woman who leaves the country life to set up home in Dublin. Also worth reading is *The House in Clewe Street* (Virago, 1987). A family saga which uncovers the problems and pitfalls of an Irish Catholic upbringing.

Deirdre Madden, *Hidden Symptoms* (Faber, 1987). A brilliant, hauntingly evocative novel that centres around a woman's attempt to reconcile herself to the sectarian murder of her twin brother.

Julia O'Faolain, *No Country for Young Men* (Penguin, 1980). Devastating story of human and political relations in contemporary Ireland.

Italy

Many Italians regard Italy as two distinct countries: the north and the south. The first, ending at Rome, enjoys an image of prosperity and innovation; the second, encompassing the notorious Mafia strongholds of Calabria and Sicily, is considered poor, corrupt, backward and, at least in the minds of most southerners, cruelly neglected. Compared to the thriving industrial centres in and around Turin or Milan, the south is indeed desperately poor. It's also more traditional and conservative and, in this respect, less easy for travellers.

As a people, the Italians are hospitable and talkative, and it takes little to be drawn into long conversations, however poor your grasp of the language. Train journeys provide the perfect setting and, perhaps surprisingly in the light of widespread street harassment, several women report these as among their most enjoyable experiences. Fellow passengers like practising their English and everyone tends to pool their efforts to keep a conversation going. Travelling with a child, you'll be made even more welcome. All over Italy children are doted on and fussed over, providing a wonderful passport for meeting people and gaining their respect. It's quite common in a restaurant for your child to be whisked off to the kitchen and showered with kisses and treats for a couple of hours while you enjoy your meal.

Travelling alone, or with a female companion, you'll be treated as a curiosity. But the attention you receive can vary from quite genuine concern about your isolation (and possible loneliness) to incredibly brazen and persistent harassment. The cat-calls, propositions and kerb-crawling tend to get worse as you head further south and in Sicily, especially, it takes a tough skin and plenty of determination to stick out a holiday on your own. As usual the hassles and misconceptions fade as you become known in a place and even the most frustrating moments can be tempered by singular acts of great warmth and generosity.

Italian society (with the weight of the Catholic Church behind it) is so strongly family-oriented that it's hard for the older generation, at least, to understand any female desire for independence. Mamma may appear to reign at home, but outside *machismo* is irritatingly prevalent. Italian men are stereotypically proud, vain, and not easily rejected, and in any situation like to at least be *seen* to have the upper hand.

Italian women have a lot to battle against and today every city has at least one **feminist organisation**; several have their own bookshops (also meeting places) and documentation centres. The roots of the movement lie in the generation referred to as the "Sixty-eighters", political activists who, during that period of social turmoil, gradually saw the need for women to organise separately from men. Many did and still do belong to the huge Italian Communist Party (PCI)*; feminism and communism have always been strongly linked in Italy. *Noi Donne*, the country's first feminist magazine, was started as an organ of the PCI in the 1940s – but campaigns for divorce rights and against rape, the successful fight to legalise abortion, and a more recent women's peace movement, all indicate a firm belief in the importance of autonomous organisation.

---

*At the time of writing, the PCI, in the wake of events in Eastern Europe, are considering changing the "Communist" part of their name.

Singled Out

· · · · · · · · · · · ·

Celia Woolfrey has travelled widely in Italy, both north and south, most recently to research and write a *Rough Guide* to the country.

I first went to Italy about ten years ago on holiday and have kept going back ever since. However, researching the *Rough Guide* took me to areas less well known to British tourists and revealed a lot more about Italian life. I travelled mainly on my own, though friends came out to join me for the occasional week and I had contacts to look up while I was there. I spent most of my time finding good places to eat and stay, checking out the tourist sights, visiting art galleries and museums, and occasionally sampling Italian nightlife.

My mode of travel covered the range, from walking and hitching my way through the Dolomites – my best lifts were got by accosting people at petrol stations – to travelling by Vespa in the hinterland of the Riviera. In practical terms it's no problem travelling on your own. Buses and trains are cheap, and in summer there are other women doing the same thing, so if you want company you can meet up with people in Youth Hostels and campsites on the tourist circuit. It's the reaction you get which is difficult.

Actually choosing to go to places on your own can lead people to make strange assumptions about you; Italians are sociable and often go around in big gaggles of family or friends so that being solitary is seen as something weird, and pitiable. People often couldn't work out what I was doing. They would relax visibly when I told them I was in Italy to do a guidebook, but often they weren't convinced. However, there is a positive side to travelling on your own in that you're too much of an oddball to hassle, as people don't know what they are going to get in return.

"Now that I'm 27 and old enough to be called Signora, I've entered a new phase of life"

I was attracted back to Italy not so much by the landscape and architecture, but more by the style and grace with which things are done. Among friends there is a lightness of touch, even when someone is telling you off. Add to this the café life, the posing, women dressing up in furs to eat ice cream . . . it's a very glamorous place. If you are backpacking on a low budget it is worth bearing in mind that Italy today is a far from cheap country and one where appearances hold great store. You get caught out it you're on the way back from a beach holiday with only shorts and espadrilles to wear. Nobody actually turns you away because you're wearing the wrong clothes, but they do something much worse – they feel sorry for you for not having any pride in yourself.

Age makes a big difference; now that I'm 27 and old enough to be called Signora, I've entered a new phase of life. People talk to me completely differently, as though I deserve automatic respect. Conversely, you know there's going to be trouble if someone says "Mah, Signorina . . .", as they begin to explain why you can't do what you were about to. The reaction I got from women of different ages altered too. Older women I chatted to on buses would say "brava" ("well done") when I

told them what I was doing, though I got the feeling they thought I was completely mad. Women younger than me didn't bat an eyelid and were amazingly helpful and open; they would give me lots of information and talk about anything.

It was people my own age who made the most assumptions about me; the question "So what are you really doing here?" would underlie a conversation, as though researching a guidebook must be a cover. For what? Stealing someone's husband? Finding a lover? Messing around before I went back to where I came from and settled down? I came off badly in what one woman wanted to turn into a gladiatorial conversation when we were talking about "courting". She asked what the English word was for the Italian verb *corteggiare*, to which I replied that there was an English verb "to court" but that it wasn't used a lot nowadays. "And what do English women do these days," she retorted, "jump into bed with a man on the first night?" This was an assumption which I came across on other occasions – frustrating in that it's an argument which you can't hope to win. However, you are just as likely to find newspaper articles referring to "Thatcher's Victorian Britain" – a nation of prudes, paranoid about AIDS.

"At a couple of places women hotel proprietors pursed their lips and looked me up and down before telling me that they didn't have a single room"

Attitudes towards me varied greatly from place to place. Big cities and isolated mountains were no problem; it was at family resorts that I had the strangest time. I didn't always get a good reception at some of the seaside towns on the Riviera and the Adriatic. At a couple of places women hotel proprietors pursed their lips and looked me up and down before telling me that they didn't have a single room and that no, they didn't have any double rooms either, at least until next year. The problems occurred when people placed me out of context: what was I doing on my own in a family resort? (They were very sure they knew.)

And family resorts mean just that: holiday towns full of numbered rows of sunbeds, crammed together so the extended family can observe at close quarters other versions of itself. Here tradition and continuity are all important. One Italian women who ran a seaside pension for years told me that the same families came back to her year after year and that some were in tears last season when she told them she was closing down.

In these and regular Italian towns, I was surprised how often the place virtually closed up at night, with shutters pulled down over shops and few signs of life except the occasional bar. This was the time when I was most harassed by men, who tended to assume I was a prostitute if I was walking along the street on my own. This aggravated me a lot because it meant I had to look as if I was on my way to somewhere, even when I wasn't.

In La Spezia, on the Ligurian coast, I was bothered by endless tooting cars as I waited for a bus. It reached extremes in the resort of Rimini after about 8pm, where cars crawl along the main street from the station to the beach, the front passenger door mysteriously springing open as you pass by. Apart from this I was surprised to get more catcalls and stupid comments travelling with a woman friend than when I was alone. I think this was because people just assumed we were on the pick-up – we were obviously tourists.

Most of the time I've felt safe on my own and confident about initiating conversations with people. Comments or overtures from strangers tend to be less offensive than in London, and politely declining someone's offer to accompany me on my way has never

lead to threats, as it has done in Britain and other countries. I often ate alone in restaurants or sat in a bar I felt comfortable in.

Conforming to family life is still a big deal for most of the people I met. It's harder in a practical sense to leave home, and I met quite a few people in their thirties who still lived with their parents because places to rent with friends hardly exist and mortgage arrangements for buying property are quite different from Britain. It was those who had broken away from the rituals of conforming who were most generous with their time and spare rooms, and a lot of fun.

"Many of the assertive women I met would rather have died than call themselves feminists"

Women my age who I met through friends of friends were generally very career oriented, had married to subdue family pressure and were childless. The all-providing mother seemed to be a bit of a spectre for the men as well as the women who have actively rebelled against big dinners and domesticity. This to the extent that they were horrified when I said I liked cooking and eating. "Reactionary women!" they screamed.

As in the rest of Europe, Italian feminism seems to have gone through a quiet patch since the Seventies and many of the assertive women I met would rather have died than call themselves feminists. At the same time, Italian women have achieved some of the most progressive legislation in Europe surrounding maternity benefits and childcare.

Italians have a very positive attitude towards children; they love them dearly which is why they want the best facilities for them to grow up in. Ninety percent of the under-threes are in full-time nurseries, lessening the burden for women who are working outside the home. Even small villages in the Emilia

Romagna region (admittedly more progressive than most) have purpose-built nurseries. An enlightened communist administration and a slow political process have brought this about. It is ironic indeed that the woman politician with the highest media profile is Scicciolina (Llona Staller), dubbed the *pornodiva* by the press and a whore by her Radical party boss.

Living in the City of Fashion

. . . .

After two years teaching at a women's university in Hiroshima, Japan, Valerie Waterhouse travelled extensively around the Far East. She has since moved to Milan, where she teaches English at the British Council.

Milan is thought of as the Italian capital of industry and of fashion. The "industrial" label makes the visitor expect a city of high-rise blocks and of factories belching out evil smoke. Yet the centre of the city, dominated by the elaborate Gothic cathedral, is surprisingly grand and beautiful. Wandering through the Saturday markets or exploring the nightlife along the canals inspires excitement, even passion.

It is a city where north meets south, where *casinisti*, chaotic attitudes, combine with a strong work ethic. The Milanese work like maniacs too. For me, these conflicting elements are epitomised in the frivolous extravagance of the cathedral, the Duomo, which took 500 years of hard work to build. Significantly, it took a Frenchman, Napoleon, to get it completed.

Industrial activity is hidden around the outskirts of the city, but it creeps into your nose and lungs invidiously in the form of Milan's most serious problem – pollution. Milan is the most polluted city in Europe and people here regularly develop irritating coughs or bronchitis. Having to wash your hair twice as often as normal can also become wearisome. In early 1989 there was a drought and the pollution build-up became so serious that an emergency was declared. On certain days it was recommended that babies and young children should not be taken outside, and people could be seen in the streets wearing smog masks. No cars were permitted in the centre and people were asked to turn off their central heating. As a result, pollution was reduced; but whether these changes continue to operate once the "pollution emergency" is forgotten remains to be seen.

The fashion industry in Milan is both more attractive and more visible. Milan is an essential stepping stone on the career path of any model wishing to make it big. Models, mostly Americans, come here to collect "tear sheets", photographs in the glossies. Photo shoots near the Duomo or in the glass-roofed arcades nearby are frequent, and tall, pale models of both sexes drift through the streets of the "Golden Rectangle" of expensively labelled designer shops.

Despite this reputation for sophistication, Milan is not as liberal as you might expect. One of the largest differences for a British person lies in the attitudes towards the family. For both social and financial reasons, young people tend to live with their parents until they marry. Students and the unemployed, without state support, cannot afford to live by themselves, and working people see comfort, convenience, and being able to own a car as more important than independence.

In general, less importance is placed on independence than in Anglo-Saxon countries and this is reflected in attitudes to travel. When I told friends or neighbours that my sister was moving to Tanzania, the most common reaction was: "How terrible!" Among older people, the next question was: "How do your parents feel about both of you living abroad?" Even young people were sometimes horrified.

"The 'Latin lover' in a man usually manifests itself in the first, or possibly second, meeting"

Living with another woman teacher, like me in her twenties, provokes some odd reactions. Our neighbour, a middle-aged housewife, thinks nothing of wandering in if the door is open, and commenting if we haven't done the washing up. This of course is double-edged. It is irritating when neighbourly gossip starts intruding on your privacy, but wonderful when you want someone to water your plants, or discover that you've just run out of eggs.

The friendliness displayed by neighbours or people in the street lends justification to the hospitable Italian stereotype. Ask someone on the bus for directions and you will be overwhelmed by people offering you advice. Local shopkeepers are always willing to chat to you about the lack of rain, "La Thatcher", or how your Italian is coming along.

Not surprisingly, friendly social invitations are not uncommon for women. But acceptance of an invitation to a party or to the theatre, even in a group, is often taken as equalling interest in sexual involvement, and it can be hard to counter this macho assumption. The "Latin lover" in a man usually manifests itself in the first, or possibly second, meeting, and with a directness not usually encountered in colder climates. Platonic relationships, as an Italian male I met sadly commented, are extremely difficult to achieve. Of course, not all men behave in this way, but it's in this area that you experience the biggest cultural gulf. Italian women have told me that it is the image of the sexually liberated northern blonde which attracts this sort of behaviour.

In terms of street harassment, approaches are usually verbal. Men do sometimes press up against you in a crowded tram, but no more so than in Britain. However, standing alone or with a female friend at a bus stop at night is taken as an invitation. Men in cars will stop at five-minute intervals and utter those ubiquitous words "Vuoi un passagio?" ("Do you want a lift?"). Generally speaking, a short sharp "no" soon causes them to drive away. If you take the usual precautions, Milan is not an unsafe city to travel in. Public transport is extensive, efficient and safe, and runs until 1.30am. The only place to avoid is the *Circonvallazione*, the city ring road. Prostitutes – many of them transvestites – operate here, so the number of kerb-crawlers can become more than a nuisance, as can harassment from flashers.

Perhaps because it is unusual for women to socialise alone together, I have rarely received a social invitation from a Milanese woman. Riding on a winter tram, you might well think that all women here have fur coats, long hair, shoulder pads and jangling jewellery. Bodily conscious femininity is highly prized and foreign women with short hair, flat masculine shoes and ankle-length coats are a definite oddity, though not unacceptable. My closest Milanese friend is Cinzia, a thirty-year-old bilingual Italian who works for an air freight forwarding company. Unlike most women of her age, Cinzia is single and lives alone, since her immediate family have emigrated to Australia. Her Australian connections and perfect English make her untypical, but her example proves that independent women who do not fit the stereotype do exist in Milan.

Amelia, a silk buyer, is another exception. At 35, she is a junior partner in her company and is sent regularly to China, Thailand or India on business trips. Pregnant for the first time, she is still working and intends to return to work soon after the baby is born; she is fortunate in that her career to date has been a successful one. Other women find the path to promotion blocked and feel that less capable men are valued more highly.

Though advanced compared to Britain, Italy lags behind some countries in its provision of crèches, and professional childminders are not always easy to find. But this is partly because of the strength of the family support system. Maternity benefit, on the other hand, is much better than in Britain. Female employees can take six months paid leave, a further six months at seventy percent of their salary, and have a job guaranteed on their return.

Some Italian feminists now believe, however, that fighting for such concrete rights as provisions for small children or abortion on demand should no longer be the primary concern of the Women's Movement. In Milan there is a women's bookshop, run by a group of voluntary workers, whose main activities are political discussion and the publication of feminist books and magazines. The Milan group feel that in society as it is, women are not motivated to become involved or to realise their full potential. We must look within or at our relationships with other women if society is to change. Co-operation between women, for example teachers and pupils in schools, is more important than fighting for individual rights which, in any case, not all women will think worth fighting for. When I asked whether social liberation

for Italian women matched theoretical advancement, the woman in the bookshop said she couldn't comment. "Every woman is different. It depends on the individual."

"For Italians, racism extends to anyone coloured, including their own compatriots south of Rome"

The women's bookshop has a noticeboard containing personal ads and information about cultural events of interest to women. There is a similar noticeboard at Milan's Women's Club, *Cicip e Ciciap*. The club was established by three women, involved in the Women's Movement of the Seventies, to provide an atmosphere where "feminism could flourish". Daniela, a founder member, told us that it is the only club of its kind in Italy, although similar places are planned to open in Turin and Rome. No importance is placed on the sexual preferences of the clientele and in the club women sit talking, their short hair and jeans in this city of fur coats lending truth to the idea that it is ridiculous to talk about women as a homogeneous group with the same needs and wants.

One issue just emerging into media discussion in Milan, as elsewhere in Italy, is racism. Italians I spoke to often mentioned the British reputation for racism, but to my mind the only difference between the two countries is that Italians have yet to confront the problem. And for Italians, racism extends to anyone coloured, including their own compatriots south of Rome. When seeking accommodation, we found that, as white, foreign females in stable jobs, we were perceived as ideal tenants. (It is illegal for landlords to evict their tenants, and they hope that foreigners will not be as well informed about their rights.) However, attitudes may well have been different had we been a different colour. At one accommodation agency, a landlady had specifically requested foreign girls, but "non di colore". We wondered what would have happened when our black or Asian British friends had come to stay.

The issue of racism is one which many Milanese cannot afford to ignore for much longer. There are a growing number of poor black Moroccans, Algerians and Ethiopians living here now. Often we see them sleeping in the parks, where they store their few belongings under bushes. Public reactions vary from sympathy to downright hostility. As a tourist, of course, you will mostly be met with friendliness.

A Chinese Traveller in Sicily

. . . .

Helen Lee, a British woman of Hong Kong descent, spent six months in Sicily with her English husband. Only through giving English lessons did she begin to feel at all accepted.

When the opportunity arose to travel to Sicily for six months with my husband, Jules, I leapt at the chance. It seemed a perfect opening to dispose of the stifling, mundane day-to-day activities of work and life, and to pack my home into one rucksack. This would also be the first time I had travelled with a man and I saw it as a chance to explore a new country with security and ease. It's annoyingly ironic that to escape likely sexual harassment and nuisances from men, you are forced to travel with one of them. However, my experience wasn't as straightforward as that. Although I initially enjoyed the novel sense of relief and safety, and life undoubtedly became smoother, we remained items of fascinating doorstep gossip owing to our unusual pact. This, coupled with my inexplicable "Englishness", not only caused a riot, but seemed to block any further attempts to understand us.

We chose for the first month to live in Taormina, a medieval hill town overlooking the Ionian sea on a spur of Monte Tauro, Sicily's most exuberant holiday resort (mainly for wealthy Germans). I loved strolling through the main Corso Umberto, lined with beautiful palaces transformed into bars, *pasticcerias*, restaurants and expensive clothes shops, and I found it easier to start off living in a tourist resort where people knew English and were accustomed to foreigners.

"Despite this lazy and agreeable life, I still felt an undercurrent of tension on account of my colour"

We had no trouble finding accommodation. All we had to do was ask at the tourist office and keep our eyes open for notices with the word *affitasi* (to rent) displayed on doors and shop windows. An Italian friend gave me the useful tip that rent can often be reduced by straight away offering the landlord a few months' payment in full.

Later, when we decided to move again and I felt more confident about speaking Italian, I found a place through an *Agenzia Immobiliare* (estate agent). This was a beautiful two-bedroomed flat in the nearby town of Giardini-Naxos and commanded gorgeous views of Mount Etna from one window and the beach from another – a far cry from our dark, cold and cramped London flat.

It may be a cliché but Sicilians are renowned for their joyous love of life, for their great enjoyment of the simple sensual pleasures of eating, drinking, sleeping, and idle banter with the neighbours. I spent the next few months completely indulging in all my favourite senses: waking to the early morning sounds of the *carciofini* (artichokes) man, calling out his goods as he wheeled his cart through the streets; the aroma of fresh ground coffee and the fragrance of freshly baked pizza and pasta drifting from homes at mealtimes; the flamboyant fish stalls displaying the catch of the day, whole swordfish, heaps of flesh-coloured prawns and great slabs of tuna; the *pasticcerias* with their wicked cakes, pastries and dazzling array of homemade Sicilian sweets; and, best of all, the brilliant sweet-smelling flowers that Sicily is so famous for. Being vegetarian, I loved the wide range of fruit and vegetables available – ruby tomatoes tasting of sunshine.

I grew to thrive on the afternoon siestas, the perfect antidote to our usual substantial three-course lunch of pasta, fish and fruit. And there were many aspects of Sicilian culture that I could identify with, as a Chinese, such as the importance of the family, especially at mealtimes, with their chaotic loud chatterings and adoration of food. In the evenings I'd put on my finest rags, and look forward to the ritual *passeggiata* – a time to stroll leisurely and to admire the beautiful women and frown at their fur coats. The men were even more dashing in their sharp suits, hair greased back, sauntering along the pavements or else driving beaten-up cars or riding wildly, usually in pairs, on noisy mopeds.

Despite this lazy and agreeable life I still felt an undercurrent of tension on account of my colour. It became unsettling to walk into a bar or *trattoria* and always be greeted by hard stares and be aware of people nudging one another. I grew to rely on Jules being with me and could feel my independence dwindling. It was easier travelling in larger cities like the island's capital, Palermo, where I could disappear among the crowds. With its stupendous churches, cathedrals and fountains. I found this a powerful and impressive place. I loved the markets – the confusion of stalls brimming with food and shopkeepers eagerly competing against each other, singing out their prices – which reminded me of the streets in Hong Kong. The many warnings I'd received from tourists about Palermo seemed quite ill-founded and I never came across even a hint of the Mafia.

"Theirs was a familiar story of being hemmed in by groups of men clustering around them, leering and touching"

I spent many days travelling by train along the coast and deep into the countryside, but despite all the horror stories I had also been told about Italian trains, I never encountered an unpleasant situation. Although trains were nearly always late and inevitably overcrowded, passengers were generally friendly and I found this one of the most relaxing ways to travel. Only going inland, where I was more of a curiosity, proved strenuous at times; not to mention frustrating, as Jules's personal experience was so different, he couldn't always understand what I was suffering.

It was a relief when I met a group of American women students at Taormina bus terminal. Homeless and penniless, they ended up spending the Easter holiday with us and in that short time we formed a strong friendship. I vividly recall one incident when they went into the village to shop, excited at the prospect of eating ice cream and practising their Italian, only to return an hour later, angry, flustered and humiliated. Theirs was a familiar story of being hemmed in by groups of men clustering around them, leering and touching. During their stay I noticed that only one woman, of Mexican origin, was repeatedly left alone; Sicilian men seemed to disregard her in the same way that they look down upon Arab women as racially inferior.

My worries about an increasing cultural gap – the Sicilians' misunderstandings of me and my steady intolerance of their ways – were to be proved wrong. As a way of improving my Italian and at the same time earning money, I began advertising English lessons and to my astonishment soon gained a handful of private students.

These ranged from an initially reluctant six-year-old girl to an enthusiastic bank clerk who was determined to develop her vocabulary beyond the monotonous bank conversations with tourists. I was overwhelmed by the generosity of my students who, at the end of each hourly lesson, would nearly always present me with flowers, chocolates or some other gift.

The girl's parents would insist I eat lunch with them twice a week before lessons. Farida was an adopted Sri Lankan and an only child. Because of her colour she had problems with other children at school, so perhaps the parents thought I might provide some comfort. We spent many happy hours sketching and playing together in a mixture of Italian and English. Being with a child, I had less worries about making a fool of myself and learned many new words and expressions.

With these new responsibilities I regained my sense of independence and began to really enjoy myself. I noticed that people were beginning to take me seriously and whenever I walked into the bank to change money, I found myself greeted with nods and whispers no longer of "Chinese" but of "English teacher". It was far too premature to assume their respect, but at least people seemed less suspicious and more willing to accept me.

TRAVEL NOTES

Languages Italian, with strong regional dialects. If you can't speak Italian, French is useful. People working in tourist services usually speak some English.

Transport Trains and buses are reasonably cheap and efficient. Hitching is easy enough but risky, especially in the south.

Accommodation *Pensioni* (and more expensive hotels) are plentiful throughout the country.

Special Problems *Machismo* rules and harassment can be a problem, especially in the south which some women find quite unbearable. Railway stations everywhere are particularly hazardous. You should spend the least possible time in them, and never sleep in a station; you run the risk of theft and sexual assault. In general the most obvious strategy is to avoid eye contact. Whatever clothes you wear, you're still likely to be followed, pushed and touched and have your route blocked. Italians are quite amazing at identifying foreigners.

Beware of the police, too. According to Diana Pritchard who has lived and travelled extensively in Italy: "Their conduct is an unpleasant combination of abuse of authority (even the Italian public are cautious of them) and an apparent lack of respect for foreign women. Some of my worst experiences have involved the *Carabinieri* – the armed police – ranging from the indiscreet fondle of my breast as I walked by, to a time when a group of *Carabinieri* demanded that I open the door of a tiny bedroom in which a female friend and I were staying. Although I eventually managed to get them out of the room, we were followed the next day until we left town."

Guides *Rough Guides* to Italy, Sicily and Venice (Harrap Columbus), all recommended.

Contacts

The following is a selected list of **women's centres and bookshops**. Often bookshops (*librerie*) and centres (*case*) are combined in the same building. A *biblioteca* is a library and suggests a more academic place.

ALESSANDRIA: **Casa delle Donne**, Via Solero 24, 15100.

L'AQUILA: **Biblioteca delle Donne**, c/o A.I.E.D., Corso Federico 11 58.

ANCONA: **Biblioteca delle Donne**, Via Cialdini 26.

BOLOGNA: **Librellula, Libreria delle Donne**, Strada Maggiore 23/e. **Centro di Documentazione Ricerca e Iniziativa delle Donne**, Via Galliera 4. Open from 8am–2pm, the centre promotes research on women's issues and includes a small but growing feminist library. **Circulo Culturale "28" Giugno**, Piazza di Porta Saragozzae, ☎43 33 92. Gay centre, bookshop and library that often holds lesbian meetings, social events, etc.

CIVITAVECCHIA: **Centro Donna 'Terradilet'**, V.G. Abruzzeze, 00053.

FIRENZE: **Libreria delle Donne**, Via Fiesolana 2B; **Casa delle Donne**, Via Carraia 2.

MILANO: **Libreria delle Donne**, Via Dogana 2; **Casa delle Donne**, Via Lanzone 32; **Centro per la Difesa dei Diritti del Donne**, Via Tadino 23. **La Nuova Idea**, via de Castiglia 3, ☎68 92 73. Gay bar. Thursday is lesbian only.

MODENA: **Casa delle Donne**, Via Cesana 43.

PARMA: **Biblioteca delle Donne**, Via XX Settembre 31.

PISA: **Centro Documentazione Donne**, Via Puccini 15.

REGGIO EMILIA: **Casa della Donna**, Viale Isonzo 76.

ROMA: **Libreria delle Donne**, Piazza Farnese 103; **Centro Studi Elsa Bergamaschi**, c/o UDI, Via Colonna Antonina 41, 3rd Floor. Feminist library and archives.

TORINO: **Casa delle Donne**, Vía Fiocchetto 13.

Books

Sibilla Alermo, *A Woman* (Virago, 1979). A classic in Italy, first published in 1906, the semi-autobiographical story of a girl growing up, dominated by her love for her father, but determined to break away and forge her own life.

Dacia Maraini, *Woman at War* (Lighthouse Books, London, 1984). By one of Italy's best known contemporary writers, it records, in diary form, a woman's growing self-awareness, beginning on holiday with her husband. The book encompasses weird characters, political argument and a wealth of sensual detail. Also by the same author, ***The Train*** (Camden Press, 1989). This brilliant satire on student life in the 1960s follows a group of friends on their way to an international socialist gathering in Helsinki.

Natalia Ginzburg, *The Road into the City* and ***The Dry Heart*** (1963; Carcanet, 1989) and others. The constraints of family life are a dominant theme in Ginzburg's writing, and her own upbringing is the source for this rigorous yet lyrical work. A radical politician who sits in the Senate in Rome, she is Italy's best-known woman writer, and most of her books are available in translation from Carcanet.

Elsa Morante, *History* (Penguin, 1980). Capturing the experience of daily Roman life during the last war, this is probably the most vivid fictional picture of the conflict as seen from the city.

Mary Taylor Simeti, *On Persephone's Island* (Penguin, 1988). Sympathetic record of a typical year in Sicily by an American who married a Sicilian professor and has lived on the island since the early 1960s.

Lucia C Birnbaum, *"Liberazione Della Donna": Feminism in Italy* (Weslyan U. Press, US, 1983). Good general survey – focuses on post-war developments.

Judith Hellman, *Journeys amnog Women: Feminism in Five Italian Cities* (OUP, 1987). Good, readable study of the womens' movements since 1968 in Turin, Milan, Reggio Emilia, Verona and Casserta. Slightly limited focus – mostly on the activities of the *Unione Donne Italiane* (*UDI*).

Fiona Pitt-Kethley, *Journeys to the Underworld* (Chatto and Windus, 1988). English poet searches Italy for the sibylline sites, a good third of her time in Sicily – though Pitt-Kethley's salacious appetite for sexual adventure often distracts from the real interest.

Thanks to Diana Pritchard and Jane Harkess for useful insights, and Susan Bassnett, who obtained most of the addresses listed above.

Jamaica

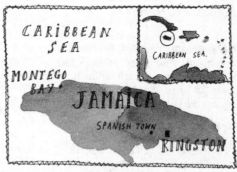

ountains, beaches and a tropical climate attract tourists all year round to Jamaica. Tourism is integral to the island's economy, and strings of discotheques, expensive restaurants and watersports centres line the coast roads. At the same time beaches are never crowded, and outside major resorts like Montego Bay there's plenty of scope for more adventurous travel, though it won't be cheap.

Safety is mainly a hazard in and around the capital, Kingston. The people of Jamaica are mostly very poor; unemployment is high and violence, much of it politically motivated, has become a regular feature of city life. No traveller is advised to walk there alone, especially at night, but tension fades visibly as you move away from the area. You can expect comments from men wherever you go, but no general threat of sexual attack. Communication, however, can prove an unexpected problem. Although British colonisation has left English as the official language, most people speak a local patois which is very difficult for outsiders to understand. It's much easier and probably safer to travel with someone who knows "Jamaica talk".

The importance of reggae music amongst young people, the practice of Rastafarianism (a cult based on the divinity of the late Emperor Haile Selassie of Ethiopia), and moves to achieve official recognition of Jamaican dialect as a language in its own right, are all signs of a nation struggling to define its cultural identity. **Women** are integral to this process, for they have always been greatly responsible for preserving African tradition in the passing down of customs through the family. Recognition of the hitherto submerged role of women in Caribbean history lies at the core of Jamaica's most radical women's group, *Sistren* (meaning sisters), a theatre collective for working-class women. According to founder-member, Honor Ford-Smith, the groups use drama as a consciousness-raising tool, "a means of breaking silence, of stimulating discussion, of posing problems and experimenting with their solutions." This approach is far removed from other women's organisations which tend to focus on domestic and handicraft schemes which do little to challenge the actual position of women in society.

Encounter with a Rastawoman

. . . .

Mara Benetti travelled to Jamaica with friends. During her ten-week stay she found that, though difficult at times, it was more rewarding to explore the island alone.

My first three weeks were a gentle breaking-in period during which I got used to being shouted at in the street – "Ehi! Whitie! Whitie!" – from passing cars and lorries, and learned how to cope with the constant hassling which tourists can expect to suffer. With time I felt stronger within myself and decided to travel around the island.

With its eruptive vitality and alien ways, Jamaica is an intimidating country for a woman to travel alone. However, in the end I much preferred it to travelling with white friends. Alone it was easier to divorce myself from the wealthy tourist hordes and, although I certainly felt insecure and threatened at times, I always ended up having some interesting encounter. I learned to get used to the men who swarm around almost any white woman with caressing looks and sweet words. They are different from, say, the Italian *pappagallo* or the North African male champion; in Jamaica attitudes to sex are more free and easy, sexual taboos appear to be less strong, and I came to the conclusion that the dominant reason behind these seductive approaches was the "subtle charm of the bourgeoisie"

which white skin exerts on people who are very poor. If you go out with a Jamaican man don't be surprised to find yourself paying for two.

Contacts with women in Jamaica aren't easy. Unlike the men, they aren't particularly inclined to strike up a conversation, partly because they're too busy making ends meet, and partly because they see Western women, with the allure exerted on Jamaican men by their wealth, as dangerous competition. From a distance I was struck by the preponderance of strong "mother" figures, mainly a result of the high number of "baby mothers", that is women who are single parents. Relatively little importance is placed on the institution of marriage, but womanhood in Jamaica seems to revolve around children.

"Rastawomen struck me with their strength of character, confidence and self-possession"

With its total rejection of birth control, this emphasis on children is especially strong within the Rastafarian community. The rasta queen is meant to be entirely subordinate to her king. Yet the rastawomen I met struck me with their strength of character, confidence and self-possession. They stood firm and independent. Many lived with their children without men in their lives. The community was generally supportive and the baby's father gave some erratic contribution to the upbringing of his offspring, but it was the women who provided for most of their needs and ran the household.

This was the life of one of the few rasta-women I had the chance to meet.

My encounter dated back to the very beginning of my stay when I made a trip north with Tekula, an American black dreadlock woman I had met through a friend. Tekula was incredibly beautiful and, with her unusual light blue eyes, aroused great interest in everyone she met. She was also very stylish, always dressed in clothes dyed and designed by herself with great inventiveness and skill.

Something must have attracted the rastawoman who approached us as we sat on the beach at Orange Bay. With a sense of purpose she walked straight up to Tekula and, after exchanging a few words, invited her to her hut in the bush. I was taken along as a sort of special concession for the woman took one look at me and announced: "The Bible says woman shall not wear men's clothing," staring at my baggy trousers which, up to that moment, I'd thought very respectable.

Our guide, who was tall, well-built and in about her mid-thirties, led the way up a hill along a path which soon disappeared to leave us scrambling through tropical vegetation. After the first hill we descended into a valley covered with small coconut trees, then up again, past another valley in which grazed half a dozen goats, then up yet another hill.

I can hardly remember how many hills and valleys we walked, but we finally made our way along the edge of a mound at the end of which a couple of bamboo sheds stood on a flattened open space. The first, largish and built on a raised platform, had a couple of beds in it and most of her belongings – a plastic bag full of rags, clothes and several blankets – as well as a wooden table cluttered with tobacco leaves and small parcels of *ganja* characteristically wrapped in brown paper. The other hut was her kitchen, open on two sides, with an open fire and a few makeshift seats made of old beer barrels.

The woman lived alone, although that day several of her men friends were present, all young rastas looking proud and dignified despite their unkempt appearance. They were poorly dressed and no one wore shoes. We were ushered into the first hut and told to make ourselves comfortable and take a seat on her bed. She rolled up a massive joint for herself and offered me some tobacco when I said that *ganja* was too strong.

> *"As the only white woman and a 'bald head' . . . I felt so out of place I could only sit in silence and soak up the scene"*

It began to rain and everyone came to take shelter and the hut became really crowded. As the only white woman and a "bald head" (the rasta expression for all non-Rastafarians) I felt so out of place I could only sit in silence and soak up the scene. The conversation was in patois, double-dutch to me, and I could only under-stand the usual "Praise Jah, Rastafari", repeated by everyone so often and regularly that it gave a musical rhyth-mic quality to what was being said.

Our hostess seemed to rule like a queen. She pointed to the banana and the coconut trees that grew around the hut; at the yam, the green breadfruit she had just collected from the lower branches of a tree, and launched into a thanksgiving litany to Jah. At some point – I didn't understand why or what in the conversation had prompted it – she started to undo her flowery head-scarf. It was an automatic movement, one gesture after another, as she kept on talking to her attentive public. Finally her dreadlocks tumbled down from the top of her head, heavy, long, twenty years of them perhaps? She looked suddenly younger and gave us all a proud satisfied smile before wrap-ping her hair up again and folding everything into place.

TRAVEL NOTES

Languages Most people speak patois or "Jamaica talk" amongst themselves, but can easily switch into English. Language problems usually depend on the situation you find yourself in.

Transport Buses are cheap, but slow, and the driving can be pretty wild. Minibuses also operate on all the main routes, always jam-packed since they only set off when full. Some taxis have meters, but it's wise to sort out the fare before you set off. Hitching is not recommended.

Accommodation Hotels tend to be expensive and it's usually better to try to find a room for rent. There are lots of houses on the beach at Negril which offer inexpensive rooms.

Special Problems There are varying reports about the safety of Kingston – the shanty-town areas in the southwest of the capital are definitely to be avoided – but provided you feel confident and carry very little money it's worth a visit. Market prices shoot up one hundred percent at the sight of a white face, so bargaining is a must.

Standard medical care is very dubious and medicines expensive, so make sure you are insured and, as far as possible, take your own supplies. *Ganja* or marijuana is widely grown and smoked, but it's illegal. It's also very, very strong.

Guides *Caribbean Islands Handbook* (Trade and Travel Publications) is from the publishers of the excellent *South American Handbook* and includes a good section on Jamaica.

Contacts

Sistren Theatre Collective, 20 Kensington Crescent, Kingston 5. The group works mainly in the shanty-towns and in rural areas, but it's worth getting in touch to try to see them in action.

Books

Sistren, *Lionheart Gal – Life Stories of Jamaican Women* (The Women's Press, 1986). Edited by Sistren's long-standing artistic director, Honor Ford-Smith, this book is based on testimonies collected in the course of the theatre collective's work with ordinary Jamaican women.

Pat Ellis, ed., *Women of the Caribbean* (Zed Books, 1987). This collection of essays provides a good general introduction to the history and lives of Caribbean women.

Michelle Cliff, *Abeng* (The Crossing Press, New York, 1984). Explores the life of a young girl growing up among the contradictions of class, colour, blood and Jamaica's history of colonisation and slavery.

Erna Brodber, *Jane and Louisa Will Soon Come Home* (New Beacon Books, 1980). The author's first novel, written in the form of a long prose poem about life in Jamaica.

Ziggi Alexander and Audrey Dewjee, eds., *The Wonderful Adventures of Mrs Seacole in Many Lands* (1957; Falling Wall Press, 1984). Mary Seacole, who was born into Jamaican slave society, writes about her life and travels.

Pamela Mordecai and Marvyn Morris, eds., *Jamaica Woman* (Heinemann, 1982). Exciting anthology of poems by fifteen Jamaican women.

Also look out for the work of Jamaica's best-known woman poet, **Miss Louise Bennett**.

Japan

F or some years now Japan
has been asserting its power as
the world's richest nation, the
pivotal force of international
commerce, technology and fashion. Alongside this, a new nationalistic pride has emerged – one
that increasingly relegates visitors from less successful nations
to a second-class status. This is
less of a problem for white
Westerners, who tend to be
treated with traditional hospitality and courtesy, but black or
Asian visitors (of whatever
nationality) face fairly blatant
discrimination.

The country is an expensive
place to visit and the crowds and
hectic pace of the cities can be hard to adjust to. However, Japan does have a
reputation for safety. Sexual harassment and violence are relatively rare (at
least on the streets) and, even wandering around at night, you're unlikely to
feel personally threatened. It is however, easy to feel isolated. People might
be curious about you, and want to question you about Western culture or
practise their English, but few follow this up. Westerners have a reputation
for being clumsy, confrontational, ignorant of etiquette, and very much out of
step with Japan's peaceful and harmonious way of life. Even if you speak
Japanese you'll find it difficult to cross the cultural divide.

Living and working in the country you'll also come up against a deeply
entrenched sexism and conservatism. Pornography is evident and available
everywhere – in newspapers, advertisements, even early evening television –
and prostitution is a well established industry. So much so, that even a business deal is incomplete without a visit to the nightclub for "hostess"
entertainment.

Women in Japan are expected to take a subservient role. The renowned
work ethic, the devotion to a company and a job, is greatly dependent on
women's unpaid labour as housewives. Women are heavily discriminated
against in the workplace and are often only taken on by companies as tempo-

rary, supplementary labour with less pay and none of the security and benefits available for full-time workers. It is also quite common for female employees to be pressurised to retire "voluntarily" when they reach thirty. Much the same level of discrimination has existed in education and, until very recently, in almost all levels of government.

This is now changing. After an almost constant stream of government sex and corruption scandals the Japanese electorate has been casting about for new political figures. It was in this context that Takako Doi, leader of the Japan Socialist Party, appointed 200 new women candidates and launched a serious challenge against the ruling conservative coalition at the last national election. As a counter-move the Liberal Democratic Party appointed a woman, Mrs Moriyama, as chief cabinet secretary, a choice that would have been unthinkable only a year or so ago. Whether this impetus will continue, and women politicians will be able to make a significant impact, is still uncertain. Undoubtedly this political shift has provided a major boost to the **Japanese feminist movement**, which through an expanding network of grass-roots organisations has been campaigning against sexual discrimination at work, sexual violence in the home, and pornography. There are also groups campaigning against Japanese participation in the sex tourism industry in Asia.

Finding a place in Kyoto

. . . .

Riki Therivel went to Japan on an American scholarship to study civil engineering. She lived for almost one-and-a-half years with a Japanese family, did a variety of teaching jobs to boost her savings and travelled extensively throughout the country and also into China.

When I left the US for an eighteen-month stay in Kyoto, I knew almost nothing about Japan. But I planned to rectify that by living as much like a Japanese person as possible. In my fantasies this involved spending long hours cross-legged in a remote Zen monastery and communicating predominantly in haiku verse.

This vision faded more or less as soon as I arrived. I was taken, at 10pm, from the airport to the university, where my fellow students (all men) were waiting to greet me. Over the next few weeks I set about learning how to read and speak Japanese. The other students were pleasant and polite, and we got on in very slow and simple sentences. I noticed, however, that they seemed uncomfortable with direct questions and invariably called to their friends to confirm their opinions. No one seemed willing to express a personal view or even enter into a discussion on their own, although they asked me many questions, especially about my views of Japan. At that point I started understanding how very group-oriented the Japanese are, and also how easily the group casts out members who do not conform. As a foreigner, I wasn't expected to understand the group "rules", but, equally, I couldn't expect to be completely accepted.

People in Japan work long hours, usually six days a week, and generally take only a few days' holiday a year. In the evenings, the men often go out to dinner and then to the bar with their fellow workers, spending little time at home. This leaves little space for other things, like travelling around the country, which I also wanted to do. So after a month of living Japanese-style I started going to lunch with other friends and taking Saturdays off to travel around. Unfortunately this seemed to alienate the other students, and the tentative friendships that had begun chilled quickly. Luckily the university soon matched me up with a host family who had volunteered to help a foreigner to adapt to Japan; the Sueishis took me to festivals, taught me to cook Japanese meals, lent me their sewing machine, and really did become my "family".

I had been provided with an apartment in a foreign students' housing block, a modern Western-style affair, and very luxurious considering that Japanese students usually live in tiny seven foot by seven foot rooms. But three of us soon tired of what we considered to be a gilded cage, so we moved to a Japanese-style house. The move itself was an exercise in formality and ritual: the house had been rented by friends-of-friends who were willing to recommend us, then my host mother and I visited the landlady with presents, and the negotiations reached a crescendo of innumerable phone calls before we were deemed acceptable tenants.

Living in a Japanese neighbourhood was a wonderful way of learning about everyday life. Each morning the women would wave off first their husbands then their children. On my morning shopping trip I would see them all in the street, sweeping the already-clean tarmac, and by the time I returned they would all be in their houses again. The recycling truck would come by with blaring loudspeakers and we would scuttle out with our newspaper bundles. The garbagemen, in turn, were greeted with beautiful piles of neat blue plastic bags. According to a Japanese proverb, "the wife is happy when her husband is healthy and out of the house"; the women in my neighbourhood were happy most of the time.

What struck me was the uniformity of the women's lives. Girls are expected to finish high school and perhaps study English or cooking or fashion at a two-year college. Then they work for a few years and marry. The usual age for marriage is between 23 and 25 and about half are arranged. This initially shocked me, but my host mother reasoned that people from similar backgrounds who have the support of both families will develop love, or at least what she called "warm currents between them".

"I learnt that women walk through doors after men, only after several collisions, with much subsequent apologetic bowing"

The first child comes a few years after the marriage, and the second a few years after that. There is a lot of social pressure to stick to this format. My host mother said that, despite her agreement with feminist principles, she would still suggest this traditional path to a daughter, simply because not conforming would lead her into so many difficulties.

Women in Japan hold their cups and food bowls differently from men, bow more deeply, and use different verb endings. I learnt that women walk through doors after men, only after several collisions, with much subsequent apologetic bowing. Women rarely wear shorts or sleeveless blouses, or even anything very colourful; black and white were definitely *de rigeur* while I was there. Traditional events like tea ceremonies, visits to temples, or trips to the bathhouse also involve etiquette which is best learned from someone who has been before. Foreigners *can* get away with almost any infringement of etiquette and are not expected to master more than the simplest Japanese words. But this only serves to confirm preconceptions that we're invading barbarians.

During my stay I met a lot of Japanese people, but the cultural differences were so strong that I made few friends. The Japanese express themselves predominantly in allusions, ritual phrases and body positions; very different to more verbal and confrontational style of communication I was used to. Also I was brought up with an entrenched belief in egalitarianism, whereas Japan is very hierarchy-oriented, so we had different preconceptions of what friendship should be.

Foreigners have their place in the hierarchy, usually at one of the extremes. White Americans are treated with a mixture of admiration and contempt; admiration, strangely enough, because of their victory in the war, and contempt because Japan is now beating them economically. The Germans are widely respected because of their own post-war achievements, while blacks and Asians are seen as inferior; if Japan could rise from economic obscurity why couldn't they?

Women in Japan are trained (externally at least) to buttress, build up, and coddle their menfolk, and are simply not expected to have any opinions of their own. My conversations with women of my age (mid-twenties) consisted of their questions and my answers, or my questions and their deflections of them. Of course, there were exceptions: the open-minded and incredibly charming Japanese woman who joined me on a journey through China; the woman I met in a crowded and steamy cafeteria who involved me in a wonderful and unintelligible discussion about nuclear war (I think); and my host mother who is one of the most energetic, self-assured and lovable people I have met. But generally the women I met treated me deferentially, tentatively, and often shied away, as though I were a tall and unpredictable extra-terrestrial.

"Foreign women, with their strong opinions and aggressive mannerisms, are considered threatening"

Foreign residents in Tokyo and Kyoto have founded women's groups, and their meeting times are listed in the English-language papers. Japanese women's organisations exist, but these are more like special interest clubs than support groups. Because foreign women tend to be viewed primarily as foreigners and only secondarily as women, I don't think that they would provide much help for the woman traveller in Japan.

Because Japanese women are expected to be so submissive, foreign women, with their strong opinions and aggressive mannerisms, are considered threatening, especially by men. On the other hand, foreign women are also attractive because they are different, and possibly because they are thought to be more sexually available than Japanese women. A Japanese male friend said to me "You're American which puts you above me, but a woman which puts you below me, so we must be equal." One man used to send me and several Western friends an endless stream of postcards and presents, as though we were movie stars. My supervisor asserted his control over me shortly after I arrived by insisting that I go home with him after a drinking party. He woke up his sixty-year-old wife at midnight so that she could prepare snacks for us and then politely insisted that I stay the night as a guest; from then on I avoided the office drinking parties.

However, as unpleasant and frustrating as the sexual discrimination often was, it was never translated into physical harassment. Japan prides itself on its low crime rate, and one can walk around safely anywhere at any time. Public transport is invariably clean, punctual, and safe. The occasional drunken man may mumble "you are beautiful" or "speak English to me", but I never had to go beyond a polite "no" to stop it. Because crime is so rare in their country, many Japanese see other countries, and especially America, as highly dangerous places where drug abuse is rampant and gun-toting hoodlums lurk on every street corner. They were much more afraid of me than I was of them.

I travelled around a lot, predominantly by bicycle. Japan is dotted with beautiful rural villages tucked between steep mountains, and I spent many pleasant afternoons sweating my way up to them and careering back down. The roads are clogged with cars near the cities, making cycling dangerous, but an hour's ride got me away from the traffic and into as much countryside as Japan still has. There aren't many cyclists in Japan, and even fewer women cyclists, but they were friendly and always yelled out a greeting as they sped past.

Hitchhiking in Japan is easy and safe, even for a lone woman. The difficult part is explaining what is wanted, since few Japanese hitchhike themselves. We made big signs, in Japanese, "please take us with you", and never had problems getting picked up, even with a bike. In fact, once they picked us up, the drivers seemed to feel responsible for the outcome of our journey, and often drove us directly to our destination. We finally learned to ask the drivers where they were going first, and rearrange our journey to save them the sometimes very lengthy detour.

Finding a job in Japan was easy, especially once I had made a few connections. I taught English to schoolchildren, office workers and doctors, corrected translations of Japanese articles, and worked as an assistant at an international Zen Buddhism symposium. English teachers are in high demand and the pay is quite good.

The Zen symposium took place only a week before I left the country and somehow fulfilled my initial romantic vision of Japan. I had worked for the symposium committee for several months, so that when the foreign scholars arrived I felt like a host rather than a visitor. We all went to a traditional tea ceremony and, kneeling to be served by a kimono-clad woman, with a view of a rock garden and pond, I felt that maybe I had learned a lot in Japan after all. I still didn't feel at home and would probably always be treated as a foreigner, but I had learned how to cope with loneliness and a thoroughly foreign culture.

TRAVEL NOTES

Languages Japanese. Little English is spoken outside the cities,

Transport Extensive, efficient and expensive. Hitching is very unusual but fairly safe.

Special Problems The underground is one of the few places where physical harassment is likely. It's worth standing with other women. Racial harassment is more of an upfront problem and applies to all non-Japanese, who may have problems using bathhouses, etc.

You should bring any contraception you need. The pill is illegal and virtually unobtainable and the diaphragm almost unheard of.

Accommodation Japanese-style hotels (*ryokan*) are difficult to cope with and, unless you have knowledge of the language, it's best to go to the tourist office for advice. Look out for "business hotels" which can be up to fifty percent cheaper than normal ones. "Love Hotels" are best avoided although they are not only used for illicit sex – privacy can be hard to come by in Japan's overcrowded cities and people are willing to rent rooms by the hour.

Guide *Japan – A Travel Survival Kit* (Lonely Planet) is comprehensive and useful.

Contacts

TWIN (Tokyo Women's Information Network), c/o BOC Publishing, Shinjuku 1-9-6, Shinjuku-ku, Tokyo 167, ☎358 3941. The best source of information on feminist groups in Japan (both Japanese and English-speaking). Organises feminist English classes and produces a biannual journal, *Agora Agoramini*.

International Feminists of Japan, Fujin Joho Centre, Shinjuku Ku, nr Akebonobashi Station, Exit 4a (meets the first Sunday of every month). Aims to forge better links between Japanese feminist groups and their counterparts abroad. Publishes monthly newsletter, *Feminist Forum*.

Fusen Kaikan (Women's Suffrage), 21-11 Yoyogi 2 Chrome, Shibuya-ku, Tokyo 151, ☎370 0238. Centre for education, research and publishing, with a library and a good permanent exhibition of the life of journalist and political activist Ishikawa Fusae (1893–1980), who was active in the Women's Suffrage League in the 1920s. The staff speak some English.

Gayon House Bookshop, next to Tokyo Union Church (nearest station Omote Sando), Tokyo. Feminist and anti-nuclear books.

Asian Women's Association, Shibuya Coop Rm 211, 14-10-211 Sakuragaokacho, Shbuya-ku, Tokyo 150, ☎592 4950. Campaigning group opposed to the use of cheap female labour in Japan and South East Asia, and also against Japanese sex tourism in Seoul, Taipei and Bangkok. Publishes *Asian Women's Liberation*, a quarterly journal in English and Japanese.

Kyoto Feminist Group, Kyoto YWCA, Muromachi, Demizu-agaru, Kyoto, ☎722 0686. Mainly foreign residents who meet weekly.

National Women's Education Centre, 728 Sugaya, Ranzan-machi, Hiki-gun, Saitama-Ken, ☎355 02. An information centre for study and research, with space for local women's groups.

Lesbian Groups. There is a fairly well established lesbian network in Japan, but Japanese and foreign women tend to organise separately. The main meeting points are lesbian weekends arranged every public holiday. For information, write to **Lesbian Contact**, CPO Box 1780, Tokyo 100-91 (send an International Reply Coupon). The group publishes a regular newsletter, *DD*, with articles, listings and events. There are a few **lesbian bars**, all in the Shinjuku Sanchome area of Tokyo.

Books

Yukio Tanaka, ed., *To Live and to Write: Selections by Japanese Women Writers 1913–1938* (Seal Press, US, 1988). Essays by the first major women writers in Japan, dealing with subjects traditionally taboo for women.

Susan Pharr, *Political Women in Japan: The Search for a Place in Political Life* (California UP, 1981). Exploration of women's images of self and society and of expectations, from first-hand interviews.

Liza Crihfield Dalby, *Geisha* (California UP, 1983). Contemporary study of a living phenomenon. The author, an anthropologist, became a geisha during her stay in Kyoto.

Leonie Caldecott, At the Foot of the Mountain: The Shibokusa Women of Kita Fuji, in **Lynne Jones, ed., *Keeping the Peace*** (The Women's Press, 1983). Moving and extraordinary account of a rural and local peace group at the foot of Mount Fuji and their defence of their community through disrupting military exercises in the region.

Shizuko Go, *Requiem* (1973; The Women's Press, 1986). Diary narrative of the last months of World War II, as experienced by the "daughters of military Japan".

Sachiko Ariyoshi, *Letters from Sachiko* (Abacus, 1984). Letters to the author's sister in the West highlight the constraints faced by women in contemporary Japanese society.

Fiction

Yuko Tsushima, *Child of Fortune* (The Women's Press, 1986); ***The Shooting Gallery and Other Stories*** (The Women's Press, 1988). Lucid pictures of the lives and aspirations of contemporary Japanese women and the pressures they face to accept a subservient role.

Michiko Yamamoto, *Betty San: Four Stories* (1973; Kodansha, 1985). Again addresses the subservient domestic roles of Japanese women – and also East-West incompatibilities.

Junichiro Tanizaki, *The Makioka Sisters* (Picador, 1983). A very well-known novel in Japan, with a quintessential heroine struggling between passivity and self-will.

Thanks to Sylph and Marilyn Haywood for information.

Kenya

Since gaining independence from the British in 1963, Kenya has developed an image of Westernisation and affluence. Its capital, Nairobi, is a major commercial centre crowded with British and multinational firms. Britons also make up a major slice of the country's lucrative and well established tourist trade, attracted by accessible gameparks, beaches, and the country's reputation for political stability. But the economic advantages, which are rapidly levelling off in the context of world recession, have benefited only a small minority. Stretching north from Nairobi into the Mathare valley there are vast urban slums, with up to 100,000 people living in cardboard, tin and plastic bag shanty huts. In the north, the edge of the Sahel region, there are areas devastated by drought.

The country has been ruled as a one-party state since 1982, under President Daniel arap Moi, leader of *KANU* (Kenya African National Union). His government has consolidated its power by ruthless suppression of oppositional groups – literally hundreds have been detained without trial and reports of torture and death in custody are common. In 1989, against a background of international condemnation of widespread human rights violations, an amnesty was announced for political detainees. There are no other signs, however, of a political change of heart and many dissidents, convicted of political subversion, continue to suffer appalling conditions in prison.

Tourism is heavily promoted and, although geared mainly towards expensive safari packages, there are plenty of facilities for independent travellers. Most women, however, tend to travel in pairs rather than alone. Sexual harassment is a fairly persistent problem, especially along the predominantly

Muslim coastline where the experience of mass tourism has fuelled stereo-types of Western women as "loose" and "available". The continual comments and propositions can at times feel personally threatening and on the beaches it's never a good idea to isolate yourself. Statistics for violent robbery are also high, and carrying any symbol of wealth (in fact anything but the bare necessities) can make you a target.

There are numerous **women's groups** throughout the country. Many of them are associated with *Maedeleo ya Wanawake* (Progress of Women), a popular and autonomous organisation responsible for setting up multi-purpose centres for health education, skills training and literacy groups (in the 1970s only ten percent of women were literate). In addition to this the *National Council of Women of Kenya*, which is partially funded by the government, campaigns to abolish the practice of female genital mutilation, reform legislation on abortion, and increase women's knowledge of contraception. A continuing scandal is the extent to which untested contraceptives (or those banned in the West) are being foisted on Kenyan women.

Knowing Nairobi
. . . .

Lindsey Hilsum is a journalist and foreign correspondent for the BBC. When she wrote this she had been working in Nairobi as a freelance writer and Information Officer for the United Nations Children's Fund.

It was my first solo walk through the streets of Nairobi. Having just arrived from Latin America, where I learnt that streetwise means ready to run or ready to fend off catcalls, comments and unwelcome hands, I was on my guard. But in Nairobi no man bothered me. I was proffered the occasional elephant-hair bracelet, the odd batik, but no one tried to touch or waylay me. Some months later, a Norwegian woman friend arrived on her first trip outside Europe. As I showed her around Nairobi that afternoon, men shouted and stared at her. Talking to other

women later, I understood the problem; because I had already learned to walk with confidence and aggression, no one perceived that I was vulnerable. But my friend gave off an aura of uncertainty – she was obviously a newcomer, a tour-ist and, as such, was fair game.

It is possible to travel widely in Kenya using public transport. There are hotels and campsites scattered throughout, and people usually go out of their way to help. A lone woman is something of a curiosity in small towns and rural areas but people are more likely to be sympathetic than hostile. "Isn't it sad to be without a husband and children?" I have been asked. My reply that I prefer it that way has started many good conversations. People like to talk – a smattering of Swahili helps, but there are many Kenyans who speak English.

For most visitors, going to a game-park is a high priority. The most comfortable way to go is on an organ-ised tour. I went on one to Masai Mara, and found myself ensconced in a Volkswagen minibus with two cowboy-hatted Texans who were "in oil" in Saudi Arabia, an American couple plus toddler also from Saudi, and a lone geriatric British bird-watcher. Other people have found themselves crushed between Germans and Japanese, straining for a glimpse of a lion through the forest of telephoto lenses, and my sister ended up in the Abedares with a busload of Americans wearing name-badges who turned out to have won the trip by being "workers of the year" at a Coca-Cola factory.

"Hacking my way through the forest at night, in search of two friends and two small children who had not returned from a walk, I realised how threatening the forest can be"

It's more fun to go independently, but only with a reliable, preferably four-wheel drive vehicle. I spent one hot, frustrating, exhausting week trying to get to Lake Turkana in an ancient Landrover, the remnants of a long-since discarded Ministry of Livestock Development Sheep and Goat project. Accompanied by a friend as mechanically incompetent as myself, I never made it to the lake, but now know all the amateur motor mechanics between Baringo and Barogoi.

Only an hour's drive from Nairobi, you reach the natural rainforest. If you want to explore this region you should go with a guide. It's easy and very dangerous to get lost. Hacking my way through the forest at night, in search of two friends and two small children who had not returned from a walk, I realised how threatening the forest can be. One moment luxuriant and enticing, the next, when every coughing sound could be a leopard and every thud an elephant, it becomes sinister. We found our friends, who had lit a fire and tucked the children snugly into the forked foot of a tree when they realised at dusk that they were lost. We would

never have found them without the local Forest Rest House warden, who searched with us as a guide.

One place which has become popular with low-budget tourists is the largely Muslim island of Lamu. With its white sand beaches and curious melée of backstreets, downmarket restaurants and mosques, it is closer in culture and history to Zanzibar and Ilha de Mozambique than to the rest of Kenya. Sometimes I think I'm just prejudiced against it. The first time I went, my friend Laura and I took the sweltering eight-hour bus ride from Malindi, and then the boat. The sun blazed down as we left the shore, my period started, and I passed out. Stumbling to the quay at Lamu, I collapsed in the dirt. Laura, pursued by a young man informing her of a nice cheap hotel he was sure she'd like, went in search of liquid. She found a bottle of bright orange Fanta. I took one glance and then vomited. All around me were male voices, saying things like, "get her to hospital" and "why don't you go back to your own country?" Needless to say, it was two women who helped us find a place to stay.

Personal experience apart, Lamu can be difficult for women. The traditional Muslim culture has been sent reeling by the advent of beer and bikinis and while women tourists bathe topless, Lamu women walk the streets clad in black robes from head to foot. Concerned about the corruption of local youth and the rising numbers of "beach boys" who hang around tourists, the local authorities are reported to have forbidden young local men from talking to visiting women. The clash in culture has found expression in sexual violence, and there have been several incidents of rape on the beach. I would never bathe topless, and never lose sight of other people on the beach, however solitary and tempting it may appear.

Back on the mainland at Malindi the beach is fringed with luxurious hotels, complete with bar service, butler service, air conditioning, chilled wine and four-course meals. Not so far away, the town crumbles into ramshackle mud and wooden dwellings where sewage runs along open drains, and household electricity and water are just promises the municipal council has yet to fulfil.

It's this divide between rich and poor that shocks the first-time visitor to Africa. Personally I avoid staying in tourist hotels, not only because the luxury jars alongside such evident poverty, but because guests are alienated from "Africa", as alive in a tourist town like Malindi as in any upcountry village where *mzungu* (white people) are rarely seen.

Generally, I stay in a *hoteli*, a small guesthouse found in any town. They are cheap, occasionally clean, and almost invariably the people who run them will be friendly. But single women sometimes have problems with men knocking on their bedroom door (this happens in upmarket hotels too), so I always make sure that my room can be firmly locked from inside.

I think the only way I've come to understand anything about "ordinary" Kenyan women is by frequenting local bars. In many countries, bars are a male preserve, but in Kenya there are usually women about – barmaids, prostitutes, and in some places women doing their crochet over a bottle of beer. Not many *mzungu* women go into bars, except in tourist hotels, so those that do attract a fair amount of attention. "People say it is dangerous to come here," said the proprietor of one bar in Kisumu, "but you are safe." I agreed with him, and he bought me a beer simply because I'd dared to be there. As I left, some Asian youths cruised by in their Mercedes. "Wanna fuck?" they called. That was when I felt nervous and wished I could find a taxi back to my hotel.

The women tend to assume a protective role. In one bar in downtown Nairobi, a woman kept me by her side all evening. "No one speaks to my sister without my permission!" she insisted, glaring at anyone, male or female, reckless enough to look at me. As I entered a bar in Kisumu, Jane the barmaid, came to sit with me. A young man slouched towards us from the counter. "My friend is talking to *me*," said Jane, and he shrugged and walked away.

"Opening gambits like 'Tell me about free love in your country' are irritatingly common"

Women like Jane have interesting stories, and they usually like to talk. Many come from rural backgrounds, left home to look for a job in the big city, got pregnant, and have been trapped in the circle of barmaiding and prostitution ever since. Options for women are few once you leave the village; with no education and no money, and with children to support, prostitution is often the only way.

These women may ask you for an address, hoping for a job as a housemaid, or some money to pay school fees, or some clothes. But they're not talking to you because they want something, but because it feels good to talk, and because they're curious, and there is a sympathetic link between women of different cultures, and it is somehow comforting to find common ground with a stranger. "You can so easily end up in a maternity," lamented one woman I know, who hangs around the same bar in Nairobi every evening. "I could be pregnant again. So could you." Later she took a male friend of mine aside. "Don't you get my sister pregnant," she admonished him, "That would be a very terrible thing to do!" Kenyan men do tend to look upon foreign women as an easy lay, and opening gambits like "Tell me about free love in your country" are irritatingly common.

If you have any problems, women around will usually help. But beware "big" men in small towns. If it's the local police chief or councillor who is making advances, it may not be possible for other local people to help out, because of his power and influence. If in doubt get out; preferably accompanied, preferably in a vehicle. I never walk alone at night in Nairobi, because mugging and rape are quite common, and it's always worth the taxi fare to be safe.

I don't think that Kenyan men are intrinsically any more sexist than men from my own country, England. As a person unfettered by family, educated and employed and travelling unaccompanied, I get treated in some ways as an honorary man. But underneath it all, a woman is a woman is a woman, and most Kenyan men I've met agree with their president, who announced in September 1984 that God had made man the head of the family, and challenging that was tantamount to criticising God. And certainly when I've expressed my doubts, the response is generally that in *my* culture we may have different notions, but *their* women like it that way. I'm not so sure about that.

Throughout Kenya there are large numbers of women's groups which have banded together to earn some money, by making handicrafts, growing crops, keeping bees or goats, or other small-scale businesses. Their success is variable. Some groups have made profits and shared them; in other cases the men have sabotaged the group when they felt threatened by the women's success or have appropriated the money. In others, lack of organisation, inexperience, or simply the lack of time among women already overburdened by the day-to-day tasks of survival have built in failure from the beginning.

Women do want better healthcare, contraception, education for themselves and their children, and a higher income. But their needs and wants come a poor second to the concept of "development" which a male-dominated government and which predominantly male-dominated aid agencies promote. The rhetoric of the UN Decade for Women has resounded throughout Kenya, and we all know that small-scale water projects, reforestation, support to women as farmers and access to credit are important. But agricultural extensionists are still men; although it's women who dig the land, women are rarely consulted, and there is a tendency to start "women's projects" as a sideline to the more serious business of "nation building".

Women leaders in Kenya tend to take the attitude that gentle persuasion works better than protest. Many of them are middle-class urban women, whose ideas and problems are often seen as divorced from the reality of ordinary Kenyan women. With their emphasis on education, welfare and income-generating projects they have been criticised for supporting the status quo and denying the possibilities of radical change.

"The widespread denunciation of feminism . . . is a way of keeping women down, by telling them that any change is 'un-African'"

A Western feminist is often resented. There is good reason for this – many Western women simply do not know about the issues which affect Kenyan women, but nonetheless push their own priorities. On the other hand, the widespread denunciation of feminism (which finds its most outrageous expression in the letters pages of the newspapers) is a way of keeping women down, by telling them that any change is "un-African". I have come to believe that issues such as accessible clean water and getting more girls into school are more important to most Kenyan women than free abortion on demand or the acceptance of lesbianism – and many Kenyan women oppose the latter two. Other issues, such as male violence and access to healthcare and contraception are as important in Kenya as in any Western country, although the starting point for pushing to achieve these things is different.

Foreign women who have lived in small towns and villages, usually as anthropologists or volunteers, have a deeper understanding of Kenyan women than I do. Many such women leave the country thoroughly depressed, as they see Kenyan women, year after year, accepting violent husbands, one pregnancy after another, children dying, endless work and little reward. Most visitors can't see all that, because it takes time, and nor do they get to see the other side of things, such as the sense of community amongst women and the strength of character that outward acceptance and seeming submissiveness belie.

It's not possible to understand so much on a short visit, but I think that many women coming to Kenya could see and understand a lot more if they dared. It took me a year to dare to travel Kenya alone, on *matatus* (collective taxis) and buses; hitchhiking, going to small towns, being open, talking to people. There's no need for every woman to take a year to pluck up courage – it's fun, it's interesting and it's worth it. I haven't had nearly enough yet.

TRAVEL NOTES

Languages Swahili is the official language; also Kikuyu, Luo and Maa. English is widely spoken.

Transport Public transport (buses and a small train network) is reasonable and safe. On well-worn tourist routes there are also collective taxis, usually big Peugeots. *Matatus*, impromptu communal trucks, need more confidence. Hitching isn't advisable.

Accommodation Board and Lodgings (B&Ls) can be found in any town and are good value. In gameparks there are very expensive lodges but also *bandas* (small wooden huts with cooking facilities; you bring your own food and sleeping bag) and "tented camps" (tents provided and set up within lodge compounds).

Guide The Rough Guide: Kenya (Harrap Columbus) gives an excellent run-through of just about everything you'll need to know about the country.

Contacts

Maedeleo ya Wanawake (Progress of Women), PO Box 44412, Nairobi. Largest and best-known women's organisation with numerous local groups.

National Council of Women of Kenya, PO Box 43741, Nairobi. Produces the publication *Kenyan Women*.

Kenya Association of University Women, PO Box 47010, Nairobi.

African Women Link (AWL), PO Box 50795, Nairobi. A development newsletter aimed at linking development groups and agencies that involve African women.

Viva, PO Box 46319, Nairobi. Monthly magazine combining feminism and fashion in a glossy but appealing package.

Books

Anonymous, In Dependant Kenya (Zed Books, 1982). A strident book which you shouldn't take with you, condemning the status quo and Kenya's involvement in the neo-colonial web.

Patrick Marnham, Fantastic Invasion: Dispatches from Africa (Penguin, 1986). Sharp, incisive essays on development and politics, concerned in large part with Kenya.

Fiction

Marjorie Oludhe MacGoye, Coming to Birth (Virago, 1987). Acclaimed story of a young woman's arranged marriage, its failure and her new life in post-Uhuru Kenya. Set during and just after the Mau Mau emergency.

Rebeka Njau, Ripples in the Pool (Heinemann, 1978). Novel, full of myth and menace, about the building of a village clinic.

Toril Brekke, *The Jacaranda Flower* (Methuen, 1987). A dozen short stories most of which touch on the lives of women.

Muthoni Likimani, *Passbook Number F 47927: Women and Mau Mau in Kenya* (Macmillan, 1986). Describes, in ten fictional-ised episodes, the impact of the 1950s Mau Mau revolt in Kenya on women's daily lives.

Beryl Markham, *West with the Night* (Virago, 1984; illustrated version, 1989). In 1936 Beryl Markham became the first person to fly solo across the Atlantic. Her biography tells of her upbringing and adventures in colonial Kenya.

Martha Gellhorn, *The Weather in Africa* (Eland, 1985). Three novellas, each set in Kenya and dealing absorbingly with aspects of the European-African relationship.

Karen Blixen, *Out of Africa* (1936; Penguin, 1986). A bestseller and cult book covering Blixen's experiences on a coffee farm in the Ngong Hills between the wars. Evocative, lyri-cal, sometimes obnoxiously racist, but a lot better than the film.

South Korea

Under the glare of publicity surrounding the 1988 Olympic Games in Seoul, South Korea emerged as a major economic power and centre of commerce. For many years a protegé of the United States, and currently forging close economic links with Japan, the country's foreign trade continues to flourish in the newly built luxury hotels and conference centres. The tourist industry is overtly geared towards the male business traveller, and like Thailand and the Philippines, relies heavily on the exploitation of women as prostitutes, the price of a *Kisaeng* or hostess often being included as part of a package deal. Promoted as a male paradise, South Korea attracts literally thousands of (mainly Japanese) sex tourists every year, many of them arriving in group tours, paid for as part of company incentive schemes. Despite the massive revenue this generates, the hostesses themselves earn notoriously little.

Whilst Korean women frequently face harassment from male tourists, the picture is very different for Western women. People tend to show a great deal of interest in foreigners, but even amongst the hostess bars of Seoul this is rarely intimidating or threatening. Relatively few tourists venture beyond the capital, and travelling alone around the rural areas you are bound to be seen as something of a curiosity. Again this is relatively easy to cope with – you'll most likely be treated with courtesy as a stranger and guest. Without a few words of Korean, however, communication can be a problem.

Tourists have always been very carefully cushioned from the' effects of political dissent. Yet it is hard to ignore the atmosphere of political transition that has begun to take hold of the country. Since the elections of 1988, Korea's new president Roh Tae Woo – the hand-picked successor of the former rigidly authoritarian regime – has initiated a surprising number of reforms. Besides promising various democratic changes, he has begun to pursue charges of past corruption, torture, and general illegality within his own political party. How far he will be able to control the impetus for change, after thirty years of right-wing rule, remains uncertain. An enduring demand amongst many students in the country has been reunification with the Democratic People's Republic of Korea in the north.

Korean culture owes much to Chinese influences but has its own distinctive features, like its unique female *shamans* (religious leaders). In general, the position of women is still dictated by Confucianism, and the disparity in the way daughters are valued in comparison to sons is so glaring that there has been an educational campaign to try and redress the balance.

Conditions of work for South Korean women have long been exceptionally grim – the major employers being the multinational factories that moved to Korea to take advantage of the very low wages and often cut costs further, with unsafe, poorly lit and unhygienic workplaces. Whilst the new regime has introduced an Equal Opportunity Employment Act, with fines imposed for the more blatant discriminatory practices, this has relatively little effect on sweat-shop work, where women comprise most of the workforce. However, attitudes appear to be changing, if very gradually. **Women's groups** both within South Korea and Japan have been militating against sex tourism.

Accepting the Rules

. . . .

Jane Richardson has been living and working in Seoul since June 1988. After a year teaching at a private language institute she moved to a job with the British Council. Throughout her stay she has travelled extensively around the country.

When I accepted a teaching job in Korea I knew little about the country and had only a vague idea of where it was. I knew it was to be the host of the 1988 Olympics, and that, according to the British media, half the population was involved in riots. After many

months here I feel I'm just beginning to know Korea and the Korean people.

The most difficult thing to adjust to initially was the sheer number of people; everywhere I went, pushing, elbowing, jostling, staring, laughing. There were days when I dreaded leaving my apartment or when I would miss my subway stop because I didn't want to push anyone to get off.

After a while I became much more assertive, and also learnt how to avoid, or at least ignore, the staring. The advantage of people staring is that I can also stare without having to worry about offending anyone. I've also learnt what kind of behaviour I should accept from Koreans. A few weeks after I arrived a woman waiting for a subway with me noticed that I had hairs on my arms. She called her friends over to have a look and I ended up with five women trying to pull the hairs out – perhaps to see if they were real. A Korean friend was horrified by this and told me that the women were being very rude. In a country like Korea, with so many customs and social rules, it's very easy to accept things passively out of fear of offending someone.

I lived in an apartment building in a tiny one-bedroomed flat. For me it was a luxury, but for the families and couples living on the estate it must have been impossibly cramped. There were half a dozen other teachers living in the neighbourhood and it was always possible to tell when one was coming home, as the children shouted "Migguk saraam. (American person) Hello. Goodbye. Thank you." They never seemed to get tired of this and were really delighted if you replied to them, rushing off to tell their friends about it.

"One day they decided to take me on a 'girls' trip out' after class, and sent all the men home"

There were also a few people living in the complex who spoke fairly good English – housewives who'd lived in the States, a man who sold eggs in the market, and a delivery boy from a Chinese restaurant. The delivery boy always shouted "hello my teacher", when he saw me, and was convinced that one of the other teachers was my mother simply because she was about 25 years older than me.

As a foreign woman it was very easy to meet people in Korea, but not so easy to make friends. I found that, among my students, the women I had most in common with were the older housewives or the students. However, friendship in Korea is a time-consuming business. Most of the housewives were too busy with their homes and children to go out and the women students were often not allowed to stay out after school hours.

With the men too it was difficult, simply because of the gossip network in the school – if you went to lunch

with a student everyone would know about it. It was also difficult, as a woman teacher, knowing that some of my ideas and way of life could be not exactly shocking, but certainly surprising to some students, and could cause them to lose respect for me.

I usually relied on intuition to tell me what I could say to one student and what to another, but it also depended on how open and interested the students seemed. I had one class which consisted mainly of housewives. One day they decided to take me on a "girls' trip out" after class, and sent all the men home. We went to Imjinga, near the Demilitarised Zone, and they talked about their memories of the Korean War, and also about their husbands and children. I felt privileged that they wanted to discuss these issues with me but it was also depressing – so many of them had been to university and had nurtured ambitions and dreams they had no way of fulfilling once they became married.

One woman I remained friendly with after she had left school, and through her I came to know more about the position of women in Korea. She was evidently unhappy in her marriage, which had been arranged, yet knowing that her own needs and desires would be considered unimport-ant she had decided to try and forget these and live through her children. It struck me that, much more than in the West, women are expected to hide their feelings and be seen to be happy with their lot in life. Complaining seems to be viewed almost as a moral defect, to be frowned upon even by close friends and family.

But the influence of the Women's Movement is growing. More and more women are entering the workforce and demanding better working conditions. Perhaps the increased openness to the West has also made people more aware and receptive to Western ideas about women's rights. In 1983 the Korean Women's Development Institute was set up to provide education and resources, undertake research, and generally attempt to improve women's status. It also provides a counselling service for Korean women and a regular newsletter in English. The atmosphere at the film forum and at the Institute in general was friendly and supportive.

If you're looking for a relaxing, women-only atmosphere, go to the *mogyoktang*, or sauna. These are found in every town and city in Korea, and are indicated by a flame symbol. You can spend, and Korean women frequently do, many hours here, simply getting clean. However, washing seems to be the secondary purpose, the main object being to talk, exchange gossip, and generally relax. As a foreigner you will inevitably attract attention, but it is only friendly curiosity. The women are more than willing to show you what to do.

First you have to wash sitting at a low hand-shower, then you enter the sauna, followed by a plunge in the cold tub, back to the sauna again, and eventually soak in the hot tub or jacuzzi. Later you will be called by a masseuse (mine was bizarrely dressed in black underwear). You lie on a bench and she scrubs you, with something resembling a Brillo pad, until your skin falls off in big grey lumps. A grated cucumber mask is put on your face and oil poured on your body which the masseuse then hits, slaps, pummels and kneads free of aches and pains. The whole process ends with a rinse in warm milk before you stagger, dazed but amazingly clean, to the shower.

In Confucianism women are considered inferior to men and are expected to be submissive, obedient, and to produce sons. A number of incidents illustrate the pervasive nature of these beliefs. In March 1989 a 13-year-old girl and her three sisters from a poor family attempted suicide in order that their parents might have enough money to educate the youngest son. The family had obviously continued to have children until a son was produced, and the girls had internalised the feeling of inferiority. This created an outcry in the country as people started to acknowledge and protest against the sexism in Korean society.

"My biggest problem in terms of harassment comes from drunk businessmen, usually on the subway"

As another example, at the institute where I work, during a money crisis, the manager paid everyone's wages except the female secretaries. After the secretaries went on strike they were fired, rehired, and eventually paid. The very fact that they and their wages were seen as dispensable says a lot about the way women are treated here.

As a Western women, you are also affected by these attitudes. In a shop an assistant will stop serving you if a man wants to be served; men are given empty seats on subways; and some older male students in my classes are obviously disturbed at having a woman teacher. Western women face an additional problem in that the only contact many Koreans have had with foreign women is through soft-porn films, shown regularly at the cinemas here.

Many Korean men assume that all Western women jump into bed with the first man they see. This can cause some harassment, though usually opportunistic rather than intimidating, along the lines of "Do you live alone? You are beautiful. What's your telephone number?" It is very unusual to live alone in Korea – the only women who do so are considered "bad", ie prostitutes.

My biggest problem in terms of harassment comes from drunk businessmen, usually on the subway. From the expressions on their faces and from the reaction of other passengers I presume they are making suggestions about what we could do if we got together. Korean friends have advised me to stare through the men as if they weren't there which causes them to "lose face". "Face" is a key concept of Korean society, and maintaining it is essential to one's feeling of self-esteem and general well-being.

Apart from prostitution, there are various other forms of sex-oriented entertainment in Seoul. "Adult" discos offer strip shows and dancers – young, bored girls wearing swimsuits and white high-heeled boots, who dance on raised podiums between your tables. Both men and women attend these type of discos. Korean women seem angry but accepting of this aspect of Korean life – "It's her job, she has to do it."

If you go to a disco in one of the large hotels you will see countless hostesses – women who are paid to sit with men, drink with them, and, sometimes, have sex. It is difficult to find anywhere in Seoul where entertainment is not provided by women. Even some coffee shops are actually *room salons*, which, like the hotels, have hostesses. I have heard about similar places where women can be entertained by male "hosts", but these are illegal and often raided by police; men's *room salons* are a social necessity, women's are immoral.

Despite all this, travelling in Korea is relatively safe, if not exactly easy. Outside Seoul few people speak English, and most local bus timetables are written in Hangul, or Korean script. Even if you can read Korean it's not always much help since the writing is sometimes handwritten and hence illegible. What does help is if you can pronounce the name of the place where you want to go. People are always really helpful. Take out a map or stand around looking puzzled and at least five people will appear and offer to help you.

The first time I travelled alone, to Tedun mountain, near Taejon, in the middle of winter, I discovered just how unusual it is to travel alone. Everybody I met offered me food, drink, help getting up the mountain, and insisted on taking my photograph. On another occasion, I travelled with another woman teacher to Cheju island, off the south coast, famous for its women divers. These women dive all year round, for shellfish and seaweed, and stay under water for minutes at a time. Postcards show them wearing bikinis, posed provocatively on rocks. Actually they are strong skilled women, proud of their professional skills and reluctant to be photographed, even wearing wetsuits.

TRAVEL NOTES

Languages Korean which has its own alphabet, *Hangul*. Despite the strong American influence, English is spoken in only the large hotels and commercial districts of Seoul.

Transport In Seoul the subway is cheap, easy and safe, though crowded. There are also plenty of taxis and buses. Express coaches, trains and internal flights are all efficient and quite cheap methods of getting round the country.

Accommodation There are plenty of cheap, basic options, including renting private rooms. Camping is possible in more tourist-oriented areas. Many hotels are "Love Hotels", renting rooms by the hour as well as overnight; they are usually quite safe for visitors.

Guide *Korea – A Travel Survival Kit* (Lonely Planet) is the most useful, but don't rely on the maps!

Contacts

Korean Women's Development Institute, C.P.O.Box 2267, Seoul 100, ☎783 7341/7271.

Books

In Korea, look out for the contemporary and historical studies on the position of women from the **Ewha Women's University Press**.

From the Womb of Han: Stories of Korean Women Workers (CCA-URM, 57 Peking Road, Kowloon, Hong Kong, 1982). Collection of stories, many direct transcriptions.

Laura Kendall and Mark Peterson, eds., *Korean Women: Views from the Inner Room* (East Rock Press, US, 1983). Slightly patchy collection, good on Korean women's history, but a bit limited in its portrayal of women's contemporary position and status.

Malawi

F or many years Malawi has been an outcast amongst the African frontline states, condemned for its close links with South Africa and for the dictatorial and incredibly repressive regime of its president-for-life, Dr Hastings Banda.

Recently, under pressure to ensure safe passage for his country's exports and imports, Banda has made moves to ease relations with the neighbour states of Zambia, Zimbabwe and Mozambique, but his diplomatic ventures have been by no means matched by any improvement on human rights. Opposition of any sort is dealt with swiftly and harshly. Pogroms are waged against any group strong enough to pose a threat, thousands are imprisoned or have fled the country, and an all-pervasive network of informers and spies ensure that all criticism – even the most trivial – is silenced.

At the same time, much of Malawi's wealth – its agricultural and mineral resources – have been placed in the hands of a newly formed elite (government ministers, foreign investors and those in favour with Banda); while large estates, cleared of peasant farmers, have been given over to ex-pat "Rhodesian" managers, who have transplanted intact their privileged and isolated lifestyles. For the majority of Malawians, healthcare and educational provisions are minimal and poverty an enduring way of life.

Malawi is the sort of destination that divides independent travellers. There are plenty who visit the country (many of them South African students) attracted by the beauty of its lakeside beaches and its reputation as a more than usually safe place for women travelling alone. Many boycott it, preferring not to sink their foreign cash into such an authoritarian regime. Obviously the decision is yours. The only rules that seem to apply to travellers is that skirts and trousers must, by law, cover the knees and that no attempt should be made to engage Malawians in political discussion. You'll find that most people are extremely friendly and hospitable in their approach to visitors and that harassment of any kind is exceptionally rare.

In keeping with the blanket repression operating in Malawi no autonomous **women's groups** have been allowed. The one official women's organisation is run by Banda's "official hostess" (he is unmarried) and is geared towards reminding women of their traditional role in society. In general terms, women form the backbone of the economy as traders and food producers, but have less status and much less access to education than men.

A Part of the Truth

. . . .

Jessie Carline first heard about Malawi when she was offered a place there as a volunteer for VSO; two years later she is still working in the country. As she intends to stay, she has had to avoid making any comment about the political situation.

When I was told that my two years voluntary service were to be spent in Malawi I had to look it up in an atlas. Now that Mrs Thatcher and the Pope have visited, it may be more commonly known that it is a small (by African standards), thin, landlocked country, wedged in between Tanzania, Zambia and Mozambique. It does not make the headlines because (again by African standards) there is no large-scale famine or fighting.

My job here involves running a department of twenty and it has taken me many, many months to get accustomed to all that this entails. I was apprehensive from the start about being a boss – never having been in that position before – and from this viewpoint alone I knew the post would be challenging. I remember having the list of everyone's names and trying desperately to pronounce them correctly in case I made a fool of myself, only to discover that my name

was equally impossible for my colleagues to say.

There turned out to be many other parts to this post that I had never considered and found myself totally bewildered by. The first was the enormous amount of requests from people for time off work. The range of requests was also startling: "Madam" (being called this was also something to get used to!), "My uncle/mother/son is ill in Balaka so may I go and visit?"; "Madam, I need to go to Liwonde to buy some maize"; "Madam, it's raining may I go and plant my seeds?"; "Madam, I have malaria"; "Madam, someone in my village has died, may I go to the funeral?". How could I refuse?

And perhaps more difficult to cope with were the requests for money: "Madam, my child is unable to go to school because I cannot afford the fees"; "Madam, I would like to buy a bicycle"; "Madam, my brother/daughter/aunt is ill and needs transport to the hospital"; "Madam, my wife is having her fourth child and we have no clothes for the baby". How could I refuse these, either?

After a few weeks I realised half my staff were either away or owing me money and this didn't seem to be a situation that I was in control of. Plucking up courage to ask my Malawian colleagues for their advice, they explained that I'd have to set my own limits. The problems brought to me were real enough – Malawi is one of the poorest countries in the world – but they suggested that it wasn't a good idea to be seen as an endless source of ready cash.

"Being 'rich' means that I have leisure time – there is no need to spend hours hoeing a field or walking miles to the nearest clean water"

Ironically, VSO attempts to pay volunteers a "local wage" so that we are not seen as wealthy ex-pats with more money than sense. But this just doesn't work. However little I earn, I am rich. All my possessions announce my wealth: clothes, motorbike (loaned to me by VSO), radio/cassette player, camera, etc. And at the weekend my time is spent playing tennis or walking up Mulanje because being "rich" means that I have leisure time – there is no need to spend hours hoeing a field or walking miles to the nearest clean water. At the beginning I used to ask my colleagues "And what did you do at the weekend?" I've stopped doing that now.

How I have actually coped with the situation is difficult to explain, but somehow the requests are fewer. Maybe it was because I began to say no, maybe because people began to understand my situation and, perhaps, realise how little I do earn! I'm not so sure about the latter, though. Most of the non-volunteer ex-pats earn a small fortune, plus they receive hard currency back home, so to most Malawians we are all white and rich.

After eighteen months here, however, I am beginning to feel part of the community at work and less of an outsider. It has taken me a long time to make friends. A woman's role in Malawi is in the kitchen, on the land and with the children, and all, bar one, of my professional colleagues are men. It does not make sense to either women or men that I am thirty, single and childless and so far from home (my mother would agree!), and it would be unheard of for any of the male professional staff at work to invite me round to their house to meet their wife. But the one woman in my department has become my friend and, through her, people have seen that I won't turn my nose up at local food and that I am more than willing to socialise. Without her I'm not sure that I would have coped when I had to go to my first funeral.

That was after a close member of staff lost his wife. She had been admitted to hospital with high blood pressure and heavily pregnant. She gave birth and the high blood pressure continued. This in itself is not unusual and with rest all should be fine. However the hospital needed the "bed" (there are four patients to every mattress on the floor) and so she was dismissed two days later. Having to walk, with her new baby, to the bus station, she began to feel ill – so instead of continuing home she decided to come to the clinic opposite work, where she died soon after arrival. She was in her early twenties and this was her second child.

Everyone at work attended the funeral, along with all the nearby villagers, so it was big affair. I clung on to my friend's hand as we slowly and silently made our way through endless seated women who alternated between great wailing and soft song. We stopped outside the mud hut where the woman had lived and sat on the ground amongst all the other women from work – secretaries, cleaners and canteen staff. I felt horribly conspicuous as the only white woman amongst so many Malawians, but that was something that came from me; I was treated as one of the many mourners and it was appreciated that I had come.

It surprised me that the atmosphere at the end was not heavy and depressing. Mourners had begun to chat and people were smiling. It was a tragic and preventable death but somehow the will to survive, regardless of the daily catastrophes, was paramount. The grave itself was in a cemetery – in land put aside for graves, which is completely untouched and where it is forbidden to cut down and remove the trees. The body then had been lain in an indigenous forest and would not be visited – the woman had been returned to the land, the cycle had been completed. Life continues.

One of the things that I had been forewarned about were the frustrations that I would experience at work – and this has certainly shown to be the case. The problems and difficulties that give rise to frustration are varied, ranging from the telephones being out of order for days on end to the mile of road to work being transformed by a heavy night's rain into a muddy swamp. The machinery I inherited looked impressive until I discovered that four out of the six UN-donated photocopiers lay idle because we cannot afford the spare parts. Other UN machines costing thousands of pounds have not ever been used as there is no-one experienced enough here to operate them, and the UN refuses to let South African technicians show us how, even though they are here to work on non-UN equipment.

"In Africa, you'll find the Malawian lecturers in Tanzania and Botswana"

Lack of foreign exchange means Malawi is in the hands of donor agencies, who at any moment might decide that the way forward is inappropriate new technology that costs a fortune. If the phones don't work, how can desktop publishing? In practical terms, I do not feel that I have achieved a lot and any hopes and aspirations that accompanied me out here have certainly disappeared. I can see others achieving a great deal, but I am increasingly sceptical of the role of the volunteer and aid agencies.

As I write this, Malawi celebrates 25 years of independence. Why then, you ask yourself, are more than fifty percent of the university staff ex-pats when there are qualified Malawians who could do as well? It's the same with the medical service, and the answer is the same, too. A fully qualified Malawian doctor prefers to stay in Manchester rather than to return to a pitiful salary back home. So doctors here are recruited from Europe, thus perpetuating the myth that whites are more capable. In Africa, you'll find the Malawian lecturers in Tanzania and Botswana.

The extreme of Malawian education is represented by Kamuzu Academy – the so-called "Eton of Africa". This has only white staff and Latin is a compulsory subject for study. The children, after taking their A-levels, will go on to foreign universities. But will they return? If not, Malawi will continue to be one of the few countries left in the world where it is socially acceptable for the minority white population to live in the biggest houses, surrounded by beautiful gardens (plus pool), and serviced by black nannies, workers, gardeners and night watchmen.

If I am fed up at all about working in this country, this is not the case with living here. Malawi calls herself "the warm heart of Africa" and this is certainly true. Malawians are the friendliest and most hospitable people I have ever met (a fact that was reinforced after visiting neighbouring countries). And, on top of this, the country is astonishingly beautiful, with efficient transport and good tarmac roads. Any tourist brochure will elucidate on the mountains, game parks and the stunning lake, where you would be forgiven if you thought you were swimming in an aquarium. And it's all true!

For a woman, Malawi is an easy country to travel alone, without fear of harassment or intimidation. My only caution is that night time travelling, for both men and women, is not recommended, especially in the bigger towns, as the occasional mugging (often accompanied by violence) does occur.

Once, when I found myself travelling alone on the last bus, which didn't take me as far as my destination, the bus conductor himself made sure that, if the hitching didn't pay off, there was some place where I could be put up for the night safely. There aren't many cars on the road late at night.

"For a woman, Malawi is an easy country to travel alone"

Other times I have found it annoying when men have incessantly questioned me whilst waiting for a bus – but it has only been a friendly and inquisitive approach, nothing to do with being "chatted-up", and privacy is an unusual thing to want. And you will be stared at! Staring is not considered rude, so be prepared, especially away from the larger towns, to be the centre of attraction. This is perhaps most trying when, after a long day's travelling, you find yourself surrounded by silent, staring children when all you want to do is relax.

Living, as I do, in one of the larger towns, there is reasonable access to a wide variety of food. Most of it, the *Lillets* or *Tampax*, the tinned coffee and, of course, the wine, comes from South Africa. It was very strange for me coming from London, where I boycotted South African goods, to find myself in a black African store full of South African produce. And it is doubly strange to realise that Malawi's precious foreign exchange is being spent on luxury items for the ex-pat community (me!) instead of paper for the children's school exercise books. In fact, I feel more guilty living here than I did back home – especially as my living standards have shot up: no dingy London flat on a busy main road for me, but a three- bedroomed house with all mod cons!

TRAVEL NOTES

Languages English and Chichewa and a number of other African languages.

Transport Roads have been improved and there's a reasonably efficient network of express buses. Steamers ply up and down Lake Malawi – which is also one of the few areas where women hitch alone.

Accommodation There are plenty of government rest houses or council rest houses. This is also an easy country for camping.

Special Problems People do not discuss politics with strangers. Attempts to do so are seen as incriminating and compromising. Also be aware that the laws about dress (you should wear skirts that cover the knees) are strictly enforced. Any literature considered critical to the state might be confiscated at the border.

Guide *Africa on a Shoestring* (Lonely Planet) gives a fairly clear overview and has therefore been banned.

Contacts

There are no autonomous women's groups operating within the country.

Books

We've been unable to track down any books by or about Malawian women. *"**Malawi from Both Sides**"*, in **Joseph Hanlon, Beggar Your Neighbours** (CIIR, London, 1986), is a lucid and concise account of the political situation.

David Rubadiri, No Bride Price (E. African Pub. House, 1967). A novel of urban Africa centred around the strange and tenacious relationship between Lombe (the main character) and Muria, his town mistress.

Legson Kayira, The Detainees (Heinemann, 1984). A remarkable and stylish novel by a Malawian political refugee.

Mali

. . . .

Mali stands at the edge of the Sahara desert and for overland travellers is the traditional gateway to West Africa. Even during the critical years of the Sahelian drought, travellers would arrive on the desert route from Algeria, attracted by the country's distinctly West African culture and atmosphere, the spectacular Bandigari Escarpment and the views of the great river Niger flowing between its desert banks.

As a predominantly Muslim country, Mali can be difficult for a woman travelling alone – and it becomes a lot easier if you join up with other travellers or an overland expedition. For many Malians, struggling to maintain a subsistence living, travellers now represent an essential source of income. In the cities, especially, you will be continually approached for money and this, coupled with the fairly common experiences of harassment, can become quite oppressive. The police particularly can give you a hard time and it's almost always worth getting someone to go with you if you have to report at a local station. Outside the tourist areas the atmosphere changes. People greet strangers with open hospitality and friendliness – and it's important to carry gifts with you as a means of reciprocating.

For the last two decades, the country has been governed by a succession of Marxist-inspired military regimes. Whilst many of the bureaucratic constraints on foreigners have been lifted in an effort to encourage tourism, travel is still closely regulated. There are restrictions on camping and staying with local people, and accommodation is expensive. Without your own vehicle, journeys can be incredibly slow and arduous.

A **women's movement** is developing in Mali though at present it is predominantly urban-based, made up of well-educated, middle-class women.

The *UNFM (Union Nationale des Femmes du Mali)* is the central organisation and its members campaign for women's rights and participate in meetings abroad. There are also various development centres set up in and around Bamako, mainly co-ordinated by the *Centre Djoliba*, which provide training skills for girls and women as well as education on nutrition and health, and talks on the health hazards of female circumcision.

"In and Out of People's Lives"

. . . .

Stephanie Newell travelled to Mali as part of a six-month overland expedition in a truck heading from Ramsgate, England, to Nigeria.

A fading wooden placard announced our entrance into Mali, and splintered arrows pointed vague tracks across the desert. With the compass as our only guide we headed towards Gao amid rising excitement at the prospect of letters from home. A thick layer of sand covered my scalp from the previous night's sandstorm; I had slept out – the power of the Sahara night sky is impossible to resist.

I was travelling with 25 other people as part of an overland expedition, the cheapest way of covering an unusual route. It started at 4am on the cold front of Ramsgate harbour and took us through many different African countries and climates, ending six months later in the concrete jungle of Nairobi. There were more women than men in our group and we shared tasks equally on a rota basis. We camped out every night, cooked over an open fire, and tried to buy fresh fruit and vegetables from local markets whenever possible. It was not easy travelling with so many new companions, our only common experience being Africa itself. But

when we stopped in a place for any length of time we could always wander off alone, or even leave the truck and meet up with it in another town.

"Arriving in Timbuctou, the group, especially the women, were constantly harassed"

We entered Mali through Tessalit, a desolate area with arid plains all around and the silence of a vast space. Small thick-walled houses crouched at the mercy of black slag-heaps that dominated the bleak landscape. It was difficult for the Western eye to assimilate – flat, orange sand-and-water buildings, a constant haze of dust in the air and a bright, white sun in a white hot sky. In a country that has been devastated by fifteen years of drought I had mixed feelings when we were offered American soft drinks and Dutch lager as an alternative to the tasteless water we had been drinking over the past four days. Overseas companies are dominating a continent where simple, low-cost improvements of water purification facilities could solve so many problems.

The women changed into long skirts as the sprawling town of Gao grew larger on the horizon. Young boys jumped on to the truck, giggling and stumbling as they kicked each other aside to view the new arrivals, calling out for "cadeau" as they fell off and raced behind. The desert's spell of silence became an equally powerful flurry of noise. Our white skins signalled wealth, and we were bombarded with offers of jewellery, metalwork and cloth.

We camped on the outskirts of the spacious town, alongside a mass of Tuareg huts – home to a traditionally nomadic people who have been forced towards the relative security of towns by the widespread drought.

The energy and spirit of these people was overwhelming. Their welcome and curiosity led to constant companionship in whatever we did, whether washing, eating or writing. The young girls were transfixed as a friend applied Moroccan henna to my hair; they watched as it set hard in the sun, then cried out for some as my hair turned from dull brown to bright orange. Likewise the strange ceremony of cleaning teeth with a toothbrush and paste was hilarious to a race who use the far more efficient method of chewing on bark and creating a paste from the sap.

The women and young girls of Gao stayed within the confines of their market stalls, mimicking our high-pitched European female voices, and collapsing with giggles at our hurt looks. They then extended smiles of friendship as we admired their clothes and made appointments to have our hair plaited.

From Gao we turned back into the desert for the three-day drive up to Timbuctou: we navigated the dried riverbeds, stopping to fill our water containers at tall wind-powered pumps gently turning in the winds that sweep along the flat plains. Camels and donkeys were herded to the supply to drink from goatskin watersacks. Arriving in Timbuctou, the group, especially the women, were constantly harassed, so much so that we left after only four hours. Two of us took refuge in the ancient mosque; taking off our shoes, we entered the vast building, climbed some crumbling steps on to a flat roof and then ducked low to climb to the top of the minaret overlooking

the town. We descended from the cool breeze to bowls of clear water from huge earthenware casks before reluctantly joining the bustle outside.

"The circle of tents went up slowly as the group realised that we could be stuck for quite a while; nobody knew where we were and there were no trucks large enough to haul us out"

Speeding on through the ever more green countryside, beside the river Niger, we became more and more lost. A truckload of village men eventually guided us towards Mopti and then turned off as we approached a ford. Our twenty-ton truck ground to a halt in the soft mudbanks midway between shores. The inhabitants of nomadic settlements on either side of the river clustered into the water at this sudden new source of entertainment, leaving their vast herds of cattle to pick at the dried grass. The engine roared and the truck gently tilted to a 45-degree angle at which it remained for almost a week.

The circle of tents went up slowly as the group realised that we could be stuck for quite a while; nobody knew where we were and there were no trucks large enough to haul us out. By dusk, news had spread and running figures approached through herds of cattle. We had 24-hour companions to our shifts of 24-hour guards. Perhaps, to the local people, we were wealthy nomads, certainly we were considered doctors with cures for every ailment. A woman came forward leading another by the hand, blinded by conjunctivitis, infected by the lack of clean water. One of the women in our group couldn't bear to touch this woman, her eyes were so bad; it took twenty minutes to thoroughly clean them with swabs of boiled water and eye drops.

Crowds of people looked in at our first meal by the river, watching in astonishment as we munched our way through soup, then plates of mince, mashed potato and vegetables. A baby was brought to see me, the fifth, sixth, seventh, umpteenth conjunctivitis case in one evening. As its mother opened its eyes for the drops to go in, they looked so sore, almost blind; I broke down, dashing away from the camp in tears. I could never come to terms with the lack of basic health facilities on the shores of the river Niger: a cow keeled over and died in the water as the herd passed through. Eight hours later it was still there, swollen and bloated as the sun beat down.

"We seemed to be a bubble of Englishness with our plentiful fall-back supplies of tinned foods, dehydrated vegetables and packet mixes"

Meanwhile, work on the truck continued as we tried to dig the axle and wheels clear. The vast, yellow lorry had almost become a part of the landscape. Cattle would pass through the river beside it as they were herded across before nightfall; *pirogues* (like gondolas), loaded with baskets and people, navigated around it shouting greetings; and flocks of pelicans would survey the scene from the air as dusk fell over our camp. We seemed to be a bubble of Englishness with our plentiful fall-back supplies of tinned foods, dehydrated vegetables and packet mixes, travelling through communities that had to rely on being self-sufficient. Water and wood, however, are the dictators of health in Mali, and as both ran out for us, we too experienced the discomfort of diarrhoea and conjunctivitis in a relentlessly hot country.

Children pounced on the things we discarded. It was traumatic to watch our waste become prized and fought over; our tins would be thrust forwards through the tight circle of tents as we served up food in the evenings.

Then, in contrast, a group of travelling artists crossed the river and stopped near us one evening. They were on their way to Mopti for a festival of traditional song and dance, and their tuneful passionate singing and relaxed dancing drew some bolder members of our group towards them. We sat in awe at the swaying patchwork of bright African cloth, the togetherness of the musicians who had only a regular drumbeat to set the tempo. The leader of the group sat on the only foam mat and plucked a battered guitar, its three remaining strings held together by elastic bands and the body of a biro. A young boy was called to the front after the main song was over and, strong and rhythmical, his voice rang out in a new song he had created for the group. A young woman with a bold, deep voice that matched her stature joined in with a chorus and presently the whole group were again swaying and singing. We were motioned to leave by the seated man as a passing truck stopped and took them off to Mopti for the festival.

One day three of us negotiated the loan of two donkeys and set out for the local village in search of bread. A young boy was appointed to escort us, or rather the donkeys, who were constantly trying to head back for their owner's hut. Having got used to the rocking movement of the animals we relaxed into the two-mile journey, progressing slowly past the laughing "hellos" of local people and through the occasional herds of cattle. At the edge of the river we scrambled off the donkeys into a *pirogue*, having first spent a while agreeing on a price with the boat owner. I was not wearing shoes and hid from the sun under a long strip of cloth wrapped around my neck and shoulders as we clambered out into the mud on the opposite bank, to be greeted by an excited crowd of people.

The villagers seemed delighted to have three white women visit them and showed us into many one-roomed houses before asking us to take shelter for a while. Our escort of children hovered uncertainly in the doorways, awaiting our exit. Younger children rubbed our arms to prove to themselves that our colour really was not an elaborate paint. All over Africa the children would do this, very softly rubbing our skins, then holding their arms up to ours with wide-eyed enjoyment at finding such a difference.

We came away clasping tiny hands, but no bread. The ovens are fired by the heat of the sun and as it was not yet hot enough for baking to begin we were asked to return later on the following day. The women on the river banks pointed to my bare feet in concern as we climbed back into the narrow wooden boat to leave. Perhaps this was because as a wealthy person I should have been wearing shoes, or maybe because there are so many diseases that can pass up through the soles of one's feet. However, by that time we were drinking and washing in the same river water, but with the knowledge of antibiotics back home.

The truck was eventually heaved out of the river after an SOS message was conveyed via a foreign aid truck to another overland group we had heard was passing through. By this time we had made special friends by the river and seemed to have been accepted as curious residents. It was sad to wave goodbye to the proud people whose world we had somehow stepped in and out of. Our destination was Mopti, where it was encouraging to see variousnew foreign aid agencies working in conjunction with each other on agricultural and health projects. They seemed optimistic about the future of Mali – "All we need now is rain."

A Walk along the Niger River

. . . .

Over several years, Jo Hanson has travelled to many countries in Africa. In the course of one overland trip across the Sahara, she spent a month walking along the Niger River.

If you look presentable, you might easily fall into the foreign aid circuit in Bamako, which consists of men of many nationalities living in styles to which they are probably unaccustomed at home. Exasperated by the two-hour lunches and afternoons beside the swimming pool, I set off to walk up the Niger River towards its source in Guinea.

As soon as I left Bamako and the tarmac road became laterite, good things began to happen. A young man carried my sleeping bag roll and showed me where to buy a cup of condensed-milk coffee, then a half-blind woman took over the bag and led me into a large compound, where I was the centre of attention for several minutes while I put ointment into her eyes (I always carry a few tubes) and lamented the fact that she was in such a plight only a couple of kilometres from the capital. "I can't afford to send her to the hospital," said her husband, but as he was sitting on a good chair surrounded by various sheep and cattle, I wondered where his priorities lay.

Later, in the heat of the day, I was invited to rest by a farmer whose wife was cooking beside the river a delicious-looking fish and groundnut stew.

I was looking forward to a taste of this when he pedalled to the village shop and brought back two tins of sardines and four loaves of French bread, obviously thinking that this was what white people must have! When the heat had lessened he led me back to the road (another thing I didn't really want) and proudly showed me the new table-football game a local entrepreneur had set up, penny-a-go. It was the kind where you manipulate handles at high speed to move model players from side to side, and looked a bit bizarre under a baobab tree with a field of maize nearby.

That night I slept on a handy pile of straw at the edge of an aid project (you can always tell them by the huge size of the fields and the large machinery that is used). Next morning I noticed a Frenchman trying to mend a diesel water-pump, but being an advocate of intermediate technology, I preferred the *shaduf*, an ancient Egyptian device with pole and weight, which was being operated by a market gardener further along the river.

I was invited to a fish stew lunch by a family who this time, far from buying French bread for me, eagerly shared the remains of mine. The six sons seemed to be thriving, but at the expense of their mother who looked utterly sapped as well as pregnant. I couldn't speak her language; even if I could, what would I say? I gave her as many iron and vitamin tablets as I could spare, using sign language to tell her "One a day – only for you"; I often found that men appropriated the little benefits I gave to their women.

All along the way I was repeatedly asked into huts and given rides on bikes, mobylettes, a donkey cart, and even in the car of a gang of hunters out shooting partridges. I met many strange types: a Jehovah's Witness who tried to convert me in French, a Nigerian seaman who had got stranded and was earning enough to get home by selling face cream made from the boiled root of a tree, and a student of English on a motorbike who stopped me to chat about Dickens. Small-scale trading went on in every village, but there was little enough to buy – maybe a few oranges, bananas or water melons or a bowl of rice and groundnut stew in a "café" (a mud hut containing a bench).

"I walked all one afternoon in the shallows of the river wearing only bra and pants, with wading birds hopping round and hippos sighing"

After five days' walking, I had a rest in a metropolis (well, it had a pharmacy and a man who sold matches) called Kangaba. I was adopted by a young unmarried woman called Fatika who was the local community health worker. She took me to the community centre, a large shed where all kinds of classes presumably went on since the walls were plastered with posters about nutritious food and clean, boiled water. I asked Fatika for a drink, thinking this was the right place to be, and she brought me a black cupful from a fetid pot in the corner. As it took so long for my sterilising tablets to dissolve, I surreptitiously threw it away. This gap between theory and practice is often evident in Africa. I saw it again when Fatika's brother showed me his school books, pages full of neat writing in French about hygiene – yet they both had dysentery and pleaded with me for a remedy (the pharmacy had run out).

I stayed the night with a couple of Dutch volunteers. They were marvellous people, up at dawn and out to remote villages with a cold box full of children's vaccines strapped to the back of their motor scooters. For the next couple of days many people I met asked me if I knew "Nelly-et-Harry"!

I crossed over the river by canoe when I reached the border with Guinea (which was closed to tourists at that time), and started to walk back down the other side. This was a wilder part with less population; in fact I walked all one afternoon in the shallows of the river wearing only bra and pants, with wading birds hopping round and hippos sighing and not a soul in sight. The water was so clear I drank straight from the river.

Reaching another large village opposite Kangaba I stayed with a nurse-midwife. She was obviously more committed and practical than Fatika, but stymied by an almost complete lack of medicines and supplies. In the evening she had to make two trips to the river to fetch water, carrying on her head a tin tub that I couldn't even lift when it was full. Other women did the same, many of them pregnant, one even saying that her labour pains had started! That night there was a total eclipse of the moon, marked by much drumming and dancing amongst the population who had been forewarned by news on the radio.

Next day I found myself climbing up a wooded plateau and after several hours' walking through wild, dry scrub, I came upon a gold-mining village. Gold is Mali's principal mineral export, but the people who did the labour obviously had no status at all: they were dressed in rags with no school, clinic or facility of any kind in the place. While I was watching the miners lower themselves into deep holes in the ground, a young man on a bike came wobbling through the trees and introduced himself in French as a gold-dealer. He took me on to his father's village, wading over a rushing cold tributary of the Niger, then bike riding *à deux* amongst a wide area of termite hills like a forest of pointed witches' hats. It would certainly have been a tourist attraction if SMERT (the state tourist agency) had known about it!

After that I paid an old man to pole me a dreamy fifteen kilometres down the river in the evening to a rice-processing factory. I expected to find it a hub of activity, but instead it was empty, deserted, thousands of francs (or dollars, or pounds, or deutsch-marks) just rusting away. Bats and mosquitoes abounded, and for the first time I had to use my net as I spent the night there.

Although the small town attached to the factory had a road back to Bamako and a once-weekly minibus, it wasn't that day, so I resumed my riverside walk. Gradually it got more and more difficult. I followed lonely cattle tracks over rocks and into small fertile areas, but these petered out and I was faced with a huge area of high elephant grass with no way through. I could walk no further – in any case by now I had given away all my spare clothes and presents. I noticed a man standing on a spit of sand and he told me that a ferry-*pirogue* might come across some time. I knew I could get a lift or a squashed paying ride on the laterite road back on the other side of the river, so decided to wait with him.

He was most solicitous, sharing his food and finding a soft place for me to sit and read, his attitude being typical of all the men I had met. Yet I had never seen one offer a bike ride, carry a heavy load or take the hoe out of the hand of his wife, sister or even mother. It is not difficult to find an explanation for this, but I still regret that the friendly assistance I was lucky enough to receive from men did not touch the visibly arduous lives of the women that I saw on my journey.

TRAVEL NOTES

Languages French and various African languages. The most common is Bambara. Some students speak English.

Transport There is only one railway line, connecting Bamako (the capital) with Dakar (Senegal). Roads are fairly rough – tarmac up to certain points out of Bamako, the rest sandy tracks. Hitching is difficult as there are few private cars but you can get rides with lorries where you're expected to pay. Shared taxis are also available as well as *taxis brousses* (crowded minibuses/vans) which go from town to town. When the river is high enough (usually August–December) riverboats run between Mopti, Timbuktu, Gao and sometimes on to Koulikoro, near Bamako.

Accommodation Small hotels are relatively expensive. Travelling outside the towns and tourist areas you will have to rely on local hospitality – you should offer something (money/gifts) in return for your keep.

Special problems Visas are required by all except nationals of France, and can be quite hard to get hold of. Once in, you have to register with the police in each town that you stay in overnight. Sometimes you might be hassled for bribe money – it's best if you check in with another traveller. It can be hard coming to terms with the degree of poverty in Mali. Begging is seen as a necessary part of the social system and you should set money aside for this.

Guide *The Rough Guide: West Africa* (Harrap Columbus) has a good chapter on Mali.

Contacts

Union Nationale des Femmes du Mali, BP1740, Bamako. Formed in 1974 to fight for women's rights, the Union organises literacy programmes, promotes the participation of women in development work, and campaigns against female circumcision.

Books

We have not managed to trace any books dealing specifically with Mali. See other African countries and the General Bibliography for general works on Africa.

Thanks to Jo Hanson who provided much of the information for the Travel Notes.

Mexico

. . . .

Mexico is a chaotic and exciting country with a tremendous amount to offer the traveller. Between the highly developed resorts lie miles of untouched beaches, but most of the interest lies inland. Large areas of central and southern Mexico are steeped in Spanish colonial history and are rich in Indian traditions and the relics of ancient civilisations – not to mention magnificent scenery. An extensive bus network makes it easy to get around and, depending on the exchange rate (Mexico is in a permanent state of economic crisis), there's plenty of cheap accommodation.

After a very stormy past, Mexico is nowadays regarded as one of the most stable countries in Latin America. This stability is based more on its strength as an advanced industrial power than on just or democratic government. Despite efforts to present a radical face to the outside world, the Institutional Revolutionary Party, in power for over forty years, is deeply conservative. Little has been done to implement the kind of social changes symbolised by the famous 1911 Revolution.

The bulk of the population are very poor and there is considerable resentment of the affluence of their northern neighbours in the United States. This is sometimes focused on tourists, which can be hard to cope with. *Gringas* (foreign women), representing both wealth and a type of sexuality denied to Mexican men, are easy targets for resentment. Approaches from men tend to be aggressive, so you need to feel strong. It's also worth making a great effort to learn at least some Spanish – a relatively easy language – before you go.

Not only foreigners need to arm themselves against *machismo*. **Mexican feminists** have long recognised it as a deep-rooted obstacle in their struggle for equality and freedom. However, as in the rest of Latin America, more urgent concern is given to the denial of basic economic and social rights. Since it began in 1970, a large section of the Women's Movement has had close links with various political parties of the Left. At the same time there is an autonomous movement, for which abortion is a central issue, and there are several organised lesbian groups. Although certain reforms, such as the elimination of discriminatory laws, have been passed on paper, Mexican women see themselves as having a lot more to fight for.

Alone on the Northern Circuit

· · · · · · · · · · · · ·

Esther Berick lives in San Francisco and has made several trips to Mexico, most recently travelling by bus and train in the north and central regions.

After four trips to Mexico with friends, I felt confident enough in my ability to speak and understand Spanish to travel by myself. I wanted to experience the train ride through the Barranca del Cobre, the Copper Canyon, which I'd read was the most spectacular rail trip in all of North America. The canyon, which is in the Sierra Madre of the northern state of Chihuahua, is larger than the famous Grand Canyon of Arizona and home to the Tarahumara, the least assimilated indigenous people in Mexico. The photographs I'd seen of the Tarahumara – the women in their

voluminous, brightly coloured skirts and blouses, the men in their traditional baggy white pants and shirts – fascinated me. This, I told myself, was worth setting off alone for.

My trip began with a flight from San Francisco to El Paso, Texas, a city which shares a border with Ciudad Juarez, Mexico. It's about a six-hour bus ride from El Paso to Chihuahua, Mexico, where I purchased my ticket for the train ride through the canyon. On the way down to Chihuahua I sat next to a young Mexican named Teresa – a woman of about 25, with black, wavy hair and a wonderful, wide smile.

Teresa was from Chihuahua but lived in El Paso with a wealthy American family, cleaning their house and caring for their children. Her own three young daughters lived in Chihuahua with her mother and every other weekend she made the six-hour trip to visit them. She carried small gifts for her little girls: a child's comb and brush set, candy, a doll. She proudly showed me photos of her daughters and lamented how she had to live and work so far away from them.

The small salary she made in El Paso, however, was more than she could ever hope to earn in Chihuahua. Despite living and working in an American city, she barely spoke English, but was eager to learn. She cajoled me into giving her an impromptu English lesson by promising that she would teach me some Spanish words that weren't in the dictionary. I was glad we had something to share.

> **"'You must be a writer,' she said, 'there is no other reason for a woman to be travelling by herself'"**

Chihuahua City is the capital of the richest state in all of Mexico and this prosperity attracts a broad ethnic mix of people. In the wide streets you see cowboys in their boots and ten-gallon hats, Mennonite women in long sombre skirts and bonnets and, occasionally, some colourfully dressed Tarahumara. This is cattle country, and I'd never been in a Mexican town with so many steak-houses before. I was starving when I got off the bus from El Paso and, after searching unsuccessfully for a café that served simple rice and beans, I ended up at a healthfood restaurant eating a tofu burger with alfalfa sprouts – a unique eating experience in my many trips to Mexico!

The train ride from Chihuahua through the Copper Canyon to Los Mochis, at the other end of the line, takes twelve hours. I decided to break the trip by spending a few nights in Creel, a very small town that serves as a jumping-off point for excursions into the canyon. Creel has unpaved streets, lots of cowboys driving big Ford pick-up trucks, and Mexican country-and-western music blaring from every radio.

It's hot and dusty in the summer and, I was told, cold and snow-bound in the winter. There's a bank, a post office, a pharmacy and a small store, run by the local Catholic mission, where the Tarahumara bring their crafts to be sold to tourists. Here one can purchase woven baskets, wooden dolls dressed in traditional indigenous clothing, blankets and excellent, sensitive photographs of the Tarahumara, taken by a Jesuit priest whom they know and trust. The availability of these pictures compensates for not taking your own; the Tarahumara are extremely shy and any attempt to photograph them would be seen as an intrusion.

I arrived in Creel hoping to meet other women travellers, but was disappointed to find that I was one of only three people staying at my hotel. The other two were a Mexican couple on their honeymoon. "Where are your travelling companions?" they wanted to know. The young bride looked at me curiously when I told them I was on my own, then gave me a quick smile: "Well, you must be a writer," she said, "there is no other reason for a woman to be travelling by herself." Thinking of all the years I'd spent travelling and writing in my journal, I thanked her for the compliment.

Because of the dearth of tourists in Creel, none of the fantastic tours I'd read about in my guidebook were being offered. However, the train on to Los Mochis was everything my travel literature promised. The scenery, as we passed through lovely wooded canyons, twisted around sharp mountain curves and chugged over high bridges, was truly spectacular. The train, though primarily a tourist attraction, also serves the local people who live in the tiny towns scattered in the mountains: the men in their ubiquitous cowboy hats and jeans, the women in simple dresses, and nearly everyone holding packages and young children.

It was on this train that I met two Dutch women travelling together, the only women I would meet during my whole time in Mexico who were not travelling with men. I was often looked at with curiosity by the Mexicans I met, though I was never treated rudely. "Pobrecita," (poor little thing) the older women would say when I told them I was on a solo journey through their country. After too many "pobrecitas", I started telling people that I was a student on holiday from my studies in Mexico City. To them that seemed more legitimate than being simply a traveller and quite frankly it got very depressing always having people feel sorry for me.

The men, in general, were bolder in approaching me than the women, and would often ask me about my job in San Francisco and how much money I made. My reply invariably provoked a whistle and the exclamation "That's a lot of money!" followed immediately by the question of whether I was married. At these times I always said yes, and that I was on my way to meet my husband and two darling children in the next town. I made a vow to wear a fake wedding band the next time I travelled to Mexico. Many of the men I met had worked in San Francisco and we would talk about the neighbourhoods and businesses we both knew. These conversations always left me with a warm feeling that I wasn't really so far from home, alone.

There were times, however, when it was very lonely being in a culture that put so much emphasis on a woman always being with her family, or at the very least with an escort. As a result I found myself accepting invitations from men that could have been dangerous. In one situation, I went out to dinner with a man I met at the Guadalajara bus station. We went to a famous *mariachi* nightclub where I seemed to be the only foreigner, and I was delighted when the whole place joined in singing the high-spirited romantic songs along with the performers. My "date" had the idea that the romance would continue in the taxi on the way back to my hotel.

"Just say the word," he told me, trying to pull me close, "and I'll cancel all my business plans just to spend the night with you."

"I dealt with both of these situations by acting the part of an incredibly modest and shy young woman"

On another occasion I hired a guide to take me to see some pyramids in Tzintzuntzan, a small town outside Patzcuaro in the state of Michoacan. We'd met the day before at the Regional Museum of Popular Art in Patzcuaro where he worked explaining the folk-art exhibits to tourists. He told me he often took visitors on excursions to see the pyramids, and thinking it would be safer to go with a guide than alone, I agreed to the plan. The pyramids are in an isolated spot on top of a hill and do not receive many visitors. After climbing the hill we sat and chatted for a few minutes; then he surprised me by putting his arms round me and kissing me.

I dealt with both of these situations by acting the part of an incredibly modest and shy young woman. I clearly had no chance of winning a physical struggle, in fact it would probably have made me a more exciting challenge: the feisty *gringa*. It was much safer to appeal to their protective instincts and adopt the role of little sister. How I would have coped if they'd pushed me further I don't know. I'm glad it never happened.

I strongly recommend any woman planning to visit Mexico to have a good working knowledge of Spanish, as relatively few Mexicans speak English, especially in the smaller towns. The conversations I had with local people on buses and in the market places could make the difference between a very good day and a very bad one. Youth Hostels are few and far between, so it helps to have a companion along to share the cost of a hotel room. Although there are some extremely low-cost hotels in Mexico, I often chose to stay in more moderately priced ones as the very cheapest are usually in parts of town that I wouldn't risk going into alone. I avoided being hassled in restaurants by always picking the type of places where families go to eat. While waiting for my meal, I would either read a book or write in my diary. Besides keeping myself busy, it gave the impression that I was comfortable being alone and did not want to be bothered.

A Place to Return To

. . . .

Valerie Walkerdine is a psychologist, writer and artist living in London. Fascinated by Mexico, she has visited the country five times in recent years to travel, work and extend friendships she has made there.

I first had the idea of going to Mexico when I was working for the summer in Canada, from which (like the US) it is possible to get very cheap flights. Although clear that I wanted to see America's so-called back yard for myself, I found it difficult at first to work out where to go. This being the first real solo trip I had made, I suppose I was also slightly afraid.

Cheap flights from North America to Mexico all tend to focus on very Americanised holiday resorts, which are not the best places to go unless you like observing imperialism at work in a particularly obnoxious way. A Mexican woman in one airline office was helpful and found me some literature, but other travel agents just wanted to shunt me off to the beach resorts.

People also suggested that it would be too hot for me in the summer – I have very fair skin – as Mexico is chiefly known as a winter resort. Basic knowledge of the Mexican seasons, however, would have cleared up this mistake; it rains a lot in July and is certainly no hotter in the summer than in winter or spring, though the climate varies according to region.

In the end I decided to start with the city of Oaxaca, some 500km south of Mexico City. My guidebook made it sound interesting, not too full of *gringos*, off the tourist beach scene, and with a strong, relatively intact Indian heritage. It turned out to be a very attractive town, though not exactly off the tourist trail. The surrounding state of Oaxaca was stunning, offering a combination of pre-Columbian remains, tropical forests, mountains and a beautiful coastline, though visiting some of the more remote coastal areas with a friend, I felt that, while they looked inviting, they might well prove dangerous for a woman on her own.

"Men will ask outrageous questions about your sex life"

Getting around Mexico is cheap if you have a European or North American income. For Mexicans it is very expensive, as is the general cost of living. I travelled by plane and bus – trains are very slow, hire cars extortionate. It helps considerably to speak Spanish. On my first trip I spoke none, but can now hold a reasonable conversation, which really repays the effort of learning. I found people on buses eager to talk. Unlike Europeans, who hide themselves in books on journeys, Mexicans like to sit together and chat.

A woman alone, however, is considered an oddity in this patriarchal country and everyone wants to know if you are married and have children. Men will ask outrageous questions about your sex life. It's easy to pass this off as proof of the blatant sexism only to be expected of a macho culture, but it's not as simple as that. Attitudes to *gringos* and *gringas* are also about the hate and envy of an oppressed and exploited people.

White women, especially with fair hair, are about the most hated, envied and desired of all. Any glance at the television screen makes it immediately obvious that white skin equals wealth and class in the Mexican popular imagination. Hence many Mexican men's desire to "have" a white woman is matched by their secret (or sometimes not so secret) contempt.

Travelling alone, the attentions of Mexican men can be both irritating and flattering.

As the Canadian film, *A Winter Tan*, demonstrates, Mexico can feel like a place to let go of the strictures of European morality, but the relationship of the *gringa* tourist to Mexican patriarchy requires some reflection. The film painfully documents the "adventures" and eventual death of a North American woman looking for sex in Mexico. In quite a racist way, it presents the pain of a white woman in search of sexual freedom and, unable to find what she is looking for at home, she is left to pursue the fantasy through another of escape and Otherness. Of course, tales of the promiscuity of *gringa* women abound in Mexico and it is important to try and reflect upon the complex relationship between not only capitalism and patriarchy, but of power and powerlessness between white women and Mexican men.

I have to say that these are issues which I have thought about as I have got to know Mexico and Mexicans better. I was not actually frightened by the harassment at any time, but I do advise caution, for instance when travelling on the metro in Mexico City. The public transport system is stunningly efficient in carrying millions of people at low cost, consequently the trains are always crowded. Where they are available it's wise to travel in women's compartments. You also need to hold on very carefully to your money. In this respect it obviously helps not to go around saying loudly in English (or Spanish for that matter) how cheap everything is: it is only cheap to us.

"It was perhaps the first time in many years that I had actually felt able to let go of some of the attachments to work and begin to recognise that I could relax, that there were other things in life"

Mexico exists with an overt level of corruption and danger in its political and everyday life which can be frightening and shocking. To gain more insight into this complex country it is well worth trying to make contact with feminist groups and to find out what is going on politically. The strongest current is socialist feminism, but the talks I went to were overwhelmingly run by white, middle-class women. However, in both these discussions and the political meetings I attended, people were friendly and more than willing to talk about what was going on. On my last visit, in the summer of 1988, feelings were running especially high in the aftermath of the latest round of corrupt elections. Zapatistas (supporters of the politics of Emilio Zapata, principal hero of the Revolution) marched in the streets of Mexico City and beyond. Elsewhere ordinary people laughed at the very mention of the word *revolucion*. "We call it *robolucion*", was a common remark.

Mexico is beautiful in a way that makes you never want to return to northern winters (or summers). There is something about the quality of light and the big skies that is easy to romanticise – as it is to exoticise the country's rich and varied culture. The mixture of indigenous and Spanish cultures can quite take your breath away and makes the West seem horribly obsessive in its post-modernist hype and materialism. I remember stopping in New York on the way home from my first visit in the summer of 1987, having been relaxing with friends north of Mexico City. It was perhaps the first time in many years that I had actually felt able to let go of some of the attachments to work and begin to recognise that I could relax, that there were other things in life. New York after this seemed gross.

For all these reasons and more, it didn't take long for me to dream up an excuse to return. This was provided a few months later by the chance to do some research for a short film about the Mexican painter, Frida Kahlo. My Spanish had improved and I found it fairly easy to wander alone around Mexico City – even with a Super-8 movie camera complete with tripod! I also travelled to Guanjuato and Patzcuaro to the north. The former is a colonial town of great beauty where, in my memory, the golden yellow walls of houses blend with the winter sunshine. In the glorious December light, Patzcuaro, built on the shores of a huge lake, was spectacular. Many Mexicans were on holiday, eating meals of freshly cooked fish overlooking the water. The boat trip out to the central island is lovely, though everything, from the fishermen lifting their nets for the tourist cameras to the souvenir stalls on the island itself, shows how tourism has become a central means of survival for local inhabitants.

I was fascinated by Mexico and yet, as an academic and visual artist, I was aware of how much writing about and seeing of Mexico there had already been through European eyes. D.H.

Lawrence, Malcolm Lowrie and Graham Greene have all set novels here, and all, in one way or another, use the country to explore the fascination and exoticisation of European "man" for the "other" – the uncivilised and primitive, the hot passion against civilised European coldness.

"The women I met in a street market picking through the thrown away rotten produce; they wanted above all not to be photographed in the humiliation of their poverty"

It is all too easy to see Mexico like this, as well as the other version, the big holiday playground south of the border. Of course, there are also writers and artists who want to see and to document oppression and poverty. But this is equally problematic in its way. The role of voyeuristic observer, looking to report to the affluent West, does nothing for, say, the women I met in a street market picking through the thrown away rotten produce; they wanted above all not to be photographed in the humiliation of their poverty.

In the end I made a tape-slide about the relationship between my geographical journey, the problem of the voyeuristic aspects of observing and reporting on other cultures' oppression and poverty, and my own history and personal journey towards liberation. Mexico is an exciting country which makes you look again at all those things most of us take for granted in Europe. The diversity of its cultures, the stunning remains of pre-Columbian civilisations, the wonderful revolutionary artistic heritage, mixed with the complexities and oppression of its present, make it seem both wonderful and terrible. I will keep on going back.

TRAVEL NOTES

Languages Spanish and various Indian dialects.

Transport Buses are the best means of getting around. Trains are cheaper but limited and very slow. Hitching is more hassle than it's worth, with the additional threat of police harassment.

Accommodation Cheap hotels are usually easy to find and it's worth haggling if you feel you're being overcharged. In cities you'll find most of them concentrated around the central square or *zocalo*.

Special Problems Many women have enjoyed travelling alone through Mexico, in spite of sexual harassment. Self-confidence and some knowledge of Spanish seems to help.

Don't get involved with or ever trust the police. Police bribery is a common racket (especially if you're driving). If approached it's best to act as if you don't know a word of Spanish. Talk a lot in English about the British Embassy and *Sectur* (a government agency in charge of looking after tourists), offer them less than half of what they ask and only pay once a reasonable price has been reached. Don't touch drugs. It's usual for a dealer to sell them to someone, sell the information to the police and then get half the drugs once his victim has been arrested.

Guides *The Rough Guide: Mexico* (Harrap Columbus) is one of the best in the series — practical, informed and often amusing. *The South American Handbook* (Trade and Travel Publications) also has a good Mexican section.

Contacts

Movimiento Nacional Para Mujeres, San Juan de Letran 11-411, Mexico DF, ☎512-58 41. National women's organisation, useful for contacts throughout the country.

Colectivo Cine Mujer, Angelas Negoechea, Penunuri 19, Sede Casa Oyoacan, Mexico DF. Women's film collective, established in 1974 and, as far as we know, still going strong.

CIDHAL, Apartado 579, Cuernavaca, Morelos. Women's documentation centre primarily concerned with popular education among working-class women.

For information on the lesbian scene in Mexico, write to *Places of Interest to Women*, PO Box 35575, Phoenix, AZ 85069, USA, ☎602-863 2408.

Books

Sybille Bedford, *A Visit to Don Otavio* (1953; Eland Books, 1984). An extremely enjoyable and surprisingly relevant account of travels in 1950s Mexico.

Hayden Herrera, *Frida: A Biography* (Bloomsbury Press, 1989). Biography of the extraordinary Mexican painter who died in 1953.

Oscar Lewis, *The Children of Sanchez* (Penguin, 1982). Chronicles the lives of a working-class family in Mexico City in the 1940s. Oral history at its best.

Octavio Paz, *The Labyrinth of Solitude* (Grove Press, US, 1983). Collection of essays exploring the social and political state of modern Mexico, by one of the country's leading philosophers.

Gisela Espinosa Damián, "Feminism and Social Struggle in Mexico" in **Miranda Davies, ed., *Third World – Second Sex 2*** (Zed Books, 1987). This article, by a former *CIDHAL* worker, discusses the experience of coordinating workshops on sexuality in a poor neighbourhood of Mexico City.

Morocco

Only an hour's ferry ride from southern Spain, Morocco is easily the most accessible and certainly the most popular of the North African states. The fact that it's so close to the well trodden Mediterranean routes, and has the familiar feel of recent French colonialism, can however be a disadvantage – leaving you little time to adjust to an Islamic, essentially Third World culture. In line with the precepts of Islam, women keep a low profile, particularly in urban life, and travelling alone (or with other women) you may well find yourself

labelled as a "loose" and "immodest" Westerner, your freedom to travel and mix with men placing you in a broadly similar category to a Moroccan prostitute.

These attitudes are at their most stiflingly apparent in the main resorts and cities where contact with tourists is greatest and where sexual harassment easily merges with the continual and persistent approaches from hustlers and "guides" (many Moroccans have to depend on tourists for economic survival). Tangier, the main point of entry for most travellers, is perhaps the hardest to contend with, and many women stay just a couple of days and then take the ferry back.

To do this, however, would be to miss a great deal. The tradition of hospitality towards strangers runs much deeper than the mutual exploitations of tourism, and just as you can experience harassment you can also experience great friendship and generosity. It's essential to remain polite and even-mannered in all your dealings. At its best – in the high Atlas mountains, in Marrakesh and throughout the southern desert routes – Morocco can be a great country to visit.

Since Independence from the French in 1956, women have looked to the state to take over the traditional functions of providing welfare and educational services for the family. A small proportion of women have managed to gain access to higher education and, despite intense discrimination, professional employment. For the majority, however, modernisation has brought only the erosion of traditional networks of support, with few alternatives provided. This has very much increased women's vulnerability to isolation and poverty.

There is an official government **women's organisation**, the *Women's Union*, which has centres running skills training classes in most of the large cities. More recently, a feminist group, linked to the Left opposition movement, has also emerged in Rabat, printing a women's paper *The 8th of March*; distribution is increasing and the group has also organised various conferences, seminars and events in other cities.

Running through Fes

. . . .

Margaret Hubbard, who works as an English teacher in Scotland, set off to Morocco for a month's holiday. Although she had long been interested in Islamic culture and had already travelled in the Middle East, this was her first trip alone to a Muslim country.

I knew that there were likely to be difficulties in travelling as a woman alone around Morocco. I'd been warned by numerous sources about hustling and harassment and I was already well aware of the constraints imposed upon women travellers within Islamic cultures. But above and beyond this I knew I'd be fascinated by the country. I

had picked up a smattering of Arabic and the impetus to study Islamic religion and culture during trips to Damascus and Amman (both times with a male companion). Also I already had enough experience of travelling alone to know that I could live well with myself should I meet up with no one else. So, a little apprehensive but very much more determined and excited, I arrived at Tangier, took the first train out to Casablanca and found a room for the night. It was not until I emerged the next morning into the bright daylight of Casablanca that I experienced my first reaction to Morocco.

Nothing could have prepared me for it. Almost instantly I was assailed by a barrage of "voulez-vous coucher avec moi . . . Avez-vous jamais fait l'amour au Maroc . . . Venez avec moi madame . . . Viens m'selle". Whatever I had to say was ignored at will and wherever I went I felt constantly scrutinised by men. Fighting down the panic I headed for the bus station where, after a lot of frantic rushing to and fro (I couldn't decipher the Arabic signs), I climbed on to a coach for Marrakesh.

It wasn't that the harassment was less, in fact it was almost as constant as in Tangier. But wandering through the Djemaa el Fna (the main square and centre of all life in Marrakesh) amongst the snake charmers, kebab sellers, blanket weavers, water sellers, monkey trainers, merchants of everything from false teeth to handwoven rugs, I became ensnared to such an extent that my response to the men who approached me was no longer one of fear but rather a feeling of irrelevance.

Marrakesh proved to me that I was right to come to Morocco. There was too much to be learned to shut out contact with people and I heard myself utter, as if it were the most normal reply in the world, "Non, monsieur, je ne veux pas coucher avec vous, mais pouvez-vous me dire pourquoi ils vendent false teeth/combien d'années il faut pour faire des tapis a main/pourquoi les singes (monkeys)". That first night I returned to my room at 2am more alive than I had felt for months.

I'd also stumbled upon a possible strategy for pre-empting, perhaps even preventing, harassment. Moroccan hustlers know a lot about tourists and have reason to expect one of two reactions from them – fear or a sort of resigned acceptance. What they don't expect is for you to move quickly through the opening gambits and launch into a serious conversation about Moroccan life. Using a mixture of French and Arabic, I developed the persona of a "serious woman" and from Marrakesh to Figuig discussed the politics of the Maghreb, maternity rights, housing costs, or the Koran, with almost anyone who wanted my attention.

It became exhausting but any attempt at more desultory chat was treated as an open invitation and

seemed to make any harassment more determined. That isn't to say that it's impossible to have a more relaxed relationship with Moroccan men. I made good friends on two occasions with Arab men and I'm still corresponding with one of them. But I think this was made easier by my defining the terms of our friendship fairly early on in the conversation. As a general rule whenever I arranged to meet up with someone I didn't know very well, I chose well lit public places. I was also careful about my clothes – I found it really did help to look as inconspicuous as possible and almost always wore loose-fitting blouses, longish skirts and occasionally also a headscarf.

"'Is it true that women are opened up by machine?' is a question that worries me still"

After exploring Marrakesh for five days I took a bus out over the Atlas mountain range to Zagora. The journey took twelve hours and the bus was hot and cramped but, wedged between a group of Moroccan mothers, jostling their babies on my lap and sharing whatever food and drink was going round, I felt reassured, more a participant than an outsider.

This was also one of the few occasions that I'd had any sort of meaningful contact with Moroccan women. For the most part women tend to have a low profile in public, moving in very separate spheres to the tourists. There are some women's cafés but they're well hidden and not for foreigners. For me, the most likely meeting place was the *hammam*, or steambath, which I habitually sought out in each stopping place.

Apart from the undoubted pleasures of plentiful hot water, *hammams* became a place of refuge for me. It was a relief to be surrounded by women and to be an object of curiosity without any element of threat. Any ideas about Western status I might have had were lost in the face of explaining in French, Arabic and sign language to an old Moroccan woman with 24 grand-children the sexual practices and methods of contraception used in the West. "Is it true that women are opened up by machine?" is a question that worries me still.

I arrived in Zagora on the last night of the festival of the King's birthday. It was pure chance. The town was packed with Moroccans who had travelled in from nearby oases, but I met only one other tourist – a German man. We were both of us swept along, as insignificant as any other single people in the crowd, dancing and singing in time to the echoing North African sounds. At the main event of the night, the crowd was divided by a long rope with women on one side and men on the other, with only the German and I standing side by side. I felt overwhelmed with a feeling of excitement and well being, simply because I was there.

From Zagora I headed for Figuig and the desert, stopping overnight en route at Tinerhir. It's possible that I chose a bad hotel for that stop but it was about the worst night that I spent in the entire trip. The men in and around the hotel jeered, even spat at me when I politely refused to accompany them, and throughout the night I had men banging on the door and shutters of my room. For twelve hours I stood guard, tense, afraid, and stifled by the locked in heat of that dismal hotel room. I escaped on the first bus out.

Further south I met up with a Danish man in a Landrover and travelled on with him to spend four days in the desert. It was a simple, businesslike arrangement: he wanted someone to look after the van while he slept and I wanted someone to look out for me while I slept. I can find no terms that will sufficiently describe the effect that the desert had on me. It was awesome and inspiring and it silenced both of us. On the rare occasions that we spoke we did so in whispers.

I also found that the more recent preoccupations that I had about my life, work and relationships had entirely slipped from my mind, yet strangely I could recall with absolute clarity images from over ten years ago. I remain convinced that the desert, in its simplicity, its expansiveness and its power changed me in some way.

At Figuig I parted company with the Dane and made my way in various stages to Fes. I tended to find myself becoming dissatisfied after travelling for a while with a male companion. Not because I didn't enjoy the company, which was more often than not a luxury for me, but I used to feel cheated that I was no longer at the forefront and that any contact with Moroccans would have to be made through him. This is often the case in Islamic countries where any approaches or offers of hospitality are proffered man-to-man, with the woman treated more or less as an appendage. I was prepared to go on alone however uncomfortable it might become as long as I was being treated as a person in my own right.

"I found that Moroccans have such a high regard for sport that the very men who had hustled me in the morning looked on with respectful interest . . . as I hurtled by in the cool of the evening"

In Fes I discovered yet another, perhaps even more effective, strategy for changing my status with Moroccan men. I am a runner and compete regularly in marathons and I'm used to keeping up with my training in almost any conditions. Up until Fes I'd held back, uncertain of how I'd be greeted if I dashed out of the hotel in only a track-suit bottom and T-shirt. My usual outfit, a long skirt and blouse, was hardly suitable for the exercise I had in mind.

After seriously considering confining myself to laps around the hotel bedroom, I recovered my sanity and sense of adventure, changed my clothes and set off. The harassment and the hustling all melted away. I found that Moroccans have such a high regard for sport that the very men who had hustled me in the morning looked on with a respectful interest, offering encouragement and advice as I hurtled by in the cool of the evening. Furthermore I became known as "the runner" and was left more or less in peace for the rest of my stay. After this I made it a rule to train in all the villages and towns I stayed in on the way back to Tangier. Now when I run I conjure up the image of pacing out of Chaouen towards the shrine on the hillside, keeping time with the chants of the muezzin at dawn.

Returning to Tangier I felt as far removed as it is possible to feel from the apprehensive new arrival of the month before. I felt less intimidated by and more stoical about my status as an outsider and I had long since come to accept the fact that I was a source of income to many people whose options for earning a living are sorely limited.

Walking out of the bus station I was surrounded by a group of hustlers. I listened in silence and then said, in the fairly decent Arabic that I had picked up, that I had been in the Sahara and had not got lost so I didn't think I needed a guide in Tangier; furthermore, that I had talked to some Tuareg in Zagora who told me that it is a lie that Moroccans buy their women with camels; please would they excuse me, I had arrangements. I spent the next few days wandering freely around the town, totally immersed in plotting how soon I could return.

Three Kinds of Women

. . . .

Pat Chell lived for two years in Fes, teaching English at the university.

"In Morocco, there are only three kinds of women," I was often told, "virgins, wives and whores." It is as useful a proverb as any to keep in mind when you visit, and a start to understanding the core of the country's culture – Islam and the family.

A woman in Morocco must be a virgin when she marries, and usually she is expected to prove this on consummation of the marriage by showing evidence of hymenal blood. I have known "Westernised", bourgeois women, no longer virgins but about to marry, who have gone to a doctor in Casablanca to have the hymen restitched. This has not necessarily been done to deceive their prospective husbands, with whom they may have been sleeping in any case, but to "observe form" and keep the two families happy.

"All unmarried Moroccan men whom I spoke to about sex had had their only experiences with prostitutes (apart from those who had been 'lucky' enough to meet tourists who would oblige)"

I have also known of liberal families who have given their consent for a couple to sleep together, after the marriage contract has been made but before the wedding ceremony, yet have "satisfied themselves" that the woman was a virgin upon the first occasion.

The only legitimate reason for a woman not being a virgin is if she is a wife. If she is known to be neither, then she will be considered a prostitute. Indeed, once a girl's virginity is lost and her marriage prospects become virtually nil, without family support, she may well have to resort to prostitution as a means of making enough money to live. Prostitution is very common in Morocco. All unmarried Moroccan men whom I spoke to about sex had had their only experiences with prostitutes (apart from those who had been "lucky" enough to meet tourists who would oblige).

On the first occasion this was almost always as an adolescent with a prostitute known for her experience in dealing with "virgins", though Moroccans would laugh at that expression, as the concept of male virginity does not exist. Indeed, many regard childhood circumcision as equivalent to the taking away of virginity. A bridegroom is tacitly expected to be sexually experienced and one who is not is seen as something of a joke.

Homosexuality, though it does exist as a sexual preference, is more likely to be thought of as a substitute for the "real" thing; tourists sometimes misinterpret Moroccan men's show of physical affection for each other as sexual, but this is simply a cultural norm. As for women, I'm not so sure that the concept of sexual satisfaction (let alone sexual preference) even exists. Amongst my students at the university, presumably an intellectual elite, the idea of choosing lesbianism, either for physical or political reasons, was inconceivable. If anything, it was regarded as another example of Western decadence.

Some of my students did have relationships with men but this was a very risky business indeed. If the relationship was "known about" and then ended, the woman could be branded as a whore and her life made a misery. I have met female students who have

been beaten by fathers or brothers simply for being seen talking to a man. Another, who had been raped, did nothing about the attack even though the assailant was known to her, because she was sure that if her family found out she would be taken from the university. Many families are reluctant to allow their daughters to go to university, not because they don't want them educated – they often do as job prospects for women continue to improve – but because they don't want them to be at risk by being in a situation where they can have contact with men.

"Many students . . . equated feminism with danger because they saw it as anti-Islamic"

A number of students, male and female, were obviously dissatisfied with the status quo. A married student I knew attempted to help his working wife with chores until he was forbidden to do so by his mother, and his wife was severely reprimanded for failing in her wifely duties. They, like most young Moroccans, were not in a financial position to have a home of their own, even if the family constraints against doing so had not been there. Others of my students wanted to marry Europeans, not so much to have a more equal relationship, nor the financial benefits, but because there was more likelihood of their being able to free themselves from family restraints.

I was only ever aware of one student who did not want to marry. This was Saloua; she was very intelligent and studious, determined to further her studies, which would have meant leaving Morocco, and then returning as a university teacher. She saw this as the best way in which she could help the women of her country.

Although Saloua had a very supportive family, she knew that she had to have a strategy to allow her to carry out her plans. She dressed in Western clothes but very demurely – rather middle-aged "Marks and Spencers". She was rarely seen alone, thus denying any man an opportunity to talk to her. When with women, she avoided the usual "gossip" and "scheming". In a mixed teaching group she spoke only when invited to do so. If she did become involved in a classroom discussion with males, she would be pleasant but distant, humourless and polite. In other words, she always kept a low profile. She was aware of walking a very tenuous tightrope to freedom. She was the most courageous Moroccan woman that I met and I wish her well.

Many students, however, equated feminism with danger because they saw it as anti-Islamic. Some of the most politically active women that I came across were involved in Islamic fundamentalism and wanted nothing to do with Western decadence and therefore nothing to do with me.

Moroccans form their ideas of Western women from two main sources, the media and tourists. The cinema is very popular and there is an abundance of trashy European soft-porn films. I have heard great cheers in the cinema when the "macho" hero has torn off a woman's clothes or physically abused her prior to her becoming a willing sexual partner.

"No father would put his daughter at risk by letting her travel unless she was already 'worthless'"

One of the biggest culture shocks I had in this respect occurred in a very poor home with no running water, toilet or electricity. There was, however, a television and a wire would be run over the roof to a neighbour's when we wanted an evening's viewing. Every Wednesday, neighbours would gather to watch *Dallas*. It was the first time they had spent time socially with a European and so naturally they were curious. My host had to go to great lengths to explain that I was not a "Pamela" or a "Sue Ellen" and that

neither were the majority of Western women. I don't think they were very convinced.

If a woman is alone or only with women, what kind of woman can she be? No father would put his daughter at risk by letting her travel unless she was already "worthless". Her nearest equivalent in Moroccan society is the prostitute. She sits in cafés, drinks alcohol, smokes cigarettes or hashish and will even comb her hair in public. She often dresses "indecently" – not even a prostitute would do this. Why should a woman want to "flaunt" her body? She will also often be prepared to have sex if you can charm her into it. These are the kinds of attitudes I heard so frequently.

And, as a traveller, these are the attitudes which you can expect to meet. The forms the inevitable sexual harassment take vary from the relatively innocuous to the absolutely obscene. The most persistent and annoying is a clicking noise made with the tongue every time you walk past a café, for example. Not terribly serious, you might think, but the cumulative effect is very degrading.

Then there are more direct, verbal approaches. I would strongly advise against confronting anyone who pesters you, as your remonstrations only provide unexpected entertainment. I've never yet seen a woman come out of one of these confrontations without feeling foolish and humiliated. Your anger will simply not be understood. You are unlikely to receive much sympathy from Moroccan women, either. They will either disapprove of you and think that you must be prepared to accept the consequences of being out in public (ie in the man's world) or they will fail to understand your annoyance as there are many young Moroccan women who seek this kind of attention. It is proof of their attractiveness and may be the only kind of contact they have ever known with men.

I don't think as a tourist you can ever avoid sexual harassment completely, but there are certain compromises that reduce its extent. You can dress "appropriately", in skirts, rather than trousers, and in sleeved, loose-fitting tops. You should avoid making eye contact too, and not start up a "casual" conversation with a man – there is no such thing in Morocco. Above all, be as polite and even tempered as possible. Moroccans have a highly ritualised, elaborate etiquette, which you will not be able to learn in a short time, but they do respect politeness. Loss of temper equals loss of face, no matter what the provocation.

What I have written are generalisations. There are Moroccan men and women who do not share these attitudes. There are many students who genuinely want to practise their English and can only do so with travellers. Unfortunately, on a short stay, the Moroccans you're most likely to encounter are street hustlers only after your money or your body. Sometimes, particularly if you are feeling threatened or insecure, it is difficult to tell whether people are being genuine or "hustling". But if you are cautiously optimistic and rely on your instincts, then you might find, as I did, that Moroccans are incredibly hospitable people, many of whom love to have Westerners to stay.

I hope that I haven't put you off travelling to Morocco. Too often, sadly, I met travellers who judged the society with Western values: they saw the men as villains and the women as martyrs.

With a Toddler in Tow

. . . .

Jo Crowson, a single mother, travelled to Morocco from Britain with her two-year-old daughter, Merry. Whilst most of the Moroccans she met seemed very positive in their attitudes towards her and her child, she found that fellow male travellers could be surprisingly critical and unsupportive.

I had already spent some time in Morocco with a group of friends, both male and female, and had a pretty bad time – entirely our own fault. For a start we went in July (temperatures at 31°C plus) and we went straight to the Rif mountains where one of our party immediately got caught with hashish.

We spent the next two weeks trying to get him out of prison and virtually all our combined funds on his fine. So I had a good idea what not to do in Morocco.

Six years later, I found myself a single parent in great need of a winter adventure and my thoughts turned again to Morocco. It was not too far (in case Merry, my two-year-old daughter got ill), it was accessible overland (I wouldn't have to pay for two flights), it was cheap and it was definitely different. I decided to go for it, but with so many doubts, fears and reservations, that I thought I was probably completely mad.

In the following weeks I read as many guidebooks and travel books on Morocco as I could find in the library. This did little to ease my fears. All included warnings about sexual harassment, and the incredibly persistent street hustlers, and they all, without exception, advised women against travelling alone. I decided that if, after a couple of days, I found that travelling with a child was just as difficult as travelling alone, I would go back to Spain and spend my time there. Having established this "escape clause", I felt a lot better.

I managed to get a lift with friends as far as Northern Portugal, which I thought would make the journey cheaper. I'm not sure that it did in the end, but it is good to see the land you're travelling over and watch the gradual changes as they happen. (As a result of this journey I have many tips to pass on to anyone planning to spend three days in the back of a car with a two-year-old.) I was also lucky enough to get a letter sent poste restante from some women friends who were already travelling in Morocco with their children, suggesting a couple of good places to visit and saying what a wonderful time they were having.

"Feeling very brave and excited we boarded the ferry, had our passport checked, and kept a look out for dolphins"

After we left our friends in Portugal we had a great journey into Spain and down to Algeciras, where there are ferries to Morocco. It gave us a chance to get adjusted to our new lifestyle and to gain confidence. It also gave me a bit longer to feel apprehensive about how we'd cope. Finally the great moment arrived and feeling very brave and excited we boarded the ferry, had our passport checked, and kept a look out for dolphins.

I'd decided we'd go to Tangier as it's better connected than Ceuta and I could get a train straight out to Rabat. The south is supposed to be slightly easier for travellers than the north and Rabat sounded like the least problematic (as well as the least exciting) place to acclimatise in.

Despite all my fears, arriving at Tangier was astonishingly easy. We were waved through customs, while most of the other people were emptying out their luggage, shown where to buy our train ticket and pointed in the right direction for the station. There, two unofficial porters grabbed my bags and charged five dirhams for help I didn't need. Ah well. I'd managed the first obstacle although I was still pretty nervous – what if my carriage fills up with men?

At the next stop three young men got on, followed by two women. I began to relax a bit. One of the three started talking to me in English, eating away at my reserves of confidence (not difficult) by saying that we wouldn't be getting to Rabat until very late, it was a terrible city, all the hotels would be full and so on. He was attempting to persuade me to get off at his home town which he described as a beautiful seaside resort full of tourists. This put me off. I looked it up in my guidebook and was put off even more. It was when he insisted that the Youth Hostel where I planned to stay at Rabat would close at 6pm that I suddenly realised I was having my first encounter with a dedicated "hustler". He left the compartment and the women seated opposite me warned me that he was a "bad Moroccan" – a phrase I heard frequently during my stay.

From then on I communicated with my fellow passengers in abysmal French, with the help of an exchange of bananas for biscuits. They were delighted by Merry but seemed very anxious when she fell asleep that she should keep her legs fully covered. I'm not sure if it was fear of her catching cold or the glimpse of bare flesh that particularly disturbed them, but I covered her anyway. Moroccan girls wear loose trousers under their skirts from babyhood onwards and although I had thought about keeping myself covered up, I hadn't considered Merry. From then on I made sure that she wore trousers and/or longish skirts everywhere except at the beach and no one else ever commented.

"Their attitudes ranged from praise for my bravery to criticism of my mothering instincts. More than one warned me of the danger of Merry being stolen and sold into slavery"

When we arrived in Rabat I stomped off, trying to look more confident than I felt. I was a bit worried that the Youth Hostel might not let us stay as, according to the handbook, children under five were not admitted. Either the manager didn't know that or didn't care and we got a place for only a few dirhams a night. The bunk beds were a great hit with Merry and I wanted an uncomplicated place to stay with contact with other travellers for first-hand, up-to-the-minute information. The other travellers at the hostel seemed shocked that I was travelling alone with a small child. Their attitudes ranged from praise for my bravery to criticism of my mothering instincts. More than one warned me of the danger of Merry being stolen and sold into slavery. I treated this prejudice with the contempt it deserved, but I did wonder how they could bring themselves to travel in a place where they believed such things were common. At this point I was still wondering myself what I was doing there, but then one man went too far in his criticisms and I retreated angry but fortified by it. (There were no women staying at the hostel that night.)

Rabat was indeed a mellow city and we wandered around the Medina without hindrance or offers of a guide. At the Kasbah, however, a man approached us and offered to show us around although he said he wasn't a guide. "Good," I said, "as I'm not going to pay you." It was all very amiable and the Kasbah was lovely, like a village within the city, and everyone seemed to know my "not a guide". I relaxed into

chatting while he showed me where he lived and we drank mint tea. He invited me to an evening meal of *couscous* and after I accepted it he went off.

Left to my own devices I began to regret having accepted as I didn't feel completely happy about going to his house alone after dark. I decided to leave a note for him saying I couldn't make it and hoped he would get it. I felt pretty bad about not trusting him, but, with Merry there I had become more than usually cautious and was simply not prepared to launch into any situation where I felt our safety was in doubt. (I still felt bad though.)

All the time I was in Morocco I masqueraded as a married woman. I felt there was nothing to gain in explaining my real circumstances as they would inevitably be misunderstood. Over the course of my stay my "husband" got ever closer. Whilst in Rabat he had been working in England, but on the advice of my Moroccan friend I moved him to Tangier. Later on I occasionally said I was meeting him in a café. (I met a woman who pretended she was pregnant whenever she felt harassed and said it worked.)

Back at the hostel I was happy to meet a woman who had been travelling around Europe on her own. Before coming to Morocco, however, she had gone to a Youth Hostel in Malaga to find someone to travel with. She found a man who was also travelling alone and seemed to have enjoyed her stay. Also at the hostel was a young Moroccan visiting Rabat in order to get a US visa. He was a devout Muslim and we had a friendly and completely uncomplicated conversation about America, the country he was aiming to visit, before he was suddenly and quite aggressively thrown out by the manager. This was despite his being there at the invitation of one of the guests. It seemed to me he was thrown out because he was a Moroccan.

As I spent more time in Morocco I became more relaxed, told "lies" more readily, became better tempered and began to learn who to avoid. Sexual harassment is a problem for women in Morocco, but I seemed to experience less than a lot of other women I met who were travelling with men. I think perhaps having a child labels you as some man's property. "Hustlers", however, still made approaches – and proved incredibly persistent, innovative and subtle. It is important to remember that it is need that spurs them on to such great lengths to part you and your money. Tourists in Morocco are viewed as rich, and in many ways it's true. We're certainly privileged.

Both Merry and I loved Marrakesh immediately. We found a room in a cheap but fairly clean hotel just off the Place Djemaa el Fna, from where we could wander out amongst the stalls, entertainers, travellers and coachtrippers or climb up to the terraces to look out at the views and sip mint tea. I found it fascinating and enjoyed the anonymity of the crowds, while Merry adored the snake charmers and other entertainers. She also loved stopping to buy fruit here, nuts there, and freshly made egg sandwiches from the woman who ran the hard-boiled egg stall. She soon, however, began to miss the freedom to run about and play, and wanted to go to the coast – whilst I would have preferred to stay longer.

"The best part of travelling with my daughter was the contact she brought with Moroccan women"

We went on to a small village just north of Agadir called Taghazoute and rented a room from a Berber family; a mother, grandmother, two sons and two daughters. Although communication was hard – I couldn't speak Berber and they had very few words of French – we smiled a lot at each other. They seemed especially pleased with Merry and would take her out to show her their animals or bring small children in

to see her, and every now and then Yasmina, the mother, would offer us food. It was an ideal place to stay and the beach itself was wide and fairly empty.

I was worried about how safe it would be to swim alone, but resolved this by asking a couple if we could join them for a bit. Later on I became more confident about swimming alone and was happy just to site myself near family groups. I tried to make sure that I was never completely alone with no one in sight, as a woman friend had earlier been assaulted on an isolated bit of beach not far up the coast.

The best part of travelling with my daughter was the contact she brought with Moroccan women. In Essaouira I met a woman called Barka who offered me a room in her house. Again communication was a little difficult but we seemed to manage well on a mixture of French, Arabic, and empathy. She lived alone with her eight-year-old son – her husband was working somewhere in the north (fishing, I think) and didn't come home very often. Eating meals and watching TV together, we soon became very close. Her son Mohammed loved Merry and wanted us to stay much longer than we could. The only problem I had with Barka was that she would refuse to let me help with any chores and wanted to do all of my own work as well. I ended up having to hide in the toilet to wash my clothes.

When it was time for us to leave, she came with us to say goodbye at the bus station. On the way we dropped her son off at school where she introduced us to some of her friends. It was a scorching day and all the women were covered from head to foot in thick white blankets with just their hennaed hands and feet showing and their eyes peeping through above the black veils they wore. I was hot in my light clothing. We were so different in our dress, customs and language and yet somehow we all managed to communicate about our kids and school just as I suppose women all over the world do. Later Barka kissed me goodbye through her veil at the station and made me promise to come back and visit her. I felt I didn't want to leave.

"We were so different in our dress, customs and language and yet somehow we all managed to communicate about our kids and school just as I suppose women all over the world do"

We spent a couple of days exploring Tangier before catching the ferry. For part of this time, we joined up with a couple of English men and I was surprised to find that, with them, I experienced more harassment than I'd ever encountered alone with Merry. I also had my first and only offer to buy hashish.

In the end leaving Morocco wasn't so much of a wrench as Merry caught some sort of stomach bug which made her sick and incredibly tired. Travelling back through Spain to Portugal was awful for us both, although marginally worse for me (she slept through a lot of it). One of the worst aspects of it was the amount of criticism I got from other travellers just when I could have used a little support. I'm not sure why I encountered so much unhelpfulness, especially from male travellers, but fortunately there were exceptions. And Moroccan, Spanish and Portuguese people have a great attitude towards children.

Travelling with a child, I found I couldn't live on as tight a budget as I'd planned, due mainly to the need for odd, expensive, treats. I also felt pretty isolated at night when Merry was asleep but I still wanted to be out and about. Before I went I didn't expect night-time to be a problem as at home Merry is capable of staying up till all hours. I don't know if it was the fresh air and excitement but her pattern certainly changed and she was asleep by eight every night. I took a pushchair with me so that I could push her around if she slept but this wasn't practical. The roads and paths anywhere other than in the cities were so bad that I would have to carry the pushchair as well as Merry most of the time. Even in the cities there are usually many steps to negotiate. Her pushchair was only useful for carrying our stuff from the bus to the train station. (The lack of personal space will be familiar to all single parents as will the exhaustion you occasionally feel.)

Overall, I think it's a great idea to travel with a child in Morocco, though I wouldn't recommend it to someone wanting a "holiday". It's an adventure above all else and requires a certain amount of work. Other women I know have travelled in Morocco with their children and all agreed that they had a great time. One friend managed to borrow someone else's daughter as well as take her own and so travelled with two ten-year-olds – that has to be the perfect arrangement. And in a way all my earlier fears have left me feeling that I have really accomplished something. When I wasn't feeling a bit scared about what I was taking on I felt incredibly strong and extraordinary – it's not often women get to feel that in their lives.

TRAVEL NOTES

Languages Moroccan Arabic (a considerable variant of "classical" Egyptian/Gulf Arabic) and three distinct Berber languages. French is widely spoken and is taught in schools.

Transport There's a small but useful rail network. Travel otherwise is by bus (plentiful and cheap) or collective taxi (*grand taxi*), which run between towns according to demand. In the Atlas and sub-Sahara you can negotiate lifts on trucks — some of which operate like buses. Hitching is inadvisable, though fellow tourists are sometimes worth approaching at campsites.

Accommodation Very rarely a problem — there are all categories of hotels graded by the state and other (even cheaper) options below them.

Special Problems Arrival can be daunting at both Tangier and Tetouan, where you'll find the country's most persistent, aggressive and experienced hustlers. If it's your first visit it makes sense to move straight on — it only takes a couple of days to get used to things. Many tourists come to Morocco to smoke hashish (*kif*). Although officially illegal, the police tend to turn a blind eye: the main trouble lies with the dealers, who have developed some nasty tricks (like selling you hash then sending friends round to threaten to turn you in to the police unless you pay them off). It's best to avoid the *kif* growing areas of the Rif mountains and the drug centre, Ketama.

Guide *The Rough Guide: Morocco* (Harrap Columbus) is a well-deserved classic.

Contacts

Centre de Documentation et d'action Féminin, 46 Rue Aboudest-Agdal, Rabat. Recently formed and very small feminist group.

8th of March. A feminist journal produced at the Mohammed V University, Rabat.

Books

Fatima Mernissi, *Beyond the Veil: The Sexual Ideology of Women* (1975; Al Saqi, 1985). Enlightening study by Morocco's leading sociologist.

Fatima Mernissi, *Doing Daily Battle: Interviews with Moroccan Women* (The Women's Press, 1988). Eleven Moroccan women, from a range of backgrounds, talk candidly about their lives.

Vanessa Maher, *Women and Property in Morocco* (Cambridge UP, 1974). Respected academic study.

Nancy Phelan, *Morocco is a Lion* (Quartet, 1982). Ordinary, lightweight travelogue — but well observed and includes a variety of interviews/experiences with Moroccan women, both rural and urban.

Works by the Moroccan-resident American writer **Paul Bowles** provide an interesting insight into the country. The best of his novels, *The Spider's House* (1955; Abacus, 1988) is set in Fes during the struggle for independence. Bowles's other Moroccan novels, and especially his translations of Moroccan storytellers (notably Mohammed Mrabet), are also worthwhile.

Nepal

For the first half of this century Nepal was virtually untouched by the outside world, an isolated mountain kingdom and a highly traditional Hindu and Buddhist society. Since the Sixties it has been caught up in a full-scale tourist boom, with travellers pouring into the capital, Kathmandu, and, accompanied by local guides, out along its spectacular Himalayan trekking routes.

As a primarily rural and Hindu society, Nepal is a relatively safe place to travel; Kathmandu has its share of hustlers, eager to gain custom, but they are rarely aggressive in their approach and violent crime, even theft, is uncommon. You'll find that you are treated first and foremost as a foreigner, rather than a woman and, as such, the atmosphere is tolerant. However, it is important to be sensitive to local customs – shorts and skimpy clothes are considered offensive.

A growing number of women trek alone and on the well-trodden, shorter treks this is considered reasonably safe; it would be advisable to have company if you're planning anything longer or more adventurous. What is disturbing, however, is the pattern that tourism is creating; Kathmandu has been transformed into a commercial and cosmopolitan capital, and the trekking industry, for all its supposed "contact with local people", is as prepared as any other to exploit workers with low wages and poor conditions. If you want to feel good about trekking, you'll need to choose your tour with care.

At present the government of King Birenda is locked in a trade dispute with India. Recently this manifested itself in an Indian fuel blockade which has affected transport within the country, but more seriously has caused an escalation in the already critical problem of deforestation as wood is used for fuel in the capital. It is hard to predict what will happen if the blockade continues – such is the importance of tourism that trekking agencies are given priority rations of kerosene and petrol.

Under the partyless political system, autonomous **women's groups** are considered divisive. (It is illegal for any political group to function without prior government consent.) The few officially sanctioned bodies – notably the *Nepal Women's Organisation* – are orientated mainly towards providing educational and social welfare services. They have initiated campaigns on issues of property rights, polygamy, and child and forced marriages, but these have been criticised by Nepalese feminists as being largely tokenistic. The bulk of Nepalese women live in rural villages where their lives are dominated by the demands of subsistence farming and the traditional roles of domestic work and child-rearing. With the recent trend of modernisation, more urban middle-class women are, however, getting access to higher education and the professions. Women are also gaining employment (albeit low-paid) within the tourist industry.

Home in a Hindu Valley

. . . .

Deborah Rutter, a post-graduate student in Social Anthropology, went to Nepal to complete research for her PhD. She took along her male partner and thirteen-year-old daughter. None of them had lived abroad before.

The first thing that struck me on arrival in Kathmandu was the filth in the streets; the city had been transformed into a sea of mud by out-of-season rains. Like all first time visitors we headed straight for Thamel, the tourist district, where we picked our way between the small hotels and souvenir shops selling Buddhist wall hangings, Tibetan carpets, bags and outlandish hippy clothing – anything from tie dyes and brocades to cotton ten-tone draw-string trousers and jackets. Young Nepali men took it in turns to try and grab some custom; "Change money? Buy carpet, madam? Clean hotel? Good trekking guide?" As elsewhere in Asia there's a commission on everything. It was a relief to find that there were few beggars although children, with no other English vocabulary, would immediately strike up a chorus of "one rupee, one rupee!"

Staying in Thamel you begin to feel that you are participating simultaneously in several different time-zones. Despite all the recent incursions of tourism, the traditional Newar architecture and way of life still holds sway. Nepalese women wearing traditional dress and ornamentation come outside to wash their clothes and hair at the standpipes, bargain for fruit and vegetables at the stalls around the larger shrines, and make offerings to the street deities. At harvest time city and countryside merge into one another as the streets are used to thresh and dry the grain and you'll find that most urban residents have a home called "my village".

Nepalese custom dictates that women are treated with respect and even a casual acquaintance is referred to as elder or younger sister. This doesn't necessarily apply to Western women. There's a flourishing video trade via Bangkok and many young male aficionados apparently cannot distinguish between female tourists and the soft-porn starlets of the screen. My thirteen-year-old daughter had to put up with a public commentary on her anatomy every time she walked down the street. (On only one occasion was she actually touched, being pushed into a sewage-filled gutter.) She regarded these elaborately coiffeured youths with great scorn, dismissing them as ignorant and racist, but it was hard for me, hearing loud and offensive remarks directed at my daughter, not to react in fury.

These incidents are not common, but they are unpleasant and can feel threatening, especially as the antagonisers are always in groups. I realised that such aspects were just another manifestation of being "different", and that the situation had not been helped by some tourists' insistence on wearing transparent clothing or shorts cut above the buttock. Nepali people have little experience of external mores and I suspect that they assume that if you break one taboo you are likely to have no moral sense at all.

As usual it is women's dress and behaviour that attracts the most scrutiny and criticism. If you are interested in meeting Nepalese people, you may need to make concessions, such as covering shoulders and legs: many women wear loose skirts for trekking, instead of shorts, with elasticated waists so that, like the indigenous petticoat, they can be drawn up over the breasts to allow privacy while washing.

Of course, most people come to Nepal to trek. How you choose to go about it is very much up to you, but it's worth remembering that the company with the glossy brochure is likely to supply the same standard of food and accommodation on trek as you would get if you just picked up your pack and walked. We did just that, choosing a route which took only seven days of walking into the Annapurna sanctuary region, renowned for its 360-degree panoramas.

"I found it impossible to overcome my reluctance to employ someone to do my 'dirty work', whether washing or carrying"

But we did not get off the ground without the customary debate as to whether we would need to hire a guide. Everywhere we turned we encountered horror stories of fraudulent foreigners with imperialist ideas but dollar deficiency, expecting their guides to struggle under fifty-kilo loads on a bowl of rice a day; or *raksi* (rice wine) crazed guides abandoning their clients in snowstorms, having first relieved them of their Swiss-down trekking clobber.

We ventured only as far as Ghorepani, the most trodden part of the Jomosom–Muktinath trail, and really didn't need a guide. But, in common with many other trekkers, we had a very expansive idea of "necessities" and did wish that we had hired a porter. I found it impossible, however, to overcome my reluctance to employ someone to do my "dirty work", whether washing or carrying: I hated to be called, or treated as, a *memsahib*.

Treks into the Annapurna region normally start with a bus ride to Pokhara in west-central Nepal. Buses and roads, where they exist at all, are appalling. Our first trip involved nine hours of bouncing around with miscellaneous bits of metal stabbing our calves, bottoms stuck with sweat to the plastic seats; we were stunned by heat; and we were starving – having contracted salmonella in the capital's poshest restaurant, we'd become incredibly wary of eating cooked food.

But hunger got the better of us and we joined the other Nepali travellers for a lunch of boiled rice, daal, and vegetable curry at a roadside stop. It was a good nourishing meal and a welcome relief from the pizzas and buffalo, cut up as steak, that the enterprising caterers of Kathmandu are now serving up for foreigners.

"We began to feel ludicrously under-equipped, in our trainers, with a set of thermal underwear and a sweater; all those paperback novels and first-aid kits were just so much dead weight"

Back on the road to Pokhara, cursing the corrupt engineers who applied such a thin layer of tarmac to this important supply route that most of it had worn or washed away, we gazed out at the scenery. Very little of Nepal's mountainous surface is cultivable but every slope where a seed might possibly survive is terraced – the most amazing achievement in human ingenuity and effort. Depending on the season, there are teams of water buffalo churning the flooded rice terraces in preparation for the new seedlings, or teams of scarlet-clad women planting or weeding.

Pokhara was breathtakingly beautiful, the white-iced Himalayas rising like a mirage above the lush vegetation and green waters of its lake. After a day's browsing among the Tibetan-owned stalls (there are several refugee camps in the area), we set off along what's known as the "apple pie trek". The name is a bit of an exaggeration, though the lodges do attempt to satisfy the Western palate with peculiar variants of well-known vegetarian staples – porridge, chips, vegetable omelettes, vegetable soup – and the ubiquitous Coca-Cola. These became progressively more expensive as we climbed the trail, reminding us of the porters who lug the crates up on their backs.

The mountains were as stunning as expected, although the weather proved unreliable and cloud obscured the views for large parts of the day. Still, the English are used to such occurrences and the sheer effort of keeping going left me with little mental energy to contemplate disappointment. I had thought I was quite fit, but I'd never experienced the hills of Nepal.

When you are climbing up you long for a downhill stretch, only to find that every muscle screams and every joint jars going down, so that struggling up seems by far the easier option. I found it a severe challenge, especially for the first three days and my daughter claimed to be too exhausted to even frame the anticipated complaints. For most of the trek we were battling with the heat but as soon as we came to the Ghorepani pass it became foggy, cold and damp. We began to feel ludicrously under-equipped, in our trainers, with a set of thermal underwear and a sweater; all those paperback novels and first-aid kits were just so much dead weight.

It's strange how preoccupied you become by the physical aspects of life on trek but for many, including us, this was the first experience of day-to-day living without any mod cons. You learn that you don't smell any worse after three days without a shower than you did after one. You learn what is really important for human survival, like finding water for drinking, and you get a very real sense of what environmental depletion is all about. I was incensed by those trekkers who accepted the offer of hot water for bathing, knowing that yet more trees would need to be cut down to feed the wood-burning stoves. Of course I didn't cast off the habits of a lifetime, but I did begin to question them.

Equally, the Nepalese need to learn how to deal with the debris of industrial society. They do not seem to realise that the non-biodegradable materials that have flooded into the country in the wake of tourism cannot simply be dropped on the ground. Who of us does not entertain the surreptitious wish that the Nepalese would remain charmingly different and ethnic, unpolluted by the trappings of industrial capitalism. Well, tough luck, it's their choice, not ours, and the convenience of two-minute noodles and plastic bags is much appreciated.

In autumn and spring, the Himalayas are visible from most parts of the Kathmandu valley and there is nothing like the sight of a snow-covered peak to raise the spirits. I don't know why this proof of humanity's insignificance should be so comforting to the soul. But it was for me, and, being stuck in the capital trying to get a research visa, I was often in need of comfort. For six months I traipsed from Ministry to Ministry, grovelling to officials and getting increasingly anxious and frustrated, until eventually I got my permit and was able to set off for the valley slopes. My plan was to live in a small Hindu village for a year in order to see through a full agricultural cycle.

Initially, life in the village was difficult. I knew very little about the practicalities of subsistence living and depended, like a child, on the village women for instruction and help. They never seemed to resent this, claiming that we were a welcome source of amusement and distraction, and showed us great hospitality – offering a constant flow of gifts of food, milk and curd, as we had no cows.

Although we rented our own house, we suffered greatly from lack of privacy; it isn't the Nepalese way to expect great intimacy and intellectual companionship between husband and wife. As a young female, our daughter often felt excluded from conversations with our nightly visitors, but on the whole, having approached the entire trip with dread, she fitted in amazingly well. She would pop in and out of people's houses and kitchens with a freedom only accorded to non-adults, asking about the animals, comparing prize possessions with the girls next

door, and often returning with an infant on her hip.

While I began to feel more weary and, at times, even paranoid about the endless necessity of being "on show", she became more sociable, took part in the rice-planting and did her washing at the tap. Many tears were shed when she returned to England and school; at the awkward age of thirteen, such a radical shift is no joke. In the village she was everyone's sister or daughter and happily free of many of the contradictions about sexuality and behaviour that afflict our own society.

"Initially, life in the village was difficult. I knew very little about the practicalities of subsistence living and depended, like a child, on the village women for instruction and help"

Nepal is a very poor country. Our village was privileged, since they had nearly enough grain to feed themselves, but if there was no starvation there was plenty of malnutrition. Rice is given precedence over vegetables and as a result many people suffer from stomach and eye infections and sores, exacerbated by local remedies. I tried, as far as possible, not to interfere in medical treatment, except with antiseptic cream, or in translating English dosage instructions on medicines haphazardly dispensed at the child health clinic. The only time that I did intervene, when I gave a neighbour some aspirin to soothe her toothache, I felt responsible for a rash that suddenly (and, as it turned out, coincidentally) appeared all over her body. People had very little understanding of our preoccupation with diagnosis; it is assumed that because we all look so healthy we must have the universal panacea.

This is all part of the general assumptions made about foreigners, the most obvious one being that we are rich. The fact of having paid the airfare is proof enough although, knowing that we did not have a house, nor rice fields, our friends were quite puzzled as to where our wealth, not to mention our priorities, lay. I always found myself trying to play down my wealth, by wearing only cheap, cotton dresses and living as simply as possible. But the pressure to keep up an endless round of small gifts, and the even-handedness needed to do this without creating jealousies, would sometimes become a strain.

"At 5am, I would try to ignore the cockerel . . . desperate to delay the barrage of questions from early morning visitors, including every child in the village"

Throughout my stay I had many periods of travelling on my own, especially when I was searching for a site for my fieldwork. Invariably it would be women who would invite me home with them; the Nepalese sense of hospitality and general curiosity towards strangers meant that I always had a roof over my head. We would sleep fully clothed on an uncovered rice mat. At 5am, I would try to ignore the cockerel (once, perched at the end of the bed), desperate to delay the barrage of questions from early morning visitors, including every child in the village. I hated the constant observation, the sense of

being alien, and stared at by all, though usually without hostility. But I valued the bridges of shared experiences which I found with Nepali women.

There is only one feasible path for Nepali rural women – marriage and work within the fields and at home. Work is very rigidly divided and, though women have much more to do than men, they rarely complain. My impression was that they placed a high value on cheerfulness and resilience, but this did not make them naturally submissive; a woman might drop to the ground to kiss her husband's feet for religious reasons but she could also be quick to contradict him. For the most part, socialising is segregated and women depend on each other for support and friendship. It helped that I too was married and had a child (though not the son that is so important in Nepali culture) and could take some part in discussions of motherhood and married life.

Leaving was hard. I realised how much I appreciated the bond I had formed with these women, when it became necessary to break it. It is strange now to remember with what trust they took me into their kitchens to feed me. They would wave aside any thanks and say, "if we came as strangers to your country, you would feed us, wouldn't you?"

TRAVEL NOTES

Languages Nepali and regional dialects: some English is spoken on tourist circuits.

Transport Within the Kathmandu Valley there are buses; further north trekking is the only option, other than a small network of flights (expensive and unreliable, though if time is tight you can fly out into the Himalayas and trek back). The recent introduced rationing of petrol has meant that buses are more irregular and crowded – be prepared for long waits.

Accommodation Plenty of cheap places to stay in Kathmandu and surrounding areas; also

small hotels on regular trekking routes. On more remote routes, there are virtually no tourist facilities and you'll have to carry your own tent or join a trekking party with porters. The Nepalese are incredibly hospitable and often invite foreigners to sleep in their homes – you should reciprocate with a small gift or some money.

Special Problems Although many tourists wear short summer gear, this is seen as disrespectful. In the more orthodox Hindu areas you may be asked – as a foreigner (and therefore untouchable) – to sleep outside the main living room. Everywhere you should try to avoid touching cooking utensils or food that is being prepared, and if you're given water to drink from a communal vessel avoid any contact with your lips.

For trekking, proper clothing and equipment are absolutely necessary. Altitude sickness is a common problem and should be taken very seriously. There is no clean drinking water, so infections are incredibly common; the numerous stool test laboratories in Kathmandu are an entrepreneurial innovation and have a poor record for reliability.

Guides A *Rough Guide* to Nepal (Harrap Columbus) is forthcoming and should give the best overall view of the country, with information about the many different ethnic minorities and current environmental issues. Best of the specific trekking guides is *Trekking in Nepal* (Mountaineers, US).

Contacts

Centre for Women and Development, PO Box 3637, Kathmandu. A non-governmental organisation established by a group of professional women which collects and disseminates information on women's issues and development projects.

Books

Lynn Bennett, *Dangerous Wives and Sacred Sisters* (Columbia University Press, New York, 1983). Good insight into the life and position of Hindu women in Nepal.

Karuna Kar Varilya, *Nepalese Short Stories* (Gallery Press, US, 1976). A collection of stories by some of Nepal's best writers, on a wide variety of themes.

Lynn Bennett, ed.; *The Status of Women in Nepal* (CEDA, Tribhuvan University, Nepal). Lengthier, more academic study.

The Netherlands

The Netherlands can be regarded as virtually two separate countries: Amsterdam and the rest. As the centre of West European counter-culture and a gateway to Europe and North America, Amsterdam attracts thousands of visitors every year. The city has a reputation for tolerance – an easy acceptance of race and sexuality – and, compared with other Western capitals, it does feel noticeably relaxed and safe. You can sit on your own in most cafés and bars without feeling conspicuous and there are plenty of women-only resources (bookshops

and bars) to tap into. The obvious exception is the red light district where, even in daylight, you can get hassled to buy drugs and may well have to face a stream of comments, catcalls and propositions.

Amsterdam's image as a permissive, "alternative" capital has waned only slightly since its heyday in the Sixties. The municipal authorities have been actively trying to divert attention and funds to more mainstream attractions, such as conference centres, hotel complexes and prestigious arts projects, but the city's progressive politics and policies remain well defended. Squatters continue to oppose urban development plans, the gay community maintains its high profile with plenty of venues and some of the best nightlife in Europe, and the sale of cannabis is still sanctioned in bars and cafés. One disturbing hangover of the "liberated" Sixties has been the proliferation of pornography, seen on newsstands and billboards throughout the city.

All of this stands in marked contrast to the entrenched conservatism of the provinces, where women are largely expected to follow the traditional path as home-makers and child-rearers, and where life can seem parochial and dull. People remain open and hospitable to visitors but it can be hard to gain acceptance as a foreign resident. However, getting around is very easy and Dutch women routinely travel alone. Your major problem will probably be the high standard of living which makes existing in The Netherlands very expensive.

For its size and population, the Netherlands has an expansive and wide-reaching **women's movement**. Since the Sixties, it has staged some impressive and well-publicised campaigns – notably, in the 1970s, to legalise abortion. There are now many local groups, organised around specific issues like sexual violence, unequal education, healthcare and pornography, and many women are active in the peace movement and various squatting campaigns. The Women's Union, a recognised trade union, was set up to improve the position of housewives and unpaid carers by agitating for improved state childcare and benefits.

Behind the Progressive Myth

. . . .

Suzie Brocker, a New Zealander, has been living in The Hague for the past three years. She works as a freelance writer and boosts her income with nannying and cleaning work for Dutch families.

Arriving in Holland is a bit like entering a warm, cosy room which makes you feel comfortable and at home straight away. There's something intimate about the country which I miss elsewhere; from the gabled houses with their overflowing gardens to the little cafés and old-fashioned black bicycles parked outside. People seem friendly and open-hearted, a far cry from the stereotyped image I had of dour-faced Dutch. But then, after living and travelling here for four years, I've had to question a lot of my preconceptions about Holland.

Before coming to live here, the image I had of the country was of a progressive nation at the forefront of moves for social change and equality. I therefore expected that the position of women would be far more advanced than that of many other Western countries. It came as a shock when, on my first day here, I faced a bank manager who was reluctant to open an account for me in my own name, separate from my husband's. Since then I have experienced numerous other incidents which illustrate the problems that many Dutch women face every day.

Dutch women are up against some fairly entrenched attitudes and, surprisingly, less than half of them work – a percentage well below the European Community average. Although the number has been rising gradually, and more and more women would like to work, many services and regulations in Dutch society remain based on the traditional family model, which hinders any attempt to move away from the home. There's a drastic shortage of both public and private childcare facilities, parental leave arrangements are virtually non-existent, and stores and government services are closed outside of regular office hours. I was amazed to find that the school down the road from my house closed between twelve and one, and that mothers were expected to collect and look after their children during this time.

Upon arriving here I advertised for work as a childminder in order to supplement my income, and the number of calls I got from working mums desperate for help was staggering. Most were married women attempting to juggle a career, child-rearing and domestic responsibilities, with little or no help from their husbands. I was perplexed therefore to read a recent survey which showed that eighty percent of the population favoured men and women sharing responsibility for running the house and raising children. From my experiences here there seems to be a big gap between the ideals expressed and actual practice.

"It's nice to be able to walk into a café alone without feeling as if you've invaded a male sanctuary"

I've often wondered why the position of Dutch women is behind that of their North European contemporaries. I think the long-standing influence of the church has had an impact, but beyond that I believe it has something to do with the importance the Dutch have always placed on family life. They are first and foremost home-loving people. They even have a special word for the cosy, comfortable elements of domestic life they treasure so dearly – "gezellig", a word which really has no equivalent in English. And the responsibility for keeping this home together and functioning has always fallen upon the women.

This notion is carried over into Dutch social life too. The small, intimate cafés of Holland which I love aren't intended to supplant the home but duplicate it. Unlike in Greece or Spain where cafés tend to be filled with men flicking ash on the floor and passing comment about any woman that

walks in, cafés in Holland are open to everyone, young and old, alone or in groups, to eat, drink, and mostly just enjoy each other's company. It's nice to be able to walk into a café alone without feeling as if you've invaded a male sanctuary and without having to deal with unwanted attention.

Living in such a tiny country with a population of over fourteen million, the Dutch appreciate the importance of individual privacy, and it's very rare that you'll be hassled. The only time I've ever felt unsafe was when I inadvertently wandered into the red light district of Amsterdam, and then the cause of my unease was a male tourist. The attitude towards pornography and prostitution does mean that certain areas of major cities in Holland, the worst being in Amsterdam, can be hostile places for women, but in response to this, cafés, restaurants and nightclubs have been set up by women and for women almost everywhere.

While there may be many frustrations for a woman living in The Netherlands, I've found travelling on my own here a great experience. The Dutch are incredibly hospitable to travellers and, as English is very widely spoken, language is hardly ever a barrier. The flat countryside lends itself to active holidays, with miles of specially built cycle tracks and walkways leading to the more picturesque areas of Holland not so accessible by car. It's excellently set up for camping, with over 2000 campsites throughout, including several women-only sites.

I've really enjoyed the few camping-biking holidays I've been on as it's an activity in which all age groups and combinations of people are involved, and therefore a good way of feeling part of the place.

One of the most memorable trips I made was a boating holiday on the canals of Friesland in North Holland. Four of us hired an old-fashioned *tjalk*, a sort of flat-bottomed houseboat and set off for a few weeks. We did, however, meet with a lot of sexist flak, even if it was good-natured. Men worldwide seem to think that water is an exclusively male domain, and Dutchmen are no exception. The charter company nearly balked at hiring the boat out when they discovered I'd be the skipper, and men in the villages we stopped at along the way insisted on mooring us up so that it was done "properly". Apart from that it was still magical – there's something very special about the Dutch countryside from the water.

Basking in Tolerance

. . . .

Louise Simmons drove to Amsterdam in a dilapidated VW van, found a job as a secretary and stayed there for nine months. She is now working her way across South East Asia en route from India to Australia.

I left Britain in a flurry of snow and freezing winds. Having driven my fifteen-year-old VW Camper from Birmingham to Harwich in arctic conditions – and in a hurry – I could feel little more emotion at leaving my beloved homeland than relief that sensation was beginning to return to my numbed limbs. I wanted to spend the next few years (extendable) of my life working my way round the world, and chose The Netherlands as my first venture. I hoped to learn something more about this flat land of windmills and finger-in-dike fame (by the way, I never met a Dutch person who knew that story).

Why The Netherlands? It would perhaps be more appropriate to ask "Why Amsterdam?" and make a clear differentiation from the start. During a previous holiday there I'd fallen in love with the intimate atmosphere and romantic architecture of the city; narrowly missed falling in one of the many canals; and had come away with an impression of a laid-back paradise for (ex-)hippies and all lovers of moral and racial freedom. There are reputed to be more different nationalities living in Amsterdam than in any other European city. I have to admit that my own rose-tinted memories, coupled with assurances from a woman friend living there of limitless employment, and an awareness of pro-people legislation from the Sixties had created an idealistic image of the city which seemed unlikely to survive. My woman friend, of Liverpool origin, talked keenly of the equal status of women and the ease of living happily and safely in a single state.

Anyway, I was in such an optimistic mood that not even the manic lurchings of ferry and stomach could upset me. The drive from Hoek van Holland to Amsterdam was relatively trouble-free. For the majority of the time I managed to stay on the right side of the road and trundled through beautifully clean towns and villages, low houses hugging the flat land and canals everywhere I looked.

Living and working as a foreigner in Holland is, in practice, not quite as straightforward as the EC would have us believe. You need an "Eligible for Employment" stamp in your passport to obtain legal employment, which you get from the Foreign Police office. This is a routine procedure (a lengthy wait being the main inconvenience) but you need to have an official residential address (not a hostel) in order to qualify. This can all too easily throw you into the "no money = no flat = no job = no money" pit.

The flat agencies were my first brush with anyone in "authority" in Holland and it was a refreshing experience. Everything was direct and open with none of the patronising comments and questions I've come to expect in these situations. Couples are rarely questioned about their marital status; all Dutch women are automatically the equivalent of "Mrs" after eighteen; and I was told that there was little overt discrimination against gay couples. I had the same positive experience with the private landlord, from whom I finally rented a small studio flat that had been advertised (in English!) in a newspaper.

It just remained to find work! The majority of legal jobs for non-Dutch-speaking women are in the hotel and catering industry – the same exploitative labour as in any other country, but with the comfort of an official (and rigidly enforced) minimum wage. Plodding round job agencies was a depressing task. Not surprisingly, many are loath to consider non-Dutch speakers in view of their own worsening economic situation. I eventually found a job with an academic publishing company (having luckily walked into the right place at the right time) and prepared myself to face the horrors of an office environment.

Living in Amsterdam was surprisingly easy. Virtually everyone can speak English, but this has its drawbacks. Although I took Dutch lessons and spoke Dutch whenever I could, I encountered a problem that seemed common to many foreigners, even those who'd been living in Amsterdam for many years. If people hear an English accent they will often switch into English – and the chances are that their English is far better than your Dutch. Unfortunately, I also found that in Amsterdam the response from shop-keepers to broken, slowly-spoken Dutch is not as friendly as when you just speak English and they assume you're a tourist. But travelling in the more rural areas of The Netherlands my limited knowledge of Dutch did help, and it was warmly welcomed at work where, with justification, my Dutch colleagues sometimes felt like foreigners in their own country.

Working in a Dutch office was a sharp contrast to what I had known in England. The Dutch women were all strong-minded, independent people and, although it would be hard to say which was cause and which effect, there were none of the inter-sex power games that have infuriated me in English offices. Never once was I asked to make coffee by some smiling male superior. Never once was I assumed to have less intelligence than my typewriter. Never once was I verbally "patted on the head" for my apparently amazing ability to do the most mundane of tasks. (Never ever was I patted on any other part of my anatomy!)

"I sought out women's cafés and spent some peaceful, friendly evenings in the **Saarein**, *one of the best known of the women-only bars"*

Instead, women and men dealt with each other as colleagues and hierarchy was kept to a minimum. Dress was casual with people wearing whatever they felt most comfortable in. It seemed to me that the Dutch had grasped the point, still missed by many in English commercial life, that a woman doesn't have to wear a skirt and nylons for her brain to function. As such, the office was both cheerful and colourful.

People I met were friendly and helpful and, whilst it was very easy to fall into English-speaking cliques due to the number of English, Irish and Scottish people living in Amsterdam, I did have Dutch women friends who were enthusiastic to include me in their lives. If you live there long enough to have a reasonable grasp of Dutch, there are numerous political, spiritual or environmental organisations and a strong network of women's groups that you can tap into.

The rights of the individual was one of the things that struck me most during my nine months in The Netherlands. People know their rights and, on the whole, seem to respect others'. If I wanted to sit on the pavement and watch the world go by, I could. The police, whilst cutting a frightening figure with guns strapped to thighs, seemed far more interested in towing away illegally-parked cars than hassling harmless drifters.

Women held hands and kissed. Men held hands and kissed. Couples, regardless of colour and age differences, seemed able to show affection in public. I sought out women's cafés and spent some peaceful, friendly evenings in the *Saarein*, one of the best known of the women-only bars (Elandsgracht 119), but this was some way from where I lived in the eastern part of the city and I soon discovered that I could as easily sit and read a book without harassment (if I felt like solitude rather than sisterhood) in a mixed café as in a single-sex one. This didn't mean I was pointedly ignored, but if people spoke to me it was generally in a chatty, friendly manner without any sexual overtones. I travelled freely on my own late at night, but perhaps it is wrong to draw too many conclusions from this: my own conditioning leads me to avoid places or situations I have come to regard as "dangerous".

It took a while to realise that my mood of well-being was due in part to the atmosphere pervading the capital. As opposed to the rat-race of English cities where most people you see look preoccupied, or, at least, determinedly pursuing some goal, people in Amsterdam seemed more relaxed. The rich/poor divide is not as visually apparent as it is in the UK and, as far as

I could gather from my Dutch friends, the standard of living was generally quite high – taxes might be heavier but then there are more benefits available.

"Whilst frightened of the dark alleyways and bodies leaning in doorways, I was only ever hassled as a consumer, urged to buy some drugs"

This must sound as though I was living in some socialist paradise for nine months. Indeed not. The Netherlands is as capitalistic and consumerist as Britain and the two countries have much in common ideologically. Some older (and younger) members of the Dutch community that I met were voicing just the same prejudices about colour and sexuality that you come across in the UK. In the red light district, women's bodies are readily available for men's pleasure and it seemed to me that adjacent windows were offering animal flesh and female flesh for sale with very little discrimination. Whilst perhaps preferable to the street-corner hypocrisy of English prostitution, the extent to which this fundamentally exploitative industry has taken root in the city came as a shock.

From my own point of view, however, whilst frightened of the dark alleyways and bodies leaning in doorways, I was only ever hassled as a consumer, urged to buy some drugs. Thankfully, a "no" was always enough. But I only felt safe when I was back in the better-lit and busier streets of the city, away from the rows of neon flashing lights promising "real fucky fucky".

Of all the happy days I spent there, one deserves a special mention. The 30th April is "Queen's Day". This is the Queen's official birthday, but it is certainly not royal pageantry. The whole city is a "free market" on that day and, from dawn to dusk, the streets are full of makeshift stalls or flung-down blankets offering every conceivable sort of item for sale. The smell of foods from many different parts of the world hangs in the air, buskers are out in force and bands, whether reggae or classical, play well into the night. This is Glastonbury in the city, but what amazed me most of all was that, despite the heaving crowds, I never had a moment's worry about drunken violence or street aggression.

TRAVEL NOTES

Language Dutch. But very many people speak fluent English, German and French.

Transport Easy in such a compact country: bus and train routes complement each other and stations are usually adjacent. Hitching is good. Bikes can be hired at all main train stations.

Accommodation Hotels are expensive: pensions less so. In Amsterdam and other cities you'll find *Sleep-ins*, dormitory accommodation heavily subsidised by local councils, and some Youth-Student hotels. There are also a few women-only hotels, guesthouses and campsites (see listings below).

Special Problems The only area where you are likely to experience street harassment is the Amsterdam red light district. There's a growing number of foreign women who get immersed in the Amsterdam drugs scene and resort to prostitution to support their habit. Outside of Amsterdam attitudes are noticeably more conservative – you could feel uncomfortable expressing lesbian sexuality. Bicycle stealing is big business in Holland, especially in Amsterdam (use the bike-pound at the Central Station); there are pickpockets working the Amsterdam's trams.

Guides *The Rough Guide: Amsterdam* (Harrap Columbus) gives an excellent run-through of everything you might need to know about the capital and environs. *The Rough Guide: Holland, Belgium and Luxembourg* (Harrap Columbus) contains a thorough section.

Contacts

Although there are many feminist and lesbian groups throughout The Netherlands they are not necessarily open to casual visitors. Unless you've lived in the country for some time your contacts will mainly be limited to other foreigners. There are however, plenty of **women's centres, bookshops, cafés and bars** that are open to newcomers, only a selection of which are listed below.

Amsterdam

Vrouwenhuis, Nieuwe Herengracht 95. Women's Centre. The best overall contact for local groups and campaigns. Hosts all kinds of cultural events, including regular rock'n'roll

Xantippe, Prinsengracht 290, ☎235854 (closed Sun and Mon). The capital's main feminist bookshop and a good source of local information.

Internationaal Archief voor de Vrouwenbeweging, Keizersgracht 10, ☎244268. International archives for the Women's Movement. Also acts as a referral service for women's studies.

Amazone, Singel 72, ☎279000 (closed Sundays and Mondays). Women's contemporary art gallery and exhibition centre.

COC, National Gay Centre, Rozenstraat 14, ☎268300. Information centre with some congenial bars and a women-only disco on Saturday nights.

Café Saarein, Elandsstraat 119, 1016 RX, ☎234901; **Bar Vivelavie**, Amstelstraat 7. Two of the best known women-only bars.

Françoise, Kerkstraat 176, ☎240145. A women-only café with art gallery and music. Serves lunches as well as snacks.

Amsterdam has a few **hotels and guesthouses** which welcome gay women. None of them are cheap. You could try **The Quentin Hotel** Leidsekade 89, 1017, ☎262187; **ITC Hotel** Prisengracht 1051, 1017 JE, ☎20 230230; and **Hotel New York**, Herengracht 13, ☎243066.

Elsewhere

THE HAGUE: **Vrouwenhuis** (Women's House), Prins Hendrikstraat 33, ☎653844. A meeting place and information centre. **Trix** (feminist bookshop), Prinsestraat 122, ☎645014.

UTRECHT: **Savannah Bay** (feminist bookshop and women's bar), Teelingstraat 13, ☎314410.

ROTTERDAM: **Vrouwencafé Omnoord** (women's café), Sigrid Unsedweg 100, ☎212722. **Krities Boekwerk** (feminist bookshop), Nieuw Binnenweg 115a, ☎4364412.

Camping Holidays

For **women-only camping** contact *Vrouwenkampeerplaats de Hooimijt*, Pieterzijlsterweg 4, 9844 TA, Pieterzijl, Groningen, ☎05948 357. They have a large house with rooms for rent and a number of tents already set up. You can also rent bicycles and boats.

Books

Anja Meulenbelt et al., *A Creative Tension: Exploration in Socialist Feminism* (Pluto Press, 1985). Writings of Dutch feminists ranging across the socialist feminist debate.

Marga Minco, *The Glass Bridge* (Peter Owen, 1989) and *An Empty House* (Peter Owen, 1990). First British publication of a popular saga following the life of a Dutch Jewish woman during and immediately after the second world war.

Anja Meulenbelt, *The Shame is Over* (The Women's Press, 1980). Introspective account of becoming a feminist.

Journals

Katijf, Postbus 16572, Amsterdam 10001 RB, ☎020 240382. A bi-monthly socialist-feminist magazine with articles and events.

Lover (pronounced Lowver), Keizersgracht 10, 1015 CN Amsterdam. Review and resources quarterly for the Women's Movement (Dutch and foreign).

Opzij, Raamgracht 4, 1011 KK Amsterdam, ☎10 262375. Feminist monthly.

Lesbian Information Booklet, COC-Magazijn, Rosenstraat 8, 1016 NJ Amsterdam. Annual directory of lesbian resources throughout The Netherlands.

New Zealand

N ew Zealand (Aotearoa) comprises two main islands – North and South – as well as the much smaller Stewart and Chatham Islands. Despite the huge distances separating it from Europe and America, strong links are retained with both, although increasingly the cultural influence of the Pacific is replacing these traditional ties.

Almost all of the indigenous Maori population live on the North Island. Maori society is tribal, traditionally associated in complete harmony with land and sea, and tied closely to the bonds of family life and the village community. Although far more integrated into white European immigrant (*pakeha*) society than, say, the Australian Aboriginals, Maori society has been badly disrupted by rapid urbanisation. Together with age-old land grievances, high unemployment, discrimination in work and education, and low standards of health and housing have contributed to the rapid acceleration of Maori protest in recent years.

New Zealand is a great place if you like the outdoor life. The countryside is wild and beautiful, far more varied than the common image of acres of grazing sheep would suggest. Many travellers are struck by the variety of terrain – mountain, lake and seashore often lie within close proximity. New Zealanders themselves are widely regarded as hospitable and it's generally safe to travel around alone, though hitching on your own is not recommended. Another area for caution is pubs; any unaccompanied woman entering a pub can expect persistent pestering from men, who will refuse to accept that you are not on the look-out for male company.

There is a remarkably strong **women's movement** in New Zealand, illustrated by a range of organisations from Maori women's groups to broad-based women's resource centres and groups working to support the current Labour government's anti-nuclear stance. Campaigns against French nuclear testing and the dumping of nuclear waste in the Pacific are widely supported – particularly as pressure from Britain and the US mounts for New Zealand to abandon its anti-nuclear policy in the Pacific.

Back to the "Home Country"

· · · · · · · · · · · · ·

Amanda Gaynor is British, though, having a New Zealand mother, she was brought up with tales of the "home country". After an initial visit as a teenager, she returned to spend three years living in Auckland, where she worked as a teacher in a large multicultural school.

A customary vision of New Zealand is sheep, burly farmers, thick-set Maori performing *poi* dances and "tourist" *haka*, all backdropped by magnificent rugged scenery. This is the way the country has been marketed, as a kind of outdoor wonderland accompanied by the quaint anachronisms of a cosy "never, never land Britain" of forty years ago. In fact, this was pretty much my impression on my first trip to New Zealand eight years ago at the age of eighteen.

Returning to teach presented me with much more of a paradox. I had a sense of a country in limbo, moving uncomfortably away from its colonial heritage and struggling to emerge as a Pacific nation – compelled to do so, in fact, by dwindling European markets if

not desire. Nowhere is this tension between the Pacific and the European felt more keenly than in the northern North Island city of Auckland, which is now billed as the largest Polynesian city in the world. The city sprawls in an ungainly fashion across a complex network of harbours and inlets, creating an atmosphere of disunity. Yet a broad division between north and south Auckland persists, the former being mainly European and the latter predominantly Polynesian. In general terms, the difference is that between wealth and poverty and respectively low and high unemployment.

I have a New Zealand mother (although I was born and brought up in Britain) and was raised on her Elysian belief in the myth of racial harmony between black and white in New Zealand. So a part of what interested me in coming to this country was to try to gain an insight into the practice of race relations. Owing to the current teacher shortage, I had no problems picking up work in a large, multicultural and rigidly streamed school.

It was immediately apparent that the Maori and Pacific Island pupils made up the majority in classes at the lower end of the ability range (clearly reflecting a discriminatory system) and were hardly present in the top three bands. I was even more startled by the low expectations that many Islander and Maori girls had of themselves; that marrying and having children would take the place of a career. Indeed, for many, the concept of a career hardly figured and the stereotype of homemaker was strongly endorsed by the boys.

However, as I began to understand the differing structures upon which their family groupings were based, I began to question whether it would be appropriate for me to impose upon these children a Western feminist ideal of what constitutes freedom. Historically, Maori women have always held an important and publicly recognised role as homemakers within the *marae* (meeting house). They are endorsed and commended within Maori art as powerful, fertile lifegivers – as women they are creators.

So, it seems that although the urban Maori may have moved away from the traditional lifestyle, they carry with them a cultural heritage of strong womanhood which is then in danger of negation by Western liberal concepts of equality – a system that condemns large families and urges material success in a competitive society.

"European reserve can often be interpreted as rudeness"

By contrast, it has been interesting to step outside my own niche and to go to the mainly Polynesian preserve of the Otara market in South Auckland. The somewhat inauspicious setting of a supermarket car park soon fades amidst the thronging mass of people out shopping and socialising on a Saturday morning. Here, amongst piles of *puha* (a popular edible green) and long earthy kava roots, Samoan music blares and little English is spoken. For me it is the chance to feel in the minority and to catch a glimpse of another way of living. Few white people use the market and, until I started taking my nine-month-old son, I was treated with caution. It was partly because I stood

out and partly because European reserve can often be misinterpreted as rudeness by more outward-going Polynesian people. But now, accompanied by Daniel in backpack, I find a tacit support, especially from women, and a more open friendliness.

Another area in which to experience differing cultures is at the local beach; here an unwritten apartheid seems to operate, whereby black and white gravitate to opposite ends, perhaps because the former tend to come for family picnics and the latter for water sports like jet-skiing. Amongst the picnicking, garlanded Samoans it is rare to find women bathing with their legs uncovered once they have reached puberty, as thighs are regarded as erogenous. From respect I often wrap a towel around me, dropping it only at the water's edge. I enjoy the sense of festivity of these beach outings and the feeling of large family groups settling in for the day with their rugs, windbreaks, fires and volleyball nets.

Yet it is not only the contrast between European and Pacific to which I have had to adapt but also the unexpected differences between me and *pakeha* (white) New Zealanders. "We share the same language but that's about all", was the way one woman put it to me. Again I found fundamental differences in the way we communicated and I am sure that, at times, what I construed as rudeness was in fact a blunter kind of directness with which I was unfamiliar. There are fewer codes of courtesy here, gushing thanks are seldom forthcoming, and consequently I have at times been left feeling taken for granted when this was not the intention. Likewise in performing public transactions it took me quite some time to get away from the "excuse me . . . I wonder if you could possibly tell/help me . . . ?" to the more colloquial and perfunctory "hey, where's the . . . ?". People often visibly stiffened to the former, whereas I was greeted with warm helpfulness by the latter.

Once accustomed to this, I discovered that I made better progress. In my discussions with women I noted frequent reference to the "Kiwi male", often accompanied by a disparaging shrug of the shoulders. When pressed, women are particularly critical of what they view as (white) men's inability to express themselves on an emotional plane and their reluctance to analyse their actions. Many women argue that, by and large, men still maintain traditional attitudes to women. Certainly, from staff-room conversations, I was surprised by the number of women who were still expected to bear sole responsibility for looking after the home, in addition to full-time jobs. But to me the problems seemed comparable to those in England, and the New Zealand Women's Movement correspondingly active and vocal.

"By and large, men still maintain traditional attitudes to women"

What is evident is the solidarity that exists between women in New Zealand. There is a strong sense of companionship that seems to spring from the old pioneer settler mentality. Indeed, there is a practicality about New Zealand women that is reflected in the most popular of the women's magazines, the *New Zealand Women's Weekly*. I have been impressed by the breadth of articles that it runs and the refreshing absence of romantic pap. Women I have spoken to suggest that it is because they are interested in the real issues affecting their lives rather than in escapist fantasies centred on men.

New Zealand is diverse in its facilities for women. In Auckland and other major cities there are women's centres, women-only discos and women's reading rooms at the university. Yet in the rural areas it is not uncommon to receive an invitation to, say, a dance, with the peculiar addendum "and ladies a plate". I was mystified by this on my first encounter but my host explained

to me that it was the woman's responsibility to provide the food. Such traditions die hard in rural communities and the division of labour within the farming sector remains largely clear-cut, with the woman staying in and around the home, preparing food for the men. On farms I have visited it was unusual to see men do more than make a cup of tea when at home. Change is certainly coming, but slowly.

In my travels around both North and South Island I have been astounded by the warmth of strangers toward me. People are eager to meet foreigners and have been happy to go out of their way to help me. But sadly it is no longer as safe as it once was for women to hitch alone, and this is particularly true of more remote areas of the South Island, where there has been an increase in the occurrence of violent rape.

However, there is only one situation in which I have felt directly threatened by men, and that is on my own in pubs. Pubs tend to be utilitarian drinking houses with plastic seating and glaring overhead lighting. They are generally male dominated and the arrival of a sole woman seldom passes without notice. There's the overwhelming assumption that you have come to meet a man, and polite rebuffs are frequently ignored. Men in this situation can be persistent and will sometimes involve others in the bar into the goading of the "reluctant" woman. If possible, it is better to arrange to meet somewhere more neutral and then go on to a pub in a group. Having said this, there are of course pubs where there are more convivial atmospheres and lively bands.

One good way, I found, of discovering what there is to offer in Auckland is to look at the noticeboards of the numerous small health-food cafés. Here I have found adverts for feminist flatshares, womanlines, notices for various discussion groups and alternative women's medicine. If you're looking for accommodation this is an easy place to start and far less bewildering than the reams of adverts in the Saturday *New Zealand Herald*. For me, living in New Zealand for the past two years has been "a looking-glass" experience, by turns frustrating and rewarding. What has been satisfying is the chance to get away from the image of a little England in the South Pacific and come to a recognition of New Zealand as a poly-glot society, striving to achieve a distinct identity. But it is an identity beleaguered at present by an insecure heritage of racial tensions and restrained by the desire to look back to Europe for national origins – as symbol-ised in the plethora of mock-Elizabethan motels that greet you on the journey from the airport.

"Whose side do you think I'm on?"

. . . .

Viki Radden is a black American, currently living in Japan, where she is working on her first novel, due for publication in 1990. She has both lived and worked in New Zealand.

I first went to New Zealand for love. While living in San Francisco, I fell in love with a man who lived there, and after he returned to New Zealand, I quit school and followed him back. I had certain preconceptions. As everyone knows, New Zealand is an agricultural country, and you see more sheep there in one day than in an entire lifetime else-where. I expected to see green, rolling hills; long, endless beaches on the North Island, and alps and fjords on the South; and I was not disappointed. For physical beauty, few countries can equal New Zealand. Two things I did not expect to see, however, were a thriv-ing Women's Movement and a strong indigenous struggle among the Maori, the native Polynesians of New Zealand.

Although racial tensions and prob-lems exist (and they're getting worse rather than better), New Zealand is still serene and safe when compared with other Western countries. It was refresh-ing to be able to come and go virtually free of the debilitating fear of violence that haunts me as a black American woman. I had a feeling during my last visit, however, in 1989, that New Zealand society is now at a critical point in its history. The country is either going to have to extricate itself from its problems – including the new phenom-enon of unemployment – or go into an acute tailspin. In 1988, more than 38,000 New Zealanders left the country, hoping for better times in Australia, where jobs are more plentiful, and where the rights of the Aborigines are so restricted that it is easy for whites to lull themselves into thinking that there is no "race problem".

For the visitor, New Zealand is an ideal country in which to travel. Getting around is easy; there are good bus and train services, and hitchhiking, though always risky, is generally a breeze. Picking up seasonal jobs is no problem either. Though New Zealand govern-ment policy states that visitors who enter the country on a tourist visa are not allowed to work, jobs like fruit pick-ing (in Hawke's Bay, Northland and Central Otago) and sheep shearing are relatively easy to obtain. Employers, as well as the government, seem to turn a blind eye to the rules when it comes to this type of employment.

There are also few problems in trav-elling alone. A well-established women's community makes it easy to forge contacts. All one needs to do is visit one of the feminist bookstores, located in Auckland, Hamilton, Wellington and Christchurch; *Broadsheet*, a wonderful feminist magazine, is a good place for locating women doing political work. As an American, however, you should be prepared for the occasionally frosty reception. Americans are stereotypically viewed as arrogant, money-ridden, and ignorant about how to behave in this country. A particular cause of tension, during my visit, was the US government's threat to place an embargo on New Zealand exports, after it began refusing entry to nuclear-weaponed and nuclear-powered ships. New Zealanders are justly proud of their nuclear-free policy.

"People reacted first to my being an American and a tourist, and then to the fact that I was black"

My experience was in many ways representative of what might happen to any woman traveller who lives and works in New Zealand. People reacted first to my being an American and a tourist, and then to the fact that I was black. This was a new, but not altogether refreshing experience, as white New Zealanders would often complain to me about the Maori, using the same racist terminology I'd heard about black Americans back at home. They assumed that, since I was American, I would sympathise with their feelings. "Look at me," I told the boss of the blueberry orchard where I worked, when she complained that the Maori workers were likely to spend their pay cheques buying beer and marijuana and that they all were violent and carried knives. "Look at the colour of my skin. Whose side do you think I'm going to be on?"

There was one experience which both disturbed and frightened me. My lover and I were on the west coast of the South Island, a wild, beautiful and sparsely inhabited part of the country. In an incident which I can't help believing was racially motivated, a car with two surly-looking men pulled alongside our car and, without the men saying a word, they stayed beside us for miles, sneering and brandishing a tyre-iron at us.

I had some experiences which changed my life, most notably through my contact with Maori women. I was able to go to several *hui* meetings on Maori land, where problems affecting the Maori community were discussed. The most inspiring of these was a national black women's rape crisis *hui*, followed by an all-women's music concert. Maori events are commonplace in New Zealand but a visitor will be lucky indeed if she is allowed to participate in them. Through this contact, I was able to gain some first-hand knowledge of the deplorable living and working conditions of the Maori – something every visitor should be made aware of.

Time spent in New Zealand will certainly be worthwhile. The sheer beauty of the scenery, most of it pristine and unpolluted, will lighten the spirit and infuse new energy into one's life. Eating is a joy. Never have I tasted such delicious fruit and fresh vegetables; the milk and cream are the best in the world. There really is nothing quite like the thrill of sitting alone on a beautiful beach in the middle of summer, slowly licking an ice cream cone so delicious that it must have been dropped straight from heaven.

TRAVEL NOTES

Languages English and Maori.

Transport The two islands are connected by ferry between Picton and Wellington. If you can afford the hire, a camper van is much the best way of seeing the country. Trains are limited, but buses operate to most outlying areas and quite a few women hitch, though seldom alone.

Accommodation Hotels, lodges and hostels (with dormitories or private rooms) are reasonably priced by Western, or Australian, standards. Camping is very popular and many motor camps have cabins and caravans for hire as well as providing camping facilities.

Guide *New Zealand – A Travel Survival Kit* (Lonely Planet) is practical and comprehensive.

Contacts

The main feminist magazine is *Broadsheet*, based in Auckland. Individual groups include:

AUCKLAND: **The Women's Bookshop**, 228 Dominion Rd., ☎608 583. **Auckland Women's Health Collective**, 63 Ponsonby Rd., ☎764 506/766 838. **Lesbian Support Group**, PO Box 47-090, Ponsonby Rd., ☎888 325. **West Auckland Women's Centre**, 11 McLeod Rd., Henderson., ☎836 6381. **Womanline** (telephone information and referral service), open Mon–Thurs, 9am–noon, 6–9pm, ☎765-173.

CHRISTCHURCH: **Kate Sheppard Women's Bookshop**, 145 Manchester St., ☎790 784. **Lesbian Line**, ☎794 796. **The Health Alternative for Women** (THAW), ☎796 970.

DUNEDIN: **Lesbian Line**, Mondays, 7.30–10 pm, ☎778 765. **Women's Resource Centre** (books, space, coffee), Room 10, Regent Chambers, Octagon.

HAMILTON: **Dimensions Women's Bookshop**, NZI Arcade, Garden Place, ☎80 656.

NEW PLYMOUTH: **Women's Centre**, Liardet St., ☎82 407.

PALMERSTON NORTH: **Women's Shop** (books, music, arts), Square Edge, PO Box 509.

TAURANGA: **Women's Centre**, 92 Devonport Rd., ☎783 530.

WELLINGTON: **Access Radio** (783 khz), Woman Zone 10am Sundays, Lesbian programme 11am. Contact the collective via Radio NZ, ☎721 777. **Lesbian Line**, Tues–Thurs, 7–10pm, ☎898 082.

Books

Lady Barker, *Station Life in New Zealand* (Virago, 1984). First published in 1870, this is a classic story of early colonial life told with warmth and a real feeling of adventure.

Claudia Orange, *The Treaty of Waitangi* (Allen and Unwin, 1988). An award-winning account of the history and implications of the treaty signed by the British government and the Maori in 1840, which gave British sovereignty to New Zealand – an important book for understanding the roots of current Maori grievances.

The Maori of New Zealand (Minority Rights Group Report, No 70, 1986). Excellent background to Maori history and grievances up to the present. Obtainable from good bookshops or MRG, 36 Craven Street, London WC2N 5NG.

Fiction

Keri Hulme, *The Bone People* (Picador, 1985). Extraordinary semi-autobiographical novel weaving in Maori myth, custom and magic, and a wonderful evocation of place. Originally published by a New Zealand feminist co-operative it went on to win the British Booker Prize and international distribution.

Janet Frame, *Owls Do Cry, Living in the Maniototo* (The Women's Press, 1985, 1990), and others. Often psychological novels by arguably New Zealand's finest writer. Also look out for her autobiography in three volumes, starting with *To the Is-Land* (The Women's Press, 1985), a haunting tale of growing up in the New Zealand of the 1920s and 1930s.

Rosie Scott, *Glory Days* (The Women's Press, 1988). A gritty, hard-hitting thriller set in Auckland's underworld, and with a marvellously realised heroine.

MacDonald Jackson and Vincent O'Sullivan, eds., *New Zealand Writing Since 1945* (Oxford University Press, 1983). A collection of prose and poetry which brings together the work of many of New Zealand's finest contemporary writers.

Yvonne du Fresne, *The Bear from the North* (The Women's Press, 1989). Spirited stories of pioneering days in New Zealand through the eyes of a child.

Nicaragua

At the time of going to press, Nicaragua is braced for a change of government. The ruling Sandinistas' ten-year struggle to uphold the momentum of revolution against persistent US-backed destabilisation has ended in a surprise electoral defeat. True to his reputation for political integrity, the Sandinista leader Daniel Ortega has pledged to respect the popular mandate and support a process of peace and reconciliation under the new government – to be formed by the politically obscure Violeta Chamorro, "moderate" leader of the broad and disparate coalition party, UNO. How she will manage to reconcile the conflicting claims of commu-

nist and ultra-right factions within her alliance (or contend with the strong Sandinista support within the army and police) is hard to imagine. The only certainty to conjure with is that the US will lift trade sanctions, withdraw from the *contra* war and provide some degree of aid.

For the last decade travel to Nicaragua has taken the form of a personal political statement of solidarity with the Revolution. The country itself had become a powerful symbol of resistance to US intervention and of self-determination in Central America. Foreigners arrived to contribute much-needed skills and labour, or to learn from the initiatives taken in land reform and the massive improvements taken in health and education provisions. As it was assumed that you had a purpose in being in Nicaragua you were unlikely to be considered an oddity travelling alone. Transport and accommodation were cheap, if not the most comfortable. *Machismo* was still prevalent, despite the impressive participation of women in the Revolution, but there was little threat of sexual harassment.

Now that the impetus to express solidarity has gone it seems unlikely that war-torn Nicaragua will get many foreign visitors. It's certainly too early to tell how travellers will be welcomed under the new administration.

The huge involvement of **women in the Nicaraguan Revolution** – at one stage they made up thirty percent of the army including some in high command – has made it a case study for feminists and women in national liberation movements everywhere. Nicaragua has long had an independent women's organisation. Since 1978 this has been the Luisa Amanda Espinoza Nicaraguan Women's Association (AMNLAE), bearing the name of the first women to be killed in the battle against Somoza. At AMNLAE's third congress in 1987, the ruling FSLN presented a policy document stating that discrimination against women would not be "put off or separated from defence of the Revolution" and that *machismo* and other elements had to be immediately combatted as they "inhibit the development of the whole society". AMNLAE was subsequently reorganised and acquired a new status as a "movement" instead of an organisation. The new brief was to work more closely at a regional level within mass organisations, such as trade unions, the Sandinista Youth movement, agrarian workers' co-operatives and the neighbourhood-based Sandinista Defence Committees, including having representatives in each at an executive level. It was also decided to open women's centres (*Casas de la Mujer*) in all regions to offer training courses and provide a focal point for organising social activities. Again we have no notion how this will change under the new administration. AMNLAE is, however, likely to continue its work in opposition.

The piece below was written before the 1990 election. We felt that in its description of Managua life it would have some enduring relevance.

Welcome to the Republic of Sandino

. . . .

Helen Tetlow spent three months working at the University of America in Nicaragua's capital, Managua.

"Nicaragua will get into your blood," said the voice at the other end of the phone, one of a number of people who asked me to deliver letters in Managua, the only sure way of knowing that mail would arrive. I was due to leave in four days and in too much of a panic about an overnight stay in Miami, a five-hour wait in Honduras (where lengthy questioning of passengers in transit to Nicaragua is not unknown), and about coping with the heat and humidity of Managua, to feel particularly reassured. But she was right.

Probably the main reason I was going to Nicaragua was that it had "got into the blood" of a good friend who had taken out my CV to the university in Managua. Until then I had only felt passive curiosity about this small Central American country whose

Revolution had survived despite all efforts by the US to destroy it; I also had a rather vague notion that I wanted to use my teaching skills in a country which not only desperately needed them, but which was committed to building a society based on socialist principles.

I had been reasonably well briefed about what to expect before I went but, as most of my previous travelling had been confined to fairly developed countries, no amount of words describing the hardship, the food shortages, the minimal transport system and the poverty could have prepared me for the culture shock of my first night in Managua.

"'It's like Los Angeles after the holocaust.' A friend's description of the capital was beginning to make sense"

My very first feeling, however, was of tremendous relief. I had arrived safely without becoming a Miami crime statistic and with nothing more threatening in Honduras than a sticky, five-hour, non air-conditioned wait in Tegucigalpa departure lounge. Then came optimism and excitement as I stepped off the plane to face the enormous placard, "Welcome to the Republic of Sandino".

I joined my first long, slow-moving Nicaraguan queue to change the statutory sixty dollars into córdobas. Like many transactions in Nicaragua, this was done without modern technology and took a frustratingly long time. At last I wandered out into the concourse to see if anyone from the university had got hold of a car and enough petrol to come and meet me. They hadn't. Not, it later transpired, because of petrol rations, but because my letter giving arrival times had not arrived and, like several envelopes of tea bags and cassettes, never did.

As I took my first step out of the air-conditioned airport building into the hot, soupy Managuan night, and peered through the extremely minimal street lighting at a couple of very derelict-looking taxis standing on a road with more holes than surface, I wondered with despair where on earth I had come to. "It's like Los Angeles after the holocaust." A friend's description of the capital was beginning to make sense.

This lack of someone to meet me could have been very unnerving, but I had got talking with four other *internacionalistas* on the plane (two Canadian students and two North American nuns) and shared a taxi with the students to a *hospedaje* (hostel) where they had stayed on a previous visit. It's worth saying that you are unlikely ever to feel isolated travelling alone in Nicaragua. There are a large number of people from many different countries working in solidarity on short and long term projects, making it relatively easy to find a hitching, room or taxi companion with whom you are likely to have something in common.

After the US$48 a night Miami motel room with king sized beds, knee-deep carpet, colour TV, private bathroom with courtesy shampoo and conditioner, the Managua *hospedaje*, which was to be my home for the next three weeks, was a shock. We entered what looked like an untidy back yard surrounded by ramshackle huts.

I remember thinking that I would soon be able to take my crippling rucksack off and then standing paralysed when I was shown my room: bare brick and plasterboard walls, a dusty concrete floor, a tin roof which didn't quite keep out the tropical rain, two very old bedsteads with thin, old, lumpy mattresses, a rickety table and stool, and a piece of string tied across the room to hang my clothes on. I was hot and sticky from a day's travelling in the tropics, but still too accustomed to tiled bathrooms to venture out into one of the unlit tin shower cubicles, where the water supply was a sawn-off pipe running across the top and you could only guess at what insects might be lurking inside.

My stomach turned over many times during my first few days in Managua as I acclimatised from the relative material comfort of my life in London to the hardship and poverty here. I'm glad that I kept a diary to record my first impressions of things which so quickly became familiar. Things which shocked me, like the poor *barrios* (neighbourhoods) with houses built of scraps of wood and metal; pigs and barefoot children everywhere; cars with doors and windows missing, held together with bits of wire; small pick-up trucks bouncing over enormous pot-holes with sometimes thirty people standing in the back, drenched to the skin by a tropical downpour.

And there was my leaky room in the *hospedaje* which soon became home. Here I met *internacionalistas* from Iceland, Finland, West Germany, the USA, Switzerland, involved in anything from journalism and printing to health-care. I was sorry to leave when I eventually found a room in a university colleague's house.

"I lived in Managua for three months and I would say, without hesitation, that it is the most unmanageable city I have ever visited"

Besides the shock, there were aspects of Nicaragua which I found mesmerising: the beauty of the landscape with its volcanos and lagunas; the giant, lush foliage; people's faces with their mixture of Indian, Spanish and African blood; walls covered in political slogans or reminders of vaccination campaigns so that walking round Managua was like walking through a social history book; the enormous billboards with posters about breastfeeding or slogans about the current political situations: "Reagan is going but the Revolution continues".

I lived in Managua for three months and I would say, without hesitation, that it is the most unmanageable city I have ever visited. Destroyed by an earthquake in 1972, severely bombed during the last months of the Somoza regime, what was apparently a beautiful capital city is now little more than a series of neighbourhoods separated by vast open spaces of scrub and joined by a network of very wide and dangerously pot-holed roads. It is unbelievably difficult to find your way around because very few of the roads have names, only about a third of the houses are numbered, and so addresses are calculated in blocks away from local landmarks: "Two blocks north, one block south of the shop selling yoghurt" or, even more difficult, "two blocks south, one block north from where the grey tank stood before the earthquake"!

Add to this the vast area now covered by Managua, the debilitating heat and humidity, the skeletal, desperately overcrowded and extremely erratic bus service, the almost non-existent street lighting in a city which is plunged into tropical darkness at 6.30pm, and you will begin to understand that coping with Managua is a bit of an endurance test.

I would not like to have arrived alone in Managua without relatively good Spanish and colleagues at the university to help me find my feet. Having said that, I did meet lone women travellers who, though unprepared, seemed fine having made contacts and discovered Managua "survival techniques" at the *hospedajes*.

Unless you have a car, travelling in Nicaragua is another endurance test. Because of the desperate economic situation, there are few buses and most of these are in bad condition. Usually packed beyond belief, they are rich hunting grounds for razor blade thieves. By day two in Managua, I had heard so many horror stories about rucksacks, bags and even moneybelts under shirts being slashed, that I made my first bus trip carrying nothing more than the two small coins I needed for the journey and a photocopy of my passport tucked in my knickers.

But I quickly mastered the art of bus travel: how to catapult myself on to a bus already bursting at the seams; how to have everything of value wrapped up in a thick towel inside my small rucksack which I would clasp manically to my chest; how to start preparing to worm my way off at least three stops in advance, and how to develop extrasensory perception about where to get off at night.

"When I hitched alone I didn't have any problems but I did worry, more about being robbed than being sexually harassed"

If you manage to get on a bus, it's a very cheap way of travelling, as is the train which runs between Leon, Managua and Granada. However, the trains have open carriages which means that passengers travelling in the dry season – from January to May – will arrive coated in a layer of dust and, if wearing contact lenses, with streaming eyes. Because of the dire public transport system hitching is very common, particularly at the weekends when many Nicaraguans hitch home to visit families. This can mean long hot or long wet waits.

My experience was that you get there in the end – even if it is on a horse or on the top of a truck load of logs! When I hitched alone I didn't have any problems but I did worry, more about being robbed than being sexually harassed. Nicaragua's desperate economic problems are leading to an increase in robbery, and *internacionalistas* with dollars are an obvious target.

The prospect of surviving alone in Nicaragua was in fact much more frightening than the reality. I had been worried about living in a country at war. However, working in Managua, with only the weekends for travel, meant

that I only visited the Pacific Coast side of the country, well away from the war zones, though I must admit that the *contra* ambushing of a civilian bus and boat put me off trying to squeeze in a visit to the north.

Of course, the effects of the war and the US economic blockade are all too evident. There is a huge military presence and all males over sixteen do two years compulsory military service. But strangely enough, unlike in other Central American countries and indeed Britain, I never felt at all threatened by the army or police in Nicaragua. The Sandinista soldiers really did seem to be the People's Army.

Once, hot, lost and dehydrated in Managua, a soldier walked me home. It's quite customary for army trucks to pick up groups of hitchers and one of my students, who had returned recently from military service, told me that as well as active defence work, he had been involved in literacy work and building projects in some of the villages.

The economy is a disaster, with the country's already battered human and economic resources having to be poured into the battle to maintain the Revolution. Inflation rockets from week to week. When I arrived in May 1988, the exchange rate was one dollar to eleven córdobas. By the time I left in September, it was one dollar to 400.

One week, petrol went up from seventeen to 175 córdobas a litre overnight and bread from ten to forty. The supermarkets and chemists closed without warning for a day to adjust all prices, and for two weeks before the government could implement and backdate a thirty percent salary increase for state workers, some of my Nicaraguan colleagues at the university (who were earning substantially more than school teachers, nurses, the police) were going without meals in order to feed their children.

"Quien sabe?" (Who knows?) is a typical Nicaraguan answer and I think for me it was the uncertainty that even the most basic aspects of daily life would continue to function, which made life so unnerving. There were daily power cuts, water cuts, tropical storms which would paralyse transport, no milk for two weeks, days when there would be little but cheap loo paper and plastic plates in the supermarket, and days when there would be three types of cheese and jelly – but no loo paper!

"I was astounded by the machismo of many Nicaraguan men"

Politics is never far away from any conversation. I heard many moving accounts of people's memories of the fight against Somoza, of participation in the mammoth literacy campaign in the six months after the Triumph when all the schools and universities were closed to release thousands of students and teachers to work in the villages. But I also found it depressing to hear many people, who clearly had been supporters of the Sandinistas, now criticising the government and looking for ways to leave Nicaragua – not because they don't support the basic principles of the Revolution, but because they've had enough hardship. The US may not be able to defuse the Revolution militarily, but economically they are having a profound effect.

I was astounded by the *machismo* of many Nicaraguan men. While producing children and thus proving virility seemed to be a major preoccupation, according to my women colleagues it is rare for a Nicaraguan man to offer any help in the house or with the children, and male infidelity is a hobby. Though I never exactly felt threatened on the streets of Managua, it was hard to take the constant stream of "my queen", "beauty", "my little love", either whispered or shouted by passing men. The women at work were amazed that I objected to these "compliments" and like everything else I got used to them.

The resilience, generosity and good nature of people (and especially women, who face seemingly endless hardship) was something I found extraordinary and inspiring. It is not uncommon for a mother to be supporting three children, possibly by different fathers. "How do you survive?" I asked one woman doing a full-time teaching job at the university, a part-time postgraduate course, and bringing up four children alone. "I make shorts in my spare time," she laughed. In one household to which I was invited to lunch, even though there wasn't enough cutlery to go round, the mother had lost her son in a *contra* ambush, been deserted by her husband and, despite her meagre income, had still adopted a five-year-old war orphan to bring up alongside her own daughters.

One of my students made a special six-hour journey to his mother's house to retrieve a silver pen, clearly one of his treasures, to give me as a farewell present. The pen was presented to me at a very impromptu party which nevertheless included a series of formal and very moving speeches. I was always struck by the Nicaraguans' ability to move from informality to formality without sounding either pompous or self-conscious. Perhaps this has something to do with the very important role poetry plays in this "land of poets". My students loved having parties, which were usually organised at about five minutes notice and always in the middle of the rum and salsa, someone would request a poem.

TRAVEL NOTES

Languages Spanish, with one of the harder accents to understand in Latin America. Creole-English is spoken by a minority on the Atlantic Coast.

Transport Buses are very cheap but over-crowded and uncomfortable. Beware of pickpockets on buses in Managua. Taxis are safe and reasonably cheap, though be sure to negotiate a price in advance. Hitching is very popular and reportedly safe.

Accommodation There are quite a few clean, cheap hotels or *hospedajes* in Managua, though they tend to fill up quickly. Elsewhere accommodation gets more and more basic the further you are from the capital.

Special Problems Dress modestly and avoid wearing shorts, not worn by Nicaraguans despite the intense heat. They are poor but proud dressers and always like to look clean and neat. Don't change money on the black market. It's illegal and there's little difference from the official rate. Bring dollars and make sure you change them into local currency in Managua as you'll only be charged the exorbitant "airport official rate" outside. Take a torch with you. Power cuts are frequent and you'll really appreciate having your own light.

Guide *The South American Handbook* (Trade and Travel Publications) has accurate but limited coverage.

Contacts

For up-to-date information and details of study tours, including a yearly two-week tour for women, contact the **Nicaragua Solidarity Campaign**, 23 Bevenden St., London N1 6BH, ☎071-253 2464. Also, **Progressive Tours**, 12 Porchester Place, London W2 2BS, ☎071-262 1676.

Any contact with women's groups is best made through the central office of **AMNLAE**, Apt. Postal A238, Managua.

Books

Adriana Angel and Fiona McIntosh, *The Tiger's Milk: Women of Nicaragua* (Virago, 1987). A photographic record of people's lives since the Revolution, backed up by testimonies from a range of Nicaraguan women.

Cain et al., *Sweet Ramparts* (NSC/War on Want, 1983). Traces the history of the Nicaraguan Revolution and assesses achievements and their limitations for women since 1979. Unfortunately out of print, but worth hunting for.

Margaret Randall, *Sandino's Daughters* (Zed Books, 1981). Tells the story of women's participation in the Revolution through a number of interviews made shortly after 1979.

For a general historical summary of Nicaraguan history up to that period, read **George Black, *Triumph of the People*** (Zed Books, 1981).

For an introduction to Nicaragua, it's also worth looking at the handbook ***Nicaraguans Talking*** by Duncan Green (LAB, 1989).

Special thanks to Marta Rodriguez for her contribution to the introduction and Travel Notes.

Nigeria

Nigeria has virtually no tourism. The difficulties of obtaining a visa, political instability, and the legendary armed robbers who roam the highways between cities are enough to put off all but the most determined traveller. However, those who do make it often find that the sheer vitality of the country, coupled with the overwhelming hospitality of the people, are enough to make them want to return.

In the thirty years since Independence, Nigeria's progress has been scarred by civil war, assassinations, plummeting oil revenues, economic crises and a succession of repressive mili-

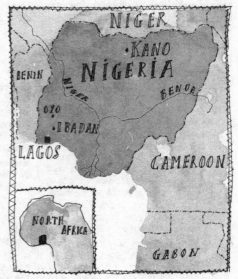

tary coups. Nigerians are a highly divided people, speaking over 200 languages, and there seems little chance of finding an enduring political solution to their tribal and ethnic conflicts. General Babangida, the current leader of the Armed Forces Ruling Council, has held power since the coup of 1985. While his commitment to widen political freedoms and open the way for national elections in 1990 has been welcomed, he faces considerable dissent over the introduction of widespread and stringent austerity measures – including a fourfold devaluation of the nation's currency.

Women, who have borne the brunt of high prices as consumers and as market traders, are often seen at the forefront of protest. In general, however, Nigerian **women's organisations** seem relatively moderate in their demands. The *Nigerian Council for Women's Societies*, one of the most established bodies, renamed the 1985 International Women's Day "Family Day" to reflect their priorities. These have barely changed. Although many of the women are middle class, professional, and financially independent (the group is often accused of elitism), marriage and bearing children are central to almost all their lives. An infertile woman is likely to be rejected by her husband and fall prey to the many private infertility clinics which advertise every few hundred yards along the roadside.

The country's most radical organisation is *WIN* (*Women in Nigeria*), which was launched in 1983 with the aim of overcoming women's problems within the context of the "exploitative and oppressive character of Nigerian society". Through a nationwide network of state branches and co-ordinators WIN is currently carrying out a plan of action on issues such as domestic violence, sexism in the media and in education, shared housework and childcare with men, and the need for non-sexist alternatives to government and institutional policies. Although men are incorporated into the organisational structure, this programme indicates a radical departure from the traditional, institutionalised and often church-based women's groups.

A Very Nigerian Coup

. . . .

Jane Bryce is white and in her early thirties. She went to Nigeria on a Commonwealth scholarship in order to research African women's writing at the University of Ile-Ife. She stayed five years, married a Nigerian and worked as a freelance journalist. Besides various trips to Lagos, to attend conferences and seminars, she travelled incessantly around the country.

I was so terrified of going to Nigeria that I drank heavily for a month beforehand and arrived in a state of advanced alcohol poisoning. The popular image abroad was of a country riven by extreme violence, lawlessness, and political infighting with a leadership held in place by bribery. I went, however, because I wanted to research a book on African women writers and had decided the best way was to enrol for a PhD at a Nigerian university.

I had lived in Africa before, in Tanzania, I had Nigerian friends, I had read books, but I still felt as if I was severing all ties and jumping off into the unknown, alone. And I was right. Nothing can prepare you for Nigeria; it simply isn't like anywhere else. Or if it is, it's so much bigger, so much more complex, varied, crowded and contradictory, that comparisons seem ludicrous.

Arriving at dawn, I felt utterly elated and totally exhausted. The sun rising red through the seasonal harmattan smog over Lagos, the palm trees, the unmistakable smell of Africa, of my childhood, hit me like a belly punch. I flung myself down by the hotel swimming pool and let the African sun drain the poisons from my body. I lay in a stupor all day, speaking to no one.

In the evening I got dressed and ventured out on to the street. It was New Year's Eve and I wanted to party. I had friends in Festac Village, built for the Festival of Arts and Culture in 1977. All I knew was that it was somewhere in Lagos, so I set out, looking for a taxi.

It was dusk, that sensual, soft, velvety tropical dusk, which caresses your skin and holds you and everything else in its warm embrace . . . the alcohol had left me and instead I was drunk with a feeling of homecoming.

"I spent that New Year's Eve sitting with the other hotel guests . . . listening to radio music interspersed with martial music"

I noticed there were few cars, and they were rushing by at break-neck speed. Nor was there anyone on the street, except a group of armed soldiers guarding a road block, casually wielding menacing-looking machine-guns. "Oh well," I thought happily, "perhaps that's what they do in Nigeria on New Year's Eve." I walked on, flagging taxis. None stopped, though most were empty. Suddenly a car materialised beside me, two anxious male faces peering out.

"Where are you going?"

"To Festac."

"At *this* time? Don't you know there's a curfew?"

"Curfew? Why?"

"Because of the coup."

"Coup? What coup?"

"The government was overthrown today. The soldiers have taken over."

Realisation dawned. The armed soldiers, the empty speeding cars . . . I stood in the road and laughed aloud. I had just arrived and there had been a coup. Nigeria . . . The two men bundled me into the car, turned with a screech of tyres, and drove furiously back to the hotel, where they dropped me off, with just enough time to beat the curfew home. I spent that New Year's Eve sitting with the other hotel guests in the outdoor bar, listening to radio bulletins interspersed with martial music.

Dodan Barracks, the scene of the coup, was a stone's throw from the hotel, the other side of the elite Ikoyi Club and golf course. I was an ignorant outsider with no idea of the significance of the events I had stumbled on: the end of a corrupt civilian regime which had squandered and stolen the country's massive oil revenues, leaving its people no better off than before.

The next morning at breakfast, I was sitting in the dining room when a man entered, dressed in *agbada*, the flowing Yoruba traditional dress. With a dramatic gesture he threw back the folds upon folds of richly coloured cloth, hitching them on to his shoulders and spreading his arms wide to take in the entire room. Enjoying his moment, he shouted to a waiter: "Bring me porridge . . . and champagne!"

Everybody clapped. The universal greeting that morning was, "Happy New Year, happy new government!" I understood, at least, that the civilians had been unpopular. As time went by, I came to understand why. Nigeria's much-vaunted democracy was a sham, the elections had been rigged, huge amounts of money had been spent buying the voters, with unparalleled ostentation and flagrant corruption. Ordinary people, sickened by the display and the waste, and by being forced to look on while their own condition remained unchanged, were all too happy to see the soldiers back. It was not the first time, and it wouldn't be the last.

Unknowingly, my arrival had coincided with an historic moment: the end of the era of oil wealth, the beginning of austerity, foreign debt and IMF-imposed economic stringency. By the time I left, five years later, I had not only seen, I had experienced the effects. Living and working, not as a highly paid "expatriate", but as an honorary member of the Nigerian middle class, I shared the agonising process of impoverishment and the struggle for survival, and I learnt some of the Nigerian strategies for dealing with it – patience, a philosophical outlook, opportunism, and above all, humour.

I've told this story because it illustrates so much about Nigeria, and about the expectations of people who go there: the volatility of the political situation, the love of display and performance, the danger, the humour and warmth, the material disparities. On my side, the ignorance, the shock, the delight and disillusionment, the gradual change of consciousness every sympathetic foreigner undergoes, emerging, in some fundamental way, changed. As a woman and a foreigner, you are exposed in a way both uncomfortable and inescapable. If you're white, you hear everywhere you go:

> *"Oyibo pepe*
> *If you chop pepe*
> *you go yellow more-more!"*
> *(White person, like red pepper,*
> *if you eat pepper,*
> *you'll get more yellow).*

You can never, never be anonymous, you're constantly being reminded of your difference. Even if you're black, if you dress and talk differently, you'll be called "Oyibo" (or outside of the Yoruba areas, "Batoure" or "Amingo"). When I was feeling strong, I could deal with it by laughter, join in the fun. But on bad days, when all I wanted was to be left alone, it could reduce me to tears.

Then as a foreign *woman*, you're a source of curiosity, a challenge to men. There are two roles for women vis à vis men: "wife" and "girlfriend". Polygamy, a fact of life in the Muslim north, was officially ousted by Christianity in the south. Southern peoples – Yoruba, Igbo and numerous minority groups – instead practice a less institutionalised form, often having one or more wives and multiple girlfriends.

The effect of this on relationships between the sexes is, to a Western outlook, almost impossible to accept. It means that ordinary, disinterested friendship (though I did eventually achieve this with a handful of men) is almost impossible. For a start, public opinion doesn't allow it. Then, it means that women are perpetually in competition with each other, regarding each other with jealousy and suspicion. As a single foreign woman, your role is automatically that of "girlfriend", since

marriage is a liaison between families, and most families won't countenance a foreign wife.

Having said this, there's a surprisingly large network of foreign wives, with their own organisation, *Nigerwives*. You can go to their meetings as a visitor and they'll be friendly and supportive – often more so than married middle-class Nigerian women, who see you as a threat.

Though, again, I eventually made deep and lasting friendships with several Nigerian women, married and single, it was perhaps my greatest source of loneliness and dismay that women's friendship was so hard to come by. I found myself forced back on the company of men, who were invariably available, eager, and willing to befriend me.

"Like modern Nigerian women, the trick is to learn how to appear to conform, in order to do what you want"

Over and over again, my naive, Western assumptions and open behaviour let me down. At last, I learnt to copy Nigerian women – by not believing anything men told me till it had been proved; by being prepared for sexual advances and not allowing the circumstances to develop where things would get out of control; by standing on my dignity and demanding respect. It was all very alien at first, but it worked, and life became easier.

Like modern Nigerian women, the trick is to learn how to appear to conform, in order to do what you want. And one thing you notice, except in the north where, due to the practice of *purdah*, women are invisible, is how dominant and outspoken women generally are. The markets, epicentre of trade and commodity flows, are ruled by women, who have power over prices and availability.

Trade is second nature to West African women, and many professional women also engage in business, from selling soft drinks to importing luxury goods. There are more women in so-called male professions like law and banking than is common in Europe – indeed the president of United Bank for Africa is a woman. On a more basic level, many women make a living from processing and selling food, whether frying *akara* (bean cakes) on the street, or providing hot spicy pepper soup and beer in the *bukas* and beer parlours.

Overt sexual harassment is rare. In parts of Europe you can't even get on a bus without having your bottom pinched. In Nigeria, this *never* happens. Rape occurs, of course, far more than people will admit, because it's considered a disgrace to the woman and generally hushed up. But as a foreigner you are, to an extent, granted extra licence, and allowed to be eccentric.

I did all sorts of dangerous things before I knew better. Like hitching 400 miles north to Kano, starting so late in the day I had to be rescued and taken home by a man who turned out to have worked on a forestry project in Zaria with my father and introduced me to all his friends as a "very old family friend"; like riding pillion on a motorbike and without a crash helmet from Kano to Benin in the south, sleeping two nights in the bush; like taking *kabu kabu* (unlicensed) taxis to Fela's Shrine at midnight and coming home at three or four in the morning, when fear of armed robbers had driven everyone else off the streets.

I hardly ever felt afraid for my personal safety. Arbitrary accidents, like a blowout on the expressway at 140km per hour, or being caught in the undertow at the beach and breaking my shoulder on the sea bed, could happen to anybody. But the sexual threat was mostly absent.

Deeply entrenched in all Nigerian cultures, though being eroded now by the economic situation, is the automatic protection and assistance of strangers. This manifests itself in all sorts of ways.

In the dreadful discomfort of an over-crowded *danfo* minibus, I would find someone had anonymously paid my 20 kobo fare. Arriving in another city and asking the way, a passer-by would carry my bag half a mile to where I wanted to go. The poorest households would mobilise all their resources to lay on the kind of food they thought appropriate, and exclaim with disbelief and delight if you expressed a preference for "our food".

"Cashing a cheque can take a whole morning – if the bank hasn't run out of money"

The great advantage of the unreal exchange rate of the naira – a contrast to the early 1980s when Nigeria was the most expensive country in Africa – is that anyone with foreign exchange is rich in Nigeria. As a visitor, you can afford to reciprocate such generosity, because to you, everything will be cheap. When my sister came to visit, for two weeks we stayed in the best hotels and flew from place to place, before I reverted to a naira based existence. There's so much to see, such a variety of cultures and traditions, such vitality and creativity, that travel inside Nigeria remained a source of continual excitement.

To some extent, it offset the frustrations of intermittent electricity, phones that didn't work, the unreliability of "Nigerian time" which means that everyone's always late, the sheer *difficulty* of getting simple things done. Cashing a cheque can take a whole morning – if the bank hasn't run out of money. But you can always cool off afterwards in the shade of a palmwine shack, roofed with palm fronds, where you sip from a calabash while eating that great delicacy, bushmeat – wild animals trapped in the bush and smoked over an open fire.

The one certain thing about Nigeria is that you can never predict what's going to happen next, either in politics or everyday life. The president can declare at 6pm that the following day will be a public holiday because the national football team is playing somewhere. Or, you can stand for half an hour in an office while a clerk, being paid to do a job, insolently ignores you while he narrates a story in a language you can't understand to his colleagues,

then tells you indifferently that the boss is "not on seat".

As you splutter with speechless rage, he'll turn to you with a winning smile, holding out a paperful of freshly roasted groundnuts. If his invitation to "Oyibo, come chop!" doesn't melt your fury and make you join in the communal laughter, you shouldn't be in Nigeria.

TRAVEL NOTES

Languages Quite a few people in cities speak English, the official language. Of the 200 indigenous languages, Hausa is commonly used in the north, Yoruba in the southwest, and Ibo in the southeast. Pidgin is the best language to get you around in the south.

Transport Shared taxis run between all major cities. There is also a limited rail service. Internal flights are reasonably cheap. There are long distance buses run by private companies, no cheaper than taxis but considerably safer.

Accommodation Hotels are now inexpensive. Missions also offer accommodation in some large towns for a reasonable price; *ECWA* (Evangelical Church of West Africa) are the most common. Also, universities often have guest-houses where visitors can stay.

Special problems Nigeria is under military rule and there is the constant presence of army and police checks in the street. You should expect to be stopped and questioned frequently, and occasionally asked for money (bribes are a routine expense). You may get away with innocently misunderstanding this but you should never show anger. Try to avoid travelling between cities or walking around anywhere alone after nightfall. Nigeria's reputation for violent robbery is no myth. In the predominantly Muslim areas, particularly in the north, women are seen much less in public and can be hard to meet. In these areas it's advisable to wear clothes that cover the arms and knees and to avoid wearing trousers. In the Old City at Kano, women have been thrown off public transport or had stones hurled at them for dressing "immodestly".

Nigerians are very dress conscious and you could embarrass yourself and your hosts by

looking scruffy. It's good to try and look as smart as possible.

Guide *The Rough Guide: West Africa* (Harrap Columbus) gives a full and useful rundown of the country.

Contacts

Women in Nigeria, PO Box 253, Samaru-Zaria. Write for details of WIN groups around the country.

National Council for Women's Societies, Tafawa Balewa Square, Lagos. An NGO umbrella group and a focus for many different women's groups throughout Nigeria, which campaigns around issues of marriage and divorce.

University Groups. There are various women's groups forming at the universities who would welcome contact with western feminists. One such group is **Obafemi Awolowo University** (Ile-Ife) Women's Studies Group (contact Mrs Simi Afonja, Faculty of Social Sciences).

Nigerwives, PO Box 54664, Falomo, Lagos. A network organisation of foreign women married to Nigerian men, which operates as an extended family for attendance at weddings, funerals, etc, and as a pressure group for immigration issues, information and support. They also publish a newsletter.

Books

Women in Nigeria, *Women in Nigeria Today* (Zed Books, 1985). A selection of theoretical papers on women's subordination in Nigeria from the Women in Nigeria (WIN) conference.

S. Ardener, ed., *Perceiving Women* (John Wiley and Sons, New York, 1975). Revealing essays on Ibo women.

Mary Kingsley, *Travel in West Africa* (1897; Virago, 1982). British woman's journals of her travels in West Africa in the 1890s.

Molara Ogundipe-Leslie, *"Nigeria: Not Spinning on the Axis of Maleness"*, in ***Sisterhood is Global*** (Penguin, 1986; see General Bibliography).

West Africa magazine, published weekly in London, has up-to-date and in-depth news on Nigerian events, as well as many advertisements for cheap flights.

Fiction

Buchi Emecheta, *The Joys of Motherhood* (Heinemann, 1980). Powerful story about the strains of living in a society where women are denied any identity unless they bear children.

Flora Nwapa, *Efuru* (Heinemann, 1966), ***Idu*** (Heinemann, 1970), ***One is Enough*** (Tana Press, Eguru, 1981). Nigeria's first published woman novelist, all of whose work in some way concerns the constraints which marriage has on women. Nwapa now runs her own publishing house as an outlet for African writers.

Ifeoman Okaoye, *Men Without Ears* (Longman, 1984). The frantic chase for money and the obsession with prestige in urban Nigeria today.

Zaynab Alkali, *Stillborn* (Longman, 1984). Story of a young girl in rural Nigeria torn between village life and the lure of the city.

Thanks to Jane Bryce and Deborah Birkett who provided much of the information for the introduction and Travel Notes.

Norway

Like most of Scandinavia, Norway is a relaxed and easy country to travel around. Norwegians would see nothing noteworthy about a woman travelling alone or with other women, and whether you choose to hike across the justly famous coastline of the western fjords or sit in a bar in Oslo or Bergen you're unlikely to feel hassled or intruded upon. The country is, however, expensive, and most visitors resort to camping to make ends meet – though given the spectacular scenery and general outdoors culture this is little hardship. More of a problem can be the feeling of isolation that comes from travelling in a sparsely populated country with vast, uninhabited stretches, and where communities can seem insular and exclusive. Norwegians tend not to strike up conversations with strangers, foreign or otherwise, so if you want to make contact you have to take the initiative.

Oslo is often dismissed as a bland, unprepossessing capital. It does, however, have a surprisingly cosmopolitan atmosphere and a lively street culture. Bars and cafés are usually well mixed and easy places to enter alone, although alcoholism, despite high costs and legal restrictions on drink, continues to be a mounting problem for both sexes. There's also a fair scattering of women-only venues. Again, the lack of people can be a little unnerving; Oslo has only half a million inhabitants with plenty of room for all, which means you may well find yourself wandering alone in near-deserted city streets. The problem is in shifting your perception of city life. Crimes against women are extremely rare and taxis are an expensive and for the most part unnecessary luxury.

After more than three decades of persistent and effective campaigning, the **women's movement** in Norway appears to have entered a quieter, less politicised phase. Women's societies and study centres are well established (the latter internationally renowned) but they no longer have the activist profile that typified earlier years. In part, this reflects the advanced state of equality already achieved within Norwegian society. The last government (which lost office in 1989) was led by a woman, Dr Gro Harlem Brundtland, and parliament has more than 25 percent women representatives. Women are clearly established in most areas of political and public life and, for a new generation of Norwegian women, equal opportunity (enforced via a strict quota system for education and employment) is an accepted legal right. Health and welfare policies are similarly progressive – there are extensive childcare facilities with additional help for single mothers, and abortion is available on demand in the first twelve weeks of pregnancy. Although Norway lags behind Sweden and Denmark in that it has not yet passed equal rights legislation for gay women and men, attitudes towards sexuality are generally permissive, particularly in Oslo and Bergen.

Perhaps one of the more telling examples of women's improved status was a landmark court ruling in 1983, when a pornographer was convicted of slander of a particular feminist activist and of women as a class.

Breaking the Ice
. . . .

Belinda Rhodes followed up an undergraduate degree in Scandinavian studies with a year's postgraduate research at the University of Bergen. When time and money permitted she travelled, mainly on her own, around the southern region and the western fjords.

I had spent time in Norway before and knew more or less what to expect. Nonetheless I arrived exhausted and bewildered after a serious bout of seasickness on the 25-hour ferry crossing from Newcastle to Bergen. The last

two hours of the voyage were by far the most pleasant as the boat turned inland, gliding between the superb scenery of the fjord, leaving the high seas behind.

I disembarked with a feeling that I had somehow arrived by accident. The research scholarship I'd applied for, but never really expected to get, had come through suddenly, leaving me very little time to sort out my travel arrangements. It was great, however, to be on firm ground again and to take in the colourful port, harbourside houses and cobbled streets of Bergen, surrounded by a magnificent sweep of Norwegian mountains.

The sight of the student residence where I was to live was far less inspiring. With its eighteen storeys of grey concrete and hundred-metre-long corridors, it reminded me of a prison, and the staff did not seem particularly friendly or helpful either. The latter fact did not really surprise me. The Norwegians are not known for their courtesy to foreigners and, although I had been determined to avoid generalisations when I came here, "cold", "brusque" and "distant" seemed to fit my first impressions of the women and men I met. It is unfair, however, to make such judgements on the basis of what you are used to at home. To a Norwegian there is nothing particularly rude about jostling someone in a queue, not saying "good morning" or "thank you", and there is no word in the Norwegian language for "please". Women are just as likely as men to be elbowed in crowded places, in fact I often found offending elbows belonged to women, but none of this is intended to show hostility or discourtesy, it is simply their way.

Having had previous experience of the unfriendly exterior of the Norwegians (and I must stress that it's only the exterior), I knew it would be up to me to make the effort to meet people and make friends, and I knew it would be worth my while. English is widely spoken so there need never be a language problem. As a foreign student it is always very easy and therefore tempting to get involved with the kind of foreign student subculture which seems to exist at every university.

As I speak Norwegian, I had made a conscious decision to avoid the English-speaking foreigners and to throw myself fully into the Norwegian way of life. Having said that, one of my first friends was an Icelandic woman who was on the same scholarship programme as myself. She was possibly one of the warmest, most liberated and aware women I have ever met, but in a way so natural and non-militant that it suggested to me that feminism must be even more advanced in Iceland than in Norway.

On most occasions I found my knowledge of the language a huge advantage, not only as a means of conversation but also as a talking point. Norwegians were fascinated to find someone who wanted to learn their language. I found the university had a warm, lively atmosphere, though I was surprised to discover that most of my colleagues were men and that there was not a single female teacher in the department of Scandinavian studies where I was to do my research. However, I was always treated as an equal and offered a great deal of help on an academic level. I did spend some very lonely weeks in the library before I began to meet up with any of my co-students socially, but later discovered that, as I hadn't actually approached anyone, it was assumed that I must have already sorted out my own social life.

> *"I also came across a large number of student single mothers who seemed to feel that they were supported and encouraged to continue their studies"*

One of the reasons for the apparent absence of women in the department was that several lecturers had left to set up their own Centre For Women's Studies in the Arts. There the work focused mainly on modern European literature by women, and I attended several of their excellent seminars and talks – often led by notable authors such as Fay Weldon and Angela Carter. It was during a debate in which these authors took part that we discussed why British feminism seemed more politicised than Scandinavian – the conclusion was that it still needs to be in Britain, whereas in Norway many of the goals have already been achieved. I found that many younger women took the great degree of social equality they enjoy for granted, while those in their forties could well remember the period of intense struggle which led to changes in legislation and attitudes in the Fifties and Sixties.

On a social level there were very few women-only events but this was possibly a progressive sign, indicating the ease with which men and women students share whatever's available – most exercise classes, for example, would be mixed. I also came across a large number of student single mothers who seemed to feel that they were supported and encouraged to continue their studies. The local women's group in Bergen was campaigning for less universal causes than we are used to, focusing instead on local issues, like the closure of one particular nightclub in the city, identified as a "meat-market", due to the promotional strategies of the management.

After a couple of months at the stony, silent student residence I decided I would be better off moving into the city. I was lucky enough to find a nice flat in the centre, close to the harbour, which made it a lot easier for me to get involved in the social life of the place. In general I was quite impressed with Bergen after dark. Although it is a busy port and has its large and inevitable quota of drunken sailors and ex-sailors, I never felt threatened when walking home at night. When they are not being hauled off in police vans to sober up in the cells (a regular occurrence), the drunks seem to keep themselves to themselves. The only sexual harassment I remember experiencing was of a very mild nature, and it was only ever from drunks. That Norwegian women are incredulous when they come to Britain and get whistled at by builders would bear out my impression that sexual harassment is relatively rare in Norway.

There were only one or two bars near the harbour where I would generally avoid going alone, and these were extremely easy to spot. Generally, Norwegian bars and cafés have a very relaxed atmosphere and the locals wouldn't find anything strange about a woman going in alone. Tourists are often wary of the strict Norwegian laws on drinking, but in fact these only amount to exorbitant prices and a law in some areas that you have to eat to order a drink. In such places you will often be supplied with a token prawn on a morsel of bread and get a rubber stamp on your hand to show you have consumed something. Beer can be purchased in shops but anything stronger, including wine, is only available at the *Vinmonopol*, the state monopoly store for spirits.

> *"I enjoyed experiencing life in a society more liberated than my own and where women do appear to have more respect, opportunities and greater freedoms"*

Prohibitive prices do not seem, however, to have much effect. Although one might be frowned upon for drinking during the week, people do drink quite heavily at weekends – and always to get very drunk. My impression was that women are just as likely to get very drunk as men, and for this reason, though it may sound odd, I felt much less vulnerable in crowded bars than I would in Britain.

Travelling in Norway should not be a problem for a woman alone. Major hindrances, however, are costs and long distances, although the hours spent on a train are easily compensated for by spectacular scenery. More than once I chose to make the eight-hour journey from Oslo to Bergen by day rather than night for the sake of staring at the landscape and on each occasion found it quite easy to get talking to the other passengers. Norwegians, being very patriotic, are always willing to tell you stories and give you information about any part of their country. Unfortunately there is a limit to where you can actually get to by rail. I occasionally hitched short distances and though it was never easy to get a lift – traffic can be very thin on the more interesting roads – the drivers who did pick me up were very friendly and helpful. I felt that Norway was a relatively safe country to hitchhike in.

One form of travel worth recommending is the *hurtigruta* or coastal steamer which starts at Bergen and calls at all major ports the length of the coast as far as Nordkapp (north of the Arctic Circle). I have yet to experience the midnight sun, but as far as I can gather it is very special. It apparently has something of a magical effect on those living in the far north. Their attitudes and lifestyles change dramatically with the arrival of summer – they sleep less and party more.

Even in Bergen, where it only gets dark for three or four hours in the summer, it was easy to talk the short hours of darkness away or remain at a party until dawn. The whole personality of the city changed dramatically when spring came, the foliage returned to the trees almost overnight, people opened up and the streets became suddenly much more lively. It seemed a more light-hearted place than it had been in the winter.

Overall, Norway was a very agreeable place to live and travel as a woman, and I enjoyed experiencing life in a society more liberated than my own and where women do appear to have more respect, opportunities and greater freedoms. Of course there are areas, particularly in the rural isolated regions, where the traditional way of life still holds firm and where you still come across shepherdesses and "dairymaids", proud of the fact that they represent the "old Norway". One woman I met high in the mountains on a trip from Bergen to Oslo told me with extreme pride that she made the only real goats' cheese to be found in Norway today. It's the peculiar mix of radical social change and valued traditions that makes Norway such a fascinating country to live and travel in and I certainly intend to return to find out more.

TRAVEL NOTES

Languages *Riksmal* or *Bokmal* (book language) are the official Norwegian languages although almost everyone, especially younger Norwegians, speaks some English.

Transport Expensive but very efficient public transport. Some trains have a play space for children. Hitching is apparently safe but slow going, with little traffic even on main routes.

Accommodation Again very expensive – cheap options are university campus rooms and camping (there seems little problem in camping alone even in the more isolated areas).

Guide *The Rough Guide: Scandinavia* (Harrap-Columbus) has a fine, enthusiastic section on Norway.

Contacts

Women's House (Kvindehuset), Rådhusgatan 2, Oslo, ☎41.2864 (Mon–Fri 5–10pm, Sat 11am–5pm, closed in the summer). A good place to pick up information regarding the range of women's groups and resources.

Oslo Bookcafe, C.J.Hambros Plass 2, Oslo. Co-operatively run radical bookshop and café.

Women's University (*Kunneuniversitetet*). Contact Berit Aas (Director), Kunneuniversitetet, Joernstadveien 30, NI 360 Nesbru. Courses are exclusively for women.

Books

Bjorg Vik, *Aquarium of Women* (Norvik Press, 1986). A collection of short stories by one of Norway's best known feminist authors.

Ebba Haslund, *Nothing Happened* (1948; Seal Press, 1988). First English translation of an early Norwegian novel dealing with lesbian love and friendship.

Gerd Brantenburg, *Egalia's Daughters* (Seal Press, 1988). A satire on sex roles by a highly popular feminist writer.

Pacific Islands

· · · · · · · · · · · · · · · · · ·

The South Pacific is an immense area, dotted with thousands of mostly tiny islands. The main exceptions are the vast island of New Guinea, north of Australia, and the two principal islands of New Zealand in the southeast. The many clusters which lie in between make up the countries of **Fiji**, **Western and American Samoa**, **French Polynesia** (the largest island of which is **Tahiti**), **Tonga**, **Vanuatu** and **New Caledonia**, to name just a few.

New Zealand, with its predominantly white-settler population, is unique in sharing more affinities with Australia than with its Pacific neighbours – whose inaccessibility and limited facilities have kept them relatively unknown, until recently, both to package tourists and independent travellers. Nowadays, a growing number of islands threaten to follow the fate of Tahiti, which commercial interests have succeeded in virtually transforming from a Pacific paradise to a tourist nightmare. In some countries, however, most notably Fiji, New Caledonia and Papua New Guinea, political unrest has reversed the trend, causing travellers to shy away from once lucrative tourist resorts. In the case of Fiji, especially, such caution is not necessarily warranted, but sensitivity to the political climate throughout the South Pacific is necessary, and worth learning about in more detail before you set off.

Of the two countries featured in the following accounts, **Fiji** (consisting of 332 islands) is one of the largest and most developed Pacific Island states. It also stands out in having a majority Indian population, whose presence stems from the days of British sovereignty when indentured Indians were brought in to work the sugar plantations. It was the predominance of Indians in the newly elected government of 1987 which provoked a coup by the military who demanded that Fijians be given permanent political control of the country. In contrast, **Vanuatu**, colonised at once by the British and the French, has managed to maintain a degree of political stability – despite mounting Francophone opposition to the chiefly Anglophone government.

Depending on where you go, your choice of accommodation in the South Pacific will vary from luxury hotel to village hut; the cost of food and transport will also fluctuate. In terms of safety, it's again hard to generalise, but provided you're careful and respect local customs there shouldn't be much problem of sexual harassment, at least from the indigenous inhabitants.

A few Pacific nations, among them **American Samoa** and **French Polynesia**, have quite large foreign communities, for they have been maintained as overseas territories by the countries which colonised them. Colonialism is a key political issue, along with escalating concern about French and American nuclear tests and the dumping of foreign nuclear waste into the ocean. In recent decades a vast network of nuclear bases, ports and airfields was set up throughout the region with little, if any, consultation with the indigenous people. Today, heralded by the example of Vanuatu, there is an impressively united and growing movement for a nuclear-free and independent Pacific, a movement in which women play a leading role.

From 1975, when the First Pacific Women's Regional Conference took place in Fiji, the **Pacific women's movement** has spread to more and more countries. Much of its work is co-ordinated by the Pacific Women's Resource Centre which links up groups and spreads information with the help of a satellite communications system. As well as the vital nuclear issue, the concerns of the movement include violence against women, racist and sexist use of experimental contraception, tourist exploitation, and the need for a feminist approach to development projects.

Adventures of a "Snail Woman"

. . . .

Linda Hill, a forty-year-old New Zealander, spent two months in the Pacific islands of Tonga, Samoa and the Cook Islands, before travelling on for another seven weeks to Vanuatu: "Nuclear free, independent, and a different world."

Vanuatu is a scattering of Melanesian islands between New Caledonia and the Solomons. It is too far from the rich tourist markets of the First World to get many visitors. A few package tourists arrive to stay in the overpriced hotels, and regular cruise ships stop for day visits, releasing a flood of very white Australians over Port Vila or Champagne Beach. But backpackers are still virtually unknown – in a six-week stay, I met one Japanese guy waiting out his visa renewal for Tuvalu, and two Australian nurses exploring Vanuatu largely by trading ship, as I was myself. And I would say, from the way news of their later movements reached me through the locals, we five were the only ones in the country at that time.

"It seemed acceptable that, having no family responsibilities, I should be free to do as I pleased"

The crews of the trading ships seemed familiar with the ways of backpackers. Outside Vial and Sano, however, people stopped what they were doing and came over to investigate. "Where are you going? Who are you visiting? Are you a teacher, a nurse or a missionary? And where is your husband?" The Australian women told me that in Hogg Harbour the village women had gone into a huddle at the sight of them and come out giggling. "You are snail women," they were told. "You carry your house on your back and you walk slow!" Though my pack was light and I carried no tent, I was delighted to think of myself as a snail woman too.

My standard answer to the recurrent question, "Where is your husband?" was, "No husband, they're too much work." The women would laugh and agree. It seemed acceptable that, having no family responsibilities, I should be free to do as I pleased. There don't seem to be possible penalties attached to a woman walking or travelling on her own, as in, say Samoa, where a woman who doesn't take her sister along might meet difficulties, especially after sundown.

Certainly, I always felt very safe and welcome – a pleasant novelty for the locals rather than an intruder. The women I met were very friendly and generous and the "house on my back" slowly filled with beautiful hand-made baskets and grass skirts. The best I could do in return was to take addresses and photos, inevitably posed, and send copies when I got home.

As in Polynesia, hospitality is given on the assumption that it will be returned. Where this is unlikely it is important to try and redress the balance of obligation, and not to leave people the poorer. Take enough food with you: tea, sugar, coffee, rice, tinned beef or fresh meat from the town are suitable gifts to offer if you are invited to visit someone's family or village for a few days. If you're uncertain you can always ask another *ni-Vanuatu* (literally, born Vanuatu) to advise you on what is appropriate.

Exploring on your own, accommodation can often be found in one village or the next if you ask around. A church may have a room for guests or there may be a women's committee house, perhaps doubling as their kindergarten, where visitors can be put up. There may be a fixed charge for an overnight stay, but where this is not specified, it is appropriate to make a donation of about the going rate, say, 200–300 vatu, to the women's committee, church or chief.

Interest in you will include concern that you are eating. If you have your own food, it is advisable to make that clear or someone will turn up with a plate of *taro* and "Vanuatu tinned fish" (land crab!). You could share your supplies or contribute some from the village co-op store, or accept whatever arrangement will be made for you and make sure your donation redresses the balance. Someone will show you where women and men go to wash. If camping, it is nearly always proper to check with the nearest village about a campsite. Perhaps safest, too, to be in a way under the villagers' wing, since people will certainly come to see what you are up to.

The 105 languages spoken in Vanuatu present a problem to locals rather than to the traveller, but it is quite usual for totally "uneducated" people to speak two or three languages besides their own. Those with schooling will speak either French or English, as well as the *lingua franca* preferred by independent Vanuatu – Bislama.

Bislama is largely a corrupted English vocabulary, on a Polynesian grammar base, and can be learned easily enough by English speakers with the aid of books available in Vila. People tend to ask standard questions about background and family, and I was soon able to conduct the basic social conversation in Bislama and understand a remarkable amount on more complex subjects. I speak French and met many English- and French-speaking *ni-Vanuatu* with whom I could communicate at a very satisfactory level. I found that I learned a great deal about the country and current opinions and politics.

> *"I very quickly had to revise any notion that this society was less socially advanced than my own"*

Choice of language is a political question in modern Vanuatu. Under the old colonial condominium there were areas of strong French (Catholic, Francophone) and British (Anglican in the north, Presbyterian in the south, Anglophone) influence which still structure politics today. The present Vanua'aku Party government reflects mainly the Anglophone communities, while the gradually consolidating main opposition comes from Francophones.

But large areas are still *kustom*. These villages should not be regarded as "backward" or merely left behind by modernisation. Theirs is often a deliberate political choice, reflecting condemnation of both sides for undermining age-old conventions and traditional forms of leadership by introducing the colonial system of electoral government. There are various expressions of this view, but it has been associated with rejection of churches and education, always the thin edge of the colonial/imperialistic wedge. A recent solution by less remote *kustom* villages has been to send most children to a French-speaking school since the present government is Anglophone, but a few children to an English-speaking school, just in case. This may be supplemented with a *kustom* school to preserve the old ways.

I very quickly had to revise any notion that this society was less socially advanced than my own. Most of the people I met lived in communal, non-cash, village economies, still only peripherally connected to the money economy of capitalism through need for tools, kitchen equipment, clothes, modern building materials, transport, fuel and – less fortunately – tinned goods, tailor-made cigarettes and Fosters lager. A comfortable basis for village life is still provided by food and materials from gardens, sea and bush. "We don't have to pay money for everything, like you," my friend Ernestine told me. "We can take two or three weeks' holiday anytime and there'll still be plenty to feed the kids."

Other criteria of supposed "backwardness" stem from simple lack of access to information and knowledge that our world takes for granted. Access to radio is recent and *battery* (cash) dependent. Books and even writing materials are largely non-existent outside Vila and Santo. Take copies of the government newspaper with you from Vila and pass on any spare magazines, maps, or other material in English or French.

My church affiliation was something I was asked about constantly. Each Sunday I was in Vanuatu I seemed to go to a different denominational church with the different people I met. I had resurrected a brief Anglican background for conversational purposes, but then found myself very embar-

rassed at being the only person at a
service who didn't know the Anglican
prayerbook responses by heart, especially as I was the only mother-tongue
English speaker.

In the past, bits of information, and
missionary teaching, and such bizarre
experiences as the sudden arrival and
equally rapid departure of Uncle Sam
with World War II, led to some ingenious philosophical explanations of the
world, such as the still popular *Jon
Frum* cargo cult in Tanna.

Cargo cults mushroomed throughout Melanesia with the arrival of
European-manufactured goods, which
being inexplicable according to local
technology, were understood in spiritual and millenial terms: "Our ancestors
must be sending us things. These
Europeans try to make us pay but one
day our ship will come." The *Jon Frum*
("frum" means American) variation on
this theme seems to have been sparked
off by a US pilot's decision to redistrib-
ute goods meant for the war front to
Tanna locals.

In the more remote islands and
villages, people just don't get to hear
about things and have no way of checking what they do hear. You will meet
with some fascinating opinions and you
yourself will be a source of information
for people. One thing *ni-Vanuatu* like is
a "good story" and I had to repeat again
and again the different things that had
happened to me on my trip.

I was able to relate first-hand news of
the devastation still being caused to
villages by the volcano in East Tanna. I
told about going to the Friday night *Jon
Frum* cargo cult service at Sulphur Bay
and dancing with the women in a grass
skirt that they gave me to the wonderful funky music. Then there was the
walk home in pitch dark across an
eerie moonscape of black ash, lit only
by thunderous flashes from the
volcano, and the deaf man who nearly
jumped out of his skin when I tapped
him on the arm and pushed my white
face into his to ask directions.

My white face often had a similar
effect on toddlers, who no doubt associated me with doctors, nurses, injections and nasty tastes. Smiling didn't
help – they all do that before they hurt
you.

> *"The sisters were still talking about
> a young German woman who had
> turned up in 1978 and stayed a fort-
> night with them"*

Another very popular story I told was
about dancing at a Vanuatu wedding in
North Ambrym. I had arrived by trading ship at Ranon and walked up to the
French-speaking villages around Olal.
When I asked about accommodation, I
was offered a bed in the New Zealand-
donated leper hospital at St Jean's
Mission, now just a clinic. But I should
just drop my things and hurry, I was
told, because the entire village was
going to a wedding nearby.

The male teacher from the mission
turned me over to some women my
age, who talked to me in French, translating for others. With them I joined the
line to kiss the beflowered bride and
groom sitting under a canopy, leave a
small present in a growing pile and
have my head sprinkled with talcum
powder. With Ernestine, her sister and
her four children, I shared a large
banana leaf parcel of earth-oven cooked
taro, kumara, pork and beef, flavoured
with fern leaves. The sisters were still
talking about a young German woman
who had turned up in 1978 and stayed a
fortnight with them, just "doing what
the women do".

That evening there was a wedding
disco, with Western pop music, reggae
and the local bands in Vila, tea with
bread and butter, and *kava* out the
back. Everyone was there; men and
women danced in separate groups and
I got up with the women I had met
earlier. When I teased one for dropping
out before I did, a man sprang over
from the other side of the floor to
sweep me off in a foxtrot. My tired part-

ner at once started to beat him about the legs for the impudence of dancing with a woman, and everybody roared with laughter. This was a story that delighted *ni-Vanuatu* elsewhere: that I should have been dancing "Vanuatu-style" with the women. Europeans danced "modern-style" with a man, like people did in Vila. I tried to tell them their way suited me very well.

The "men's house" culture recorded by ethnographers and anthropologists throughout Melanesia seems to be paralleled by an unrecorded but strong women's culture. Women tend to work together in groups (much as they do in the factories, typing pools and other sex-segregated work in the West) and interact socially in groups of girls or women. Women approached me very easily and small groups of girls wanted to accompany me and show me everything. This women's culture is being supported by the liberal Vanua'aku Party government, with a few strong women's rights advocates such as Grace Molisa. Feminism seems at its beginning stages and, like the rest of Vanuatu's development, will, I hope, be a home-grown product.

I came back from Vanuatu with a strong desire to go back in a couple of years, not to be a "snail woman" again but to stay in one of the villages for a month or so, just "doing what the women do". In the meantime I have a plan for subsistence agriculture in my Auckland garden!

A Nice Life . . . for a Tourist

· · · · · · · · · · · · · · ·

Carol Stetser is an American artist and founder of Padma Press. After living for fifteen years in rural Arizona, she and her partner sold their house and decided to spend a year travelling and doing independent art studies in the Pacific. They began their trip in Fiji.

We arrived in Fiji at five in the morning, tired after an eleven-hour flight and not ready for the onslaught of taxi drivers who surrounded us as soon as we emerged from customs.

Our destination was a hotel on Saweni Beach, north of the Nadi airport and south of Lautoka. We drove past barren hillsides covered only with brown grass. Was this the South Pacific? Not a palm tree in sight. The valleys were all cultivated with sugar-cane. We saw long-horned bullocks pulling wooden ploughs followed by Sari-clad Indians. Trucks piled high with cut cane passed us on the road. Narrow-gauge tracks ran parallel to the road, and periodically the long, slow-moving cane train, its flatbed cars piled high with cane, chugged by. We felt like we were in India.

Saweni Beach turned out to be a good place to rest after the long flight, and to unwind into Fijian time. Our room looked out on to a wide green lawn with coconut palms and beyond this were field after field of sugar cane with green leaves standing eight to ten feet high. We could hear the loud horn of the sugar train as it switched back and forth across road junctions on its way to the mill at Lautoka, the sugar capital, the noise rising easily above the crowing of roosters and the bellowing of cows tethered nearby. Early every morning the fishermen would paddle ashore in their fifteen-foot wooden boats to sell their fish from the beach.

There was also a small store where we could buy eggs, bread and beer.

Time is measured in Fiji in terms of the coup of 1987. Before the coup there was a restaurant at Saweni Beach; before the coup the pool was operational; before the coup the taxi driver brought his family to the beach on Sunday. But now the foreign owner doesn't want to put any money into a hotel and the cooking staff has been sent home. Taxis cannot run on Sunday so the taxi driver without a second car must stay at home. All small businesses are closed on Sunday – since the coup.

Only sugar cane mills are supposed to run and this directive has sparked revolt, with workers refusing to harvest their cane on Sunday. Inflation and a devalued dollar has more or less doubled the price of everything. Tourism is down fifty percent since the coup, when the rooms at Saweni Beach were full. Now the lobby and dining areas were empty and maybe half the rooms were rented. Who knows what is going to happen?

It made us uneasy being this close to Lautoka where so much of the trouble had erupted. There were more Indians here than Fijians and an undercurrent of tension was apparent to even the casual tourist. An internal security measure was passed a month before our visit and an amnesty was in effect for the return of weapons shipped illegally into Fiji since the coup. We didn't want to be here when the amnesty ended in July 1988.

We bargained for a taxi to drive us south to the Coral Coast, through the concrete boulevard of duty-free shops and hustle that is Nadi, through the Polynesian Fijian villages, over a mountain pass covered with pine trees, and down into the coconut-fringed coast where the locals and tourists alike come to play.

Our destination, Tumbakula Beach Cottages, was full; so was Sandy Point; the Reef was too expensive; Waratah Lodge was full. The cabby was getting edgy and so were we – tired and hungry after the two-hour drive. The Fijian manager of the Lodge told us of a house for rent. We were sceptical but in desperation decided to give it a look. What luck! It was a luxurious *palangi* house, owned by a New Zealander, right on the beach in Korotogo and set in a compound landscaped in a true Polynesian fantasy: coconut palms and ornamental plants, grass lawn and lovely flowers, even a lily pond with magnificent large pink blooms and a multitude of grotesque bullfrogs that would plop into the pad-covered water whenever anyone approached. "Life doesn't get much better than this," we sighed, as we unpacked our clothes.

A block from the house was the Korotogo store and a bus stop on the Nadi–Suva highway. The buses are an experience. Local buses are air-cooled, and have no glass in the windows; when it rains, a large plastic curtain is rolled down to cover the openings. I have seen the passengers climb out of the windows of a full bus when it stops at the beach with a load of picnickers. The bus crawls along the Queen's Road from Lautoka to Suva so it's a great way to go sightseeing.

"We wondered how all the small shops ever stay in business until we saw the tour buses arrive, full of Australasians"

Once a week we went to town, crossing the Sigatoka River over an old one-lane bridge whose traffic was regulated by a street light that worked periodically. Main Street paralleled the river: hardware stores, sporting goods, banks, tourist tee-shirt shops, handicraft centres, the ubiquitous duty-free shops, milk bars and refreshment stands. A block away from this main thoroughfare was the small bus terminal and the covered market, dark and chaotic, where the smell of curry overpowered the aroma of bananas. We wondered how all the small shops ever stay in business until we saw the tour buses arrive, full of Australasians.

Fiji in July (winter in the Pacific) is pretty hot and humid but not unbearable. We couldn't imagine what the summers must be like. Most of the other tourists seemed to restrict themselves to the hotel pools or shopping in Sigatoka, so we had the beach more or less to ourselves. At low tide I could walk for miles from our house, observing all the marine life to be found along the water's edge: coral hiding a blue starfish or the long brown sea snakes, transparent small fish darting away from my shadow, crabs scurrying from my approach to hide in the sand, and big fat slugs.

At full moon, when the tide was exceptionally low, the Fijian women would hike up their skirts and, bending double, root for clams or octopus along the reef. The men, meanwhile, sat in the shade on the beach and drank beer. When their sacks were full the fisherwomen would heave them onto their backs and head back to the village, while the children frolicked in the water and the men shuffled empty-handed behind them.

We rented a car for a week to drive southeast along the highway toward Suva, the capital. Here the lush, verdant jungle was such a contrast to the dry, brown hills of the west. Along the road we visited all the $200-a-day luxury resorts; we browsed in the lobby shops and sat around on their beaches. It was a disorienting experience. There were no Fijians staying in these resorts, only white tourists served by smiling Fijian waiters. "Bula Bula" and "Welcome" to the Fijian or the Sheraton or the Hyatt.

Not a mile down the road from this opulence was a village of thatched *bures*, one-room tin shacks with screenless windows and outhouses; barefoot, often naked children; unpenned animals; and women washing their clothes while squatting in the river. The mind boggles at trying to reconcile these two extremes.

TRAVEL NOTES

Language More than 700 languages are spoken throughout the South Pacific, but you're sure to find someone who speaks English, especially in Fiji. Here the main languages are Fijian and Hindustani, while in Vanuatu it is Bislama.

Accommodation Available in all price ranges on Fiji's main island, though hotels fill up very quickly in winter. Elsewhere you will often have no choice but to accept village hospitality. Such invitations are a privilege and require at least some understanding of local culture and traditions.

Transport A limited selection of trading and cargo ships, and domestic airlines will carry you between the islands. Of the two domestic airlines, Dovair is slightly cheaper. Cargo ship is about half the cost of an airfare and includes meals. Take a radio to check the shipping news and keep your fingers crossed. They go by cargoes, not schedules. Transport on land varies from place to place, but anywhere of any size has a bus service.

Special Problems Be careful not to offend local customs by your dress. A woman's thighs are considered more erotic than her breasts and are not meant to be exposed in public, so shorts are definitely out.

Guides *South Pacific Handbook* (Moon Publications, US) is very practical and covers even quite remote places. Lonely Planet have individual *Travel Survival Kits* to *Tonga, Samoa, New Caledonia, Raratonga & the Cook Islands, Tahiti & French Polynesia, Fiji, Micronesia* and *The Solomon Islands*.

Contacts

The following organisations are all based in Fiji, but should be able to provide information about women's activities in the rest of the South Pacific.

Tok Blong Oi Meri/YWCA, Pacific office, Box 3940, Samabula, Suva. Dedicated to promoting improvements for women in the region, the Fiji office also produces a newsletter, *Ofis Blong Oi Meri*.

The **Pacific Women's Resource Centre**, PO Box 534, Suva. As well as housing resources, the centre publishes a magazine, *Women Speak Out*.

The **National Council for Women**, PO Box 840, Suva. National co-ordinating body for non-governmental women's organisations.

Books

Jan Dibblin, *Day of Two Suns: US Nuclear Testing and the Pacific Islanders* (Virago, 1989). Account of protest amid the atolls and in the international courts against the inhuman appropriation and use of land by the US military. Draws widely on the personal experiences of women and men of the Marshall Islands.

Grace Mara Molisa, *Colonised People*, (Black Stone Publications, Port Vila, 1987). Poetry plus statistics on women in Vanuatu.

Margaret Sinclair, *The Path of the Ocean: Traditional Poetry of Polynesia* (Hawaii U. Press, US, 1982). Fascinating transcription of traditional oral verse.

Thanks to Carol Stetser and Linda Hill for help with the introduction and Travel Notes.

Pakistan

. . . .

Benazir Bhutto's accession to power in Pakistan in November 1988 was one of the decade's most extraordinary events: a woman elected to the most powerful office of a neo-fundamentalist Islamic state. Yet, almost from the moment of taking her seat at the head of the ruling Pakistan's People's Party, her administration has been under siege, with mounting opposition from the army and growing fundamentalist factions, constitutional wrangles over her prime ministerial powers, and deep divisions and dissent

within her own party. Her landmark post-election promise to remove discriminatory laws against women (more particularly to repeal the restrictive Hudood Ordinance that effectively defines a woman as a permanent minor) appears to have sunk without trace, while many other radical policies have floundered in compromise and political concessions. Significantly, she has also changed the image she presents to the public, assuming the more submissive stance of a traditional wife (accepting an arranged marriage) and mother. Calls for another general election are intensifying and it seems unlikely that Benazir Bhutto will be able to retain her mandate.

The atmosphere of political instability (violence has erupted in the province of Sind and along the border with Afghanistan) coupled with widespread and intense sexual harassment makes this a very difficult country to travel around alone. Westerners are viewed stereotypically as morally lax and promiscuous, a notion that's confirmed by the fact that they choose to leave the protection of their homes and mix freely with men in public. Away from the luxury star hotels it takes a fair amount of resilience to cope with the continual propositions, leering and comments. Dressing with extreme modesty helps – for instance wearing the traditional *shalwaar kameez* (loose fitting trousers and tunic) – as does travelling with a man. But unless you're escorted by Pakistani friends, your chances of avoiding unpleasantness are very slim. For some, however, the spectacular scenery of Pakistan's mountains and ravines make it all worthwhile.

The Islamicisation programme introduced during the Zia years ushered in a wave of legislation that very clearly limited women's freedoms and undermined their security at the heart of the family. These rules are still being implemented, most forcefully against working-class women, who cannot protect themselves with bribes or family influence. Under the notorious Hudood Ordinance, women are no longer allowed to testify in a murder case, cannot secure a rape conviction without four *male* witnesses and, unless rape is proved, run the risk of being themselves imprisoned, flogged or stoned for the crime of *zina* (adultery or unlawful sexual intercourse).

Opposition to these laws remains strong. The *Pakistan Women's Action Forum* (*WAF*), the main **feminist organisation**, has set up groups in all the major towns and spearheads campaigns for the laws to be repealed. Large demonstrations were staged in Lahore and Karachi even under Zia, though they were dispersed by mass arrests and a brutal show of force. Perhaps the saddest aspect of Bhutto's compromised politics is that having endorsed the WAF charter of demands she has been unable either to prevent or condemn the use of police force in breaking up continuing women's demonstrations.

A Cautious Enjoyment

. . . .

Sarah Wetherall spent six weeks in Pakistan, squeezing in the trip on her way back from India, where she had been working as a volunteer. She is a student of fine art and uses her experiences of travel in her work.

Arriving from India, I had been used to the cultural and social restrictions on women, Indian and Western, and I expected to see few women on the streets and stricter segregation of the sexes in public areas. At first, I was pleasantly surprised to find women walking around Lahore dressed in *shalwaar kameez* (a long sleeved shirt with loose trousers) with a *dupati* (a long scarf) over their head, rather than the full *burqua* that covers the body from head to toe. But my initial impression of freedom proved to be deceptive.

Arriving at the YWCA I found fellow travellers complaining that it was almost impossible to wander out alone; slipping past the matron took hours of intrigue and once on the streets there were continual problems of harassment to contend with. The YWCA had become both a welcome retreat and a prison. It was like some British Victorian boarding house, where middle-class women led chaperoned lives. Piano and typing lessons were held at the beginning of the day and the professional women who lodged at the hostel would go out to teach school-children in the mornings. One woman was allowed to meet her fiancé in a small room in the hostel for an hour each evening and, despite the fact that they were good friends, the door to the room had to be left open. All lights were out at ten.

The mosque and fort in Lahore were the main recreation areas for the Friday holiday. Children played cricket on the grass outside and families picnicked and bought ice creams. The amplified chants from the mosque resounding over the miniature orange trees seemed to conjure up the image that most Westerners hold of Asian Islam. I sat under a tree, nursing a headache, with my *dupati* pulled over my head, and tried to ignore the fact that men were staring at me. A carefully aimed cricket ball landed in my lap, not once but three times, and each time a girl ran across to collect it and gave me a friendly smile. Finally, her mother came up and tried to explain about the attention I was attracting.

"Pakistan men not OK" (*teek ne he*), she explained. Her husband and brother had sent her over to save me from the stares. Her son was sent to get me a cup of tea for my headache and I was taken around the old fort with the family. Her husband and sons paid me the customary compliment of not acknowledging or addressing me except to make sure that I wasn't getting lost in the crowd. The family was the first in a long line of people who were to help me out. My vulnera-bility was double edged. As a woman, I was open to harassment but also equally open to great hospitality and kindness from people amazed to find me travelling alone and unprotected in their country.

The question of religion constantly came up. Before arriving in Pakistan I had been advised not to attempt to explain the casual Western agnostic view. This proved sound advice as your religion defines who you are. I opted for Christianity. One or two women actually approached me to talk about their faith after finding out that I was a Christian too. Their opposition to Islam was whispered as, under the Islamicisation laws, blasphemy is punishable by death. However, I was unsure whether their antipathy to Islam was towards the religion itself or the cruelty that women are beginning to suffer under the fundamentalists.

"The women I met were polite in their bewilderment at my presence in their country"

When I asked for directions in the street, I always approached women first and would act as though affronted if any strange man tried to strike up a conversation with me. But I also made mistakes in this area. At a guesthouse in 'Pindi, I began to wonder at the heavy sighs of the waiters when I sat down for my evening meal. It was only after two days that I understood. I was sitting at the wrong table – a table for four – and, as no man could share it with me, was taking up precious space. I eventually banished myself to the small segregated women's tables, where we ate together below the TV in the corner of the room. My views of the test match were, consequently, coupled with a severely cricked neck.

However, I certainly didn't resent the women's segregation in the buses and minibuses whilst travelling on long journeys. A happy camaraderie exists, at the very back or front of the bus. My huge supply of art materials and draw-ing pads were soon whittled away as kids energetically pounced on my felt tips and leafed through the pictures in my guidebook.

The actual vehicles were certainly different after India. Auto rickshaws were a uniform blue and decorated with paintings and stickers of animals noted for their prowess, such as tigers and falcons. Shiny Islamic stickers replaced Hindu imagery and there was also a Muslim pin-up of women in lipstick and mascara, pouting through a thin veiled *dupati*. Minibuses were my favourite form of transport, their interiors decorated with pictures of Imrahn Khan, Bhutto and Zia. Outside, Pakistan rolled by – abandoned donkeys next to multistorey car parks, grey-pink sunsets with a train of camels on the horizon, women carrying children and bundles of grass with a herd of goats in tow.

The women I met were polite in their bewilderment at my presence in their country. I had four brothers and sisters, so why was I alone in Pakistan? This incomprehension was also partly the reason for being refused a room at guesthouse counters. What was wrong with me, I despaired. I was polite, I was well-mannered, I was conservatively dressed. The difficulty was in fact twofold. Firstly, if a single room was refused, I would have to stay in a double room at twice the price. The second reason for rejection was wariness of single foreign women for, simply by being there, I would attract men hanging around the hotel. (This seemed to apply only to smaller guesthouses and only in the more rural areas.)

Though I had been advised in advance by a British Pakistani woman to stick to the main cities, I felt more relaxed in the smaller, more remote areas. It was easier to find my way around and the atmosphere was friendlier. I especially enjoyed my time in the Northern Hunza Valley, though this was partly because I spent most of my time with a Western man.

After staggering into a guesthouse in Bhawalpur in the South Cholistan desert, with rucksack and painting materials and being very politely refused a room, I sat down dispiritedly and didn't move.

"You are single?" the manager asked. I affirmed, and a worried discussion ensued with a group of men casting anxious glances at me. I eventually asked the manager what the problem was.

"In Pakistan women never single," he replied.

They eventually gave me the room because I was an artist. "A painter!" they all said in relief.

Bhawalpur was getting used to single women after Zia's assassination nearby. I later cashed in on this and became a self-appointed journalist. My profession gave me a certain amount of respectability. I also learned the key to getting around safely and seeing as much as possible outside of the major cities.

"The tourist office in Bhawalpur provided me with a guide whom they proudly asserted was the only man they would trust in the whole town"

Anywhere vaguely official, such as smarter hotels, newspaper offices or tourist offices, could somehow provide a reliable male escort. The tourist office in Bhawalpur provided me with a guide whom they proudly asserted was the only man they would trust in the whole town. We motorbiked through the desert and I even managed to get some painting done. Resorting to male escorts – in reality, bodyguards – may seem to be copping out, but the alternative, staying in self imposed *purdah* within four walls of a hotel room, seemed a worse defeat. My escort from the tourist office had helped out women travellers before. Two other girls had once come to the office, depressed, upset and terrified of Pakistan. I sympathised with their story. The continual harassment by Pakistani men; low wolf whistles in my ear, oppressive attention, verbal abuse ("fuck me baby"), made my hotel room seem distinctly inviting.

The combination of sexually liberated women in the bygone age of the hippy trail and widely circulated Western pornography make up a formidable myth of the Western woman as a whore. A myth that cannot be exploded by a single woman traveller wearing a *dupati* for protection. Women, on the other hand, did not seem to hold this view of Westerners and were kind, warm, and anxious to gently correct mistakes that I made in public so that I wouldn't put myself in embarrassing or dangerous situations, saying "sit here with us", "queue here for your tickets", etc. I met women everywhere, in the telephone exchange, on buses, in post offices where friendliness and concern bridged all language and cultural barriers. Travelling alone often brings about strong swings of mood and I didn't want my impressions of Pakistan to be coloured by stressful harassment. Women certainly made my time easier in Pakistan. The occasional male escort enabled me to enjoy my time there – albeit a cautious enjoyment.

The codes of hospitality are very strict and it is a delicate task to accept but not take advantage of hospitality, as your hosts adopt your concerns as their own. Soon I learnt not to mention my intention to do anything, or that I was thirsty or hungry, as it resulted in an embarrassing flurry of hospitality that I couldn't accept. Having mistimed my arrival in a desert town, I got off a bus in the middle of the night and was escorted by a couple *and* the bus driver to a "good" hotel. There were no rooms free but instead of turning me away, I was put up in the manager's office with the words: "You are a visitor to our country, it is an honour."

Obviously relying on hospitality is not the best way to travel. I saw few Westerners and only two Western women on their way back to work in Peshawar. There was so much that was regrettably too difficult to see or do, such as eating out at night, walking in the Chitral district, going scuba diving in Karachi, etc. In replying to my letter of thanks after returning to Britain, my escort from the desert wrote that it was a great pleasure to help a "good girl" like myself.

I think back on the restrictions that were formidable, numerous and often trivial. Lighting up a cigarette on a bus on my first day in Pakistan almost caused a traffic pile-up as the driver turned round to gasp! The careful constraint I had to use was quite difficult for a chain smoker and a "good girl" such as myself.

Alone on the Overland Route

· · · · · · · · · · ·

Wendy Dison has been travelling since 1980 when she realised that a career in administration was not for her. She crossed through Pakistan on her way from Iran to India.

Where the eastern Iranian desert meets the Baluchistan desert of Pakistan a wire fence runs across the sand to mark the border. In the Pakistan frontier town of Taftan a warm wind whipped up the dust in the main street where goats chewed pieces of cardboard and wild-looking men with dark skins squatted in the shade.

Proprietors of shops made of packing cases watched me with friendly interest. One man with a gold-embroidered pill-box hat and a ready smile that revealed large white teeth invited me to rest in his shop until my bus left. During the afternoon he brought bowls of stewed meat and potatoes from the cookshop over the road and showed me how to eat using only a *chapati*. I found it difficult but he encouraged me, ignoring the mess I was making.

A loud two-tone horn announced the departure of the Quetta bus waiting in the bazaar, brilliantly decorated with coloured lights, chrome, plastic cut-out shapes and rows of chains dangling from the bumpers. Men swarmed up and down the ladder at the back to load boxes and bundles on the roof while inside I scrambled for a seat, climbing over enormous quantities of luggage and stools in the aisle. The men stared at me and I was too overwhelmed to do more than stare back.

We travelled east on a dirt road with bone-rattling ridges across the vast stony Baluchistan desert where everything – rocks, bushes, people – had been bleached and burnt to the colour of the earth. The sun set spectacularly and as soon as it touched the horizon we stopped for prayers. The men dispersed, purified themselves with a symbolic "wash" in sand, faced Mecca and started the ritual of praying – bowing and touching their foreheads to the ground, kneeling in the last rays of the sun with their shoes beside them and their loose clothing blowing in the wind.

"After three days in the country I saw my first Pakistani women"

Around midnight we stopped in a small village. In a pool of lamplight outside a restaurant groups of people squatted on rush matting around teapots and bowls. Huge pans simmered on a mudbrick fireplace and unglazed pots of water stood on straw rings with drinking bowls balanced on top. Two men wearing wide Afghan

turbans invited me to join them and we ate in a friendly silence, dipping our *chapatis* into a communal dish of meat and drinking bowl after bowl of green tea.

In Quetta, the capital of Baluchistan, the broad avenues lined with plane trees and houses set in walled gardens are unmistakably British but the bazaars, I was relieved to find, are colourful, bustling and very much Asian. On the pavements men are shaved, tailors work at sewing machines and cooks stir smoking pans of *samosas* and sell them in bags made from used school exercise books. Lorries decorated with exotic paintings of tigers and mosques trundle past raising clouds of dust and heavy black bicycles, carrying three people, weave amongst camel-drawn carts and buses groaning under the weight of men clinging on to the outside. I ate in a restaurant with smoke-blackened walls and a choice of either tables and chairs or a raised platform for those who preferred to squat. Men watched me curiously and when I looked up from my spiced spinach they held their gaze. Pakistani men look each other in the eye without embarrassment but I found their steady gaze disconcerting.

After three days in the country I saw my first Pakistani women. Travelling in the ladies' compartment of the Quetta Express the women emerged from their sombre veils and the carriage was filled with glittering colourful fabrics, gold earrings, jewelled nose studs and smiling faces. Delighted to meet a foreigner they spoke to me in Urdu, teasing me when I couldn't understand and enjoying my attempts to pronounce their names. My photos from home fascinated them and one woman, married only two months, showed me her wedding album. They offered me *pan* – a mixture of spices and mild intoxicants wrapped in a betal leaf – and laughed when I screwed up my face at the bitter taste then, in my ignorance, swallowed it with watering eyes. At the stations we reached through the windows and bought hard-boiled eggs, bananas, and tea in disposable clay cups. Later, when it grew dark and sleeping shapes draped with shawls sprawled on the hard wooden seats and carriage floor, the women offered me a turn on the luggage rack and I slept. '

Multan, a traditional religious city, came as a shock. Women wore the *burka*, a garment that fits tightly round the crown of the head, completely covering all but the woman's feet. She sees the world through a net visor. In traditional society women turn their backs on male strangers. Hurrying along the back streets of the towns they turned away as I passed, mistaking me for a man. My behaviour rather than my appearance was to blame for the misconception; I was doing things that Muslim women didn't do. It saddened me to see them pull their veils over their faces and retreat into the shadows.

"That night, lying awake with men peeping at me through knot holes in the door, my spirits were low"

The men were clearly unused to seeing Western women. Youths trailed me, giggling and jostling, leering rickshaw drivers kerb-crawled, men followed me making kissing sounds and suggestive comments, and boys nearly fell off their bikes in their efforts to turn and watch me. I felt so uncomfortable that I returned to my hotel.

That night, lying awake with men peeping at me through knot holes in the door, my spirits were low. It seemed that the dire warnings I'd been given about Pakistani men were justified. How could I hope to travel in this country? I was heading for the mountains and experience led me to hope that it would be different there. Yet my guidebook gave the disheartening advice that it was dangerous to travel alone in the Himalayas – for women, of course. I left

for Lahore early in the morning, hating myself for giving in but unable to face another day in Multan.

Lahore felt much more European. Unlike their drab veiled country sisters the women of Lahore wear brilliant colours and their *shalwaar kameez* are more tightly fitting – some even have short sleeves, though legs are always covered. However, it was difficult to look around the city. I attracted whistles and leers even though I was modestly dressed. Men stood close to me, staring, oblivious to my feelings, and everybody asked questions, always the same, about my country, my name, my age, my occupation, my qualifications. Few people bothered to listen to the answers.

By the time I left for the mountains I loathed men. The *chai* shop at the bus station smelt of diesel fumes and was crowded with men sheltering from the rains. The wails of a baby came from behind a curtain where women could sit in private. The waiter, confused by my anomalous status, did not seat me with the women but cleared a table for me and protectively kept away any man who tried to sit with me. Outside the rain poured, streaming from the plastic sheeting that vendors rigged up over their stalls and filling potholes in the bus yard through which motor rickshaws lurched. People struggled in the mud in plastic slip-on shoes.

After a twenty-hour bus journey up the Indus gorge we emerged in Gilgit, isolated amongst the high mountains of the Karakorams. In the dusty bazaar swarthy men wearing dun-coloured blankets over their *shalwaar kameez* stared at me curiously. In tiny shops bargaining sessions were conducted over glasses of tea, the customers sitting on sacks of lentils or squatting against piles of rock-salt, smoking cigarettes through clenched fists. If the draped figures of women were seen at all they disappeared quickly.

In the *chai* shop, men lounging on string beds turned to look as I entered.

The sight of a foreigner, let alone a female one, was enough to attract attention and it was impossible for me to break through the barrier of staring eyes and speak to anyone. Maybe the men weren't unfriendly, just ill at ease when a woman invaded their preserve. But the result was the same; I drank alone.

"Maybe the men weren't unfriendly, just ill at ease when a woman invaded their preserve"

Away from the town it was different. Walking on tracks between villages I was stared at by children and tongue-tied youths and young women giggled at me, but everyone greeted me with "Salaam". In the villages so many people invited me in for tea it was difficult to choose one house without offending.

At the end of the day the smell of wood smoke heralded a settlement. Children came whooping down the terraces shouting "angrezi" (foreigner) and led me to an old man sitting outside his house, presumably the headman. Inside, orders were given to his wife and daughters and a meal of *chapatis*, chillied potatoes and rice was prepared on the stove. The women held a water jug for the man and I to wash our hands, then served the meal to us, waiting until we had finished before they ate. I hated the deference they showed me. As a foreigner and an honorary male I felt I was betraying these women.

These women had little variety in their lives and seemed to enjoy my visits as a break in their routine. Away from men they relaxed. Though we had no common language they managed to ask many questions: "Was I alone? Why did I have short hair? How many children had I?" In a land where children are highly valued, I was pitied for being childless. Once I was admonished for my immodesty and advised to roll my sleeves down and button my shirt higher at my neck. Often I was gently teased and it didn't matter that I couldn't understand. It was frustrating however, not to be able to talk to the women other than in sign language. The Urdu I was learning was little use when every village spoke a different dialect, and as girls have only recently started to receive education, few women spoke English.

Being invited into people's homes, forbidden to men outside the family, was one of the privileges I enjoyed in Pakistan. But it didn't outweigh the disadvantages. In many areas I felt threatened. Probably there was no real danger although once I was forced to turn back when a man blocked my way, masturbating. Conflicting emotions confused me as I left. In this country I had felt oppressed even while I was humbled by the hospitality. And three months of being treated as a second-class citizen, albeit often graciously, had left me resentful of being a woman. This was the hardest thing to bear. I can't imagine that Benazir Bhutto's election success will make any difference. It will take more than one woman, powerful but far removed from the lives of ordinary women, to change the attitude of the Muslim male.

TRAVEL NOTES

Languages Urdu, Pushtu and many others. You will find many people speak English in the main towns.

Transport Most buses and trains have special seats or compartments for women and children. There are also different queues for women to buy tickets.

Accommodation A wide range, from top-class international-style hotels to small, very basic inns. Some of the smaller hotels refuse to let out rooms to single women.

Special Problems Harassment can become restrictive and oppressive. It helps to dress conservatively in long, loose clothes or the traditional *shalwaar kameez* (long-sleeved tunic and trousers). It's also possible to hire a guide from a hotel. If you ever feel uneasy you should seek help from Pakistani women.

Guide *Pakistan – A Travel Survival Kit* (Lonely Planet) is the best researched, but you'll need to get local information on areas that are closed off by the military.

Contacts

Women's Action Forum (WAF), 103 Basement Raja centre, Main Market, Gulberg 2, Lahore (postal address: PO Box 3287, Gulberg, Lahore). Holds monthly public meetings, and organises workshops, seminars and discussion groups in both Urdu and English.

Asian Women's Institute, c/o Association of Kinnaird College for Women, Lahore-3. Active in the field of education and women's studies, also in rural development projects for women which emphasise consciousness-raising as well as economic growth.

Simorgh (Women's Resource and Publication Centre), 1st floor, Shiraz Plaza, Main Market, Gulberg 2, Lahore (postal address: PO Box 3328). A new women's centre aimed at providing resources, documentation, research etc, for the Women's Movement.

Books

Benazir Bhutto, *Daughter of the East* (Mandarin, 1988). Benazir describes her fabulously privileged upbringing in Pakistan, her Oxford years and the traumatic events surrounding her father's death. There's little that could be considered self-revealing although it's worth reading as a loose chronicle of the more obvious influences on her life.

Khawar Mumtaz and Farida Shaheed, *Women of Pakistan* (Zed Books, 1986). Concise account of women's determined resistance under the Zia regime.

Dervla Murphy, *Where the Indus is Young* (1976; Century, 1985). Lively account of a journey through the more remote parts of northern Pakistan which the author made with her seven-year-old daughter.

Paraguay

Paraguay is something of a backwater and is rarely visited in comparison to its Latin American neighbours. This fact is entirely to your advantage. There is little of the *gringa* mentality, and, even as a woman alone, you are unlikely to be intimidated by men. The kind of violence and theft against tourists associated with, say, Colombia, Peru or Brazil, is also virtually unknown.

Two bitter wars and several autocratic dictatorships have, however, left their scars on this remote, landlocked country, whose population includes a high

proportion of people of Guarani Indian descent. During 34 years of military rule under the notorious General Alfredo Stroessner, when hundreds of political dissenters were killed, imprisoned, or disappeared, indigenous peoples faced extinction as their lands were seized to make way for cattle ranching, intensive agriculture and foreign speculators. At the same time Paraguay became known as a tax-free haven for infamous right-wing pariahs, including the deposed Nicaraguan dictator Anastasio Somoza and several Nazi war criminals. It also became known as an important staging post for drug traffickers.

Recently, however, the country has seen dramatic changes. In February 1989 Stroessner's former right-hand man, General Andreas Rodriguez, mounted a successful coup. Promising democracy and respect for human rights, he had little trouble in winning the presidential elections hastily thrown together some three months later. As he denies widespread accusations of involvement in the lucrative cocaine trade and people wait for signs of concrete reform, there is still hope that the fall of one of the world's most repressive dictatorships has opened up the way for a process of genuine democratisation.

The sleepiness and isolation of Paraguay is reflected in a set of outdated, patriarchal laws that discriminate blatantly against women. A woman found guilty of adultery receives a prison sentence twice as long as a man in the same situation, and, in the eyes of the law, rape of a single woman is a less serious crime than that of a married woman. Women were only accorded the right to vote in 1961 and as recently as 1987 the government passed a law prohibiting women from working outside the home without their husband's permission.

Although **women's groups** have started campaigning for legal changes in the last decade, on the whole they have been nowhere near as vociferous and radical as their sister organisations in the rest of South America. However, the Women's Movement does seem to be gaining momentum and groups have multiplied in the last five years. Since the fall of Stroessner the once censored progressive Radio Nanduti is back on the air and transmits a regular "woman's hour", known as "Palabra de Mujer", which provides women with an invaluable forum to air their views.

"Land of Peace and Sunshine"

. . . .

Mary Durran spent two months in Paraguay at the invitation of a missionary friend, towards the end of the Stroessner dictatorship. She now works for the London-based El Salvador and Guatemala Committees for Human Rights.

In spite of the claims in official tourist leaflets, there wasn't a great deal of sun when I arrived at Asunción airport. But the city was bathed in a wintry haze, dusk was approaching, and there was certainly an air of tranquillity, if not peace, about the place. Bored-looking officials stood around leaning on airport counters, grunting to each other in Guarani, Paraguay's indigenous language. Two of them welcomed the diversion of a thorough search through my rucksack.

I hadn't chosen Paraguay for any specific interest in the country's culture or politics. I had simply followed up the offer of a friend, Paco, who was sent there as a missionary shortly after being ordained as a priest. Caught up with sitting final exams and with my last long summer before me, I had vaguely suggested visiting him to "help with whatever I could", but had made no definite plans as to how I'd spend my time.

As we drove from the airport through the cobbled streets, swerving to avoid potholes, towards the suburb of Lambare, dishevelled-looking barefoot children approached us at traffic lights to sell us newspapers, crying their wares in the curious nasal tones that only a Guarani speaker could utter. I caught a glimpse of a weather-beaten old Indian woman, her wrinkled face blackened by constant exposure to the elements, her headdress a sad mass of flopping, dirty feathers. Cows grazed placidly on grass verges and squalid tumbledown shacks stood beside spacious white houses with gardens and swimming pools. Every street corner displayed the regulation poster of the ailing president of the republic with the slogan "Peace and progress with General Stroessner".

I was later to discover the Asunción depicted by the tourist leaflets: the grandiose white government palace, home to the president and a few dignitaries, which stands only a few yards away from the mosquito-infested shanty town on the edge of the River Paraguay; the impressive Hotel Guarani and its fashion shows featuring the latest European collections for the Paraguayan jet set; exclusive discotheques where elegant bow-tied waiters address customers in the indigenous language, yet a beer would cost the average Paraguayan at least a day's wages. There was something faintly ridiculous about the sombre grandeur of the dark and cool interior of the Heroes' Pantheon, where the bodies of former dictators are interred.

A few days after my arrival, we drove along a dirt track road, pitted by ditches and potholes. Red sand flew everywhere. I was on my way to Yhu, a small town in the east of the country and home to about 1500 people. As we passed the *ranchitos* (wooden huts with thatched roofs) of the smallholders, old men raised their ruddy hands in greeting, their palms reddened by seasons of contact with the dark soil. The red sand contrasted with the verdant green of the surrounding *estancias* and beautiful brightly coloured butterflies basked in the hot sun.

Having done my homework, I knew that about 80,000 people, mainly smallholders and their families, lived in the district surrounding Yhu. There were only two doctors in this area, about the size of Wales, and I had been invited to stay with a family who were determined to improve the standard of healthcare in their community. Chiquita was a 23-year-old voluntary rural health worker living with her family in San Juan, a

small community. Trained by missionary sisters in basic first aid and preventive healthcare, her main task was running the health club which had been set up to encourage villagers to take measures to prevent disease.

> *"From the advertising and television I saw in Asunción, European women and European lifestyles are presented as the models to aspire to"*

As I was introduced to Chiquita's parents, her numerous brothers and sisters and in-laws, I took in what were to be my immediate surroundings for the next few days. The family was housed in four straw-roofed wooden huts in the middle of a plot of land where bananas and manioc (a starchy root crop) were cultivated. A couple of black piglets ran around squealing and several hens pecked at the ground. A crackly old wireless set played the latest American disco sounds alternated with the inimitable strains of Paraguayan polkas – popular folkloric music brought over by German settlers at the beginning of the century. Most of the words were in Guarani, and sang of the beauty of the Paraguayan countryside and the charms of the indigenous *cunatái* – young women. There's some irony in such eulogies, since from the advertising and television I saw in Asunción, European women and European lifestyles are in reality presented as the models to aspire to.

A log fire in one of the huts served as the kitchen. To prepare a meal (often manioc and cornflour omelettes), water had to be drawn from the well and food was cooked in a pot hanging over the fire. There was no chimney. The fire burned from dawn to dusk providing light, warmth and comfort during the long winter evenings. Its earthy smell permeated everything – clothes, hair and sleeping bag – and remains one of my most vivid impressions of the few days spent with Chiquita and her family.

I was made to feel very welcome. Although not speaking Guarani was a distinct disadvantage (as it is everywhere in Paraguay), Chiquita's parents made sure their Spanish-speaking children translated their greetings and questions. Her teenage sisters and brother were intensely curious about me and never seemed to tire of staring while I wrote letters or read. This made me feel rather uncomfortable, though I tried to bear in mind that, for them, to stare was simply a natural expression of interest and curiosity.

"The family insisted on providing one of the younger brothers as a chaperone every time I went anywhere"

I very quickly became aware that I was an object of absolute fascination for most of the villagers too, many of whom had never been any further than Caaguazu, the main provincial town some sixty miles away. "Did I have a husband?" No, I answered patiently, to at least twenty different people. "Why then, was I not accompanied by at least one of my parents?" (I had to smile at the idea of my ageing parents accompanying me over gruelling dirt tracks to a hamlet where there was neither post, newspapers nor electricity!)

Since I was unaccompanied, the family insisted on providing one of the younger brothers as a chaperone every time I went anywhere, even if it were only a few yards away. I found this quite amusing if sometimes irritating, but realised that the family were genuinely concerned about my welfare and simply couldn't understand the notion that I didn't mind, and sometimes even preferred, going out on my own. Norma, Chiquita's sister, explained to me that women who went out alone were generally badly thought of, considered by men to be trying to attract their attention.

Eighteen-year-old Norma had a boyfriend from a nearby village, who would come to visit her on the traditional courting days: Tuesdays, Thursdays, Saturdays and Sundays. Why such a rigid code? "Normally, the girl's parents would think badly of a *novio* (boyfriend) who disregarded tradition," she explained. The young couple would often sit in the dusk outside the huts, but always within sight of Norma's mother or one of her older brothers. And for them to go to one of the travelling dances without a chaperone was unthinkable – mother or older brother had to go too. I was surprised to learn that in spite of this strict moral code, there were several single mothers in San Juan and the surrounding area. But it did seem that most families required their daughters to adhere to this convention.

Although Paraguay is unquestionably a male-dominated society, I actually felt very safe as a lone female traveller. I found most Paraguayans gentle and softly-spoken, and if there is a grain of truth in the myth propagated by Stroessner that Paraguay is an "oasis of peace", it lies in the fact that the traveller in Paraguay does not have to be obsessive about devising ingenious methods of hiding money and valuables in their shoes and underwear. The violence and theft that tourists experience in many other Latin American countries are virtually unheard of in Paraguay. Neither are women travellers likely to be intimidated by men on city streets or in the countryside. Paraguayans welcome travellers, who are generally treated with friendliness and curiosity, foreign women receiving probably much more respect than their Paraguayan counterparts.

Almost inevitably, during my stay in San Juan I never once saw a man do any of the traditionally female household tasks. On top of housework, the women seemed to do most of the back-breaking work in the *chacra*, each smallholder's plot of land, a lifeline for the survival of the family.

Chiquita's family were lucky enough to possess title deeds to their land. I met a family who had no documents proving "ownership" of the tiny plot of land that had housed and fed their ancestors for centuries. Their peace had been shattered one day by the agents of a foreign absentee landowner who had bought the land from the government. Some of the neighbours had refused to move from their plots and were subsequently continually harassed by agents of the landowner. One man had been shot dead in a violent scuffle.

I later found out that Paraguay's land distribution problem is acute. Although there are vast expanses of land available for cultivation, there are approximately 300,000 landless families in the country and eighty percent of the national territory is owned by one percent of the population. Many people in eastern Paraguay had been driven to occupy uncultivated land owned by absentee landlords, and these occupations, although legal under Paraguayan law, have led to several violent conflicts between squatters and army or police-backed landowners.

Malnutrition is also a severe problem. On my first day in San Juan, I woke to the din of cocks crowing and the smell of the fire. I itched all over from mosquito bites. We rose at 6am and walked three miles along the red sand path to the health centre. Already, a queue of patients had formed – old men, mothers with crying children, a man whose arm was in a makeshift sling. I watched Chiquita administer a salt and water solution to a scrawny baby with chronic diarrhoea. She then recommended a simple diet to the mother.

Chiquita explained that many families lived for several months of the year just on manioc, especially if the price of cotton had been low at harvest time. This explained why most of the children were undernourished. Attempts by local farmers to organise to beat the middlemen's price monopolies on cotton had been met with brutal

government repression. Several peasant leaders had been imprisoned and tortured for their efforts.

"Lesson one began: 'William Shakspeer borned in Stratford-upon-Avon'. I reckoned I could at least do better than that"

I left San Juan amazed at Chiquita's dedication and commitment to what was a never-ending task, with few rewards. I returned to Yhu, and spent three weeks living in relative luxury, in a house belonging to missionaries, which had running water, and electricity for a few hours in the evening! During the day, I taught a variety of subjects to some of the 165 pupils at the only secondary school in the district.

Not having come prepared to teach in a school, when this was suggested I felt somewhat daunted by the prospect – until one of the sisters showed me a school 1950s-produced dog-eared English language textbook. Lesson One began: "William Shakspeer borned in Stratford-upon-Avon". I reckoned I could at least do better than that and decided to have a go. I tried to organise my lessons on an exchange basis: I would teach my class an English or a Spanish song, then I'd ask the pupils, aged between 13 and 27, to teach me a Paraguayan song in Guarani. This way, I hoped to place equal value on their culture, and to make the point that things European weren't necessarily better, as many of them believed.

Many were intensely curious about the lifestyle and material goods I had in England; they were very disappointed to discover that my parents lived in an ordinary semi-detached house and not a *Dynasty*-style mansion which they assumed was the norm in Europe. I often asked the young women about their feelings about the status of women in the Paraguayan countryside. What did they think of the fact that the women did all the work in the house, often on the *chacra* and looked after the children as well? Most shrugged and said, "that's the way things are". One girl of about fourteen said, "women are lucky, because if there's a war, it's the men who've got to do the fighting."

There is one image of the national school in Yhu that has stayed with me. Every day, before school began, the pupils would line up outside the building and halfheartedly sing the national anthem. One of the lines referred to

Paraguay as the republic "where union and equality reign". I thought of the Asunción elite and their white houses with swimming pools and contraband Mercedes, and then of the peasant families in their cramped huts who eked out the year with a meagre diet of manioc. That was the reality behind the veneer of the "land of peace and sunshine". There was a very hollow ring to that anthem.

TRAVEL NOTES

Languages Spanish is the official language though most of the population express themselves more fluently in Guarani. Seventeen Indian tribes speak variations of another five different languages.

Transport Buses run between all major destinations, but more remote parts of the country are very hard to get to, even if you hire a jeep. Hitching, though probably safer than in other Latin American countries, carries the obvious risks.

Accommodation Good cheap accommodation is plentiful in Asunción and, apart from some of the *residenciales* around the railway station, hotels are generally clean and safe. The same applies to the roadside hostels which you'll find along all major roads. It's more difficult to find somewhere to stay once you get off the beaten track.

Guide *The South American Handbook* (Trade and Travel Publications) has around 25 pages on Paraguay.

Contacts

For more information write to the **Paraguay Committee for Human Rights**, Latin America House, Kingsgate Place, London NW6.

The only women's organisation we have been able to locate in Paraguay is the women's studies group, **Grupo de Estudios de la Mujer Paraguaya**, Eligio Ayala 973, Asunción, who produce a publication, *Enfoquer de Mujer*.

Books

We have found no books on Paraguay, but the **Latin America Bureau**, 1 Amwell St., London EC1R 1UL, has published 2 reports: *Dominion ... for ever Secured?*, a report of a mission to Paraguay by the British Parliamentary Human Rights Group, May 1987, and *Paraguay: Power Game* (1980). A more recent booklet, *Decline of the Dictator: Paraguay's Crossroads* is available from the **Washington Office on Latin America**, 110 Maryland Ave., NE, Washington DC 20002, USA. Cost US$8.

Special thanks to Mary Durran for background information.

Peru

eru is one of the most travelled countries in South America, largely due to its magnificent Inca sites. It also, however, has one of the poorest and most isolated Indian populations in the entire continent. Erratic changes in government, combined with the development of the coast and the Amazon (rich in oil) at the expense of the sierra have restricted any positive moves to improve their position in recent years.

Since the early 1980s, the country has been in the grips of a devastating financial crisis. Inflation has been running at a staggering 5000 percent and, with the denial of any new international loans, the standard of living for those still in employment has plummeted. The embattled young president, Alan García Perez, a social democrat, is leaving office in April 1990. Novelist Mario Vargas Llosa looks set to be his successor on a centre-right coalition ticket, promising to restructure the economy by dismantling state bureaucracy and selling off state-owned companies, increasing prices and devaluing currency.

All this financial chaos and uncertainty is taking place against a background of continuing guerrilla activity, terror and disruption by the *Sendero Luminoso* (Shining Path), a Maoist group allegedly dedicated to achieving self-sufficiency for Peru's largely Indian peasant population. Whatever its motives, *Sendero*'s continuing campaign of bomb attacks, coupled with the government's violent response, have led to a wave of unrest previously unknown in Peru. For the traveller this means that at least one section of the country, the mountainous area around Ayacucho, is completely out of bounds. Most recently, there are reports that Colombian drug barons have begun to transplant their cocaine enterprises across the border into Peru, and in so doing are forging alliances with the guerrillas and the peasant coca producers, beyond the reach of government.

Besides the danger of being caught up in escalating guerrilla activity – the *Sendero Luminoso* have very little sympathy for foreign travellers – Peru is notorious for the skill of its thieves who will try almost any trick to distract you from guarding your belongings. Heed warnings carefully and avoid travelling at night. Women don't report any general sexual threat, but take care: you may well seem a more vulnerable target for robbery.

Peru has a relatively active **women's movement**. As in all Latin American countries, most of its groups are socialist-feminist in outlook, meaning that they are based on the belief that the majority of Peruvian women (seventy percent of the illiterate population) are doubly oppressed, as women and as members of the poorest socio-economic class. At the same time, they are concerned with issues such as the legalisation of free abortion on demand, the right to contraception, and the campaign against male violence, all of which have been consistently neglected by the traditional Left.

An Uncluttered Trip

· · · · · · · · · · · ·

After a disastrous start, Margaret Hubbard spent a rewarding few weeks travelling alone by bus and train to all the better-known destinations in Peru.

My journey from Europe to South America lasted forever. At every refuelling stop the passengers changed – only a handful of worthies who had got on the plane in London seemed destined for Lima. Only then did I feel how very far away South America is.

Perhaps because it does not have for us the strategic importance it does to "Uncle Sam", most Europeans have limited knowledge of South American life and politics. Our media carry little news, so my ideas were shaky and stereotyped. I had one contact in Lima and it was she, along with simple curiosity, who had taken me there.

At Lima airport I faced the nightmare that all travellers dread. My luggage had been lost in transit. Thirty-six hours of travel and only a sparse knowledge of Spanish is not the recipe for dealing calmly with this catastrophe. I stood in Lima airport with nothing but my documents, my money, a camera, one film and a book. The airline assured me the luggage would arrive on Saturday, Monday, Wednesday, mañana; it was in Bogotá, Buenos Aires, wherever. I never saw it again and coping with this disaster turned out to be the key to my holiday and to some lovely moments I would never otherwise have had.

Peru is a difficult place to travel, but being alone did not of itself seem to be a problem. Nor did being a woman; the *machismo* was little different to that in Mediterranean Europe. But being a foreigner, and by definition wealthy in the eyes of the inhabitants of a Third World country, the situation was constantly uneasy and at times positively harrowing. Theft is a big problem. Rucksacks are slit. Thieves jump on to the trains at the switchbacks and the stations to steal luggage not securely tied or chained down. Jewellery is a prime target.

There is a resulting paranoia which sets in and grows worse the longer that you stay. I finished up constantly alert and wary and I met others unwilling or unable to relax their wariness enough even to chat to local people or fellow travellers in case it distracted from the business in hand of protecting their belongings. I was constantly warned to take no notice of any display of local folk culture, children singing or dancing, for example; it was almost certainly a set-up for theft. These warnings were in the guidebooks, but they were also coming from Peruvians that I met.

"In choosing to travel by train I accidentally fell upon a solution to my luggageless state"

The combination of locals warning foreigners against their own people, and an unease about watching some of the attractions of the country became in the end very wearing. I reached the point in Puno of wondering whether the apparently friendly warnings of the apparently friendly locals were themselves part of a set-up. They weren't but that level of unease and distrust is something I have never experienced before in many years of travelling.

Getting around, the roads proved rough and the bus journeys shaky, so trains seemed a better option. In choosing to travel by train I accidentally fell upon the solution to my luggageless state. I had bought the bare minimum of replacement clothing in Lima, the airline constantly assuring me that my

luggage would turn up. On the train to Huancayo, the highest railway station in the world, I told a fellow traveller my tale. She and others in the carriage immediately gave me items I needed. A T-shirt here, three diarrhoea pills there, a pair of socks, a map. All vital items, so carefully planned and packed at home.

That was only the beginning. All along the journeys to Cuyo, Puno, La Paz, people gave or loaned me items. In some ways the loans were most valuable of all. To allow a total stranger use of an item you want to keep is an act of trust seldom met in this world. I spent many happy hours back in Scotland packing up borrowed items and boxes of Edinburgh rock. In some ways I think this could only have happened in a place so fraught with danger.

The journey to Huancayo was exciting. I had read Paul Theroux's *The Old Patagonian Express* and he seemed less than happy on this journey – I loved it. Desemparados Station was a colonial architectural gem, and the train even more fascinating. Up we went on the switchbacks, going forwards, reversing, forward, reverse, and always gaining more height. I began to get breathless and overwhelmed with tiredness. The air was raw and thin.

Huancayo itself is an Indian town, and, despite the fame of the journey, not that heavily geared to tourists. I spent a week up there and used the local buses to get to the villages roundabout. The fertility of the valley astonished me. It also felt safe to walk in the hills alone, although I never went too far off the path. It was cold. Anyone travelling to South America in winter should not underestimate how cold it is at these heights. Proximity to the tropic is irrelevant. During the day it is often in the seventies and at night below freezing.

A friend in Lima afforded me an opportunity to participate in a very different Peru. Very quickly I saw how extensive is the control of the country in the hands of a very few Europeans and their wealthy Peruvian counterparts. The suburban mansions of San Isidro and Miraflores, their shops, cafés, life-styles and values are completely European. The Lima Cricket and Tennis Club is an enclave of a colonial past where you can drink pisco sours and read *The Times*. The ex-pats I met were very friendly and went out of their way to show me around. But I was struck by how small a community it is and how hungry they were for news from home.

"Sadly, this has affected Peruvians' attitude to their own culture, which they regard as second rate"

Peruvian folk culture is a casualty of the country's ambivalent attitude to the USA. Despite a political wariness of its influence and power, North America still symbolises wealth and a better way of life. Sadly, this has affected Peruvians' attitude to their own culture, which, in general, they regard as second rate – a great shame in a country so rich in indigenous music and art.

The centre of folk culture is Ayacucho. However, this city is also a centre of *Sendero Luminoso* activity and thus to be avoided by foreign travellers. I was lucky to see a group of Ayacucho musicians performing in Lima. It was fascinating and I left sad that this music was not more easily available. The lost luggage meant severe tightening of the financial belt, but tapes of Peruvian music were high on the list of necessities to bring home.

For most people, Cuzco, Machu Picchu and Lake Titicaca are the mecca of a trip to Peru. Sooner or later, most, if not all, South American travellers finish up at these sights, and the first two at least were for me no disappointment. I loved Cuzco. It had such charm. The Spanish churches and the halls built on Inca foundations were a mind-bending architectural combination. Through narrow cobbled lanes, up the hill to Sacsayhuamán, the fortress on the hilltop keeping watch over the valley below. Only the columns of Egypt have previously dwarfed me into silence. These massive Inca stones cut

with only the most basic of tools and transported without the wheel left me gazing in awe.

Machu Picchu, too, was everything I hoped for, and more. Stripped of tent, boots, etc, I had to go by train. The Inca trail was no longer possible. I took the local train to Aguas Calientes, a little village one mile before Machu Picchu where there are thermal springs. It was hot and had all the steaminess of high jungle. In the early morning I walked up the railway line to the foot of the mountain and began the climb. It seemed almost indecent to go up any other way. At the top I was seized by a childish unwillingness to look in case it was a let-down. I had nothing to fear. The tiny houses and narrow streets had a sense of identity quite impossible to catch in the photos. The ruins would have been impressive anywhere. But it is the setting which leaves the spectator breathless. Set on a mountain saddle which falls off on each side to the Urubamba river, the ruins are surrounded by a bowl of jungle-covered peaks. It is so remote and so moving that it is difficult to leave behind. Somehow I wanted to parcel it up and take it with me.

I am glad I felt this about Machu Picchu because sadly I felt quite different about the floating islands on Lake Titicaca. There is always an unhealthy contradiction in the juxtaposition of tourism and traditional culture, but at the Lake it verged on the obscene. In one of the most desolate and beautiful places on this planet, I felt a captive source of income, gazing at a human zoo. It disturbed me very deeply indeed.

Peru was for me a strange holiday of dichotomy; stress and beauty, loneli-ness and moments of rich companion-ship. I felt a sense of relief when I left to be alive and going home, but back in Britain, months later, Peru haunts me and I search the pages of the news-papers for its news. To me it is no longer on the other side of the world. It is now in me, part of me, and I feel a richer person for having been there.

TRAVEL NOTES

Languages Spanish, Quechua and Aymara.

Transport A fairly comprehensive network of long-distance buses covers all but the most remote Andean towns and the Amazon region. There is no railway in the mountains except between Lima and Huancayo and across the flat *altiplano* between Cuzco and Lake Titicaca. As well as being potentially dangerous, hitching is difficult and you are expected to pay.

Accommodation There are plenty of hotels, most of them cheap but fairly basic. Camping is free since there are only a couple of official campgrounds but you'd be advised not to sleep out alone in remote areas.

Special Problems Peru is the home of very skilled pickpockets and grab-and-run thieves so take care everywhere, especially when arriving in towns at night by public transport. Remember that thieves often work in groups – sometimes families – where *gringas* are caught off-guard by the distracting appealing glances of a small wide-eyed child. It is a livelihood.

Coca leaves, the raw material of cocaine, are freely and legally available for chewing and brewing. However the government, with American help, has mounted a big campaign against smuggling and production of the drug itself. Police have a habit of arresting *gringos*, especially in Lima, and demanding a ransom for their release – otherwise drug-handling charges are threatened. Five years in a Peruvian jail is no joke, so make sure there is absolutely no reason for you to be under suspicion.

The *Sendero Luminoso*, whose activities are spreading, have no love of foreign tourists, so take care to avoid areas where they are active.

Guides *The Rough Guide: Peru* (Harrap Columbus) is probably the best guidebook to any individual South American country, practical and culturally sensitive. Otherwise the *South American Handbook* (Trade and Travel Publications) is always recommended.

Contacts

For up-to-date information on the situation in Peru, contact the **Peru Support Group**, 20 Compton Terrace, London N1 2UN, ☎359 2270.

Among the most longstanding **women's organisations** are:

Flora Tristán, Centro de la Mujer Peruana Av. Arenales 601, Lima. Women's centre dedicated to the growth, development and strengthening of the feminist movement in Peru. Allied to the United Left (*Apron*) party, with the basic tenet "first socialism, then the feminist revolution".

Movimiento Manuela Ramos, Camana 280-Oficina 305, Apartado Postal 11176, Lima 14. Mainly concerned with co-ordinating projects with working-class women. Write first.

There are quite a few **feminist publications** in Peru, published in Spanish. Watch out for *Mujer y Sociedad, La Tortuga* and *La Manzana*. For help, literature, or advice try *Flora Tristán*, the *Libreria de la Mujer* **bookshop** (near the women's centre in Quilca, just half a block from Av. Wilson), which is run by nuns.

Books

Dervla Murphy, *Eight Feet in the Andes* (John Murray, 1983). Describes the author's journey with her nine-year-old daughter and a mule 1,300 miles through the Andes.

Audrey Bronstein, ed., *The Triple Struggle: Latin American Peasant Women* (War on Want Campaigns, London, 1982). See General Bibliography.

Carol Andreas, *The Rise of Popular Feminism in Peru* (Lawrence Hill, US, 1985). Accessible account of the gradual rise of the Peruvian Women's Movement.

Ximena Bunster and Elsa Chaney, *Sellers and Servants: Working Women in Lima, Peru* (Bergin and Garvey, US, 1989). Using an innovative "talking pictures" technique, presents the lives of women street peddlers and domestic servants from their own words.

Michael Reid, *Peru – Paths to Poverty* (Latin America Bureau, London, 1985). Good account of the political situation from the 1950s. The author is currently working on a book about the García years, to be published in 1990.

Mario Vargas Llosa, *Aunt Julia* and the *Scriptwriter* (Picador, 1984), ***Conversations in the Cathedral*** (Faber, 1986), and others. Llosa is Peru's best-known novelist – highly readable with incidental, sometimes crazy insights into life in Lima.

The Philippines

Tourists are beginning to steer clear of the Philippines. Its image as a collection of tropical island paradises (replete with luxury hotels and private beaches) has become more than tarnished by the country's obvious political instability. Since being swept into office by the extraordinary "People Power" revolution of 1986, President Corazon Aquino has faced six coup attempts (the latest involving pitched battles with rebel army factions on the streets of Manila), a plummeting economy, and a continuing war in the southern islands with the communist New People's Army.

Although Aquino herself still claims some popularity, the optimism that greeted the end of the twenty-year Marcos dictatorship has become submerged by disillusion that little has really changed. Unemployment has continued to rise and the sprawling poverty-stricken slums that border most cities have been swelled by a new wave of rural poor. Aquino's failure to institute promised land reforms, deal with government corruption, or curb US intervention (from long-established US military bases in the country), are sources of mounting resentment.

Americans tourists particularly, and many luxury holidaymakers, are staying away. But there are still a fair number of European budget travellers stopping off at the Philippines as part of a long haul journey to East Asia. Tourists have in fact never been an ostensible target of hostilities, but travel is limited by army restrictions. However, it's essential to get up-to-date information before choosing to set off.

Uniquely in Asia, the islands of the Philippines are predominantly Catholic and Westernised – the indigenous Malay culture having been subsumed first by Spanish and then American influences – and English is widely spoken as a second language. In general terms Filipino men and women have a reputation for great courtesy and hospitality towards foreign visitors, and women particularly can be incredibly generous with their help and advice. Travelling on your own, anywhere other than the obvious tourist enclaves, you may well attract attention but you'll find that most people who approach you have a genuine (if disconcerting) interest in meeting a Western foreigner.

Sexual harassment from men does occur but it's usually in the form of catcalls and propositions and is rarely personally threatening. If you do have a problem you should turn to the nearest woman for help – it's likely that she'll take you under her wing. It's not unusual to be invited to stay in people's homes, either; in accepting you do need to be sensitive to the costs you impose and look for opportunities to reciprocate.

Women in the Philippines have for many years faced discrimination and exploitation at work. In the Marcos years cheap female labour was used explicitly to attract foreign investment for labour-intensive textiles and electronics industries, with promotional packages advertising the nimble fingers and docile nature of the workforce. Working conditions in these factories were, and continue to be, exceptionally grim. With much of the land taken over by vast agribusiness conglomerates, rural women had little choice but to look for work in the factories or otherwise join the service industries and prostitution rackets that flourished with the tourist trade and around the US military bases. Sex tourism, where the services of a prostitute would be included in the hotel and tour itinerary, became big business in the 1970s and "hostess bars" remain a common sight in Manila and the major tourist enclaves.

As unemployment and poverty have worsened, thousands of women have been leaving the country to find better paid, but often appallingly insecure, work as foreign domestic servants in Asia, the Middle East and Europe. In many countries – Saudi Arabia being a notorious example – Filipina women routinely face harassment and abuse as the bottom-of-the-heap of migrant workers. There are also a growing number of women who work as prostitutes in Japan on short-term entertainment visas – an inverted form of Japanese sex tourism.

In the name of national pride, Corazon Aquino declared a ban on all foreign recruitment of Filipino domestic servants in 1988. This was revoked shortly after as a result of pressure from the women themselves, who felt she was missing the point of their struggle to gain recognition and protection. The main campaigning force for women's rights in the Philippines is the umbrella organisation *Gabriela*. As well as implementing local campaigns against the sexual and economic exploitation of women it has highlighted the problems of women working within the "hospitality industry". The group continues to pressurise the government to bring about the necessary social and economic changes that will provide Filipinas with more equitable options. However, like many other legal organisations associated with the Left, it has to contend with continual suspicion and threat from the army.

Adjusting to the Sight of Guns

. . . .

Jackie Mutter visited the Philippines "out of sheer curiosity", almost a year after the overthrow of Ferdinand Marcos. She spent ten weeks in the country, on the first stage of a long solo trip via Asia to Australia.

As I boarded the plane for Manila, it occurred to me that I knew very little about my destination beyond its image as an exotic group of islands, famous for their palm-fringed beaches and, despite political upheaval, still coveted by many as an idyllic holiday location.

Armed with rucksack and carrying a copy of James Fenton's *Snap Revolution*, which offered a restricted though topical insight into the current state of affairs, I arrived in Manila alone, greeted by the onslaught of vivid first impressions that inevitably accompany one's immediate experience of Asia. This was my first "longhaul" trip outside Europe and the Soviet Union and, at 25 years old, I was travelling alone for the first time in my life. I felt apprehensive but my anxieties were lost in the excitement and anticipation of exploring unknown territory and at finally having escaped from the fetters of nine-to-five drudge in London.

My first few days were spent in a constant state of amazement as I survived, one by one, a steady stream of culture shocks. These started with my arrival at the airport and the surge of people who came at me from all angles as I left the arrival hall. Then came a hair-raising taxi ride, where I sat dazed and frozen, watching the suburbs of Manila fly past as if on a some giant 3-D movie screen. As we screeched to a halt at each junction, I caught a glimpse of the barefooted boys dodging in and out of the traffic, selling newspapers, chewing gum and cigarettes to drivers. I gradually became aware of people sitting on the grass verges in the middle of major roadways and the sudden realisation that these people were in fact living on these verges in makeshift homes left me feeling very, very naive. I was riddled with a guilt of decadence as I walked past people lying on pavements, too weak to move, and approached by young children begging and tugging at my clothes. The sight of young armed men guarding the banks, shops and money-changers was totally unfamiliar to me and yet was to become part of the everyday scenery in the Philippines.

"I soon found myself adjusting to the sight of guns and the aggression and underlying tensions that went with them"

Although I never experienced any violence during my two and a half months in the country, I remember being woken one night in Baguio by the sound of gunfire, and seeing a friend return one evening in a state of shock after having witnessed a man being shot dead in the streets of Ermita. One picture that sticks in my mind is that of a child, no more than eight or nine years old, playing with his father's automatic rifle as if it were nothing more harmful than a toy.

However, in the words of a friend, the Philippines is a political time-bomb and I soon found myself adjusting to the sight of guns and the aggression and underlying tensions that went with them. It became apparent after a few days of travelling around and talking to various people in the provinces of Zambales and Pangasinan, northwest of Manila, that life on an individual basis had much less value in a country where people were struggling to survive, where the majority of the population are living under the national poverty line and where "salvaging" (politically motivated murders) were daily occurrences.

Purely by coincidence, I had arrived in the Philippines almost a year after the Revolution which had ousted the repressive dictatorship of Ferdinand Marcos and his notorious wife, Imelda, and replaced them with the extremely tentative government of Corazon Aquino. I was interested in finding out how people felt about their release from the manacles of a dictatorship and was surprised to learn that Marcos still had many supporters, not only amongst the wealthy landowners, but also amongst the rural population. There was a general atmosphere of impatience and disillusionment with the new regime and the distinct lack of political and economic reforms which had been promised before the Revolution.

The long-awaited land reforms were conspicuous by their absence and the majority of peasants remained as tenants or hired agricultural workers. Furthermore, the Philippines has had for many years an export-orientated economy which has made the country a haven for multinational corporations, and consequent bad working conditions and wages which the people are powerless to change. Foreign control of the economy, feudal conflicts, and lack of social welfare seem to be the three major obstacles to redevelopment in the Philippines.

Despite their problems, the Filipinos are among the most friendly and welcoming people I have come across in my travels and I was frequently overwhelmed by kindness. Most of my time was spent in Northern Luzon, although this had not been my original intention. I left Manila after just a couple of days and headed north to Iba and Bolinao, where I was met with endless warmth and hospitality, being invited into homes to meet families, share meals, and spend the night exchanging stories, all of which gradually gave me an insight into Filipino lifestyles.

I discovered that this hospitality was customary and that refusing to share food or a drink would cause deep offence. Of course, there were the very occasional invitations that seemed to have an "ulterior" motive but on the whole – and to my embarrassment – I found that people were "honoured" to be visited by a Westerner.

"It was undoubtedly a trial at times, being a fair-haired, fair-skinned and blue-eyed single woman"

I travelled around the country by bus and *jeepney* (brightly coloured taxi jeeps) and, although crowded and bumpy at times, these journeys were never unbearable and certainly never dull. Sharing my limited space with chickens, pigs, and various other livestock, as well as all manner of produce, was a completely new experience and one that followed me throughout my travels in Asia. Although comfort was not comparable with Western standards, the only major discomforts were usually caused by lack of suspension and dusty roads! Besides, the attitude of the Filipinos was such that they would always create enough space for me and would go out of their way to ensure that I had a pleasant journey.

It was undoubtedly a trial at times, being a fair-haired, fair-skinned and blue-eyed single woman, and my patience and tolerance were frequently put to the test. In Manila there were very few instances when I ventured out into the city and returned without being followed or harassed in some form or other. On one occasion, I was actually kerbcrawled by police officers in a patrol car in the middle of the city! There were many other similar incidences too numerous to mention (one or two of them quite unpleasant) although none impossible to deal with. Being chased around my room early one morning by the 76-year-old hostel owner, who had let himself into my room with the master key, was one incident I found hard to take seriously. Nonetheless it can be a problem and one to be aware of.

My overall impression was that *machismo* seems to rate very highly among the characteristics of the Filipino male. A firm refusal, though, would usually work and I have experienced a far more brutal and arrogant type of sexual harassment in certain other countries. On the whole, I felt quite safe travelling alone and this feeling was reinforced by the attitudes of the Filipinas, who would always come to my aid when necessary and seemed to consider it their responsibility to protect me. I soon built up enormous respect for these women and was keen to learn more about their lives and the conditions in which they lived.

Consequently, I leapt at the opportunity, while in Baguio, Northern Luzon, to attend the first Congress of the Cordillera Women's Movement. The Cordillera is a collective name for the mountain provinces in Northern Luzon and incorporates villages where the cultural minorities of the region continue to practise their own laws and customs. There is an ongoing struggle to maintain their autonomy in the face of various pressures from the government and also from national and international corporations, who have made frequent attempts to take their land over in order to mine its precious metals deposits.

"Around fifty women attended the conference, most of them clothed in traditional dress"

I was introduced to the Congress by Leah, an active feminist who works at Baguio University and who was at the time trying to establish a centre for women in the area. This centre was to act as a much needed refuge, a rape crisis centre, and also as a means to educate women on their rights and the opportunities available to them. Violence against women in the Philippines is a widespread social problem and there is little within the law to protect women and provide them with

financial support, should they need it. Entrenched sexual inequality is aggravated by inadequate childcare and maternity benefits, lack of effective family planning, and lack of access to accurate information, as well as the additional hurdle created by corruption and waylaying of funds by local bureaucrats.

The Congress itself was to take place during the three days leading up to International Women's Day and turned out to be the most memorable part of my visit as it gave me the opportunity to listen to and learn about the women in these indigenous groups. I was also given a chance to participate in the conference myself, talking to the women about the Women's Movement in the West, its aims and achievements so far . . . I had to cover a fair amount of ground, needless to say!

Around fifty women attended the conference, most of them clothed in traditional dress, which was usually made up of bright red and black embroidered skirts, with some wearing headbands made from snake vertebrae and others dressed in brightly coloured beads with arms covered in ritual tattoos. The conference was conducted in Ilocano, the local, most commonly used dialect of Tagalog, and was translated for us by one of the conference organisers. We sang songs to start with – a very important aspect of Filipino culture – then various speakers discussed the general situation of women in the country.

However, the most interesting aspect of the conference was the workshops, where we were divided into groups to discuss and exchange our ideas and personal experiences. Women talked about the appalling work conditions within factories and mines, which are generally owned by multinational corporations, and consequent damage to their health (women frequently suffered from urinary infections due to working without breaks, even to visit the toilet), and horrific stories emerged of rape and various forms of sexual abuse. As for maternity benefits, in many cases the sack was almost inevitable for a pregnant woman working in a factory or mine.

Birth control was out of the question for most of the minority women as they have to consult their husbands first and, in some of the villages, lack of children within a marriage is grounds for divorce. On a national scale, even whilst I was there, an Executive Order, endorsed by the Minister of Social Services, had been passed whereby the government would only implement natural methods of family planning – yet another hurdle in women's uphill struggle to achieve some sort of independence.

Undoubtedly, the Philippines will always remain a special place for me: a country of spectacular and varied scenery, exotic rainforests and coastline, and home to a variety of cultures. I left with a profound admiration and respect for the women, in particular, whose courage enables them to maintain their hardworking, generous and kind disposition in spite of the suppression and abuse they endure in their daily lives.

Working as "One of the Boys"

· · · · · · · · · · · · · · · ·

Journalist Kate Barker spent five weeks in Manila in 1989 with a film crew, making a documentary about Freddie Aguilar, the Philippines' best-loved popular singer. She has since returned to explore the country on her own.

I never considered my big nose an asset until I arrived in the Philippines. People would come up to me in the street and say, "Hello ma'am. Your nose is so beautiful." Women I met would ask for my photograph to show their friends. The ideal is to be pale-skinned and pointy-nosed, a hankering after Western appearance that is part of the love of things foreign which President Corazon Aquino and her supporters are trying to tackle with a determined promotion of Filipino nationalism. But years of American interference in the country cannot be wiped away so easily. A foreign car, husband or friend remains a status symbol.

I was offered roles in television commercials during my stay, too, despite having absolutely no acting ability or experience. Film-makers are desperate for "white talent" to appear in advertisements, to give the impression that whatever is being pushed is imported, even if it is not.

"Every bar door we opened led on to the same scene: skimpily-clad women dancing on bar-tops"

I don't know if it was this attraction to all things foreign, the natural Filipino amiability, or the fact that I was meeting people through work rather than travelling as a tourist, but I found it very easy to make friends. I have spent a great deal of the last seven years abroad, in Europe, India, the Soviet Union and Turkey, but nowhere have I found myself so quickly accepted, and so few inhibitions or cultural differences acting as a block to friendship.

I was staying with two members of the film crew in a flat in Makati, the business area of Manila, which is also home to the most up-market of the capital's three red light districts. Many of the women working in the *girlie* bars had children to support. While they danced for the tourists, their mothers or sisters looked after the youngsters.

Soon after we arrived, I and another (male) journalist tried to find somewhere to have a beer. Every bar door we opened led on to the same scene: skimpily-clad women dancing on bar-tops, while their colleagues fawned over middle-aged European or American businessmen. Eventually we settled on a bar with an outside terrace and ordered drinks, with me feeling incredibly self-conscious. After a few visits, however, my qualms were eased. "Hello si-ir, hello ma'am," the girls used to shout as we entered. They were always very friendly towards me. They wanted to know how old I was, did I have a boyfriend, what did I think of the Philippines, and could they have my picture?

They often looked incredibly bored as they made flirtatious conversation with the punters. The men could take them away from the bar if they paid a bar fine to the management of between 300 and 500 pesos (roughly £8–14). The women got the money spent on their "ladies' drinks" – about £1.50 for each tiny glass of orange juice – and anything else the client gave them.

Many dreamed of marrying a Western man, or meeting someone who would send them an allowance so they could escape the bars. One such was Benjy who had only been working in the bars for three weeks to pay for her studies in computing. She said her father had died, leaving most of his money to his mistress, and there was nothing left to fund her studies. Benjy struck lucky while we were there and found an Englishman to pay for her education.

Appearances were sometimes deceptive. Not all the women were available for a bar fine. In one place, where the girls arrived for work in red satin knickers and vests, high heels and fishnets, the Western owner prided himself on employing only virgins and married women. Joy fell into the first category. She was nineteen and a student. She worked in the bar from 3pm to 3am before travelling the two hours' journey home to the provinces, where she went to school for the morning, then returned straight to Manila. She slept when she could. If there were no punters in the bar, the women got out their books to study. Joy wanted to be a doctor. She told me I looked like the Virgin Mary because I had "tantalising eyes". The remark seemed to sum up the happy-go-lucky attitude to sex and religion. In another bar, Rosa, the Madam, sang the praises of Cory Aquino as a devout family woman. In the next breath, she offered to procure girls for my two companions.

"This is the kind of hardship which drives thousands of Filipinas to Japan each year as 'entertainers'"

Despite their often desperate situation, the bar-girls remained stoically cheerful and optimistic. The same was true wherever we went. Even on Smoky Mountain, an enormous rubbish dump where over 22,000 of Manila's poor eke out a living by scavenging, there appeared to be no resentment towards myself and a friend as we were shown around by a church worker. No one asked us for money. They just wanted to know our names, and asked us to take their picture.

I spent a long time talking to a former cycle rickshaw driver who worked on the heap with his wife and children. They made just over the equivalent of £1 a day, each sorting out baskets of paper, glass, plastic and metal from the garbage. It was easy to see why large families were prevalent when a child could earn as much from scavenging as an adult.

Eva, our guide, said that typically the urban poor married young, did not finish their schooling, and had between six and eight children. Many came to Manila from the provinces hoping to find employment. A mother might work as a maid earning about £12 a month, while her husband could make about £17 a month as a driver. Their combined incomes still put them way below the poverty line. This is the kind of hardship which drives thousands of Filipinas to Japan each year as "entertainers" and to Hong Kong as maids.

"I always felt as if I was going out honorarily as 'one of the boys'"

The capital is bustling, dirty, and not particularly prepossessing, having been extensively bombed during the Second World War. Most tourists seem to head straight out to the fantastic beaches and natural landmarks which abound in the 7107-island archipelago.

Manila's main tourist attraction these days is the Marcos's presidential palace, where Imelda's thousands of shoes and dresses, gallon bottles of perfume, and bedroom modelled on Marie Antoinette's can be seen. But what makes the city fun is just spending time relaxing with Filipino friends. The Philippines is not the place to visit if you want a solitary trip.

Our film crew, all Filipino men, soon adopted the three of us – the director, another reporter and myself – who had come from England, and decided to show us the city, which basically meant the bars and restaurants. Filipinos are incredibly laid back, nothing is rushed and there is time for everything. We soon picked up the expression "Filipino time", which means, as we discovered when filming began four days behind schedule, "late".

I was the only woman involved in the production, and generally the only woman in the group when we went out in the evenings. Young Filipinas do not seem to go out much in mixed parties even after they are married and the crew found it hard to understand that I was staying in a flat with two men who were neither relatives nor boyfriends. They could not believe that in England I lived away from home and did not have a boyfriend. I always felt as if I was going out honorarily as "one of the boys". The crew were surprised when I drank beer and looked shocked if the occasional swear word crept into my conversation.

Nearly all the single men and women we met were still living at home, and so were quite a few of the married ones. Older couples claimed Filipinos mature late as they stay with their parents for so long. Families are particularly strict with the daughters.

Women, however, tend to dominate the family both in looking after the money and having the final say. Of all the couples I met who had any connection with business, it was always the wife who took financial control. One woman running an export company with her husband told me she even preferred to employ women as they worked harder. Of the Filipino man, she said: "Show him a leg and give him a bottle, and nothing gets done."

"There is no need for women's lib here. The Filipina has always been considered equal, even dominant, by the Filipino," Lorena, the Filipino wife of our English lighting director, told me, pointing out that many women worked and occupied high positions. But, without sensing the contradiction, Lorena admitted there was a double standard of morality for men and women. "It is quite acceptable for the husband to play around, but if it is the woman who plays around, she gets into a lot of trouble," she said.

I never found any problems going out on my own despite dire warning from Filipino and Western friends about taking taxis alone and travelling late at night. The nearest thing to sexual harassment came from the rank of tricycle drivers waiting for clients outside our apartment. "I love you ma'am," they called out every time I passed.

TRAVEL NOTES

Languages Filipino (Tagalog) and numerous local dialects. English and Spanish are spoken quite widely in cities and tourist areas.

Transport Boats between islands, and buses around them, are very cheap though far from comfortable. *Jeepneys* (taxis) in towns are also inexpensive.

Accommodation There are few cheap hotels. In Manila and other cities you can usually find dormitories in the university area. Elsewhere negotiate locally for rooms.

Special Problems Due to the continuing NPA guerrilla action, or occupation, many of the southern islands are now impossible (and perhaps unsafe) to visit. On gaining a visa you'll be given an up-to-date list of restricted areas (and activities) and once in the country will have to gain permission from the army for travel to areas outside the main cities and tourist spots.

The evident exploitation of women in the "hospitality" industry is deeply unsettling, so too are the extremes of poverty. Filipina women frequently face problems of harassment, particularly from GIs and foreign tourists in search of cheap sex. You have much less to contend with as a Westerner.

Although people are well used to Western tourists wandering about in shorts and T-shirts, you should remember that this is an inherently conservative society and that you are much more likely to gain respect if you dress modestly.

Guides *The Philippines – A Travel Survival Kit* (Lonely Planet) and, more recently updated, *South-East Asia on a Shoestring* (Lonely Planet).

Contacts

For up-to-date information on what's happening in the country, including women's activities, contact the **Philippine Resource Centre**, 1 Grangeway, London NW6, ☎624 0270.

Gabriela (Women's Movement), PO Box 4386, Manila 2800.

TO-MAE-W (Third World Movement Against the Exploitation of Women), PO Box SM-366, Manila. Very dynamic organisation, established in 1961 to co-ordinate research and action on issues such as tourism/prostitution, sexism in the media, and the plight of women workers throughout the region and the Third World.

Books

Linda Ty-Casper, *Awaiting Trespass (A Pasión)* (Readers International, 1986). the first of Ty-Casper's novels to be published in the West (and a book which could not be published in Marcos's time). Set in the days before the pope is due to visit Manila, it combines a personal awakening with powerful social satire.

Committee for Asian Women, *Tales of Filipino Working Women* and *Our Rightful Share* (both 1984). These two excellent short books, available from the Committee for Asian Women, 57 Peking Road, 5.F, Kowloon, Hong Kong, use the personal stories of Filipina factory-workers to describe their working conditions and struggles to stand up for their rights.

James Fenton, *The Snap Revolution* in *Granta 18* (Penguin, 1986). Fenton arrived in Manila to cover the phoney election called by Marcos and found himself charting the progress of a Revolution. A sensitive, moving and wild account.

Women Writers in Media Now staff, *Filipina, I: Poetry, Drama, Fiction* (Cellar, US, 1984) and *II: An Anthology of Contemporary Women Writers in the Philippines* (Cellar, US, 1985). Two good anthologies of Filipina writers, that draw on the experiences of women from all walks of society.

Rowena Tiempo-Torrevillas, *Upon the Williows and Other Stories* (Cellar, US, 1979). Well-crafted short stories by a female novelist, if from a rather upper-middle-class and Americanised perspective.

Poland

. . . .

These are deeply uncertain times for Poland. Having ousted the Communist Party from its "leading role" and voted in a Solidarity-led coalition, the Polish electorate are now anxious to feel the benefits of reform. However, faced with a worsening economic crisis, crippling austerity measures, spiralling inflation and widespread food shortages, optimism is wearing thin and support for the new government of Prime Minister Tadeusz Maziwiecki is already

dwindling. Predictably, young Poles are leaving the country – a trend that is steadily mounting. Meanwhile, back at home, people are more than ever having to rely on the black market even for basic commodities.

Western travellers are largely cushioned from these hardships (hotels and "dollar shops" are always well stocked) and, with the new atmosphere of political openness, tourism is on the increase. In general terms Poland is a safe and easy country to travel around alone. Outside the main centres, such as the beautiful city of Krakow, people might seem curious about you as a rare Western visitor, but this is unlikely to feel threatening or intrusive. Harassment, other than the occasional hassle from drunks and illegal money-changers, is rare, and, if you do encounter problems, you'll invariably find other Poles stepping in to help. The Polish people are renowned for their hospitality to strangers and will sacrifice much to make you feel welcome.

As with many Eastern bloc countries it's likely that you'll socialise mainly with men; women tend to have much less time to spend with visitors. It can be hard to come to terms with the entrenched (and largely unchallenged) sexism that you find at all levels of Polish society, even in quite progressive circles. Men still tend to approach women with a degree of old-style gallantry and much is made of hand-kissing and the giving of flowers.

Socially and politically, Poland remains a profoundly Catholic country, and **women's roles** as mothers and homemakers are deeply ingrained. Most women have to combine the tasks of queuing for food and hard domestic labour with full-time jobs – a double burden made increasingly untenable by the worsening shortages. Men for the most part consider themselves exempt from work in the home and, whilst these attitudes persist, the legislative reforms, such as maternity leave (extended to two years by the efforts of Solidarity) and the provision of day nurseries in most workplaces, seem unlikely to bring much relief. There is no feminist movement in the Western sense of the word, and you'll find that feminism has acquired fairly negative connotations, being linked in many people's minds to Soviet propaganda. Under the new Catholic coalition, moves are being made towards repealing the 1956 abortion laws to make abortion illegal. In a political climate that so strongly asserts Catholic values it is proving difficult for women to voice dissent.

Guests in Krakow

. . . .

Krystyna Gajda is British but of Polish descent. She spent a month in Krakow as a guest of an elderly family friend, with an English companion who had never visited the country before.

I was only eleven years old when I had last visited Poland and the idea of rediscovering the country through adult eyes seemed momentous. In many ways I felt as new to the country as the English friend I was travelling with, though my knowledge of Polish was undoubtedly a buffer when it came to dealing with customs officials on the long rail journey across Europe and with people such as taxi drivers once we reached our destination.

Anyone from the West, however, is at once recognised as such. East Germans and Poles homed in on us on the train journey with a mixture of warmth and curiosity and were bowled over that one of us spoke Polish. As our visit went on, I found myself asserting my Polishness to the point of wearing our hostess's fur hats. I became very conscious of my anglicised Polish language and of being seen as a Westerner who had Polish origins, feeling guilty for what I without a doubt viewed as my affluent British lifestyle. I wanted to be accepted as a Pole by the people I met, to dispel any notions of theirs that they had to prove something to me. Unlike my friend, Alison, I was in the curious position of being viewed as a Western outsider *and* a Pole, and I was always aware of this ambivalent identity.

Concerned that my friend might be feeling left out, I worked hard as her interpreter for the duration of our stay. We were based in Krakow, staying with Anna, an old family friend who lived alone. The presence of an "all-English" person put her under something of a strain. She, too, was anxious that my friend did not come away with a bleak, negative image of her country and went to great lengths to provide the best food she could find – bartering, black marketing, stocking up on ration cards and, of course, queueing.

Before long I realised that she was sharing these chores with her closest friend, a woman called Czesia. While Anna whirled us around theatres, art galleries, monasteries and churches, Czesia was organising the food for us all, so it was on the table when we came home. Yet I am sure that we still don't know the *full* extent of the sacrifices made so that we were not forced to take part, or to witness, the difficulties of everyday living.

Travelling around with Anna, I sensed that she became uncomfortable whenever we laughed loudly or behaved flamboyantly. Similarly, when we were shown Krakow's many churches – which are open all day, every day, and are always full of the Faithful – I felt that I was never fervent enough for her liking. It's not unusual for people to attend mass every day of the week. Anna would rise at 6am for church and be back on time to give us her whole day. Even though Alison, like myself, is a Catholic, I know that she found Poland's brand of Catholicism, which is enmeshed in the Polish national identity, overwhelming. I found myself wondering how a non-Catholic, or an unmarried mother, or a homosexual, would cope in a society where one is expected to be Catholic to the letter.

It was quite staggering to walk past Anna's room and see her praying on her knees before a huge portrait of the Virgin Mary. Prayers were always said before meals. Alison was very balanced and detached about all this but it made me feel like an emotional and spiritual cart-horse and not a "proper" Pole.

We travelled to Auschwitz (now called Oswiecim) to visit the camp's museum of martyrdom with a young Polish woman, Basia, a friend of Anna's and a lecturer in English at the university. Basia is married but has no children. As a professional woman she has more chances to travel abroad and more contacts when it comes to finding "luxury" items. She is viewed as a "modern" woman; when Anna found what she thought was a contraceptive device on the floor (I didn't recognise it myself!) she showed it to me and said it was Basia's. When I said I didn't know what it was, she said: "That's good, that's very good. People should have more self-control." It was a view that I realised was quite commonly held.

"Cafés serving alcohol are usually run-down, sleazy looking places filled with men"

There seemed to be a lot of pressure on women to maintain traditional roles although a few professional women have gained some reprieve. But there is no pleasant place – no pubs or clubs – where women from all backgrounds can meet and socialise; when women are not earning money they are queueing for food and running a home; menfolk are "chivalrous" but offer little help in the home. As a result there is little time or opportunity for women to socialise outside of the family circle.

Cafés serving alcohol are usually run-down, sleazy looking places, filled with men – women never darken the doorstep. Spirits are about the only commodity that's cheap and in plentiful supply. Anna told me that alcoholism was an endemic social problem and that it was common for men to drink away their wages.

Foreigners are always welcomed very warmly and are an object of great interest. But they are invariably viewed as well off. Whenever my parents visited their relations, I was always aware of the fact that they never felt they were giving enough. Money always creates tension in our family group. Although anything that is given is gratefully received it must be given with care, as Poles are very proud and want you to have a good impression of what their country has to offer.

I never succumbed to selling dollars on the black market for huge sums of zlotys, as I felt that it would only reinforce the stereotype of the exploitative, wealthy Westerner, only interested in accumulating money to buy furs and crystal. Nor did I shop at the Pewex stores, which accept only Western currency. I will never forget the evening when a chance shipment of oranges made the national TV news bulletin, or the peculiar short propaganda shots shown in between programmes. I soon realised why my cousins loved British TV commercials on their visits!

Most Poles live in tower blocks, which are seen as quite a comfortable and safe form of accommodation. Space, however, is incredibly limited; whole families might live in one partitioned room and there's seldom any choice about which flat you'll be allocated. Czesia, for instance, had to cope with living on the fourth floor despite the fact that her legs were so bad she could barely climb the stairs. Anna told me (she was less concerned about hiding facts from me) that if too many people did their laundry on one day, the water would run out.

Despite the daily limitations they face, Poles do know how to let their hair down. Guests are toasted with plum liqueur (even at breakfast!) and evening gatherings can be pretty wild occasions – with music and conversation rising to fever pitch, and brimming over with fervent political discussion. The exuberance and energy of these impromptu gatherings is in complete contrast to the subdued atmosphere and cold, huddled faces of people commuting to work on the trams. My impression was that the Poles are a vital, lively people who make full use of their dry, almost black, sense of humour to cope with the harsh realities of life.

As a visitor, you'll find this contagious and the famous Polish hospitality unforgettable. Beware of saying you like something in someone's home: I mentioned to Anna that I liked her glasses, and before I could blink she was wrapping them in paper for me to take away, saying that I was doing her a favour by solving her dilemma of what to get as a leaving present.

TRAVEL NOTES

Languages Polish. Almost everybody learns Russian at school, although most don't like admitting to it. Some people speak English and older people often speak German.

Transport Mostly by train: make sure you take the *expresobowe* as the alternatives are incredibly slow. Hitching is quite safe but uncommon, and you should expect to contribute towards (rationed) petrol. Public transport in towns is cheap and frequent and so are taxis.

Accommodation You have to stay in state-run hotels, which can be booked through the official travel agency, *Orbis*. Some may only accept payment in foreign currency.

Special Problems Shortages – things you take for granted are unavailable, including: sanitary towels, tampons, paper tissues, toilet paper, shampoo, washing powder, contraceptives, aspirin, coffee, toothpaste, toothbrushes. Western medicines can only be bought from the Pewex shops – most Poles have to rely on herbal remedies. How you deal with the relative privileges you have as a Western visitor is a personal issue. You'll need persistence and

ingenuity to reciprocate the hospitality you receive. You might encounter some harassment from illegal money-changers but it is neither persistent nor threatening.

Guides *Eastern Europe – A Travel Survival Kit* (Lonely Planet) has an adequate section on Poland, good on the bureaucracy. A *Rough Guide* is in the making.

Contacts

No information on any women's groups.

Books

Jnina Baumann, *Winter in the Morning, A Young Girl's Life in the Warsaw Ghetto and Beyond* (Virago, 1986). Account of resilience and courage during the Warsaw siege and Nazi occupation.

Wislawa Szymborska, *Sounds, Feelings, Thoughts: 70 Poems by Wislawa Szymborska* (Princeton U. Press, US, 1981). Beautiful poems on simple observations of everyday life.

Portugal

Portugal may be technically an Atlantic country, but its character is – like neighbouring Spain – essentially Mediterranean. The climate is warm, the people a mix of Latin and Celt, and, for visitors, the attractions are a mix of beaches, lush countryside and good, cheap food and wine. It is also distinctively rural, with few sizeable towns beyond the historic capitals of Lisbon and Porto. The culture is relaxed and traditional: the Portuguese talk of themselves as a country of *brandos costumes* – "gentle ways".

The compact size of the country and an efficient network of buses and trains make exploration easy and straightforward, while *machismo* is less rampant here than in other Latin countries; men may hiss and make comments in the streets of Lisbon, but elsewhere traditional courtesy is generally accompanied by welcome male restraint. It is one of the safest countries in Europe.

Given the persistent strength of tradition, it's sometimes hard to believe that Portugal not so long ago experienced a dramatic and quite extraordinary Revolution. On 25 April 1974 several decades of dictatorship came to an end in an almost bloodless coup, engineered by the army. On top of economic stagnation at home, much of its impetus came from the politicisation of soldiers returning from Africa where their government had sent them, at great expense, to combat the escalating wars of liberation in its colonies. As well as sudden independence for these colonies, the Revolution meant massive changes inside the country; amongst them the redistribution of land, the achievement of workers' rights, better social and living conditions, and alterations in the family law. Portugal also showed an impressive tolerance – in stark contrast to its appalling colonial administration – in coping with the influx of over a million refugees from the former colonies. In the 1980s there has been something of a conservative backlash in politics, with the emphasis placed firmly on handling the economy – the most backward in the EC.

Throughout the period of the Revolution, women campaigned and organised alongside men. Gradually, however, political change seemed to reach a deadlock and with it came the familiar realisation that women's specific needs had been submerged. Despite positive legal reforms, the brief emergence of a woman prime minister, and the high profile of women in higher education, old attitudes die hard and the Portuguese **women's movement** has had difficulties mobilising on any large scale. Compared with, say, Italy or Spain, the movement today is small. However, there are at least a couple of central organisations in Lisbon which can put you in touch with what's happening around the country.

"What You Do and What You Don't"

. . . .

Elizabeth Mullett has lived and studied in Lisbon, as well as travelled throughout the country.

Lisbon is one of the most attractive capitals in the world: a breezy, dazzlingly white city which has somehow escaped the worst of urban expansion. I lived there for a while, with a thesis to research, a long list of archives to visit and an irredeemably student income on which to do it. Not quite a resident, nor quite a tourist, I hired a room and traipsed between libraries and the city sights. I explored the frantic covered market on the river front in the early mornings and, from my landlady, learned to cook the sweet rice desserts and the rich stews, brimming with pigs' ears and calves' shinbones.

I also learned to duck the harassment experienced by most young women in the city, finding in museum gardens and monastery cloisters the perfect places to read or write letters undisturbed. Following the example of other students, I used to take my books and newspapers to one of the big town cafés in the evenings and sit there with a coffee, half-studying, half-watching the world. Local incomes are low but the habit of an evening out universal. I acquired an ability to stay up until four in the morning to listen to the city's *fado* music (a kind of national blues – worth hearing), to eat breakfast standing up in the busy *pastelerias*, to look people back in the eye and to take lunch seriously.

I was so energetically absorbing a new culture that it took me some time to feel a foreigner's isolation. It wasn't that most Portuguese women of my age were locked into family life, married with several children already; more that, despite the relaxing of social attitudes since the 1974 Revolution, women are still essentially seen in the image of their family relationships; somebody's daughter, wife, mother or widow. Acute housing shortages in Lisbon and Porto and a national minimum wage of less than £100 a month mean that most children leave home only after marriage and often not even then.

To be sure, women achieved paper equality within five years of the

Revolution, but male socialism has tended to view women's needs and aims as secondary and feminism has had little institutional and popular support. A liberal family background makes more difference than any legislation and if the corridors of the universities are full of women students, access to higher education (gained by under two percent of the population) is still largely a privilege of the middle classes. Talking to feminists, I found that the most highly valued opportunity had been to travel, either through work or study, and that way gain a sideways look at their culture and sense of themselves as individuals.

My work took me to Evora, a white-washed Moorish town in the Alentejo, a region which seemed to me one of the most fascinating. Since Roman times it has been an area of vast rural estates, most of which were seized from the landowners and transformed into collective farms after the Revolution. Governments responded first by extending, then restricting, agricultural credits needed by these new farms, and now big families are being allowed to return to parts of their estates.

The towns are therefore a focus of both the region's poverty and its provincial bourgeoisie. If the narrow convoluted streets are still lined with sixteenth- and seventeenth-century houses, it's because they have mostly escaped redevelopment; and if the sky on summer nights has more stars than you've ever seen before, it's because electricity has not reached every house in every town.

Every Tuesday, Evora's main square is full of livestock farmers in dark suits and black hats, negotiating business. At lunchtime they swarm into the local restaurants and fall upon the goat stews, dishes of pork cooked with shellfish, and great steaming plates of salt cod boiled with chickpeas. This is a profoundly masculine society – the characteristic music of the region is that of the male voice miners' choirs –

and if you travel from Evora to any of the medieval towns beyond you will find cafés the meeting places of men after dinner. It's rare to see women on the streets after nightfall.

As I moved around the north, to the granite and down-to-earth city of Porto and to Vila Real and the castellated hill towns of the Spanish frontier in Tras-os-Montes, I was confronted with a quite different world. This is the area of the great vineyards, but also of small subsistence farming. On the terraces of the River Douro and in the handkerchief-sized plots, there are jumbles of cows, cabbages and vines, each family holding infinitely subdivided among families by the inheritance divisions of the Minho district. For the visitor, it's an area which repays a good eye for changing styles of domestic architecture – the granite boulders of the Beiras and the drystone walling of Tras-os-Montes; a stomach for the egg-yolk and sugar confections, different in each town; and a taste for the Dão wines and the delicious semi-sparkling *vinhos verdes*.

"The survival of gentle and courteous social attitudes make Portugal one of the easiest Latin countries in which to travel alone"

To the east of the Douro, the journey from Chaves to Bragança takes you through some of the most spectacular scenery in the country, wild and empty. From time to time you pass through villages desiccated by emigration, communities of old people, women and children, whose men work in the cities of Central Europe, returning only for visits in the summer months. It's the most conservative area of Portugal, where adherence to the Church and respect for authority have remained strongest. As "widows of the living", the wives remain rigidly subject to popular criticism of their social behaviour – as one woman put it, "what you do and what you don't".

What you do and what you don't, as a visitor, is very much up to you. There are excellent detailed guidebooks and the tourist offices are friendly and helpful about all sorts of unusual requests – where to go to find the country's remarkable wild flowers, for example, or where to nurse a particular ailment or allergy at a spa. Whatever you can learn of this strangest of the romantic languages in advance will help immeasurably, but many Portuguese speak some English or French and understand Spanish. And the survival of gentle and courteous social attitudes make Portugal, beyond Lisbon or the busy beaches, one of the easiest Latin countries in which to travel alone.

Family Life in the Alentejo

. . . .

After travelling by Landrover around Africa with her husband and three young sons (see Algeria), Jan Wright has settled in a remote part of the Alentejo. Here the family have thrown themselves whole-heartedly into the local peasant life.

A gust of hot air singes my eyebrows and I duck back before swabbing out the clay oven and beginning to shovel in the loaves. One after the other: ten three-pounders, a pizza, a flan, a couple of cakes and a dozen sweet potatoes. Get them in as fast as possible before the oven cools and then relax. Relax? I'll be lucky! Sometimes the weekly bake is a disaster, bread charred on the outside or soggy on the inside. But I'm learning and the disasters are the exception now and not the rule. A small handful of flour on the oven floor – if it goes dark brown the oven's too hot; a knowing tap on the bottom of the first loaf out – if it's too soon pop it back in for another ten minutes. Even the neighbours have to agree it's good.

The neighbours love to help and advise. Even more they love us to be wrong. We are doubly strangers:

foreigners and city people. We are ignorant of everything that to them is basic knowledge learned in the early years of life from father or mother. Or more likely grandfather or grandmother, for in this society child-rearing is usually passed back to the older generation to free the parents for the relentless toil which all too often leaves them old beyond their years. "Kill the pig next Saturday?" They look at us in horror. Have we offended some religious festival? We look at each other, at a loss, and eventually they deign to explain: "It's the waning moon." We all look at each other, time travellers, by some fluke caught in the same place at the same time.

Portugal, in the twentieth century. Closer to Africa than to Northern Europe, the Alentejo was, up to fifteen years ago, a semi-feudal society where most people were too poor to afford shoes, where the old starved if they had no family to support them. It's one of the last examples of the peasant society in Europe – a society doomed to extinction among the red tape of EC grants and the glitter of the world on the other side of the TV screen.

Five miles from the west coast and just north of the border with the Algarve, we have a valley to ourselves. Its elements are a continuing wonder to me: native Portuguese trees, Imperial eagles circling overhead in spring, wild flowers, and lots of butterflies. There are no main services and no prospect of ever having them. A track deters all but the most determined visitors. Our building has thick clay walls and a tiled roof; small windows to keep out the sun; an open fireplace and, outside, the great clay bread oven. There's a stream which runs dry in the summer and spills out in furious flood once or twice a year, when we get half the annual rainfall in a few hours. "The worst rain for forty years," they assure us as we all huddle in the local bar. They said that last time, too.

"The prevalent machismo *can turn male children into strutting, demanding brats"*

We've been here three years now, myself, my husband and our three children. We drive the boys four kilometres up to school in the morning because it's a long steep hill, and who wants to go to school? They make their own way home, stopping to play with friends, getting a freshly baked bun from the old couple who live in the last house of the scattered village, spotting wild flowers and butterflies, birds of prey, the occasional snake. We are a significant minority in the school. There are only ten children, aged from six to ten, including our three. There is just one teacher, an unwilling exile from Porto, who responds to her enforced sojourn in the back of beyond with frequent absences "on business in Odemira".

Predictably it is Sam, our eldest, who has had the most problems settling into our life here. He knew the greater stimulation of primary school in England. He's a great reader and took a long time to develop the skill in Portuguese sufficiently to be able to read the books that interested him. He has had several confrontations with the teacher. "Copy out this passage." "What does it mean?" "I'll tell you later. Copy it out." "I won't copy it out until I know what it means." A sudden reminder of how authoritar-

ian a society Portugal was, and therefore is. After fifty years of fascism many people had forgotten, or had never learned, to think for themselves.

Now, fifteen years after the Revolution, the same attitudes and ideas persist, even though the physical compulsion has disappeared. We can only explain both points of view: that he is right, but that while he is in the school he must go towards the teacher's point of view. The other two boys always have the stimulation of their older brother. Sam suffers from our isolation. Eddie, the youngest, is almost more Portuguese than English. He takes his imaginary cigarettes out of his imaginary breast pocket and taps them on the table: the stance and gestures are completely Portuguese. He was under three when we came here. When we help him with his homework, it's usually in Portuguese. We hope they will all be fully bilingual when they are older and, in their turn, exercise the choice we made of where we would live. Can we also protect them from or show them an alternative to the prevalent *machismo* that can turn male children into strutting, demanding brats?

In choosing the Alentejo, we chose a pre-consumer and almost pre-money society. We all have plastic carrier bags, but the shops charge for them and so we wash and re-use them. There is practically no visible rubbish: anything edible goes to the pig; anything organic disappears in the manure heap; oil cans and paint tins reappear as plant pots. The council provides big square bins at strategic places on the road and we drop off the few bits that are left. Our neighbours usually have one or two money-making lines: peanuts, maize, beans or potatoes, goats, pigs or cheese.

If there is a surplus of something, it is for giving not selling. Giving to family, giving to visitors, giving to those amazing English who are so incompetent that they don't have cabbages coming out of their ears when everybody else does. In return we give the one thing that we have and they don't: transport. Recently I was hailed by one of the ladies of the village and told there was a funeral that after-noon and would I take some of the ladies. Eight elderly ladies in black chose the Landrover in preference to the taxis that were taking the rest of the villagers. I felt rather flattered.

The poorer of our neighbours have very few cash outgoings: they live entirely on their own produce. When they kill a pig, of which every scrap is used, they eat meat; the bulk is salted down to keep them going for months. Potatoes, beans and bread are eaten in quantity and so are a lot of vegetables in season. The cool dark back rooms of the clay houses are ideal for storing vegetables. We were astounded to be given tomatoes in February – they had kept perfectly since the previous October. Cash is spent on alcohol, occa-sional clothes, and very little else. In the house of our nearest neighbours up-valley there is a bed, a rough wooden table, and a crate for a chair. They cook over an open fire and the only light is a candle.

"My neighbours, Edite and Ze, started with nothing but a couple of goats and a rented house"

The rest of Portugal sees the Alentejans as stupid and lazy. There are Alentejo jokes, just as England has Irish jokes. Lazy perhaps, because they might have seen the Alentejan farmer from their cars, sitting with his back against the cool white walls of his house, looking at the distant sea. They were still in bed when the peasant did half his day's work before breakfast.

My neighbours, Edite and Ze, started with nothing but a couple of goats and a rented house. In a lifetime's work, during which the holidays can be counted on one hand, they increased the herd to 150 goats and 50 cows. The

kids and calves are sold once a year; Edite sells goat's cheese of high repute. By local standards they are now wealthy people. Over the years they paid for two daughters at university and now, in their fifties, have bought and paid for the house and acres to which they will retire when a few more calves, a few more goats have added to the security in the bank. The only machine which assists their farming operation is a petrol pump; they do not own a vehi-cle. A black-and-white TV runs off a car battery; a gas light and the open fire illuminate the kitchen where the life of the family revolves. In an unusually hopeful sign for this way of life, the youngest daughter, after trying several city jobs, has come home to work alongside her parents.

True, the trend is away from the country. The young people want elec-tricity and the tarmac road, and the government encourages this move which pulls people into the money-spending, tax-paying economy. Portugal as a whole is poised between the past and the EC dream of the future. Car ownership increased by eighty percent over the last twelve months, but with a high cost in people defaulting on credit, which was all too easy to arrange.

The older people, though, do not only hold to their way of life through ignorance of any other. Antonio, the local contractor, worked for several years in France to pay for his tractor. Mario, who runs the local garage as a sort of semi-charity for the usually decrepit vehicles around, can afford to do so because of the money he made in Africa and the Middle East. Like many other Mediterranean countries, there are few families who don't have some-one working abroad, providing for the present or the future. When the emigrants return they don't want to bring back the ways of more "advanced" countries: they appreciate the way of life here, the importance of the family and friends, the simple pleasures of good company, the beauty of a countryside largely unscarred by man.

It's half-past eight. Still cold at this time of year, and as we mutter greetings to our neighbours, one of the grandmothers, less than five feet tall and dressed in black (she is a widow and widows wear black for life), comes forward with cake and a tiny glass of the local *medronho* spirit, distilled from the fruit of the strawberry tree which grows wild over the hills. Down it in one, and give the ritual exhalation as the spirit burns. We are here to help our neighbours kill a pig: an excuse for a two-day celebration of eating and drinking, music and dance.

The pig is enticed out of the sty, seized firmly by six men and walked to a low table. The fearsome jaw is tied. The pig is lifted bodily on to the table. Two men hold each back leg and one the front against the death throes. The knife goes in deep twists, and within three or four minutes of leaving the sty the pig is dead. We pause for another glass of spirits; nobody enjoys the act of killing and few of the local *matadores* will kill more than once in a day. The women collect and stir the blood for black pudding and the men burn off the hair with a gas burner. (Edite and Ze use burning gorse, but here we are modern.) Then the men scrape the skin white again with the razor sharp penknife that every countryman carries. The pig is opened and the women take the guts and organs for sorting and grading and making into sausages.

My stomach turns as I wash out the intestines, turn them inside out and wash them again. The balance of the work is with us now. Great cauldrons steam over the open fire as the pork fat is rendered down and the skin cut into pork scratchings and the sausages prepared. Meanwhile, since early morning, a separate group of women have been preparing the feast that marks the first major stage of the job; the pig has been halved and the sides separated

from the head and the spine. The men lounge around drinking and smoking. Until the meat sets and they can joint it they have nothing else to do.

> **"Cassimira . . . found herself insulted by some men at the well. She took down her father's shotgun and fired two rounds over their heads"**

As in many rural societies, the division of roles is very marked: women tend to socialise with women, men with men. Some jobs are women's jobs, others men's. The women are strong and often run the families and the farms while the men go away or abroad to work. Cassimira, Edite and Ze's daughter, found herself insulted by some men at the well. She walked back up the hill, took down her father's shotgun and fired two rounds over their heads. She was fifteen. She describes with relish their hasty retreat to their car. Having seen the ease with which she hoists a hundred-weight sack of animal food on to her shoulder, I would prefer to be on her side in any fight!

Interestingly, both men and women are known by their Christian names, with or without the equivalent of Mr or Mrs. So I am Jan or Senhora Jan and my husband is Chris or Senhor Chris, an external sign, perhaps, of the degree to which people keep their own identity.

Our society is poised at a crossroads, firmly divided between the generations. At the moment it's a land of windmills and watermills, of cobblers and cartwrights, blacksmiths and coopers. A way of life very close to nature and based on the village. With a lifetime of immense hard work, the older generation have scraped together a sufficiency and in many cases considerable wealth. The fruits of that thrift are now being lavished on their children.

Our neighbours down the valley have bought their son the car they never allowed themselves. Next they will buy him a plot of land and build him a house. It is almost certain that the son will never return to till the family land.

The alternatives for the future are all too obvious. The paradise that the Algarve once was has been destroyed by piecemeal development, soaking up easy foreign money. The danger is very real that this development will spread up the more austere but totally unspoilt west coast. Inland, as the people move away from the land, the eucalyptus trees move in: mile after mile of mono-culture – the fastest growing tree in the world which, after three crops and thirty years, totally depletes the soil. Many of the plantations are there to guarantee IMF loans, providing secure hard cash in terms of pulp for Northern Europe.

Our own property is an island in this sea. We feel privileged to be experiencing and sharing this life. It seems likely that soon the waves will close over a way of living that has been self-sustaining for the last 2000 years.

TRAVEL NOTES

Languages Portuguese is a difficult language, especially when it comes to pronunciation, but if you know some French and/or Spanish you shouldn't find it too hard to read. English and French are quite widely spoken in cities and most people understand Spanish (albeit reluctantly).

Transport A slow but reasonably cheap and efficient network of buses and trains covers most of the country. Taxis are cheap and reliable; everyone uses them all the time in Lisbon, though outside city boundaries negotiate fares in advance. Bicycle hire is a good, if exhausting, way of exploring the countryside.

Accommodation Reasonably cheap hotels and *pensões* are available, even at the height of summer. In smaller towns it's often best to ask the nearest friendly-looking woman, who will know who lets rooms; it's quite accepted. Youth Hostels are cheaper (there are about a dozen in Portugal, most of them open all year round), but you won't meet Portuguese people that way. There are also about a hundred authorised campsites, mostly small and attractive.

Guide *The Rough Guide: Portugal* (Harrap Columbus) is reliable and up-to-date.

Contacts

There are relatively few **women's organisations** in Portugal. The following addresses, all in Lisbon, are good initial contacts.

Comisão da Condicão Feminina, Avenida de República, 32-1 Lisbon 1093. Researches and maintains a watching brief on all aspects of women's lives in Portugal; organises meetings and conferences, and is very active in areas of social and legal reform. Also a good library and connections with feminists throughout the country.

Informação, Documentação Mulheres (IDM). Rua Filipe de Mata, 115A, Lisbon, ☎720598. Women's centre incorporating a small library and the one women-only café in Lisbon. Run by a collective of lesbian and heterosexual women, very keen to welcome foreign travellers and publicise the activities of the centre. French, German and English spoken.

Editora das Mulheres, Rua da Conceição 17 (4th floor), right in the centre of Lisbon. Feminist bookshop.

Espaço-Mulheres, Rua Pedro Nunes 9a, Lisbon. Art gallery and meeting place for women. Open every day, 3–7pm.

Books

Maria Velho da Costa, Maria Isabel Barreno and Maria Teresa Horta, *The Three Marias: Portuguese Letters* (Paladin, 1975). Collage of letters, stories and poems by three feminist writers. Hard to obtain, but worth the effort.

Few other Portuguese women writers have been translated into English but we'd appreciate any recommendations.

Thanks to Elizabeth Mullet for supplying much of the information for these Travel Notes.

Saudi Arabia

$\cdot$ $\cdot$ $\cdot$ $\cdot$ $\cdot$ $\cdot$ $\cdot$ $\cdot$ $\cdot$ $\cdot$ $\cdot$ $\cdot$ $\cdot$ $\cdot$ $\cdot$ $\cdot$ $\cdot$ $\cdot$

Islam of the stern Wahabite tradition dominates all aspects of life in Saudi Arabia. Although Western technology is welcome, its culture most clearly is not. The country permits no tourism. With the exception of Muslims, who can obtain pilgrimage visas to visit the holy sites of Mecca and Medina, foreigners can only enter the country on work or family visas.

However, due to Saudi Arabia's oil industry – the country is the world's leading exporter – foreign workers make up a significant part of its population. Amongst this large community, the vast majority migrant workers from the Arab world, are several thousand Westerners. Most women among them are on family visas, accompanying their husbands, but a significant number come independently as teachers, doctors, nannies and nurses.

Western women living in Saudi Arabia are faced with numerous restrictions. It is illegal for a woman to drive; it is essential to dress extremely modestly and to keep to the areas marked out for women – the rear of buses, the "family section" of a restaurant, etc. Failure to observe these and many other practices (see Travel Notes) can lead to severe reprimands or arrest by the stick-wielding *mutawa*, the religious police. At the same time, Western women, particularly single workers, are vulnerable to harassment – both from Saudi men for failing to conform to the role expected of women, and from the large numbers of foreign men with bachelor status.

Westerners are usually housed in special compounds, often luxuriously equipped; however, with strict curfews for women, these can become stiflingly insular. Reports are that the various rules and regulations have an infantalising effect and many foreign wives, like their Saudi counterparts, complain of abject boredom. It's not easy to explore the cities, let alone travel around the Kingdom on your own. Most women join up with other expatriates for trips around the country.

Saudi women are expected to lead traditional, secluded lives – their roles strictly confined to that of wife and mother. On the rare occasions when they go out, they are heavily veiled and accompanied by their husbands, fathers or brothers. Their participation in the open labour force is one of the lowest in the world, though, with the widespread introduction of female education in the 1960s, changes have started to take place. Women are now encouraged to work in segregated female sectors (as teachers, doctors, social workers, nurses, etc), and the government has also begun to consider the economic advantages of employing women outside of teaching and social services instead of relying on a large foreign workforce. Moves in this direction provoke much opposition from the conservative Muslims in the country, but at the same time there is a growing movement amongst Saudi women, backed by liberal men, advocating women's greater participation in the economic and social life of the country.

Back Behind the Veil

. . . .

Alice Arndt first went to Saudi Arabia in 1975, on a two-year teaching contract; she returned ten years later to live, with her husband.

I first arrived in the Kingdom fifteen years ago, washed in on the wave of modern technology, foreign workers and petrodollars. If you had asked me then, I would have told you that, of course, in a few years Saudi women would be driving cars, veils would gradually disappear, the shops which closed their doors at prayer times would constitute an ever smaller minority. I noted the increasing educational opportunities for women, and felt certain that they would soon lead to demands from the women for further work opportunities and ultimately for emancipation in

their society. And the large number of young Saudi men who were being sent to other countries for advanced degrees would surely be infected with more liberal attitudes towards the women at home. I assumed without question that the East-West gap would gradually close up, and took it for granted that exposure to Western customs and values would lead inevitably to their adoption.

Well, it hasn't turned out that way at all. It is still illegal for a woman to drive or own an automobile or to ride a bicycle. Today, virtually every shop closes up tight during the several daily prayers, and any shopkeeper who's slow to lock his door or pull down the shutters is likely to find the *mutawa*, the religious police, brandishing a long stick in his direction. Even television programmes are interrupted by a prayer intermission.

Women in the Kingdom must dress more conservatively than they did during my first stay – and that includes foreigners as well as Saudis. My husband's company issues regular bulletins about the "Dress Code" for employees and their families. The long skirts which I used to wear are now considered to be too form-revealing because they have a waistband; a long, loose dress is preferred. For the same reason, trousers must be covered by a long tunic top. Did I really wear sleeveless blouses in the summer heat one and a half decades ago? Not today.

"When it is necessary for a man to teach a class of women, he lectures to them from behind a one-way glass which functions just like a veil: they can see him but he cannot see them"

Recently, with my family and friends, I ventured into a very old market area of a conservative town in the centre of the peninsula. Although I wore a black silk *abaya*, a long cloak that extends from the top of my head to my feet, covering all but face and hands, the local residents – both men and women – were not satisfied until I was peering out at them in astonishment through three layers of black gauze which hung before my face.

When I first arrived in Saudi Arabia, I got a job teaching English and mathematics to young Saudi men in an industrial training school. Although it was somewhat remarkable for them to have a woman teacher, my skills were needed at that time and most of my students accepted me with friendly good grace. Today, women are not permitted to teach in that school. In some women's colleges, there is a shortage of qualified instructors similar to the situation at my training centre years ago. When it is necessary for a man to teach a class of women, he lectures to them from behind a one-way glass which functions just like a veil: they can see him but he cannot see them.

This is how the Saudis always said it would be. They insisted from the very beginning that they would take

Western technology without taking Western culture. They warned that they would hire foreign workers when they needed them and send them home the minute they had trained Saudis to do their jobs. Today, with oil production at a twenty-year low, thousands of foreigners are leaving the Kingdom every month, returning to homes all over the world.

In addition to preserving their traditions and customs in the face of modernisation, the Saudis are participating in that broad political and religious conservatism which has swept across both East and West. Fundamentalist Muslims, within and without the Kingdom, are urging the Saudi government, as Guardian of the Holy Cities of Mecca and Medina, to be ever stricter in adhering to and enforcing Islamic principles.

Most of the Saudi women I met were disapproving of their sisters in the West. They see Western women as unprotected, living in dangerous cities, and unable to rely on the men of their family to escort them on the streets. A strong sense of sisterhood has always been a part of Arab culture, and constant familial support buoys Saudi women throughout their lives. In contrast, Western women's lifestyles seem full of risk – of loneliness, promiscuity, and abandonment by their children in their old age.

In public, Saudi women and men are separated. Schools are segregated by sex. All museums and public exhibits have men's days and women's days during the week. The few women who venture to worship in a mosque are confined to a special section. Even weddings are celebrated with a men's party and a women's party.

Education for females outside the home is a new phenomenon, which began only 35 years ago. Today there are girls' schools at every level, including women's programmes at several universities. Older women are included in a national literacy campaign.

Opportunities exist for women to study abroad (usually with their husbands). A woman may become a teacher (with female students) or a doctor (with female patients) or a businesswoman (whose brothers provide the interface with the male world). Several banks have established branches just for women. The government has recently begun to consider whether putting their own women to work would be less disruptive to their society than bringing in masses of foreign workers, and is looking for ways to create more "women's jobs".

"There is no political action group in Saudi Arabia, male or female"

I am acquainted with a few Saudi women who refuse to wear the veil – they are fortunate in that their families support them in this move – and a couple who rankle at government censorship and what they see as religious coercion. I know of several who feel depressed by the numerous restrictions placed on them. But they all consider themselves to be good Saudis nonetheless, and are devoted to their families, culture, religion and country. There is no political action group in Saudi Arabia, male or female. Women are not agitating for "liberation" or "equality". Change in Saudi society will come from the inside, within individual lives, homes and families, and at a pace consistent with the Middle Eastern concept of time – one profoundly different from the Western concept.

Thanks to the oil boom of the 1970s, the Saudis' material needs are basically met. The country is now self-sufficient in food production; electricity has reached a large number of towns and villages; education is free and available to anyone who wants it; hospitals are well-equipped and their number is growing as fast as the staff can be found; even the nomadic Bedouin have access to new water wells drilled here and there in the desert. These material advances can free the people to turn their thoughts and energies to the larger questions of life, to contemplate, perhaps, among other things, the role of women in this modern manifestation of their ancient culture. And that has to be good for Saudi women, for their men, and for both halves of the earth.

TRAVEL NOTES

Languages Arabic. English is widely spoken and understood.

Transport There are frequent and reasonably-priced plane services between all the main cities in the country. There is also a network of good roads and rental cars are available in all areas. However, as a single woman, you will have to obtain a driver (it is illegal for a woman to drive) and obtain written permission from your employer for trips further than thirty kilometres! The larger cities have a public bus service. Each bus has a special compartment for women, which is closed off from the rest of the vehicle and entered by a separate door. Employers of Westerners usually operate a private recreational bus service for shopping and beach trips.

Accommodation Special compounds have been built for foreigners. Women are subject to curfews and need a written invitation from a married couple in order to stay out overnight. Cohabitation is absolutely prohibited. Hotels are often reluctant to register single women and, although it is not legally required, you may be asked to produce a letter of permission from your employer, husband or father. During the *Hadj* (pilgrimage) hotels become very full and you'll need to reserve a room well in advance.

Special Problems Visitor's visas are usually only given to workers travelling to a job already obtained in the Kingdom, to women and children on family visas, and to visitors attending a conference or invited by an academic or commercial institution. Tourist visas are not available and it has become more difficult recently for single women to obtain a work permit. Customs officials search luggage thoroughly for alcohol, drugs, medicines and pornography. Penalties for attempting to bring any of these items into the country can be severe.

Western women, in particular single ones, are subjected to a wide array of both verbal and physical abuse – cars hooting, kerb crawling, staring and touching. However, penalties for all crimes are very harsh and actual physical attack (in public at least) is incredibly rare. If you feel uncomfortable you should make a fuss; few men would persist if confronted. It is illegal for a woman to spend time alone with a man who is not a relative. Dress codes are strict and rigidly enforced. Any woman considered immodestly clothed faces severe treatment from the religious police. Many foreigners find it simplest to wear the *abaya*, which covers the body from head to toe.

Guides Madge Pendleton, ed, *The Green Book; Guide for Living in Saudi Arabia* (Middle East Editorial Associates, Washington) is useful to prepare yourself for the regulation. *Saudi Arabia: A MEED Practical Guide* (Middle East Economic Digest, London) gives a good overview and details of sights.

Contacts

Saudi Arabia Women's Association, BP 6, Riyadh. The association provides information about Saudi women's organisations, most of which are organised for social and charitable purposes.

Books

Marianne Alireza, *At the Drop of a Veil* (Houghton Mifflin, US, 1971).

Eleanor Nicholson, *In the Footsteps of the Camel: A Portrait of the Bedouins of Eastern Saudi Arabia in Mid-Century* (Stacy International, 1983).

Soraya Altorki, *Women in Saudi Arabia* (Columbia U. Press, US, 1986). An analysis of life in the rich Jeddah elite. Focuses particularly on Saudi women's efforts to improve their status working within traditionally defined roles.

Useful information on Saudi women can be found in ***Sisterhood is Global*** and in the Minority Rights Group report ***Arab Women*** (see General Bibliography).

Thanks to Jean Grant Fraga for contributing to the introduction.

Senegal

enegal was the first West African country to be colonised by France and the continuing French influence is immediately apparent in the smooth road networks and transport system, and in the exclusive resorts, restaurants and private beaches along the coast. The country draws around 200,000 French package tourists a year – and it is also one of the most popular West African destinations for independent travellers.

Beneath the French veneer, Senegal has a profoundly African Muslim culture and the precepts of Islam are widely practised and felt. In comparison with the North African states this imposes relatively few restrictions on women, who maintain a high profile in public life and are easy to make everyday contact with. Politically the country is run as a multiparty democracy and despite the riots of 1988, a continuing economic crisis, and escalating racial conflicts with the Mauritanian minority, it manages to retain its reputation as one of the most stable countries in the region.

Dakar is perhaps the worst introduction to the country. Many people compete to make a living from the tourists and French ex-pats, and the constant pressure and hard-sell tactics of the street vendors and "guides" can give it a coercive atmosphere. The only real danger, however, is in the wealthy commercial centre where muggings are now common. Elsewhere in the country you experience few problems, though you will need to get used to being a symbol of affluence and to having people constantly approach you for money. How you cope with this is a personal issue; most Senegalese routinely give something to beggars and it's vital to remain friendly and polite. Sexual harassment is much less evident. It's advisable, though, and certainly more comfortable in the hot climate, to wear long, loose clothes. Travelling around the country is fairly easy – transport is good, there's a fair amount of accommodation, and the Senegalese people are renowned for their hospitality to strangers. It is quite likely that you will be invited to stay in someone's house, in which case be aware of the burdens you are imposing. There's no offence in paying for as much as you can and it's polite to offer gifts.

The main **women's organisation**, the *Fédération des Associations Feminines du Sénégal* (*FAFS*) was founded by the ruling Parti Socialiste and retains close links with the government. Its chief emphasis is on development and the provision of social welfare and educational services. Although it has a wide membership and has set up a range of local groups, its impact in the rural areas is still small. A more radical group is the *Association of African Women for Research and Development* (*AAWORD*), created by a group of African women dedicated to doing feminist research from an African perspective. Over the last decade they have assisted in numerous schemes, emphasising the need for direct participation of local women in development projects. One of AAWORD's central concerns has been to place the issue of genital mutilation firmly in context as an African problem to be resolved by African people, counteracting Western outrage and sensationalism.

Life with the Diops

• • • • • • • • • • • •

Daphne Topouzis, a founder editor member of *Africa Report*, an American bi-monthly magazine of African affairs, spent six months in Senegal researching a PhD; she lived with a Senegalese family on the outskirts of Dakar.

My original purpose in going to Senegal was to research into the impact of French colonial rule on the development of Black Politics during the 1930s and 1940s. I also wanted to collect material on the Women's Movement in the cities and on the role of women in rural development. It gradually became apparent to me, though, that living with a Senegalese family was easily the most

valuable experience of the trip. It enabled me to meet and get close to a large number of women of all ages, from all walks of life, which would have otherwise been impossible.

A friend who had also researched in West Africa helped me make contact with a Muslim family in Dakar. Though we had never met before, the Diops borrowed a couple of relatives' cars and came to meet me at the airport like an old friend. Hospitality (*teranga*) is central to Senegalese culture and hosts will go to great lengths to provide their guests with everything they possibly can, often exceeding their means.

My first days at the "Keur Diop" (Diop household) in Liberté VI, one of Dakar's suburbs, were overwhelming. Not only was this my first time in Africa but it was also the first time I had lived with a family of twenty. I shared a tiny room with two other women my age and was at once deprived of all privacy and independence, both of which had until then seemed essential to me. Differences in lifestyle and culture initially seemed both fundamental and insurmountable.

Curiosity and shyness on both sides made conversation awkward for the first couple of days, until the youngest children broke the ice. They taught me my first words of Wolof, reminded me of everybody's names, gave me directions to the bus stop and involved me in family activities. Within a week or so I had settled into a daily routine and had learnt a great deal about my host family and its expectations of me.

"We spent long hours discussing polygamy, men, and the lack of choices for women"

Marianne, aged 56, was a secretary in a Dakar hospital, the second of four wives and mother of three daughters and five sons. Just under half of all marriages in Senegal are polygamous (Muslims can have up to four wives), which is a harsh reality and nightmare for many women. It involves economic hardship, neglect of the older wife, favouritism of the younger one, jealousy (wives often share the same bedroom), oversized families and overcrowded households. We spent long hours discussing polygamy, men, and the lack of choices for women. What impressed me most was her good humour, which invariably meant that conversations about grief ended with hearty laughter.

Marianne's daughters (aged 16, 22 and 23) were enormously curious about me and soon became constant companions. One particular incident a few days after my arrival brought us together. After jokingly remarking that my long, straight hair looked dull and ugly, they began plaiting it without awaiting my reply: "Plaits can make anyone look good," they said. But, however graceful they looked on them, plaits made me

look worse than before (not to mention the fact that the children became afraid of me). We laughed about it for hours, and later in the evening, fearful that my feelings had been hurt, my closest friend, Fatou, offered me a *pagne* (square patterned fabric tied around the waist). It felt comfortable and looked good – or so was the general consensus – and I began wearing it regularly.

My relationships with the men in the family were friendly and comfortable except for an isolated misunderstanding with the eldest son. But being always a little uncertain of my status I tried to maintain a safe distance. I rarely saw Mr Diop (a retired postman) as he spent almost all of his time with his third wife. However, I always looked forward to his weekly tea gatherings with his comrades from the Second World War where colonial politics were passionately discussed. They never quite understood how I knew so much about this relatively obscure period of African history, but greatly appreciated my avid interest in their accounts as well as my endless questions and occasional contribution to the discussion.

On the whole, everyone in the family was discreet, never asking personal questions which might have been difficult to answer (on religion, politics or sex). Part of the explanation might be that I was much more curious about them than they were about me. But, like most Senegalese, they were far more tolerant of me than I had expected. For instance, though visibly puzzled by the fact that I did not have children (but less concerned by the fact that I was single), they never pressed the issue.

As a devout Muslim family, the Diops had assumed I also would be religious (the fact that I was Christian did not make us all that different in their eyes) and when I first arrived they gave me directions to the local church. I never went there, and although they realised I did not practice my religion they never held this against me. Similarly, they were perplexed by the fact that despite being white, which meant rich, I dressed relatively casually while they, despite their very tight budget, were always elegant and graceful. In this case, I began to dress visibly better as a result of living with them, but again, they never tried to talk me into it.

In fact, two months after living with the Diops, the differences in culture which had at first seemed so radical began to wane and I was treated like a member of their family: they encouraged me to learn Wolof, dance the *sabar*, wear *pagnes*, and help with the cooking and shopping.

"I was ... forced to confront why privacy and independence as I understood them were so important to me"

The only two things I found difficult to cope with were the lack of privacy and their unshakeable belief that, being white, I had an inexhaustible supply of money. The lack of privacy meant that I did not have a quiet half-hour to relax, read, or write letters. But there was no way around it as the family was large and the house overcrowded. The real challenge for me, however, was that the women with whom I was closest seemed unable to understand my professed need to be alone once in a while or my occasional spells of gloom and loneliness. I was gently scolded for my self-indulgent attitude and forced to confront why privacy and independence as I understood them were so important to me.

One particular incident has crystallised in my mind: On the last day of Ramadan, all but three young children and a couple of adults had gone to the local mosque to pray. At once, the compound which was full of activity and the noise of many children became unusually quiet. Marianne came to me

and said anxiously, "I cannot stand it when the house is empty. It feels so lonely." While in the past I would have relished this rare moment of peace and quiet, I found to my surprise that it did feel lonely and painfully silent without the usual commotion. When the children returned, Marianne was visibly happier and proudly said to me "Now you see why my children (which virtually meant the whole extended family) are my fortune."

This is not to say that I resolved the problem of privacy, but I learnt a lot from doing without it. The problem of money I never fully resolved. Even though I contributed a weekly sum to the family income, regularly bought treats, took the children to the cinema, etc, etc, I was regularly asked for cash. If there was an emergency such as medical expenses or school fees, I gave what I could. But often it was for luxuries like cosmetics, which seemed essential to them but not to me. I learnt to say I did not have money but that always created some tension. In retrospect, I believe it is wiser to give something, even if only a fraction of the amount, rather than refuse altogether and appear insensitive to needs.

Except for those relatively minor problems, my life with the family ran smoothly once I had established a routine of my own. My day began at 7am when after a cup of *kenkilabah* (local herb tea) I would take the bus to the "Building Administratif" where the government archives are held. After work I would return to Liberté VI, often stopping by on the way amid the tiny, dark market stalls, loaded with vegetables and colour.

Marianne's daughters would start to prepare the food in the courtyard while there was still daylight. Evening entertainment consisted of either visiting friends or dancing to the haunting tunes of Dakar's musical superstars Youssou N'Dour (who has now become a celebrity worldwide) and Super Diamono. Social life around the family was so enjoyable that I never went downtown to discos, restaurants or bars. I knew they existed, and they are popular amongst the Senegalese, but it never seemed worth the trip. Liberté VI was relaxing after a hectic day in Dakar. Everybody knew each other, little French was spoken, and no whites lived there. At first I felt uncomfortable being stared at in the streets but gradually people got used to me. As soon as I learnt some Wolof the barrier was broken and I began greeting neighbours regardless of whether I knew them or not.

My first trip outside Dakar was to Fatik, a small town four hours south of the capital. Marianne's son took me to visit his grandmother and her family. The further away we got from Dakar the more we could see the effects of the drought: long stretches of land with dried-up baobabs, cotton trees and abandoned villages. Around Fatik the dry earth had cracked and dead cattle in different stages of disintegration baked in the sun. We visited the local market to get *gris-gris* (protective amulets) and then went to a wrestling match. Wrestling is Senegal's national sport and worth seeing. On a Sunday afternoon you can catch up to thirty matches. They last only a few minutes each and involve mesmerising ritualistic movements.

A second trip to Touba was a little disappointing. Touba is the birthplace of the Mouridyyia – Senegal's fast-growing Muslim brotherhood. A great mosque and Koranic university dominate the town, which itself is very poor. The contrast between the incredible wealth of the mosque and the poverty surrounding it is quite disturbing. Touba has its own militia who can (and do) arrest people for drinking alcohol or smoking cigarettes within the boundaries.

On another trip, with two women friends, I took the Casamance express boat down to Ziguinchor and visited the US Peace Corps house, which is situated right behind the port. (The Peace Corps is an American voluntary development agency.) Even though I initially had reservations about the organisation and its approach to work in Africa, I found the volunteers friendly, hard-working and eager for company. Travellers can stay at the house for a small fee. Also, the volunteers are usually delighted to take travellers to their assigned villages. Their knowledge of the local languages and the fact that they are well integrated in the local community were a positive contrast to the Canadian missionaries nearby who seemed totally estranged from their surroundings.

"I began having all the symptoms of malaria: chills and flushes, headaches, hallucinations and diarrhoea"

After Ziguinchor I went to Diembering, a small village off Cap Skirring. Villagers were drying fish in the sun, mending fishing nets and repairing pirogues on the beach. I had originally planned to stay for a few days at the government *campement*. But the same evening I began having all the symptoms of malaria: chills and flushes, headaches, hallucinations and diarrhoea. Usually, the first 72 hours of malaria attacks are the worst and after that a large dose of Nivaquine begins to work. I was helped on to the boat back to Dakar and went to the Peace Corps doctor. (They usually only treat volunteers but made an exception in my case.) It took ten days for me to recover and when I returned to the Diop family they treated me as though I had been long lost, showing very real relief and concern.

Soon after that episode I was stopped in the centre of Dakar by a *gendarme* who wanted to check my passport. As I didn't have it on me I was taken to the station, where I encountered at least twenty whites picked up for the same reason. (I was later told that every once in a while the police go out on such raids to show foreigners who's boss.) After sitting for hours in the waiting room I began to feel uncomfortable and frightened. The Chief of Police asked me a long series of questions and then calmly assured me that I would be there all day. A few moments later someone offered me a cigarette and I thanked him in Wolof. Suddenly the atmosphere changed, the police became warm and apologetic and I was inundated with invitations and offers of hospitality.

These problems did not cast a shadow over my stay. They were part of the challenge of trying to lead an integrated life in a very different culture and climate to my own. I've kept contact with the family in Liberté VI, whom I consider now part of my extended family, and am returning soon for another six-month stay.

TRAVEL NOTES

Languages French and several African languages – Wolof is the most widely spoken.

Transport The basic transport throughout Senegal is the bush-taxi (*taxi-brousse*). Each passenger pays for a seat, and the taxi leaves only when it is full. Try to travel early in the morning to avoid long waits for other passengers, especially in villages. Prices are government-fixed and fairly low. In Dakar there are taxis and buses.

Accommodation The tourist hotels of Dakar are generally expensive, though you can stay in *campements* (cheap but comfortable accommodation in simple buildings) at Casamance, outside the city. In the rural areas it is likely that you'll be invited to stay in people's homes. You should offer some money or gifts towards your keep.

Special Problems You will often be approached for money by hustlers, beggars and other people who need it and have none. People have their own ways of dealing with this – most give coins or small gifts.

Guides *The Rough Guide: West Africa* (Harrap Columbus) has a major section on Senegal.

Contacts

Association of African Women in Research and Development (AAWORD), Codesria, B3304, Dakar. A pan-African women's federation which carries out research, publishes a journal, and campaigns for women's rights throughout Africa.

Council for the Development of Economic and Social Research in Africa (CODESRA), BP3304, Dakar. Research centre which works, among other themes, on women and development in Africa.

Books

Mariama Ba, *So Long a Letter* (Virago, 1982). Brilliant portrait by a Senegalese feminist of a Muslim woman living in a society of transition. Ba's second book, *The Scarlet Song* (Longman, 1986), focuses on the relationship between an educated French woman and a poor Senegalese man.

Nafissatou Diallo, *A Dakar Childhood* (Longman, 1982). Autobiographical account of growing up in Dakar.

Aminata Sow Fell, *Beggars Strike* (Longman, 1981). Fictional tale of a beggars' uprising in Dakar by Senegal's leading woman novelist.

Sierra Leone

• • • • • • • • • • • • • • • • •

Very few travellers go to Sierra Leone. The problems of an almost defunct transport system and no direct links to neighbouring Guinea and Liberia make it difficult to visit the country as part of a West African tour. And, despite having some of the finest beaches on the continent, tourism has barely developed beyond the odd, isolated resort on Freetown peninsula and a clutch of hotels in the capital.

Escalating foreign debts, high-level corruption and an almost institutionalised diamond smuggling racket have brought Sierra Leone to the verge of economic collapse. The country's British colonial infrastructure, along with many of the state institutions developed since independence from the British in 1963, have either crumbled or fallen into disarray. Education and health provisions are poor and erratic, there's a chronic lack of transport, no internal phone system and a very limited electricity supply. Even the capital, Freetown, is subjected to regular blackouts. General Momoh, who heads the civilian government, has introduced widespread austerity measures in an attempt to prevent national breakdown. But, as poverty and hardship take hold, dissent and opposition are mounting.

Although tourists are very rare, there are plenty of foreign aid workers who travel around the country and there are few obvious restrictions or dangers for women. Men may well approach you with offers of sex – the propositions are usually direct and upfront – but this rarely feels oppressive or threatening. Much the same is true about requests for money. The assumption that you are rich is inescapable and, in a country where you have to rely quite heavily on local hospitality, the onus is on you to be a generous guest. Theft is a fairly common problem, especially if you live in the country for some time, and you'll be warned against wandering alone on deserted stretches of beach.

Attitudes towards women vary as you move from the predominantly Christian and more Westernised south, dominated by the Mende and Krio ethnic groups, to the nominally Muslim and more conservative north, dominated by the Temne. Amongst the Krios, who descend from the freed slaves of the Caribbean, and the Mendes, women have greater access to education and paid work and are expected to take a much more active role in community life. The Mendes still have a fair number of female paramount chiefs, something unheard of in the north. As a foreigner, though, you're unlikely to be affected by the shifts in local customs.

In Freetown there is a fairly well established **women's movement**, set up and run by Krio women to develop and support local education and income-generating projects. But, traditionally, women gain support, solidarity and not a little prestige through membership of the so-called secret societies. Genital mutilation is a central feature of many of these societies' initiation rites and, although campaigns have been set up opposing this practice, it remains a popular and widely accepted aspect of the rites of passage to womanhood.

Working in Makeni

. . . .

Nicky Young has been living for the last eight months in Makeni, the capital of the northern province, where she works as an administrator in a school for deaf children.

When I arrived in Sierra Leone I was prepared for life without some of our normal creature comforts – running water, electricity, railways, efficient public transport, good roads, a national newspaper. What I did find a shock was that only twenty to thirty years ago most of these things were a reliable part of everyday life. The remnants of an economy that once worked is sad to see and incredibly frustrating for the nation who now have to live with it.

If first impressions are important, I can't ignore the arrival at Lungi Airport. The airport, built on a peninsula slightly north of the capital, Freetown, is small, busy and very confusing. You have to push your way through to various desks to produce visas and yellow fever certificates, fill in different coloured forms, and declare and change currency, before going through customs. And then you have to hold tight to your bags in case an over eager taxi driver grabs them and locks them in the trunk of his car. I was lucky in that I had someone to meet me.

Each year sees a small but growing number of wealthy French tourists arriving on package deals to Freetown Peninsula to soak up the hot African sun on the miles of unspoilt, tropical beaches. Besides joining an occasional tour around a "Typical African Village", few of them stray further than the local bars. Travelling up country is a difficult business and has to be treated as part of the adventure, but until you make it out of Freetown you won't really see Sierra Leone.

Hitching is a necessity. The only way of getting around is to wave at a passing car and hope that it will stop. The cars with the yellow number plates and bursting with people are supposed to be taxis, but you may get a lift from someone else, sometimes for free. Outside Freetown, most of the Western people you meet are expatriate workers and volunteers. Those who have transport are usually sympathetic to those who don't and I seem to spend much of my time scrounging lifts. People have mixed opinions of Freetown – most dislike the hassles involved in getting anything achieved, but appreciate the more frequent power and water supplies, Western foods and tropical beaches. It's a welcome break from the heat and commotion of Makeni where I live.

Makeni is about 115 miles inland from Freetown and has the reputation of being the hottest place in the country. I arrived in March, the hottest time of year, having come from frosty English weather. Sierra Leone is divided up into chiefdoms, each dominated by one of several tribes. Makeni is predominantly a Temne area. Temnes are known to be rather vociferous, and since my flat is situated right in the town centre, next to the market, I soon learnt that living in Africa wasn't going to be the peaceful experience I had hoped for.

Every morning at five I am woken by the call to prayer at the town mosque. From then onwards I hear the town stirring into life; market women setting up stalls, cocks crowing, dogs barking, and cassava leaves being pounded down into the staple soft green pulp seasoned with palm oil and fish. The mosque each morning is a constant reminder that Sierra Leone is a predominantly Muslim country. Before I arrived I was warned to dress modestly because of this. But so long as your clothes aren't brief or tight, most local people accept that you'll wear Western clothes, even shorts, and don't seem too bothered.

"When can we meet to do some loving?' is the usual opening gambit"

Local people greet one another as they pass on the street, whether they know each other or not, and it is considered rude not to return a greeting. However, my trying not to be culturally insensitive was often misinterpreted by men, who took it as an invitation to get better acquainted. Men tend to be very forward in their proposals, "When can we meet to do some loving?" is the usual opening gambit. Life would be much easier if they took no for an answer, but they seldom do and I have often ended up being equally direct. White women tourists are considered both a novelty and a source of funds.

Overall, though, there is a friendliness and openness towards visitors, and people are eager to help you out – sometimes, uncomfortably so. I am rarely allowed to pull water from a well or to weed a garden without someone stepping in to help. And there have been times when I have been given the front seat of a bus, only to find that a frail old woman has been squashed into the back.

My job, as administrator for a school for hearing-impaired children, involves training a local woman the same age as myself. Mankapr had been doing the job for several years already, was used to Westerners coming to "share their skills", and knew how the people in her country expected things to be done. My first few months were spent building up a relationship with her and learning how it all worked.

My arrival coincided with preparations for her tribal wedding. Most of her contemporaries had married long ago and now had large families, but Mankapr had an overprotective brother as a guardian, who had been reluctant to let her go. She had been raised largely by this brother, as her mother had become sick after her birth and had never quite recovered, while her father was busy with his second wife. Mankapr was pregnant on her wedding day, which she explained was a fairly standard occurrence as a man wants to ensure that his wife will be fertile before he agrees to the marriage.

"Sitting in the candlelit room, watching the cockroaches scuttle across the walls, I remember feeling very lost"

I was lucky enough to be invited to attend the wedding, which took place one evening in a dimly lit yard behind the house of the bride's father. I was met by a group of older women, all brightly dressed in batik and tie-dyed *lappas* (fabric tied around their waists and a matching top and head tie), who took me to a neighbour's house. The men, I discovered later, had gathered further down the street.

Sitting in the candlelit room, watching the cockroaches scuttle across the walls, I remember feeling very lost – not understanding any of the Krio being spoken around me. (I learnt Krio fairly quickly afterwards; having so many adapted and assimilated English words it is a fairly easy language to pick up.) Eventually we were led to a yard, lit by a sole kerosene lamp placed in the centre, where the the the male representatives of the bride's family were awaiting the entry of the groom's family. The wedding began with the

latter arriving carrying cola nuts – a gift of friendship. The bride's family pretended to be completely ignorant of who they were and why they were there. Then followed introductions of all the important people in the room – including me, because I was white – after which the nuts were accepted and the two groups settled down to negotiate the contract.

Money was discussed for all the groom's specific privileges as a married man, such as being allowed to talk to the bride, take her through the door of his house and, ultimately, to share her bed. This last caused a roar from all the guests, demanding that the price be much higher. The strangest thing throughout was that the bride wasn't even there. She was summoned only when the talks were finished. Then a young girl draped in white, obviously not the bride, was thrust forward and was rejected by the groom to everyone's amusement. Finally Mankapr appeared, was asked if she knew Hassan and if she would marry him and if he would marry her. After each "yes", money was flung in from the guests with much cheering, more cola nuts were exchanged, ground nut stew and *poyo* (palm wine) were distributed and the party began.

Several months later Mankapr and Hassan had a religious wedding, something most people have to forego because of the expense. They are now the proud parents of a healthy baby boy, with a cheeky smile, called Louis. Sierra Leone has one of the highest child mortality rates in the world, if not the highest. A teacher at my school told me that she was the only one of nine children to survive past childhood, and her story was not an uncommon one.

As I walk to school every morning along the dusty streets, children of all ages stop to chant at me, "Porto, Porto, Syrian. Are ya Syrian". The song fades as I pass but rises again with next group. "Porto" means "white". If they stop singing it's usually to greet me and ask for two *leones* (about 2p). School starts at 7.45am and, arriving at the gates, I am usually met by children rushing up for hugs. We have assembly and then Mankapr and I return to our tiny office and attempt to battle through the chaotic task of organising three schools, five bank accounts, and endless problems. It would be easy to spend days just counting out money which arrives in big bundles of old and tatty two *leone* notes – no joke when you're dividing it up for forty people's monthly wages.

"Some women have had things stolen from their rooms at night while they've been asleep, which is unnerving, though personal attacks are extremely rare"

The schoolday ends early at 1.30pm, Mankapr rushes home to cook, wash and clean. I also head home, thankful that I haven't a demanding family waiting for me. On the way I might stop at a bar for a soft drink and a *binche* sandwich (beans, palm oil, fish and onions), using the midday heat as an excuse for relaxing on the veranda with a book and delaying the walk home. Later in the afternoon I'll start to think about the main meal of the day and wander off round the market for inspiration.

Large women with babies tied to their backs, and small children clinging to their ankles, call as I walk past, "Yu no wan jibloks?" (You no want aubergines?). Spread all around in a bright array of colours are bundles of hot red peppers, piles of onions, okra, small squashy tomatoes and sweet potatoes. Green bundles of cassava and potato leaves are heaped into baskets, and rice, beans, groundnuts and spices fill large enamel basins. Dinner is usually an assortment of these vegetables served with rice. Because power is scarce there is no refrigeration and food has to be bought fresh daily. The days and weekends seem to drift past

in a routine of writing home, reading, visiting people, and watching the world pass by from the local bar.

Before I arrived, in March 1988, an economic emergency was declared. The number of checkpoints that appeared on the roads made travelling even slower than usual. These checkpoints have now decreased considerably in number, though foreign currency is strictly regulated and checked for, as well as gold and diamonds, which are frequently smuggled out. Corruption and thieving are a major problem. Makeni is supposed to be particularly vulnerable and during my first few months my flat was broken into twice. Almost all the volunteers living here have been robbed, despite having watchmen, bars on the windows and bolts on the doors. Some women have had things stolen from their rooms at night while they've been asleep, which is unnerving, though personal attacks are extremely rare.

As a volunteer, I currently manage on the weekly equivalent of about ten pounds, but the teachers I work with average only two pounds per week, on which most of them have to support a family. The worst of it is that the salaries don't always arrive. At the time of writing the teachers had been without pay for over four months. They are now on strike. It is no surprise that people resort to stealing.

It is more difficult sometimes to understand how people survive. It seems that family and friends give and share whenever they can. I also give money but it's a problem to know where to draw the line, especially as my own budget is limited. After a few months in the country I felt I was becoming very hard-hearted. I was able to walk away from beggars, people who were hungry and children dressed in rags, without feeling shrouded in guilt.

Sierra Leone is not an easy country to visit, but, once there, you'll find yourself drawn into the local way of life. It certainly makes you rethink old values.

TRAVEL NOTES

Languages Krio (partly derived from archaic English), Mende and Temne. English is widely spoken in Freetown.

Transport There are no trains, government buses are sparse, and *pode podes* (local trucks) are slow, unreliable and packed. Women routinely hitch, which is considered fairly safe.

Accommodation Freetown and the peninsula resorts have a few expensive tourist hotels; the women's hotel, run by the convent on Howe Street, Freetown, is a welcome haven. Upcountry hotels and rest houses are few and far between. If you want to stay in a village you should organise this through the paramount chief and be prepared to reciprocate hospitality with money or gifts. You might also be given sleeping space by VSO or Peace Corps workers; again, you'll be expected to contribute towards your keep.

Special Problems Theft is common. You also face frequent propositions from men, but this is rarely threatening. But there's a real danger of tourist muggings on the deserted beaches. Take everything you'll need by way of sanitary protection, contraception and medical supplies. Supplies are erratic.

Guide *The Rough Guide: West Africa* (Harrap-Columbus) includes a full section on Sierra Leone.

Contacts

Sierra Leone Women's Movement, The Retreat, 40 Main Road, Conge Cross, Freetown. **National Federation of Sierra Leone Women's Organisations**, PO Box 811, Freetown. Both organisations give out information on local development projects involving women, and education and health campaigns.

Books

Olayinka Koso-Thoma, *The Circumcision of Women – a Strategy for Eradication* (Zed Books, 1987). Detailed research and thoughtful analysis focusing on Sierra Leone's powerful women's societies.

Adelaide M. Cromwell, *An African Victorian Feminist – the Life and Times of Adelaide Smith Casely Hayford 1868–1960* (Frank Cass, US, 1986). The compelling biography of an early Krio activist and campaigner.

E. Frances White, *Sierra Leone's Settler Women Traders* (Michigan UP, US, 1987). Charts the historical role of Freetown's "Big Market" women.

Donald Cosentino, *Defiant Maids and Stubborn Farmers: Tradition and Invention in Mende Story Performance* (CUP, US, 1982). Academic study of oral literary traditions amongst the Mende people. Includes analysis of how women are represented.

Soviet Union

$\mathbf{A}$t the time of writing surmise is starting to give way to certainty that the Soviet Union is breaking up. *Perestroika* has clearly taken on a momentum of its own, unleashing a wave of nationalism, urgent demands for self-determination from many of the federation's fifteen republics – and, with it, age-old and bloody ethnic conflicts and border disputes (the Azerbaijan-Armenian war being only one of many potential sites for the outbreak of hostilities). Many of us in the West have only begun to recognise and appreciate the vastly contrasting races, cultures and religions that exist within Soviet borders as a result of headlines switching from one area of popular dissent and unrest to another.

Yet the explosion of nationalism is only one amongst many of the challenges that threatens to destabilise Mikhail Gorbachev's reforms. Within the Soviet Union, where economic crisis is taking its toll in renewed hardship and shortages, popular support for the president is waning fast. *Glasnost* has

lifted the lid on the abuses, shortcomings and incompetence of the old monolithic and centralised Communist system (blamed for all current ills – from
Chernobyl to train crashes), while *perestroika* has provided the means to
express dissent through newly legalised oppositional groups.

As far as the West is concerned, much of the excitement generated by the
opening up of the Soviet Union has been reined in by anxiety about its future.
To a frightening degree this seems to depend as much on the abilities and
stamina of Gorbachev himself as on the extent to which the Soviet people can
go on enduring the hardships they face. Gorbachev has stressed that the
changes made (in terms of improved civil and human rights, democratisation,
and moves towards a more market-oriented system) are irreversible – and
that there can be no sudden clampdown and purge of dissenters. To a large
extent he is believed, but the guarantee that there will be no return to a
fortress mentality rests largely on what links can be forged with the outside
world in cultural, economic, political, and simply human terms.

Ironically, at a time when travel is becoming much more open, republics
are being wiped off the tourist map by instability and unrest. Azerbaijan and
Armenia are obvious examples, but many other destinations – the Baltic
states, the Transcaucasian republics, even the Trans-Siberian express – seem
to be hanging in the balance. Obviously it's important to get up-to-date information before deciding to set off. In general terms, though, travel is by no
means the restricted or one-way industry it used to be. More than at any
other time Soviet citizens are being allowed to view the West for themselves
(the US embassy has been so swamped by visa applications that it no longer
treats Soviet immigrants as "political refugees"), while Westerners are being
presented with a range of options for travel.

It is possible to travel without a tour group but it's expensive and you'll be
expected to work out and declare your itinerary well in advance. The most
usual, and still the most popular, way to visit is a package deal arranged
either through *Intourist*, the main Soviet travel organisation, or *Sputnick*, the
youth wing. There are also new co-operatives being formed, however, that
run their own private tours and, more surprisingly, have gained permission to
rent out private rooms. At present these operate exclusively through travel
agencies but they may well soon be on offer to independent travellers.
Already, it is pretty routine to arrange a semi-independent visit through
Finland to the Baltic states.

In the past, state tourist guides were anxious to promote the Party line and
edgy about people wandering off on their own. This is no longer the case.
Itineraries might suddenly change as a result of political unrest but once you
arrive somewhere you are more or less allowed to explore at will, talk to
whoever you wish and even accept invitations to people's homes. If you do,
you will experience first-hand the justly famous hospitality of Russians (or
citizens of the other Soviet republics). It's important, however, to be sensitive
to the burden that hospitality creates and to reciprocate where you can.

Obviously your experience of the Soviet Union depends on where you go –
the European and predominantly Protestant Baltic republics can seem as far
removed from, say, Islamic Uzbekistan, as Holland is from Iraq. Sexism in
the European republics is much more likely to show itself in the form of an

old-fashioned "gallantry" while in the Islamic eastern republics Western visitors, like European Soviets, can come up against fairly persistent street harassment (being propositioned, followed home, etc).

Travelling around, alone or with a group, presents few problems of safety. Crime is on the increase throughout the Soviet Union but these are mainly "economic crimes". You might feel pressurised to change money or barter goods, but sexual assault is incredibly rare. More of a problem can be the feeling of unwarranted privilege that you have as a hard currency tourist. The creation of new and flashy dollar shops and hotels have been amongst the least relevant (but most publicised) of the East-West co-operative ventures and are often pitched well beyond the means of most Soviet citizens. However, there seems to be little resentment shown towards foreigners, and people generally seem interested to meet and talk about their country's pitfalls and promises.

The **position of women** in the Soviet Union is shaped by the different traditions and cultures of its republics. In Russia and the other European republics women have the highest participation in the labour force of any modern industrial society, but they are concentrated in low-pay, low-status jobs. Articles 35 and 53, which instituted sexual equality, have had little impact on sexual relations and the division of domestic, unpaid labour. The double burden of domestic and paid work is an entrenched feature of many women's lives and, in a society where the logistics of looking after a home and family are both complex and time-consuming, can be crippling.

The legislation on maternity leave (one year on full pay and the option of six months unpaid leave) and childcare may seem exemplary, too, but reality again falls far short of the ideal. Daycare centres are understaffed, overcrowded and hotbeds of childhood diseases, and many women prefer to either leave their child with a *Babushka* (granny) or make private arrangements. Abortions are easily available but contraception and sex education are not. Women clearly feel abused by a family planning system centred on the provision of abortions (with poor healthcare and follow-up) at the expense of a safer, more comprehensive, approach to birth control – the average European Soviet woman undergoes six to eight abortions in her lifetime.

In response to concern about the falling birth rate in the European republics, attempts are being made to revive and officially promote the role of the full-time housewife. Women are facing much more social pressure than before to have children, and to take their full quota of maternity leave when they do – articles have suddenly started to appear in state journals alerting society to the problems of maternal deprivation. Whilst there are certainly women who see this as retrogressive, and who have responded with letters and articles defending their right to pursue a career, many are desperate to reduce their appalling workloads and support any move that brings with it flexible work schedules.

A very different picture emerges in the eastern republics. Women tend to follow the traditional pattern of marrying at a very young age, bearing many children (the average being six) and working unpaid on the land or in the home. Poverty is often intense and, for all the claims of the Soviet healthcare system, the infant mortality rate in some areas ranks amongst the worst in the world. The Soviet press has recently started to draw attention to the continuation of outlawed Islamic practices such as arranged marriages and the use of dowry and bride-price. The authorities are similarly running family-planning campaigns in these republics and local activists are trying to persuade women to take up their rightful places in the workforce. Whilst these initiatives might overtly seem pro-women they are understandably viewed as an attempt to lower the birth rate and infringe upon the traditions and strength of Islam. And, as such, they are met largely with hostility.

We realise that in these rapidly shifting times there's little that can be said about the experience of travel in the Soviet Union that would not in some way seem dated – even by the time of publication. The pieces below obviously tell of a particular historical moment but in their descriptions of meetings with Soviet women have, we hope, some enduring relevance.

Touring the Republics

· · · · · · · · · ·

Lynne Attwood works as a guide and interpreter for American student trips to the Soviet Union. Her fascination for the country has stood the test of innumerable visits. She has also completed a PhD in Soviet Studies.

I first visited the Soviet Union on a whim, a spur-of-the-moment response to an advert about a New Year student tour to Moscow and Leningrad. Thus began what promises to be a lifetime of fascination with the place. Ten years and more than twenty visits later, I have a PhD in Soviet Studies and a job which takes me to different corners of the country several times a year, as a guide and interpreter to groups of American students.

It has been a love-hate relationship. On the one hand there has been the welter of Soviet bureaucracy to contend with – red tape, delays, rejections, a mass of petty frustrations. On the other there is the warmth of Russian friendships, the coolness of crisp white winters, the delight of coming to understand the rich complexity of the country's cultures.

"I suppose we were some kind of 'exotica' for you!" suggested my friend Larisa, attempting to understand my long-term attachment. (Russians generally seem rather confused by the interest Westerners take in them – or at least they were, until *perestroika* opened the floodgates of media attention and they had to get used to it.) That was probably the case, at least in the beginning. But the Soviet Union – or at least Russia, Georgia, or other of its component parts – just seems to get under some people's skin.

Moscow was blanketed in snow on my first visit, the white pierced by the bright red of New Year decorations. The group I was with was booked into a restaurant for a New Year's Eve dinner, but there were some hours till we were due to meet and I set off to explore the city by myself. Struggling to work out the metro map, I sought the help of a young Russian who spoke some English. His name was Igor. He had a bottle of Soviet champagne tucked under one arm and was on his way to a New Year party.

The champagne did not make it with him. We drank it on a park bench, surrounded by snow-encrusted pine trees, exchanging life histories in painfully fractured English. It was already dark but I was struck by the fact that the curfew which many women in Western cities impose on themselves was not in force here. A number of women strolled past our bench. Some were in twos, arms linked, relaxed and laughing. Others were alone, short-cutting through the park with their shopping bags. I have always felt relatively safe in the streets and parks of Russian cities, a feeling I evidently share with local women. This has to be one of the big advantages of the place.

Two days later I was invited to Igor's home, and was exposed to my first taste of Russian hospitality. Around a table groaning with food and drink (this was some years before Gorbachev would launch his anti-alcohol campaign) I forged friendships which have outlived almost all of those I had at the time at home. Like most people I know, I have lost old friends and gained new ones in the process of growing and changing, so my British friends are a fairly homogeneous bunch with a broad similarity of views. Not so in Russia. Our lives, the ideas we have been exposed to, and our responses to them, have been completely different. We discuss these differences, we argue and marvel over them, but they do not dislodge our mutual affection.

Larisa, Igor's sister, was a seventeen-year-old student when I first met her. Now she is married with a three-year-old child and has become one of a new breed of Soviet women – the rehabilitated housewife. She gently mocks me for my feminism. To her, as to many Russian women, "equality" means that women have ended up with twice as much work. Their full-time professional activities have just been heaped on top of their traditional domestic duties. They get little help from men, nor from the labour-saving devices we take for granted in the West. This has made them a receptive audience for the pro-family propaganda which has been pouring out of the Soviet press since the mid-1970s.

"How long will it be – if glasnost continues – before a Russian version of The Women's Room or The Captive Housewife appears on the shelves?"

It is claimed that women's "equality" in the European part of the Soviet Union has had a number of negative consequences – the divorce rate has risen, the number of births has dropped, and teenage delinquency has increased because children were packed off too young to creches and kindergartens. The catch phrase now is that "being equal does not mean being the same", and unless women are exceptionally career-minded they are being urged to put their paid work in second place and spend more time at home looking after their children.

Larisa admits she sometimes feels bored and isolated in this role, but she insists that her mother – who was the head of a team of architects before she retired – regrets the limited time she spent with her children when they were small. In any case, the women she knows who do leave their children in creches are constantly having to take time off work as their children come home with childhood ailments. She is adamant that she is doing the right thing and I no longer argue with her. But how long will it be – if *glasnost* continues – before a Russian version of *The Women's Room* or *The Captive Housewife* appears on the shelves?

The Soviet Union is the largest country in the world, and a mass of cultural, linguistic and religious variations. Keep moving East, and you'll find that life – particularly for women – undergoes considerable changes. This is certainly the case in the Caucasian republics.

The first time I travelled through the Caucasus was with three British friends, two women and a man, in a hired car. Women drivers are a rarity in that part of the world, and evidently pose a challenge to local manhood. The response was to race past us, horn honking, and then come to a virtual standstill so that we had no choice but to overtake. Then the game would be repeated. We lurched along in this mechanised leap-frog for miles, narrowly avoiding oncoming traffic, on roads which hung precariously over the edge of mountains.

Georgia is the most accessible of the Caucasian republics. Fair-skinned women certainly get a lot of attention there, but in much the same way as they do in Italy. It can be annoying, but it is not threatening. Wandering round Tbilisi alone, I was approached by a succession of men offering to "show me the city". But when I did accept I found the offer was usually genuine, while a refusal was accepted graciously enough. The Georgians are, in any case, a supremely hospitable people. If this characteristic is particularly pronounced when it comes to women, it is not confined to them. I have had some equally friendly encounters in male company.

Our drive through Georgia introduced us into a social whirlwind. When we stopped to sunbathe on a crowded Black Sea beach, we found ourselves the centre of attention. A queue of people formed to practise their English, ask us to find penfriends for their children, and compare notes on problems of everyday life. Turning off the road to have a picnic by a rural stream in the Caucasian foothills we were joined by a group of Georgians on their lunch break from tending the nearby bee hives. Immediately their bottle of vodka was pressed into our hands. In Tbilisi I looked up a complete stranger, a friend of a friend, who at a moment's notice prepared a sumptious banquet.

Sexism certainly flourishes in Georgia, but women do not passively accept it. One of the Soviet Union's finest film makers, Lana Gogoberidze, is from Tbilisi. Her film *Several interviews on Personal Problems*, which has won awards both in the Soviet Union and the West, is a wonderful testament to the strength and resilience of women in the face of the mass of problems and dilemmas they have to deal with.

Armenia is harder to cope with for a woman traveller. I have been there twice, before the uprisings and the tragedy of the earthquake put the republic virtually off limits. I spent one miserable afternoon trying to explore Erevan alone and being pursued relentlessly by one man after another. If I sat down on a bench for just a moment to consult my guidebook, I immediately had company. I was trailed for more than an hour by two men, who followed me on and off a bus and in and out of a shop and took it in turns to make unambiguous advances.

"They thought you were Russian – Russian girls have a reputation here for being loose"

That evening I had dinner with a family who were friends of a friend. As honoured guest, I was placed at one end of the table with the men of the family – two brothers, their father and the older sons. I had little chance to talk to the women, who, after a full day at work, still had to spend all evening cooking and serving and cleaning up. I recounted the story of my day, and, after expressing sympathy, one of the brothers explained "they thought you were Russian – Russian girls have a reputation here for being loose". Not relishing the thought of more battles that night, I accepted an offer to sleep on the sofa – and in the morning, once everyone else had gone to work, was subjected to an unmistakable sexual come-on by this same man.

The republics of Soviet Central Asia present the biggest contrast to life in the Russian republic, though the larger cities bear some heavy imprints of modern Russia. In Tashkent, in particular, the office buildings and apartment blocks which emerged out of the rubble of the 1966 earthquake have stepped straight from a Russian blueprint, and the metro looks identical to the one in Leningrad. But, between the mosques, minarets and bazaars of the Old Town, Asia can still be found. In the labyrinth of dusty alleys, the ramshackle mud houses seem to turn their backs on visitors – they were built around hidden courtyards, and their windows overlook these instead of the streets. Visitors, however, are often invited in.

Walking through Bukhara, I got talking to three teenage girls who told me that there was a wedding in their street. They invited me to come. No questions were asked when I arrived: a plate of food was pressed into my hands and a place made for me on one of the rugs strewn on the ground, on which the guests sat cross-legged. Another time, in the old town in Tashkent, my female companion and I stopped to ask directions from a man leaning against the sun-baked wall of his home. He invited us in to meet his family and "see how we live".

We found ourselves in a courtyard bordered by three low huts and shaded by a cherry tree. There we sat cross-legged with our host, Ahkmet, on the distinctive Uzbeki seat which looks like a huge wooden bedstead. One of the huts had only three walls and served as the kitchen: Ahkmet's wife brought us bowls of soup, *non* (large flat loaves of bread), and green tea. Two small sons sprawled on the ground and played backgammon, while an older daughter sat shyly on the edge of the seat and listened to our conversation.

It was largely about the misguided policies of the Russians. *Perestroika*, Ahkmet felt, was a Russian phenomenon which had nothing to do with Central Asia. He was scathing about most of the Russian innovations in the area, particularly the attempt to moder-

nise housing. Convinced that no-one actually wants to live in these ancient houses, Russian bureaucrats are forcing people into faceless blocks of flats. Yet few people want to move. These houses are cool in the summer and warm in the winter; the courtyards contain vegetable plots and fruit trees, which are a vital counterbalance to the high prices in the markets. They are also the centre of community life.

"While women in the European republics of the Soviet Union seem set to move back into the arms of the family, few Central Asian women have had the chance to leave them"

Ahkmet spoke eloquently and passionately about the benefits of traditional life in Central Asia. It is this kind of attitude which has disturbed the Russians since the time of the Revolution, and now stands in stark contrast to the perceived need to restructure the whole of Soviet society. Yet there is a darker side to the continuation of tradition. The Soviet press has recently drawn attention to the growth of Islamic influence in rural Central Asia, which denies women any control over their own lives, forces them into arranged marriages, and commits them to a life of constant pregnancy and child care. The contrast between the socialist promise of equality for women, and the reality of their own lives, has apparently led to an alarming number of suicides amongst young women.

Certainly the desire to discredit Islam is likely to underlie much of this sudden media interest in the plight of Central Asian women. But published statistics, as well as personal observation, make it clear that outside of the cities, Central Asian women have yet to break out of the traditional mould. While women in the European republics of the Soviet Union seem set to move back into the arms of the family, few Central Asian women have had the chance to leave them.

A Friendship Visit to Moscow and Riga

. . . .

Sheena Phillips, who works for the Campaign for Nuclear Disarmament, visited the Soviet Union on a trip organised by the Quaker Peace Service and the GB-USSR Friendship Society. The official part of her tour included a series of meetings in Moscow and Riga with Soviet officials and researchers on European affairs.

My first view of Moscow was from the air, as the plane started its descent. The city suddenly appeared on the horizon, looking like a white island in a dark green expanse of forest and water. Its isolation and the huge flatness of the surrounding landscape were quite different from anything I had seen before, and this sheer physical strangeness was one of the most exciting things about being there.

Having read books by people like Solzhenitsyn and Kafka (who's Czech, mind you!), I was predisposed to find the Soviet Union dark, dismal and generally downtrodden. As if to confirm my prejudices, it was dark when we arrived, the lighting in the airport was dim, the air was acrid from pollution, and the streets were very bare-looking. Outside the hotel, unsmiling cab drivers stood around sharing cigarettes. Inside, we hung around for ages waiting for our rooms and baggage to be sorted out.

Later, most of these impressions got reinterpreted as aspects of the Soviet Union's economy rather than anything more sinister. Compared to most of Western Europe, the Soviet Union is a strikingly poor country. There is a generally lower standard of amenities like electricity, telephones and plumbing. The supply of most consumer goods, even in the capital city, is erratic. There is also a lot of bad housing. Moscow is surrounded by miles of high-rise apartment blocks and in Riga I visited the most stinking and badly lit block of tenements I had ever been to (though I'm sure parts of Glasgow have rivalled them, at least in the past).

> *"I also experienced the terrifying privilege of being ferried around at high speed in huge black government cars"*

My own accommodation, along with the rest of the group I travelled with, was in a variety of hotels, all booked for us by our hosts. Our first stop was the large and rather ugly Hotel Rossiya in the centre of Moscow, of which my chief memories are faulty telephones, over-heated rooms and large quantities of food (especially bread, meat, yoghurt and fizzy drinks). In Riga we stayed in a much smaller hotel, with better food and some striking local paintings. Then on our return to Moscow we were allocated to a large Trade Union hotel several miles from the centre, crowded with throngs of chattering people from many different parts of the Soviet Union.

In all hotels you are issued with a card that identifies you as a tourist and allows you to eat in other hotels too. You exchange it whenever you come in for your room keys, generally with the *dezhurnaya* – the woman (as it always seems to be) who organises cleaning and other services (sometimes including baby-sitting) on your floor of the hotel. All the hotels I stayed in were clean, comfortable and spacious, and they seemed to have a very unfair share of local food supplies.

Part of my time in the Soviet Union was spent in meetings with researchers and Communist Party officials, discussing disarmament and other issues on the East-West political agenda. I encountered an interesting mixture of frank and restricted conversation – officials are still ideologically bound on some issues, but not nearly as much as they would have been just a few years ago. I also experienced VIP treatment, including delicious (though alcohol-free) lunches and the terrifying privilege of being ferried around at high speed in huge black government cars called *chaiki* (seagulls).

The rest of my time was spent in walking around, sampling sights and wayside snacks and visiting people. Art galleries, museums and swimming pools are all very cheap, and staring at buildings is free! Red Square was stunning, especially at night. There is also some beautiful art in some of the churches open to the public, though in Moscow most are either closed or used as offices. In Riga both the rain and the architecture were more familiar; there was even a true Victorian red-brick church, built by the British in the nineteenth century to serve diplomats and traders.

I also went to a film, which was an interesting experience. The dialogue was in Georgian, but with Turkish sub-titles and an occasional voice-over in Russian given by the projectionist, some of which was then relayed to me in a loud English whisper. I wouldn't even have got in without native help. The film had sold out but my Russian companion spotted a ticket-shark and managed to buy tickets (at twice cover price). In general, I was told, it's hard to get tickets without someone who knows the system. Most outings for groups of tourists are arranged days in advance by their Soviet hosts.

Public transport is cheap and on the whole good, though there were long bus queues on some of the main roads in from the residential areas. There are also numerous taxis. The only problem with getting around on your own is likely to be persuading your hosts or official tour guides that you want to; this simply requires firmness. It's a good idea to try and learn the Cyrillic script so that you can make sense of maps and station names more easily –

this is especially useful on the Moscow Underground.

I felt safe everywhere I travelled (and safer than in Britain), including at night, though attitudes vary as to the wisdom of women hitching alone. I have read reports of Moscow street gangs but I didn't see any violence and there was surprisingly little evidence of vandalism. At night, in fact, there was surprisingly little evidence of anything; apart from clusters of artists and musicians in and around the Arbat, Moscow's famous pedestrian precinct, there were few places open and few people on the streets.

"For anyone who wants to, it's easy to make contact with Soviet people"

Walking around, I felt self-conscious as a Westerner looking in on a society out of which many people still cannot easily travel. Westerners are also conspicuous simply by their clothing. On buses and trains I received a few stares and I felt particularly conspicuous in a small café in Riga where my only means of ordering was by pointing at the things I wanted. At least I managed to say "thank you" in Lettish! I didn't ever feel unwelcome, rather as if I had come from a different planet.

For anyone who wants to, it's easy to make contact with Soviet people. English is the first foreign language taught in most schools and people are very interested in speaking to foreign visitors. I was in Russia with people who had personal contacts to follow up in Moscow and we made telephone arrangements to meet. If you have no contacts, one strategy for meeting people (which I am assured works) is simply to sit down somewhere public with a Western brand-name carrier bag, and wait.

I was not travelling alone, so I cannot write in detail about what it would be like to do so as a single woman. But I spent a lot of time talking to women, especially to our translator Tanya and to other women whom we met in their own homes.

From her appearance, I thought Tanya would be a rather formal and conservative person: she was in her mid-thirties, very neatly dressed and made-up, and her speech was very precise and proper. But this was a misjudgement. Soviet codes of dress, hair styles, etc, are very different from those in the West. To us, most styles seem fairly conservative – and faintly Sixties or Seventies – but there is simply not enough choice of clothing for "fashion" to be a sign of social class or personality. Tanya turned out to be very warm, serious and thoughtful. She also treasured the opportunity to meet and work with us: it gave her a break from her normal teaching job, which she described (as always in perfect idiomatic English) as "humdrum".

"Like Tanya, most people seemed very emotional about meeting us: moved that we should have wanted to visit the Soviet Union and eager to tell us about their lives"

The private houses I saw were all tiny but lovingly kept pockets of individuality in the anonymity of the large housing districts. We were always greeted with great warmth and generosity, even in the poorest of conditions. Invariably, tea would be made: first brewed in a small pot until very strong, then diluted. Tea, by the way, is a good thing to take as a gift, as are things like soap, nuts, vitamin pills, batteries, even biros – many of which are hard to get hold of – and almost any Western magazines.

Like Tanya, most people seemed very emotional about meeting us: moved that we should have wanted to visit the Soviet Union and eager to tell us about their lives and to suggest other people we could visit. All our meetings were also tinged, I think, with an awareness of a gulf between our basic experience of everyday life. "You are richer, in every sense," one woman said. At our partings the separateness of our fates seemed accentuated and I sometimes felt almost guilty about my freedom and, as they saw it, my wealth.

People did not always comment on things in the way I expected. In Riga a young woman studying languages described the distribution of students between the polytechnic (chiefly women taking arts subjects) and the university (chiefly men studying sciences); but she saw this in a very positive light. She was proud of what she was doing and had a cheerful disdain for the university. Another woman, a psychologist, explained that there has been a reaction against the pressures of full-time work while having children. If they can, many women are now choosing to spend more time at home.

Other things also surprised me – like the teams of women painters, decorators and street labourers. I was also disconcerted by the almost sullen manner in which transactions such as money-changing, handing over room keys, and restaurant service, which in the West would be accompanied by professional servility, were carried out.

Except in small pockets of academia there is nothing comparable to the feminist movement in the USSR. According to Tanya, there are various sorts of women's organisations, from the National Committee of Soviet Women to women's councils at nearly all workplaces employing women. They organise things such as daycare facilities and holiday entertainments for children, and clubs for activities – from knitting to aerobics and lectures on family psychology, home economics and fashion. However, these are statutory bodies, not voluntary organisations, and are certainly not feminist in inspiration.

It was hard even to put across the idea of the breadth and diversity of the Women's Movement in the West. A male academic to whom I spoke in

Moscow seemed to think feminism must be an organised political sect with a clear ideology, leaders and virtually a card-carrying membership! In Latvia, which is geographically and culturally fairly close to parts of northern Europe, our guide was a self-confident, casually dressed young woman who had just finished studying English at university. She said she was "probably a feminist" and seemed to know what we meant by it. But, even to her, Latvian nationalism was a much more important issue.

"Patterns of sexuality have changed in the Soviet Union very much as they have done in the West"

With or without an explicit feminist revolution, however, patterns of sexuality have changed in the Soviet Union very much as they have done in the West. Tanya said that people generally live together before getting married. The divorce rate has increased. Tanya herself is divorced but has her own flat, which she said reduced the pressure on her to find a new partner. Contraception is widely used, though the pill is not as popular as condoms or the IUD. There are reportedly a few gay and lesbian orientated bars in Moscow.

One of the best conversations I had with Tanya, sitting on a wall in the popular Latvian seaside resort of Jurmala and eating sickly confections from one of the street stalls, was about Soviet attitudes to the West. To her, first of all, the West meant wealth and choice – though also materialism, which she compared unfavourably with Russian generosity and sentimentality. The word *"firma"* is used, mainly of clothing, to mean "good quality – made in the West" – and people, especially women, go to great lengths to get and flaunt Western goods. To Tanya this was humiliating, though she envied my freedom of choice and was clearly exasperated by the difficulty of buying the things she wanted.

She, and many other people to whom I spoke, expressed shame about the Soviet Union. Several apologised for the laziness of the Russian people. Latvians, on the other hand, pride themselves on their stronger work ethic and their higher standard of living. Some of the talk about "scroungers" could have been taken straight from Britain, though it was very hard to explain this and many people seemed to have an unrealistically rosy image of material conditions in the West: they saw things like motivation as a peculiarly Soviet problem.

It was also striking, in meetings with Soviet officials and researchers, how closely Western policies on economic management, taxation, etc, are being studied. There is a huge amount of criticism of existing models of state provision: we were told at the new Institute of Europe that Sweden was not a country of much interest to Soviet planners because it was so heavily committed to the idea of the welfare state! Britain's free market approach, on the other hand, was more in vogue.

The watchwords of change under Gorbachev – *perestroika* (restructuring) and *glasnost* (openness) – were very much in evidence, particularly in terms of a much freer and more critical media. But the air of excitement and change that permeated the political think-tanks and some of the newly spawned political clubs did not extend to most of the people we met privately, at least in Moscow. The dominant attitudes were: "it's good, but let's wait and see . . . in this country, you never know what will happen in five minutes . . . maybe in three hundred years you will notice a big difference". For most Moscovites, improvements such as better housing, better consumer goods and (especially for women) less time spent in searching for them, are at least as important as an increase in political freedom. Yet in the short term, at least, the standard of living is likely to sink even lower as the state grapples with an ever more pressing economic crisis.

Most of the people I met who were involved in politics were men (they were also the ones who did most of the talking on television). This left me with a familiar and unwelcome impression! The dominant issues being debated: democracy, law and how to enable the growth of a "civil society", in which certain activities are unregulated by the state, are all important to tackle. But while men took on the task of tussling with the state, I wondered, what happened to the people with no time for late-night meetings and no grounding in political philosophy?

I was more moved and impressed by my meeting with a woman who, at considerable risk to herself, was trying to publish an account she has written of the terrible experiences of many young men, including her son, in national military service – or in trying to avoid it. If published, her book will speak directly to many, many Soviets. However, I don't want to sound too critical of the more

formal political developments – the flourishing of discussion and argument in what has been such a closed and tightly controlled society is amazing.

Our last evening was spent in tasting some of the fruits of *perestroika* in a new co-operative restaurant whose profits are shared by its owners and the state. We sat down at a table covered with beautifully prepared cold dishes, drank some wine, listened to a fiddler as he paraded around performing various ingenious feats with his violin, and were presented several hours later with a very handsome bill. The atmosphere was as bourgeois as anything you could find in Hampstead. That left me with mixed feelings. I couldn't help hoping that some of the more useless trappings of consumerism would never reach the Soviet Union – and I shall keep the flimsy wrapping paper from the hard currency export shop as a sentimental reminder of how things were at the end of the Eighties.

A Trans-Siberian Ambition

. . . .

After years of dreaming, planning and vacillating, Catherine Grace finally set off for the Soviet Union to travel on the Trans-Siberian Express.

From the time I first heard about it, I had wanted to travel on the Trans-Siberian Railway. I even, hopefully, learned Russian at school. When I was planning nine months' travelling, the Soviet Union was the place to start.

I went on my own, catching the train from Liverpool Street. They called out "Mos-Cow" as though it was a huge

joke. I felt scornful and brave. My friends thought I was mad, and would I please send a telegram when I got out safely at Japan.

I started to feel lonely in Holland, solitary in a compartment in the only carriage going to Moscow. Then Olga Petrovna arrived – an enormous Russian with an immense amount of luggage. She had been staying with her sister in the West, and the ten vast bundles (including a carpet) were "presents". She was crude, she was kind, she was overwhelming. My limited Russian was not nearly adequate; we shared food and laughed a lot, mostly through incomprehension.

The Polish-Soviet border was my introduction to Russia's other face. The East German and Polish crossings had been no more than a brief disturbance in the night, a quick passport check. Expecting something similar, I was in my nightdress, a full-length ribboned affair which clearly halved my apparent age. A succession of inspectors looked disbelievingly at me. The food inspector (Olga lost all her fresh food), ticket inspector, customs and immigration officers all passed me by and pounced upon Olga, who became more and more flustered. She and all her baggage were taken off for examination.

> *"I only realised later how generous she had been. Most importantly, I had my first taste of the warmth and generosity of individual Soviet people"*

Before we were eventually reunited, I pattered around watching the event of the night – the changing of wheels for the entire train. The Soviet Union retains a different gauge railway system as a defence precaution, even from its closest allies.

This slow introduction to the Soviet Union was useful. I had had no idea how separate and final the Soviet border was compared to other Eastern bloc countries. And the number of officials at the border was just a foretaste of the bureaucracy to come. I was issued with new tickets at every point along my way, retaining the last one (for the boat to Japan) as long as an hour. Similarly, the sheer quantity of consumer goods and food that Olga had brought back gave me an inkling of shortages: I only realised later how generous she had been. Most importantly, I had my first taste of the warmth and generosity of individual Soviet people.

Arriving at the Hotel Metropole in Moscow, I assumed that *Intourist* would be at least a little interested in me and might even tell me what to do. However, once they had my passport, I was left severely alone. I overheard someone talking (in English) and asked them what to do about theatre tickets. Thus began my rapid disillusionment as the *Intourist* staff demanded "hard" Western currency. They weren't pleased when I produced the exact money – no chance of fiddling the change.

Leningrad lovers don't have a good word to say for Moscow; it's not beautiful, people are dwarfed by the gigantism of streets, squares and monuments. I am not in a position to make the comparison: I loved Moscow. I didn't know what I wanted from this new place and I got a little bit of everything. I suspect it is a very Russian city.

A visit to the Kremlin was an initial shock. It is not a great, grey, grim fortress. It contains some stunningly beautiful buildings; from a distance the white towers and golden domes of the cathedral gleam and glint like a fantasy castle. The Kremlin Wall in Red Square looks as though it came from an Italian Renaissance picture (it was in fact designed by an Italian), and Saint Basil's, preposterous onion domes and all, is for real.

It's worth branching out, though, from the city's sights and architecture. The centre of Moscow has lots of cinemas and theatres and you can use the workers' restaurants as well as the hotels. You'll have to queue, of course. But queues and waiting are a basic part of everyday life in the Soviet Union. People on buses and in the street were unfailingly kind and helpful when I asked the way; people in food queues were friendly. The only thing there were no queues for was bread.

The longest queue of all, stretching through Red Square and around the Kremlin, was to Lenin's tomb; many of the people were from outside Moscow. As we entered Red Square we were directed to leave anything we were carrying in a cloakroom, made to tidy up our appearance and put in an orderly two-by-two line. The guards

hushed us when we entered the mausoleum, we descended reverently into the
gloom and filed past the body. Early
training will out, and I had to restrain
an impulse to make the sign of the
cross. The evident significance of that
visit for the people around me helped
me to make sense of the huge images
of Lenin found in every Soviet city and
main street.

"It was, I think, one of the most sociable times of my life"

Rejoining the Trans-Siberian, the
journey took over again. It was, I think,
one of the most sociable times of my
life. The landscape across the Soviet
Union is not striking, and you inevitably spend much of the time talking.
There were many other Western travellers on the train and I discovered for
the first time that to travel alone is to
be vulnerable to the needs of people
travelling in couples who are bored
with each other and not necessarily
interested in you. The same people also
dish out unwanted sympathy for the
(chosen) state of being alone.

I enjoyed myself much more when I
struck up a friendship with a Russian
family in the next compartment. Galia
and Seriozha, a married couple, and
Galia's sister Valia, were travelling the
whole way to Vladivostock to new jobs.
Seriozha had been a chauffeur, Galia a
housebuilder and Valia had been at
school. They did not know what they
would be doing in the east and had had
to leave most of their belongings, but
they were remarkably cheerful about it.
They were also very sweet to me, and
enormously excited at the prospect of
having their photographs taken; there
were kisses and tears when we said
goodbye. I later met Laura, a singing
teacher, who was shy but generous.
We exchanged little gifts every day,
and she attempted the almost hopeless
task of trying to teach me a Russian
song.

Life on the train was complicated by
the fact that it ran on Moscow time,
though we were in fact crossing a time
zone every day. This affected the
restaurant car and you could never
quite predict when it would be open.
Once we were in Siberia I stopped
using it; whenever the train stopped at
a station we would all get out and see
what was for sale. Middle-aged women
would be standing behind stalls selling
cabbage salads, potatoes and onions –
whatever was local. Once it was excellent carrots; once potato pancakes;
another time there were nothing but
pine cones, which aggravated me until I
made the connection with pine nuts
and joined the Soviet passengers who
had rushed out to buy them.

It was important to get out at the
stations as it was the only form of exercise available and it meant fresh air.
Our conductress would never allow us
to open the windows; all carriages were
heated separately by a coal-burning
stove, and it was each conductress's
responsibility to get the coal. There
was, however, hot water available from
urns most of the time, and cups of tea
were brought round at regular intervals. Though there was no hot water for
washing, and the lavatories were grim,
I gathered from more seasoned Soviet
travellers that we should be grateful
they were in working order at all. The
Trans-Siberian is a prestige train.

At Khabarovok all Westerners have
to leave the train, which in fact goes on
to Vladivostock, a military port closed
to foreigners, for a connection to the
ferry across to Japan. We had one more
day and night in the Soviet Union, travelling along the Chinese border.
Autumn was nearly over, the trees on
the horizon were bare and we had seen
our first snow. Crossing the frontier
and leaving the frontier was an anti-
climax. I felt sad, knowing that if I'd
understood more, if I'd been better
prepared, I'd have got much more from
my stay. I knew that I wanted to return.

TRAVEL NOTES

Languages Varies according to republic (Russian, Moldavian, Uzbeki, Georgian, etc), though Russian is the language of higher education, centralised politics and commerce. (Russian linguistic imperialism is fiercely resented and is a major issue behind the nationalist protests.) English is the second language taught in most schools.

Transport Generally by train, with attendant bureaucracy in booking seats through *Intourist*. Internal flights are cheap and are often included in package tours taking in Samarkand, etc. It is possible to rent a car or drive your own, but petrol is expensive and you have to plan and declare routes in advance.

Accommodation Usually arranged through a tour (*Sputnick* being the cheapest). As part of an East-West collaborative venture hotels are being refurbished and new hotels are being built in Moscow and Leningrad; at present, however, standards are pretty basic. A co-operative in Rostov-na-Dony has recently got permission to run tours and arrange accommodation in private homes; more look set to follow. The cheapest option for accommodation (and a good way to meet Soviet rather than Western tourists) are the *Intourist* campsites. They generally have wooden huts if you prefer not to take a tent.

Special Problems Bureaucracy – from getting a visa on. You have to be prepared for sudden changes in your itinerary as a result of unrest.

Sexual harassment can be a problem in the Caucasian and eastern republics, but this is not the case in the Baltic republics and Russia. All foreigners are approached for hard currency and to buy and exchange goods. It's wise to firmly, but politely, steer clear of black-market dealings – both parties can still get arrested.

It's easy to underestimate the conservatism of Soviet society. *Babushkas* (grannies) seem to have the self-appointed role of social police and won't hesitate to put you right if they take issue with your clothes or behaviour. Although there are reports that some gay venues are opening up, any public display of gay sexuality is still extremely risky.

Guides The Motorists' Guide to the Soviet Union (Progress Publishers, Moscow) is essen-tial for independent travellers, and the individual city guides produced by Progress Publishers are probably the most detailed you'll find. Most of these are available at *Collets International Bookshop*, 129 Charing Cross Road, London WC2.

Contacts

Soviet Women's Committee, Nemirovitch-Danchenko Street 6, Moscow. Co-ordinates many of the (official) local groups and campaigns. Russian readers should look out for *Rabotnitsa* (Woman Worker) which has begun to include a fair number of radical articles and letters.

Lotus, c/o Anastasia Posadskaya, Institute of Socioeconomic studies of Population, USSR Academy of Sciences, Krasikova 27, Moscow 117218, ☎129 0653. A small feminist research group, who would welcome books, articles or research papers from the West.

The USSR-GB Friendship Society, House of Friendship, 14 Prospect Kalinina, Moscow. (See Sheena Phillips' piece.)

We've been unable to track down any autonomous women's groups or venues. Further information would be welcome.

Books

Tatavana Mamonova ed., *Writings from the Soviet Union* (Blackwell, 1984). A collection of articles and essays that were first printed secretly in Russia by a group known as the *Leningrad Feminists*. Exploding the myth of women's so-called equality, they speak out about the sexism inherent in Soviet society, the untenable pressures of work women suffer and the abuse of a healthcare system that provides abortions but not contraception. The group was forced to disband under duress from the authorities. Five years later much the same issues are being aired – but this time in the national press.

Barbara Holland, ed., *Soviet Sisterhood* (Fourth Estate, London, 1985). A good, if slightly dated, overview of the position of women in Soviet society. Includes a chapter by Lynne Attwood.

Mikhail Gorbachev, *Perestroika: Our Hopes for Our Country and Our World* (Fontana, 1988). The manifesto for reform. Gorbachev lays out his ideas for the New World, including his thoughts on racial and religious differences, and the emancipation of women.

Martin Walker, *Russia* (Abacus, 1988). A collection of pieces from the Moscow diary of the *Guardian* correspondent. Recommended as an easy but informative glimpse of life in the post-*glasnost* republics.

Fiction

Tatyana Tolstoya, *On Golden Porch* (Virago, 1989). Highly acclaimed collection of short stories that draw on a wealth of Russian characters and settings.

Julia Voznesenskaya, *The Women's Decameron* (Methuen, 1986). This debut novel by a Soviet dissident, now resident in West Germany, became an immediate bestseller. Combining humour with blunt realism it compares the lives of ten women brought together on a Russian labour ward. Voznesenskaya's latest novel, *The Star*

Chernobyl (Methuen, 1988), deals with the human cost of the 1986 nuclear disaster.

Natalia Baranskya, *A Week Like Any Other* (Virago, 1989). A novella and collection of short stories that passionately and poetically reveal the everyday realities of women's lives in the Soviet Union.

Alexandra Kollontai, *Love of Worker Bees* (1923; Virago, 1977) and *A Great Love* (1930; Virago, 1981). One of the most remarkable figures of the Revolution, Alexandra Kollontai was the only woman member of the Bolshevik Central Committee. She fled to Norway, at the height of Stalin's purges, where she wrote these two collections.

Tania Alexander, *An Estonian Childhood* (Heinemann, 1989). A remarkable memoir of the last decades of Tsarist Russia.

Irina Ratushinskaya, *Grey is the Colour of Hope* (Hodder, 1988), *In the Beginning* (Hodder, 1990). The first book describes the dissident poet's experiences in a labour camp; the second explores her childhood and faith.

Thanks to Lynne Attwood for her help with the introduction and Travel Notes.

Sudan

. . . .

For the last six years Sudan has been in the throes of a guerrilla war. The Sudanese People's Liberation Army, predominantly Black African (Christian and Aminist) southerners, have been fighting to end domination by the richer and more populous Arab Muslim groups in the north. It is a conflict which has cost many thousands of lives, draining an already fragile economy and leaving the country open to political instability and corruption. Added to this, thousands of people – many of them refugees from neighbouring Chad and Ethiopia – have been placed at risk by droughts and plagues of locusts. At the time of writing, General Beshir, who recently seized power in the second military coup in five years, has initiated peace negotiations and a ceasefire. Should these fail he appears committed to resuming full-scale military confrontation.

Whilst there seems little place at present for tourism, there are a fair number of independent travellers, foreign workers and volunteers still entering the country. With the south effectively off limits, travel is restricted to the predominantly Muslim areas of the north. The Sudanese are renowned for their courtesy and kindness to strangers, and though a woman travelling alone is clearly seen as a phenomenon, reports are that it's easier to cope with the attention this attracts, and to accept hospitality and friendship, than it is in neighbouring Egypt. Harassment certainly occurs, though, and with relatively few other travellers around it's easy to feel isolated and vulnerable. Dressing inconspicuously in loose, long clothes helps, and you can always insist on the option of joining in with the segregated groups of women and children on trains, buses etc. Travelling with a man you are unlikely to experience many problems.

Women in Sudan bear the brunt of economic hardships, both as providers in the home and as agricultural workers. Whilst cultural constraints vary between the different religious groups, there are widespread problems of illiteracy, poor access to paid employment, and minimal political representation. Sharia Law (introduced as part of a general shift towards Islamicisation in the north) clearly limits the power and status of women to the domestic sphere; although there are still a few middle-class Muslim women in professional roles, their future is uncertain. For many years the most powerful autonomous **women's organisation** has been the *Sudanese Women's Union*. Despite frequent repression it has continued to campaign vociferously against genital mutilation, divorce by verbal denunciation, polygyny, and discrimination in work and pay. Along with various other government-funded groups it has also promoted income-generating projects and launched literacy schemes.

Cycling across the Nubian Desert

· · · · · · · · · · · · ·

Terri Donovan, a 36-year-old New Zealander, spent a month travelling by bicycle in Sudan in early 1988, as part of a journey which took her through Europe and Africa. Pushing, riding and hauling her bike across the open stretches of the Nubian desert, she found herself relying more and more on the hospitality of Sudanese workers at the remote railway maintenance stations.

I had already been cycling solo for seven months from London when I arrived at Wadi Halfa, by steamer across Lake Nasser from Egypt. Two months' cycle touring in the Upper Delta, around Sinai and down the Nile Valley to Aswan, had provided an introduction to Muslim customs and Arab culture and also to desert conditions.

I had learnt that it is anathema for women to be seen going about freely and unveiled, and that, although as a non-Muslim I was under less pressure to comply with these strictures, I had to be careful not to cause offence. I found

I could escape censorious reactions, as well as the worst effects of sun, by wearing light, loose cotton trousers or skirt and sleeved tops. Entering strange situations, I would try to avoid prolonged eye contact with men (considered an open invitation) and assume an air of quiet purposefulness in what I was doing. Background reading (for example, on the teachings of the Koran) and simple observation helped best in learning to attune myself to cultural and religious nuances.

Everywhere, too, people responded positively to genuine curiosity about their customs and circumstances and, in return, showed an unfailing interest in mine – it was assumed that I had a husband and children and they wanted to know where they were. Most significantly, I had discovered that in places which were popular meccas for tourists, you were much more likely to experience what one guidebook described as "the hustle, the hassle and the hard sell". I anticipated Sudan's culture to be less diluted by Western tourism, but hoped to encounter the same Arab openness and basic good will to travellers.

Overall, I probably experienced less overt propositioning than in Europe, and no more sexual harassment (or hassles generally) travelling alone in Muslim society without the fetters of male patronage than those women I met who did journey with companions. Women travelling with companions sometimes expressed to me the desire to try solo ventures, yet frequently assumed themselves in possession of fewer inner resources to do so than was probably the case. Having travelled both ways, I am aware that responsibility shared can mean initiative halved, and my experiences of solo travel are that confidence soon builds on itself.

"I was amazed to see the shimmering, mirage-like outline of another bicycle approaching from afar along the railway line"

So, with very limited scope for cycle touring in Sudan, owing to restrictions imposed by political circumstances and the sheer lack of roads, I expected that travel would, of necessity, be largely "off the beaten track". I was also prepared to make my way in a much harsher environment amidst more widespread human suffering. I felt an initial trepidation disembarking on to a stark foreshore, bustling with predominantly male, djellaba-clad figures, and seeing only arid desert beyond.

In the township I found a hotel and was directed to the women's quarters – dark, shuttered rooms facing on to an open courtyard in which other women were washing and hanging out laundry. My room-mate, whose husband was in separate men's quarters, was a shy Egyptian woman with a six-month-old baby. She had also arrived on the steamer and, though communication was limited by my rather basic Arabic and her lack of English, we smiled and exchanged food. I welcomed this rare opportunity to meet and talk with other women, and particularly Muslim women, whose traditionally low public profile makes contact very difficult.

The morning after the twice-weekly train had departed to Khartoum, I rose

before the sun to begin my intended cycle trek along the same route across the Nubian Desert. There are no discernible roads and Betty (my bicycle) and I juddered along precariously between the rails, attempting to avoid sinking into the sand by riding over the wooden sleepers.

After several hours I was amazed to see the shimmering, mirage-like outline of another bicycle approaching from afar along the railway line. I had been misguidedly warned by dubious locals in Wadi Halfa about the dangers of lions and hyenas, but had not expected to meet another cyclist in the vast open spaces. I had also received a veiled warning about men I might encounter in the desert: "These are men without women . . ." It was a worker from the first maintenance station returning the thirty kilometres or so to the main station for supplies.

We greeted one another like old friends and I continued on to Station Number One, where the remaining three workers overcame their double astonishment at the sight of the laden bicycle and strange, cloth-swathed figure with cropped red hair who turned out to be a woman. They immediately proffered *chai* (tea) and shade. I began to wonder if I was as crazy as the anxious expressions of the men suggested as I could not cycle self-assuredly away but had to resort to pushing and even dragging Betty through the now loosely packed sand in the direction of Station Number Two.

An hour or more later, as I squatted hunched by the edge of the rail, bike leaning against my back to provide shade while I lunched on a boiled egg, biscuits and fruit, a figure approached.

It was one of the men from Station Number One, carrying a container of water and clearly sent to try gently to dissuade me from continuing. I was touched by the gesture and struck by the fact that I had made as little progress as I would have had I been walking. But I was far from ready to give up. I had more than ample food supplies, and knew that with the maintenance stations located approximately thirty to forty kilometres apart, I could obtain additional water to supplement what I had. I thanked him and sent him back to the station with packets of Egyptian cigarettes for his kindness.

It took all my concentration to keep Betty upright and on course, steering a track, alternately riding over the sleepers or when jarring caused my hands and wrists to ache – parallel to the rails. There was the additional difficulty of a strong, side-buffeting wind, and compensating for that meant little energy for anything else. Occasionally I would stop to absorb my surroundings. Alone in this vast expanse with just the railway line, wind mocking eerily along the telegraph wires, hazy unrelenting sun, and sand stretching *ad infinitum*, Peter Mathiessen's description came to mind: "The Nubian Desert, an hallucinatory void burned by bright winds" (*The Tree Where Man Was Born*). I was glad to be there and felt an inner peace.

"Looks of amazement came from a group of workers passing on a jigger, each one reaching down solemnly to shake my hand"

Progress to the third station proved just as difficult, with the tyres sinking and slithering after short intervals of riding. Hordes of flies clamoured about me whenever I stopped and, attracted by the moisture in the eyes, tried to get behind my goggles. My head and face were shielded by a light muslin shesh, protecting me from the sun and containing condensation from breathing, so reducing dehydration. More looks of amazement came from a group of workers passing on a jigger, each one reaching down solemnly to shake my hand.

One of them introduced himself as the son of the cyclist encountered the previous day and said in English, "Welcome, sister!". The wind at last

turned to tail, the sand became firmer and I rattled happily along for several effortless kilometres, singing desert songs as I pulled into the next station.

I was shown the same unstinting welcome and warned that the winds would worsen. I was told I should remain and accept shelter in one of the men's huts rather than risk having my tent flattened. Two of the three men amused themselves by trying on my safety helmet and goggles and directing invisible armies while I took photos.

An extra rope-strung bed was hauled inside one of the conical-shaped outhuts, empty except for a transistor radio and a crucifix on the wall. These were the sleeping quarters of a young man named Belo. I realised he had offered me his own more comfortable bed, and my sudden qualms about sharing the room and lack of privacy were dispelled as he cheerily bid me goodnight and curled up to sleep. The door and window were well shuttered, but sleep was elusive as the wind gathered force during the night.

Next morning, after a shared breakfast of *chai* and a packet of biscuits contributed by me, the men indulged my lifelong whim to ride a jigger. We careered wildly southward, pumping the handle two by two and laughing loudly into the wind. The men laughed even more loudly as I tried to persuade them to join Betty and me in hijacking the jigger to complete the desert journey.

Another man, Khiddr, complained of persistent stomach upsets and diarrhoea, and I dispensed homeopathic and medicinal remedies from my first-aid kit. More difficult to explain than how much to take, and when, was the importance of boiling the brackish water which the men drank. I politely declined to share a communal bowl of okra simmered with spices and eaten with pancake bread – though it looked tasty – for fear of unhealthy repercussions.

Suddenly the air was thick with blinding, choking dust. Less than 300m away, the main station had disappeared. This was the beginning of a weather phenomenon I had heard of: fierce inter-seasonal windstorms which can rage unabated for ten days at a time. The strong winds which had impeded my progress from Wadi Halfa were only a mild precursor. Further movement was impossible and I passed a companionable day under siege with the men, illustrating English and Arabic words and telling stories graphically on the sand floor. The civil conflict between the Arab, mainly Islamic north, and the socialist, mainly Christian/Animist south, did not reflect in the easy compatibility of this mix of Muslim and Christian men.

"The spectre of a single vulture hunched on the overhead wires to spur me on"

With the wind somewhat abated, I experienced the same difficulties in riding with over-thin tyres on wind-loosened sand. Progress towards the next station was confined to pushing, with my usual halo of flies for company and the spectre of a single vulture hunched on the overhead wires to spur me on. There were exhilarating stretches where I could make some speed, and these made it all worthwhile as I sailed along on a sea of sand, alone with lofty thoughts.

Occasionally these were brought to an abrupt halt as I hit a loose patch of sand and was thrown clear off the bike. At the journey's worst, approaching another station, I could manoeuvre Betty through the sand only by balancing both wheels on one of the rails. This required a steady eye (not easy with the loss of one contact lens), and necessitated bending low to push. The picture this must have presented brought out a hasty rescue party of two men carrying water, obviously unprepared for my reaction as I stood tall with a broad grin

and greeted them, clearly far from staggering in on my last legs.

Among the eight or ten men at this station, one young man was aggressively insistent that I should supply him with medication (which I did not have) for a persistent cough. His demeanour was in marked contrast to the excessively polite and unobtrusive manners and easy humour of the Sudanese men I had met so far. The expressions of the others were apologetic, and I later learned that his agitation was a consequence of having suffered from cerebral malaria.

An invitation to join the group for a lunch of freshly chopped tomato and onion salad tossed with oil and seasonings and scooped up with fresh-baked pancake bread was more than I could resist. I squatted eagerly beside the men, scooping heartily from the bowl and remembering in time to keep my left hand away from the food, as this would be considered contaminating. Walking toward the outback toilet (a walled, raised concrete platform with a hole over a bucket), the young man with the pushy manner stepped forward and thoughtfully provided me with a plastic container of water. I was, however, still conditioned to use my dwindling supply of toilet paper from Egypt.

A welcome had been extended to me to stay and wait for the next through train if I wished. Philosophising to myself that had I set out to walk most of the distance, and would have done so unencumbered by my ill-suited companion, Betty, I decided to rail the remaining distance, and passed the interim days in the relaxed company of the isolated railwaymen.

I shared a hut with two mild-mannered men who, like Belo, were from the same area near Djuba in the south. Again, one of them insisted on giving up his own bed for me. Akedj (29) was close on seven feet tall – characteristic of the Dinka tribe – yet the bed was designed for someone my height – five feet six inches. I was aware of how little these men had and the starkness of their existence at these stations. Waal (37) explained his ambition to work at the larger station at Abu Hamed because of its access to the *souk* (market) and the availability of fresh fruit and vegetables to supplement their meagre diet. Akedj expressed a wish to go to London to study, but had neither passport nor financial prospects of doing so.

"In their hospitality these men were unstinting and I was made to feel comfortable and accepted"

In their hospitality these men were unstinting and I was made to feel comfortable and accepted. As at the other stations I found small tokens in my panniers to show my appreciation: mint tea, biscuits, tins of beans and nail clippers.

Before and after meals the three of us would draw water in turns from a clay pitcher outside and pour while the others washed. I was conscious of hiding hands blackened the previous evening from endeavours with my temperamental paraffin camping stove. Despite the largely insanitary conditions in which the men lived, their rituals of washing face and hands were fastidious. We enjoyed the early-morning warmth over games of Ludo in the sand before the sun rose too high and we had to retreat from the gathering forces of wind and flies.

It was curious to be shown a well-thumbed *Oxford English Reader*, adapted for Africa by English speakers, yet with illustrations and references to British Royalty and English lifestyles, outdated and inappropriate to the African context. Akedj and Waal listened attentively to a radio broadcast in both Arabic and English by the Sudanese People's Liberation Movement. It advocated multi-racial harmony, the uniting by law of all national groups in Sudan, and the right of all minorities to an equal say in the National Assembly. The SPLM declared itself committed to the armed struggle against what it called the religious bigotry and racism of Islamic Sharia Law, and to liberating the country from all forms of sectarianism. The men's exuberant reactions after the broadcast provided a suitable opening to explore (within the bounds of the language barrier) the topic.

The late-evening arrival of the train to Khartoum barely left time to say a hurried goodbye as I leaned out the open window to shake hands with Akedj, laughing and easily running apace with the departing train.

There was no time to dwell on sadness; the man behind me in the cramped, unlit compartment put his arm on my shoulder and pressed full body against me. Sinking feeling: it was the first hint of any untoward advances from anyone in this country. When he tried to bustle me backwards to a prone position on the seat behind, under the guise of gauche chivalry offering his place, I sensed differently and reacted swiftly with a firm "No!" and a vice-like grip and twist to his wrists. It effectively repelled him and I had no further trouble.

I soon discovered that the Michelin-marked road from Atbara does not in fact begin until the outskirts of the capital. Reports of bandit activity and a spinal meningitis epidemic weighed the balance in favour of accepting Land-rover rides, first to Shendi and then to Khartoum itself, from British engineers working in the area and concerned to obtain vaccinations. This opportunity provided insight into the shabby splendour and colonial relics of Kitchener's rail-building era in the town of Atbara, and the chance to inspect irrigation projects based on the Nile, designed to overcome the spread of desert into the surrounding parched settlements.

Khartoum at the time was beset with an uneasy tension, exacerbated by the epidemic which was claiming many lives, governmental discord, and, shortly after I left, bombings in which English tourists were killed. It was possible to remain impervious to this whilst wandering the city, tourist fashion, during the daytime, enjoying the delights of fresh mango juice stalls or queuing for fresh-baked bread rolls. However, permits for travel outside the capital were being restrictively issued, as were permits for taking photographs, and travel in the south was prohibited.

Through development workers for aid agencies came the news that starvation and drought were becoming more widespread in the northwest. Families displaced and fleeing from war in the south were being forced to sell their children into contractual slavery in order to raise money to reach Khartoum. But prospects for employment in a city already besieged by the homeless and destitute, many of them refugees from neighbouring Chad, Ethiopia and Somalia, were grim.

Flying north several months later, after touring Kenya and Tanzania, poignant memories of Sudan returned as the plane descended for a brief stopover in Khartoum and we had a bird's-eye view of areas afflicted by recent flooding. The following day even this sight would have been obscured as I read in newspapers of the sky over the capital darkened by a plague of locusts.

TRAVEL NOTES

Languages Arabic and tribal dialects. English, the old colonial language, is taught in schools and quite widely spoken.

Transport Slow and unreliable – expect long delays. Buses are marginally better than trains: *boxes* (collective taxis) are useful. If you're travelling alone it's always best to sit with Sudanese women – they often use separate compartments to men.

Accommodation Outside Khartoum, the capital, hotels tend to be of the dormitory type; many of them have separate women's quarters. Most Sudanese stay with relatives when they travel and hotels are usually a last resort! Catholic resthouses (at Juba, for instance) are good refuges.

Special Problems The southwest of the country is at present in a critical position, devastated by drought and guerrilla war. To visit Sudan at all is probably not realistic or useful other than for work. Visas are granted by the Sudanese Embassy in London but not generally in Egypt or any other transit points. If you do visit the north be very sensitive to the strong Islamic culture, both in dress (cover upper arms

and knees) and habit (very harsh penalties for use of alcohol).

Guide *Sudan – No Frills Guide* (Bradt) is good on the basics. *Egypt and the Sudan – A Travel Survival Kit* (Lonely Planet) is also useful.

Contacts

Sudanese Women's National Assembly (SWNA), PO Box 301, Omdurman. The autonomous women's union active in development campaigns with rural women.

Ahrad, University College for Women, PO Box 167, Omdurman. Twice-yearly journal on status of women in developing countries.

Books

Marjorie Hall and Bakhita Amin Ismail, *Sisters Under the Sun: the Story of Sudanese Women* (Longman, 1981). Regional study with thorough historical background on the position of women in the Sudan today.

Eric Hoagland, *African Calliope* (Penguin, 1982). Anecdotal stories of Sudanese life.

Thanks for general help in putting together this chapter to Debbie Garlick and Pat Yale.

Taiwan

ot least among the many anachronisms of Taiwan is its pretensions to be the legitimate Republic of China. At the end of the 1949 Revolution the defeated nationalists fled the mainland for the island and took full political and economic control. Their party, the Kuomintang, has remained in power ever since and, under the guise of securing the country from Communist invasion, held it under martial law for close on four decades. This has now been lifted, and a certain element of electoral reform has been introduced, but many Kuomintang deputies remain those who were voted in on the mainland in pre-revolution ballots. Significant change is unlikely.

Political rights, however, have not been a predominant issue in Taiwan. This is first and foremost an entrepreneurial society – money is an abiding obsession and consumerism rampant. Visitors expecting a harmonious and gentle taste of the East will be sorely disappointed. The massive overdevelopment of the main cities, crowded with ugly high-rise blocks and choked with traffic and pollution, can come as a shock, as can the incredibly high cost of living. Taiwan is second only to Tokyo in expense.

Travelling alone, however, is relatively safe. The strong military presence has meant that street crime is uncommon and Western foreigners are generally treated with great courtesy and kindness. Although the country has a fairly large community of expatriates (mainly American businessmen and itinerant English teachers), most tend to lead rarefied and isolated lives. In the less commercial districts of the main cities and throughout the countryside you are likely to attract a great deal of attention. People may well stare and point at you but this rarely leads to more than friendly interest.

As in Hong Kong and South Korea, **women in Taiwan** are caught between the conflicting demands of a modern, Westernised and highly competitive culture and traditional Confucianist values. In constitutional terms women are supposed to have equal rights in work and education but the reality is that they face entrenched discrimination, are ghettoised in poorly paid jobs and are expected to take a subservient role within marriage. Prostitution is illegal but exists on a massive scale (you'll be warned against wandering alone in the red light district of Taipei) and Taiwan has remained a fairly popular destination for Japanese businessmen in search of cheap sex. Under the authoritarian rule of the Kuomintang, autonomous political groups, including feminist initiatives, have been suppressed.

Taipei without Maps

. . . .

Kate Hanniker travelled to Taiwan to stay with a friend who was working there on a temporary contract. She spent a month exploring the capital, Taipei, and made a few trips to the south of the island.

Taiwan is a little island with big ideas. Physically it is half the size of Ireland, with a population of only nineteen million, yet the Nationalist Kuomintang Government still considers itself the only legitimate ruler of the vast mainland and it convenes regularly to pass legislation for the Peoples' Republic. In spite of, or perhaps because of, its exaggerated sense of self importance, it is extremely successful in other ways.

Within the last forty years the country has leapt from rags to riches. Its people are a disconcerting mixture of those men and women who have been caught up in the whirlpool of money-making activity and of those – largely the older generation – whom this frenzied activity has utterly passed by. Life

for this latter category is noticeably more comfortable than it was thirty years ago but essentially their lifestyles remain little altered by the new wave of consumerism.

The bulk of the wealth is concentrated in the five major Taiwanese cities, and especially in Taipei, where the women are streets ahead of their country cousins in their Western dress. For the nouveau riche, life in Taiwan is luxurious and massively consumer-oriented with all shops open daily until 10pm. Unemployment stands at two percent and beggars, touts and pimps are noticeable by their absence. Towards the end of my visit I was thrown by the sight of a beggar and the word suddenly reeled back into my vocabulary (though squalor had not left it).

The cost, inevitably, of this surge of economic growth is overdevelopment, scant accommodation and appalling pollution. In Taipei, apartment blocks stand high and virtually back to back. On the outskirts of the city, homes are little more inviting than chicken shacks and three generations of a family are often crammed into one flat. Traffic is choking and anarchic. The Taiwanese prefer to call it "flamboyant" and the surprisingly low level of road accidents indicate that they employ not a little skill in getting about as quickly and as economically as possible. This same sixth sense is used by the Taiwanese when conducting their business affairs.

What struck me most during my four-week stay was how immediately secure I felt, despite the fact that I had only a limited Chinese vocabulary and a roughly sketched street-plan in English characters which at times impeded, rather than guided, my progress. Being able to roam freely and unaccosted was something I had not expected in Asia.

"Since I was possibly the only redhead in Taipei, I caused something of a stir"

On one of the numerous occasions when I lost not only my way, but also all sense of direction, I felt safe enough to accept a lift from a man I had asked for directions. He spoke no English and was kind enough to leave his work and drive me to my destination on the other side of Taipei.

Whenever I asked the way (most people speak Chinglish to match my Englinese) I would be drawn into a lengthy confab and on occasions an entire family joined me on the street to mull over my map. At times the sense of obligation the Chinese showed towards me as a stranger transcended my (cynical) belief. Finally they would point me in any direction to save the important Chinese "face" and I would embark unknowingly on a vast detour. Yet again I'd have to hail a taxi, defeating my purpose of familiarising myself with the city. With time I came to accept this as simply the most reliable method of getting from A to B without travelling via C and D.

My novelty value as a foreigner was seemingly endless. And since I was possibly the only redhead in Taipei, I caused something of a stir. Children ran up to me grinning as if I was a long lost friend. "Hey, Okay, Number One," they would holler. All foreigners are American to the Taiwanese. "Ingwor" ("I'm English") was a phrase I soon mastered, but it made no odds, their reaction was still as fervent.

Westerners seem to embody some kind of utopia for the Taiwanese. The fashionable Chinese women have rejected their traditional clothing, opting instead for bolstered shoulder pads. And Western images and models are used to promote even the most oriental of products. It's easy to see how this emulation is interpreted as adulation by the resident ex-pats, who live in isolated splendour in the north of Taipei. Their arrogance translates itself into maudlin attempts to recreate mini-Europes and USAs, epitomised by the disconcerting appearance of a pub or *bierkeller*.

As a European woman I seemed to inspire respect and admiration, especially since I was negotiating the city by myself, unescorted. This is quite contrary to Chinese custom, rooted as it is in Confucianism and chauvinism. Attitudes, I'm assured, are gradually changing, but beyond the more sophisticated work places, sexual discrimination and harassment are still everyday problems. Women may rule over the home, traditionally a power base in Taiwanese society, but they have much less status in public life and double standards are very obvious. For example, it is accepted that men will have "other women" – prostitutes or mistresses – but a wife will be reviled and cast out if she is found to be "unfaithful".

In custodial cases the children will automatically stay with their father. And even where a woman has been subjected to domestic violence, she is ill-advised to seek a divorce, which may result in her social ostracism. Although Taiwanese businesswomen wield considerable power, they are often paid less and work longer hours than their male counterparts and many working-class women suffer harsh conditions in the nation's sweatshops.

The only time that I felt ill at ease in Taiwan was on my final morning when I visited the Lungshan Temple area. There was no obvious threat but the atmosphere unnerved me. A dog twitched to death on the sidewalk and a crowd of old men looked on and shouted useless encouragement. Younger men in string vests stood entranced around a streethawk who measured up a white powder in brass scales. Schoolgirls hovered half-naked in doorways. Later I learnt that I was a street away from the notorious Snake Alley, where women are sold to Japanese businessmen for $1.25 a day and where turtles are tortured for their blood, which is guzzled by the same men to increase their virility.

"Hairdressers and tearooms often operate as hostess-type joints"

The sex industry is big business in Taiwan. All except the most expensive hotels increase their profit margins by letting out rooms by the afternoon and by transmitting soft porn day and night. Hairdressers and tearooms often operate as hostess-type joints, not necessarily brothels, but places where the lonely businessman can fork out large sums of money in exchange for a few hours of female company.

My great joy in Taipei was looking around the temples. The Confucian Temple seemed to be the only public place to have escaped the rest of the city's haphazard development. The Taoist temples on the other hand were home to the same bedlam to be found in the streets. Chickens, children and dogs run amok through the endless passages, up into the small sub-temples. The tiered levels offer panoramic views of the city.

The temples throw up constant surprises to the Western eye accustomed to uniform architecture and solemn devotion. On one floor multi-coloured puppets rotate in a perpetual electronic parade, offering gifts to the gods. Somewhere in the grounds an opera may break out. Old men sit around a table playing cards and watching TV rigged up precariously on an altar. A businessman waves joss sticks and throws crescent-shaped pieces of wood to find out if he should change his car.

The state is just beginning to invest money in tourism but as yet there are few concessions to the Western traveller. This has its advantages and its drawbacks. It is pleasant to find areas of natural beauty still unspoilt by the commercialism which has so ravaged the cities. But it can be frustrating when travelling to be faced with the options of a state-run tour or of getting lost trying to decipher Chinese town names. The tours are blatantly commercial, whisking you from site to site with a final compulsory stop at a local factory, where you will be assailed by pretty girls hoping to persuade you to part with your money.

Initially I was irritated by the persistence of the sales people, not only in the tourist shops but also in the village stores, where the shopkeepers wave excitedly and shout at any foreigner passing within ten metres of their shops to come inside and spend. Finally I learnt to laugh at the unashamedness of it all.

Getting around by public transport is cheap and efficient but you're restricted in where you go and what you see. I hired a car which is relatively inexpensive. Cheaper are the mopeds which clog up the streets of Taipei (and often with an entire family aboard one bike), but you have to be brave to contend with the traffic. Driving down the East Coast I found wild and untouched beaches. Central Taiwan was a visual feast – the tranquility of the huge mountains chilling the lakes and paddy fields by night gave way to the intense heat of the March sun and lizards and creepers and luscious foliage.

TRAVEL NOTES

Languages Mandarin is the official language but most people use Taiwanese. English is widely taught although people tend to be shy of trying it out in public.

Transport Taxis are abundant and relatively cheap. There's an efficient bus and train network covering most of the island.

Accommodation The international hotels are very expensive but there are plenty of cheaper and reasonably comfortable youth hostels.

Special Problems Expense. You'll have to fork out for accommodation and food. Harassment is rarely a problem although few women wander alone into the red light districts of Taipei and Kaohsiung, where drug peddling and prostitution breed their own violence. Although the government is now toeing a softer political line you should be careful not to compromise others in political discussions. The Taiwanese are still exhorted to inform on potential "communist agents".

Guide *Taiwan: A Travel Survival Kit* (Lonely Planet) is the best general guide, though like most books on Taiwan it doesn't really explain why you should want to go there.

Contacts

Women's Research Programme, Population Studies Centre, National Taiwan University, Roosevelt Road, Section 4, No.1, Taipei. A resource for information on women's issues, although most of the literature published is in Chinese.

A useful place to look for contacts, information about jobs, language courses, accommodation etc, is the common-room noticeboard of **The Mandarin Training Centre**, National Taiwan Normal University, 162 Hoping East Road, Section 1, Taipei.

Thanks to Lidi Van-Gool and Luisetta Mudie for help with the Travel Notes.

Tanzania

• • • • • • • • • • • • • •

Compared with Kenya, tourism in Tanzania is relatively low-key. Few travellers venture beyond the "northern circuit" of Dar es Salaam, the island of Zanzibar, Arusha (for the ascent of Mount Kilimanjaro), the Ngorongoro crater and the Serengeti. It is in fact a huge country and independent travel, without the money to hire a jeep or a small plane, can be slow and arduous. Most women, however, find the country reasonably relaxed, once outside of the capital, Dar es Salaam, which has definite no-go areas. As a general rule you should dress modestly, particularly in predominantly Muslim areas like the island of Zanzibar.

The population is made up of a diverse range of tribes and cultures – Muslim, Christian, Animist, Hindu. No single group dominates and the official language of Kiswahili affords a very tenuous communal link. Since gaining independence from the British in 1961 the country's politics and policies have been moulded by Julius Nyerere, one of Africa's longest running elder statesmen. He finally stepped down as president in 1985 but continues as chairman of his party, *Chama Cha Mapinduzi* (*CCM*), and still features alongside the current ruler, Ali Hassan Mwinyi, in all government office photos.

Throughout his long rule, Nyerere introduced and determinedly pursued his own brand of Christian Socialism, the most central and ambitious policy of which was *ujamaa*, literally villagisation. This involved the compulsory resettlement of populations on a massive scale with the intention of raising agricultural production through local collective farming. The experiment floundered amidst claims of local and central government corruption, low-level productivity in the villages and increasing scarcity of basic (imported) commodities. Hard hit by the Seventies oil recession, a war with Uganda and a refusal to compromise the country by trade with South Africa, poverty and shortages have become an enduring fact of life. Unsurprisingly theft is a widespread problem and travellers who flaunt their relative wealth are an obvious target.

The **Union of Women of Tanzania** is a government-aligned organisation which was set up to provide and expand education and welfare projects. Its leaders are predominantly urban, middle-class women who work alongside trainers and teachers provided by VSO and other development agencies. Women attached to the church have traditionally had a high social status and are now often seen working at the forefront of education and medicine. Many women community leaders first learnt their organisational skills in the Church. We have been unable to find any additional information regarding autonomous feminist activity.

Slowly, Slowly, Kilimanjaro

. . . .

Sara Oliver describes her ascent of Africa's highest mountain, Kilimanjaro.

Kilimanjaro was given by Queen Victoria to Kaiser Wilhelm as a birthday present, but later reverted to British colonial rule. In the evening sun the magnificent monster looks calm, its white top sparkling out of a shroud of cloud, the foothills dark with forest shadows. An injured young German who had just descended groaned, "Not for a million dollars! Never again", as he limped by.

The National Park entrance at Marangu has a "going up" book and a "coming down" book. Here we begin. With our guide, Anasion Mabando, three porters (who carry warmer clothing and supplies for five days in baskets on their heads), a Dutch volunteer returning from Zambia, and myself, we are a party of six.

The porters soon disappear ahead. The well-trodden path leads past euca-

lyptus trees and Japanese cherry blossom. Singing birds are hidden among dense trees and butterflies fly across the stony track. The walk is pleasant, though warm, and we pause where a deep green, shaded stream falls among rocks, refreshing us. After three and a half hours we reach Mandara hut, 9000ft above sea level, where we will stay the night.

We sit watching the lights of Moshi town and the mass of stars. Anasion cooks onion soup, goat, cabbage and potatoes – "food for white people". He urges us to eat a lot as at higher altitudes we may lose our appetites. He has climbed the mountain over 800 times and has progressed from being a junior porter at fourteen to a senior guide. His experience is comforting. We sleep in the wooden huts, well wrapped up against the cold night.

Anasion brings sweet tea at 7am. The morning is clear and quiet but for birds singing, bees humming, and two large white-naped ravens scavenging. We breakfast on paw-paw, porridge and eggs and Anasion suggests we drink a lot of tea. He plans five hours' slow walking. We plod up the path into the forest again while the porters leap ahead with their loads.

The rainforest is dense and dark, with drooping creepers hanging from every branch. Loud screeches come from turacos and red-headed parrots which flash in front of us. Suddenly we are out of the forest and on to high savanna. Blinking in the sun, we see Mawenzi peak and further over, the snow of Kilimanjaro.

Here ferns and long grasses replace the wet green of the forest and the sun burns through the dry thin air. We walk slowly, and stop to watch buck and eland. We meet some porters dashing downward with a radio playing. They are followed by some rotund Norwegians who declare that most of their party reached the top.

Then comes the sound of panting and a group of people appears, running. Two rush by, carrying a grey-faced boy on a stretcher; his companions pause to explain that he has a pulmonary oedema and the only way to save his life is to *run* down to a lower altitude and then take him to hospital. These are fit eighteen-year-old students. Anasion shakes his head and sighs and warns us to move slowly.

Cloud comes rushing towards us and we are engulfed in cold, damp mist. A piercing whistle from Anasion brings back a porter with the down jackets we hired at Marangu. We don gloves and hoods and plod on through the air which shows our breath. We take frequent rests as the track becomes steeper, and I begin to notice the altitude, as any violent movement results in lightheadedness.

We walk silently in single file, saving our breath. Anasion, last in line, walks at the pace of the slowest, which is me. The mist swirls and we seem to be utterly alone on the way to the top of the world. My sinuses ache and my throat thumps strangely, so I realise I must rest.

At last, through the mist, we see the shapes of the huts of Horombo, where we will stay our second night. It is 2pm and we have walked for five hours,

climbing 3000ft. We sleep fully clothed, with hats on inside sleeping bags, tossing and turning fitfully. Breakfast is maize porridge again. Then we start walking. We pass the last water source where we fill our bottles. We cross the saddle between Mawenzi and Kilimanjaro, a vast stretch of empty terrain. We walk for five hours and the last part, just before Kibo hut at 15,520ft, takes a long time; we rest frequently and pant with the effort of moving upwards.

"A German woman vomits continuously and another drifts in and out of consciousness"

We arrive, tired, and eat goulash, which Anasion is delighted we can still manage. We rest, listening to our racing pulses. I sneeze and my nose bleeds. A German woman vomits continuously and another drifts in and out of consciousness, gasping for oxygen.

Anasion rouses us at 1am. We drink sugary tea and put on our warmest clothing. It has been snowing and the bright moonbeams cast shadows as clear as daylight. Anasion leads, instructing us to tell him if we feel unwell. We shuffle off into the night, walking on volcanic scree, using our long sticks to stop sliding backwards on loose gravel. The moonlight is enchanting, the night clear and quiet; our rasping breath sounds insultingly loud.

At about 4.30am a cloud covers the moon and an icy wind begins to batter us; between rests we now take eight paces, then six, then four with our leadlike feet. My lungs ache and I feel very tired. Anasion urges us on, chanting "Slowly, Slowly, Kilimanjaro", and we follow. Nothing matters but the next step.

Anasion points to a thin red line in the cloud. "Alleluya!" he shouts, his voice echoing across the mountain. "It is morning! Alleluya! Thank you, God!" I am thankful too. The sun's rays warm us and give us courage to continue as we see the beautiful brilliant dawn of Kilimanjaro. In the growing light Anasion points to something white in the rock. It is not snow. It is a flagpole. It is the top.

Painfully and slowly we ascend the rock, encouraged by Anasion's chanting, scrambling with our hands over the last little bit. Shaking with the strain but enormously exhilarated I look down on huge glaciers, giant steps of brilliant ice dazzling white in the morning sun. The steaming volcano reminds me of my puniness. A wooden box was wedged between the rocks, inside a book full of triumphant signatures. We had no pen.

We had taken eight hours to climb the peak; coming down took only one hour. At Kibo hut the Chaga mountain rescue men congratulated us. "Two white women! Really, that is surprising. It's good, very good." I felt angry, indignant, and pleased.

TRAVEL NOTES

Languages Kiswahili, English, and numerous tribal languages. It helps to speak even a little Swahili, which is far more necessary than in neighbouring Kenya.

Transport Buses, trains and planes are all stricken by shortages of fuel and spare parts. It is often easier to hitch, or, for a small sum, cadge a spare seat on someone else's safari vehicle. Ask around the Asian travel agents who can be helpful. It is possible to go by ferry from Dar to Zanzibar and from other towns like Bagamoyo and Tanga, but can be difficult to arrange as it is thought to threaten national security.

Accommodation The YMCAs are cheap, friendly and admit women too; the YWCA in Dar is a good and secure meeting place. Hotels and guesthouses are similar to Kenya, though fewer and less developed.

Special problems Shortages. Dispensaries and hospitals often lack vital drug supplies, so take your own (Tanzania is in a high risk malarial zone), plus tampons, toiletries, any contraceptives, etc; be prepared, too, for food and drink shortages, even of Tanzanian products. Official currency rates are abysmal, the black market up to eight times better; but deal at your own risk, penalties are severe on both sides. If you take any photographs ask first and expect to pay.

Guides *Guide to East Africa* (Travelaid) and *East Africa – A Travel Survival Kit* (Lonely Planet) both have fair sections on Tanzania. *Backpacker's Africa* (Bradt Publications) is useful for hikes.

Contacts

Tanzania Women's Organisation (UWT), Ofisi Kun ndogo SLP 1473, Dar es Salaam, Tanzania. The longest running women's group. Established in 1962, it aims to promote political, economic and social equality.

Women Communicators, PO Box 9033, Dar es Salaam. A Church organisation affiliated to the Msimbazi Centre. Its aim is to promote women's participation in nation-building activities.

Books

Laetitia Mukarasi, Post Abolished: One Woman's Struggle for Employment Rights in Tanzania (The Women's Press, 1990). Brave and fascinating account, not just of the right to work, but of the dynamics of respect within family life.

Goran Hyden, *Beyond Ujamaa in Tanzania: Underdevelopment and an Uncaptured Peasantry* (Heinemann, 1980).

Tepilit Ole Saitoti and Carol Beckwith, *Maasai* (Elm Tree Books, 1980). Photo record with interesting text.

Ophelia Macarenhas and Marjorie Mbilinyi, *Women in Tanzania: An analytical bibliography* (Scandinavian Institute of African Studies, 1983).

Look out too for the work of **Tanzanian writers** like Hanza Sokko, W.E. Mkufya, Agoro Anduru and Prince Kagwema. Also for the writings of Julius Nyerere – essential insights into the present social structure.

Trinidad

The largest island in the Eastern Caribbean, Trinidad has a population of around one million. Outside carnival there is little tourism. Trinidadians themselves take their holidays on the much smaller sister island of Tobago which, as the classic "tropical island paradise", has far more tourist facilities.

Trinidad itself is an oil state, though the collapse of oil prices since the boom period of the 1970s has left the island in bad financial trouble. Even so, the middle classes continue to live a comfortable life, driving around in large gas-guzzling American cars (petrol, despite the odd price increase, is still cheap), eating in overpriced restaurants boasting international cuisine, and building large sprawling houses along the coastal strips beside the capital, Port of Spain, and San Fernando in the south. The poor have been hard hit. Bullock-drawn carts and ploughs co-exist with expensive imported cars and tractors, and many smallholders live in tumbledown shacks in the hills.

Travelling around can be quite a problem since out-of-town bus services are very limited. Without a car, it's almost impossible to get to the beautiful wild beaches and even to established tourist sites such as the mangrove swamps, where stunning flocks of scarlet ibis arrive at dusk to roost. In addition, wherever you go, even staying in small guesthouses or with local families, the cost of living is high. But people are generally friendly and hospitable and, if you love music and dancing (this is the home of the calypso and the steel band), there's lots of cheap entertainment. A drawback is that without a male companion you can expect endless propositions from local men.

Although there are some vociferous feminists within the trade unions, the **women's movement** has been slow to develop. The Secretariat of the *Caribbean Association for Feminist Research and Action* (*CAFRA*), formed in 1985, is based in Trinidad, but it is not easy to gauge how far the organisation has improved the lives of ordinary women. The island is ethnically very mixed – a combination of people of African, Indian and, to a much lesser extent, European, Chinese and Syrian descent. While relations are superficially harmonious, people are always aware of the possibilities of friction between the different groups, especially with rising unemployment. The political parties tend to be split along racial lines, but an attempt is always made to keep some balance of races within the government. People are far more conscious of this issue than they are of sexism.

A Health Worker in Port of Spain

. . . .

Patricia Jacob spent three months working in Trinidad as part of her final year's study at medical school. Wanting medical experience in a tropical country, she chose the island for its comparatively low profile as a tourist resort.

Armed with a Medical Research Council grant, I arrived in Trinidad to help establish a community-based health project. The aim of the project was to teach mothers how to rehydrate their babies at home when they developed gastroenteritis, so avoiding a long, difficult and expensive journey to hospital. Long stretches of deserted palm fringed beaches, copious quantities of rum punch, and the magic of steel pan were also frequently listed on my timetable. But, a little unexpectedly, it was my opportunity to work in the community rather than holiday in the

sun that gave me most joy and satisfaction.

My project took me to areas where, as a tourist, I would probably never have gone: the downtown areas of the poor; shanty-towns of cardboard and corrugated iron cluttering the edges of the main city, Port of Spain; old, ramshackle wooden huts perched erratically around the hillsides, clinging desperately to the worn and litter-strewn slopes. In East Dry River, where I was based, there were no roads, no house numbers but always bright-eyed barefoot children to lead you up and down the tumbling paths. Here name and family were your only rank and everyone was related.

"As a doctor . . . I was given a passage into people's houses and treated with a hospitality and intimacy I could never otherwise have expected"

I was surprised how readily the women of these communities accepted and confided in me – for, despite Trinidad's incredibly cosmopolitan people, there is still a powerful racial tension throughout the island. Many whites consider themselves to be superior, while the black population tends to look down on the Indians, who, in turn, condemn the Chinese; finally, everyone seems to hate the Syrians, perhaps because of their remarkable success in business. Even within each race there is racism – or perhaps more accurately "colourism", for the paler black people often mock their darker skinned neighbours and the wealthy Indians in the city use cruel nicknames to taunt their country cousins.

As a white woman venturing into a black ghetto, I was more than a little apprehensive about my reception. But I needn't have worried. In my role as a doctor, going out to help children, I was given a passage into people's houses and treated with a hospitality and intimacy I could never otherwise have expected.

Walking through some of the poorest areas I was often stopped by groups of cold-faced men, especially young Rastas who hang around in clusters on the street, a national habit. As they grilled me about where I was going, and what I was doing, I would explain nervously until their faces relaxed, sometimes smiles broke out, and I was pointed in the right direction for my charge.

In general these areas, like shanty towns in most big cities, aren't safe to wander alone. I was warned, many times too, about going unaccompanied into the countryside, especially into the hills in the middle of the island. Stories of strange goings-on, with hints of black magic and wild half-man, half-beast creatures were wound up into hysteria by the mythical story-telling that Trinidadians love so much. I was sufficiently scared not to go in search of the truth.

I soon learned to master the local taxi service, which runs throughout the city and, in fact, I even looked forward

to moving about this way. The taxis (recognisable by their number plates and not to be confused with tourist taxis which carry a proper sign) are shared and thus reasonably cheap. Sitting squashed in the backseat of a vehicle with several strangers soon starts up a conversation and is a great way of hearing local opinion about everything under the sun.

However, getting around the rest of the island is almost impossible; a few buses connect the main towns, but the only railways were ripped up years ago. Hitching is definitely not worth the risk and hiring a car prohibitively expensive; I found myself relying on the excessive Trinidadian hospitality showered on me in order to go further afield.

"Women's stories reflected the ease with which many Trinidadians slip in and out of relationships"

Unlike the men, women I met in the course of my work were always delighted with the opportunity to have someone new to talk to, whatever the colour of their skin. My visits provided just another chance for a chat and a laugh about children, men, rivals, love and sex – the last being a favourite topic everywhere and discussed with surprising frankness.

Women's stories reflected the ease with which many Trinidadians slip in and out of relationships. More children are born out of wedlock than in it, but the problems of the one-parent family are nothing like those in England. In Trinidad there always seems to be someone – grandmother, sisters, cousins, neighbours, friends – to look after the children. At the same time the man's macho role reigns supreme, especially among the poorer communities, and women are often left to cope on their own with the house and children. Even among the wealthier and more educated, women have yet to attain the degree of freedom that many of their Western sisters enjoy.

For much of my stay I lived with a black Trinidadian family, the Bernards, in St Annes, a pleasant district in Port of Spain. Susan, Sandra and Jill-Anne, the three daughters still living at home, were a riot of fun and continual chatter. They adopted me like a long lost member of the family and took me around with them to meet their friends, neighbours and boyfriends; to endless parties and discos; on political rallies, pop concerts, shopping trips, cricket matches, even for a weekend on Trinidad's sister island, Tobago. Life was a constant social whirl and not just for my benefit; the girls lead the same crazy social life as most Trinidadians.

I had my own room in their pretty, if rather chaotic, house and, after initial protest, was allowed to muck in with the rest of the family for chores such as cleaning and shopping. Cooking, however, remained the domain of Mrs Bernard. Meal times were completely relaxed: she would prepare great bowls of traditional food like curry *callalloo* and spicy chicken, to which we just helped ourselves when we felt hungry. Once or twice a week, for a treat, someone would bring home a takeaway; fast foods have caught on in a big way in Trinidad and the influences of both Canada and the USA pervade many aspects of life on the island.

In general the girls had the opportunity to pursue what they wanted to do and seemed to live a modern Western lifestyle. All had good jobs – in banking, as a personal assistant, and with a national airline – but underneath it all they were ultimately expected to fulfil traditional family expectations to settle down (though not necessarily marry), have several children and look after man and home. As in other sides of island life there still hovered an empty promise of something more exciting. The girls' parents, like most of their generation, had been brought up in a rural old-fashioned way.

Modern life only hit Trinidad comparatively recently with the sudden development of the oil industry. Nowadays the shops may sell almost all the material things you could want (provided someone can be bribed to bring it into the country), but it will take much longer for the social structure of Trinidadian life to change. At least the girls I was staying with were able to work in a job of their choice and had money of their own.

Many of the women in my project area had little chance of escape from the drudgery of household chores and childcare. They had to look after every family need on a minuscule income which they only saw if their man hadn't already spent it on gambling and beer. Luckily a close network of family and friends could usually be relied upon to bail them out, but a number had small choice but to struggle from debt to debt.

"Marianne sometimes used to accompany me on my forays into the slums, I think partly because she feared for my safety and partly to pursue her own mission to publicise the health centre"

One woman who had managed to break free from traditional restraints was a beautiful young nurse, called Marianne, half French West Indian, half Scottish. She had trained in England and returned to the island with a determination to improve the lot of Trinidad's women. Together with others in the Catholic community she had helped to establish a community centre in Port of Spain, offering medical help where necessary and tea and coffee to the lonely. The centre provided a welcome bolt-hole, since, while men haunt the streets and bars, there are few places where women can meet and talk outside of their own four walls.

Marianne sometimes used to accompany me on my forays into the slums, I think partly because she feared for my safety and partly to pursue her own mission to publicise the health centre. Commandeering her boyfriend's battered old car, we would drive to the fringes of East Dry River and abandon our escape vehicle to set out on foot along the dusty winding paths.

One visit in particular remains clear in my memory. To enter the house required a careful manoeuvre around a partially collapsed and exceedingly delicate porch platform, the whole hut being raised well above the steep hillside. A slightly insipid smell wafted out to greet us but inside it was pleasantly cool. In the little parlour sat several large and cheery women, dressed in bright but ragged old clothes, slightly faded by the sun and held together in crucial places by safety pins. Gathered pinnis covered their ample laps and gay scarves caught up the bobbly rollers in their hair. Children, probably grandchildren, tumbled and crawled around them as they talked and laughed. Pride of place in the crowded two-roomed hut stood three large, framed certificates, awarded for the best carnival costumes in 1977.

As proof, stunningly colourful intricate masks and headdresses hung from the tatty walls, commanding all attention away from the shabbiness of an old settee, the ragged curtains and mounting rubbish. It was as if all their scarce income had been concentrated on the wild, wonderful, drunken, dancing two days of carnival, a small investment for a momentary release from poverty. During the months leading up to each carnival, people's thoughts overflow with dreams and preparations for the forthcoming spree, while memories of all the fun provide food for months afterwards.

I found Trinidad so full of these contradictions: the wealth amidst the poverty, the gleaming children neatly dressed for school, hair uniformly ribboned, emerging from the smallest hut; the scorching sun followed so rapidly by refreshing torrential rain. The most rickety home would regularly reveal a huge, shiny fridge, trembling gently on the wafer-thin, gaping floorboards and laden with the local brew.

Almost everywhere I was invited to, from shacks to the house of a consultant surgeon, there was always an open invitation to help yourself; in other words march up to the fridge, have a nose around and take whatever you fancied.

Unfortunately the easygoing attitude of the people seems to have a link with their many problems. In a country soused with oil wealth, inefficiency, corruption, and apathetic disorder have contributed to persistent poverty, appalling facilities and massive wastage of precious resources. Nowhere was this more evident than in the government-run General Hospital.

"Patients were sharing beds, head to toe; the place had run out of clean sheets; and the mortuary fridge had broken down"

It's common for expensive equipment, imported into the country with great effort and manipulation of red tape, to lie unused in cupboards, rotting because some simple part can't be found, or the official has run off with his bribe to get it through customs. Even if the equipment was intact, the lack of air conditioning would cause it to blow up in the heat, when it would simply return to the cupboard to await supplies for spare parts. While I was out there, patients were sharing beds, head to toe; the place had run out of clean sheets; and the mortuary fridge had broken down, leaving hundreds of corpses to rot, piled up in the courtyard.

A popular saying that I heard several times suggests that Trinidadians are like trees in the forest, growing prolifically in carefree abandon. There is plenty of room for the strong to grow while the weak fall into their shadow. Wherever I went, people offered advice on how to negotiate this forest, telling me about the hundred-and-one things that every Trinidadian needs to know from the day they are born in order to survive in their country: the benefits of goat curry and cow-heel soup, who is planting *ganja*, how to get a brand new car within a week without booking.

Everyone seemed to know how to get items in and money out, legally and illegally; what not to do; where not to go; who not to see. Every Trini, it seems, is a consultant in domestic and foreign affairs, with an ear to the groundbeat and an eye to whatever opportunities a visitor might bring.

Leaving aside the chaos, indulgent hospitality was the most memorable aspect of my trip. No one in the world knows how to look after a visitor like a Trinidadian (it's also said that no people know more how to party, as I surely found out). I came home determined to try my best to emulate their friendliness in Britain's cold climate.

TRAVEL NOTES

Languages English is the main language, though, laced with Creole expressions, it can be hard to understand. In some areas Spanish and a French patois are spoken.

Transport Buses are cheap, but tend to be overcrowded. Out-of-town services are limited, so, if you can decipher the complicated system, it's often best to get a taxi. Make sure you pay after local people in order to determine the fare, or else agree a price in advance. It's not worth hitching. As well as being risky, you'll probably be picked up by a pirate taxi anyway. The *Caribbean Islands Handbook* includes a good run-down on how the taxi system works.

Accommodation Like everything, hotels are expensive and prices more than double at Carnival times. The Trinidad and Tobago Tourist Board (56 Frederick Street, Port of Spain) is very helpful, providing information on a range of places to stay, including guest-houses which are more reasonably priced.

Guide The *Caribbean Islands Handbook* (Trade and Travel Publications) has a good section on Trinidad and Tobago.

Contacts

Caribbean Association for Feminist Research and Action (CAFRA), PO Box 442, Tuniapuna PO, Tuniapuna, Trinidad and Tobago (see introduction).

Books

Pat Ellis, ed., *Women of the Caribbean* (Zed Books, 1987). Collection of essays providing a good general background to the history and lives of Caribbean women.

Merle Hodge, *Crick Crack Monkey* (Heinemann, 1981). Revealing novel about growing up and coping with the caste system in Trinidad.

It's well worth looking out for books by **Michael Anthony**, one of Trinidad's best known novelists, published in the UK by Heinemann. His most recent work, ***All That Glitters*** (Heinemann, 1983), is the story of an adolescent boy infatuated with two different older women.

Tunisia

· · · · · · · · · · · · · · ·

Tunisia has developed a highly successful package holiday industry over the last fifteen years, centred on its Mediterranean beaches and aided by a comparatively liberal Muslim culture. Most of these visitors, however, stay in or around their resorts – mainly at Cap Bon and the "desert island" of Djerba, and the country sees relatively few independent travellers.

The attention you receive varies greatly between areas with or without tourism. Sexual harassment can be persistent in the more developed resorts and in the Westernised capital, Tunis, though scarcely different to the sort of pestering you find throughout Mediterranean Europe. In the desert south, where you are defined and limited according to Islamic custom, attitudes are harsher. Most women travelling to the sub-Sahara choose to join up with a mixed group. And in these areas, as an independent traveller, you're more likely to be offered hospitality (and you'll find it much easier to accept) if you're travelling with a man.

The official **status of women** in Tunisia has changed radically over the last 35 years. This is due mainly to the liberalising influence of Habib Bourguiba, who led the country to independence from the French in 1956 and remained president until 1987 – when, virtually senile, he was ousted in a palace coup by General Ben Ali, the current president. Bourguiba justified improving women's rights from within original Islamic texts, thus securing the support of Tunisia's religious leaders. Polygamy was outlawed (as Mohammed's stipulation that each wife was to be treated equally was held to be impossible), the marriage age was raised to nineteen, and divorce by *talaq* (verbal repudiation) was outlawed. Legislation was passed on equal pay, and opportunities for work widened considerably following the departure of the French.

Actual social change has, however, been slow to follow these comparatively radical laws – a frequent assertion nowadays being that women have "too much power". It's doubtful, too, whether many of the rural poor are aware of their statutory rights. There remain disparities between the sexes in education and many more women than men are illiterate. In recent years the economic recession, coupled with the rise of Muslim Fundamentalism in the Arab world, have led to an incipient form of reaction. Though many more women work, their wages are often paid directly to husbands or used for dowry. Since 1979 increasing numbers of women have taken to wearing the *chador*, the Iranian headscarf-veil. As this apparent backlash continues, the overall process of social change is likely to become increasingly complicated. Women are finding themselves caught between, on the one hand, the break-up of the extended family – already causing problems of isolation in the cities – and, on the other, new pressures to conform to a traditional way of life.

A Surface Liberalism

. . . .

Linda Cooley has been working as a teacher in Tunisia for the last six years; she has travelled extensively around the country.

Tunisian women enjoy a measure of freedom and equality under the law unknown in many other Arab countries. Polygamy was abolished in the mid-1950s when Tunisia became independent. Divorce laws have been altered in women's favour. Most girls attend school. A reasonably large percentage of women are in higher education. Many women work outside the home and there are women in the professions and two women ministers in the government.

But the presence of so many women in public can be misleading. It may lull you into a false sense of security when you first arrive and lead to false expectations of what you can and cannot do. If you walk around the capital, you will see women in jeans and the latest fashions, sometimes sitting in cafés, even girls walking along holding hands with their boyfriends. But what you cannot see and should know is that these same fashionably dressed girls have fathers who expect them to be home by 8pm at the latest, who expect them to be virgins when they marry, and who often expect them to marry a relative chosen by the parent.

The clothes may have changed in recent years; the amount of women at work may have changed; but, deep down, social attitudes have not altered. Tunisia remains a traditional Arab society where the idea of a woman travelling abroad alone is still considered as rather strange. It is changing, but very slowly.

It is important, also, to realise how much the Europeanised image, even in Tunis, is superficial. A bar in Tunisia is not like one in France: it's an exclusively male domain and wandering in for a rest and a beer, you are bound to be stared at. Similarly, you can't expect to be able to chat to the man at the next table in the café about the best place to have lunch or the best time to visit the mosque, without your conversation being taken as a sexual invitation. Western movies have done an excellent job in persuading Tunisian men that all Western women are only too keen to have casual sex with any willing male.

"I learnt to cope by evading direct eye contact with men, and above all never smiling at a stranger"

All this must sound somewhat offputting. Yet, in six years of living in Tunisia, I have often travelled alone; I have travelled with my son; I have travelled with another woman. Perhaps I've been lucky, but, apart from the unwanted attentions of a few men, nothing has happened to me. There is no part of the country that it is unsafe to visit. (Though, unless you are enamoured of international hotel architecture – miles and miles and miles of it – you may as well avoid Hammamet and Nabeul, the most developed tourist regions.) You can see the ruins of Carthage, the underground dwellings in tranquil Matmata, the fruitful oases of the south, and beautiful Arab architecture all around. You can generally stay in cheap hotels without trouble. The *Mahalas* in particular are very good value and the ones in Djerba and Kairouan are extremely lovely buildings. You can see everything. But, travelling alone, it's incredibly hard to get to know the people.

You will also find it hard to relax, never being sure about how your behaviour will be interpreted if you do. I learnt to cope by evading direct eye contact with men, and above all never smiling at a stranger. I once found myself being followed home after inadvertently smiling at a man as we simultaneously reached for the same tin of tomato sauce in the supermarket!

Really persistent harassment, however, is not common. It may irk you to keep your silence; not to answer like with like; not to show your disdain; but in the long run it will make your day pleasanter. After a while the ignoring game becomes a reality; you really don't notice that anyone has spoken to you!

If you cannot learn to ignore the hassle from men, you will probably find yourself impatient to leave after a very short time, taking with you an awful image of the country and vowing never to return. It is, in fact, an easy country for a woman on her own to dislike.

Travelling with a man makes it all much simpler. The stereotyped images on both sides – yours of macho Arab men and theirs of loose foreign women – can be dispensed with and everyone can act naturally. Men will talk to you both as you're sitting in a café or waiting for a bus. And they're not all hustlers, they often just want someone different to talk to. You may well get invited home to meet their families, where you will be able to talk freely to the women as, unlike in many Arab countries, Tunisian women and men eat together.

You can also go to the *hammam* (public baths) with the women of the house. This is well worth a visit as it is the one place where women meet traditionally as a group, away from all the pressures of what is still a male-dominated society. Unless you speak Arabic it is difficult to talk to the older women there, who rarely speak French, but they are more than willing to show you how to remove the hairs from your body (and I mean your whole body!), to henna your hair, to use *tfal* (a shampoo made from mud), and to give you a thorough scrub with a sort of loofah mitten (and can they scrub thoroughly!). You could, of course, take yourself to the *hammam* travelling alone, but it's much better to go with a Tunisian woman and, as I've said before, introductions are almost exclusively made through men.

Another possibility is that, if you ask around the women, you may well find that you can get yourself invited to a wedding. You don't have to know the bride or groom – hundreds of people attend Arab weddings who hardly know the couple. Total strangers can be very hospitable when it comes to sharing their local customs and food with you. I once had the most beautiful couscous brought out to the field where I was eating my picnic of cheese sandwiches. But then, I was with my son and a man.

Alone or with another woman it is possible to enjoy yourself, but you will miss a great deal of what is, essentially, Tunisian life. Hopefully, through more contact between foreign women and Tunisians, a greater understanding will ensue on both sides, and the lone woman traveller will become more easily accepted.

TRAVEL NOTES

Languages Arabic. French is widely spoken.

Transport Buses cover most of the country, and there's a limited train network. *Louages* (collective taxis) are the fastest form of long-distance transport and operate non-stop. Hitching is a common form of transport, though few women would consider hitching alone.

Accommodation *Hotels Tunisiens* are cheap alternatives to the officially graded establishments but some can be on the rough side, occasionally with dormitory accommodation only – unavailable to women. *Pensions familiales* are beginning to appear on the coast, and you are unlikely to leave the country without at least once being offered hospitality for a night.

Special Problems The relative scarcity of foreigners and the more strict Islamic culture of the south can make this an uneasy region to travel around alone.

Guide *The Rough Guide: Tunisia* (Harrap Columbus) is practical, informed and culturally sensitive. It includes an interesting section on women in Tunisia and post-independence reforms.

Contacts

National Union of Women, 56 Boulevard de Bab Benat, Tunis.

All of Tunis Women (Resources and Information on Women), 7 rue Sinam Pacha, Tunis.

Alliance of Tunisian Women for Research and Information on Women, University of Tunis, Tunis.

Books

Norma Salem, *Habib Bourguiba, Islam and the Creation of Tunisia* (Croom Helm, 1985). An uncritical but useful biography of the man at the heart of the modern nation.

Wilfrid Knapp, *Tunisia* (Thames & Hudson, 1971). The best of several history-cum-background books.

Albert Memmi, *The Pillar of Salt* (1956; out of print). Tunisia's most distinguished novelist, and virtually the only one to be translated into English. As a North African Jew, Memmi's work is preoccupied with the problem of identity.

Turkey

. . . .

Since the military coup of 1980 brought its so-called political "stabilisation", Turkey has been in the grips of a tourist boom. Tour companies, turning their attentions from overexploited Greece, have already transformed vast stretches of the Aegean/Mediterranean coast into a concrete mass of hotels and holiday apartment blocks catering for thousands of Europeans every year. Yet the carefree, Westernised image of the tourist enclaves is misleading. You don't have to venture far to discover a deeply traditional and predominantly rural way of life or witness the strong military presence and atmosphere of political suppression that continues to hang over the country despite its much vaunted transition to democracy.

Although Turkey is officially a secular state, women are expected to conform to Islamic customs and values. Westerners who flaunt these by asserting their freedom to travel independently and mix freely with men are stereotypically viewed as "immodest" – a myth encouraged by the portrayal of bikini-clad tourists in the popular press. Travelling alone you may have to contend with fairly persistent sexual harassment. As usual, this is at its most oppressive around the main tourist areas – the coastal resorts, circuit of major sights, and the commercial districts of Istanbul – where men collect in search

of the "easy" tourist. Yet to close yourself off or react suspiciously to all approaches would be to miss a great deal. The Turkish people have a reputation for great hospitality and friendliness and many will go to great lengths to make you feel welcome.

Whilst you can't completely escape unwanted attention, it can help to follow the lead of more Westernised Turkish women, and adopt a fairly conservative style of dress and behaviour. Similarly, if you suffer from any overt harassment you should make your predicament clear to passers-by or fellow passengers. You'll find that Turkish women will be only too happy to take you under their wing.

Under Turkey's secular laws women have been greatly encouraged to take an active role in public life; veiling is officially frowned upon, and in some areas actually prohibited; opportunities in education and work have been expanded and a growing minority of women are entering the professions. But in doing so women are aware of walking a tightrope between meeting the demands of a recently imposed Western capitalist system and upholding the cherished traditions of a suppressed Islamic culture. The contradictions this involves were highlighted in 1988 when veiled students marched with feminists to demand their right to wear headscarves in the classroom.

Despite the repression of all kinds of political organisation in Turkey, an autonomous **women's movement** is gradually becoming established. *Kadin Cevresi* (Women's Circle), a group responsible for setting up the country's first feminist publishing house, has spearheaded many campaigns against sexual discrimination and recently led a demonstration protesting the introduction of compulsory virginity tests for civil servants in the Ministry of Defence. Their activities are currently focused on providing a network of support for battered wives. Women are also taking a leading role in trade union disputes (a woman led the successful *Nigros* grocery store strike) and have been the main force behind *TAYAD* (association of families of prisoners and detainees), a pressure group that highlights the brutal conditions faced by the regime's political prisoners.

The Turkish Left, traditionally hostile to feminism because of its espousal by a "Westernised" bourgeoisie, is now taking a greater interest in mobilising women and the underground Turkish Communist Party recently opened a well-equipped women's centre in Istanbul. The first national women's conference was held in Turkey in 1989 and, despite divisions emerging about priorities for women and the need to organise separately, a manifesto of demands was agreed.

In at the Deep End

. . . .

Rosie Ayliffe spent three years working in Istanbul, as a university teacher, freelance writer and tour leader. She has since returned to Turkey to research and write a *Rough Guide* to the country.

I went to Turkey because I couldn't think how I had finished my formal education without knowing quite where Istanbul was. I was in the university careers library, wondering if I could get one out on loan, when I happened on an advertisement for jobs teaching English in Istanbul. I thought the best way of discovering where the place was and who lived there would be to answer the advertisement.

That same day I was given a job and found myself surveying the prospect of going to Turkey. I "knew" more about Istanbul than I had realised. I knew that it was a Muslim city, and that it was therefore inhabited by people with a sympathy for the Iranian revolution. I knew that the Turks or "infidel" had failed to conquer Vienna in 1683 and that this had been a great relief to the civilised West. I knew from my wide-ranging knowledge of Turkish cinema that Turkish men beat their wives, and from British cinema that you would be arrested and made to walk around a pole indefinitely if you irritated Turkish customs officials.

I arranged accommodation before I went out. A friend who had been living in Istanbul offered to put in a good word with Zahide and Mustafa, who owned the house he was living in. I thought he was joking when he warned me to keep a bottle down the toilet against rats.

September was blistering hot but I sweated cold terror on the flight over. Was I carrying anything that could possibly cause offence to the customs officials? Would the university give me a job if they knew of my political sympathies? At the time I didn't know that I would have to work for over three months before I saw my first pay packet, not because there was really any serious vetting procedure in operation, but simply because of the sheer inefficiency of a bureaucracy that makes our DSS look like the Starship Enterprise.

"I (always kept) a whisky bottle in the hole in the floor covering an open drain which served as my toilet, but it didn't stop the rats coming in through a hole in the roof"

I arrived on the sixth anniversary of the 1980 military coup. I wasn't surprised to be greeted by machine-gun-toting soldiers, I was only surprised to be allowed to walk freely through passport control. Again, it would be a matter of time before I realised that Western visitors to Turkey are nowadays treated with care and respect by the officials, in a cosmetic attempt to improve a deservedly unprepossessing image.

My new home was situated on the Asian side of the city in the hills overlooking the Bosphorous. One rusty tap sometimes gave me cold clean water. More often it jetted forth a stream of shit-coloured fluid, thick with oxidised iron, or didn't work at all. I did always keep a whisky bottle in the hole in the floor covering an open drain which served as my toilet, but it didn't stop the rats from coming in through a hole in the roof.

The house was what is known as a *gecekondu*, a home "built in the night". An ancient law states that when a roof is put on a house it becomes a legal dwelling place. Contractors have devised methods of building apartments so that the roof is virtually on before the walls are up, and shacks spring up all over the city, literally overnight, before the authorities have time to interfere.

I learnt some Turkish through necessity. None of my neighbours or my landlady spoke any English and nor did the local shopkeepers or restaurateurs. Rather too proud to use sign language, I was hungry by the time I mastered "Could I have a . . . ?" and "Have you got any . . . ?".

Mustafa and Zahide were ancient siblings celebrating their approaching dotage in occasional outbursts of screaming, resembling either song or rage as best suited the prevailing circumstance. She was as mean as he was foolish, but they were kind enough to me, and screamed with laughter and "Masallahs!" every time I learnt a new Turkish word.

A rather more interesting companion was the doctor, their older brother, who lived in another wooden house in the same complex. While I watched him go crazy, he had moments of lucidity which seemed to suggest that insanity was a kind of refuge from the glaring injustices of the society in which he had found himself.

He sometimes spoke to me in guarded terms about torture in Turkish prisons and I learnt from him what had happened to the radicals and intellectuals in Turkish universities. Periodically he would rush out while I was doing my washing and implore me not to use detergent in the water since it would do untold destruction to the food chain. I ignored him until three years later, when the press exposed the scandal of phosphates in Turkish detergents.

About eight months after arriving I was told that new neighbours were moving into the compound and was delighted when a young and friendly couple turned up to clean the tiny wooden shack which I had previously taken for an outhouse. The woman, Cybele, was eighteen, and a friend of the doctor's. They had met at English classes in the military academy down in Cengelkoy.

We became friends, helping each other with housework, brewing up pots of tea together and sometimes, when two of her old-crone aunts came to visit from a neighbouring village, we would put on a tape of jangly arabesque music and us two youngsters would be forced to dance while the old women banged on drums, shook tambourines and cackled.

"Many of the women I met had been forced through the pain and humiliation of one or more abortions"

I went to visit her family home one day, in order to take photographs of a new baby for its father who was doing his military service. Three families and countless children appeared to live in a two-bedroom shack and off less than an acre of land. Although it was Ramadan and they were all fasting except Cybele, I was proudly served with a large meal. According to Islamic tradition a guest is given the best food in the house, and I have no doubt that as elsewhere in Turkey this rule was rigidly adhered to in that household, but the food was still virtually inedible.

On the way home I asked Cybele why she wasn't fasting. She was evasive, and it was only when she began to discuss babies that I realised that she was pregnant. Not long after this she came to my house clutching at her stomach. Her aunts arrived and took over, and throughout the evening issued a running commentary on her miscarriage. Cybele and her husband left and I never saw them again. Many of the women I met subsequently stated that they had been forced through the pain and humiliation of one or more abortions before marriage and that this was an accepted form of birth control.

Despite the fact that I was living off the beaten "Stamboul" tourist track, I provoked no more than a passing interest in the village. Perhaps Zahide and Mustafa kept the inhabitants so well informed of my day-to-day activities that there was little left for them to learn from source, but I also suspect that I had developed a well-deserved reputation for haughtiness.

For the first few weeks I seriously expected that unless I behaved with the utmost decorum my house would be surrounded by lusty youths until the early hours of the morning; and I stared rigidly ahead of me at all times rather than risk giving someone an excuse to talk to me. In time I began to realise that my attitudes to Turkish men were shaped by the same degree of unfounded prejudice that served to inform their attitudes toward Western women.

The first incident to bring this home to me happened within a few days of my arrival. Completely lost and miles from home in the street around the covered Bazaar in Cagaoglu, I went into a workshop to ask directions. A boy came out with me, and I imagined he would start to point and gesticulate. Instead he accompanied me down to the ferry port, boarded the ferry with me, then found me the right bus and took me to the bottom of my hill in Cengelkoy. Before I had found any of the words to tell him that I really didn't think it would be terribly wise of me to invite him up to my house, he had grinned, said goodbye, and set off on the two-hour journey back to his workplace. That was the last I saw of him but the first of countless occasions when I was party to acts of altruistic kindness from Turkish men.

While I never felt relaxed enough to make friends with men in the village, this was as much a result of their own personal taboos as of any misconception on my part, and I was quite happy to be assimilated to such an extent that I became *harem*, "forbidden territory".

When I travelled around Turkey I think I was afforded some protection by my appearance. As I learnt more Turkish my manner must have become more confident, and this combined with a dark complexion meant that I was continually mistaken for a Turk, or at least, cast enough doubt over my nationality to evoke the possibility of a spectral elder brother in the minds of would-be aggressors. My short hair, masculine dress and "boyish" figure further added to the confusion and I was often treated to the familiar epithet of "Agabey"'or "big brother".

"Most foreign women I met were rather less fortunate in their experiences with Turkish men"

Only on one occasion did I feel at all threatened by a man, and that was in Trabzon bus station at three in the morning, when I was put into the care of someone who was evidently less than psychologically stable. After escaping from his clutches I took refuge in the company of a group of bus drivers, who realised what was wrong and demanded to know what he had done. They must have taken the matter into their own hands, and a few weeks later some friends travelling through the city returned with the news that my would-be molester had lost his job as a result of the incident.

Most foreign women I met were rather less fortunate in their experiences with Turkish men, and the only advice I could give was to seek the company of women at every opportunity, simply by showing and responding to friendliness. I found I was more comfortable in the company of Turkish women – to whom sisterhood seems a natural concept – and I was especially grateful for the matronly protection I received from older women wherever I travelled in Turkey. While they questioned me about my marital status and wondered at such freedom of movement afforded by independence from any family, I rarely felt that this curiosity had a perjorative edge and by the end of my stay I had been adopted into several Turkish families.

During the first year of my stay I taught English to students of Islamic theology at the university. I had been disappointed in my belief that Turkey would be peopled with religious zealots screaming for their own Islamic revolution, since most people seemed only too happy with the secular state and access to Western commodities and culture. I was warned by teachers in other faculties, however, to expect the worst of my new students.

These people, I was told, wished to annex Turkey to Iran. They were enemies of the Republic and the only English they would ever need would be the vocabulary required to hijack an aeroplane. Islamic fundamentalism is regarded with distrust and distaste among the middle classes in the big cities in Turkey. Most of my students were from villages in the east, from backgrounds of extreme poverty. For many of them, the only form of education they had known to date was religious instruction: rote learning of the Koran, the life and teachings of the Prophet and some Arabic.

I arrived on the first day to find that the students had voluntarily segregated themselves by sex, the women seated in two silent rows on the furthest side of the classroom. Contrary to the rules of *Yok*, the controversial Higher Education Council established after the coup in 1980 in order to depoliticise the universities, their heads were covered in long silk scarves, and most of them wore thick woollen stockings and calf-length coats buttoned at the neck and wrists.

I rapidly discovered that the Western textbook I was using was not suited to the task in hand. There was no way these people were going to mill around a classroom shaking hands with each other. When one of the male students presented me with a picture of Chris Evert Lloyd on which he had biroed a *carsaf* (the black garment worn by fundamentalist women throughout the Islamic world), I conceded that it was time to forego the trendy TEFL teaching text and work on material which might prove more relevant in the prevailing atmosphere.

Pointing to a picture of Ataturk, founder of the Turkish Republic and official national hero, whose picture must be displayed in all public places, I asked the students what kind of man he had been. My question was greeted by silence and I concluded that this was a taboo subject.

I learnt later that even among devout Muslims there is divided opinion concerning Ataturk and his efforts to Westernise Turkey. Some say that he destroyed Islamic intellectualism and rendered their cultural heritage inaccessible by changing the Turkish alphabet. Others felt that there was no contradiction between Islam and economic and cultural progress. The students were naturally wary of expressing their feelings on such controversial issues since some classrooms retained bullet holes as a result of fights that had broken out before the military coup in 1980.

"I found nothing to argue with in their determination not to be regarded as sex objects"

The majority of the women were serious academics, and some intended to continue their education in other faculties when they had finished their religious studies. They were proud of the emphasis that Islam places on education for men and women, and they didn't feel that Western feminism had much to offer them.

I found nothing to argue with in their determination not to be regarded as sex objects (the reason they gave for covering their bodies in public), nor with a justifiable pride in their academic or artistic achievements. A couple of years after I left the faculty, it was Ilahiyat women who staged the biggest political demonstration since the coup at Istanbul university, when they protested against a ban on covered women in the classroom.

The only aspect of their lives that I couldn't agree with was that the women refused to attend services in the mosque. This was a reaction against feminism in Turkey. By staying away they reaffirmed that the mosque, the traditional forum for political as well as religious debate, was male territory.

I stayed another two years in Turkey after I left my *gecekondu* slum-dwelling and my similarly humble teaching post. I found jobs that required rather less explanation among the leftist and cultural elite, and apartments which required rather less housework.

Most visitors to Turkey opt as I did for a lifestyle which is somewhat more comfortable than that experienced by the majority of Turks. With the possible exception of decent plumbing, all modern conveniences and European commodities are now available in the major resorts and the cities in the west of Turkey. The Turkish people who service and maintain the tourist industry have a better grasp of Western values and behaviour than most of their visitors have of Turkish attitudes.

The people who make money out of tourism may have more time for driving jeeps and drinking Coke than for reading the Koran. The veneer of Western liberalism in Turkey's cities and the process of rapid cosmetic change to which this new generation of Turks is a party, cannot however disguise from them that poverty, year-round physical discomfort, sexual tension and Islamic fundamentalism are the basics of Turkish life for the majority of its population. Most Turks welcome tourism as their most valuable growth industry, but many young people also see tourists as their most valuable allies, as they attempt to improve their country's record on human rights and bring about lasting social change.

Keeping a Political Perspective

· · · · · · · · · · ·

Jane Schwartz, a feminist journalist, first went to Turkey on a package tour. She has since returned to travel independently round the country, including the east (Kurdistan), south and the Black Sea coast.

I fell in love with Turkey the first night I arrived. It was June 1987 and I'd come on a package, because I was scared of being hassled on my own. I found my carefully chosen destination was a basement room on a concrete construction site in Turkish Benidorm.

After an hour's hysterics I walked out behind the bus station into the town and found a whole street of little shops, all selling delicious food – spices, nuts, dried apricots, roasted corn, watermelons, gold-rimmed glasses of tea. Everything was brightly lit at ten o'clock at night; everyone wanted to talk; Turkish families, from grandmothers to small boys, were touring the streets along with visitors from other countries. Everything was totally safe.

I think I guessed then what I'm almost sure of now: that tourism can only be a kind of ribbon development on a country as huge and old as this. There's a row of Benettons along the seafront in Alanya, but there are goats tethered round the back – one for each household's yoghurt supply – and once a week in front of the blank-faced hotels there'll pass a procession of country people going to market, each one more amazingly and differently costumed than the last.

There are tower blocks in Antalya, but there's also a beautiful Old Town where antique ruins crumble alongside nineteenth-century plaster villas. There are wall to wall discos in Bodrum, but there are also pensions where you can eat your own meals in the centre of a silent orange grove. And next to Kusadasi – that Turkish Benidorm – there's Snake Island, and nothing but a little beach hut where a friendly Kurdish owner will grill you fish caught minutes before.

In Turkey there can be soldiers with machine guns in front of the local bank; there's a growing and nastily complacent class who've got rich quick under President Turgut Ozal – Margaret Thatcher's biggest fan. But there is an enormous culture of resistance, which you will meet in cafés and souvenir shops as much as in radical publishers or on the picket lines, which even springs up at the gates of the Topkapi Palace itself.

At the time of writing, this is a country with 30,000 people on strike. Officially inflation runs at 65 percent and unofficially at over 100 percent. In the big cities the squatted *gecekondu* districts have graduated from shanties to whole boroughs with their own water and power, housing more than a quarter of the town's population. When the new entrepreneurs try to bulldoze this prime building space, women are the ones who link arms in front of the bulldozers.

These were all shocks to my expectations. As, too, were the country's beauty; the Muslim tradition of hospitality to outsiders that extends to women as well as men; and an incredible historical generosity that can leave half the Wonders of the World safely unlocked on their hillsides. Each aspect makes Turkey an extraordinary place for me to visit.

That first year I left my package and went off down the coast: after Kusadasi the market town of Soke, then Ephesus with its wonderful museum tracing the temple of Diana through Cybele to the prehistoric mother goddess. (Her costume, as she squats between her leopards to give birth, is just like the traditional trousers that women wear today.) I went on down the Aegean coast to Bodrum, to a little Turkish resort called Ortakent, and then to the start of the Mediterranean at Fethiye. I didn't want to go home.

"Men cooked me food, carried my heaviest bags, gave me presents, showed me the sights"

The next year I came out for three months, to Istanbul, the south coast, then the east (Kurdistan), Ankara and finally the Black Sea. Although I went to many places and met many different kinds of people, the country is over 400,000 miles square, so I feel very humble trying to describe it. I can only say what I saw.

I had heard about Turkey and its beauty from my sister and her friends, who travelled there in the early Seventies. But they had told me, as well, things that were pretty frightening. They described it as the most hellish stop on the road to India – a place where men pinched you black and blue as you walked the city streets in daylight, and where you had to barricade your hotel door against staff at night.

A lot must have happened to Turkish men since the Sixties (and to me – I'm 42 now). Men cooked me food, carried my heaviest bags, gave me presents, showed me the sights. Very seldom did they even ask – and certainly never seemed to expect – anything in return. Quite a contrast with life in other countries. Undoubtedly, I had rarity value because so many Turkish women are still confined to the home, so my good times were linked to their bad times. Life for emancipated Turkish women is extremely difficult. I was told several times that the expensive Taksim district is the only safe place for a single woman, or even several women, to set up house without a man. Single women buy wedding rings to give themselves a sort of protection in their home neighbourhood.

The feminists I met in Istanbul were all exceptional people. Their march against male violence in 1985 was also the very first event anywhere in the country to break the ban on legal demonstrations imposed by the 1980 military coup. Now the feminists aim to set up Turkey's first refuge, combined with a co-op to give training and a livelihood. They recognise that with no social security and few opportunities for working outside the home, leaving a violent man can be as frightening as staying.

"On the coast there's the beginning of a gigolo syndrome as Northern European women sweep through in search of tourist sex"

I loved these feminists' concern to link *all* women – something which seems to inspire the start of every Women's Movement, but gets lost as the activists become professionals. On International Women's Day, the feminists held a fair, with soapboxes for any woman to speak from, and stalls to sell things that they had made. The Turkish feminist publishing house opened their first bookfair stall with no books but a big mirror: they invited every woman who came to "write your life here". Four books later, the publishing house's future is threatened by a new government tax of half a million Turkish lira per month.

Sometimes a rich visitor seems able to reverse the sexual roles in a nasty way. On the coast there's the beginnings of a gigolo syndrome as Northern European women sweep through in search of tourist sex. I met men who'd been picked up and left by German women without another word. The English have a more romantic reputation (and perhaps less money), sometimes marrying Turks or setting up a tourist shop.

"Ordinary" Turkish women were lovely towards me, treating me as an extra daughter or aunt to be invited in for a meal. They were fascinated by the fact that I wasn't married, and by my age – which they'd often underestimate by about twenty years. I think it was helpful to my relations with women that I brought a modest one-piece bathing suit (an old gym leotard) for non-tourist beaches. I also learned to tie a cotton scarf with the ends hanging down in front, to hide the fact that I wasn't wearing a bra. These printed scarves, which cost very little, also make useful headbands. The countrywomen use them for a serious head cover, but it's a measure of Turkey's civilisation that everyone I met was charmed to see them worn by a foreigner, not offended.

The born-again Muslims, whose rise so scares the majority of Turks, would regard the ordinary costume of the country as equally immodest. In the fundamentalist parts of Istanbul and the northeast, women are covered in black from head to ankle – then come nylon tights and stiletto heels, like some S&M fantasy. I noticed that the men got away with Western summer clothes.

I was lucky as a single woman traveller, but you can get pestered in Istanbul and the coastal resorts, especially if you ever take a taxi. I personally never had more than words to worry about, no physical harassment. The east, particularly the fiercely religious northeast, is a weird place for a woman to visit – I was told unsafe by some, quite safe by others. Part of the Turkish racism against Kurds is to give them a sex-mad reputation; but Dervla Murphy has also written that eastern Turkey was the only Muslim country where she got harassed. (She specially resented women trying to get into her bed!)

If you want to look at mosques you'll need trousers or a below-knee skirt, a shirt or jacket with sleeves, a headscarf, and shoes that come off and on easily. I found that sort of costume was convenient and cool most of the time I was travelling, anyway. On the coast, all the visitors wear shorts as so do some Turkish women. For swimming Turkish women wear anything from bikinis to full length whiteshifts, according to the location. The famous tourist beach at Olu Deniz and a few others have topless bathing. Nude bathing – male or female – would cause considerable trouble.

But maybe some of you reading this have bigger problems in mind. For you the unanswered question will be – should we go to Turkey on holiday at all? Kenan Evren, held to be a mass murderer on a level with the Colonels of Greece or Argentina or Chile, is still chief of the military. And during the 1988 "democratic elections", exiled politicians, human rights campaigners and trades union organisers went back home and were arrested as soon as they walked off their planes, in full view of foreign journalists and photographers. From the outside, what does this regime seem to care about world opinion, as long as the pounds, dollars and deutschmarks keep rolling into the seaside resorts?

Well, should we go? The best authority I can think of is the Committee for Defence of Democratic Rights in Turkey, whose English newsletter is crammed with exciting and inspiring as well as horrifying items. This is what they've written:

This year an estimated 400,000 tourists from Britain alone will visit Turkey. Many people, aware of the monstrous violations of human rights in that country, have called for a boycott of holidays.

Our position is based on the views of the victims of the regime – democrats working and struggling in Turkey and those forced into exile. We do not call for a boycott of holidays or visits.

In the darkest days of the junta, from 1980 to 1984, there was some justification for arguing for a boycott of Turkey – just as there is for South Africa today. A boycott was one of the few concrete ways one could protest at a brutal and monolithic fascist state.

However today things are different. There are still torture, political show trials, political prisoners and denial of many rights. But the big difference is the peoples of Turkey are now fighting *increasingly openly* for real democracy. Today the trade unions and human rights bodies need contact with and support from all democratic forces in the world.

A flood of foreign visitors helps to prevent any move to turn Turkey back into a "closed society" where oppression can be conducted on a massive scale unhindered by foreign witnesses and where the population is unaware of new thoughts and outlooks, not to mention world events. The movement of large numbers of people also hinders the regime's attempts to restrict the movement of its own nationals. For Turkey, seeking international respectability and its material benefits, open repression in front of the tourists is not something to make a habit of.

There is one proviso in all this. Foreign visitors to Turkey must be aware of the truth. The tourist enjoying the "sun, sea and smiles" at Bodrum must know that for the millions of Turkish people huddled in shanty towns trying not to starve, holiday is a foreign word.

When tourists go on guided tours or meet people in Turkey they should ask about the human rights situation, and unions. They should express their views on these things so as to leave no doubt in their hosts' minds as to their condemnation of the regime and its crimes . . .

Perhaps this sounds difficult, or joyless, or embarassing. But in Turkey you don't go looking for politics, it comes to you. My own holiday experiences led naturally into "politics". When I visited the Topkapi Palace, I ended up drinking tea with striking printers under the giant plane trees of the courtyard-cum-coachpark. In the south, the owners of a tourist shop took me to visit friends in jail, and I was lucky enough to be able to buy the beautiful bead toys that the prisoners make to support their families. These meetings were as friendly and lively, and as much a part of my trip as bargaining in the bazaar, or taking tea with Turkish families, or chatting with children eager to practise their English.

Not many people are going to tell you their life history in the first five minutes, but at the level of ideas, political conversation in Turkey is amazingly open. My own fears that writing down addresses and contacts might bring trouble on my new friends were waved away.

I'm only a tourist, I didn't share the lives of the people I met. As a visitor I was sheltered, and even fervent

supporters of their government (and ours) would listen politely to my opinions. I won't say I had no nasty experiences – from stomach bugs upwards – and living in Turkey might be much less happy than passing through. But the three months I spent there have made me love the place and the people, and believe they're struggling through to a future where the world will look to them for a lot more than sun, sea and sand.

TRAVEL NOTES

Languages Turkish. Some English is spoken but German is more common.

Transport Most people travel by bus; the service is extensive, efficient and cheap. Trains tend to be slower and cover less ground. Shared minibuses (*dolmuses*) are also available – they cost little more than buses and go to even very remote villages. Hitching is not recommended.

Accommodation All main resorts and cities have plenty of cheap accommodation. Some women carry their own padlocks to secure hotel doors. In the east, you'll be able to find places to stay but the choice is far more limited.

Special Problems Sexual harassment – especially in the east, which can be dangerous for women travelling alone. Anywhere in Turkey it helps to dress reasonably modestly, ie cover your shoulders and don't wear shorts. A recent worrying trend has been the rise in tourist muggings – it's wise to avoid any display of wealth. Also avoid drugs; severe penalties are enforced even for possession of a small amount of cannabis.

Guides *Guide to Aegean Turkey* and *Guide to Eastern Turkey* (Michael Haag) are good on historical background and have a fair amount of practical information and listings. Rosie Ayliffe is currently putting together a *Rough Guide: Turkey* (Harrap Columbus, 1991).

Contacts

Kadin Cevresi Yayincilik (Women's Circle), c/o Handan Koc, Klodfarer Caddesi 41/36, Servet Han Cagaloglu, Istanbul. A group of radical feminists and the main point of contact with other autonomous groups. They have a

publishing house and produce a magazine called *Feminist*. The group welcomes the donation of international feminist literature.

Demkad (Union of Democratic Women), Tiryaki Hasanpasa Caddesi 60, Toprak Han Kat 4, Akseray, Istanbul. Part of the Turkish left and hostile to radical feminism. They work with women in the shanty towns and with the prisoners' support group **Tayad**.

Bilsak (cultural centre), Siraselviler Cad, Sogaci Sok 7, Taksim, Istanbul. Regularly hosts feminist events.

Committee for Defence of Democratic Rights in Turkey (CDDRT), 84 Balls Pond Road, London N1. Publishes the *Turkey Newsletter* which includes news of women's campaigns and demonstrations.

Books

Pembenaz Yorgun, "The Women's Question and Difficulties of Feminism in Turkey", in *Modern Turkey – Development and Crisis* (Ithaca Press, US, 1984).

S Tekeli, *Emergence of the New Feminist Movement in Turkey*, in **D Dahlerup ed.,** *The New Women's Movement* (Beverley Hills: Sage, 1986).

Freya Stark, *Alexander's Path* (1956; Century, 1984). Classic travels in Asia Minor.

Rose Macaulay, *The Towers of Trebizond* (1956; Futura, 1981). Beautiful, quirky novel of camel-travelling and High Anglican angst.

Thanks to Rosie Ayliffe and Jane Schwartz for help with introduction and Travel Notes.

USA

. . . .

Anyone travelling to the USA from Europe will feel a sense of familiarity about the place: all the exposure to American film, TV and culture does form a preparation. However, it's equally likely that, on a first-time visit, this will be accompanied by considerable culture shock. It takes a while to get to grips with a country that is, genuinely, a continent. A continent where extremes of wealth and poverty can be just a couple of blocks apart – and where whole neighbourhoods, even whole towns, are formed by particular and highly diverse ethnic populations.

The hardest place to arrive, by general consent, is New York City, whose pace and hustle (all part of its appeal) can leave you feeling too vulnerable and too small. The West Coast – Washington State, Oregon and California – is perhaps the gentlest place to adapt, with its more relaxed and laid back ethos an enduring (but true) cliché. But this is only to scratch at the edges. The vastness of Middle America, the distinctiveness of the South, the quieter East Coast cities: all make for a staggering variety of travel or living experience.

As far as issues go, it's important – especially if you're travelling coast-to-coast – to get a grip on the strength of regional chauvinism. Each state has its own legislation as well as political affiliations and, between them, attitudes towards women (and God) vary greatly. On sexual issues, the Moral Majority and associated groups like the Pro-Lifers are continuing to strengthen and

extend their base, proving effective as an anti-abortion lobby and in the simmering climate of hysteria over the spread of AIDS, are receiving growing support for their tough line on "sexual deviance". In terms of race, colour discrimination, notorious in the South, remains an enduring fact of life. Black and Hispanic urban ghettos tend to be the poorest, most deprived in the country, and the recent rehabilitation of Native American culture has done little to halt the erosion of Indian territories and lifestyles. Considering the size and number of America's ethnic minorities, integration remains a reality for comparatively few.

Travel, however, presents few problems in itself. So many American women travel from state to state that you won't generally be given a second glance, and only in situations where you really stand out as a tourist is there likely to be persistent trouble from hustlers. In this case the main thing is to look confident, be firm and at least seem to know where you're going. Big cities can sometimes feel unsafe – all have definite no-go areas – and travelling anywhere in urban America it is always wise to avoid carrying more cash than you need for the day.

It clearly depends on the going exchange rate, but the USA does tend to be expensive for foreign visitors. There are many cheap motels, but these can be pretty sparse, not to mention seedy, catering as they do for migrant people at the bottom of the social heap. On the plus side, the American reputation for hospitality is well deserved and even the briefest encounter can lead to offers of floorspace or a bed for the night. Hitching is considered fairly risky, though quite a few women still do it, especially in Oregon and California, and you may have little other option in some rural areas. Otherwise a choice of *Greyhound, Trailway* bus or the alternative *Green Tortoise* will usually get you to whichever town you want. Flights, too, should be considered – there are always a range of special deals available and, by European standards, they can work out surprisingly cheap.

There is a feeling, shared by many women in the US, that the **women's movement** slumbered its way through the dead weight of the Reagan years. While an embattled group of activists tried to tell women that their rights – reproductive freedom, equal pay, the Equal Rights Amendment – were under threat, many American women, feminists and non-feminists alike, experienced the Eighties as an era of private reassessment and reappraisal. It was a defiantly "me-oriented" decade in which activism in any form was unfashionable, and in which personal and independent struggles for success and fulfilment were a priority.

The onset of the 1990s, as Reagan left Washington and his chosen successor, Pro-Life advocate George Bush, came into office, seems to be bringing changes. In April 1989, an estimated 600,000 women, men and children converged on Washington to march for women's rights and reproductive freedom. The immediate inspiration for the march was an impending Supreme Court case which threatened to overturn a woman's constitutional right to have an abortion. The march was an expression of the silent majority finally finding its voice; women who had never before participated in any kind of political activism were marching – mothers, daughters, granddaughters, and men, of all ages – raising their fists and shouting "My body. Not yours".

If the Women's Movement seemed to be in retreat during the Eighties, it may well be that such protest and the participation of thousands of women, young and old, heralds a less introspective, more dynamic new decade.

Just Jump In and Get Cracking
. . . .

Deborah Bosley and Melanie Jones have made several trips to the States, travelling around and occasionally working. Deborah's account concentrates on their experiences of New York and, to a lesser extent, New Orleans.

Perhaps the most maligned and the most adored city in the world, New York is forever on the discussion table. The plethora of information on the city, the media exposure, and stories from friends who have visited, will give you at least a sense of it. Nothing, however, can ever prepare you for arrival.

Reactions vary, so expect every and any: to our minds there are two ways of approaching New York and between us we tried them both. Either, like Melanie, you can remain closeted in your arrival bubble, that haze of defences that is not the result of neurosis but simply the fear of a city whose reputation eclipses the possibility of ever meeting it on neutral ground. Or you can, like me – and I was also scared to death – just jump in and get cracking.

Our experiences, as yours will be, were shaped by circumstances; in a perfect world you would be smack in the middle of Manhattan and able to stay in a roach-free zone in one of the racier neighbourhoods. The outer boroughs may at first seem a more economical option, but commuting back and forth to Manhattan will be a drain on both your time and resources.

Fortunately Americans (even New Yorkers) have a well-earned reputation for extending offers of a place to stay to friends and friends of friends, and we were not about to turn down the promise of a bed in Greenwich Village, even if the offer was third-hand by the time it reached us. An address to head for can make the first few hours in New York infinitely more reassuring. Bearing this in mind, we would definitely recommend that, in the absence of a friend or contact, you book a hotel ahead. Don't just turn up and hope for the best; for women especially this can be a recipe for major headaches and a safe place to stay is vital until you've reached a degree of acclimatisation and are feeling less overwhelmed by the place.

> *"Gay club fiends, though common enough in Manhattan, do nonetheless live in a somewhat self-contained world"*

That said, our own advance arrangements did not make the first few hours in New York any easier. We arrived around midnight to our predestined apartment block only to find a note pinned to the door saying: "Back at 8am – Sorry, Frank". Resigned to a long night, we camped in the lobby, cracked open the duty-free Jack Daniels and decided to ride it out. Bemused apartment dwellers nodded us cautious hellos on their way in and out, and one chap, having walked past us six times or so, heard our story and invited us up to his place to finish the JD in comfort.

We crept back down at the appointed hour and finally met Frank, our host. He was a walking contradiction – at once a man of stifling geniality and, equally, acerbic bitchiness. Only the fortuitous circumstances of immediate shelter; employment (working the stalls in the Soho flea markets of which Frank was a proprietor) and free food (he was also a catering manager at New York University), caused us to pause and reconsider our immediate inclination to get the hell out.

Fifty dollars a day for as long as we liked – we couldn't believe our luck. Not that working, living, eating, sleeping and socialising with Frank wasn't about to test us to our limits. But we believed that his condition, as with many New Yorkers, was symptomatic of where he was and of the survival skills he had acquired in order to exist without being completely discordant from New York's perverse scheme of things.

Our two months with Frank exposed us to a New York we might otherwise have missed and almost certainly steered us away from simpler experiences we might have enjoyed. Gay club fiends, though common enough in Manhattan, do nonetheless live in a somewhat self-contained world. For me this was New York at its best: highly strung, living completely beyond my means and energies and feeling (falsely) secure in the company of strangers who cared little or nothing for my welfare beyond novelty value.

I flourished, using every dexterous social skill at my disposal to charm my way into the circle of New York's terminally trendy and inevitably transient night-time life. One of my more useful acquisitions at the time was a fabulous cliché named Buddy, who was manager of New York's then hot-spot, the Palladium. Like the unfolding of some tacky movie, his character was revealed in all its ungloriousness when he opened the cupboard above his bed and produced a 26 foot python. Too much.

Meanwhile, Melanie was finding the city a little harder to swallow. Ever the realist, she arrived defensive and bristling with indignation at the rudeness and hostility of New Yorkers she had tried and sentenced before arrival. It's hard to take a back seat and feel easy about things in New York unless you're heavily sedated, and for Melanie the experience proved too crushing. Her belief in human sincerity was obscured by too many five-minute friendships: intimacy on contact, and then goodbye. It was all too fast, furious and unfriendly, and she took to adopting a foetal position in the centre of the only air-conditioned room in Frank's smelly apartment for much of the two months.

"Violent crimes against women are high, but your bearing and approach will determine much"

Indeed, New York is weird. Unless you've lived there for years, you can't even really trust your friends. On one particular occasion we were carousing in the Lower East Side's Pyramid Club and could only look on in amazement as Frank removed his shoes and socks and, with both hands full, gently manoeuvred his agile feet to the back pocket of a nearby pair of 501's and from an innocent night creature softly prised a $100 bill with his nimble toes. Not that his altruistic nature didn't surface occasionally; but even the sight of Frank thrusting $20 bills into the outstretched palms of passing tramps did little to redeem him in our eyes.

So, seeking some less hurried, more meaningful social contact, we decided to try out New York's women's scene. At the end of our street was a lesbian bar called The Cubbyhole, which strictly prohibited men. It had been recommended to us several times and we arrived with high hopes. But on arrival we found that even getting through the door was a test. Squeezing past the massive, glaring woman who was guarding the entrance shook our confidence, and it wasn't much better inside.

Rather than finding here a good-humoured, supportive and relaxed environment in which to sit and get ploughed with impunity, we found instead a tense gathering of seemingly competitive women pitched against each other, sitting steadfastly in the groups or couples with whom they had arrived. There was little cross-group chit-chat and banter such as you would expect in a place of this kind. Maybe we went on an off-night, but our experience of other women's bars in New York wasn't dissimilar and we were later to find them diametrically opposed in attitude to their far more relaxed (and to our minds superior) counterparts in California.

But New York is known for its extremes, and again we believed that, all things being symptomatic and circumstantial, fear for one's safety surely plays a part. It's a fact: you do have to watch out. Violent crimes against women are high, but your bearing and approach to New York will determine much. The usual rules apply: never walk alone after dark in unfamiliar places; look people straight in the eye, etc – but don't make too much of an issue of it. "There's nothing to fear but fear itself" is pretty applicable here. It really is no more menacing than other large cities and you should be aware of the confidence-destroying vibes of paranoia. Having said that, go on your hunches; everything happens

so fast in New York that you'll have to assimilate many of your experiences in so few moments that your instinctive reactions will be important.

It won't take much to knock your confidence. I'd been riding high for months in New York, felt I had it sussed and knew how to handle myself. Working in the markets in Soho and on Broadway had opened up contacts and engendered a feeling of belonging until, on the day before I left, I took a subway from Broadway alone. Nothing heavy at four in the afternoon, but across the platform from me stood, or rather staggered, a rangy, thin black boy, staring at me. Behind him was a huge poster giving information about AIDS. Suddenly he screamed across at me: "Suck my dick and die." Of course he was completely smashed, or cracked out of his head, and couldn't get to me because of the track between us, so there was no immediate danger. But the experience was chilling and one that has stuck.

To me this typifies some of the completely unbridled aggression that runs beneath everything in New York. Naturalness seems in short supply in the city. Maybe it's not the fault of the people. The madness which surrounds them is absolutely to blame for the rise of neuroses, which feed neuroses, and so it goes on. So don't let it get to you; put yourself in the driving seat and treat New York as an adventure. Lose yourself for a while, and be somebody else.

South to New Orleans
. . . .

After the mania and motion of New York, New Orleans shocked with its stillness. It's the heat. Nothing can move fast; even when it does, it feels

unhurried. But it has its own kind of intensity, like a Tennessee Williams play. This is the Deep South and you'd have to have been living in a cave not to be aware of the implications of racism, oppression and suffering of this unique part of the Americas.

We flew to New Orleans and were sent, through a room-finding service, to a Bed and Breakfast about ten minutes from the French Quarter. At twenty dollars a night per person, we reckoned it was about the best we could do. It was palatial. Jacob, the owner, was renovating the entire house, room by room, to create a period, mid-1800s colonial feel. An antique dealer by trade, he was letting out several of the rooms to help finance the refurbishment. Our room was high-ceilinged with big roof-to-floor windows on one side of the room – quite the place for losing yourself in a few good books, with the overhead fan creaking above.

Not realising that arriving outside of Mardi Gras in February would make much of a difference, we were shocked to find a slightly depressed, mid-sized American city. Instead of all the joviality and celebrations, we found a tacky assortment of bars and shops in the French Quarter, which, without their seasonal crowds, looked bereft and even a little pathetic. Our only real joy was finding the outlawed absinthe (the stuff that sent Verlaine mad and has been responsible for many unwanted hallucinations) on tap.

"Women, black or white, do not walk the streets alone at night"

Otherwise, the French Quarter didn't conform at all to our expectations. Bourbon Street is a row of sad-looking tourist traps, and the once famous Basin Street is now a concrete freeway. But, to be fair, much of New Orleans is startlingly beautiful. In the better parts of town the houses are grandiose structures with pillared entrances, long driveways, and probably a whole squadron of black staff catering to the whims of the white householders. The implications of such wealth were such that they sullied our enjoyment of the more pleasing parts.

Getting over our initial disappointment, we remained largely neighbourhood bound – about ten minutes by trolley-car from the centre, we preferred more local activities. Across

the street was our second home, a bar called the C-Lounge where we often whiled away the afternoons, writing postcards, chatting to the few lizards at the bar and playing over and over our favourite juke box song, "If The Drinking Don't Kill Me, Her Memory Will". Simple pleasures – for us.

In our month there we didn't once find other women out socialising independently. It struck us that white women socialised from the grandeur of their big houses, and black women slaved in the privacy of their little ones. You can't get away from it: black people in New Orleans are massively oppressed. In the street where we were staying, it was literally a case of big houses occupied by whites on one side and shanty-like dwellings for the blacks on the other. The atmosphere at night was heavy. Women, black or white, do not walk the streets alone at night – for very different reasons, but the result is the same.

And so we attracted much attention, most of it unwanted and all of it incredulous that girls really did this kind of thing. Travelling without men? Incredible! We often wondered if maybe the last fifty years had passed this town by and we were amazed that two states in the same country could differ so vastly.

We became friendly with a black girl from New York who was staying in the same house and commanded our rapt attention with her tales of who said what to her that day and the amount of stick she was receiving for being a black girl daring to go it alone in this town. One night she arrived home in tears after being jostled around on the street corner by a gang of young black men, teasing her for her independence. It all seemed a bit too nightmarish.

I'd also stress that there were occasions when we felt easy in mixed company, though this was only in the tourist-hardened French Quarter, and beyond that we found attitudes a little too strained.

Biking from Coast to Coast

. . . .

After twenty years of factory work, Ann Stirk drew out her life savings and fulfilled a lifelong ambition to tour the land of the pioneers. Her account of driving a motorbike alone, from coast to coast, is aimed as a "story of encouragement to all women bored with their everyday existence".

In July 1986, my kids had flown the nest and were fending adequately for themselves. I was 38 years old and free; time was rushing by with reckless speed and my greatest ambition, to visit the land of the Pilgrim Fathers, had yet to be fulfilled. Come August, my mind was made up to tackle this adventure alone. Against the advice of all my friends I drew out my savings, handed in my notice at work, paid three months' rent on my flat and bought a ticket for New York.

I arrived at John F. Kennedy Airport carrying a holdall complete with tent, sleeping bag and an assortment of clothing, and with my crash helmet hanging over my free arm. Altogether I spent three days in the "Big Apple", sightseeing and purchasing a Honda Rebel 450. The motorcycle was more powerful than any I'd previously owned. It had five gears, overdrive and to comply with US law the lights came on with the ignition. Somehow I managed to avoid the entreaties of salesmen on commission, eager to sell me even larger vehicles. This bike was big enough; my feet firmly touched the ground and I could lift it if it should fall over.

The New Yorkers I came into contact with were obliging and friendly, but I didn't tempt fate by walking in Central Park, down 42nd Street or in alleyways. I stayed at Sloane House YMCA, a mixed hostel on 34th Street, and paid reduced rate with my Youth Hostel card. After spending half my travellers' cheques on the Rebel, I worked out a strict budget which I vowed to stick to before setting off.

"He was typical of the people I met all across the States: hospitable, generous and full of useful advice"

Having roughly planned my route, I set out for Plymouth, Massachusetts. Luck was with me in the shape of a guy named Don from Augusta, Georgia, who I met at the first tollbooth. A lot of highways in the East charge tolls and motorcycles pay the same as cars. Don was on his way to Maine and we rode together to Providence, Rhode Island. He was typical of the people I met all across the States: hospitable, generous and full of useful advice. I came into contact with few of the other kind, who tried to take advantage of me, and found common sense by far my best ally.

I spent my first night ever under canvas in a campsite at Plymouth and viewed the plantation the following day. "Plimoth Village" is a reconstruction of the village of 1627, situated inside a high wooden palisade. The interior of the houses is dark and smoky but alive with characters in period costume pursuing the daily tasks of seventeenth-century people. They even take on the speech, attitudes and manner of the time. It was a stifling hot day and my heart went out to the women in their woollen dresses and many petticoats, and the men in their thick hose, jackets and high leather boots, but nonetheless the place lived up to all my expectations. I truly felt as if I had stepped back in time and was hugely impressed by these efforts to retain the aura of seventeenth-century living.

After Plymouth I paid a brief visit to Niagara Falls, the journey marred by a bee which flew up my sleeve and stung me. In my haste to dislodge it my bike toppled over on the hard shoulder and I thanked my lucky stars that I'd used my own judgement and not been persuaded to buy a heavier machine. Arm throbbing, I viewed the Falls and took the boat ride on the river. A year later, if I close my eyes, I can still hear the deafening roar of water, shot through with a multitude of rainbows, and can almost feel the cold spray splashing my face.

My route then took me south along the shores of Lake Erie to Cleveland where the Rebel was due her first service. I had already covered more than 600 miles. Riding through a poor part of town I was struck heavily in the back. I pulled to a halt to discover that some little kids had thrown a soda pop bottle, hitting my bike and dislodging the elastic strap which was holding my camping gear on the pillion. The strap had walloped me. Were they envious of the new bike, I wondered, or was this a national pastime in poor communities? I spent only the time it took to have the bike serviced and ascertain that the YWCA was full before leaving Cleveland to search for a cheap motel. By the time I had found one darkness had fallen. Still the price of a room – $28 – was too high for my $30 a day budget and I moved on. Eventually I noticed a small daytime YWCA, drove round the back of it and camped on the lawn, making sure I was up and away before anyone arrived in the morning.

I camped most nights. State parks are the best places: with showers, toilets and camping shops, they are clean and cheap, as well as being good places to meet people. At a "Kampground of America" in Arkansas, two bikers on Honda Goldwings sprayed my tent with insect repellent after I'd been repeatedly stung. In return I gave them moisturiser for their sunburnt arms. I breakfasted with a couple in Oklahoma who introduced me to hash browns (fried shredded potatoes) and grits (thick white porridge) in their trailer; and I spent the night adjacent to a Cherokee Indian who elaborated on the Trail of Tears, a true story about the cruel resettlement of several Indian tribes, which had touched me so much at the National Cowboy Hall of Fame in Oklahoma City.

People on the road warned me of possible dangers, such as being surrounded by motorcycle gangs and herded to some lonely spot. They feared for me and commented that my skin wasn't tough enough to withstand extreme weather conditions. I was recommended places to visit and advised to eat in fast-food diners where the food is usually fresh: "Eat where the truckers do. They have the best places sussed out." The Americans I met were generally interested in where I had been and admired my courage.

"After twenty years working in the confines of a noisy factory, the hours spent riding alone across vast spaces gave me a wonderful sense of freedom"

It was some time before I witnessed the violent weather I had been told about. Leaving Albuquerque, New Mexico, to head north, having driven west for many days, I was suddenly frightened by a terrific thunderstorm. My fingers on the clutch tingled from the static as bright streaks of lightning flashed from behind and in front of me. As soon as I could I abandoned the main highway to follow a deserted twisting road that traced the shores of the Rio Grande river. By raising my feet to the petrol tank and putting the bike in first gear I managed to plough shakily through the torrents of red mud and grit that threatened to block my path. It was with a great sigh of relief that I managed to reach that night's destination.

After twenty years working in the confines of a noisy factory, the hours spent riding alone across vast spaces gave me a wonderful sense of freedom and I greatly valued my own company. I took the Rebel high into the Rocky

Mountains, yawning frequently on account of the air's thin quality at 11,000ft. I rode across a grassy saucer-shaped valley which, millions of years ago, had been the crater of a volcano and erupted on a scale ten times that of Mount St Helens. The winding road was quite frightening, with sheer drops into canyons on one side and solid rock walls on the other. Interstate Highway 40 through Arizona is an especially lonely stretch: miles of emptiness and only the distant wind-eroded hills for company. How I loved it. I revelled in the wide open spaces of the Petrified Forest and the Painted Desert, and sat alone on the rim of the Grand Canyon at sunset, at peace with myself.

Bad luck finally struck in Las Vegas, where, suffering from dehydration after crossing miles of arid, stifling desert, I checked into the first motel with a pool. As I lay there, refreshed by a swim and drinking Coke, someone entered my room and stole everything, leaving me stranded 5000 miles from home with nothing but a bikini and a motorbike with no keys.

"Las Vegas must be one of the best places in the world to be destitute"

The cops weren't interested – it takes at least rape or murder to stir them into action. I made a report over the phone, later visiting the police station to pick up a copy of my statement as it is illegal in the States to drive without a licence on you. It wasn't hard to get a replacement set of keys made for the bike, and, three days later, new travellers' cheques arrived and I bought moisturiser for my cracked lips and dried-up face (temperatures reach 120°F in the afternoon). The motel staff were good to me at first, giving me jeans and a shirt, but they wouldn't accept responsibility for my loss and after a week I was thrown out, refusing to pay my bill.

I took refuge in the local Youth Hostel where I was able to work as an assistant until my new passport arrived from the British Consul in Los Angeles. I enjoyed the work, checking in travellers from all over the world, advising them where to eat and suggesting attractions to visit. Las Vegas must be one of the best places in the world to be destitute; if you can prove that you're from out of town, as I could with my English accent and police report, it's not hard to get free or very cheap meals in luxury casino-hotels, as well as the use of facilities. All you need is the nerve to look as if you have a right to be there.

My passport finally arrived and having swapped addresses with my new friends I set off to cross the Sierra Nevada into California. It was far from easy negotiating the high mountain pass. The relentless winds, used to power the army of metal windmills which generate electricity and pump water to the formerly parched terrain, cut through me like a knife, forcing me to ride at a 45-degree angle in order to make any progress at all. By the time I reached Yosemite, to be met by people in ski outfits and dire warnings about impassable mountain roads, I'd caught a bad cold and was forced to lie up for a couple of days. With familiar American kindness the hostel warden dosed me with remedies until I felt well enough to move on.

I only spent a day in San Francisco after crossing the Golden Gate Bridge, for I was impatient to see the ocean and know that I'd achieved my goal. The Youth Hostel I found was in a lighthouse and, that evening, after weeks of observing the sun set behind hills, I was able to watch it silently drop into the magnificent Pacific Ocean. I had made it from coast to coast.

It was now important that I find somewhere under cover to sleep each night. I hadn't replaced the stolen tent and summer was officially over; Youth Hostels were closing down for the winter and I hadn't enough cash to stay in motels.

Chance introduced me to a guy I got chatting to in a coffee shop off the Pacific Coast Highway. He needed temporary help on his secluded ranch in the hills and I accepted his offer of work. I simply kept house, fed the stock and admired the glorious landscape while he conducted business with the various people who called. I never felt threatened, but as my employer spent more and more time away I couldn't shake off the feeling that all was not as it should be.

My instincts were proved right in the early hours of one morning when I was woken by shouts of euphoria coming from downstairs. There I found him with a group of guys celebrating a haul of marijuana which they had just got off a boat from Thailand. Shaking off offers to become involved in future plans, I slipped away, not stopping for gas until I reached Los Angeles.

Here I enjoyed lazy October days on the beach, which was quiet after the exodus of summer visitors, and took in the tourist sights of Hollywood and beyond before selling the Rebel to raise my fare home via New Orleans. By the time I reached cold, damp New York I felt tired but replete. My tour had lasted ten weeks in all, cramming more miles in than many people do in a lifetime. I learned my strengths and my weaknesses. I experienced the exhilaration of the ups and the despair of the lows and most of the feelings in between. Like the lion in *The Wizard of Oz*, I learned courage and I learned it by myself.

New Age Travel
. . . .

After travelling all over the USA and living in San Francisco, Lucy Ackroyd helped to write and research the Oregon chapter of the *Rough Guide: California and the West Coast*.

America definitively isn't the homogenous mass that the media leads us to believe. Reaganite politics, TV soaps and Hollywood glamour are hardly representative of the American lifestyle and nor does most of the population live in New York or Los Angeles. The West Coast is, however, undoubtedly different. Comprised of the most socially progressive of America's 50 states – with Washington on the Canadian border, California neighbouring Mexico and Oregon sandwiched in between – it is perhaps the most hasslefree destination for female travellers in the big, bad US of A.

The little known northwestern states of Oregon and Washington, so often ignored by California sun seekers, offer a physical and spiritual prize for those who deign to visit. New Age philosophy prevails. Caring communities retrace the footsteps of native American Indian forefathers, moving back to the Mother Earth ideology in an attempt to reverse the self-destruction of Planet Earth. Forerunners in concepts such as environmental groups, organic farming, wholefood co-operatives, arts and crafts revival, Waldorf/Steiner schools, alternative medicine and natural homebirth (which, incidentally, is illegal in most states), and being "green", have long been a way of life.

In some respects this can be seen as a natural progression from the "hippy" communes of the Sixties, an era which played a hugely important role in the establishment of the Women's Movement and other sexual/racial equalities. Also, maybe, as a result of the strong matriarchal role women played back in the pioneer days, when a few brave European immigrants trekked across an unknown continent to settle in the West. Even northwest yokels don't seem to suffer from the small town mentality and bigotry so rife in Midwest and Deep South America.

"I found it comforting to meet many women, like myself, travelling alone"

Whilst travelling around the West Coast I stayed mainly in the Youth Hostels conveniently dotted along Highway 1, the scenic coastal route. I was amazed at the high standard of accommodation for such a humble price ($5 to $10 per night). They are certainly a far cry from the institutionalised Girl Guide specimens located in England's green and pleasant land. My favourite one, in Bandon, Oregon, even had a unique 24-hour open door policy and permitted alcohol on the premises – pretty lax laws for a hostel which, contrary to inviting abuse and wild parties, created a very congenial atmosphere and led to its being the most popular hostel in the state. Of course, its added attractions were spectacular scenery, friendly natives and an interestingly eclectic crowd of visitors. Such hostels are ideal if you want to meet someone to travel with, hitch a ride, or offer someone a lift in exchange for gas money. They are also useful places for gaining first-hand information about areas you're planning to visit from people who have just been there. I found it comforting to meet many women, like myself, travelling alone, with whom to swap travel tips and generally boost each other's confidence from the fact of knowing we weren't the only ones doing it.

Although I usually drove a car or hitched, I did meet quite a few women cycling the West Coast, especially in Oregon, where the famed Highway 1 follows the Pacific Coast through giant redwood forests, atop sheerfaced cliffs and along miles of deserted beaches.

It's ideal for cycling as the route is interspersed with small friendly seaside towns and well used campsites – all of which dispel the threat of isolation usually so unavoidable in America's vast expanses.

In my experience, hitchhiking, alone or with another woman, proved to be a safe and reliable method of travel. Despite the obvious degree of risk involved, it's a good means of getting around the problem of almost non-existent public transport in rural areas. Hitching on quiet back roads guaranteed short rides from locals going about their daily business, but the slowness was more than compensated for by the interesting anecdotes told along the way.

One day, covering a distance of only a hundred kilometres from Bandon-By-the-Sea to Eugene, a college town inland over the Oregon Cascade Mountains, I learnt how to hunt brown bear (apparently quite tasty unless it's been eating skunk cabbage); which of the local lighthouses were haunted; the best place to find magic mushrooms, and what kind of educational exchanges the US Rotary Club organises.

Invariably, lifts will be from single men to whom you're an uncanny reminder of their granddaughter/sister-in-law/second-cousin-twice-removed. But over the past three years and countless rides I have never had a bad time.

Another interesting mode of transport I experienced was the *Green Tortoise*, an alternative bus company based in San Francisco which runs regular trips up and down the West Coast from Los Angeles to Seattle, as well as routes all across the US, including to Alaska and Mexico. *Tortoises* began life in the hippy heydays of the early Seventies and basically go where *Greyhounds* fear to tread. Their converted camper-style coaches are ideal if you can't drive yourself off the beaten track, or just if you fancy some company; unlike most public transport, fellow passengers become instant acquaintances or even close friends as you share the cooking and washing up of communal campfire meals. It really is the answer to laid-back stress free travel for solo females and has enabled a much larger cross section of women to satiate their wanderlust. Grandmas and single mothers are not uncommon riders of the *Tortoise*, as children under the age of twelve get discounts.

"I joined a motley crew of mainly San Franciscan residents ... a British born private eye ... another character who taught Tai Chi on a nudist camp in Southern France every summer; a Jewish/Buddhist witch with her daughter Kaili"

My first experience of *Tortoise* travel was a timid fifteen-hour trip from San Francisco to southern Oregon on their regular West Coast route from Los Angeles to Seattle. Leaving the city at 6pm meant we could have a few beers and a chat to fellow passengers before getting a good night's kip whilst we whizzed up the Highway 15 corridor. The buses are surprisingly comfortable and $5 buys a cook-out meal which everyone helps to prepare. We stopped for breakfast by a creek hidden in the hills, where someone had built a sauna, which my braver companions followed with a dip in the icy creek. I busied myself making blueberry pancakes and fresh fruit salad to provide an excuse for not going skinny dipping (well it was November), but thankfully no one seemed to notice and our only punishment was being left to do the washing up.

This gentle introduction to travel by *Tortoise* inspired me to take a longer trip to Baja California at Christmas. It proved to be a perfect way for a single woman to spend the festive season. I joined a motley crew of mainly San Franciscan residents escaping from the hype associated with this stressful time.

They included a British born private eye investigating a nine-million dollar pistachio swindle; another character who taught Tai Chi on a nudist camp in Southern France every summer; a Jewish/Buddhist witch with her daughter Kaili (which has nothing to do with Australian soap but means "Ocean Spray" in Hawaiian, as she was born on a beach in Maui); and the infamous Mr Tortoise (aka Gardner Kent), who, needless to say, was quite a character and described himself as a cross between Fred Flintstone and Yogi (smarter than the average) Bear. Christmas came and went in a whirl of windsurfing, snorkelling, clam digging, sunbathing and campfire singing, topped off by an all night Marguerita party. It definitely beat turkey, Xmas pud and a re-run of *The Sound of Music*.

Being homebase for the *Green Tortoise* – and perhaps America's most beautiful major metropolis – are perhaps reasons enough to visit the Golden Gate city of San Francisco. However, its main attraction, for me at any rate, lies not in its physical location, atop seven rolling hills overlooking the Pacific Ocean, but in its cosmopolitan and carefree attitude. I had first visited "Baghdad-by-the-Bay" during a 10,000 mile whirlwind tour of the States, travelling with some friends in a Chevy and Jack Kerouac in my bag, and immediately fell in love with this birthplace of Beat, to which I promised to return as soon as possible. My second visit was a much lengthier affair and as I got to know the city more intimately I discovered many more tangible charms.

The prevailing charm of San Francisco is undoubtedly its laid back, *laissez faire* lifestyle, which allows for racial and sexual harmony to exist in a way no other city has managed to achieve. Undeniably the gay capital of the world, it has matured from the wildly homosexual "sin city" of the early Seventies to a calmly progressive place where all sexuality is accepted.

The current gay scene in San Francisco is such that there are very few strictly men/women only bars and clubs and most welcome anyone of either sex and sexuality. The atmosphere is far more relaxed than the equivalent in, say, London. Perhaps because of this liberal atmosphere, and the high percentage of gay men, San Francisco must be one of the safest cities in the world for women. I really enjoyed the freedom of going out alone at night without male hassle. Previously prohibited pastimes, such as going down to the local bar for a few beers and a game of pool, or to a favourite disco for a good boogie (alone), are just two examples of evening entertainment which men don't have to think twice about and which, in San Francisco, neither did I.

Of course San Francisco isn't a paradise and there are certain areas, as with all big cities, where extra care must be taken, such as the Tenderloin and parts of Mission. But when living in both of these so-called unsavoury districts I never experienced any danger. After finishing work around midnight I often went out dancing with friends to unwind and walked home alone in the early hours without suffering anything worse than a cut foot when I once took my shoes off. Maybe I was lucky but my advice is to heed warnings, but don't take middle-class American opinions as gospel because many tend to overdramatise possible threats to their somewhat cocooned lifestyles. Few will contemplate eating un-prepackaged vegetables, never mind venturing into neighbourhoods like Mission, where Spanish is the leading language and fast-food joints sell *burritos* instead of Big Macs.

Indeed, Mission bears more resemblance to South than North America and is a treat not to be missed, despite the annoying manifestations of Latin *machismo* culture – though these usually amount to nothing worse than verbal abuse about being blond. Although the quarter is as fascinating as Chinatown, the largest Chinese community outside of Asia, or North Beach, the authentically Italian sector, Mission remains well off the tourist track, a fact reflected in the neighbourhood's down-to-earth attitudes and prices. For some reason it's also the sunniest part of town, making the parks full of palm trees as well as people and creating a site for the city's only open-air swimming pool.

Running parallel to Mission is the city's main feminist area of Valencia Street, full of excellent bookshops and cafés. A place I found very useful was the Women's Needs Center, which provides free healthcare and contraceptive advice, charging only the cost price of any medicine prescribed and asking for donations from those who can afford it. This kind of health centre, cheap and friendly, is unusual in the USA, where astronomic medical costs can make going to the doctor a frightening experience. Medical insurance is now compulsory for visitors and residents alike and although expensive it's worth making sure you get comprehensive cover.

Part of San Francisco's magic is that these particular concentrations of ethnic or sexual minorities has not led to a ghetto situation or any noticeable neighbourhood friction as is the case in so many other inner cities.

The city is also a good example of American openness – which can come as quite a surprise to visitors conditioned by the stiff upper lip mentality and insular coldness which pervades parts of Europe. Americans seem to like a great deal of social interaction and it often made my day to be greeted on the street by total strangers. A friendly "Hi, how ya doin?", said in passing, is not a chat-up or come-on line and should be classed in the same category as "Have a nice day" – which, despite its crass reputation, is usually said with sincerity. Unlike the anonymity of large European cities, striking up conversations with strangers on a bus, in a store or at a bar is not uncommon. And although the male chauvinistic slimeball is far from extinct, don't be too quick to assume a defensive stance or refuse the invariably genuine and often very generous American hospitality.

TRAVEL NOTES

Language English – but there's a significant first-generation immigrant population who don't necessarily speak it. This is particularly true of the Spanish-speaking Americans in California, New Mexico and New York.

Accommodation Generally cheaper than Britain though beware of seedy, budget-price hotels in "unsafe" parts of of town. New York and other major cities have a few women-only hotels. Across the country, Youth Hostels, which don't usually require membership, are a good bet. There's also a well-organised network of campsites.

Transport *Greyhound* and *Trailway* buses cover all major destinations; the alternative *Green Tortoise* is more limited, but efficient, fun and a great way of meeting people. Internal flights and car hire are relatively cheap. Hitching, though recommended on the West Coast by Lucy Ackroyd, is reputedly dodgy for both sexes.

Special Problems The cost and bureaucracy of US healthcare is horrific. You must take out medical insurance and if there's any chance you may need gynaecological care, be sure to double-check your policy. Some don't cover it and it's very expensive (as are contraceptive pills).

Guides The *Rough Guides* to New York and California and the West Coast (both Harrap Columbus) are invaluable as ever – both Deborah Bosley and Lucy Ackroyd were involved in research on the latter. For travelling coast-to-coast, *Let's Go USA* (Pan) is dependable.

Contacts

Two important resources:

The Index/Directory of Women's Media (published by the Women's Institute for Freedom of the Press, 3306 Ross Place, NW Washington DC 20008, ☎202 966 7783). Lists women's periodicals, presses and publishers, bookshops, theatre groups, film and music groups, women's news services, writers' groups, media organisations, women's radio, special library collections, and more. Invaluable and updated yearly.

The National Organisation for Women, 15 W. 18th St., 9th Floor, New York 10011 and 425 13th St., NW Washington DC 20004. With groups all over the country, this is a good organisation to get referrals for specific concerns: rape crisis centres and counselling services, feminist bookshops and lesbian bars.

The select listings below comprises mainly **feminist bookshops**, which are nearly always a good source of other local contacts/activities.

ALASKA: **Alaska Women's Bookstore**, 2440 East Tudor Rd., No. 304, Anchorage 99507. Also a resource centre and music store.

ARIZONA: **Women's Place Bookstore**, Dept U, 2401, N 32nd Street, Phoenix, Arizona 85008.

LOS ANGELES: **Sisterhood Bookstore**, 1351 Westwood Blvd. Bookshop and resource centre. **Lesbian Political Action Center**, 1428 Fuller Avenue, Hollywood 90046, ☎874 8312. **A Different Light Bookstore**, 4014 Santa Monica Blvd., Hollywood 90029, ☎668 0629. Lesbian and gay books.

OAKLAND: **Mama Bears**, 6536 Telegraph Avenue. Bookshop, coffeehouse and arts and crafts gallery. **A Woman's Place**, 4015 Broadway. Women's art and bookshop.

SACRAMENTO: **Lioness Books**, 2224 J. St. Feminist and children's books.

SAN DIEGO: **Center for Women's Studies and Services**, 908 E. St. Centre for studies, women's health and therapy services, advice and information; organises educational and cultural activities like free feminist university.

SAN FRANCISCO: **Women's Needs Center**, 1825 Haight St., ☎221 7371. Provides free healthcare and contraception advice, charging only the cost price of any medicine prescribed and asking for donations from those who can afford it. **Old Wives' Tales**, 1009 Valencia St. Feminist, lesbian, Third World books.

SAN JOSE: **Sisterspirit**, 1040 Park Avenue. Non-profit women's bookshop and coffeehouse featuring live entertainment every other week.

FLORIDA: **Pagoda's Women's Space**, Coastal Highway, St Augustine 32084, ☎829 2970. Holiday centre for women; plus **Ellies Nest**, (women's guesthouse) 1414 Newton St., Key West, ☎296 5757.

CHICAGO: **North-Western University Women's Center**, 619 Emerson, Evanston 60201, ☎492 3146. Information about local women's groups. **Jane Addam's Bookstore**, 5 South Wabbash, Room 1508, ☎782 9798.

DETROIT: **Women's Liberation News and Letter** (branches throughout US), 2832 East Grand Blvd., Room 316, MI 43211. **Herself Bookstore** – recently moved, for address call information Detroit.

MINNEAPOLIS: **Amazon Bookstore Inc.**, 2607 Hennepin Avenue South, ☎374 5507. List of rooms, apartments, housing and other interests available. **A Women's Coffee House**, 1 Groveland, nr Franklin.

NEW MEXICO: **Full Circle Books**, 2205 Silver S.E. Albuquerque. New Mexico's only feminist bookshop.

NEW YORK: **Barnard College Women's Center**, 117th Broadway, ☎212 280 2067. Clearinghouse for information on women's organisations, studies, conferences etc. **Womanbooks**, 210 W.92nd St., ☎873 4121. Bookshop, record shop and community centre run by women and stocking a wide range of feminist and lesbian titles; pick up the city's monthly feminist paper, *Womanews*. **Qui Travel**, 165 W.74th St., ☎496 5110. Women's/gay travel agent. **The Saint Mark's Women's Health Collective**, 9 Second Avenue, ☎228 7482. One of the foundations of the New York women's community, offering traditional and alternative medicine at sliding-scale prices.

OREGON: **A Woman's Place**, 1431 NE Broadway, Portland 97232. Resource centre and bookshop carrying over 10,000 titles, plus art, jewellery, music etc.

PENNSYLVANIA: **Women's Center**, 616 North Highland Avenue, Pittsburgh 15206, ☎212-661 6066.

TEXAS: **Book Woman**, 324 E. Sixth St., Austin 78701. Feminist books, records and posters.

WASHINGTON: **Lammas Women's Bookstore**, 321 7th St. SE, ☎546 7299; and 1426 21st St. NW. Bookshop and information centre, with two branches. **Bethune Museum and Archives National Historic Site**, 1318 Vermont Ave. NW. Archive of educational resources on black women and organisations.

WISCONSIN: **A Room of One's Own**, 317 West Johnson St., Madison 53703. Bookshop.

Feminist magazines include:
New York: *Womanews, New Directions, Quest.*
Washington: *Off Our Backs.*
Boston: *Sojourner.*
San Francisco: *Plexus.*
Nationwide (and almost mainstream): *Ms.*

Books

Starting with non-fiction, this is inevitably more an idiosyncratic dip into the pile than any sort of "representative sample".

Maya Angelou, *I Know Why the Caged Bird Sings* (Virago, 1984). First and arguably the best volume of this ongoing (five volumes so far) autobiography by one of America's most extraordinary multi-talented black women writers.

Djuna Barnes, *Djuna Barnes' New York* (Virago, 1990). Collection of essays by a legendary literary figure of the Twenties and Thirties.

Angela Davis, *Women, Culture and Politics* (The Women's Press, 1990). New collection of essays by one of America's leading black activists. Davis's **An Autobiography** (1975; reissued by The Women's Press, 1990, with a new introduction) is also fascinating.

Betty Friedan, *"It Changed My Life"* (Norton, US, 1986). Collection of influential writings, and now historic speeches, that provides a first-hand account of the development and continuing impact of the American Women's Movement.

Zora Neale Hurston, *Dust Tracks on a Road* (Virago, 1989). Reissued autobiography of one of America's most prolific black women writers, folklorists and critics; Hurston is an acknowledged inspiration to most black American women writing today.

Joyce Johnson, *Minor Characters* (Picador, 1983). Gripping memoir of a life as part of the wild 1950s Beat generation growing up in the world of jazz, poetry and black-stockinged New York Bohemia.

June Jordan, *Moving Towards Home* (Virago, 1989). Powerful political essays by yet another multi-talented black American woman activist and writer.

Cherie Moraga and Gloria Anzaldua, eds., *This Bridge Called My Back: Writings by*

Radical Women of Color (Kitchen Table: Women of Color Press, 1983). Includes prose, poetry, personal narrative and analysis by Afro American, Asian, American, Latina and Native American Women.

Adrienne Rich, *On Lies, Secrets and Silence – Selected Prose 1966-78* (Virago, 1980). Feminist and lesbian essays, speeches and reviews.

Lillian Schlissel, *Women's Diaries of the Westward Journey* (Schlocken Books, US, 1982). Women's experiences of migrating West in the middle of the last century.

Gloria Steinem, *Outrageous Acts and Everyday Rebellions* (1983, Flamingo 1985). Illuminating journalist/feminist writings of 1960s and 1970s.

Fiction

Toni Cade Bambara, *The Salt Eaters* (1960; The Women's Press, 1982). This brilliant novel by one of America's leading black women writers, is followed by the collection of short stories, *Gorilla, My Love* (The Women's Press, 1984). Bambara writes in a wonderful, racy style, described as "reading like jazz".

Maud Farrell, *Skid* (The Women's Press, 1990). Thriller set among the lesbian dives of New York.

Maxine Hong Kingston, *The Woman Warrior* (Picador, 1981). A beautifully crafted book unravelling the Chinese cultural traditions and myths that helped form Kingston's identity as a first generation Chinese American.

Audre Lorde, *Zami* (Sheba, 1984). Powerful evocation of what it's like to be black and lesbian in a white heterosexual society.

Alison Lurie, *The Nowhere City* (Abacus). Centring on the breakdown of a couple's marriage on moving West for the husband's work, this novel paints an astute, often funny, picture of Los Angeles in the Sixties.

Toni Morrison, *Beloved* (Picador, 1987). Pulitzer prize winning novel centred on the tragedy of slavery. *Song of Solomon* (1970, Triad/Granada, 1982). Complex, beautifully told fable set in the deep south of America. Also recommended is her first novel, *The Bluest Eye* (Triad/Granada, 1981), which chronicles the tragic lives of a poor black family in Ohio through the eyes of a young girl.

Tillie Olsen, *Tell Me a Riddle* (1960; Virago, 1983); *Yonnondio* (1974; Virago, 1980). The first is a collection of four short stories exploring some of the "pain and promise of fundamental American experience"; the second, her only novel, tells the story of a working-class family struggling to better their lives in the Midwest during the Depression.

Marge Piercy, *Braided Lives* (Penguin, 1984). Semi-autobiographical novel covering the youth, adolescence and "college days" of a girl seeking to escape working-class Detroit and the repressions of the McCarthy era. Other Marge Piercy novels include *Vida* (The Women's Press, 1980), the tale of a political activist forced underground in the Sixties, and, most recently, *Gone to Soldiers* (Penguin, 1987), an epic panorama spanning the lives of women and men caught up in a world at war.

Ntozake Shange, *Sassafrass, Cypress and Indigo* (Methuen, 1984). Story of three sisters by author of the great play *For Colored girls who Considered Suicide when the Rainbow is Enuf*.

Mona Simpson, *Anywhere But Here* (Abacus, 1988). Bizarre and unforgettable saga of a young girl and her ambitious mother as they pursue LA stardom for their daughter.

Betty Smith, *A Tree Grows in Brooklyn* (Pan, 1989). Classic tale set in pre-war Brooklyn of a courageous Irish girl making good.

Amy Tan, *The Joy Luck Club* (Heinemann, 1989). Best-selling novel based on a Chinese American woman's experience of growing up in San Francisco.

Alice Walker, *The Color Purple* (The Women's Press, 1983). Engrossing, deservedly prize-winning novel about two sisters growing up in the Deep South between the wars. Walker's other works include two volumes of short stories and three novels. The latest, *The Temple of My Familiar* (The Women's Press, 1989), is described by the author as "a romance of the last 500,000 years".

Other women writers to look out for include **Joan Didion, Louise Erdrich, Rosa Guy, Tama Janowitz, Paule Marshall, Grace Paley** and **Anne Tyler**. Finally, crime fiction fans must read the novels of **Sarah Paretsky** (published by Penguin), set in Chicago and featuring the indomitable female private detective, V.I. Warshawski.

Vietnam

Fifteen years on from the Communist victory, Vietnam has had little chance to recover from the ravages of war. Immediately after unification, the US imposed an economic blockade which, to their lasting shame, was joined by all other Western nations in 1979. In consequence, this, the country that receives the world's least development aid, is one of the world's poorest. Over the last five years, the well-publicised "Boat People" emigrants have left in a constant, desperate stream, while, at home, the legacies of the war are still everywhere to be seen.

Most Vietnamese refer to the years of fighting, which wrecked so many lives, as the "American War", fuelled as it was by the American government's determination to ward off any southward extension of Communist influence from North Vietnam. In the ten years of fighting up to 1975 over six million tons of bombs and 370,000 tons of napalm were dropped by the Americans (and their Australian allies) on Vietnam; 9000 villages were destroyed and much land is still unusable owing to long-term pollution, craters and unexploded bombs. Close on two million Vietnamese (and 56,000 Americans) lost their lives. Today, women still suffer miscarriages and the tragedy of children born with disabilities as a direct result of chemical warfare.

Despite its bleak economic situation, and painful history, Vietnam is emerging as a destination for tourists. The government, in dire need of international aid and recognition, has liberalised its economic and foreign policies and now welcomes foreign visitors, including Americans. Previously, visitors were pretty much limited to the old Eastern bloc countries. However, independent travellers remain officially frowned upon and, unless you can afford the luxury of hiring your own interpreter and driver, you'll probably have to explore the country from the basis of a group tour. This can still be rewarding, and, as visas become easier to obtain, the opportunities for individual travel are likely to open up. Wherever you go, people will usually be eager to meet you and tell their stories, sometimes in the hope of a passport to the West. Be prepared for an often gruelling experience, but don't be put off. Vietnam is a fascinating country where, as a foreign woman, you'll be more of a curiosity than a target for harassment.

Vietnamese **women**, known as the long-haired army, were active as soldiers in both the Vietnam War and the battle against French occupation which preceded it. In fact their history as warriors goes back to pre-colonial times. But only since 1975 has their status improved and their achievements been fully recognised. Largely through the efforts of the *Women's Union*, the immediate years after reunification saw great progress in work and education opportunities, better healthcare and general women's rights. As the official national women's association, the Union (formed in 1930 and now with ten million members) continues to organise at all levels, from supporting village co-operatives to advising the Prime Minister on new policies for implementing women's rights. But like everything in Vietnam, theirs is a hard struggle. Women undoubtedly bore the brunt of the last war, both in terms of poverty, bereavement, and the hereditary physical effects of dioxin and Agent Orange, described below, and until the whole situation of the country improves there is small hope of even their basic needs being met.

A War That Can't Be Forgotten

. . . .

Sarah Furse went to Vietnam en route from Britain to Australia. It was a brief visit at a time when tourists were only granted short-stay visas for an organised tour. As a result of a meeting with the Women's Union of Ho Chi Minh City, on arrival in Australia she and two travelling companions raised several thousand dollars towards funding a gynaecological research centre for the treatment of women and children still affected by the deadly chemicals used in the Vietnam War.

Day 1: 6.30am. Toula and I are sipping weak coffee and chewing on rubbery omelettes in the coffee shop of our downmarket hotel in Bangkok. We are interrupted: the Diethelm minibus is here to whisk us away to the airport en route for Ho Chi Minh City. We trundle off through the already bustling streets of Bangkok, picking up the four other members of our tour – two German bank clerks, a Scottish farmer and an Australian psychologist – from their decidedly more upmarket hotels, and check each other out for potential camaraderie over the next week.

Two hours later, the ravaged defoliated land west of Ho Chi Minh City is a shocking sight. Alongside the runway the wrecks of military planes sit like rusting cadavers. Customs clearance takes an eternity, with umpteen forms to fill out detailing personal "luxury" effects, the purpose of the visit, etc.

Eventually we are ushered through to the exit area, to be met by our guide, Hinh, a beaming smile lighting up her face. She makes the customary welcome speech in perfect English, which she delivers to every group of Western tourists who arrive here at reasonably regular intervals. We clamber into a minibus and head off into the heart of the city (still known as Saigon), to the Doc Lap Hotel, our home for the next week.

> *"We emerge from the hotel to be immediately surrounded by a mob of children, tugging at our sleeves, calling us 'Mama, Mama'"*

First impressions are of an exhausted, dilapidated city: peeling paintwork on the facades of French colonial buildings; rusty iron gates and railings; rising damp; and thousands of Vietnamese in conical hats, riding all manner of bicycles – two-wheelers, three-wheelers, four-wheelers (with incredibly large loads precariously balanced) and *cyclos* (bicycle taxis). Everyone looks in a hurry to get somewhere.

On the sidewalks French *baguettes* are sold and bicycles are being mended: nearly everything happens on the dusty, cracked pavements of this city. Faded billboards advertise movies and political propaganda. Old women and men, dressed in the customary baggy black trousers, squat down, talking, thinking, chewing betel nuts and absent-mindedly brushing flies from their faces.

We arrive at the Doc Lap, are given room keys and instructions to meet for lunch in the "Rooftop Restaurant". Then we head off upwards in the rickety lift. A brass plaque showing the floor numbers indicates that the Australian Embassy was once lodged on our floor. After a brief glance from our tiny balcony, over the rooftops of Saigon, Toula and I are eager to step out and wander the streets for an hour or two.

Clutching our map of Ho Chi Minh City, written in Vietnamese, we emerge from the hotel to be immediately surrounded by a mob of children, tugging at our sleeves, calling us "Mama, Mama", and talking ten to the dozen in broken English about fathers in Australia and the United States. Many of these children are Amer-Asian or Austro-Asian street kids. Unwanted and undisciplined, they eke out a living by begging tourists for cigarettes to sell on the black market, and soap, towels, shampoo, disinfectant or pens to trade with. They are eager to show us their city, to tell us their stories and to receive affection and attention from us.

The traces of war are so visible in their faces looking intensely up at us. A little boy, Deng, whose father was a black GI, laughs nervously but does not come as close as the others. Later we learn that he sees himself as "bad, unclean, no good", because he is black. Racism is prevalent, even here. Feeling distraught by this, our first encounter with the children of Vietnam whose lives have been totally shaped by being born out of war, we quickly retreat to the hotel.

Half an hour later we re-emerge. This time there are fewer children and some of them have brought along "souvenirs" for us, carefully wrapped, with little notes of friendship written in shaky English. Nguyen has given me a beautiful black lacquerware vase with a goldfish on it; Thi, a gaudy plaster cat and dog ornament. They slip thin arms through our own rather fleshy ones, and take us for a walk around Saigon, telling us to look after our bags because "bad people will steal". A woman pedals up and asks if we speak French. I say "yes" and she proceeds to tell me that her fifteen-year-old son's father is called Harry Miller and lives in California. She wants to send her son over to him. Can I help? I can't and she pedals resignedly off into the crowded street.

Now the sun is setting and it is time for us to eat and retire, so we say our farewells and go back to exchange experiences with the others over a sumptuous Vietnamese dinner. There is a Russian circus staying in the Doc Lap, and on several occasions in the lift we are spoken to in Russian. I dredge up what little I can remember from my school studies fifteen years ago, to tell them that my mother is Russian but I don't speak or understand the language very well.

"A wave of nausea suddenly takes over, leaving me weeping inwardly at the horrors and perversions of this war"

Day 2: In the morning we visit the enormous, ugly Imperial Palace which once housed the South Vietnamese Government. It is now a museum and the venue for occasional Party conferences. It feels eerie to stand on the rooftop where the helicopters landed to fly the generals, ministers and other top officials off to safety at the fall of Saigon in 1975.

Then on to the Imperial War Museum. Outside it, a large group of "Young Pioneers", proudly wearing red kerchiefs and reminiscent of Boy Scouts, clamber over each other in their eagerness to be photographed next to an old tank. Inside the museum the history of Vietnam's occupation by the Chinese for a thousand years, and more recently by the French, Portuguese and Americans, is vividly displayed in blurred and dog-eared photographs with accompanying texts written in Russian, Vietnamese and English.

A display of guns, bomb shells and the containers used for spraying Agent Orange and other chemicals stands close to the grotesque guillotine which was used by the French right up until 1960. Paintings depict various methods of torture used on suspected revolutionaries. There are photographs of babies horrifically affected by Agent Orange, and a distorted foetus in a jar. An American anti-war pamphlet shows a group of GIs grinning at the camera, surrounded by the dismembered bodies and heads of captured Vietcong guerillas, the caption reading something like: "This is what they don't tell you about the war. You can come and try just to survive and get home in one piece. Or you can come and be turned into a psychopath like the GIs in this photo. They will fuck you over, whatever you do."

A wave of nausea suddenly takes over, leaving me weeping inwardly at the horrors and perversions of this war. We leave the museum emotionally drained and return to the Doc Lap for a subdued two hours at the hotel. Afterwards we are taken across town to a lacquerware factory, an industry which has survived in Vietnam since the fifteenth century. But my mind is still full of what I have just seen – images that will haunt me forever – and I can't take anything in.

In the evening we wander out to buy some books and walk by the river. An Amer-Asian boy of about thirteen, his emaciated spine bent over and twisted so badly that he can only crawl on his hands and feet, follows us, begging for cigarettes. I give him my packets and feel anger and sorrow mounting as I see yet another victim of Agent Orange struggling to survive.

Day 3: Up early, and off in the minibus through the crowded streets where syringes are sold openly to the city's thousands of heroin addicts, and out into the lush green countryside towards My Tho on the banks of the Mekong River delta. Water buffalo, harnessed to antiquated wooden ploughs, plod through the rice paddy fields that flash by the windows of the bus. Lorries pump noxious black diesel smoke from their exhaust pipes; old buses carry a hundred bicycles on top, a hundred passengers inside; neat oblongs of rice line the side of the road, drying in the humid sunshine.

At My Tho we board a tiny boat and are ferried downriver at high speed, to an island bursting with palm trees, grapefruit, coconuts and bananas. Here it is extremely fertile, indicating how the whole of South Vietnam must have looked before wartime defoliation. The islanders make a very good living from fishing, and from farming tropical fruit and vegetables in carefully irrigated jungle.

"The Vietnamese are ingenious at turning abandoned articles of war into useful tools of peace and productivity"

On the way back to My Tho we see a half-sunken US Navy battleship which has been turned into home for scores of Vietnamese people, their huts clinging precariously to the hull of this floating war memorial. The Vietnamese are ingenious at turning abandoned articles of war into useful tools of peace and productivity. GIs' helmets are used as wash basins and watering cans; bomb shells are hammered out and melted down for use in light industry on the communes; brightly coloured plastic electrical wire is woven into beautiful padded teacosies – it seems nothing is wasted.

On the way back to Ho Chi Minh City we stop at a Buddhist monastery to hear about the many monks and nuns who performed public self-immolation in protest at the war. In the evening, Hinh takes us to have dinner at *La Bibliothèque de Madame Dai*, an exclusive restaurant lodged in the former library and law office of Suzanne Dai. A former senator in the South Vietnamese government, she now runs evening classes for illiterate women and children, as well as making visitors to her establishment aware of her love of Vietnam (despite her disa-

greement with Communism) and the needs of her people.

Day 4: Today we are going to Vung Tau, a fishing village and beach resort some two hours' drive from Saigon. On the way we pass an area of scrubland where one of the biggest US Army bases now stands empty and useless on a bleak hillside. Vung Tau itself feels like any seaside town, with its souvenir shops and cafés along the promenade, women mending reams of fishing nets and the ubiquitous Soviet tourists sporting straw hats and sunburn. The Vietnamese are drilling for oil in the South China Sea, with the aid of Russian and Norwegian experts, and a big refining plant – Sovietpetro – sits prominently at the entrance to the village.

After lunch, it's on with the bathers and off to the beach, at one end of which, on top of a high hill, stands an enormous statue of Jesus on the cross, arms outstretched to the heavens. Despite Communism, the Vietnamese are still very religious: sixty percent are Buddhist, twenty percent Catholic, and the rest hold an assortment of beliefs. All seem to be free enough to practise their varying beliefs unhindered.

In the evening, Toula, Di (the psychologist we have befriended on our tour) and I head off for coffee on the promenade and end up having a fascinating, largely mime-based discussion about politics with a group of young Russian sailors.

The next morning, armed with paracetamol to temper our diabolical hangovers from one too many Vietnamese brandies, we are taken up a steep rocky track to the old lighthouse, to look out over a spectacular view and to see the remains of what was the largest Australian base in Vietnam.

Day 6: Another trip out of the city, this time westwards to the barren defoliated area around Cu Chi, centre of the extraordinary 300-km network of underground tunnels, built and maintained by the Vietcong despite numerous attempts to destroy them. Many children were born underground. Running beneath villages and even American army bases, these tunnels contained rest areas, kitchens, arms caches, booby traps and latrines.

They measured only 60 x 40cm in the connecting sections; Toula and I crawl through a 50m stretch, slightly enlarged to cope with the size of Western tourists. It is a frightening experience: the guide's torch goes out; it is overwhelmingly hot and claustrophobic, with huge cockroaches, rats and mosquitoes clambering up the walls that we can't see, can only feel. It gives us some idea of what it must have been like to spend weeks, even months underground, and we emerge gasping for air and water. We are then introduced to a woman whose husband had been stabbed to death and disembowelled because he was a Vietcong guerilla and who herself had helped build a section of the tunnel during the war.

In the afternoon we go to Bamboo Shoot 1 Orphanage, where the children learn skills such as weaving, carpentry, embroidery and dressmaking to help them obtain jobs when they leave. They seem to be well cared for and loved, but there is so much more that they need: simple things that we in the West take for granted such as pens, notebooks, milk powder, medicines, shoes, cotton thread, books, etc. How will those needs ever be met in a country that is struggling so hard with a besieged economy and enormous social problems? There is a policy not to send Vietnamese children for adoption outside Vietnam any more. It is very hard to suppress idiotic desires to take half a dozen of them home with me!

Day 7: Today is the big day for Di, Toula and myself. We have written a letter to the Womens' Association of Ho Chi Minh City, asking to meet with them to exchange information about women in Vietnam and women in Australia and England. Our request has been granted, and we leave the men in our group to amuse themselves while we spend a fascinating and very productive afternoon hearing all about life for women in Vietnam since 1975.

"It is estimated that women exposed to dioxin ... have six times more chromosome breaks than survivors of Hiroshima"

The Women's Association comprises women from all walks of life and is dedicated to fighting for women's rights in all areas and at all levels. Though linked to the government Medical Health Department, it remains an independent, self-funded body. Its work includes running rehabilitation programmes for drug addicts and prostitutes; classes for illiterate women and children; medical centres for women and children; creches, orphanages and kindergartens.

One of its greatest needs is the means to try and combat the terrible long-term effects on women and children of Agent Orange. The wartime spraying of this deadly chemical has caused – among other things – a variety of congenital cancers, miscarriages, and babies born with severe mental and physical disabilities resulting in limblessness, severe cleft palate, lack of spine, kidneys, and tear ducts. There have also been cases of women going through a seemingly normal pregnancy only to give birth to their own cancerous reproductive systems and it is estimated that women exposed to dioxin (a highly toxic component of Agent Orange) have six times more chromosome breaks than survivors of Hiroshima.

The Women's Association asked us to try and help them to set up a Gynaecological Research Centre in Ho Chi Minh City to research these affects and attempt to find solutions to a huge problem that does not end simply because the war is over. So we decide to take up their request and set up

"Orange Action", with the aim of raising at least some of the US$100,000 they need.

We left Vietnam on the eighth day, our minds full to bursting with experiences, images, ideas and emotions. More than anything, we left determined to continue the links we made with women in Vietnam and to make "Orange Action" a success.

TRAVEL NOTES

Languages Vietnamese, though quite a few people speak some English picked up during the American occupation. French is also quite widely spoken.

Transport Except on tours, visitors are forbidden to travel by train or long-distance bus. Any breach of these rules can lead to deportation. However, tourists seem free to wander in the cities with little fear of harassment. The main transport here is the *cyclo*, a form of pedal bicycle rickshaw.

Accommodation Hotels are generally cheap and pretty basic, but again you'll have no choice short of organising your own private tour.

Special Problems Vietnam has only minimal health facilities, so be sure to bring your own medicines, tampons, contraception, etc.

Guide *Guide to Vietnam* (Bradt). A bit scanty in places, but written by a photographer who really knows and loves the country and its people.

Contacts

Organised tours are increasingly popular. British operators include **Anita-Regent Holidays**, 13 Small St., Bristol, ☎0272-211 711, and **Bales Tours Ltd.**, Bales House, Barrington Rd., Dorking, Surrey RH4 3EJ, ☎306-885 991.

For more information on the **Women's Union**, write to *War On Want*, 37–39 Great Guildford St., London SE1 0YU, which recently launched a project to raise money for paper, desperately needed for the Union's publication, *Women in Vietnam*, and other educational activities.

Books

Arlene Eisen Bergman, *Women of Vietnam* (People's Press, US, 1975; available in Britain from Zed Books). Interesting material on the history of women's participation in Vietnam's centuries of struggle for liberation.

Michael Herr, *Dispatches* (Picador). Journalist's acclaimed account of the Vietnam War.

Thanks to War on Want for help with background information.

North Yemen

Mountainous and isolated, North Yemen (Yemen Arab Republic) is a society and economy in considerable flux. It is one of the world's least-developed nations, with little industry and no oil of its own. Yet due to the mass migration of (male) Yemeni workers to Saudi Arabia, it has acquired a recent veneer of booming capitalism – at least in the cities. At the time of writing, there is talk of a renewed union with neighbouring South Yemen (the Peoples' Democratic Republic), which for the last two decades has pursued a quite different course, with a socialist economy and, more interestingly, a break from the region's rigidly Islamic traditional code.

North Yemen itself is a completely traditional society. Foreigners are a rare sight, though various development agencies are active in the rural areas, and the startling Arabian architecture of the towns and villages is attracting a small but growing number of tourists. Visas are obtained without difficulty. Travel within the country can be arduous but, outside the capital Sana'a, sexual harassment is relatively rare.

North Yemeni **women** are for the most part bound by traditional social constraints; the vast majority are veiled and remain secluded from male/public spheres. The widespread migration of men to work in Saudi has made this position increasingly problematic for some women. Left behind in the villages, sometimes with no adult male workers at all, they have had to expand their work role without the social sanction to do so. Development agencies have begun to initiate a series of "home economics" projects, involving agricultural training as well as healthcare, literacy and handicrafts education, for rural women. In doing this, they have been lent support by the

Yemeni Women's Association and in some villages have met with considerable success. However the opposition of men to what they perceive as the "politicisation" of women remains a strong barrier.

Qat Country

· · · · · · · · · · · ·

Gill Hoggard spent a fortnight travelling around Yemen with a woman friend. They had arrived from Egypt where they had been living and working.

You cannot go to North Yemen without romantic baggage: travelling in the footsteps of Freya Stark, veiled women, austere mountains, clifftop fortresses and swirling cloud. But tempering romanticism with practicality, I stocked up in Cairo with insect repellent, malaria pills and appropriate clothing (baggy trousers and loose kaftans). Bleary eyed from the flight, I watched as our plane circled the mountains and flew low into Sana'a as the rising sun caught a jumble of mud-brick houses, spectacular free-standing minarets, and occasional concrete apartment blocks.

Sana'a airport was in the process of being modernised and on emerging from the concourse into the brilliant morning sun I was met by a cacophony of bulldozers, pneumatic drills and dumper trucks. I was somewhat unsettled by the people – a crowd of fierce-looking men, each of whom displayed a large dagger on his belt, and, unsure how to interpret this, fled back to the safety of a group of American missionaries I had chatted to on the plane.

It was thus, crowded Yemeni-style into a Peugeot taxi, and with the gossip of someone's high school graduation in Milwaukee flowing comfortingly around me, that I caught a first glimpse of Sana'a's extraordinary and beautiful architecture. Everywhere there was fretwork and tracery, picked out in white against the brown mudbrick. Gutters, drainpipes, latticework balconies and zigzag ramparts rioted over the house-fronts, while on the flat roofs washing flapped in the wind.

"Yemenis regard the modesty and chastity of their women as paramount"

In the course of my stay I saw few women. Like all Arabs, Yemenis regard the modesty and chastity of their women as paramount. They are required to wear not just one veil but two: the inner, covering most of the face except the eyes, and the outer, a kind of thin scarf which may be raised only for close relatives. I found it quite unsettling to attempt a conversation with, literally, an unseen person. Those women seen on the streets, shopping or (rarely) selling food, belong to the poorer classes; it is considered shameful for those of any wealth or position to venture out. Instead you see men doing the shopping and all external business.

Once, manoeuvring my way through the souk, I came upon a whole row of women, side by side, giggling and chattering and selling bread. Unusually they were only half veiled. I surreptitiously took a picture, but was angrily bumped and jostled by the men: they do not want anyone, even another woman, to take pictures of their own women.

I had ventured out into the *qat souk* – the market for the narcotic leaves which Yemenis chew for relaxation.

Serious buying begins around 11am in time for the afternoon, and everywhere earnest groups of men were bargaining over large plastic-wrapped bundles of what looked like privet. Alcohol is strictly forbidden and tobacco rarely smoked, but chewing *qat* is a national pastime. Everywhere, as the afternoon draws on, you see the unfocused eyes and vacant grin of those under the influence. *Qat* is easily grown and fetches a respectable sum in the marketplace, and whole mountainsides, which used to grow coffee, have been turned over to its production.

"Although we were often the only women on the buses and always the only Westerners, we were met by unfailing courtesy and friendliness"

Yemeni women as well as men chew *qat* and throughout one bus journey we made into the mountains, two heavily-wrapped ladies besides us plucked demurely at their bundles of leaves and slowly subsided, like the rest of the passengers, into a quiet and dreamy trance. On that occasion, as on several others, my friend and I had been ushered to the "best" seats at the front, from which we had all too clear a view of the spectacular gorges and canyons which fell away below the road.

Apart from some nerve-racking mountain roads, we didn't find it too difficult travelling around the country. Between all the major centres of population there are good tarmac roads and also a regular and punctual bus service. Although we were often the only women on the buses and always the only Westerners, we were met by unfailing courtesy and friendliness.

The place which left the strongest impression on me was the village of Al-Manakah, high up in the mountains south of Sana'a, and the objective of our *qat*-powered bus trip. Its "hotel for travellers" proved to be of ancient Yemeni design, a warren of tiny rooms, passageways and mysterious inhabi-

tants, laughing and chattering in the unseen lower quarters.

We had met, briefly, the woman who appeared to be in charge of the hotel in order to settle the business details. From then on our food was served by a heavily veiled and very timid girl of about twelve, probably her daughter, and thereafter, except for the muffled thumps, giggles and bangs emanating from downstairs, we saw no signs of anyone else. The unusual thing about this was that we had seen the woman and the girl at all: normally all strangers would deal only with the men of the house. But Al-Manakah, like so many other villages in the High Yemen, had sent its men to work in the Gulf, leaving the women in charge.

While staying there we followed the track out beyond the village and frequently encountered groups of men, either keeping an eye on their goats or more usually, squatting in the road to brew coffee over a small fire. We called out the Arabic greeting "Peace be on you", both to let it be known that we spoke the language, and to lessen the likelihood of any unpleasantness. Traditionally if one has replied "And on you be peace" it is morally unthinkable to insult or injure whoever you're speaking to. There was, however, not the slightest reason for unease: we were frequently invited to share in the coffee-drinking, or simply encouraged as to what we could find further on.

In Sana'a we met women Peace Corps members who told us differently, citing increasing incidents of sexual harassment on the city's streets after dark. They attributed this to the recent importation of pornographic videos from the West, one amongst a whole number of "luxury" goods that have started to enter the city. American chains such as Hiltons and McDonalds have also been established and the city as a whole is becoming increasingly open to Western influence. Yet it is still expected that these new and gleaming Western establishments will be exclusively staffed and patronised by men.

TRAVEL NOTES

Languages Arabic. It is definitely worth learning the basics before you go (numbers, simple questions) as very few people speak English.

Transport Within Sana'a there are shared taxis which are expensive (as is everything in Yemen) but the only means of getting around. A reasonably good bus service runs between main towns; most buses leaving early in the morning to complete the journey within daylight hours. Once a bus is full the driver will leave, no matter what the clock says, so it's worth arriving in good time. Internal air flights are also available, but besides being vastly expensive mean you miss out on the spectacular mountain scenery.

Accommodation In Sana'a there are several grades of hotels but prices are high even for quite basic accommodation. In the mountain villages you find *funduks*, ancient hostelries which now take in foreign travellers; they are reasonable but very basic – you sleep on floor cushions. Always ask people for a *funduk* and not a hotel if you want the cheaper, more basic accommodation.

Special problems Yemenis are strict Muslims and find bare flesh offensive – they particularly object to women's upper arms being uncovered. Clothing therefore should be loose and voluminous and cover the arms at least to the elbow.

Guide *Yemen – A Travel Surival Kit* (Lonely Planet) covers both North and South Yemen. Its publication is an indication of the country's increasing discovery by travellers.

Contacts

If you are interested in women's development programmes, make contact in Sana'a with either the **Yemeni Women's Association** or the UNESCO-backed **Tihama Development Authority** or **Southern Uplands Rural Development Project (SURDU)**.

Books

Carla Makhlouf, *Changing Veils: Women and Modernisation in North Yemen* (Croom Helm, 1979).

Yugoslavia

Most people think of Yugoslavia as one country: no Yugoslav ever does. The state has existed in its present form – a federation of six republics and two "autonomous regions" – since the end of World War II. Its peoples are a dauntingly complex patchwork of religions – Orthodox Christian, Roman Catholic and Muslim – and ethnic nationalities. And for most of them, the old national affiliations remain far more powerful than any unity forged by Marshall Tito or his successors in the centralised Communist government.

With the frenetic pace of change in Eastern Europe, the Western media frequently run articles on the disintegration of the Yugoslav federation. But, as one local journalist put it, the question is less whether it is going to break up but rather how it is going to be put together. The Yugoslav Communist Party is in crisis, and looks set to fracture into its component republics, but that does not mean the country will follow.

Instead, the republics are likely to pursue ever more individual paths. In the north, Slovenia and Croatia, the wealthiest and most progressive republics, are about to hold free elections, and are making overtures towards the EC for their trade; already, both belong to a trading group agreement with Italy, Austria and West Germany. In the centre, Serbia, and to a lesser extent, Montenegro, seem to be falling back upon national chauvinism, becoming ever more isolated as they attempt to maintain their federal power.

The greatest problems are in the south, where Macedonia has virtually Third World poverty, and where the largely Albanian population of Kosovo, an "autonomous region" officially part of Serbia, are in a state of near-revolution. At the time of writing, the Serbian-dominated federal government has had to bring tanks onto the streets of towns and cities in Kosovo. The state's record on civil rights is not good.

Travelling around the country, it is hard to scratch more than the surface of these complexities. You will be aware, however, of Yugoslavia's deep economic crisis. The calendar year of 1989 saw a staggering 4000 percent inflation and in 1990 the government introduced an extreme austerity budget and tied the dinar to the deutschmark. And if you leave the package resorts of the Adriatic – where the tourist industry is based – you will soon sense the differences between the republics. Like Italy, this has something of a north-south divide: the north, with its European culture and industrial muscle, subsidising the peasant farming regions of the south. But the individual nationalisms and religions play an equally significant role. You come up against a very Catholic Alpine kind of patriarchy in Slovenia and Croatia; a Balkan Orthodox brand in Serbia and Montenegro; a traditional, though far from fundamental, Muslim version in Bosnia-Hercegovina and Montenegro.

The everyday problems in travelling will be familiar to anyone with experience of the southern Mediterranean: *machismo* is a rare, unifying aspect of the various Yugoslav cultures. Attitudes vary from the package holiday mentality of the resorts, where women alone are regarded as available (the locals who swoop down on them are known as *galebovi*, or seagulls), to the Islamic and more backward regions inland where you can be treated with gallantry one minute and as if you don't exist the next. A suitably firm response – or stony silence – should be enough to cope with most situations.

The social system, on paper at least, guarantees Yugoslav **women** equal rights and equal wages in the workplace. They have long had paid maternity leave, state creches and nursery schools, all of which help towards economic independence even if they do little to change chauvinistic attitudes. Women make up a large portion of the student population and all careers are supposedly open to them. However, away from the cities, many remain dominated by fathers, brothers and husbands into a life of domestic servitude. Feminism as a movement scarcely exists, though there are isolated academics in some of the university towns of the north – Ljubljana, for example. Their debate, such as it is, concentrates on the need for open discusssion of issues like rape, health, prostitution and sexism in the media and, above all, the need to acknowledge the existence of a separate "women's question" outside the framework of party ideology.

Home from Home in Zagreb

. . . .

Ruth Ayliffe has been living in Zagreb, the capital of Croatia, since 1988. Free from family or material ties, her decision to make this move was largely inspired by the people she had got to know on a couple of previous visits.

Some four years after my first visit to Yugoslavia, I finally decided to stay. It was now or never, I argued to myself – I had no children, mortgage, or animals, it was time to change my job. So I made the move.

I have been living for two years now in Zagreb. A Yugoslav friend there had wanted to share a place with me, and I arrived to find that she had already rented a wonderfully located flat for us in the centre of town.

I was drawn to this country because I loved what I was getting to know of the people I was meeting – they felt immediately like family. But I was happily surprised by the loveliness of Zagreb itself, which proved a refreshing change from south London. For months after my arrival, every time I set foot outside I was thrilled by the great grey-trunked trees shadowing the streets below in green light; by the mercifully mild winter giving way to a hot spring; by the vaguely Austrian architecture; by the musicians playing in the streets, surrounded by people enjoying the sun.

I spent the first months labouring to learn the language – Croatian or *hrvats-kosrpski*. Grammatically it works like a mixture of German and Latin, but to begin with you feel it could take a lifetime to master even the essentials. Eventually, however, I did manage to finish a language course at the university, which qualified me to study for a degree here.

Since my arrival I have moved house a couple of times. My first flatmate had to move back to her home town and I lived for a while with a young family, who answered the advertisement I put in the newspapers. I thought this would help me to learn the language better, while causing them minimal stress. And I was also feeling the need to learn basic etiquette: how to cook, what is considered healthy here, and what isn't.

Ways of thinking and expression are surprisingly different from those in Britain. For example, when speaking with friends, the words "please" and "thank you" and "sorry" are not used very often. It seems more important when handing, for example, a drink to a friend, that you say "here you are" than that your friend answers "thank you". I was considered positively irritating when asking for favours: my friends told me it was as if I thought people don't want to help, as though they were not really friends. I didn't need to labour my requests so much, nor to be so grateful.

Living with a family – eating, working, partying and relaxing together – has made me some very firm friends, and taught me volumes about Yugoslavia. On the health angle, a number of bits of knowledge spring to mind. Walking barefoot is considered quite dangerous; any illness following will prove it. Any kind of draught risks the well-being of your kidneys, even at the height of summer in a train carriage full of smoke. This also means that at home a complicated system develops which ensures that two windows on opposite sides of the room are never open at the same time, while travelling in a car can be interesting, there being a strange law governing which windows can be open, and when, to achieve maximum comfort.

Then there are the perceptions that chilled drinks result in sore throats, and that walking about with wet hair is a health hazard. Tea is considered a medicament: if ever I drink it I'm asked if I'm feeling all right. (While I think of it, I would recommend the tea addict to bring her own. There is a wonderful selection of herb and fruit teas, but nothing resembling the tea to which we add milk – the idea of putting milk in tea is quite strange.)

"There is always someone, somewhere, who will watch you and click his tongue and chatter inanities at you as if you were a budgie"

Currently I am living alone, having found a cheap unfurnished flat with the expectation of sharing with a friend who had furniture; however, she needed to change her plans and I ended up in a flat which I really enjoy but need to furnish. Not that this has proved a problem. I have been amazed at how insistent people have been that I borrow their things: fridge, vacuum cleaner, three stoves, crockery, cooking utensils, bed linen, a table; and now I hear a washing machine is on the way!

As far as being a woman here is concerned, I have usually lived in a very male-dominated environment so am perhaps less than averagely sensitive to hassles from men. Some of the issues are all too familiar, like pornography and erotic films and magazines, which are now rife on street stalls. Socially, though, women face a harder situation than in Britain. It seems that by definition men are the ones who watch women – and that they certainly do, regardless of how many days you have been travelling and how grimy and awful you feel.

There is always someone, somewhere, who will watch you and click his tongue and chatter inanities at you as if you were a budgie. The local girls completely ignore the tongue-clickers, and it seems best to follow their example. Entering into conversation with them is usually taken as an invitation to continue with their pestering.

Other social aspects are, on the whole, refreshing. There are quite a few things that people seem to consider beneath their dignity. These include stealing personal property, taking drugs (alcohol is strongly recommended but taking drugs is generally considered pretty stupid) and, most importantly, rape. Aggressive action towards women is not an acceptable way for Yugoslav men to behave and, on that score, now that I know the language better, I feel much safer here than in London.

Men in fact tend to use ridiculous and sometimes clever tactics to try to win a woman, even for a brief relationship. Tales I've heard range from a heart-rending account of childhood misery, to unbelievable generosity, to infinite tenderness, or a long lecture linking health and psychological well-being to sexual pleasure. If your "No" is insistent, you will be treated to the whole lot. I recently heard someone tell me "I won't do anything you don't want", which, if I add the full meaning to his words, ". . . but I will do everything I can to change your mind", could summarise to date my understanding of the attitude of a man who has taken an interest in a woman.

"Being single at my age (28) is viewed by many of my friends here as a temporary illness"

There are geographical variations to this awful stereotype; the more you travel to the south and east, the more certain you can be that some crisis is going to arise. Travelling in Macedonia, men serving me in shops would give me sweets as I paid for my groceries, doing budgie talk in Macedonian. In cafés, if I was alone, I would be treated to a free drink by the owner. One such decided to fall alarmingly in love with me. He went much further than his Croatian counterparts, buying a round of drinks for my rather large bunch of friends, offering us all a boat ride along the coast, and finally bursting into tears as he told me that he had fallen in love and wanted to marry me.

Being single at my age (28) is viewed by many of my friends here as a temporary illness – and one that requires urgent attention. I was introduced to a lot of men in this way before I realised what was going on. Yugoslavs are confirmed dating agents: if there is a hint of a possible relationship, great discussions ensue and both candidates immediately receive any amount of personal advice.

Living in the family, I came across the concept of "man's work" and "woman's work". In that setting, both seemed very happy with their allotted roles; they worked alongside each other, each left the other to get on with their respective jobs, they worked fast and relaxed at length. Recently I have come across a couple whose roles are almost exactly opposite, though again they work alongside each other, doing their own jobs. I also know couples in which the woman is carrying an unbelievably heavy workload, usually because her husband is ill.

I gather I am considered a bit of a funny kind of woman because I'm interested in discovering how things work, I fix things around the house, and I ride a man's bike. No woman among my friends has ever commented on this but the men are always a bit puzzled, and, yes, they do seem to have the attitude that changing a plug is a rather difficult occupation for a woman.

At university, though, a surprising number of girls are studying what, in Britain, would be male-dominated subjects, for instance physics or engineering, and there aren't many clear distinctions between women and men's work in public office. The role of leadership, however, is usually male, and nursing continues to be monopolised by women and medicine by men.

There seem to be more pressing issues at the forefront of most people's minds than women's issues. Inflation is hitting 2000 percent, with wages lagging behind, while politically the country is in a state of flux. And there's also the matter of the day-to-day enjoyment of life. In summer, for example, all cares suddenly seem to be cast aside, as people work out how they will manage to get to the coast to escape the heat of the city. It's a quality I appreciate – that there is always time to be with friends.

TRAVEL NOTES

Languages Serbo-Croat is the main language; regional languages include Slovene and Macedonian. German is widely spoken in the north and Italian along parts of the Adriatic. An increasing number of Yugoslavs, in the larger cities and in the resorts, can speak English.

Transport Buses are plentiful and incredibly cheap, but it's best to book ahead as they get very crowded. Hitching is not recommended for the usual reasons, plus the fact that few Yugoslavs are prepared to give lifts to foreigners.

Accommodation Private rooms are the cheapest option. Hotel prices are strictly controlled but more expensive. Campsites, mainly on the coast, tend to be huge and, again, highly organised.

Special Problems Harassment from Yugoslav men can be very persistent. Be firm from the beginning and you should manage to avoid aggressive situations. If travelling alone, avoid bars and walking about late at night; even in large cities "nice" women are expected to stay indoors after 11pm.

Guides *The Rough Guide: Yugoslavia* (Harrap Columbus) has recently been overhauled and is now pretty much definitive.

Books

Rebecca West, *Black Lamb and Grey Falcon* (1938; Papermac, 1982). Erudite and all-embracing, this is the definitive work on Yugoslavia before the last war. Sections are included in *The Essential Rebecca West* (Penguin, 1987).

Edith Durham, *Through the Land of the Serbs* (out of print). Edith Durham was one of the most intrepid of women explorers and her (numerous) adventures through the Balkans in the early years of this century make captivating reading. Her *High Albania* (Virago, 1985) also contains a fair portion on Kosovo.

Stefan K. Pavlowitch, *The Improbable Survivor: Yugoslavia and Her Problems, 1918–1988* (Hurst, 1989). Forthright collection of essays on modern Yugoslavia and its federal crises by a veteran emigré historian.

Eva S. Westerlind, *Carrying the Farm on Her Back: A Portrait of Women in a Yugoslavian Village* (Rainier Books, US, 1989). An excellent study of the lives of women left to manage the village farms while their husbands work as migrant labourers in Northern Europe. Most of it is told in the villagers' own words.

Barbara Jancar-Webster, *Women and Revolution in Yugoslavia, 1941–1945* (Arden Press, US, 1989). Historical study of women's role in the Yugoslavian resistance and revolutionary movement. A clear, if slightly oversimplified, testimony to the courage and endurance of female partisans.

Zaire

· · · · · · · · · · · · · · · · · ·

With its wild tropical terrain, volcanoes, vast rivers, and totally erratic public services, Zaire is undoubtedly a place for adventure. Besides the river steamers (described below), there's very little in the way of public transport and, if you're not overlanding, you'll find hitching on trucks the only way to get around. As a traveller, however, most people will welcome you with warmth and hospitality – and, provided you don't brush with authority, you will probably escape any first-hand experience of the

unrelenting repression that has dominated the country for the past 25 years.

At the head of Zaire's brutal and corrupt regime stands President Mobutu, who, amid a turmoil of secessionist conflicts, seized power in a military coup in 1965. Having done little, if anything, to exploit the country's rich natural resources for the benefit of his people (only five percent of the mainly rural population even have access to clean water), he has amassed a personal fortune to rival any in the world. His nation, meanwhile, has been plunged more and more into debt. Incredibly, though Mobutu's corruption and political ineptitude has led to a degree of embarrassment among his Western backers, the support appears to keep coming. This is partly through a reluctance to see Zaire radicalise and thus change its position as one of the few African nations to take a "moderate" stand on issues such as sanctions against South Africa.

You'll need patience to travel in Zaire, plus a taste for the unexpected and a willingness to put up with humidity and discomfort – bumping along dirt tracks with thirty other people perched on top of boxes on the back of an open truck can be excruciating. But the sheer vastness and unspoiled beauty of the country and people's friendly acceptance of you makes it an adventurer's dream. The capital, Kinshasa, has its fair share of hustlers and it's clearly unwise to walk around alone at night, but sexual harassment doesn't appear to be a general problem.

Most of Zaire's people live in such poverty that the position of women has yet to become a priority issue. As in the rest of Africa, any **women's organisations** tend to be linked to development schemes and/or the Church. However, even these are very few for in the atmosphere of tight political control most efforts at self-help are deemed subversive and therefore swiftly stamped out.

A River Boat Adventure

. . . .

Chris Johnson, who has also written about Chad, visited Zaire as part of a year-long trip through Africa. She has travelled widely, helping to finance her trips by taking photographs for various development agencies.

By the time I reached Zaire I was more than halfway through my African trip. In all the hours of reading, thinking and planning before I set off from Britain, this was the country that I'd felt most anxious about. Something about its size worried me, and the uncertainty of transport; its reputation for being wild and for having to pay constant bribes.

I flew up to Kinshasa from Zimbabwe – my only long flight in Africa. Though preferable, to arrive overland would have taken too long. Kinshasa is a pleasant city combining tree-lined boulevards, streets of elegant, slightly decaying buildings, and a scattering of the modern constructions which house banks and oil companies. The heart of the capital has good music and warm people; but it's the township of Kimbanseke that I remember best.

Kimbanseke is the outermost of the Kinshasa suburbs and it takes the locals one and a half hours to get into the city to work. The morning I went there I awoke to rain, real equatorial rain that battered on the roofs and ran off their corrugations in steady streams. People walking to work pressed all manner of things into service as umbrellas: one man had a polythene bag large enough to cover his entire body; another, a small piece of soggy brown cardboard over his head. The roads out were full of potholes, and when I visited, were reduced to squelching, churned-up mud. But the women who took me around here, and for a day shared their lives with me, were wonderful. Like most women in Kimbanseke, they are traders, and photographing in the market was enormous fun. Everyone wanted to be in on the act, and there was much extravagant posturing, clapping and laughter.

From Kinshasa I planned to take the legendary river boat north to Lisala. Buying the ticket proved an experience in itself. The road down to the port was lined with women selling things: baskets of huge squirming snails; smoked fish; and gruesome smoked monkeys which looked horribly human, like the blackened bodies of tiny burnt babies. The boat office was inside the port and not at all easy to find but eventually someone rescued me and led me through the docks, past huge logs being unloaded, to the right building. I had intended to treat myself to a first-class ticket, which, at £25 for the eleven-day trip, including three meals a day, hardly seemed extravagant. However, all first-class tickets were booked, so it was to be eight pounds for second-class, including one meal a day. Only advance reservations were being taken and after watching my name written down on a torn off scrap of paper, I was told to return at a later date. Needless to say, I didn't feel too optimistic.

I returned on the appointed day to find a loose crowd already thronging the entrance to the ticket office, where a man and a woman sat doing very little. The woman was tall and looked magnificent. Like many Zairois women, she wore a richly coloured Java print, one length of material forming a wrap-around skirt, another making the blouse and the third being tied around the head turban-style.

I tried to find out what was happening. "Wait a moment." It could be a long wait. I propped myself up against the wall and got out my book. All around me people glistened with sweat, and in the damp heat I felt I was melting away. Suddenly someone took pity on me and waved me inside, pointing to a chair: they must have thought a white female belonged to a delicate species, and for once I was happy to take advantage of the judgement. However, it didn't signify any progress with regard to the ticket. I got out my book again. The man in the corner wrote out the

first-class tickets at the rate of one every ten minutes. The woman laughed and chatted with people.

Eventually someone emerged out of a back room bearing a scrap of paper – the reservation from my previous visit – and I was directed to another office where, after another long wait, someone came along, looked at my bit of paper, disappeared into an office and, to my surprise, produced a ticket. As I emerged back into the hall one man, looking very surprised, said "Fini?" Clearly people don't usually get served so quickly.

"But there was never any shortage of people to talk to and no problems being a woman travelling alone – apart from parrying the endless questions about why I wasn't married and had no children"

I left Kinshasa the next day. There are no roads through this part of Zaire, so unless you can afford to fly the river is the only form of transport. It forms the main link from the south to the north of Zaire and to the Central African Republic and, if you take it through to Kisangani, to the east. Apart from three American women volunteers who joined the boat at Mbandaka (about halfway) I was the only white person on board. But there was never any shortage of people to talk to and no problems being a woman travelling alone – apart from parrying the endless questions about why I wasn't married and had no children. I exchanged English lessons for ones in Lingala, read, wrote and watched the world go by.

The next eleven days were among the best of my entire African trip, chugging gently along in the hot sunshine on top of one of the flat-roofed barges which made up our convoy. There were six barges in all, each lashed to the main boat, the *Colonel Tshatshi*, which took up the rear, pushing four barges in front with a further two lashed along its left-hand side. This huge square main vessel was reserved for first-class passengers; second-class like me got the top deck of the barges, and third-class the bottom deck or any corner they could find.

In fact the roof was by far the best place to be. There must have been well over a thousand passengers below and you couldn't move without stepping over someone. With metal doors and wire mesh on the windows, the cabins were like cages and the toilets were soon foul. But up on the roof it was clean, quiet and peaceful. I looked out towards the hills patterned with trees sloping down to the river, where the occasional village nestled among palm trees at the water's edge. I watched a vast amount of vegetation floating by – great rafts of grass and water lilies, some with beautiful purple flowers. At one stage a rainbow, formed in a fine gauze of cloud, almost completely encircled the sun. The dominant motion was not that of the boat but of the river, flowing swiftly past while we seemed to remain motionless.

As we progressed upstream the scenery changed, becoming flatter and more jungley until it gave way to real equatorial rainforest, dripping with creepers. A full-scale market had sprung up on board, selling absolutely everything: plastic bowls, mugs, plates, waste paper bins; metal buckets and cooking pots; all kinds of food; clothes, new and second hand; and, as so often in Africa, all kinds of pills – out of date ones, ones that should be on prescription, ones that have been banned. On the roof of an adjacent barge a man was cutting hair; below, another man was busy decanting salt from a sack into small polythene bags – everything gets split up into smaller quantities here and even biscuits are sold individually as well as by the packet. Next to the salt vendor a man sat at a small table selling cigarettes, a single box of matches, orange plastic mugs, biscuits, mosquito coils and chicken stew. A canoe

paddled alongside the boat, its occupants buying bread, salt and beer, and selling fish which was taken straight into a refrigerated room at the bottom of the boat to be eventually taken back to Kinshasa. Someone else paddled up to sell palm wine, a white, cloudy liquid, slightly alcoholic and still fermenting.

For people living along the river, the boat is the only link with the outside world. Each time we passed a village dozens of canoes would paddle out to meet us and buy and sell – I counted as many as sixty tied up alongside us. It was a noisy, colourful scene as everyone struggled to keep the canoes steady in the slipstream of the boat. Both men and women paddled and there were several women-only boats, their occupants strong and full of laughter as they negotiated their canoes alongside, waving fish, or bunches of bananas, high in the air.

"A ferocious storm broke, the wind rose, tossing the trees and sending flecks of white foam scudding across the water . . . we retreated to the shelter of the bank, running aground in the process"

To the local people on board, the most exciting event of the trip was when, just after dark, we passed the other steamer on its way back to Kinshasa. It was bigger and even more crowded than our boat. Everyone was out on the roofs or hanging over the sides, to the extent that one of the barges looked in imminent danger of tipping over. Very slowly we drew alongside, to the accompaniment of great cheers. Then, as we touched, an even louder cheer went up and people leaped from boat to boat, embracing each other. This went on for some time, until finally our departure was heralded by much horn-blowing which sent the gathered multitude into a frenzy of shouting, waving, embracing, and jumping up and down on the roof.

By now we were right on the Equator and it was fearfully hot and humid. Finally, a ferocious storm broke, the wind rose, tossing the trees and sending flecks of white foam scudding across the water. Alongside us men and women in dugout canoes bailed frantically; we retreated to the shelter of the bank, running aground in the process. Driven inside, we went down to the bar on the front of the boat. As we pulled into a small village and the searchlights lit up the colourful crowd the wind tugged at the trees and the storm unleashed its fury once again. Through an open window a solitary palm was lit up in the night, lashed by the wind. The rain ran in through the many holes in the roof, down the rusty cream paintwork and along the wooden floor. The wild vibrant energy of the night ran through the people sitting at tables, drinking beer, talking. Music played loudly, someone shook out the rhythm on a pair of rattles and a lone dancer gyrated. Only later when the gale abated and the fronds of the palm hung limply down its trunk did we turn and go to bed. Some time in the night the boat began to move again.

The final evening on the river was magical. A huge sun hung briefly in the sky, then dropped swiftly over the horizon. It was 11.30pm before we docked at Lisala and midnight before I could finally make my way down to the lower deck, across the barges and through the chaos of people trying to get on or off the boat. José, a Zairois trader I'd met on the boat, had assigned a young lad to escort me to the local hotel. I followed him up the steep narrow path, the stars doing little to relieve the blackness of the night. The hotel proved to be firmly shut for the night but, as always in Africa, he knew someone who would put me up.

TRAVEL NOTES

Languages Lingala and French, the last being the official government language, plus Swahili and a few regional languages.

Transport Public transport is sparse and erratic – there's only one substantial tarred road – so hitching for a fee is widely accepted and – being usually on a lorry with a crowd of other people – generally safe. A journey by river boat is not to be missed.

Accommodation Like everything, most hotels and guesthouses are cheap and basic. In remote areas you can sometimes stay in mission stations; the mission guesthouse in Kinshasa is recommended for being safe and central.

Special Problems Harassment, apart from occasional hustling for money, doesn't appear to be a problem. Bring all your own supplies of tampons, contraceptives, medicaments etc, as such items are expensive and in short supply.

Guides *Central Africa: A Travel Survival Kit* (Lonely Planet) has a reasonable section on Zaire; the chapter in *Africa on a Shoestring* (Lonely Planet), however, is at present more up-to-date and helpful.

Contacts

We have only managed to trace one women's organisation, the **Women's Association of Kibanguist Church**, PO Box 7069, Kinshasa, whose main aim is to encourage women to participate in development projects.

Special thanks to Chris Johnson for her contribution to the introduction.

Zambia

Erratic transport, the increasing threat of robbery, and a paranoid military, combine to make Zambia one of the more hazardous African countries to explore. As so often there is an organised tourist circuit, in this case focusing on a handful of developed game parks and the famous Victoria Falls. But this has little to do with the "real Zambia", a chaotic nation of escalating poverty, drought, food shortages, rising crime and other problems – many of them stemming from the constant process of internal migration.

Since gaining independence in 1964, Zambia has become the most urbanised of African nations, with nearly half of the population living in towns. Rural production has been consistently neglected in favour of urban/industrial development, leaving the countryside thinly populated by a predominance of women – as chief food producers – and old men and children. This imbalance, coupled with the fallen price of Zambia's main export, copper, lies at the heart of the country's economic crisis.

Added to the problems of ecomonic turmoil are the consequences of the wars of liberation in the region. First Smith in Zimbabwe and then Botha in South Africa carried out the odd bombing raid on towns and bridges in Zambia to try and dissuade President Kaunda from supporting his southern neighbours' struggles for independence. The police and military already have a high profile to curb criminal activities, but it is these acts of sabotage that lie behind the pervasive fear of "spies" or "suspicious characters" which so many travellers comment on. It is to be hoped that a change of events in South Africa will mean transformation here, too.

Women travelling alone in Zambia, however, don't appear to encounter any particular problems – and sexual harassment of foreigners seems virtually unknown. It is the physical limitations that make travel difficult: the erratic bus services, slow trains and dearth of vehicles off the beaten track. From the point of view of people's acceptance of you, being a woman may well even prove an advantage.

In his many speeches on the virtues of humanism, President Kaunda talks continually of a "man-centred" society. Not deliberately making a sexist statement, he nevertheless sums up the position of Zambian women. Traditional attitudes prevail, as does the traditional division of labour. Despite being expected to feed their families and take care of the children, only seven percent of women are in waged employment; they have to try and survive by "informal" activities such as marketeering, beer-brewing, and to some extent prostitution. Discriminatory laws, unchanged since the days of British colonialism, determine that a woman's access to jobs, credit, contraception is controlled by her "guardian" – her husband, brother, father, uncle – and even widows are denied access to their dead husband's estate.

Women who challenge this state of affairs are more often than not branded as "promoters of Western imperialist thinking". However, things are slowly changing. Apart from the apparently ineffectual UNIP Women's League (a division of the national party), there are no political **women's organisations**. But women have an increasingly high profile in the Church, are widely respected as prophets and healers, and there is a growing movement, at least among the educated middle class, to appreciate women's central role in the development process.

In Search of Yangumwila Falls

. . . .

Ilse Mwanza works as a Research Affiliation Officer at the University of Zambia in Lusaka, where she moved in 1968 with her Zambian husband. Her quest in search of the Yangumwila Falls formed part of a two-month trip to the northern provinces, where she was mainly visiting researchers in the field.

Nobody had ever heard of the Yangumwila Falls. I just happened to be travelling south from Nsumbu National Park, where I had spent some days exploring the beautiful countryside around Lake Tanganyika, and, noting these falls on the map, decided to see them on the way. It was still the dry season, so I thought it wouldn't be too difficult.

Rolling into Mporokoso in my old Landrover, I first went to the police station to announce my presence and ask directions. I asked five different police officers, but all claimed to be new to the area and ignorant of such obscure places. They directed me to the nearest mission station on the outskirts of town. Here the Reverend Sikazwe was very kind; he asked his family, his colleagues, even the teacher of the school next door, but nobody knew anything about waterfalls. However, he remembered an old retired teacher from the Njalamimba area who lived nearby and accompanied me to his house.

"Anything out of the ordinary like a mzungu (white) woman travelling alone in the bush is treated with great caution"

Mr Chipopola was also most kind. We sat down on his favourite bench under a big mango tree and discussed my strange request. Why would I want to see these falls, he wondered? I explained that I was from the University of Zambia and keen to know more about the country, and that in over twenty years of living in Zambia I had yet to explore his home area. He agreed that this was a serious shortcoming, but it still didn't explain my interest in waterfalls. Had I any relatives there? I had to disappoint him. Being German by origin and married to a Zambian from the Eastern Province as my name implied (Zambian names are area-specific) – this was highly unlikely. He probed further. So why did I want to go to the falls area? People in Zambia have been exhorted so often to look out for suspicious characters, in the wake of nasty experiences with South African raids, that anyone out of the ordinary, like a *mzungu* (white) woman travelling alone in the bush, is treated with great caution.

I went on to explain how my job at the university was to advise researchers and that I needed to find out about the geological nature of scarp environments; that my description of remote scenic places might even perhaps attract tourists to the region. "Ah, tourists are going to come! Very good." And he finally told me that the Lupupa Falls, marked close to Yangumwila on the map, weren't very far from Njalamimba, from where Headman Chilatu would be able to direct me. He

gave me a note for the Headman and, pointing me in the right direction, wished me well.

After some stopping to ask the way, I eventually found the "clearly-marked track" beyond Njalamimba which led to Chilatu's. The track was so overgrown that I got no further than the end of the village. Screeching to a halt, I looked around helplessly, to be instantly surrounded by a crowd of children. No one understood my poor Nyanja (the language of Eastern Zambia), but someone ran off to return with an adult.

Mr Musonda, it turned out, was the greatest possible gift to travellers. Having once been the house-servant of *mzungu* teachers, he was experienced in their peculiar ways. He knew all about waterfalls, having sometimes accompanied his *bwanas* to visit them. But the Yangumwila Falls? Ah, no. They were a mystery.

By now it was late afternoon. How far at least were the Lupupa Falls? Not far. Mr Musonda willingly agreed to come along and show me the way. He dashed off to tell his wife and came back in a flash – no blanket, no nothing. Ah well, I always carry a spare sleeping bag and enough food, and off we went, through the thicket that proved to be the village exit, along various tracks, across some cassava fields to a huddle of huts that proved to be Chilatu's.

Children scampered in all directions. It later transpired that my Landrover had been mistaken for that of the game-scout who sometimes came in search of poachers, and the children were quickly sent to hide the game-meat that was being smoke-dried. The poor things reappeared with slightly scorched fingers. Headman Chilatu wasn't home; he had gone to visit a relative in town nine months ago! Never mind. After Mr Musonda had shown Mr Chipopola's note and explained my presence, I was warmly welcomed by Chilatu's three wives. The note read: "Please help Mama in her work to see Lupupa Falls. Show her the place. She will be very much pleased to be introduced to that place. She has been sent by the Government. Your brother Chipopola."

It was almost dark by now and there was no question of going on to the Falls, an hour's hike away, so we asked to stay the night. Immediately, one of the Mrs Chilatus hurried to the granary to get fingermillet, another chased the children to fetch more firewood and water, and the third graciously offered us some of their wild pigmeat for dinner. I have seldom eaten so well and, in return, gave them coffee and sugar – for them as rare a treat as wild pig is for me.

"After much talk about which Mrs Chilatu I should stay with, the one with the least children won"

We sat around the fire, talking about our different ways of life, with Mr Musonda, the only man around, acting as interpreter. Most homesteads in this region are female-headed due to male labour migration. Because Chilatu's lies so far off the beaten track, in a heavily wooded and hilly area of Northern province which still has a fair amount of game, the three women can only work small fields. They grow cassava and fingermillet as a staple, some pumpkins and rape as vegetables, and beans as a cash crop. The homestead is surrounded by mango and banana trees. They have to *kraal* (fence with thornbushes) their fields to protect the crops from game, especially wild pigs. The latter are trapped by making an opening in the *kraal* and digging a pit spiked with sharpened stakes. Any surplus game-meat is sold or bartered.

Sometimes the women go into the bush to collect wild arrowroot, a thickener for groundnut paste, much sought after in the 64km-distant Mporokoso *boma*, the nearest market and store. Unfortunately, on leaving nine months ago, Mr Chilatu had locked up his bicy-

cle so the family had no access to market at that moment. The children had to walk 26km to the nearest school, too, where they stayed during the week, fending for themselves from the age of seven. Equipped with cassava roots and dried meat, they set off from home on Sunday afternoons to return the following Saturday morning. On top of doing their own cooking and cleaning at school, they also have to help with chores in the house and fields at weekends or, in the case of boys, go off for a spot of bird or rodent hunting. This week the children hadn't gone. They hadn't felt like making the long trek and the mothers hadn't pressed them. Their school education was elementary in the strictest sense of the word and quite irrelevant to the lives they lived. What good to learn English and maths if they were simply destined to follow in the footsteps of their mothers? No one in living memory had ever heard of anyone from Njalamimba progressing even to secondary school, the only way out of village existence.

Discussion finally came round to where we were going to sleep. Mr Musonda was tucked in with the boys. My suggestion of sleeping, as usual, in the rooftop tent on top of my Landrover was dismissed outright as improper and far too dangerous on account of all the spirits and animals that lurk around at night. After much talk about which Mrs Chilatu I should stay with, the one with the least children won. She had only three to share her bed: a mat on the floor with a *chitenge* cloth as cover.

I was given the part of the room which contained bags of beans and arrowroot awaiting transport to market. With a little rearranging of bags by the light of a paraffin lamp (a vaseline jar filled with paraffin with a twisted cloth for a wick), I was able to spread out my sleeping bag. Not that I could go to sleep yet! My hosting Mrs Chilatu still had to tend the meat, bubbling in two pots on a paraffin stove to prevent spoilage. We drank more coffee and smiled a lot, no longer able to communicate through words, while the three children slept. The youngest, ill I suspected with malaria, kept waking up and crying, and when the light finally went out the rats appeared, busy working their way into the beans. I didn't care any longer and slept.

Next morning, after another meal of millet and pork, while I dished out bread and jam, we set out for the Lupupa Falls. I felt just like the Pied Piper having about twenty children in tow in single file. I was not only shown the way to the Falls, but learned how branches for *chitemene* fields (an age-old slash and burn system) are lopped off trees, what pig traps look like, and how to spot game tracks. We saw zebra and antelope spoor, but no sign of animals.

An hour's hiking took us to the river just above the Falls. Really more of a stream, the Mukubwe drops off a steep cliff in bridal veil fashion for about a hundred metres, deep down into where a circular pool has been formed, surrounded by dense rainforest, before the water disappears, a silver band between the bends of the gorge. I could make out hornbills and swallows, swifts and starlings, gyrating above the pool, and a troop of baboons that had come to drink. We all sat and watched the scenery. There was no way down.

I had asked about the Yangumwila Falls again and again without success so, with Mr Musonda quite happy to accompany me further, we decided to explore the Mumbuluma Falls instead. Back we went to the Njalamimba turn-off to pick up the Landrover.

We parked the car where others had obviously parked before us and followed a footpath along the Luangwa river, which rushes toward the Falls in a series of little rapids and cascades, divided by wooded islands. The Mumbuluma were much wider than I'd expected and about forty metres deep, surrounded by rainforest. The contrast of rushing white water fringed with dark green foliage in an otherwise yellow-brown savanna landscape is quite startling. With only birds for company, the area seemed like a perfect place for camping, but I was still determinedly looking for the elusive Yangumwila Falls and so, after a brief walk round, we resumed our original quest.

"Dense reeds now covered the warthog holes and dismembered trees; the track was totally overgrown"

We bumped along for a time through the forest reserve, narrowly avoiding big potholes and fallen logs, as the road got progressively worse. Dense reeds now covered the warthog holes and dismembered trees; the track was totally overgrown. Just as I was about to give up, Mr Musonda detected another bit of road, so we ploughed on, he running ahead of the car with me bumping after him until we miraculously emerged into open grassland. By now the sun was sinking fast – darkness always falls quickly in Africa – but the assumed proximity of our goal spurred us on. We kept going and with the last light reached a riverine forest, which I took to be that of the Itabu, on which the Falls appeared on the map. I could hear a gurgling brook and even the sound of falling water not too far away. We had made it, we thought, and pitched camp in a clearing.

Next morning we set off on foot to find the Falls. Sound becomes strangely magnified at night and what I had assumed to be the main waterfalls turned out to be only a small rapid. For two hours we walked further upstream, following poachers' tracks along the river. No sign of any falls. The countryside was flat, unlikely to contain cliffs or faults. The river ran quietly between mosses and shrubs. The air was still and the sun getting hot. Thinking the Falls might instead be downstream, we eventually turned back the way we'd come, towards the car.

I should have known better than to try to trace the river on four wheels! Half an hour out of camp I suddenly found myself in wet grassland, up to the axles in black-cotton soil, the kind of muck found in many African wetland areas and which can trap even elephants. It was no use struggling or revving the engine; we would just sink deeper. We were truly stuck, the nearest populated area about a day's walk away. There was nothing else to do but get to work: cut down branches, unload the car, jack it up and push the branches under the wheels. Slowly, very slowly, we inched the Landrover out of the mud. The sun was beating down and I kept pouring water over our heads to prevent dehydration and sunstroke. After five hours of sweating labour, plagued by heat and ants, the vehicle jumped with a last desperate lurch and was free. Was it any wonder that I gave up looking for the Yangumwila Falls?

TRAVEL NOTES

Languages A variety of tribal languages according to region, though English is still the official language and widely spoken.

Transport Slow and erratic; for overlanders, the shortage of spare parts, including tyres, is a permanent problem. Though not necessarily safe, hitching is easy if you don't mind long waits. There is a limited and similarly unpredictable train service.

Accommodation There are few budget hotels in towns though most, according to Ilse Mwanza, are "real dumps". In provincial or district centres, council rest houses sometimes have space, as do missions or secondary schools.

Special Problems Many basic consumer goods, including medicaments, are in short supply so it's important to bring your own. Avoid brushing with officialdom or taking photographs of public buildings. Police and army alike are obsessed with spies and can be very unpleasant.

Guide *Africa on a Shoestring* (Lonely Planet) includes a reliable section on Zambia.

Contacts

Organisation of University Women, PO Box 32379, Lusaka. A resource base for data and research findings on women, also responsible for the **Women's Development Network** which helps to co-ordinate women's organisations around the country.

It may also be worth getting in touch with the **UNIP Women's League**, Freedom House, PO Box 30302, Lusaka.

Books

Barbara Rogers, *The Domestication of Women* (Kogan Page, 1980). By now classic account of missionary and aid-agency influences on women's position in the development process with many examples from Zambia.

Marcia Wright, *Women in Peril: Life Stories of Four Captives* (NECZAM/Institute for African Studies, Zambia, 1984). Four old women tell of their experiences of slavery.

Many thanks to Ilse Mwanza for her contribution to the introduction and Travel Notes.

Zimbabwe

. . . .

As Zimbabwe celebrates ten years of independent, democratic rule, the internal conflict which dogged its early years appears to be over – at least for the moment. Caution is still recommended for travellers in the northwest of the country; otherwise all former trouble spots are reportedly safe. And with its "free spirit", beautiful scenery, great music and easy transport, Zimbabwe is a highly enjoyable part of Africa to explore.

Africa's youngest nation, Zimbabwe only gained independence in 1980, after a long, hard war of liberation from white minority rule. Despite overwhelming popular support for Robert Mugabe's ZANU party, shown in his landslide victory in the country's first national elections, the early years of independence saw several isolated but extremely bloody outbreaks of violence, stemming from persistent tension between ZANU and the main opposition party, ZAPU, led by Joshua Nkomo.

Fuelled by inter-tribal rivalry between the Shona (largely supporters of ZANU) and the minority Ndebele (who mainly support ZAPU), political disagreements were further worsened by intense personal animosity between the two leaders. However, tensions have been greatly reduced by a Unity Agreement, signed by both parties in January 1988. Moves like this and the later abolition of the twenty seats guaranteed to the whites in government are all part of Mugabe's long-term plan to transform Zimbabwe into a one-party state. Given the country's political complexity, this seems, at least in the short term, a pragmatic rather than autocratic solution.

British travellers will find an odd familiarity in many aspects of the country's infrastructure – the legacy of a century and a half of colonial history. Perhaps more surprising, for white travellers, is the almost total lack of animosity from the black majority: this is a hugely friendly and hospitable country. The most negative aspect is in the continued racism of white Zimbabweans; though you'll find this population, too, outgoing and generous, the hospitality or lifts that they offer too frequently carry penalties in the form of listening to impassioned racist monologues.

In the wake of a war in which **women** fought equally and as bravely as men, the government has made strident efforts to guarantee the equality of the sexes in society. Several laws have been passed to this end, the most significant being the Legal Age of Majority Act whereby a woman, like her male counterpart, ceases being a minor at eighteen. However, laws have limitations and women have a hard time battling against centuries of tradition and custom. The Ministry of Community Development and Women's Affairs has made inroads through its focus on literacy and self-help projects in rural areas, apparently met with great enthusiasm by the women concerned, and various other organisations encourage income-generating projects with the aim of strengthening women's economic power. But the tendency is still to concentrate on traditional home-based activities, which do little to change fundamental attitudes about women's inferiority. Signs of a growing Women's Movement, and continuing government commitment, indicate the possibility of much deeper, lasting changes in the future.

To Harare by Truck

· · · · · · · · · · · ·

After a spell of casual work in London, Jo Wells and her friend Emma, both in their early twenties, visited Zimbabwe as part of a low-budget trip to Africa. Five months later they returned, "different people"; Jo is now studying African history, while Emma is using her experience in textile design.

I knew Zimbabwe would be good when we arrived at Lilongwe. By this point the oppression of Malawi and its people was getting to us, and the Africans we met from Zimbabwe and Zambia seemed to have a free spirit in comparison. Having originally decided to fly to Harare, we eventually opted for a lift through Zambia with an obliging trucking company. This route was the long way round; most overlanders cut through Mozambique, but Emma and I weren't interested in challenging our bravado by facing that sad, war-torn country amid a barrage of armoured vehicles. Besides, we hoped our passage via Zambia would enlighten us on the sheer massiveness of the continent.

Our driver, aptly named Steady, had the job of transporting a gigantic oil container each week from Harare to northern Malawi. We had caught him on his return run, so he was inclined to travel at a leisurely pace. We spent three days in his truck, sleeping, eating, talking, and all the while watching the vast African landscape spread out before us. I suppose as two white women we were a bit of a novelty, sitting up there in the cab of a young black trucker, and therefore bound to generate attention as Steady stopped at small villages to trade packets of soap powder or bottles of Malawi gin. But everywhere people came out to greet us with the never-ending warm friendliness of the Africans; men and women alike called out "sisters, you're welcome!"

"It was as if we'd left the so-called Third World and crossed back into the West again"

Zambia is a poor country, its people crying out for essentials like bread, meat and vegetables. Throughout the country, we heard endless tales of crime, mainly theft, and every Zambian we met was a "businessman", indulging in various petty dealings simply to earn a crust. Despite all this, we found people to be generous, kind and trustworthy, guidebook rantings about their "dodginess" to be taken with a pinch of salt.

After a three-day diet of Pepsi and popcorn, and the potholed Zambian roads, it was a relief to cross the Zambezi into Zimbabwe. The contrast is remarkable, the first thing we noticed being the abundance of wildlife – baboons careering around the customs buildings and large grey elephants casually strolling in the background. Poor old Zambia is a devastated place. Nothing has been able to restrain the ruthlessness of the poachers who have deprived the countryside of its natural population. There's not even a bird in the sky. The richness of Zimbabwe is luxurious; the roads are straight and smooth and even have cars on them, but wait . . . the people in these cars have white skin.

We stopped at a motel to find ourselves in the grip of yet another culture shock: toasted cheese sandwiches and hamburgers on the menu. It was as if we had left the so-called Third World and crossed back into the West again. Whites were very much in evidence with their big, affluent cars, grand-looking farmhouses, and money. I turned to Steady: "What's happening here? Hasn't the situation changed between black and white since independence?" "Oh," smiles Steady, "we're all friends now; you'll see soon enough." I did see, that night in fact. It takes a while for bad memories to die.

We decided to spend the night outside Harare, so we could arrive fresh and clean in the morning. The clientele of the motel's restaurant was African, an environment in which we had begun to feel at home. As I sat there, wilting over my soup, an old man came over and began to mutter at me in Shona. Being exhausted, I hadn't the energy to try and be enthused by his attention and thought he was drunk. Before I knew it, he was abusing me in English: "White trash, scum," he said. Steady immediately leapt up and led him outside.

It was the first time that I had been insulted on racial grounds. It didn't offend me. On the contrary, I felt fortunate to have avoided it for so long. Steady and the manageress of the restaurant were unbearably apologetic over the whole scene, as I wished desperately that I didn't belong to the race that provoked these people to behave in this way.

The next morning we entered Harare, which, with its colonial mansions and wide tree-lined avenues, again exuded an air of comfort and wealth. This spacious city with its modern planned centre was more what I'd expect of Australia. We began our stay at the Youth Hostel, a fusty old house complete with batty old warden, clinging to her lost youth in Yorkshire with the aid of a few dusty mementoes. Our fellow travellers here were unfortunately fairly obnoxious, all white, and mostly consisting of strapping Afrikaaner women "doing Africa".

To their obvious disapproval, we managed to evade their company that first night by escaping to a township outside the city, accompanied by the hostel cleaner, Geoffrey, and his band of musicians.

"The entry of two whites into the crowded enclosure was an event in itself"

The township of Chitungwiza lies about thirty kilometres from the centre of Harare. Aesthetically, it's a depressing hole, the portaloo-type dwellings bearing no relation to the leafy avenues of Harare. However, despite its inaccessibility by public transport, the place is teeming with atmosphere and undoubtedly the capital's life blood.

It was Sunday afternoon and Geoffrey and his crew were due to perform an eight-hour marathon in the local beerhall. The entry of two whites into the crowded enclosure was an event in itself. We stepped out of the van into silence as people turned in genuine astonishment. Feeling uneasy, I almost climbed back in but a middle-aged woman waddled up and with drunken assertiveness purred "Relax, sisters. You're welcome." From then on we had the time of our lives. Never before had I commanded so much attention; in eight hours there wasn't a minute to collect my thoughts, let alone talk to Emma, though she too seemed to be enjoying herself.

The African crowd at a social gathering is wonderfully uninhibited, no doubt partly due to the endless buckets of *Chibuku* (African beer) that they pour down their throats. People, men and women alike, certainly know how

to "get on down". As the band played a steady rhumba, I could have watched those women swing their hips around for hours, but there were friends to be made, beers to be drunk and spliffs to be smoked.

As night set in it got pretty cold, for this was wintertime below the equator, and we gratefully accepted Geoffrey's offer to take us to warm up at his family's home. Inside the single-storey house it was warm and cosy; people sat in the living room watching *Dynasty* on a large colour television while Geoffrey's mother leapt up to fetch us tea and biscuits. We were introduced to a sister, Gladys, who worked in the city for Air Zimbabwe. Aged around nineteen, her ambition was to save up all her money and emigrate to Dallas the following year. "It's so much better there for black people," she told us, "They can earn a lot and buy nice houses." It was a bizarre dream – she in fact knew no-one who had visited America.

After we returned to the Youth Hostel, I found time to collect my muddled thoughts. This experience of Zimbabwe had touched me in a curious way. Eight years since independence, the persevering divide between races was still very much in evidence and, to a European, appeared both antiquated and crude. I remember my hackles rising when a former South African (intelligent) friend of mine once said: "A revolution could never succeed in South Africa because all the servants who work for the wealthy whites have seen the scope of money. Everyone wants their piece of the cake, even if it means depriving someone else . . ." The occasion in Chitungwiza and Gladys's words rang out in my mind. If there's one thing about Zimbabwe, it makes you think.

Caught Between Two Worlds

. . . .

Kate Kellaway spent three and a half years living as a schoolteacher in Zimbabwe. After a painful period of readjustment, she has finally settled back in London where she works for *The Observer* **newspaper.**

Independence in Zimbabwe has meant important legal gains for women. There is a Ministry of Women's Affairs, several women's groups and a steady, growing interest in the Women's Movement. But it is hard to connect these facts to the women I've known and the girls I've taught in Zimbabwe. Only a small educated minority are active in women's affairs – or able to protest – and it is still the exceptional woman who can define her oppression.

The closest I came to Zimbabwean women was when I was living and teaching in St Mary's, a black township outside Harare. The difference between Harare the town and the Harare townships, now euphemistically renamed "high-density suburbs", is so extreme that they shouldn't really share the same name. The luxurious "low-density" suburbs of Zimbabwe's capital are reminiscent of Britain's wealthy stockbroker belt, the style an inheritance of colonialism. The townships, made up of vast complexes of tiny houses, are crowded with people deprived of adequate amenities, a colonial inheritance of another kind.

When I went to live with a family in St Mary's, I was congratulating myself on breaking away from the "British" Zimbabwe to experience the "real thing". But it is terrible to make of someone else's hardship an interesting experience for yourself. Besides it wasn't as simple as that. I was there because it was the home of Moses, my boyfriend. Throughout my stay I felt a conflict between accepting hospitality and looking at what was around me.

St Mary's is the oldest of Chitungwiza townships, 25 miles from Harare yet still without electricity. Imagine row upon row of ramshackle houses, squashed together between miles of dusty streets. You are surrounded by people all day long. There are so many babies that at any given moment one will be crying. Cocks crow dementedly in the middle of the night.

"I wasn't really lazy so much as frightened by the routine of house-work that shaped the women's day"

Before I got a job at the local township school my days were spent at home with the women. Moses' sister, Rutendo, had three little girls. She got pregnant at fourteen, her husband treated her badly, and she was glad to be home again. Unlike many women in her position she managed to get custody of the children, whom she brings up with her mother. Moses' father worked far away and, apart from a brother, it was a predominantly female community. Moses' mother was a professional mother. She was my Zimbabwean mother for a while: she accepted me, welcomed and joked with me, and tried in every way to make me feel at home.

I didn't speak much Shona then, just enough to say a few essential things like "Ndipeiwo mutsvairo" (Give me the broom) or "Ndine usimbe" (I'm lazy) or "Ndaguta" (I'm full). I wasn't really lazy so much as frightened by the routine of housework that shaped the women's day. Zimbabwean women keep their houses immaculately clean, but in St Mary's it was an unending fight against dust and dirty feet. Rutendo would rise at dawn and sweep the yard with a broom made of twigs, making beautiful patterns in the dust. Moses' second sister, Musafare, applied strong-smelling wax polish to the kitchen and dining-room floor. The day was punctuated by a trickle of water as children, clothes, floors, pots, shelves, everything, was washed.

Most tasks involved bending. I picture Rutendo and Musafare bending from the hip. Rutendo taught me how to cook *nhopi*, a delicious pumpkin porridge made with peanut butter. She showed me how to scour a pot with sand and how to cook *sadza* – not easy over a wood fire, as it becomes stiff and hard to stir. Zimbabwean women have good strong arms; I felt puny and ridiculous struggling to stir a pot of *sadza* for fifteen, my eyes streaming with tears from the smoke. "Crying for *sadza*", Rutendo used to call it.

> **"What was I doing here ?... What sort of image was I trying to create with all this knitting, sewing and cooking of sadza?"**

I was the only *murungu* (white) in the township but people soon became openly friendly, shouting greetings when I passed. The men were often easier to talk to, partly because they spoke more English. I also think they felt a freedom to talk to me about subjects they wouldn't discuss with their own women.

One day Rutendo and I went to see her sister, Elizabeth. She was very pregnant – so pregnant it would have been tactless to ask when the baby was coming – and explained that she wanted to be a policewoman after the child was born but her husband was against it. She asked me to check that her application form was correctly filled in. (Later she became a policewoman and her husband beat her up because of it.)

I went to talk to Rutendo in the kitchen:

"Matimati," I stated.

"Matimati," Rutendo confirmed.

"Mafuta ekubikisa?" I asked.

"Yes, cooking oil," said Ruteno, adding it to the pan. In the small black saucepan the *sadza* began to thicken. Using the *mugoti*, a special stick, I stirred. Rutendo was delighted: "I'll tell Moses you are a good housewife now."

Later we sat outside Elizabeth's house, eating *sadza* and sour milk. The sun burnt my calves. I surveyed my pink espadrilles and the pumpkin leaves swaying in the breeze and was suddenly filled with panic. What was I doing here? What was life like for these women? I watched one of them idly stitching a border of little green checks onto a loosely woven yellow tablecloth. "Have a go," she indicated, thrusting the material into my hands. I didn't, afraid of ruining it or showing myself up as an inept needlewoman.

What sort of image was I trying to create with all this knitting, sewing, and cooking of *sadza*? By the time I reached home I felt exhausted from the strain of trying to communicate without enough words. I was so pleased to see Moses' mother, she must have sensed it for she unexpectedly reached for my hand and kissed it.

Women like Rutendo and Moses' mother are authoritative and powerful in the home. One of the most popular subjects my students asked to debate was "Who is the most powerful, the father or the mother?" There was no foregone conclusion. Other popular subjects included bride price, polygamy, and "a woman's place is in the home". Students tended to be reactionary, the girls being the most timidly conservative, although seeds of protest often lay beneath the surface. Most of them, at least, were prepared to express a distaste for polygamy, though few questioned the concept of marriage or women's domestic role in the home. I remember a boy named Launcelot saying: "Women should not go to school. I want a nice fat wife who'll keep me warm in winter and feed me *sadza* all the year round – that's all she will do." The day was saved by a boy, aptly named Blessing, who stood up and spoke passionately and eloquently in favour of women's freedom from the slavery of domesticity and cruel husbands. I'm sure that many girls will eventually gain the confidence they need to express their views themselves.

TRAVEL NOTES

Languages English is the official language. Shona is most widely spoken, followed by Sindebele.

Transport A good railway network connects all major cities. Buses are slow and usually very crowded, but they're cheap and travel almost everywhere. Hitching is easy and seems to be quite safe.

Accommodation All hotels tend to be expensive. Lodges, to be found in all the national parks, are cheaper but nearly always self-catering.

Guide *The Rough Guide: Zimbabwe and Botswana* (Harrap Columbus) has very full, practical coverage.

Contacts

Women's Action Group, Box 135, Harare or 127 Union Avenue, Harare. Initially formed in 1983, in response to a massive and widespread police round-up of women apparently suspected of being prostitutes, the group acts mainly as an advisory body for women on legal rights, health, hygiene and nutrition. It also publishes a quarterly magazine, *Speak Out*.

Zimbabwe Women's Bureau, 43 Hillside Road, Hillside, Harare, ☎734295. The Bureau's aim is to promote the economic self-sufficiency of women outside the formal waged sectors of urban and rural areas. They are helpful if you're interested in visiting various projects; try asking for Mrs Chikwavaire.

Voice, 16 Samora Machel Avenue, Harare. Co-ordinating body of non-governmental or volunteer organisations. Not a women's organisation but very useful for gathering information.

Books

Sekai Nzenza, *The Autobiography of a Zimbabwean Woman* (Karia Press, 1986). Sekai describes her life and shows the issues facing black Zimbabweans amid the contradictions resulting from the long oppression of white minority rule.

Tsitsi Dangaremga, *Nervous Conditions* (The Women's Press, 1988). Set in colonial Rhodesia during the Sixties, this excellent first novel tells of a young black girl's longing for education which, she soon learns, comes with a price.

Ellen Kuzwayo, *Call Me a Woman* (The Women's Press, 1985). This remarkable autobiography movingly reveals what it's like to be a black woman in South Africa. Much of the book, notably life in the townships, can be related to Zimbabwe. Look out, too, for Kuzwayo's first collection of stories, ***Sit Down and Listen*** (The Women's Press, forthcoming).

Zimbabwe Publishing House has a fast-expanding women's list, fiction and non-fiction. Also look out for short stories and/or novels by **Nadine Gordimer** and **Doris Lessing**.

Thanks to Andrea Jarman for additional information.

FURTHER READING

Some of the books detailed below have been included, for their specific concerns, in individual country bibliographies and, in the case of the excellent *Sisterhood is Global* and *Women: A World Report*, more than once. We would like to acknowledge our debt to the whole range of books listed (and often suggested by contributors) in the compilation of *Women Travel*.

Worldwide Concerns/ Anthologies

Robin Morgan, ed., *Sisterhood is Global* (Penguin, 1985). Anthology of articles from feminists all over the world, preceded by statistics and other little-known information on the history and status of women. Especially useful for an overview of the Women's Movement in each country, 70 in all.

New Internationalist, *Women: A World Report* (Methuen, 1985). Published to coincide with the end of the United Nations Decade for Women, this book provides a review of UN information on the status of women, followed by accounts by ten writers, each of whom visited a different country to report on women's experience: for example, Angela Davis on Egypt, Germaine Greer on Cuba and Manny Shirazi on the Soviet Union.

Miranda Davies, ed., *Third World – Second Sex: Women's Struggles and National Liberation 1 and 2* (Zed Books, 1983, 1987). Two collections featuring original material by Third World women activists from over 40 countries in Asia, Latin America, Africa and the Middle East. Topics include women, politics and organisation, the role of women in national liberation movements, the case for autonomy, and campaigns around health, sexuality and work, and against violence.

Cynthia Enloe, *Bananas, Beaches and Bases* (Pandora Press, 1989). Intriguing feminist analysis of international politics, revealing women's crucial role in implementing governments' foreign policies from Soviet *glasnost* to Britain's dealings in the EC.

Women and Development: a Resource Guide for Organisation and Action (Isis, 1983; available from *Isis-WICCE*, PO Box 2471, 1211 Geneva 2, Switzerland). Provides a much-needed feminist perspective to the whole issue of development, focussing on key areas like women's role in food production, health, communication and education, and the effects of migration, tourism and the recruitment of labour by multinational companies. Shows how women are organising and fighting to control their own lives, each chapter being followed by a comprehensive selection of books, groups and other resources.

Kumari Jayawardena, *Feminism and Nationalism in the Third World* (Zed Books, 1986). Authoritative – and pioneering – study of women's participation in the democratic and revolutionary struggles of Asia and the Middle East from the late nineteenth century onwards.

Mineke Schippel, ed., *Unheard Words: Women and Literature in Africa, the Arab World, Asia, the Caribbean and Latin America* (Allison & Busby, 1986). Informative introduction to women's literary achievement in the Third World – including proverbs, essays and interviews.

Joni Seager and Ann Olson, *Women in the World* (Pan, 1986). International atlas packed with satistics on women's position in terms of health, poverty, earnings, media representation, education etc. in different countries.

Gita Sen and Caren Grown, *Development, Crises, and Alternative Visions* (Monthly Review Press, US, 1987). Groundbreaking analysis of the impact of current global economic and political crises – debt, famine, militarisation and fundamentalism – on poor Third World women, including examples of how they are organising to help themselves.

African Women

Margaret Jean Hay and Sharon Stitcher, eds., *African Women South of the Sahara* (Longman, 1984). This coursebook for students is a comprehensive study of the economic, social and political roles of women in Africa, past and present.

Asma El Dareer *Woman, Why do You Weep? Circumcision and Its Consequences* (Zed Books, 1982). Scholarly survey based on large-scale statistical research of circumcision and infibulation in Dareer's native Sudan. She deals with both women's and men's attitudes to the issues, plus related health problems, the history of circumcision, and suggestions for concrete steps – all relevant to many other areas of Africa as well as the Sudan.

Anne Cloudsley, *Women of Omburman Victims of Circumcision* (Ethnographica, 1983, reprinted 1984). The author lived and worked with Sudanese women, learned about their rituals, celebrations, marriages, births. Important book about women in traditional societies, on the social context in which female circumcision is performed.

Charlotte H Bruner, ed., *Unwinding Threads: A Collection of African Women Writers* (Heinemann, 1983). Excellent anthology of modern African women's writing, covering wide geographical range, including the Islamic Maghreb areas. Good introductions, both general and to each region and author.

Raqiya H Dualeh Abdalla, *Sisters in Affliction: Circumcision and Infibulation of Women in Africa* (Zed Books, 1982). A good account which provides historical background and a political context to customs and practices within a Muslim framework. Also discusses the economics of marriage and provides community field studies.

Muslim Women

Lois Beck and Nikki Keddie, eds., *Women in the Muslim World* (Harvard University Press, 1978). An excellent collection of essays, predominantly by anthropologists, on women in different Muslim countries.

Ann Dearden, ed., *Arab Women* (Minority Rights Group Report no. 27, revised 1983). Useful survey on the position of women in different Arab countries.

Elizabeth Warnock Fernea and Basima Qattan Bezirgan, eds., *Middle Eastern Muslim Women Speak* (1977, University of Texas Press, 1984). Collection of autobiographical and biographical writings by and about Middle Eastern women.

Fatima Mernissi, *Beyond the Veil* (1975, Al Saqi Books 1985). Exploration of male-female relations in the Muslim world by a Moroccan feminist academic, The focus is on such themes as the pervasive and often destructive role of the mother-in-law and the constricting physical boundaries of women's lives.

Fatna A Sabbah, *Women in the Muslim Unconscious* (Pergamon Press, 1984). Detailed exposé of the elements in Islamic culture that combine to ingrain attitudes towards women in Muslim societies.

Juliete Minces, *The House of Obedience – Women in Arab Society* (Zed Books, 1982). A general study of women in the Arab world with one specific chapter on women in Algeria and Egypt.

Nawal El Saadawi, *The Hidden Face of Eve* (Zed Books, 1980). Personal, often disturbing account of what it is like to grow up as a woman in the Islamic world of the Middle East.

Germaine Tillion, *The Republic of Cousins* (1966, reprinted Al Saqi Books, 1985). Thesis by a distinguished French anthropologist on the effects of cultural prehistory of the Mediterranean region on the lives of the women.

Asian Women

Women in Asia (Minority Rights Group Report no 45, revised 1982). Survey on status, role, employment, work, political participation and issues and considerations of women of Pakistan, India, Sri Lanka, Bangladesh, Philippines, Indonesia, South Korea, Japan, China.

Sylvia Chipp and Justin Green, eds., *Asian Women in Transition* (Pennsylvania State Univ. Press, 1988). Academic but readable studies on women in East South-East and South Asia, covering economic, social and political aspects from a comparative perspective.

Caribbean and Latin American Women

Pat Ellis, ed., *Women of the Caribbean* (Zed Books, 1986). Essays by Caribbean women encompassing a very wide range of themes from trade-union organisation to women in calypso.

Alicia Partnoy, *You Can't Drown the Fire* (Virago, 1989). Collection of writings by 35 exiled Latin American women.

Audrey Bronstein *The Triple Struggle: Latin American Peasant Women* (War on Want Campaigns, 1982). Women in Bolivia, Ecuador, El Salvador, Guatemala and Peru express in their own works the struggle against the oppression of underdevelopment, poverty and the position of women in male-dominated societies.

Latin American and Caribbean Women's Collective, *Slaves of Slaves: the Challenge of Latin American Women* (Zed Books, 1982). Summary of women's struggles in a number of countries, including accounts of their historical roles in the different wars of independence.

Latin American Women (Minority Rights Group Report no. 57, 1983). Excellent survey of women's exploitation at home and in the workplace, including information on how women are organising, both on specific issues such as health and for wider revolutionary change.

Doris Meyer and Margarite Fernandez-Olmos, eds., *Contemporary Women Authors of Latin America* (Brooklyn College Press, 1984; 2 vols.). Useful general selection and commentary.

Women Travellers: History

Deborah Birkett, *Spinsters Abroad* (Blackwells, 1989). A fascinating piece of research that sheds new light on the attitudes and exploits of the "Lady Explorers" of the nineteenth century, and questions their role as feminist models.

Jane Robinson, *Wayward Women: A Guide To Women Travellers* (OUP, 1990). An annotated bibliography of travel writers ranging from the Abbess Etheria's fourth-century pilgrimage to the Holy Land to Isabella Bird's pan-global travels of the 1870s. A lucky dip of names, dates and journeys with very sketchy biographical details.

Many of the accounts discussed in these two books are published in the **"Virago Travellers"** reprint series.

Guides

Gaia's Guide International (Gaia's Guide, London). Useful, if haphazard, listings of gay and women-only venues in Europe, North America, Canada, Australia and New Zealand, with a few token contacts in "far away places".

Working Abroad

Susan Griffith (ed.), *Work Your Way Around the World* (Vacation Work; updated bi-annually). A mass of ideas and information, with brief contributor's experiences; covers the whole world with particular depth on Europe.

Working Holidays (Central Bureau; annual editions). An invaluable source book including numerous contacts for workcamps and community projects.

Hilary Sewell, *Volunteer Work* (Central Bureau, 1986; new edition in preparation). Contacts and some background on international voluntary agencies and their recruitment.

These books (and a range of other, specialised work directories) can be obtained direct from the **publishers**: *Vacation Work* (9 Park End St, Oxford OX1 1HJ) and *Central Bureau* (Seymour Mews, London W1H 9PE).

A Note on Bookshops

In Britain, the best general sources for most books detailed here are *Sisterwrite*, 190 Upper St., London, N1 (☎01-226 9782) and *Silvermoon Women's Bookshop*, 68 Charing Cross Rd. London WC2H OBB (☎01-836 7906). *The Travel Bookshop*, 13 Blenheim Crescent, London W11 (☎01-229 5260) is useful for the more esoteric guidebooks and travel literature.